Lecture Notes in Computer Science   9690

Commenced Publication in 1973
Founding and Former Series Editors:
Gerhard Goos, Juris Hartmanis, and Jan van Leeuwen

Editorial Board

David Hutchison
 Lancaster University, Lancaster, UK
Takeo Kanade
 Carnegie Mellon University, Pittsburgh, PA, USA
Josef Kittler
 University of Surrey, Guildford, UK
Jon M. Kleinberg
 Cornell University, Ithaca, NY, USA
Friedemann Mattern
 ETH Zurich, Zürich, Switzerland
John C. Mitchell
 Stanford University, Stanford, CA, USA
Moni Naor
 Weizmann Institute of Science, Rehovot, Israel
C. Pandu Rangan
 Indian Institute of Technology, Madras, India
Bernhard Steffen
 TU Dortmund University, Dortmund, Germany
Demetri Terzopoulos
 University of California, Los Angeles, CA, USA
Doug Tygar
 University of California, Berkeley, CA, USA
Gerhard Weikum
 Max Planck Institute for Informatics, Saarbrücken, Germany

T0172221

More information about this series at http://www.springer.com/series/7408

Sanjai Rayadurgam · Oksana Tkachuk (Eds.)

NASA
Formal Methods

8th International Symposium, NFM 2016
Minneapolis, MN, USA, June 7–9, 2016
Proceedings

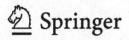 Springer

Editors
Sanjai Rayadurgam
University of Minnesota
Minneapolis, MN
USA

Oksana Tkachuk
NASA Ames Research Center
Moffett Field, CA
USA

ISSN 0302-9743   ISSN 1611-3349   (electronic)
Lecture Notes in Computer Science
ISBN 978-3-319-40647-3   ISBN 978-3-319-40648-0   (eBook)
DOI 10.1007/978-3-319-40648-0

Library of Congress Control Number: 2016941084

LNCS Sublibrary: SL2 – Programming and Software Engineering

© Springer International Publishing Switzerland 2016

Open Access Chapters 3 and 8 are distributed under the terms of the Creative Commons Attribution 4.0 International License (http://creativecommons.org/licenses/by/4.0/). For further details see license information in the chapters.
This work is subject to copyright. All rights are reserved by the Publisher, whether the whole or part of the material is concerned, specifically the rights of translation, reprinting, reuse of illustrations, recitation, broadcasting, reproduction on microfilms or in any other physical way, and transmission or information storage and retrieval, electronic adaptation, computer software, or by similar or dissimilar methodology now known or hereafter developed.
The use of general descriptive names, registered names, trademarks, service marks, etc. in this publication does not imply, even in the absence of a specific statement, that such names are exempt from the relevant protective laws and regulations and therefore free for general use.
The publisher, the authors and the editors are safe to assume that the advice and information in this book are believed to be true and accurate at the date of publication. Neither the publisher nor the authors or the editors give a warranty, express or implied, with respect to the material contained herein or for any errors or omissions that may have been made.

Printed on acid-free paper

This Springer imprint is published by Springer Nature
The registered company is Springer International Publishing AG Switzerland

Preface

The NASA Formal Methods (NFM) Symposium is a forum for theoreticians and practitioners from academia, industry, and government, with the goals of identifying challenges and providing solutions to achieving assurance in mission- and safety-critical systems. Examples of such systems at NASA include advanced separation assurance algorithms for aircraft, Next-Generation Air Transportation (NextGen), autonomous rendezvous and docking for spacecraft, on-board software for Unmanned Aerial Systems (UAS), UAS Traffic Management (UTM), autonomous robots, and systems for fault detection, diagnosis, and prognostics. The topics covered by the NASA Formal Methods Symposia include: model checking, theorem proving, SAT and SMT solving, symbolic execution, automated testing and simulation, model-based development, static and dynamic analysis techniques, runtime verification, safety assurance, fault tolerance, compositional verification techniques, cyber security, specification formalisms, requirements analysis, certification, and applications of formal methods in systems development.

This volume contains the papers presented at NFM 2016, the 8th NASA Formal Methods Symposium, co-organized by NASA Ames Research Center and the University of Minnesota Software Engineering Center, in Minneapolis, MN, June 7–9, 2016. Previous symposia were held in Pasadena, CA (2015), Houston, TX (2014), Moffett Field, CA (2013), Norfolk, VA (2012), Pasadena, CA (2011), Washington, DC (2010), and Moffett Field, CA (2009). The series started as the Langley Formal Methods Workshop, and was held under that name in 1990, 1992, 1995, 1997, 2000, and 2008. Papers were solicited for NFM 2016 under two categories: regular papers describing fully developed work and complete results or case studies, and short papers describing tools, experience reports, and work in progress or preliminary results. The symposium received 70 submissions for review (51 regular papers and 19 short papers) out of which 29 were accepted for publication (19 as regular papers and 10 as short papers). These submissions went through a rigorous reviewing process, where each paper was first independently reviewed by three reviewers and then subsequently discussed by the Program Committee.

In addition to the refereed papers, the symposium featured three invited presentations: "Using Formal Methods to Eliminate Exploitable Bugs" by Kathleen Fisher, Professor in the Computer Science Department at Tufts University; "Where Formal Methods Might Find Application on Future NASA Missions" by Michael L. Aguilar, NASA Technical Fellow in Software Engineering and the NASA Engineering and Safety Center Discipline Expert in Software, NASA Langley Research Center; and "Murphy Was Here" by Kevin Driscoll, Engineering Fellow, Honeywell. The symposium also featured breakout sessions to explore the application of formal methods to future NASA missions and to connect the dots between capabilities that need to be matured for NASA missions and formal methods.

The organizers are grateful to the authors for submitting their work to NFM 2016 and to the invited speakers for sharing their insights. NFM 2016 would not have been possible without the collaboration of the outstanding Program Committee and additional reviewers, the support of the Steering Committee, the efforts of the staff at the University of Minnesota and NASA Ames Research Center who made this event possible, and the general support of the NASA Formal Methods community.

The NFM 2016 website can be found at: http://nasaformalmethods.org.

Support for the preparation of these proceedings was provided under a contract between the NASA Ames Research Center and the University of Minnesota Software Engineering Center.

May 2016   Sanjai Rayadurgam
                                                           Oksana Tkachuk

Organization

Steering Committee

Julia Badger   NASA Johnson Space Center, USA
Ben Di Vito   NASA Langley Research Center, USA
Klaus Havelund   NASA Jet Propulsion Laboratory, USA
Gerard Holzmann   NASA Jet Propulsion Laboratory, USA
Michael Lowry   NASA Ames Research Center, USA
Kristin Yvonne Rozier University of Cincinnati, USA
Johann Schumann   SGT, Inc./NASA Ames Research Center, USA

Organizing Committee

Michael Lowry   NASA Ames Research Center, USA (NASA Liaison)
Johann Schumann   SGT, Inc./NASA Ames Research Center, USA
          (General Chair)
Oksana Tkachuk   SGT, Inc./NASA Ames Research Center, USA
          (PC Chair)
Sanjai Rayadurgam University of Minnesota, USA (PC Chair)
Mike Whalen   University of Minnesota, USA (Financial Chair)
Mats Heimdahl   University of Minnesota, USA (Local Arrangements
          Chair)

Program Committee

Julia Badger   NASA Johnson Space Center, USA
Clark Barrett   New York University, USA
Saddek Bensalem   Verimag and University Joseph Fourier, France
Dirk Beyer   University of Passau, Germany
Borzoo Bonakdarpour McMaster University, Canada
Alessandro Cimatti   FBK, Italy
Darren Cofer   Rockwell Collins, Inc., USA
Myra Cohen   University of Nebraska-Lincoln, USA
Misty Davies   NASA Ames Research Center, USA
Leonardo de Moura   Microsoft, USA
Ben Di Vito   NASA Langley Research Center, USA
Alexandre Duret-Lutz LRDE/EPITA, France
Andrew Gacek   Rockwell Collins, Inc., USA
Pierre-Loic Garoche   ONERA, France
Shalini Ghosh   SRI International, USA

Susanne Graf	Universite Joseph Fourier/CNRS/VERIMAG, France
Radu Grosu	Vienna University of Technology, Austria
Arie Gurfinkel	SEI, Carnegie Mellon University, USA
Klaus Havelund	NASA Jet Propulsion Laboratory, USA
Constance Heitmeyer	Naval Research Laboratory, USA
Gerard Holzmann	NASA Jet Propulsion Laboratory, USA
Falk Howar	TU Clausthal/IPSSE, Germany
Rajeev Joshi	NASA Jet Propulsion Laboratory, USA
Dejan Jovanović	SRI International, USA
Gerwin Klein	NICTA and University of New South Wales, Australia
Daniel Kroening	University of Oxford, UK
Rahul Kumar	NASA Jet Propulsion Laboratory, USA
Michael Lowry	NASA Ames Research Center, USA
Célia Martinie	ICS-IRIT, Université Paul Sabatier, France
Eric Mercer	Brigham Young University, USA
Cesar Munoz	NASA Langley Research Center, USA
Jorge A. Navas	SGT, Inc./NASA Ames Research Center, USA
Natasha Neogi	NASA Langley Research Center, USA
Ganesh Pai	SGT, Inc./NASA Ames Research Center, USA
Charles Pecheur	Université Catholique de Louvain, Belgium
Lee Pike	Galois, Inc., USA
Andreas Podelski	University of Freiburg, Germany
Pavithra Prabhakar	Kansas State University, USA
Venkatesh Prasad Ranganath	Kansas State University, USA
Franco Raimondi	Middlesex University, UK
Sanjai Rayadurgam	University of Minnesota, USA
Kristin Yvonne Rozier	University of Cincinnati, USA
Neha Rungta	SGT, Inc./NASA Ames Research Center, USA
Oleg Sokolsky	University of Pennsylvania, USA
Oksana Tkachuk	SGT, Inc./NASA Ames Research Center, USA
Stefano Tonetta	FBK, Italy
Willem Visser	Stellenbosch University, South Africa
Virginie Wiels	ONERA/DTIM, France
Guowei Yang	Texas State University, USA

Additional Reviewers

Archer, Myla	Dangl, Matthias
Astefanoaei, Lacramioara	David, Cristina
Backes, John	Dureja, Rohit
Brain, Martin	Dutle, Aaron
Calderon, Jose	Faghih, Fathiyeh
Cheng, Chih-Hong	Falcone, Ylies

Friedberger, Karlheinz
Goodloe, Alwyn
Kahsai, Temesghen
Kalla, Priyank
Kumar, Ramana
Kupferman, Orna
Lal, Ratan
Lukina, Anna
Mukherjee, Rajdeep
Murray, Toby
Pit-Claudel, Clément
Poplavko, Peter
Prokesch, Daniel

Roveri, Marco
Schrammel, Peter
Schäf, Martin
Selyunin, Konstantin
Sewell, Thomas
Siddique, Umair
Soto, Miriam Garcia
Svendsen, Kasper
Tomb, Aaron
Urban, Caterina
Vizel, Yakir
Wasicek, Armin

Abstracts of Invited Talks

Using Formal Methods to Eliminate Exploitable Bugs

Kathleen Fisher

Tufts University, Medford, MA 02155
kfisher@eecs.tufts.edu

Abstract. For decades, formal methods have offered the promise of software that doesn't have exploitable bugs. Until recently, however, it hasn't been possible to verify software of sufficient complexity to be useful. Recently, that situation has changed. SeL4 is an open-source operating system microkernel efficient enough to be used in a wide range of practical applications. It has been proven to be fully functionally correct, ensuring the absence of buffer overflows, null pointer exceptions, use-after-free errors, etc., and to enforce integrity and confidentiality properties. The CompCert Verifying C Compiler maps source C programs to provably equivalent assembly language, ensuring the absence of exploitable bugs in the compiler.

A number of factors have enabled this revolution in the formal methods community, including increased processor speed, better infrastructure like the Isabelle/HOL and Coq theorem provers, specialized logics for reasoning about low-level code, increasing levels of automation afforded by tactic languages and SAT/SMT solvers, and the decision to move away from trying to verify existing artifacts and instead focus on co-developing the code and the correctness proof.

In this talk, I will explore the promise and limitations of current formal methods techniques for producing useful software that provably does not contain exploitable bugs. I will discuss these issues in the context of DARPA's HACMS program, which has as its goal the creation of high-assurance software for vehicles, including quad-copters, helicopters, and automobiles.

Where Formal Methods Might Find Application on Future NASA Missions

Michael L. Aguilar

NASA Langley Research Center, Hampton, VA 23681
Michael.L.Aguilar@nasa.gov

Abstract. In many cases, formal methods are a solution looking for a problem. NASA recently released the 2015 NASA Technology Roadmaps that describe numerous possible future missions. Within these descriptions are capabilities that need to be matured in order for mission success. Many of these future capabilities could be accomplished through the use of formal methods. The future capabilities identified by NASA in these roadmaps may just be the problems formal methods have been seeking. Think of these roadmaps as "on-ramps" for engineering using formal methods.

These missions include joint robotic and human exploration of Mars, robotic probes of the icy moons of the outer planets where there is evidence of organic chemistry. Sophisticated earth-orbiting satellites to advance earth science, and possible robotic refueling and maintenance missions of these satellites.

One of the predominant cross-cutting challenges is autonomy and its verification: the capability of automation to make and execute decisions in-situ; necessitated in part by the long light-time delays from Earth for deep space spacecraft. Another challenge is the high expense of achieving high assurance for software intensive systems.

And then there are the overarching issues of budget, schedule, and design. It is highly unlikely these system-of-systems will be implemented and interfaced, tested and verified, before deployment. How could formal methods define the requirements for these systems such that the protocols and interfaces, functions and fault management execute as intended for integration that may occur for the first time off-planet?

In my experience, NASA can accept new techniques where it can be demonstrated that current practices are not sufficient. For these future system-of-systems, formal methods may prove to be not only sufficient but necessary.

Murphy Was Here

Kevin Driscoll

Honeywell, Golden Valley, Minnesota 55422
kevin.driscoll@honeywell.com

Abstract. My boss once said that "All system failures are caused by design faults." This is because, regardless of the requirements, critical systems should be designed to never fail. It is extremely rare for a critical system to fail in a way that was anticipated by the designers (e.g., redundancy exhaustion). This keynote will explore the factors that lead to designers underestimating the possibility/probabilities of certain failures. Examples of rare, but actually occurring, failures will be given. These will include Byzantine faults, component transmogrification, "evaporating" software, and exhaustively tested software that still failed. Problems that Formal Methods could have found before actual occurrence will be identified as well as problems that are still intractable with the current state of the art. The well known Murphy's Law states that: "If anything can go wrong, it will go wrong." For critical systems, the following should be added: "And, if anything can't go wrong, it will go wrong anyway."

Contents

Code Generation and Synthesis

Applications of Formal Methods

Techniques for Automated Verification

Theorem Proving and Proofs

Correctness and Certification

Requirements and Architectures

Temporal Logic Framework for Performance Analysis of Architectures of Systems

Ariane Piel[(✉)], Jean Bourrely, Stéphanie Lala, Sylvain Bertrand, and Romain Kervarc

ONERA – The French Aerospace Lab, 91123 Palaiseau, France
ariane.piel@onera.fr

Abstract. This paper presents a formal mathematical framework for performance analysis (in terms of success of given tasks) of complex systems, ATLAS. This method interestingly combines temporal aspects (for the description of the complex system) and probabilities (to represent performance). The system's task to be evaluated is described using a temporal language, the ATLAS language: the architecture of the task is decomposed into elementary functionalities and temporal operators specify their arrangement. Starting with the success probabilities of the elementary functionalities, it is then possible to compute the overall success probability of the task using mathematical formulae which are proven in this paper. The method is illustrated with a deorbitation task for a retired satellite called ENVISAT.

Keywords: Probabilistic performance analysis · Time-dependant systems · Temporal logic

1 Introduction

To keep up with the complexification of systems, novel performance analysis and evaluation methods have to be developed to validate new designs. In this context, architecture models of complex systems may be used to assess dynamic system performances with regard to the time necessary for the desired task to be fulfilled. The work presented here provides a generic formal framework and a tool designed for such performance analysis, called ATLAS (Analysis by Temporal Logic of Architectures of Systems).

The proposed approach interestingly combines temporal and probabilistic aspects by computing the success probability of the complex system's global task at a given instant in time and with respect to the beginning of the task. The task itself is described temporally. It is assumed that the system's achievements may be organised as a hierarchy of functionalities: at the top, the global functionality represents the general expected behaviour of the system, *i.e.* its task. This global functionality may generally be split into simpler sub-functionalities, and this recursively, until reaching an elementary functionality associated to an identifiable component of the system. The success probabilities of these elementary

© Springer International Publishing Switzerland 2016
S. Rayadurgam and O. Tkachuk (Eds.): NFM 2016, LNCS 9690, pp. 3–18, 2016.
DOI: 10.1007/978-3-319-40648-0_1

functionalities are supposed to be known. This system architecture is described by a temporal language, the ATLAS language, which allows expressing temporal constraints between the realisations of each functionality and is derived from Allen's interval logic [1]. According to this architecture with the associated underlying temporal constraints, the global performance of the system may be computed from the individual elementary functionalities.

The aim of this approach is to avoid extensive simulations and Monte-Carlo methods which are very costly in computing time. With this respect, the benefit of this method is two-fold. First of all, since the elementary functionalities are of smaller scale, if Monte-Carlo methods are necessary to assess their probabilities, their computing time should still be reasonable. Secondly, the division into smaller scale functionalities allows isolating the different disciplines. Thus, already existing domain-specific simulation tools may be used without having to combine them all as would have been necessary for the whole task. The level of precision of each elementary functionality may be individually adjusted.

Related Work. This approach was initiated about ten years ago with a tool called OLIGRAAL [17] which considered the average duration time of the task, along with its success probability. For a more precise expression of temporal constraints, the approach was shifted to the one presented in this paper with ATLAS which distinguishes precisely each eventuality so that individual start and end times may be considered for the verification of the temporal constraints.

An extensive overview of probabilistic performance analysis methods for large scale and time-dependant systems may be found in [19]. The most notable frameworks dealing with stochastic approaches for time-dependent systems are generally based on one of the three following approaches [5]: Bayesian networks [15], stochastic Petri nets [11,20], and fault trees [10,25] or related formalisms [7,24]. Among these approaches, those based on stochastic Petri nets, though of interest, require heavy simulation (combined for example with Monte-Carlo methods). Although the Bayesian network approach is interesting, large Bayesian networks reflecting complex systems are difficult to design and maintain, and have limited temporal expressivity. Dynamic Bayesian networks consider random variables on the state of the system with a time parameter, while ATLAS considers the timing of the functionalities as the random variables. Finally, with fault trees, the potential causes of a system hazard are recursively organised into a tree structure reflecting causality - which is a crucial notion in the framework of safety analysis - so as to figure out all of the credible ways in which the hazard may occur. The representation of temporal consistency by a modal logic allowing the expression of time may be linked to the fault tree approaches using time propagation such as [12,23] based on the Interval Temporal Logic and the Duration Calculus Interval [2,8,13]. The association of Allen's logic with probabilities as in ATLAS is natural to manipulate probabilised durations. In [14], these two approaches are coupled with the aim of diagnosing with logic formulas, by manipulating facts represented with uncertain durations. In ATLAS, the aim is shifted to the performance evaluation of a task. The time interval doesn't represent a fact but the conditional realisation of a functionality so the nature of the manipulated probabilities is different.

ATLAS is a very generic framework which has and may be applied to a wide variety of systems such as space systems' vulnerability assessment to space debris [4,16,18] and ballistic missile defence performance assessment [3].

The performance analysis performed by ATLAS allows for:

– comparing different physical or functional configurations of the system;
– assessing the sensibility of the task with regard to the external conditions.

This paper presents the formal framework behind the ATLAS tool. A case study of the deorbitation of a retired satellite serves as an illustration of the method but has no purpose of realism concerning the data used. Section 2 describes the task of the chosen case study and the system configurations to be compared. Section 3 sets the mathematical framework around ATLAS and Sect. 4 uses ATLAS to evaluate the configurations of the case study.

2 Case Study: Deorbitation of Retired Satellite ENVISAT

The case study presented here serves as an illustration of the ATLAS performance analysis method and has no purpose of realism concerning the data used. It shows what could be achieved with the intervention of technical experts to determine the data associated to each elementary functionality.

Let us consider the task of completing the deorbitation of retired satellite ENVISAT [6]. ENVISAT ("Environmental Satellite") is an inoperative Earth-observing satellite still in orbit. It was launched in 2002, into a Sun synchronous polar orbit at an altitude of 790 km, and the task ended in 2012. It is now considered as a big debris: 26 m × 10 m × 5 m and 8 200 kg. For this reason it a candidate for a space debris removal task. The aim is to study different possible ways of removing ENVISAT with a chaser. The general task may be decomposed as follows: (1) launching the chaser; (2) reaching ENVISAT's orbit; (3) placing the chaser; (4) capturing ENVISAT; (5) initiating deorbitation.

(a) ROGER net system [9]   (b) Canadarm-2 ISS operating arm principle [9]

Fig. 1. Different possible equipments for the chaser

We choose to compare the following different configurations:

- the choice of the launcher between Vega and Soyuz;
- the choice of the chaser (Fig. 1): with two nets or a robotic arm;
- the choice of the deorbitation technique: with a deorbitation kit (propulsive element appended to the debris) or by dragging the debris.

3   Formal Framework Behind ATLAS

The aim of this paper is to build a formal framework for the performance analysis of such complex systems. The studied system is characterised by a given number of functionalities. The evaluation of system performance, of its conditions of success or failure, relies on the hypothesis that the functionalities which characterise it have an uncertain and temporal behaviour.

The task to be fulfilled by the complex system is described using a temporal language derived from Allen's temporal logic [1]. This temporal description has a tree structure the root of which represents the whole task with a couple (start time t_{start}, end time t_{end}) allowing for the achievement of the task, and the leaves of which are the same kind of couples (t_{start}, t_{end}) corresponding to the elementary functionalities of the studied system. The nodes of the tree are the temporal operators which define the sequencing of the task's functionalities. To take into account the uncertainty pertaining to the realisation of each functionality, a discrete probability distribution function is associated to each t_{start}. It represents the probability that the functionality succeeds at t_{end} knowing it has started at t_{start}. Following the temporal description from the nodes of the tree, one may then compute the probability distribution functions associated to the root of the tree, *i.e.* the whole task.

In this Section, the mathematical framework for these computations is formalised. First of all, the probability space is defined, followed by the temporal language used to describe the architecture of system's task. With that foundation, the probability distribution functions used may be built and then computed for each operator of the language. The uninterrupted sequence operator "meets" is chosen as a representative operator to detail the operator-dependant definitions and proofs.

3.1   Elementary Functionalities of the System

Let Ω be a probability sample space, with its σ-algebra $\mathcal{P}(\Omega)$ and its probability measure $\mathbb{P}$. The elementary functionalities decomposing the task of the system are characterised as follows.

Definition 1 (Discrete elementary functionalities, associated random variables). *Let $\mathcal{F}$ be the set of the elementary functionalities such that:*

- *Each elementary functionality $F \in \mathcal{F}$ is characterised by three discrete random variables on Ω, where $\overline{\mathbb{R}} = \mathbb{R} \cup \infty$:*
  - *$S_F : \Omega \to \overline{\mathbb{R}}$, start time of the functionality,*
  - *$T_F : \Omega \to \overline{\mathbb{R}}$, end time of the functionality,*
  - *$B_F : \Omega \to \{0, 1\}$, success/failure indicator of the functionality.*

– *The three random variables of an elementary functionality F follow the condition that, for all $\omega \in \Omega$:*
  - $\mathbb{P}(B_F(\omega) = 1, T_F(\omega) = \infty) = 0$, i.e. *a functionality which doesn't end cannot succeed,* (C1)
  - $\mathbb{P}(S_F(\omega) > T_F(\omega)) = 0$, i.e. *a functionality may only end if it has started beforehand.* (C2)

3.2   ATLAS Formulae or Functionalities of the System

Complex functionalities of the system (*i.e.* arrangements of elementary functionalities) may be defined using temporal operators most of which are inspired from Allen's interval logic [1]. These descriptions of complex and more global functionalities of the system are called ATLAS formulae. The language is built by induction with the elementary functionalities of the system and a set of operators which lead to the tree structure of the system's task.

Table 1 graphically represents the sequencing of the intervals of the studied functionalities as expressed by the operators. The semantics of the language, presented in Sect. 3.5, formally defines these temporal arrangements. When one or two of these intervals is reduced to a point, the arrangement could be classified in several categories (for instance, at first sight, if both functionalities were reduced to one point in time, they would verify "equals" but also comply with "starts"). The semantics is defined so that the operators be strictly disjointed, and the last column of the table details the affiliation of such degenerate cases.

Definition 2 (ATLAS formula or system functionality). *Let $\mathcal{F}$ be the set of elementary system functionalities. The set of ATLAS formulae over $\mathcal{F}$, denoted $\mathcal{L}(\mathcal{F})$, is defined by induction as follows: - if $F \in \mathcal{F}$, then $F \in \mathcal{L}(\mathcal{F})$;*

– *if $F \in \mathcal{L}(\mathcal{F})$ and $G \in \mathcal{L}(\mathcal{F})$ then*
  - $F[eq]G \in \mathcal{L}(\mathcal{F})$, *"equals" i.e. exact temporal conjunction;*
  - $F[me]G \in \mathcal{L}(\mathcal{F})$, *"meets" i.e. uninterrupted sequence;*
  - $F[be]G \in \mathcal{L}(\mathcal{F})$, *"before" i.e. sequence with interruption;*
  - $F[ov]G \in \mathcal{L}(\mathcal{F})$, *"overlaps";*
  - $F[st]G \in \mathcal{L}(\mathcal{F})$, *"starts" i.e. with identical start times;*
  - $F[du]G \in \mathcal{L}(\mathcal{F})$, *"during" i.e. inclusion;*
  - $F[fi]G \in \mathcal{L}(\mathcal{F})$, *"finishes" i.e. with identical end times;*
  - $F[co]G \in \mathcal{L}(\mathcal{F})$, *"concurrent" i.e. disjunction with parallel start times.*

The random variables B_F, S_F, and T_F characterising ATLAS formulae $F \in \mathcal{L}(\mathcal{F})$ are also defined by induction:

– *if $F \in \mathcal{F}$, then B_F, S_F, and T_F are defined as in Definition 1;*
– *if $F = G \circledast H$ with $\circledast \in \{[eq], [me], [be], [ov], [st], [du], [fi], [co]\}$, the definition of B_F, S_F, and T_F depends on B_G, S_G, T_G, B_H, S_H, and T_H, and expresses the temporal constraints of operator $\circledast$. The definition corresponding to operator "meets" is given as a representative example in Sect. 3.5.*

Table 1. Graphical representation of ATLAS operators

Operator	Symbol	Sequencing	Degenerate cases
equals	$F[eq]G$		
meets	$F[me]G$		
before	$F[be]G$		
overlaps	$F[ov]G$		
starts	$F[st]G$		
during	$F[du]G$		
finishes	$F[fi]G$		
concurrent	$F[co]G$	} one succeeds	

Proposition 1 (Constraints on random variables of an ATLAS formula). *The three random variables of an ATLAS formula $F \in \mathcal{L}(\mathcal{F})$ follow both constraints (C1) and (C2) of Definition 1.*

Proof. This proof depends on the inductive definition of B_F, S_F, and T_F, and is detailed as a representative example for operator "meets" in Sect. 3.5.

From constraints (C1) and (C2), there directly results that:

Corollary 1. *The random variables B_F, S_F, and T_F of a formula $F \in \mathcal{L}(\mathcal{F})$ follow two additional constraints:*

$$\mathbb{P}(B_F(\omega)=1, S_F(\omega)=\infty)=0, \text{ if } F \text{ doesn't start it cannot succeed;} \qquad (C3)$$
$$\mathbb{P}(S_F(\omega)=\infty, T_F(\omega)\in\mathbb{R})=0, \text{ if } F \text{ doesn't start it cannot end.} \qquad (C4)$$

3.3 Conditional and Prior Probabilities

The probability functions associated to each ATLAS node, *i.e.* to each system functionality, correspond to the conditional probability of success at a given instant knowing the starting instant of the functionality.

Definition 3 (Conditional probability of success of a functionality).
The conditional probability of success *of functionality* $F \in \mathcal{L}(\mathcal{F})$ *at instant* t,
knowing starting instant s, *is a function from* $\mathbb{R} \times \mathbb{R}$ *into* $[0, 1]$:

$$\forall (s, t) \in \mathbb{R} \times \mathbb{R} \qquad \Pi_F(s, t) = \begin{cases} \dfrac{\mathbb{P}(B_F = 1, S_F = s, T_F = t)}{\mathbb{P}(S_F = s)} & \text{if } \mathbb{P}(S_F = s) \neq 0 \\[2mm] 0 & \text{otherwise} \end{cases}$$

This probability function may be extended to $\overline{\mathbb{R}} \times \overline{\mathbb{R}}$ *by taking into account*
(C1) and (C3) which imply that a functionality may not succeed if it didn't end
or didn't start: $\Pi_F(s, \infty) = \Pi_F(\infty, \infty) = 0$.

Definition 4 (Prior probability of a functionality). *The* prior probability
to start F *at a given instant is a function of* $\overline{\mathbb{R}}$ *into* $[0, 1]$: $K_F(s) = \mathbb{P}(S_F = s)$.

We now have a mathematical foundation to define, prove, and compute
recursively the conditional success probabilities for all ATLAS formulae. The
calculations now have to be done for each ATLAS operator in order to obtain
mathematical formulae which will then be available to be combined according
to the structure of the task to be analysed.

3.4 Generic Method for Operators Derived from Allen's Logic

The formalisations of the different operators derived from Allen's temporal logic
are all analogous and follow a generic method which is presented here. The
application of this method for the representative operator "meets" is detailed in
Sect. 3.5.

1. Define the three random variables as announced in Definition 2 and along the
   following guidelines, where $\circledast$ represents the studied operator:
   (a) $S_{F \circledast G}$: the temporal constraints related to S_F and S_G are expressed,
   (b) $T_{F \circledast G}$: some temporal constraints on S_F, S_G, T_F and T_G are expressed,
   (c) $B_{F \circledast G}$ is the conjunction of a generic condition $B_F B_G 1_{S_{F \circledast G} \in \mathbb{R}} 1_{T_{F \circledast G} \in \mathbb{R}}$
       (expressing that both F and G succeed, and that the temporal constraints
       from $S_{F \circledast G}$ and $T_{F \circledast G}$ are followed) and the remaining temporal con-
       straints on T_F and T_G so that all temporal constraints pertaining to
       operator $\circledast$ are imposed;
2. Check that these random variables indeed follow constraints (C1) and (C2)
   as announced in Proposition 1;
3. Calculate $\Pi_{F \circledast G}$ and $K_{F \circledast G}$, with possible particular hypotheses.

3.5 The "meets" Operator

Definition 5 ("meets" operator). $F[me]G$ *is a system functionality associ-*
ated to the following random variables:

$$- \ S_{F[me]G} : \Omega \to \overline{\mathbb{R}}, \ S_{F[me]G}(\omega) = \begin{cases} s & \text{if } S_G(\omega) > S_F(\omega) = s \in \mathbb{R} \\ \infty & \text{otherwise} \end{cases}$$

$-\ T_{F[me]G} : \Omega \to \overline{\mathbb{R}},\ T_{F[me]G}(\omega) = \begin{cases} t \text{ if } S_F(\omega) < T_F(\omega) = S_G(\omega) < T_G(\omega) = t \in \mathbb{R} \\ \infty \text{ otherwise} \end{cases}$

$-\ B_{F[me]G} : \Omega \to \{0,1\},\ B_{F[me]G}(\omega) = B_F(\omega)B_G(\omega)\mathbb{1}_{S_{F[me]G}(\omega) \in \mathbb{R}}\mathbb{1}_{T_{F[me]G}(\omega) \in \mathbb{R}}$

It is straightforward to show that constraints (C1) and (C2) are verified.

Conditional and Prior Probabilities. The direct application of the definition gives the following results:

$$\forall s \in \mathbb{R} \quad K_{F[me]G}(s) = \sum_{d>s, d \in S_G(\omega)} \mathbb{P}(S_F = s, S_G = d)$$

$$K_{F[me]G}(\infty) = \mathbb{P}(S_F = \infty, S_G = \infty) + \sum_{s \in S_F(\omega)} \sum_{d \leq s} \mathbb{P}(S_F = s, S_G = d)$$

$$\forall (s,t) \in \mathbb{R}^2 \quad \Pi_{F[me]G}(s,t) = \frac{\sum_{d>s} \mathbb{P}(B_F = 1, S_F = s, T_F = d, B_G = 1, S_G = d, T_G = t)}{\sum_{d>s, d \in S_G(\omega)} \mathbb{P}(S_F = s, S_G = d)}$$

Results with Independance Hypothesis. If an independance hypothesis is taken on the random variables of two functionalities (that is, if the random variables of the two functionalites F and G are independant), the calculations of $\Pi_{F[me]G}$ and of $K_{F[me]G}$ may be simplified.

Theorem 1. *If functionalities F and G are independant, then the success probabilities may be computed with the following formulas:*

$$\forall s \in \mathbb{R} \quad K_{F[me]G}(s) = K_F(s) \sum_{d>s, d \in S_G(\omega)} K_G(d),$$

$$K_{F[me]G}(\infty) = K_F(\infty)K_G(\infty) + \sum_{s \in S_F(\omega)} K_F(s) \sum_{d \leq s} K_G(d)$$

$$\forall (s,t) \in \mathbb{R}^2 \quad \Pi_{F[me]G}(s,t) =$$

$$\left(\frac{1}{\sum_{d>s, d \in S_G(\omega)} K_G(d)} \right) \sum_{d>s} \Pi_F(s,d)\Pi_G(d,t)K_G(d)$$

Proof. From the independance, it results that if $K_F(s) \sum_{d>s, d \in S_G(\omega)} K_G(d) \neq 0$:

$$\Pi_{F[me]G}(s,t) = \frac{\sum_{d>s} \mathbb{P}(B_F=1, S_F=s, T_F=d)\mathbb{P}(B_G=1, S_G=d, T_G=t)}{K_F(s) \sum_{d>s, d \in S_G(\omega)} K_G(d)}$$

Results with Exact Sequencing Hypothesis. In this paragraph, we study the particular case of systematic exact sequencing of functions $F \in \mathcal{L}(\mathcal{F})$ and $G \in \mathcal{L}(\mathcal{F})$ as expressed by the two following hypotheses:

Definition 6 (Exact sequencing hypothesis for "meets")

- *The success of functionality F implies the start of functionality G at the instant of success of F. Conversely, for functionality G to start at an instant, it is necessary that functionality F have succeeded at this same instant and that it not be reduced to a point ($S_F < T_F$). Formally:*

$$\forall \omega \in \Omega \; S_G(\omega) = d \in \mathbb{R} \iff B_F(\omega) = 1 \wedge S_F(\omega) < T_F(\omega) = d \in \mathbb{R} \quad (1)$$

- *The success of G only depends on the instant of success of F (and on the start of G because of (1)), but not on the start instant of F.*

$$\forall (s,t) \in \mathbb{R}^2 \; \mathbb{P}(B_G{=}1, T_G{=}t \mid S_G{=}d, S_F{=}s) = \mathbb{P}(B_G{=}1, T_G{=}t \mid S_G{=}d) \quad (2)$$

Proposition 2. *Hypothesis (1) implies that:* $\forall \omega \in \Omega \; S_F(\omega) \in \mathbb{R} \Rightarrow S_G(\omega) > S_F(\omega)$.

Proof. By case disjunction. Let $\omega \in \Omega$ such that $S_F(\omega) \in \mathbb{R}$.
  $S_G(\omega) = \infty$ Then, $S_G(\omega) \geq S_F(\omega)$;
  $S_G(\omega) \in \mathbb{R}$ Then (1) implies in particular that $S_G{=}T_F$ and $S_F{<}T_F$, so $S_F{<}S_G$.

Theorem 2. *If functionalities $F \in \mathcal{L}(\mathcal{F})$ and $G \in \mathcal{L}(\mathcal{F})$ follow hypotheses (1) and (2), then:*

$$\forall s \in \overline{\mathbb{R}} \quad K_{F[me]G}(s) = K_F(s)$$

and:

$$\forall (s,t) \in \mathbb{R}^2 \quad \Pi_{F[me]G}(s,t) = \sum_{d>s} \Pi_F(s,d)\Pi_G(d,t)$$

Proof. For all $s \in \mathbb{R}$:

$$K_{F[me]G}(s) = \sum_{d>s, d \in S_G(\omega)} \mathbb{P}(S_F = s, S_G = d)$$

$$\underset{\text{Proposition 2}}{=} \sum_{d \in S_G(\omega)} \mathbb{P}(S_F = s, S_G = d)$$

$$= \mathbb{P}(S_F = s) = K_F(s)$$

$$K_{F[me]G}(\infty) = \mathbb{P}(S_F = \infty, S_G = \infty) + \sum_{s \in S_F(\omega)} \sum_{d \leq s} \mathbb{P}(S_F = s, S_G = d)$$

$$\underset{\text{Proposition 2}}{=} \mathbb{P}(S_F = \infty, S_G = \infty)$$

$$\underset{(1)}{=} \mathbb{P}(S_F = \infty, B_F = 0) + \sum_{s \in S_F(\omega)} \mathbb{P}(S_F = \infty, B_F = 1, T_F = s)$$

$$= \mathbb{P}(S_F = \infty) = K_F(\infty)$$

For all $(s,t) \in \mathbb{R}^2$:

$$\Pi_{F[me]G}(s,t) = \frac{\sum\limits_{d>s} \mathbb{P}(B_F=1, S_F=s, T_F=d, B_G=1, S_G=d, T_G=t)}{\sum\limits_{d>s, d \in S_G(\omega)} \mathbb{P}(S_F=s, S_G=d)}$$

$$\underset{\text{Proposition 2}}{=} \frac{\sum\limits_{d>s} \mathbb{P}(B_F=1, S_F=s, T_F=d)\mathbb{P}(B_G=1, S_G=d, T_G=t \mid B_F=1, S_F=s, T_F=d)}{\sum\limits_{d \in S_G(\omega)} \mathbb{P}(S_F=s, S_G=d)}$$

$$\underset{(1)}{=} \frac{\sum\limits_{d>s} \mathbb{P}(B_F=1, S_F=s, T_F=d)\mathbb{P}(B_G=1, S_G=d, T_G=t \mid S_F=s, S_G=d)}{\mathbb{P}(S_F=s)}$$

$$= \sum\limits_{d>s} \Pi_F(s,d)\mathbb{P}(B_G=1, S_G=d, T_G=t \mid S_F=s, S_G=d)$$

$$\underset{(2)}{=} \sum\limits_{d>s} \Pi_F(s,d)\mathbb{P}(B_G=1, T_G=t \mid S_G=d)$$

$$= \sum\limits_{d>s} \Pi_F(s,d)\Pi_G(d,t)$$

This completes the formalisation of operator "meets". The semantics and calculations of the other operators are analogous and Table 2 presents the resulting formulae to compute the success probabilities for all ATLAS operators.

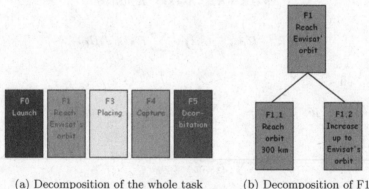

(a) Decomposition of the whole task   (b) Decomposition of F1

Fig. 2.

4 Application of ATLAS to the Case Study of ENVISAT's Deorbitation

This Section will now illustrate the use of the ATLAS method on the case study presented in Sect. 2.

Table 2. Informal summary of the formulas for K and Π

Formula H	Hypotheses to be verified	$K_H(s)$	$\Pi_H(s,t)$
$F[eq]G$	F and G independant	$K_F(s)K_G(s)$	$\Pi_F(s,t)\Pi_G(s,t)$
$F[me]G$	F and G independant $\begin{cases}S_G=d\in\mathbb{R}\iff B_F=1\wedge S_F<T_F=d\in\mathbb{R}\\\mathbb{P}(B_F=1,T_G=t\mid S_G=d,S_F=s)=\mathbb{P}(B_G=1,T_G=t\mid S_G=d)\end{cases}$	$K_F(s)\displaystyle\sum_{d\geq s,d\in S_G(\omega)}K_G(d)$ $K_F(s)$	$\left(\dfrac{\sum_{d\geq s}K_G(d)}{\sum_{d\geq s,d\in S_G(\omega)}}\right)\displaystyle\sum_{d\geq s}\Pi_F(s,d)\Pi_G(d,t)K_G(d)$ $\displaystyle\sum_{d>s}\Pi_F(s,d)\Pi_G(d,t)$
$F[be]G$	F and G independant	$K_F(s)\displaystyle\sum_{s<d,d\in S_G(\omega)}K_G(d)$	$\dfrac{1}{\sum_{d>s,d\in S_G(\omega)}K_G(d)}\displaystyle\sum_{d>s}\Pi_F(s,d)\sum_{d'>d}\Pi_G(d',t)K_G(d')$
$F[ov]G$	F and G independant	$K_F(s)\displaystyle\sum_{s<d,d\in S_G(\omega)}K_G(d)$	$\dfrac{1}{\sum_{d>s,d\in S_G(\omega)}K_G(d)}\displaystyle\sum_{d>s}\Pi_G(d,t)K_G(d)\sum_{d<d'<t}\Pi_F(s,d')$
$F[st]G$	F and G independant $\begin{cases}S_F=S_G\\\mathbb{P}(B_G=1,T_G=t\mid S_G=s,B_F=1,T_F=d)=\mathbb{P}(B_G=1,T_G=t\mid S_G=s)\end{cases}$	$K_F(s)=K_G(s)$	$\displaystyle\sum_{d<t}\Pi_F(s,d)\Pi_G(s,t)$ $\displaystyle\sum_{d\geq s}\Pi_F(s,d)\Pi_G(d,t)$
$F[du]G$	F and G independant	$K_G(s)\displaystyle\sum_{s<d,d\in S_G(\omega)}K_F(d)$	$\Pi_G(s,t)\left(\dfrac{1}{\sum_{d>s,d\in S_G(\omega)}K_F(d)}\right)\left(\displaystyle\sum_{d\geq s}K_F(d)\left(\sum_{\substack{d<d'<t\\d'\in\mathbb{R}}}\Pi_F(d,d')\right)\right)$
$F[fi]G$	F and G independant	$K_G(s)\displaystyle\sum_{s<d,d\in S_G(\omega)}K_F(d)$	$\dfrac{1}{\sum_{d>s,d\in S_G(\omega)}K_F(d)}\displaystyle\sum_{d>s}\Pi_F(d,t)K_F(d)\Pi_G(s,t)$
$F[co]G$	F and G independant $\begin{cases}S_F=S_G\\\mathbb{P}(B_G=1,T_G=t\mid S_G=s,B_F=1,T_F=d)=\mathbb{P}(B_G=1,T_G=t\mid S_G=s)\\\mathbb{P}(B_F=1,T_F=t\mid S_F=s,B_G=1,T_G=d)=\mathbb{P}(B_F=1,T_F=t\mid S_F=s)\end{cases}$	$K_F(s)K_G(s)$ $K_F(s)=K_G(s)$	$\Pi_F(s,t)\left[1-\displaystyle\sum_{d\leq t}\Pi_G(s,d)\right]+\Pi_G(s,t)\left[1-\displaystyle\sum_{d\leq t}\Pi_F(s,d)\right]$ $\Pi_F(s,t)\left[1-\displaystyle\sum_{d<t}\Pi_G(s,d)\right]+\Pi_G(s,t)\left[1-\displaystyle\sum_{d<t}\Pi_F(s,d)\right]$

4.1 Task Description

The first step is to detail each elementary functionality of the task and specify both the temporal constraints between these elementary functionalities and the success probabilities associated to them. As described in Sect. 2, the task is decomposed in five elementary functionalities displayed in Fig. 2(a). These functionalities have to exactly follow each other, so the appropriate operator to be used between all functionalities is operator "meets" detailed in Sect. 3. In addition, by definition of the elementary functionalities, they are always exactly sequenced so follow the "exact sequencing hypotheses" of Definition 6 and the corresponding formula may be applied. Each elementary functionality must now be precisely detailed to assess its associated success probabilities.

Functionality 1. The launcher launches the chaser in the orbital plane of the debris. The launching may not be operated all the time and is only possible during a 2 h period each day of the first trimester of 2020. If the task manager decides anyhow to launch out of this time-slot, the launch is operated at the beginning of the next slot. If the order is initiated inside a nominal slot, the chaser is immediately launched. Weather and other external conditions aren't considered here since they would have the same impact on the task for all studied configurations. For similar reasons, it is considered that, if the launch vehicle takes off, the probability of success of this functionality is 1.

Functionality 2. The goal of this functionality is to manoeuvre the chaser to phase it with the debris. Placing the chaser in the right orbit (ENVISAT's orbit) depends on the choice of the launcher. Vega places it on an orbit of around 300 km in about 800 s [21]. One must wait several minutes to a few hours to compensate the possible phasing difference between ENVISAT and the chaser. It is assumed that the launching slots have been judiciously chosen so that the phase difference be minimised. To simplify this example that has a strictly illustrative vocation, the 2 h time-slot is divided into three time-slots (0 to 40 min, 40 to 80 min, and 80 to 120 min). The time necessary to reach the orbit is respectively of 10 min, 20 min, and 30 min. The success probability of this function is 90 % (respectively 40 %, 30 %, and 20 % according to launching time). The situation is simpler for the Soyuz launcher since it places the chaser directly in the correct orbit (790 km) in about 60 min [22].

Functionality 3. This functionality varies depending on the equipment of the chaser. In the case of a chaser equipped with nets:

F3.1 This corresponds to the observation and debris evaluation phase and may take more or less time to succeed. A delay of one or two minutes is considered.

F3.2 The chaser manoeuvres to move closer to the debris (to reach a distance of about 100 m) and positions itself so as to be able to observe the debris with a dedicated sensor. It is assumed that the duration of this functionality is either 5 min, 7 min or 10 min and that these three durations are equiprobable.

In the case of a chaser equipped with a robotic arm:

F3.1 Greater precision is required for the operation. If necessary three attempts may be made, with delays respectively of 5 min, 10 min, and 15 min, and each with a success probability of 50 %.

F3.2 The chaser manoeuvres to reach a distance of about 1 m close to the debris and positions itself. It is assumed that the duration of this functionality is either 30 min, 40 min or 50 min and that these 3 durations are equiprobable.

Functionality 4. This functionality aims at establishing the mechanical contact with the debris. It also varies depending on the equipment used.

In the case of nets, it is considered that two nets are on-board. If the first net fails, a second net is launched 5 min later. It is assumed that both nets have the same success probability which is estimated at 60 %. The capture time is constant (about 1 min).

In the case of a robotic arm, the functionality has three chances to succeed in hitching the debris, after 5 min, 6 min, and 7 min, each of which has a probability of success or 30 %. In this case, a de-tumbling must be operated by the robotic arm. This takes about 30 min and has a high success probability of 95 %.

Functionality 5. Two options are considered here. If a deorbitation kit is chosen, it has to be attached to the debris so as to change its trajectory. It is assumed that this functionality would take about 1 min and would have a success probability of 80 %. If the debris is dragged, the success probability is evaluated to 90 %. For practical reasons, the deorbitation kit is only considered when using a robotic arm since the latter would be necessary to append it to the debris.

4.2   ATLAS Results

The results presented here do not have the vocation to provide an actual answer to the studied issue since the data used is approximative. The aim is to give an idea of the types of result the ATLAS method may offer.

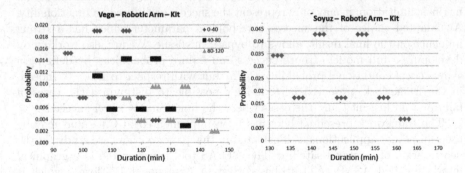

Fig. 3. Graphical representation of the ATLAS results

If M is the whole task, ATLAS provides the probability $\Pi_M(s,t)$ that the deorbitation be successful depending on the chosen configuration, at a given instant t, knowing the task has started at instant s. Different post-treatments may then be applied to the resulting data to interpret it.

For instance, since the launching 2 h time-slot has been divided into three with the Vega launcher (*cf.* Functionality 2), it may be interesting to consider the overall success probability in each time-slot, *i.e.* for the first slot: $\sum_t \sum_{0 \leq s \leq 40} \Pi_M(s,t)$. These results are presented in Table 3. If the duration of the task is crucial, it is also possible to take into account a time limit. For instance, if the duration should be limited to 100 min because of a limited quantity of propellant (so that the chaser doesn't become a debris to be deorbitised), the success probabilities are $\sum_{t,t-s \leq 100} \sum_{0 \leq s \leq 40} \Pi_M(s,t)$ presented in the last column of Table 3.

It may also be interesting to consider the success probability of the task with regard to the task duration, *i.e.* for the first time-slot $\sum_{0 \leq s \leq 40} \Pi_M(s,s+d)$ where d is the task's length. These results are presented as graphs in Fig. 3.

Beyond the straightforward conclusion that the Soyuz launcher with a robotic arm and the dragging option is the best configuration, ATLAS details the precise delays linked to the successful realisation of the overall task. Post-treatments such as presented here may thus be applied to the result data to bring to light different aspects. In addition, changes in configuration may easily be compared, which allows to study the sensitivity of the system.

5   Conclusion and Perspectives

This paper has presented a formal framework, ATLAS, to efficiently compute the probability of a successful task for complex systems. This method may be used for the evaluation and liability assessment of different system configurations. An advantage of this method is that the heterogeneity of the system (components, granularity of description, *etc.*) is not problematic since their performance is summarised by their stochastic performance. However, this representation has an intrinsic limitation: it may only represent the success or failure of a functionality. An adapted choice of the success threshold, a parameter which has a strong influence on the final result, allows to bypass this issue. We are also working on developing a full model of both success and failure probabilities by defining a symmetrical conditional probability to Π_F but with respect to $B_F = 0$. Indeed, in the framework presented here, it isn't possible to distinguish the cases of failure at an instant t and the cases where the functionality never succeeds.

The framework presented here has been implemented in C++ and may be used for actual applications as illustrated in this paper with a case study for the deorbitation of a retired satellite. The ATLAS tool is integrated in a graphical interface called ASAP (ATLAS-based System Assessment Platform) which is not described in this paper. ASAP provides two graphical interfaces for task description as well as an interface for the post-treatment of the result data.

Table 3. Success probabilities and task length of ENVISAT deorbitation

			S_M	Duration d (min)	Success	Success with $d \leq 100$
Vega	**Net**	**Drag**	0–40	30–43	29.0 %	29.0 %
			40–80	40–53	21.8 %	21.8 %
			80–120	50–63	14.6 %	14.6 %
			0–120	**30–63**	**65.4 %**	**65.4 %**
	Robotic Arm	**Drag**	0–40	93–125	26.9 %	7.7 %
			40–80	103–135	20.2 %	0 %
			80–120	113–145	13.5 %	0 %
			0–120	**93–145**	**60.6 %**	**7.7 %**
		Kit	0–40	94–126	23.9 %	6.1 %
			40–80	104–136	18.0 %	0 %
			80–120	114–146	12.0 %	0 %
			0–120	**94–146**	**53.9 %**	**6.1 %**
Soyuz	**Net**	**Drag**	0–120	67–80	72.6 %	72.6 %
	Robotic Arm	**Drag**	0–120	130–162	60.6 %	0 %
		Kit	0–120	131–163	53.9 %	0 %

In order to refine the representation of the system, we plan to introduce the notion of resources that may be produced or consumed during the task. A resource refers to a material means used during the task and which could prove to be a physical constraint and cause the failure of the task. For instance, one could consider electrical power, fuel, memory for data storage, a number of available planes, *etc.* In addition, the theoretical framework is limited to discrete probabilities. We are currently working on extending this framework to continuous probabilities, with the aim of providing a generic framework allowing for mixed probabilities, *i.e.* random variables with both discrete and continuous components, thus encompassing all situations.

References

1. Allen, J.F.: Maintaining knowledge about temporal intervals. Commun. ACM **26**(11), 832–843 (1983)
2. Allen, J.F.: Temporal reasoning and planning. In: Reasoning about Plans, pp. 1–67. Morgan Kaufmann Publishers Inc., San Francisco (1991)
3. Bertrand, S., Donath, T., Kervarc, R., Lancien, A., Louyot, C., Merit, S., Piernas, A., Prudhomme, S.: Probabilistic performance evaluation of tactical ballistic missile defence architectures. In: 6th International Conference on Missile Defence (2009)
4. Bertrand, S., Prudhomme, S., Merit, S., Jolly, C., Kervarc, R., Donath, T.: Space systems' vulnerability assessment to space debris: a methodology and a program. In: 2012 IEEE Aerospace Conference, pp. 1–15. IEEE (2012)

5. Bobbio, A., Ciancamerla, E., Franceschinis, G., Gaeta, R., Minichino, M., Portinale, L.: Sequential application of heterogeneous models for the safetyanalysis of a control system: a case study. Reliab. Eng. Syst. Saf. **81**, 269–280 (2003)

6. Bonnal, C., Ruault, J.M., Desjean, M.C.: Active debris removal: recent progress and current trends. Acta Astronaut. **85**, 51–60 (2013)

7. Chan, F.K.: Spacecraft Collision Probability. Aerospace Press El Seg., CA (2008)

8. Chaochen, Z., Hoare, C.A.R., Ravn, A.P.: A calculus of durations. Inf. Process. Lett. **40**(5), 269–276 (1991)

9. Clerc, X., Retat, I.: Astrium vision on space debris removal. In: Proceeding of the 63rd International Astronautical Congress (IAC 2012), vol. 15, Napoli, Italy (2012)

10. Dhillon, B.S.: Design Reliability: Fundamentals and Applications. CRC Press, Boca Raton (1999)

11. Dutuit, Y., Châtelet, E., Signoret, J.P., Thomas, P.: Dependability modelling and evaluation by using stochastic petri nets: application to two test cases. Reliab. Eng. Syst. Saf. **55**(2), 117–124 (1997)

12. Hansen, K.M., Ravn, A.P., Stavridou, V.: From safety analysis to software requirements. IEEE Trans. Softw. Eng. **24**(7), 573–584 (1998)

13. Hansen, M.R., Chaochen, Z.: Duration calculus: logical foundations. Formal Aspects Comput. **9**(3), 283–330 (1997)

14. van der Heijden, M., Lucas, P.J.: A probabilistic logic of qualitative time. In: Probabilistic Problem Solving in BioMedicine, p. 69 (2011)

15. Kang, C., Golay, M.: A bayesian belief network-based advisory system for operational availability focused diagnosis of complex nuclear power systems. Expert Syst. Appl. **17**(1), 21–32 (1999)

16. Kervarc, R., Bertrand, S., Prudhomme, S., Elie, A., Carle, P., Donath, T.: A functional approach to the assessment of debris effect on spatial systems. In: MASCOT&ISGG 2012 (2012)

17. Kervarc, R., Bourrely, J., Quillien, C.: A generic logical-temporal performance analysis method for complex systems. Math. Comput. Simul. **81**, 717–730 (2010)

18. Lang, T., Kervarc, R., Bertrand, S., Carle, P., Donath, T., Destefanis, R., Grassi, L., Tiboldo, F., Schäfer, F., Kempf, S., et al.: Short and long term efficiencies of debris risk reduction measures: application to a european LEO mission. Adv. Space Res. **55**(1), 282–296 (2015)

19. Morio, J., Piet-Lahanier, H., Poirion, F., Marzat, J., Seren, C., Bertrand, S., Brucy, Q., Kervarc, R., et al.: An overview of probabilistic performance analysis methods for large scale and time-dependent systems. AerospaceLab **3**(4), 1 (2012)

20. Nourelfath, M., Dutuit, Y.: A combined approach to solve the redundancy optimization problem for multi-state systems under repair policies. Reliab. Eng. Syst. Saf. **86**(3), 205–213 (2004)

21. Perez, E.: Vega users manual. ARIANESPACE (3), 154 (2012)

22. Perez, E.: Soyuz from the guiana space centre users manual. Technical report Arianespace (2012)

23. Schellhorn, G., Thums, A., Reif, W.: Formal fault tree semantics. In: Proceedings of the 6th World Conference on Integrated Design & Process Technology (2002)

24. Taylor, J.: Fault tree and cause consequence analysis for control software validation. Technical report (1982)

25. Vesely, W.E., Goldberg, F.F., Roberts, N.H., Haasl, D.F.: Fault tree handbook. Technical report, DTIC Document (1981)

On Implementing Real-Time Specification Patterns Using Observers

John D. Backes[1]([✉]), Michael W. Whalen[2], Andrew Gacek[1], and John Komp[2]

[1] Rockwell Collins, Bloomington, MN 55438, USA
john.backes@gmail.com
[2] University of Minnesota, Minneapolis, MN 55455, USA

Abstract. English language requirements are often used to specify the behavior of complex cyber-physical systems. The process of transforming these requirements to a formal specification language is often challenging, especially if the specification language does not contain constructs analogous to those used in the original requirements. For example, requirements often contain real-time constraints, but many specification languages for model checkers have discrete time semantics. Work in specification patterns helps to bridge these gaps, allowing straightforward expression of common requirements patterns in formal languages. In this work we demonstrate how we support real-time specification patterns in the Assume Guarantee Reasoning Environment (AGREE) using observers. We demonstrate that there are subtle challenges, not mentioned in previous literature, to express real-time patterns accurately using observers. We then demonstrate that these patterns are sufficient to model real-time requirements for a real-world avionics system.

1 Introduction

Natural language requirements specifications are often used to prescribe the behavior of complex cyber-physical systems. Regrettably, such specifications can be incomplete, inconsistent, or ambiguous. For these reasons, researchers have long advocated the use of formal languages, such as temporal logics to describe requirements. Unfortunately, the process of formalizing natural language requirements using formal specification languages is often challenging, especially if the specification language does not contain constructs analogous to those used in the original requirements.

Specification patterns [1,2] are an approach to ease the construction of formal specifications from natural language requirements. These patterns describe how common reasoning patterns in English language requirements can be represented in (sometimes complex) formulas in a variety of formalisms. Following the seminal work of Dwyer [1] for discrete time specification patterns, a

---

This work was sponsored by DARPA/AFRL Contract FA8750-12-9-0179, AFRL Contract FA8750-16-C-0018, and NASA Contract NNA13AA21C.

© Springer International Publishing Switzerland 2016
S. Rayadurgam and O. Tkachuk (Eds.): NFM 2016, LNCS 9690, pp. 19–33, 2016.
DOI: 10.1007/978-3-319-40648-0_2

variety of real-time specification pattern taxonomies have been developed [2–6]. An example of a timed specification pattern expressible in each is: "Globally, it is always the case that if P holds, then S holds between *low* and *high* time unit(s)."

In most of this work, the specification patterns are mapped to real-time temporal logics, such as TCTL [7], MTL [8], RTGIL [9], and TILCO-X [4]. As an alternative, researchers have investigated using *observers* to capture real-time specification patterns. Observers are code/model fragments written in the modeling or implementation language to be verified, such as timed automata, timed Petri nets, source code, and Simulink, among others. For example, Gruhn [3] and Abid [10] describe real-time specifications as state machines in timed automata and timed Petri nets, respectively. A benefit of this approach is that rather than checking complex timed temporal logic properties (which can be very expensive and may not be supported by a wide variety of analysis tools), it is possible to check simpler properties over the observer.

Despite this benefit, capturing real-time specification patterns with observers can be challenging, especially in the presence of overlapping "trigger events." That is, if P occurs multiple times before *low* time units have elapsed in the example above. For example, most of the observers in Abid [10] explicitly are not defined for 'global' scopes, and Gruhn, while stating that global properties are supported, only checks a pattern for the first occurrence of the triggering event in an infinite trace.

In this work, we examine the use of observers and invariant properties to capture specification patterns that can involve overlapping triggering events. We use the Lustre specification language [11] to describe *synchronous observers* involving a real-valued time input to represent the current system clock[1]. We describe the conditions under which we can use observers to faithfully represent the semantics of patterns, for both positive instances of patterns *and negations of patterns*. We call the former use *properties* and the latter use *constraints*.

The reason that we consider negations of patterns is that our overall goal is to use real-time specification patterns in the service of assume/guarantee compositional reasoning. In recent efforts [12,13], we have used the AGREE tool suite [14] for reasoning about discrete time behavioral properties of complex models described in the Architectural Analysis and Design Language [15][2]. Through adding support for Requirements Specification Language (RSL) patterns [16] and calendar automata [17–19], it becomes possible to lift our analysis to real-time systems. In AGREE, we prove implicative properties: given that subcomponents satisfy their contracts, then a system should satisfy its contract. This means that the RSL patterns for subsystems are used under a negation. We describe the use of these patterns in AGREE and demonstrate their use on a real avionics system. Thus, the contributions of this work are as follows:

---

[1] Although our formalisms are expressed as Lustre specifications, the concepts and proofs presented in this paper are applicable to many other popular model checking specification languages.

[2] AGREE is available at: http://loonwerks.com.

- We demonstrate a method for translating RSL Patterns into Lustre observers and system invariants.
- We prove that it is possible to efficiently capture patterns involving arbitrary overlapping intervals in Lustre using non-determinism.
- We argue that there is no method to efficiently encode a transition system in Lustre that implements the exact semantics of all of the RSL patterns when considering their negation.
- We demonstrate how to encode these patterns as Lustre constraints for *practical* systems.
- We discuss the use of these patterns to model a real-world avionics system.

2   Definitions

AGREE proves properties of architectural models compositionally by proving a series of lemmas about components at different levels in the model's hierarchy. A description of how these proofs are constructed is provided in [12,14] and a proof sketch of correctness of these rules is described in [14,20]. For the purpose of this work, it is not important that the reader has an understanding of how these proofs are constructed. The AGREE tool translates AADL models annotated with component assumptions, guarantees, and assertions into Lustre programs. Our explanations and formalizations in this paper are described by these target Lustre specifications. Most other SMT-based model checkers use a specification language that has similar expressivity as Lustre; the techniques we present in this paper can be applied generally to other model checking specification languages.

A Lustre program $\mathcal{M} = (V, T, P)$ can be thought of as a finite collection of named variables V, a transition relation T, and a finite collection of properties P. Each named variable is of type *bool*, *integer*, or *real*. The transition relation is a Boolean constraint over these variables and theory constants; the value of these variables represents the program's current *state*, and the transition relation constrains how the state changes. Each property $p \in P$ is also a Boolean constraint over the variables and theory constants. We sometimes refer to a Lustre program as a model, specification, or transition system. The AGREE constraints specified via assumptions, assertions, or guarantees in an AADL model are translated to either constraints in the transition relation or properties of the Lustre program.

The expression for T contains common arithmetic and logical operations ($+$, $-$, $*$, $\div$, $\vee$, $\wedge$, $\Rightarrow$, $\neg$, $=$) as well as the "if-then-else" expression (*ite*) and two temporal operations: $\rightarrow$ and *pre*. The $\rightarrow$ operation evaluates to its left hand side value when the program is in its initial state. Otherwise it evaluates to its right hand side value. For example, the expression: $true \rightarrow false$ is $true$ in the initial state and $false$ otherwise. The *pre* operation takes a single expression as an argument and returns the value of this expression in the previous state of the transition system. For example, the expression: $x = (0 \rightarrow pre(x) + 1)$ constrains the current value of variable x to be 0 in the initial state otherwise it is the value of x in the previous state incremented by 1.

In the model's initial state the value of the *pre* operation on any expression is undefined. Every occurrence of a *pre* operator must be in a subexpression of the right hand side of the $\rightarrow$ operator. The *pre* operation can be performed on expressions containing other *pre* operators, but there must be $\rightarrow$ operations between each occurrence of a *pre* operation. For example, the expression: $true \rightarrow pre(pre(x))$ is not well-formed, but the expression: $true \rightarrow pre(x \rightarrow pre(x))$ is well-formed.

A Lustre program models a state transition system. The current values of the program's variables are constrained by values of the program's variables in the previous state. In order to model timed systems, we introduce a real-valued variable t which represents how much time has elapsed during the previous transitions of the system. We adopt a similar model as *timeout automata* as described in [17]. The system that is modeled has a collection of *timeouts* associated with the time of each "interesting event" that will occur in the system. The current value of t is assigned to the least timeout of the system greater than the previous elapsed time. Specifically, t has the following constraint:

$$t = 0 \rightarrow pre(t) + min\_pos(t_1 - pre(t), \ldots, t_n - pre(t)) \tag{1}$$

where $t_1, \ldots, t_n$ are variables representing the timeout values of'the system. The function *min_pos* returns the value of its minimum positive argument. We constrain all the timeouts of the system to be positive. A timeout may also be assigned to positive infinity $(\infty)^3$. There should always be a timeout that is greater than the current time (and less than ∞). If this is true, then the invariant $true \rightarrow t > pre(t)$ holds for the model, i.e., time always progresses.

A sequence of states is called a *trace*. A trace is said to be *admissible* (w.r.t. a Lustre model or transition relation) if each state and its successor satisfy the transition relation. We adopt the common notation (σ, τ) to represent a trace of a timed system where σ is a sequence of states ($\sigma = \sigma_1 \sigma_2 \sigma_3 \ldots$) and τ is a sequence of time values ($\tau = \tau_1 \tau_2 \tau_3 \ldots$) such that $\forall i : \tau_i < \tau_{i+1}$. In some literature, state transitions may take place without any time progress (i.e., $\forall i : \tau_i \leq \tau_{i+1}$). We do not allow these transitions as it dramatically increases the complexity of a model's Lustre encoding.

A Lustre program implicitly describes a set of admissible traces. Each state σ_n in the sequence represents the value of the variables V in state n. Each time value τ_n represents the value of the time variable t in state n. We use the notation $\sigma_n \models e$, where e is Lustre expression over the variables V and theory constants, if the expression e is satisfied in the state σ_n. Similarly, we use $\sigma_n \not\models e$ when e is not satisfied in the state σ_n. A property p is true (or invariant) in a model if and only if for every admissible trace $\forall n : \sigma_n \models p$. For the purposes of this work, we only consider models that do not admit so-called "Zeno traces" [21]. A trace (σ, τ) is a Zeno trace if and only if $\exists v \forall i : \tau_i < v$, i.e., time never progresses beyond a fixed point.

---

[3] In practice, we allow a timeout to be a negative number to represent infinity. This maintains the correct semantics for the constraint for t in Formula 1.

3   Implementing RSL Patterns

3.1   Formalizing RSL Patterns Semantics

For this work, we chose to target the natural language patterns proposed in the CESAR project because they are representative of many types of natural language requirements [16]. These patterns are divided into a number of categories. The categories of interest for this work are the *functional patterns* and the *timing patterns*. Some examples of the functional patterns are:

1. **Whenever** event **occurs** event **occurs during** interval
2. **Whenever** event **occurs** condition **holds during** interval
3. **When** condition **holds during** interval event **occurs during** interval
4. **Always** condition

Some examples of timing patterns are:

1. Event **occurs each** period [**with jitter** jitter]
2. Event **occurs sporadic with IAT** interarrivaltime [**and jitter** jitter]

Generally speaking, the timing patterns are used to constrain how often a system is required to respond to events. For instance, a component that listens to messages on a shared bus might assume that new messages arrive at most every 50 ms. The second timing pattern listed above would be ideal to express this assumption. In AGREE, this requirement may appear as a system assumption using the pattern shown in Fig. 1.

---

new_message **occurs sporadic with IAT** 50.0

Fig. 1. An instance of a timing pattern to represent how frequently a message arrives on a shared bus.

The functional patterns can be used to describe how the system's state changes in response to external stimuli. Continuing with the previous example, suppose that the bus connected component performs some computation whenever a new message arrives. The functional patterns can be used to describe when a thread is scheduled to process this message and how long the thread takes to complete its computation. The intervals in these patterns have a specified lower and upper bound, and they may be open or closed. The time specified by the lower and upper bound corresponds to the time that progresses since the triggering event occurs. Both the lower and upper bounds must be positive real numbers, and the upper bound must be greater than or equal to the lower bound. An AGREE user may specify the instances of patterns shown in Fig. 2 as properties she would like to prove about this system. For the purposes of demonstration we assume that the thread should take 10 ms to 20 ms to execute.

> **Always** *new_message = thread_start*
> **Whenever** *thread_start* **occurs** *thread_stop* **occurs during** [10.0, 20.0]

Fig. 2. Two instances of a functional patterns used to describe when a thread begins executing, and how long it takes to execute.

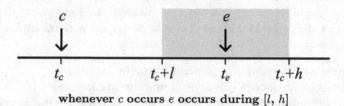

whenever *c* **occurs** *e* **occurs during** [*l, h*]

Fig. 3. A graphical representation for the RSL pattern

Figure 3 shows a graphical representation of the first functional pattern listed at the beginning of this section. The variable t_c represents the time that event c occurs. Similarly, the variable t_e represents the time that event e occurs. The formal semantics for many of the RSL patterns are described in [5]. The semantics for the pattern described in Fig. 3 are represented by the set of admissible traces $\mathcal{L}_{patt}$ described below.

$$\mathcal{L}_{patt} = \{(\sigma, \tau) \mid \forall i \exists j : \sigma_i \models c \Rightarrow (j > i) \wedge (\tau_i + l \le \tau_j \le \tau_i + h) \wedge (\sigma_j \models e)\}$$

The remainder of this section discusses how the pattern in Fig. 3 can be translated into either a Lustre property or a constraint on the admissible traces of a transition system described by Lustre. Although we discuss only this pattern, the techniques that we present can be applied generally to all except one of the functional and timing RSL patterns[4].

3.2 Implementing RSL Patterns as Lustre Properties

One can determine if a transition system described in Lustre admits only traces in $\mathcal{L}_{patt}$ by adding additional constraints over fresh variables (variables that are not already present in the program) to the model. This commonly used technique is referred to as adding an *observer* to the model. These constraints are over fresh variables: $run, timer, rec_c$ and $pass$; they are shown in Fig. 4. The constraints only restrict the values of the fresh variables, therefore they do not restrict the traces admissible by the transition relation.

The intuition behind these constraints is that one can record how much time progresses since an occurrence of c. This time is recorded in the *timer* variable. The value of the timer variable only increases if the previous value of the *run*

---

[4] The single pattern that cannot be implemented requires an independent event to occur for each of an unbounded number of causes. There are 12 functional and timing RSL patterns in total.

---

1. $run = (rec_c \rightarrow ite(pre(run) \wedge e \wedge l \leq timer \leq h,$
   $\qquad\qquad false,$
   $\qquad\qquad ite(rec_c, true, pre(run))))$
2. $timer = (0 \rightarrow ite(pre(run), pre(timer) + (t - pre(t)), 0))$
3. $rec_c \Rightarrow c$
4. $pass = (timer \leq h)$

Fig. 4. The constraints added to a transition relation to verify if only the traces of $\mathcal{L}_{patt}$ are admissible. The transition relation only admits traces of $\mathcal{L}_{patt}$ if and only if the variable *pass* is invariant.

variable is true. The *run* variable is true if an occurrence of c is *recorded* and no occurrence of e happens until after the timer counts to at least l. The variable rec_c non-deterministically records an occurrence of c. If the transition system admits a trace outside of $\mathcal{L}_{patt}$, then the rec_c variable can *choose* to record only an event that violates the conditions of $\mathcal{L}_{patt}$. In this case the *pass* variable will become false in some state.

Theorem 1. *Let $\mathcal{L}_M$ represent the admissible traces of a transition system containing the constraints of Fig. 4. The transition system admits only traces in $\mathcal{L}_{patt}$ if and only if the property pass is invariant. Formally:* $(\mathcal{L}_M \subseteq \mathcal{L}_{patt}) \Leftrightarrow (\forall \sigma, \tau, i : (\sigma, \tau) \in \mathcal{L}_M \Rightarrow \sigma_i \models pass)$

Proof. First we show that if *pass* is invariant for a trace of the transition relation, then that trace is in $\mathcal{L}_{patt}$.

Lemma 1. $(\forall \sigma, \tau, i : (\sigma, \tau) \in \mathcal{L}_M \Rightarrow \sigma_i \models pass) \Rightarrow (\mathcal{L}_M \subseteq \mathcal{L}_{patt})$.

Proof. Towards contradiction, assume $\mathcal{L}_M \nsubseteq \mathcal{L}_{patt}$. Let (σ, τ) be a trace in $\mathcal{L}_M$ but not in $\mathcal{L}_{patt}$. Since $(\sigma, \tau) \notin \mathcal{L}_{patt}$, by definition there exists i such that $\sigma_i \models c$ and

$$\forall j : (j > i) \wedge \tau_i + l \leq \tau_j \leq \tau_i + h \Rightarrow \sigma_j \nvDash e. \qquad (2)$$

Without loss of generality, we can assume that this is the only time when c is recorded. That is, $\sigma_i \models rec_c$ and $\forall k : k \neq i \Rightarrow \sigma_k \nvDash rec_c$. From constraint 1 in Fig. 4 we have

$$\forall j : ((j < i) \Rightarrow \sigma_j \nvDash run) \wedge ((\tau_i \leq \tau_j < \tau_i + l) \Rightarrow \sigma_j \models run)$$

This can actually be strengthened more. From Formula 2 the event e does not occur between $\tau_i + l$ and $\tau_i + h$. So the variable *run* will become invariant after τ_i.

$$\forall j : ((j < i) \Rightarrow \sigma_j \nvDash run) \wedge (\tau_i \leq \tau_j) \Rightarrow \sigma_j \models run)$$

From this and constraint 2 in Fig. 4, we have

$$\forall j : (j \leq i) \Rightarrow \sigma_j \models timer = 0$$

and
$$\forall j : (\tau_i < \tau_j) \Rightarrow (\sigma_j \models timer = (pre(timer) + (\tau_j - \tau_{j-1})))$$

From this and the invariant $\forall i : \tau_{i+1} > \tau_i$, we have

$$\forall j : (\tau_i < \tau_j) \Rightarrow (\sigma_j \models timer > pre(timer))$$

Therefore since the value of timer is zero before τ_i and always increasing after τ_i, and since we only consider non-Zeno traces ($\forall v \exists i : v < \tau_i$), eventually $timer > h$ and so $pass$ becomes false. This contradicts the assumption ($\forall \sigma, \tau, i : (\sigma, \tau) \in \mathcal{L}_M \Rightarrow \sigma_i \models pass$). Therefore $\mathcal{L}_M \subseteq \mathcal{L}_{patt}$. $\square$

Next we show if a trace of $\mathcal{L}_M$ is in $\mathcal{L}_{patt}$, then $pass$ is invariant for this trace.

Lemma 2. $(\mathcal{L}_M \subseteq \mathcal{L}_{patt}) \Rightarrow (\forall \sigma, \tau, i : (\sigma, \tau) \in \mathcal{L}_M \Rightarrow \sigma_i \models pass)$

Proof. Towards contradiction, assume that there exists a trace of $\mathcal{L}_M$ for which $pass$ is not invariant. This means that for some state $\sigma_j \models timer > h$. For this to be true, the timer must be running continuously since it started with some recorded occurrence of c. That is there exists i such that $\sigma_i \models timer = 0$, $\sigma_i \models rec_c$, $\sigma_i \models c$, $\forall k : i \leq k < j \Rightarrow \sigma_k \models run$, and $\tau_j - \tau_i > h$. Thus $\forall k : i \leq k \leq j \Rightarrow \sigma_k \models timer = \tau_k - \tau_i$. By the definition of $\mathcal{L}_{patt}$ we have a k such that $\tau_i + l \leq \tau_k \leq \tau_i + h$ and $\sigma_k \models e$. This means $l \leq \tau_k - \tau_i \leq h$ and so $\sigma_k \models l \leq timer \leq h$. Therefore $\sigma_k \not\models run$. We also have $\tau_k \leq \tau_i + h < \tau_j$ so that $k < j$. Thus from $\forall k : i \leq k < j \Rightarrow \sigma_k \models run$ we have $\sigma_k \models run$ which is a contradiction. Therefore, $pass$ is invariant. $\square$

From Lemmas 1 and 2 we have $(\mathcal{L}_M \subseteq \mathcal{L}_{patt}) \Leftrightarrow (\forall \sigma, \tau, i : (\sigma, \tau) \in \mathcal{L}_M \Rightarrow \sigma_i \models pass)$. $\square$

3.3   Implementing RSL Patterns as Lustre Constraints

As we demonstrated with Fig. 4, one can specify a Lustre property that verifies whether or not some transition system only admits traces of $\mathcal{L}_{patt}$. However, it is surprisingly non-trivial to actually implement a transition system that admits *exactly* the traces of $\mathcal{L}_{patt}$. Naively, one could attempt to add the constraints of Fig. 4 to a transition system and then assert that $pass$ is invariant. However, this transition system will admit all traces where every occurrence of c is never recorded ($\forall \sigma_i : \sigma_i \not\models rec_c$). Clearly some of these traces would not be in $\mathcal{L}_{patt}$.

We conjecture that given the Lustre expression language described in Sect. 2 it is not possible to model a transition system that admits only and all of the traces of $\mathcal{L}_{patt}$. The intuition behind this claim is that Lustre specifications contain a fixed number of state variables, and variables have non-recursive types. Thus a Lustre specification only has a finite amount of memory (though it can, for example, have arbitrary sized integers). If a Lustre specification has n variables we can always consider a trace in $\mathcal{L}_{patt}$ where event c occurs more than n times in a tiny interval. In order for the pattern to hold true, the Lustre specification must constrain itself so that at least one occurrence of e occurs precisely between $t_c + l$ and $t_c + h$ after each event c. This requires "more memory" than the Lustre specification has available.

Rather than model the exact semantics of this pattern, we choose to take a more pragmatic approach. We model a strengthened version of Fig. 3 which does not allow overlapping instances of the pattern. That is, after an event c there can be no more occurrences of c until the corresponding occurrence of e. We do this by proving that c cannot occur frequently enough to cause an overlapping occurrence of the pattern. Then if we constrain the system based on a simple non-overlapping check of the pattern, the resulting system is the same as if we had constrained it using the full pattern. This simple non-overlapping check and the property limiting the frequency of c are both easily expressed in Lustre since they only look back at the most recent occurrence of c. Moreover, they can both be used freely in positive and negative contexts. Formally, the property we prove is $\mathcal{L}_{prop}$ and the constraints we make are $\mathcal{L}_{cons}$:

$$\mathcal{L}_{prop} = \{(\sigma, \tau) \mid \forall i : \sigma_i \models c \Rightarrow \forall j : (j > i) \wedge (\tau_j \leq \tau_i + h) \wedge \sigma_j \models c \Rightarrow$$
$$\exists k \in (i, j] : \tau_i + l \leq \tau_k \wedge \sigma_k \models e\}$$

$$\mathcal{L}_{cons} = \{(\sigma, \tau) \mid \forall i : \sigma_i \models c \Rightarrow \exists j : (j > i) \wedge$$
$$[(\tau_i + l \leq \tau_j \leq \tau_i + h \wedge \sigma_j \models e) \vee (\tau_j \leq \tau_i + h \wedge \sigma_j \models c)]\}$$

The correctness of $\mathcal{L}_{prop}$ and $\mathcal{L}_{cons}$ are captured by the following theorem.

Theorem 2. *Let M be a transition system and $\mathcal{L}_M$ its corresponding set of admissible traces. Suppose $\mathcal{L}_M \subseteq \mathcal{L}_{prop}$. Then $\mathcal{L}_{cons}$ and $\mathcal{L}_{patt}$ are equivalent restrictions on $\mathcal{L}_M$, that is $\mathcal{L}_M \cap \mathcal{L}_{cons} = \mathcal{L}_M \cap \mathcal{L}_{patt}$.*

Proof. We prove the theorem by showing that the subset relationship between $\mathcal{L}_M \cap \mathcal{L}_{cons}$ and $\mathcal{L}_M \cap \mathcal{L}_{patt}$ holds in both directions.

Lemma 3. $\mathcal{L}_M \cap \mathcal{L}_{patt} \subseteq \mathcal{L}_M \cap \mathcal{L}_{cons}$

Proof. From the definitions of $\mathcal{L}_{patt}$ and $\mathcal{L}_{cons}$ it follows directly that $\mathcal{L}_{patt} \subseteq \mathcal{L}_{cons}$. Therefore $\mathcal{L}_M \cap \mathcal{L}_{patt} \subseteq \mathcal{L}_M \cap \mathcal{L}_{cons}$. □

Lemma 4. *Suppose $\mathcal{L}_M \subseteq \mathcal{L}_{prop}$, then $\mathcal{L}_M \cap \mathcal{L}_{cons} \subseteq \mathcal{L}_M \cap \mathcal{L}_{patt}$*

Proof. Suppose towards contradiction that $\mathcal{L}_M \cap \mathcal{L}_{cons} \nsubseteq \mathcal{L}_M \cap \mathcal{L}_{patt}$. Consider a trace $(\sigma, \tau) \in \mathcal{L}_M \cap \mathcal{L}_{cons}$ with $(\sigma, \tau) \notin \mathcal{L}_M \cap \mathcal{L}_{patt}$. Then we have $(\sigma, \tau) \in \mathcal{L}_{cons}$, $(\sigma, \tau) \in \mathcal{L}_{prop}$, and $(\sigma, \tau) \notin \mathcal{L}_{patt}$. From the definition of $\mathcal{L}_{patt}$ we have an i such that $\sigma_i \models c$ and

$$\forall j : (j > i) \wedge (\tau_i + l \leq \tau_j \leq \tau_i + h) \Rightarrow \sigma_j \nvDash e. \tag{3}$$

Then from the definition of $\mathcal{L}_{cons}$ with $\sigma_i \models c$ we have a j such that $j > i$ and either $(\tau_i + l \leq \tau_j \leq \tau_i + h \wedge \sigma_j \models e)$ or $(\tau_j \leq \tau_i + h \wedge \sigma_j \models c)$. The former option directly contradicts Formula 3; so we must have $\tau_j \leq \tau_i + h$ and $\sigma_j \models c$. From the definition of $\mathcal{L}_{prop}$ with $\sigma_i \models c$ and our j, we have a k in $(i, j]$ such that $\tau_i + l \leq \tau_k$ and $\sigma_k \models e$. From $k \leq j$ we have $\tau_k \leq \tau_j$ and thus $\tau_i + l \leq \tau_k \leq \tau_i + h$. Instantiating Formula 3 with k yields $\sigma_k \nvDash e$, a contradiction. Therefore $\mathcal{L}_M \cap \mathcal{L}_{cons} \subseteq \mathcal{L}_M \cap \mathcal{L}_{patt}$. □

From Lemmas 3 and 4 have $\mathcal{L}_M \cap \mathcal{L}_{cons} = \mathcal{L}_M \cap \mathcal{L}_{patt}$.   □

Example 1. Suppose we want to model a system of components communicating on a shared bus. The transition relation for this system must contain constraints that dictate when threads can start and stop and how frequently new messages may arrive. First we constrain the event *new_message* from occurring too frequently according to the pattern instance in Fig. 1. Let $\mathcal{L}_{nm}$ represent the set of admissible traces for this pattern. This set is defined explicitly in Formula 1.

$$\mathcal{L}_{nm} = \{(\sigma, \tau) \mid \forall i : \sigma_i \models new\_message \Rightarrow$$
$$\neg[\exists j : (j > i) \wedge (\tau_j < \tau_i + 50) \wedge (\sigma_j \models new\_message)]\}$$

Suppose we wish to constrain the system to the pattern instances in Fig. 2. The first pattern instance is represented by the set $\mathcal{L}_{start}$ and the second by $\mathcal{L}_{stop}$:

$$\mathcal{L}_{start} = \{(\sigma, \tau) \mid \forall i : \sigma_i \models new\_message \Rightarrow \sigma_i \models thread\_start\}$$

$$\mathcal{L}_{stop} = \{(\sigma, \tau) \mid \forall i \exists j : \sigma_i \models thread\_start \Rightarrow$$
$$(j > i) \wedge (\tau_i + l \leq \tau_j \leq \tau_i + h) \wedge (\sigma_j \models thread\_stop)\}$$

Let $\mathcal{L}_M$ denote the admissible traces of the transition system that is being modeled. The goal is to specify the transition system in Lustre such that $\mathcal{L}_M = \mathcal{L}_{nm} \cap \mathcal{L}_{start} \cap \mathcal{L}_{stop}$. Writing a Lustre constraint to represent the set of traces $\mathcal{L}_{start}$ is trivial. The traces that are contained in $\mathcal{L}_{start}$ are those whose states all satisfy the expression *new_message = thread_stop*. However, as we noted earlier, it is not possible to develop a set of Lustre constraints that admit only (and all of) the traces of $\mathcal{L}_{stop}$.

Note that the second pattern in Fig. 2 is an instance of the pattern described in Fig. 3. Therefore we can split the set $\mathcal{L}_{stop}$ into two sets, $\mathcal{L}_{stopc}$ and $\mathcal{L}_{stopp}$:

$$\mathcal{L}_{stopc} = \{(\sigma, \tau) \mid \forall i : \sigma_i \models thread\_start \Rightarrow \exists j : (j > i) \wedge$$
$$[(\tau_i + l \leq \tau_j \leq \tau_i + h \wedge \sigma_j \models thread\_stop) \vee$$
$$(\tau_j \leq \tau_i + h \wedge \sigma_j \models thread\_start)]\}$$

$$\mathcal{L}_{stopp} = \{(\sigma, \tau) \mid \forall i : \sigma_i \models thread\_start \Rightarrow \forall j : (j > i) \wedge$$
$$(\tau_j \leq \tau_i + h) \wedge \sigma_j \models thread\_start \Rightarrow$$
$$\exists k \in (i, j] : \tau_i + l \leq \tau_k \wedge \sigma_k \models thread\_stop\}$$

In this example, the sets of admissible traces representing the patterns happen to have the following relationship:

$$\mathcal{L}_{nm} \cap \mathcal{L}_{start} \subseteq \mathcal{L}_{stopp} \tag{4}$$

This is because for every trace in $\mathcal{L}_{nm}$ the event *new_message* only occurs at most every 50 ms. Likewise, for each state of every trace of $\mathcal{L}_{start}$ the variable *thread_start* is true if and only if *new_message* is true. Finally, the set $\mathcal{L}_{stopp}$ contains every trace where *thread_start* occurs at most every 20 ms. From Formula 4 and Theorem 2 we have $\mathcal{L}_{nm} \cap \mathcal{L}_{start} \cap \mathcal{L}_{stopc} = \mathcal{L}_{nm} \cap \mathcal{L}_{start} \cap \mathcal{L}_{stop}$. Thus the system $\mathcal{L}_{nm} \cap \mathcal{L}_{start} \cap \mathcal{L}_{stopc}$, which we can model in Lustre, is equivalent to a system constrained by the pattern instances in Figs. 1 and 2.

Example 1 is meant to demonstrate that, in practical systems, there is usually some constraint on how frequently events outside the system may occur. Systems described by the functional RSL patterns generally have some limitations on how many events they can respond to within a finite amount of time. The Lustre implementations of $\mathcal{L}_{cons}$ and $\mathcal{L}_{prop}$ are simpler than Fig. 4, and their proof of correctness is also simpler then Theorem 1, though we omit both due to space limitations.

4   Application

We implemented a number of RSL patterns into the AGREE tool. These patterns were used to reason about the behavior of a real-world avionics system. Specifically, the patterns were used to model the logic and scheduling constraints of threads running on a real-time operating system on an embedded computer on an air vehicle. Each thread in the system has a single entry point that is dispatched by some sort of event. The event may be the arrival of data from a bus or a signal from another thread. When a thread receives an event, the current state of the thread's inputs are latched. Each thread runs at the same priority as every other thread (no thread may preempt any other thread). A thread begins executing after it receives an event and no other thread is executing.

The patterns in Figs. 1 and 2 are actually fairly representative of the constraints used in this model. Figure 5 shows some of the RSL patterns that were used to describe these scheduling constraints. We added an additional tag "exclusively" before the second event in the patterns to indicate that the second event occurs only in the specified interval after the first pattern (and never any other time). We found that this was a useful shorthand because one often wants to specify a signal that only occurs under a specified condition and not at any other time.

---

assert *"thread A runtime"* : **whenever** *thread_A_start_running* **occurs**
    thread_A_finish **exclusively occurs during** [10.0, 50.0];

assert *"thread B runtime"* : **whenever** *thread_B_start_running* **occurs**
    thread_B_finish **exclusively occurs during** [10.0, 50.0];

assert *"thread C runtime"* : **whenever** *thread_C_start_running* **occurs**
    thread_C_finish **exclusively occurs during** [10.0, 50.0];

Fig. 5. Assertions about the how the operating system schedules threads

The results that each thread produces after it finishes executing are described by an assume-guarantee contract. Generally speaking, the assumptions restrict the values of inputs that the thread expects to see. Likewise, the thread's guarantees constrain the values of the thread's outputs based on it's current state and input values. The AADL component that contains the threads has assumptions about how frequently it receives inputs and has guarantees about how quickly it produces outputs. These assumptions are translated to constraints in the Lustre transition system, and the guarantees are translated to properties. Figure 6 illustrates one of these assumptions and guarantees.

The "eq" statements in Fig. 6 are used to constrain a variable to an expression. They are usually used as a convenient short hand to make AGREE contracts easier to read. In this case, the first "eq" statement is used to set the variable *change_status_request* to true if and only if a new message has arrived and the content of the message is requesting that the vehicle change its status. Likewise, the second statement is used to record the last requested change value into the *change_request* variable. The contract assumes that this new message arrives periodically (with some jitter). The contract guarantees that if a new message arrives requesting that the vehicle change its status, then the vehicle's status will be set to the requested value within 500 ms. In this application we assumed that all time units are expressed in microseconds. This means that the timing constraints expressed in Fig. 5 are also expressed in microseconds. Other constraints are used to assert that the *vehicle_status* variable corresponds to one of the state variables in the component's threads.

```
eq change_status_event : bool =
    new_message and message_content.change_vehicle_status;

eq change_request : bool =
    ite(change_status_event,
        message_content.status,
        false → pre(change_request));

assume "periodic messages" : new_message occurs
    each 10000.0 with jitter 50.0;

guarantee "new message can change vehicle status" :
    whenever change_status_event occurs
        vehicle_status = change_request during [0.0, 500.0];
```

Fig. 6. Assumptions and guarantees about the component containing the threads.

The guarantee of this component is invariant if and only if the threads in the component's implementation are scheduled in such a way that whenever a new message arrives its content is parsed and sent to the correct threads to be processed in a timely manner. The logic expressed in the contract of each thread determines how the content of this message is transmitted to other threads in the system.

4.1   Results

We had three properties of interest for the vehicle. These properties were related to timing, schedulability, and behavior of the system's threads. We ran the translated Lustre file, which contained about 1000 lines, from the AADL/AGREE model on the latest version of JKind on a Linux machine with an Intel(R) Xeon(R) E5-1650 CPU running at 3.50 GHz. JKind uses k-induction, property directed reachability, and invariant generation engines to prove properties of Lustre models. In the case of this experiment, it took about 8 h to prove all three properties. One of the properties was proved via k-induction, the other two were proved by the property directed reachability engine.

JKind allows users to export the lemmas used to prove a property. These lemmas can be exported and used again in order to speed up solving for similar models and properties. We found that when these lemmas were used again to prove the properties a second time all of the properties were proved in less than 10 s. This seems to indicate that the properties are not particularly *deep*. That is to say, to prove the properties via k-induction, the inductive step does not need to unroll over many steps. We are currently exploring techniques for lemma discovery for properties specified with RSL patterns.

5   Related Work

Our work focuses on the real-time patterns in the Requirements Specification Language (RSL) [5] that was created as part of the CESAR project [16]. This language was an extension and modularization of the Contract Specification Language (CSL) [22]. The goal of both of these projects was to provide contract-based reasoning for complex embedded systems. We chose this as our initial pattern language because of the similarity in the contract reasoning approach used by our AGREE tool suite [14].

There is considerable work on real-time specification patterns for different temporal logics. Konrad and Cheng [2] provide the first systematic study of real-time specification patterns, adapting and extending the patterns of Dwyer [1] for three different temporal logics: TCTL [7], MTL [8], and RTGIL [9]. Independently, Gruhn [3] constructed a real-time pattern language derived from Dwyer, presenting the patterns as observers in timed automata. In Konrad and Cheng, multiple (and overlapping) occurrences of patterns are defined in a trace, whereas in Gruhn, only the first occurrence of the pattern considered. This choice side-steps the question of adequacy for overlapping triggering events (as discussed in Sect. 3), but limits the expressiveness of the specification. We use a weaker specification language than Konrad [2] which allows better scaling to our analysis, but we also consider multiple occurrences of patterns, unlike Gruhn [3]. Bellini [4] creates a classification scheme for both Gruhn's and Konrad's patterns and provides a rich temporal language called TILCO-X that allows more straightforward expression of many of the real-time patterns. Like [2], this work considers multiple overlapping occurrences of trigger events.

The closest work to ours is probably that of Abid et al. [10], who encode a subset of the CSL patterns as observers in a timed extension of Petri nets called TTS, and supplement the observers with properties that involve both safety and liveness in LTL. For most of the RSL patterns considered, the patterns are only required to hold for the first triggering event, rather than globally across the input trace. In addition, the use of full LTL makes the analysis more difficult with inductive model checkers. Other recent work [6] considers very expressive real-time contracts with quantification for systems of systems. This quantification makes the language expressive, but difficult to analyze.

Other researchers including Pike [23] and Sorea [24] have explored the idea of restricting traces to disallow overlapping events in order to reason about real-time systems using safety properties. The authors of [25] independently developed a similar technique of using a *trigger* variable to specify real-time properties that quantify over events.

6   Conclusion

We have presented a method for translating RSL patterns into Lustre observers. While we only specifically discussed a single pattern in detail, the techniques we presented can be applied analogously to other functional or timing patterns. Similarly, the techniques we presented can be applied to other synchronous data flow languages. The RSL patterns have been incorporated into the AGREE plugin for the OSATE AADL integrated development environment. We used these patterns to show that we could successfully model, and prove properties about, scheduling constraints for a real-world avionics application. Future work will focus on lemma generation to improve scalability for reasoning about real-time properties.

References

1. Dwyer, M.B., Avrunin, G.S., Corbett, J.C.: Patterns in property specifications for finite-state verification. In: ICSE, pp. 411–420. IEEE (1999)
2. Konrad, S., Cheng, B.H.: Real-time specification patterns. In: Proceedings of the 27th International Conference on Software Engineering, pp. 372–381. ACM (2005)
3. Gruhn, V., Laue, R.: Patterns for timed property specifications. Electron. Notes Theoret. Comput. Sci. **153**, 117–133 (2006)
4. Bellini, P., Nesi, P., Rogai, D.: Expressing and organizing real-time specification patterns via temporal logics. J. Syst. Softw. **82**, 183–196 (2009)
5. Reinkemeier, P., Stierand, I., Rehkop, P., Henkler, S.: A pattern-based require-ment specification language: mapping automotive specific timing requirements. In: Fachtagung des GI-Fachbereichs Softwaretechnik, pp. 99–108 (2011)
6. Etzien, C., Gezgin, T., Froschle, S., Henkler, S., Rettberg, A.: Contracts for evolv-ing systems. In: ISORC, pp. 1–8 (2013)
7. Alur, R.: Techniques for automatic verification of real-time systems. Ph.D. thesis, stanford university (1991)

8. Koymans, R.: Specifying real-time properties with metric temporal logic. Real-time Syst. **2**, 255–299 (1990)
9. Moser, L.E., Ramakrishna, Y., Kutty, G., Melliar-Smith, P.M., Dillon, L.K.: A graphical environment for the design of concurrent real-time systems. ACM Trans. Softw. Eng. Methodol. (TOSEM) **6**, 31–79 (1997)
10. Abid, N., Dal Zilio, S., Le Botlan, D.: Real-time specification patterns and tools. In: Stoelinga, M., Pinger, R. (eds.) FMICS 2012. LNCS, vol. 7437, pp. 1–15. Springer, Heidelberg (2012)
11. Halbwachs, N., Caspi, P., Raymond, P., Pilaud, D.: The synchronous dataflow programming language LUSTRE. Proc. IEEE **79**, 1305–1320 (1991)
12. Backes, J., Cofer, D., Miller, S., Whalen, M.W.: Requirements analysis of a quad-redundant flight control system. In: Havelund, K., Holzmann, G., Joshi, R. (eds.) NFM 2015. LNCS, vol. 9058, pp. 82–96. Springer, Heidelberg (2015)
13. Murugesan, A., Heimdahl, M.P., Whalen, M.W., Rayadurgam, S., Komp, J., Duan, L., Kim, B.G., Sokolsky, O., Lee, I.: From requirements to code: model based development of a medical cyber physical system. SEHC (2014)
14. Cofer, D., Gacek, A., Miller, S., Whalen, M.W., LaValley, B., Sha, L.: Compositional verification of architectural models. In: Goodloe, A.E., Person, S. (eds.) NFM 2012. LNCS, vol. 7226, pp. 126–140. Springer, Heidelberg (2012)
15. Feiler, P.H., Gluch, D.P.: Model-Based Engineering with AADL: An Introduction to the SAE Architecture Analysis & Design Language, 1st edn. Addison-Wesley Professional, Reading (2012)
16. CESAR: The CESAR project (2010). http://www.cesarproject.eu/
17. Dutertre, B., Sorea, M.: Timed systems in SAL. Technical report, SRI International (2004)
18. Pike, L.: Real-time system verification by k-induction. Technical report, NASA (2005)
19. Gao, J., Whalen, M., Van Wyk, E.: Extending lustre with timeout automata. In: SLA++P (2007)
20. Gacek, A., Backes, J., Whalen, M.W., Cofer, D.: AGREE Users Guide (2014). http://github.com/smaccm/smaccm
21. Gómez, R., Bowman, H.: Efficient detection of zeno runs in timed automata. In: Raskin, J.-F., Thiagarajan, P.S. (eds.) FORMATS 2007. LNCS, vol. 4763, pp. 195–210. Springer, Heidelberg (2007)
22. Gafni, V., Benveniste, A., Caillaud, B., Graf, S., Josko, B.: Contract specification language (CSL). Technical report, SPEEDS Deliverable D.2.5.4 (2008)
23. Pike, L.: Modeling time-triggered protocols and verifying their real-time schedules. In: Formal Methods in Computer-Aided Design, pp. 231–238 (2007)
24. Sorea, M., Dutertre, B., Steiner, W.: Modeling and verification of time-triggered communication protocols. In: 2008 11th IEEE International Symposium on Object Oriented Real-Time Distributed Computing (ISORC), pp. 422–428. IEEE (2008)
25. Li, W., Grard, L., Shankar, N.: Design and verification of multi-rate distributed systems. In: 2015 ACM/IEEE International Conference on Formal Methods and Models for Codesign (MEMOCODE), pp. 20–29 (2015)

Contract-Based Verification of Complex Time-Dependent Behaviors in Avionic Systems

Devesh Bhatt[1], Arunabh Chattopadhyay[1], Wenchao Li[2], David Oglesby[1(✉)],
Sam Owre[2], and Natarajan Shankar[2]

[1] Honeywell Aerospace Labs, Golden Valley, USA
david.oglesby@honeywell.com
[2] SRI International, Silicon Valley, USA

Abstract. Avionic systems involve complex time-dependent behaviors across interacting components. This paper presents a contract-based approach for formally verifying these behaviors in a compositional manner. A unique feature of our contract-based tool is the support of architectural specification for multi-rate platforms. An abstraction technique has also been developed for properties related to variable time bounds. Preliminary results on applying this approach to the verification of an aircraft cabin pressure control system are promising.

Recent years have seen a large growth in the size and complexity of avionics systems due to increasing system functionality and closer integration among existing and new aircraft subsystems. Verifying the safety of these systems and their compliance with their intended functional requirements is a critical certification objective that is becoming prohibitively expensive due to this increasing complexity. Compositional verification approaches [1,2] manage the verification complexity by decomposing requirements into component-level contracts and applying assume-guarantee reasoning. Contract-based tools such as AGREE [3] and OCRA [2] have been used in recent effort to formally verify control modules in avionic systems. Most existing work has focused primarily on verifying safety properties, e.g., the system must not exhibit behaviors that can result in a catastrophic failure. Using such techniques to verify complex behavioral requirements of a system in a distributed setting, however, has not received much attention. In many avionics application domains such as flight controls, cockpit displays, flight management, and environment control systems, a variety of complex time-dependent behaviors are present that can cut across several components. Verifying such behaviors for compliance to the intended functional requirements is essential and has been traditionally accomplished using testing techniques that can be expensive but still not exhaustive in revealing the presence of errors. There is a strong need for a verification approach that can enable scalable use of formal verification (e.g., model checking) tools for complex time-bounded properties and the composition of such properties over components in

This research was supported in part by NASA Contract NNA13AC55C and DARPA under agreement number FA8750-16-C-0043.

© The Author(s) 2016
S. Rayadurgam and O. Tkachuk (Eds.): NFM 2016, LNCS 9690, pp. 34–40, 2016.
DOI: 10.1007/978-3-319-40648-0_3

a distributed environment. This short paper presents a compositional approach of verifying such systems involving complex time-dependent behaviors.

1 Case Study Example

The motivating case study for this work comes from aircraft cabin pressure and environment control system applications. In a typical mechanical system with sensors and actuators, it is necessary to perform calibration, initialization, or other built-in-tests on these components (e.g., a pressure sensor) only at certain specific times in successive aircraft takeoff and landing cycles. The specific signal to invoke this activity is called finalize_event in this example, and it is triggered after the aircraft door is open for a minimum amount of time. Figure 1 shows the components involved in triggering this event. The Timing Computation module computes the amount of time the door should be open before the finalize_event is triggered as a function of altitude reached during flight. The Mode Transition Logic controls the changes in aircraft modes, for example LANDING (L) to GROUND (G). The Mode Detect Logic module evaluates sensor values to determine the current aircraft state, for example, if the aircraft is on the ground or climbing. The mode, state, and timing all inform the decision when to finalize the aircraft. This example illustrates an end-to-end subsystem from sensors to actuator, even though it is only a small part of an environmental control system. Depending on the architectural platform, components in this subsystem may be physically distributed across the aircraft. For instance, each component executes periodically (with different rates) and communicates with one another over a shared bus.

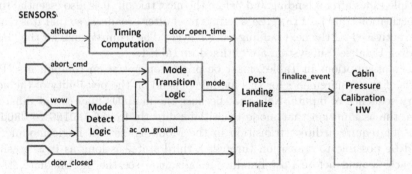

Fig. 1. Case study example – diagram of interacting component subsystems

The finalize_event signal is activated by several events and aircraft states occurring in a particular temporal sequence shown in the Simulink diagram of Fig. 2. The door may open any time after landing, and once it has been open continuously for door_open_time, the finalize_event is broadcast.

Additionally, the activation must occur only once in a landing-to-takeoff cycle even through certain states of aircraft (e.g., door opening or closing) may change

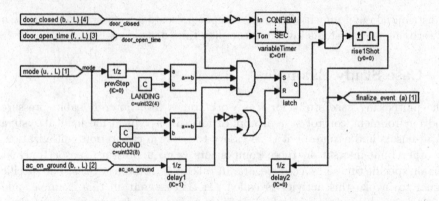

Fig. 2. Diagram of "Post Landing Finalize" subsystem

Table 1. Requirements for the "Post Landing Finalize" subsystem

Requirement 1	A finalize event will be broadcast after the aircraft door has been open continuously for `door_open_time` seconds while the aircraft is on the ground after a successful landing.
Requirement 2	A finalize event is broadcast only once while the aircraft is on the ground.
Requirement 3	The finalize event will not occur during flight.
Requirement 4	The finalize event will not be enabled while the aircraft door is closed.

multiple times after a landing and before the next takeoff. It is also essential that the activation state for `finalize_event` is reset after broadcast so that it is ready to be activated for the next landing-takeoff cycle. The requirements for the "Post Landing Finalize" subsystem are outlined in Table 1.

The assumptions in Table 2 must be proven on upstream components. The proofs of the requirements for this module depend on the possibility of the necessary sequence of inputs. Note that because the modules may run at different rates, the assumption that mode transitions directly from LANDING to GROUND does not require a direct transition in the Mode Transition Logic module. It could be possible to transition through a third state, as long as it is possible to reach Ground before Post Landing Finalize can see the intermediate state. The translation of assumptions to requirements on upstream components must take into account different rates of execution. Assumption 3 is not specific about the definition of "aircraft is on the ground." This would likely be formalized as `altitude` is within some tolerance of zero since that is the only signal into the Timing Computation module on which the proof of this assumption will fall. Assumption 4 is more of an assertion that the door will not be open during flight. As an user-driven input signal, this cannot be proven using upstream modules; but it does assure Requirement 3.

Table 2. Assumption for the "Post Landing Finalize" subsystem

Assumption 1	ac_on_ground can be true before the mode transitions to GROUND.
Assumption 2	The mode can transition directly from LANDING to GROUND as observed by "Post Landing Finalize."
Assumption 3	door_open_time does not change while the aircraft is on the ground.
Assumption 4	door_closed must be true if ac_on_ground is false.

2   Verification Techniques and Tools

2.1   Translation of Simulink Models and Contract Language

The integration of Simulink into a high-assurance design flow can bring significant benefits especially for safety-critical applications. Our tool Sim2SAL automates the generation of formal models by translating Simulink designs into transition systems in SAL. A unique feature in our tool is the support for real-time multi-rate systems. Sim2SAL allows the specification of the multi-rate architecture as annotations attached to Simulink subsystems. An example annotation is shown below that describes the timing characteristics of a periodically executing subsystem.

```
arch_begin
period: 5 ms;       /* the subsystem executes every 5 ms */
jitter: 0.1 ms;     /* max jitter of the clock is 0.1 ms */
latency[1]: 1 ms; /* max latency at input port 1 is 1 ms */
init[1]: 0;         /* initial value at input port 1 is 0 */
arch_end
```

The formal model of computation for these systems is given in [4]. Several abstractions of multi-rate systems are also possible and handled automatically, including zero communication delays and zero jitters. In this paper, we present the use of Sim2SAL in verifying the properties of the case study example in the discrete-time setting. In reality, the system is implemented on a distributed architecture with periodic components. Hence, the multi-rate model is more faithful to the actual implementation. In such a setting, conventional assume-guarantee methods are insufficient since they were developed for discrete transition systems. We explore compositional techniques for verifying these models in future work.

In short, the contract language of Sim2SAL consists of two parts – behavioral specification and architectural specification. Similar to OCRA [2], the behavioral part is based on Linear Temporal Logic (LTL) [5] over assume-guarantee pairs. In addition to the typical syntax of LTL, additional constructs are provided for simplifying expressions that involve large step sizes. For instance, we use $\mathbf{G}\_[0, 50]$ f to specify that the formula f has to hold true during the next 50 time steps including the current one. Certain real-time properties can also be specified at the system level. For example, an end-to-end property may require that a request will always be serviced by a response within some t time units, where $t \in \mathbb{R}$. Sim2SAL uses additional timer constructs and translates these properties to an equivalent LTL formula involving these timers. We refer interested readers to [4] for details of this technique. Currently, Sim2SAL can handle a subset of Simulink's discrete blocks. Sim2SAL takes the Simulink model (.mdl file) and the contract annotations as input and generates an encoding of the model and properties in SAL.

2.2   Abstraction Pattern for Variable Time Bounds

Dwyer et al. have created a Specification and Pattern System [6] for defining various types of behaviors. Tool chains have been prototyped [7] to facilitate the capture of requirements using such patterns such as minimum duration, bounded response etc. For example, the *minimum duration* pattern specifies the minimum amount of time a formula must hold once it becomes true. There are, however, practical considerations of model-checking complexity; a large time bound can translate into a large number of discrete steps to be explored, resulting in exponential growth of the search space. Another consideration in many systems is that variable time bounds are provided to a component that are dynamically computed by another component.

For example, for the "Post Landing Finalize" component, Requirement 1 in Table 1 specifies a timed response where the value of door_open_time for the response is dynamically computed by "Timing Calculation" component. The Simulink model of this component (Fig. 2) contains a block named variableTimer that receives a variable external input door_open_time. Due to the dynamic value of time, one cannot express the LTL property for this requirement as a fixed duration response. Furthermore, a proof of the requirement's property for a fixed value of time will not be valid when the value of time can be different in the dynamical system.

A Timer Abstraction Pattern. Our approach is to create a *timer abstraction pattern* to construct and verify properties related to variable time bounds in a compositional manner. Consider the changes to the states and signals in the model of Fig. 2, as the behavior for Requirement 1 is realized. Initially the state of the finalize_event is false when the aircraft is landing: the door_closed input is true and ac_on_ground is true before mode changes from LANDING to GROUND. When the door_closed input is false (the door is open), the variableTimer block starts counting. Note that the relevant state variables do not change in the time steps when the timer is just counting up. This establishes a bound on the minimum number of steps to which the timer behavior can be collapsed while still preserving the properties. Such an abstraction is useful in making the verification problem tractable for the compositional verification of interacting components with variable time bounds. For example, we can prove the properties on the "Post Landing Finalize" component using a small time bound, t_{min}, and specify that as an assumption for this component. We can then independently prove this assumption, using a static analysis tool, as a guarantee provided by the "Timing Calculation" component that it will always produce a value of door_open_time $\geq t_{min}$. This allows the application of different types of model checking and static analysis tools for proving properties for different components.

Computation of Minimum Time-Steps Bound for the Timer Abstraction. We briefly describe the algorithm to compute the minimum number of time steps $tsteps_{min}$ required to explore all possible input to output behaviors in the model while the timer (e.g., `variableTimer`) is counting. We start by noting that all states in the Simulink model of interest are expressed by `unit delay` blocks: a unit delay block stores the last value of its input and outputs that stored value in the current step (higher-level blocks such as `latch` and `rise1Shot` use `unit delay` blocks to hold a state variable). If a path from an input to an output contains a unit delay in series (e.g., block `prevStep`) then that adds 1 step to $tsteps_{min}$ since with 1 additional step one can produce a value at the output of the unit delay that is possible to be created at its input. A Boolean unit delay in a feedback loop (e.g., `delay2`) also adds 1 to $tsteps_{min}$, since the feedback of a Boolean variable creates a repeating sequence the second time around the loop. Feedback loops that create an accumulator using a numeric variable can exhibit a long non-repeating sequence of values and such models are excluded from our analysis. Our observations across avionics systems show that most instances of timer patterns do not have other accumulators in the same subgraph as the timer. The algorithm is simply to enumerate all unique paths from models inputs to relevant outputs, count the number of unit delays (including feedback) in each path, then compute $tsteps_{min}$ as the largest count across all paths. This algorithm provides a conservative bound on $tsteps_{min}$. A precise smaller bound can be derived by considering constraints on the variables used in the property. Such a computation, however, complicates the analysis algorithm while yielding little practical benefit.

3   Preliminary Results and Future Work

The LTL specifications of the properties from Sect. 1 are listed in Table 3. We have introduced two auxiliary variables. We use `latch` so we need not repeat the entire landing condition in both Property 1.2 and 1.3; it also allows arbitrary time between landing and the opening of the door. With the `timer_count` variable we can capture the properties without nested temporal operators.

Table 3. Formal requirements for "Post Landing Finalize" in LTL

Requirement 1	**Property 1.1**	$\mathbf{G} \begin{pmatrix} \texttt{ac\_on\_ground} \wedge \texttt{mode} = \texttt{L} \wedge \texttt{door\_closed} \wedge \\ \mathbf{X}(\texttt{mode} = \texttt{G} \wedge \texttt{door\_closed} \wedge \texttt{ac\_on\_ground}) \\ \Rightarrow \mathbf{X}(\texttt{latch}) \end{pmatrix}$
	Property 1.2	$\mathbf{G}(\neg\texttt{finalize\_event} \Rightarrow \texttt{timer\_count} \leq 4 \vee \neg\texttt{latch})$
	Property 1.3	$\mathbf{G} \begin{pmatrix} \texttt{timer\_count} \geq 4 \wedge \neg\texttt{door\_closed} \wedge \texttt{latch} \\ \Rightarrow \texttt{finalize\_event} \end{pmatrix}$
Requirement 2	**Property 2.1**	$\mathbf{G} \begin{pmatrix} \texttt{finalize\_event} \Rightarrow \mathbf{X}(\mathbf{G}(\neg\texttt{finalize\_event} \vee \\ (\texttt{latch} \wedge \texttt{timer\_count} \geq 4 \wedge \neg\texttt{door\_closed}))) \end{pmatrix}$
Requirement 3	**Property 4.1**	$\mathbf{G}(\texttt{door\_closed} \Rightarrow \mathbf{X}(\neg\texttt{finalize\_event}))$
Requirement 4		

In this case, `timer_count` $= x$ is equivalent to $\mathbf{G}\_[0, x]$ ($\neg$`door_closed`) because `timer_count` counts the time the door is open, and resets to 0 when the door is closed. For these properties, we used the minimum bound analysis in Sect. 2.2 to show that four time-steps are sufficient to prove any property in the model. All properties were proven in SAL using k-induction.

The assumptions in Sect. 1 implicitly underlie these proofs. As model inputs, `mode`, `ac_on_ground`, and `door_closed` are not constrained in successive values or interaction. The fact that the `finalize_event` follows the appropriate input sequence does not indicate that sequence is possible. We are working to automate the translation of those assumptions into guarantees that can be proven on the upstream components. Other future work includes feeding the computed minimum time bound directly to `Sim2SAL` to generate the timer abstraction and translate the properties to utilize the new bound, and compositional techniques for multi-rate systems.

Open Access. This chapter is distributed under the terms of the Creative Commons Attribution 4.0 International License (http://creativecommons.org/licenses/by/4.0/), which permits use, duplication, adaptation, distribution and reproduction in any medium or format, as long as you give appropriate credit to the original author(s) and the source, a link is provided to the Creative Commons license and any changes made are indicated.

The images or other third party material in this chapter are included in the work's Creative Commons license, unless indicated otherwise in the credit line; if such material is not included in the work's Creative Commons license and the respective action is not permitted by statutory regulation, users will need to obtain permission from the license holder to duplicate, adapt or reproduce the material.

References

1. Brat, G., Bushnell, D., Davies, M., Giannakopoulou, D., Howar, F., Kahsai, T.: Verifying the safety of a flight-critical system. In: Bjørner, N., de Boer, F. (eds.) FM 2015. LNCS, vol. 9109, pp. 308–324. Springer, Heidelberg (2015)
2. Bozzano, M., Cimatti, A., Fernandes Pires, A., Jones, D., Kimberly, G., Petri, T., Robinson, R., Tonetta, S.: Formal design and safety analysis of AIR6110 wheel brake system. In: Kroening, D., Păsăreanu, C.S. (eds.) CAV 2015. LNCS, vol. 9206, pp. 518–535. Springer, Heidelberg (2015)
3. Backes, J., Cofer, D., Miller, S., Whalen, M.W.: Requirements analysis of a quad-redundant flight control system. In: Havelund, K., Holzmann, G., Joshi, R. (eds.) NFM 2015. LNCS, vol. 9058, pp. 82–96. Springer, Heidelberg (2015)
4. Li, W., Gerard, L., Shankar, N.: Design and verification for multi-rate distributed systems. In: ACM/IEEE International Conference on Formal Methods and Models for Codesign, September 2015
5. Manna, Z., Pnueli, A.: The Temporal Logic of Reactive and Concurrent Systems (1992)
6. Dwyer, M.B., Avrunin, G.S., Corbett, J.C.: Patterns in property specifications for finite-state verification. In: Proceedings of the 21st International Conference on Software Engineering, ICSE 1999, New York, NY, USA, pp. 411–420. ACM (1999)
7. Barnat, J., Beran, J., Brim, L., Kratochvíla, T., Ročkai, P.: Tool chain to support automated formal verification of avionics simulink designs. In: Stoelinga, M., Pinger, R. (eds.) FMICS 2012. LNCS, vol. 7437, pp. 78–92. Springer, Heidelberg (2012)

ARSENAL: Automatic Requirements Specification Extraction from Natural Language

Shalini Ghosh[1]([✉]), Daniel Elenius[1], Wenchao Li[1], Patrick Lincoln[1], Natarajan Shankar[1], and Wilfried Steiner[2]

[1] CSL, SRI International, Menlo Park, USA
{shalini,elenius,li,lincoln,shankar}@csl.sri.com
[2] TTTech C. AG, Chip IP Design, Graz, Austria
wilfried.steiner@tttech.com

Abstract. Requirements are informal and semi-formal descriptions of the expected behavior of a complex system from the viewpoints of its stakeholders (customers, users, operators, designers, and engineers). However, for the purpose of design, testing, and verification for critical systems, we can transform requirements into formal models that can be analyzed automatically. ARSENAL is a framework and methodology for systematically transforming natural language (NL) requirements into analyzable formal models and logic specifications. These models can be analyzed for consistency and implementability. The ARSENAL methodology is specialized to individual domains, but the approach is general enough to be adapted to new domains.

1 Introduction

Requirements specify important properties of software systems, e.g., conditions required to achieve an objective, or desired system invariants. Requirements in formal languages can be cumbersome but are precise and useful for checking consistency and verifying properties. NL requirements can be written easily without burden of formal rigor, but can be inherently imprecise, incomplete, and ambiguous. The main objective of this paper is to answer the question: *"Can we design a methodology that combines the strengths of natural and formal languages for requirements engineering?"*. To this end, we present the methodology of ARSENAL: "Automatic Requirements Specification Extraction from Natural Language'. In this paper, we focus on mapping NL requirements to transition systems expressed in SAL and logic specifications in Linear Temporal Logic (LTL), for safety critical systems (e.g., in Sect. 4.1, Fig. 5 shows the SAL model corresponding to the requirements sentence REQ1).

ARSENAL is able to generate a full model from multiple requirements sentences in an automated fashion by using a combination of approaches: preprocessing, type rules, intermediate language representation, output adapters, and powerful formal methods tools. ARSENAL has two stages — Sect. 2 gives an overview of the Natural Language Processing (NLP) stage, while Sect. 3 gives an overview of the Formal Methods (FM) stage. We evaluate ARSENAL in Sect. 4 and conclude in Sect. 5.

© Springer International Publishing Switzerland 2016
S. Rayadurgam and O. Tkachuk (Eds.): NFM 2016, LNCS 9690, pp. 41–46, 2016.
DOI: 10.1007/978-3-319-40648-0_4

2   Natural Language Processing

The NLP stage takes NL requirements as input and generates a set of logical formulas as output. The different components of the NLP stage are shown in Fig. 1 — more details about the NLP stage are available in [3].

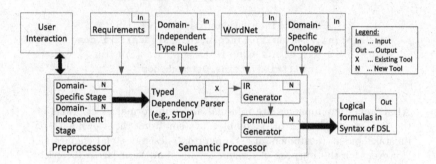

Fig. 1. NLP stage of ARSENAL pipeline.

3   Formal Analysis

In this section, we discuss the Formal Methods (FM) stage. The overall flow of the FM stage is shown in Fig. 2 — this stage takes as input the set of logical formulas as generated by the NLP stage and creates a composite formal model. The FM stage uses a combination of consistency, satisfiability and realizability checks to formally validate the completeness/correctness of the requirements.

3.1   Consistency Analysis

Requirements can be error-prone and inconsistent. In our context, inconsistencies can arise from human errors in writing the NL requirements or from inaccuracies introduced by ARSENAL. Given a set of requirements formalized as LTL formulas, we check if there exists a *model* for the formulas, i.e., they are *satisfiable*. If the formulas are *unsatisfiable*, then it can be due to errors in the specification or due to errors in the NLP stage. The problem of *LTL satisfiability checking* can be reduced to checking emptiness of Büchi automata [9]. Given an LTL formula ϕ, we can construct a Büchi automaton A_ϕ such that the language of A_ϕ is exactly equivalent to the model of ϕ. If the language of A_ϕ is empty then ϕ is unsatisfiable, indicating an inconsistency in the requirements — we report this inconsistency to the ARSENAL end-user. Otherwise, we proceed to creating the SAL model.

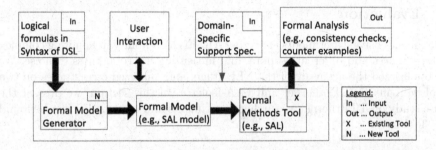

Fig. 2. FM stage of ARSENAL pipeline.

3.2 Model Checking

A transition system like SAL [2] is composed of modules, where each module consists of a *state type*, an *invariant definition*, an *initialization condition*, and a *binary transition relation* on the state type. Creating a complete SAL model directly from text with correct semantics is non-trivial, since formulas need to be categorized as definition, initialization, transition, or theorem. Each variable in SAL is also *typed*, which needs to be explicitly specified. During the model generation stage, ARSENAL gathers type evidences for each variable across all sentences, and then performs type inference by merging them into equivalence classes (details of the type merging algorithm are outlined in [3]). Further, in case of a type conflict, an inconsistency warning is generated, thus helping the user to refine their NL requirements at an early stage. When the model does not satisfy the specification, a negative answer (often in the form of a counterexample) is presented to the user as a certificate of how the system fails the specification — if SAL finds a counterexample, we know the property encoded in the requirements does not hold. If SAL does not find a counterexample at a known depth of model-checking, we next try to see if the LTL formulas are realizable. Once the specification becomes realizable, an implementation can be generated automatically, e.g., in Verilog[1].

3.3 Temporal Logic Synthesis

Given an LTL specification, it may also be possible to directly *synthesize* an implementation that satisfies the specification. It has been shown that a subclass of LTL, known as Generalized Reactivity (1) [GR(1)], is more amenable to synthesis [5] and is also expressive enough for specifying complex industrial designs. We have incorporated into ARSENAL a counterstrategy-guided assumption mining approach developed for GR(1) LTL formulas [4], which allows adding assumptions to the formulas until either the specification is realizable or all the recommendations are rejected by the user.

---

[1] An example of a synthesized Verilog model for the FAA domain is available at: http://www.csl.sri.com/users/shalini/arsenal/faa-isolette.v.

4   Evaluation

We ran extensive experiments analyzing ARSENAL's ability in handling complex NL sentences and different corpora, and measuring it's robustness to noise. We also analyzed the accuracy of the NLP stage, and analyzed case studies on two real domains — TTEthernet and FAA-Isolette. In this section, we present the case study on TTEthernet — further experiments and case studies can be found in [3] (Fig. 3).

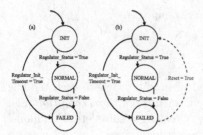

Fig. 3. Original FSM (a) and modified FSM (b) for regulator.

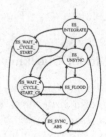

Fig. 4. Synchronization FSM in TTEthernet

4.1   Case Study: TTEthernet (TTE)

In the TTEthernet corpus, we consider the NL requirements that describe the synchronization state machine in TTEthernet. Figure 4 shows the diagram of this state machine (conditions for transitions are not shown). The machine starts at the ES_INTEGRATE state, and the ES_SYNC_ABS state indicates that the end-system has synchronized with other systems in the cluster. This corpus contains 36 sentences. ARSENAL can handle complex requirements sentences, generating the correct formula automatically. An example, describing part of the behavior in the ES_UNSYNC state, is shown below.

REQ1: *When an end system is in ES_UNSYNC state and receives a cold-start frame, it shall (a) transit to ES_FLOOD state, (b) set local_timer to es_cs_offset, (c) set local_clock to 0, (d) set local_integration_cycle to 0, and (e) set local_membership_comp to 0.*

From the overall SAL model generated automatically, the part corresponding to REQ1 is shown in Fig. 5. Observe that ARSENAL was able to infer that the end-system has an enumerated type (Type0) which contains named values ES_UNSYNC_state and ES_FLOOD_state. It was also able to set correctly the type of local_integration_cycle and local_membership_comp to INTEGER. In this example, the user asserted that all the five LOCAL variables are *state* variables. Hence, the actions over these variables were considered as state updates and mapped to the TRANSITION section. The formula generated by the SAL adapter corresponding to REQ1 is therefore placed in this section of the SAL model.

```
tte_example : CONTEXT =
BEGIN
  Type0 : TYPE = {ES_UNSYNC_state, ES_FLOOD_state};
  Type1 : TYPE = {coldstart_frame}; Type2 : TYPE = {es_cs_offset};
  main : MODULE =
  BEGIN
    LOCAL local_integration_cycle : INTEGER
    LOCAL local_membership_comp : INTEGER
    LOCAL local_clock : INTEGER
    LOCAL end_system : Type0
    LOCAL local_timer : Type2
    INPUT in_channel : Type1
    TRANSITION
      [ (end_system = ES_UNSYNC_state AND in_channel =
               coldstart_frame) --> end_system' = ES_FLOOD_state;
          local_timer' = es_cs_offset; local_clock' = 0;
          local_integration_cycle' = 0; local_membership_comp' = 0 ]
  END;
END
```

Fig. 5. SAL model for REQ1.

A formal method expert was asked to review the model and found it was compatible with (and in fact, included more information than) a similar model that he handcrafted in [8]. We then asked one of the original creators of the TTEthernet documentation to provide a high-level specification that should be verified for this model. The sentence in English is given below, followed by the corresponding LTL theorem in SAL syntax generated by ARSENAL.

REQ2: *If the end system is in ES_FLOOD state, it shall eventually not be in ES_FLOOD state.*

```
THEOREM main |- G((end_system = ES_FLOOD_state =>
F(NOT(end_system = ES_FLOOD_state))));
```

We applied bounded model checking, a model checking technique that checks if the model satisfies the requirement within a bounded number of transitions, and found a counterexample. This counterexample reveals that if the environment keeps sending a `coldstart_frame` to this module, then `local_timer`, which maintains a count to timeout in the `ES_FLOOD_state`, will keep resetting to 0 and thus preventing any transition out of the `ES_FLOOD_state` to occur. This helped us identify the missing assumption (absent in the original documentation) that was needed for system verification. In fact, modular verification is one of the most difficult tasks in verification since it requires the precise specifications of the constraints on the environment. These constraints are often implicit and undocumented. In this case, the interaction of multiple end-systems should ensure that any end-system will not receive a `coldstart_frame` infinitely often before it can exit the `ES_FLOOD_state`.

5   Conclusion and Future Work

ARSENAL converts NL requirements to formal models in an automated fashion, which can be further refined through iterations with a human in the loop. It provides an NL front-end to formal analysis that is flexible to adapt to usages in different domains. To that end, ARSENAL can be an important aid for a system designer in designing high-assurance systems, while reducing cost in the overall design and manufacturing process. The main advantages of ARSENAL over prior work [7, 10] in requirements engineering is that it has a less restrictive NL front-end, a more powerful FM analysis framework, and has the ability to generate a full formal model directly from NL text.

In the future, we want to test ARSENAL on other domains, generate other models (e.g., Markov Logic Networks), and go beyond NL text to handle flow-charts, diagrams and tables. We would also like to explore learning, e.g., in the NLP stage we currently create the type rules manually — we would like to use a learning algorithm like FOIL [6] or Propminer [1] to learn type rules. We would also like to explore active learning for incorporating user feedback.

References

1. Akbik, A., Konomi, O., Melnikov, M.: Propminer: a workflow for interactive information extraction and exploration using dependency trees. In: Proceedings of the ACL: System Demonstrations (2013)
2. Bensalem, S., Ganesh, V., Lakhnech, Y., Munoz, C., Owre, S., Rueß, H., Rushby, J., Rusu, V., Saïdi, H., Shankar, N., Singerman, E., Tiwari, A.: An overview of SAL. In: LFM (2000)
3. Ghosh, S., Elenius, D., Li, W., Lincoln, P., Shankar, N., Steiner, W.: Automatically extracting requirements specifications from natural language. CoRR abs/1403.3142 (2014)
4. Li, W., Dworkin, L., Seshia, S.: Mining assumptions for synthesis. In: MEMOCODE (2011)
5. Piterman, N., Pnueli, A., Sa'ar, Y.: Synthesis of reactive(1) designs. In: Emerson, E.A., Namjoshi, K.S. (eds.) VMCAI 2006. LNCS, vol. 3855, pp. 364–380. Springer, Heidelberg (2006)
6. Quinlan, J.R.: Learning logical definitions from relations. Mach. Learn. **5**, 239–266 (1990)
7. Roth, M., Diamantopoulos, T., Klein, E., Symeonidis, A.: Software requirements: a new domain for semantic parsers. In: Proceedings of the ACL Workshop on Semantic Parsing (2014)
8. Steiner, W., Dutertre, B.: SMT-based formal verification of a *TTEthernet* synchronization function. In: Kowalewski, S., Roveri, M. (eds.) FMICS 2010. LNCS, vol. 6371, pp. 148–163. Springer, Heidelberg (2010)
9. Vardi, M.Y.: An automata-theoretic approach to linear temporal logic. In: Moller, F., Birtwistle, G. (eds.) Logics for Concurrency. LNCS, vol. 1043, pp. 238–266. Springer, Heidelberg (1996)
10. Walter, M.R., Hemachandra, S., Homberg, B., Tellex, S., Teller, S.J.: Learning semantic maps from natural language descriptions. In: Robotics: Science and Systems (2013)

Testing and Run-Time Enforcement

Assisted Coverage Closure

Adam Nellis[1], Pascal Kesseli[2]([⊠]), Philippa Ryan Conmy[1], Daniel Kroening[2],
Peter Schrammel[2,4], and Michael Tautschnig[3]

[1] Rapita Systems Ltd, York, UK
{anellis,pconmy}@rapitasystems.com
[2] University of Oxford, Oxford, UK
{pascal.kesseli,kroening,peter.schrammel}@cs.ox.ac.uk
[3] Queen Mary University of London, London, UK
michael.tautschnig@qmul.ac.uk
[4] University of Sussex, Brighton, UK

Abstract. Malfunction of safety-critical systems may cause damage to
people and the environment. Software within those systems is rigorously designed and verified according to domain specific guidance, such
as ISO26262 for automotive safety. This paper describes academic and
industrial co-operation in tool development to support one of the most
stringent of the requirements — achieving full code coverage in requirements-driven testing. We present a verification workflow supported by
a tool that integrates the coverage measurement tool RapiCover with
the test-vector generator FShell. The tool assists closing the coverage
gap by providing the engineer with test vectors that help in debugging
coverage-related code quality issues and creating new test cases, as well
as justifying the presence of unreachable parts of the code in order to
finally achieve full *effective* coverage according to the required criteria.
We illustrate the tool's practical utility on automotive industry benchmarks. It generates 8× more MC/DC coverage than random search.

1 Introduction

Software within safety-critical systems must undergo strict design and verification procedures prior to their deployment. The ISO26262 standard [1] describes
the safety life cycle for electrical, electronic and software components in the
automotive domain. Different activities are required at different stages of the
life cycle, helping ensure that system safety requirements are met by the implemented design. The rigor to which these are carried out depends on the severity
of consequences of failure of the various components. Components with automotive safety integrity level (ASIL) D have the most stringent requirements,
and ASIL A the least strict. One of the key required activities for software is to
demonstrate the extent to which testing has exercised source code, also known
as code coverage. This can be a challenging and expensive task [4], with much
manual input required to achieve adequate coverage results.

The research leading to these results has received funding from the ARTEMIS Joint
Undertaking under grant agreement number 295311 "VeTeSS".

© Springer International Publishing Switzerland 2016
S. Rayadurgam and O. Tkachuk (Eds.): NFM 2016, LNCS 9690, pp. 49–64, 2016.
DOI: 10.1007/978-3-319-40648-0_5

This paper presents work undertaken within the **Verification** and **Testing** to Support Functional **Safety Standards** (VeTeSS) project, which develops new tools and processes to meet ISO26262. The paper contains three contributions:

1. We integrated the FShell tool [7] with an industrial code coverage tool (Rapi-Cover) in order to generate extra test cases and increase code coverage results. This work represents an effort in the integration of formal-methods based tools with industrial testing software. In the safety-critical domain these two areas are generally separated from one another, with formal methodology used only for small and critical sections of software to prove correctness and viewed as an expensive procedure. The tool is at an evaluation stage of development, assessing future improvements to prepare its commercialisation.
2. We present a discussion as to how this technology is most appropriately used within the safety life cycle. Achieving 100 % code coverage can be a complex and difficult task, so tools to assist the process are desirable, however there is a need to ensure that any additional automatically generated tests still address system safety requirements.
3. Finally, we apply the technology to three sizeable automotive benchmarks to demonstrate the utility and the limitations in practice.

Safety standards require different depths of coverage depending on the ASIL of the software. The requirements of ISO26262 are summarized in Table 1. The aim of requirements-based software testing is to ensure the different types of coverage are achieved to 100 % for each of the categories required. In practice this can be extremely difficult, e.g. defensive coding can be hard to provide test vectors for. Another example is code that may be deactivated in particular modes of operation. Sometimes there is not an obvious cause for lack of coverage after manual review. In this situation, generating test vectors automatically can be beneficial to the user providing faster turnaround and improved coverage results.

Table 1. ISO26262 Coverage Requirements (HR = highly recommended, R = recommended)

Type	Description	ASIL
Function	Each function in the code is exercised at least once	A, B (R); C, D (HR)
Statement	Each statement in the code is exercised at least once	A, B (HR); C, D (R)
Branch	Each branch in the code has been exercised for every outcome at least once	A (R); B, C, D (HR)
MC/DC	Each possible condition must be shown to independently affect a decision's outcome	A, B, C (R); D (HR)

This paper is laid out as follows. In Sect. 2 we provide background to the coverage problem being tackled, and criteria for success. In Sect. 3 we describe the specific tool integration. Sect. 4 describes an industrial automotive case study. Sect. 5 looks at both previous work and some of the lessons learnt from the implementation experience.

2   Assisted Coverage Closure

Testing has to satisfy two objectives: it has to be effective, and it has to be cost-effective. Testing is effective if it can distinguish a correct product from one that is incorrect. Testing is cost-effective if it can achieve all it needs to do at the lowest cost (which usually means the fewest tests, least amount of effort and shortest amount of time).

Safety standards like ISO26262 and DO-178B/C demand requirements-driven testing to increase confidence in correct behavior of the software implemented. Correct behavior means that the software implements the behavior specified in the requirements *and* that it does not implement any unspecified behaviors. As a quality metrics they demand the measurement of *coverage* according to certain criteria as listed in Table 1, for instance. The rationale behind using code coverage as a quality metrics for assessing the achieved requirements coverage of a test suite is the following: Suppose we have a test suite that presumably covers each case in the requirements specification, then, obviously, missing or erroneously implemented features may be observed by failing test cases, whereas the *lack of coverage*, e.g. according to the MC/DC criterion, indicates that there is behavior in the software which is not exercised by a test case. This may hint at the following software and test quality problems:

(A) Some cases in the requirements specification have been forgotten. These requirements have to be covered by additional test cases.
(B) Features have been implemented that are not needed. Unspecified features are not allowed in safety-critical software and have to be removed.
(C) The requirements specification is too vague or ambiguous to describe a feature completely. The specification must be disambiguated and refined.
(D) Parts of the code are unreachable. The reasons may be:
   (1) A programming error that has to be fixed.
   (2) Code generated from high-level models often contains unreachable code if the code generator is unable to eliminate infeasible conditionals.
   (3) It may actually be intended in case of defensive programming and error handling.
   In the latter case, fault injection testing is required to exercise these features [8]. Dependent on the policy regarding unreachable code, case (2) can be handled through justification of non-coverability, tuning the model or the code generator, or post-processing of generated code.

The difficulty for the software developer consists in distinguishing above cases. This is an extremely time consuming and, hence, expensive task that calls for tool assistance.

2.1   Coverage Closure Problem

Given

– an implementation under test (e.g. C code generated from a Simulink model),

- an initial test suite (crafted manually or generated by some other test suite generation techniques), and
- a coverage criterion (e.g. MC/DC),

we aim at increasing *effective* test coverage by automatically

- generating test vectors that help the developer debug the software in order to distinguish above reasons (A)–(D) for missing coverage;
- in particular, suggesting additional test vectors that help the developer create test cases to complete requirements coverage in case (A);
- proving infeasibility of non-covered code, thus giving evidence for arguing non-coverability.

Note that safety standards like to DO-178C [11] allow only requirements-driven test-case generation and explicitly *forbid* to achieve full structural code coverage by blindly applying automated test-vector generation. This can easily lead to confusion if the distinction between test-*case* generation and test-*vector* generation is not clearly made. Test-*vector* generation can be applied blindly to achieve full coverage, but it is without use by itself. A test vector is only a *part* of a test case because it lacks the element that provides information about the correctness of the software, i.e. the expected test result. Only the requirements can tell the test engineer what the expected test result has to be. Test-*case* generation is thus *always* based on the requirements (or a formalized model thereof if available). Our objective is to provide assistance for test-case generation to bridge the coverage gap.

2.2   Coverage Measurement

Combining a test-case generator with a coverage tool provides immediate access to test vectors needed to obtain the level of coverage required for your qualification level. Coverage tools determine which parts of the code have been executed by using instrumentation. Instrumentation points are automatically inserted at specific points in the code. If an instrumentation point is executed, this is recorded in its execution data. After test·completion, the coverage tool analyzes the execution data to determine which parts of the source code have been executed. The tool then computes the level of coverage achieved by the tests. We use the coverage tool RapiCover, which is part of the RVS tool suite developed by Rapita Systems Ltd.

2.3   Test Vector Generation by Bounded Model Checking

We use the test vector generator, FShell [7] (see Sect. 3.2 for details), which is based on the Software Bounded Model Checker for C programs, CBMC [3].

Viewing a program as a transition system with initial states described by the propositional formula *Init*, and the transition relation *Trans*, Bounded Model Checking (BMC) [2] can be used to check the existence of a path π of length k from *Init* to another set of states described by the formula ψ. This check is

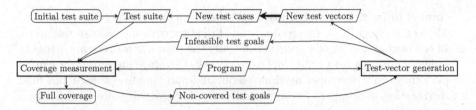

Fig. 1. The Coverage Closure Process

performed by deciding satisfiability of the following formula using a SAT or SMT solver:

$$Init(s_0) \wedge \bigwedge_{0 \leq j < k} Trans(s_j, i_j, s_{j+1}) \wedge \psi(s_k) \tag{1}$$

If the solver returns the answer "satisfiable", it also provides a satisfying assignment to the variables $(s_0, i_0, s_1, i_1, \ldots, s_{k-1}, i_{k-1}, s_k)$. The satisfying assignment represents one possible path $\pi = \langle s_0, s_1, \ldots, s_k \rangle$ from $Init$ to ψ and identifies the corresponding input sequence $\langle i_0, \ldots, i_{k-1} \rangle$.

Besides being useful for refuting safety properties (where ψ defines the error states), BMC can be used for generating test vectors (where ψ defines the test goal to be covered).

The analysis performed by CBMC is bit-exact w.r.t. the machine semantics of the execution target and CBMC provides full bit-exact support for floating point arithmetic. Architecture-specific settings can be configured via command line in FShell and RapiCover supports on-target coverage measurement. We are hence guaranteed that the generated test vectors are going to cover the test goals. In addition, using BMC in a test-vector generator permits generating the shortest test vectors possible to cover a certain test goal or even a whole group of test goals, which helps keeping test suites concise and test execution fast [12].

An advantage of using a model checker is also its ability to find test vectors for corner cases ("Under which conditions can this floating point variable take the value NaN?"). Moreover, in our experience, due to the high precision of the analysis, it is even very likely to discover inconsistencies and holes in the requirements specification during test-vector generation.

BMC can give a proof of unreachability of a test goal in certain conditions, e.g., if loops can be unrolled completely or using k-induction [13], which is a BMC-based technique for unbounded model checking.

2.4 The Coverage Closure Process

The algorithm that we implement to assist the coverage closure process is given in Fig. 1. It proceeds as follows:

1. We start with an *initial test suite* that has been crafted manually or has been generated using other test-case generation techniques like directed random testing. The initial test suite may be empty, but many test goals can be easily

covered using test-case generation methods that are cheaper than Bounded Model Checking. It is thus recommended to start with such a base test suite.

2. In the next step, this *test suite* is run using the *coverage measurement* tool in order to obtain a list of *non-covered test goals*. Coverage measurement can be performed on a developer machine to obtain approximate coverage, but final certification data has to be obtained by running the test suite on the actual target platform.

3. The *test-vector generator* takes the list of non-covered test goals and tries to compute input values to cover them. Ideally, the test-vector generator is parametrized with the architectural parameters of the target platform in order to obtain guarantees that the goals are indeed going to be covered. As our test-vector generator is a Bounded Model Checker, there will be three possible outcomes of an attempt to cover test goals:

   (a) A test goal has been covered. In this case this *new test vector* is presented to the user who has to turn it into a *new test case* to be added to the *test suite*. Note that building the new test case is the only part of the process (bold edge) that is not fully automatic since human judgment is required to identify why the corresponding test goal has not been covered in the first place, i.e. distinguishing reasons (A)–(D) in Sect. 2.

   (b) It is *infeasible to cover a test goal*. This happens when the test-vector generator comes up with a proof of unreachability of the test goal. As mentioned above, a Bounded Model Checker can provide such proofs if the loops have been unwound completely, for instance. In this case, the corresponding test goal can be annotated in the coverage report as *proven infeasible* to justify its non-coverability. This increases *effective* coverage by reducing the number of genuinely coverable test goals.

   (c) The goal has not been covered and we were unable to prove infeasibility of the test goal. With a Bounded Model Checker this can happen if the chosen bound k has been too low. In this case the test goal will remain uncovered and it can be tried to cover it with a higher value for k in the next iteration of the process.

4. Coverage of the enhanced test suite is then measured again to identify test goals that remain uncovered, and the process is repeated. Generated tests typically will cover more test goals than intended. Measuring coverage between generating tests increases cost-effectiveness of the process by eliminating unnecessary test-case generations.

5. If there are no more non-covered test goals we have achieved *full coverage* and the process terminates.

Note that the process depicted in Fig. 1 is not specific to our tool but applies in general. In particular, it does not rely on the test-vector generator to guarantee that a generated test vector covers the test goal it has been generated for, because the coverage measurement tool will check all generated test cases anyway for increasing the coverage. However, the generation of useless test cases can be avoided by using a tool such as FShell that can provide such guarantees.

Then, in theory, termination of the process achieving full coverage can be guaranteed, because embedded software is finite state. In practice, however, this depends on the reachability diameter of the system [10] and the capacity of the test-vector generator to cope with the system's size and complexity.

3 FShell Plugin for RVS Implementation

The input to the tool[1]. is a C program with an initial test suite. The output of the tool is twofold. The first output is a set of generated test vectors that augment the initial test suite to increase its coverage. The second output is a coverage report detailing the level of coverage achieved by the initial test suite, and the extra coverage added by the generated test cases.

FShell has been integrated into RapiCover as context menu option, illustrated in Fig. 3. Rapi-Cover can be used to select a single function, call, statement, decision or branch. The tool then uses FShell to generate a test vector for this element. Alternatively, the tool has a button to generate as much coverage as possible. When this option is chosen, the tool goes around the loop described in Fig. 1, using FShell to

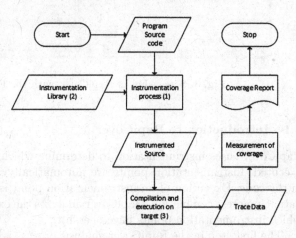

Fig. 2. RVS Process

repeatedly generate test cases to increase the coverage as much as possible, verifying the obtained coverage with RapiCover.

There is tension between the need to demonstrate that the activities prescribed by ISO26262 have been met in spirit as well as with quantifiable criteria. Recall that achieving 100 % code coverage during testing does not ensure the code meets its intent. Consequently the FShell plug-in would be provided as advisory service, generating candidate test vectors, which a user can examine to help them identify why their planned testing was inadequate. Values generated need to be assessed for being valid for the system under test, i.e. reflect real world values that could be input to a function, e.g. from a sensor.

---

[1] RVS is licensed software. An evaluation version can be requested from http://www.rapitasystems.com. The licensing policy disallows anonymous licenses. To compensate for this, we provide a video showing the plug-in here: http://www.cprover.org/coverage-closure/rvs-fshell-demo.mp4.

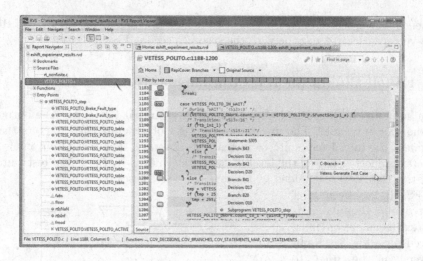

Fig. 3. Screenshot of RapiCover with the FShell Plug-in

3.1 Introduction to RapiCover

RapiCover[2] uses instrumentation to determine which program parts have been executed. Instrumentation points are automatically inserted at specific points in the code. Execution of an instrumentation point is recorded in its execution data. Upon test completion, RapiCover analyzes the execution data to determine which instrumentation points have been hit.

The first step in the RapiCover analysis process is to create an instrumented build of the application ((1) in Fig. 2). RapiCover automatically adds instrumentation points ((2) in Fig. 2) to the source code. The instrumentation code itself takes the form of very lightweight measurement code that is written for each target to ensure minimal impact on the performance of the software, and to support on target testing for environments with limited resources. The instrumented software and possibly an instrumentation library are compiled and linked using the standard compiler tool chain. The executable produced is then downloaded onto the target hardware. The executable is exercised and instrumentation data ((3) in Fig. 2) is generated and retrieved. This data is used to generate coverage metrics.

3.2 Introduction to FShell

FShell[3] is an extended testing environment for C programs supporting a rich scripting language interface. FShell's interface is designed as a database engine, dispatching queries about the program to various program analysis tools. These queries are expressed in the FShell Query Language (FQL). Users formulate test

---

[2] http://www.rapitasystems.com/products/rapicover.
[3] Available from: http://forsyte.at/software/fshell.

specifications and coverage criteria, challenging FShell to produce test suites and input assignments covering the requested patterns. The program supports a rich and extensive interface. The expressions used for the FShell plugin for RVS implementation are listed in Table 2 with syntax and examples.

@CALL(X) requires generated test cases to call function X. This is the only primitive expression used in the module. The concatenation operator . joins two expressions, requiring them to be satisfied subsequently. As an example, a test case

Table 2. FShell expressions

Expression Name	Syntax	Example
Function Call	@CALL(...)	@CALL(X)
Concatenation	.	@CALL(X).@CALL(Y)
Sequence	->	@CALL(X)->@CALL(Y)
Negation	"NOT(...)"	"NOT(@CALL(X))"
Repetition	*	@CALL(X)*
Alternative	+	(@CALL(X) + @CALL(Y))

generated by *@CALL(X).@CALL(Y)* covers a call to X immediately followed by Y. This is similar to the sequence operator ->, which requires the second call to occur eventually. *@CALL(X)->@CALL(Y)* is thus fulfilled if a call to X is eventually followed by a call to Y. The negation *"NOT(@CALL(X))"* is satisfied by every statement except a call to function X. The repetition operator is implemented along the lines of its regular expression pendant, such that *@CALL(X)** is satisfied by a series of calls to X. Finally, the alternative operator implements logical disjunction, such that $(@CALL(X) + @CALL(Y))$ will be satisfied if either a call to X or Y occurs.

The expressions and operators above are all that is used by the FShell plug-in to generate the test vectors requested by RapiCover. Section 3.3 illustrates how these expressions are used to convert test goals to equivalent FQL queries.

3.3   Use of FShell Within RapiCover

The FShell plugin for RVS translates test goals requested by Rapi-Cover into FQL queries covering these goals in FShell, as illustrated in Fig. 4. Test goals are specified using marker elements from the RapiCover instrumentation, which can identify arbitrary statements in the source code by assigning them an *instrumentation*

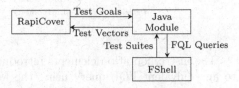

Fig. 4. Plugin Architecture

point id. In accordance with MC/DC criteria, decisions and their constituting conditions are further identified using unique *decision and condition point ids.*

Figure 5 shows an example program before and after instrumentation. The module supports two categories of test goals: *Instrumentation Point Path Test Goals* and *Condition Test Goals*. The former specifies a simple series of points to be covered by FShell. The system also permits *inclusive or* and *negation* operators in instrumentation point paths, allowing to specify a choice of instrumentation points to be covered or to make sure that a requested instrumentation point

```
int main() {                        int main() {
    // ...                              // ...
    if(a == b || b != c) {              Ipoint (1);
        printf("%d_%d\n", a, b);        if(Ipoint (4, Ipoint (2, a == b) ||
    }                                       Ipoint (3, b != c))) {
    return 0;                               Ipoint (5);
}                                           printf("%d_%d\n", a, b);
                                        }
                                        Ipoint (6);
                                        return 0;
                                    }
```

Fig. 5. Code example before and after after RapiCover instrumentation

is not covered by the provided test vector. As an example, the instrumentation point path *1->5->6* in Fig. 5 is only covered if the decision in the *if* statement evaluates to *true*. Conversely, the path *1->NOT(5)->6* is only covered if it evaluates to *false*. The former can be achieved with inputs $a=1, b=1, c=2$, whereas the latter could be covered using the input vector $a=1, b=2, c=2$. *Condition Test Goals* on the other hand are specified by a single *decision point* and multiple *condition points*, as well as the desired truth value for each decision and condition. This allows us to cover branch conditions with precise values for its sub-conditions. As an example, the condition test goal *(4,true) -> (2,false) -> (3,true)* would be covered by the input vector $a=1, b=2, c=3$.

Table 3. Test Goal Types and FShell Queries

Category	Goal	FQL
Instrumentation	Simple	@CALL(Ipoint5) ->@CALL(Ipoint6) ->...
Point Path Goal	Disjunction	(@CALL(Ipoint5) + @CALL(Ipoint6) + ...)
	Complement	@CALL(Ipoint1)."NOT(@CALL(Ipoint5))*".@CALL(Ipoint6)->...
Condition Goal	Condition	@CALL(Ipoint2f)."NOT(@CALL(Ipoint1))*".
		@CALL(Ipoint2t)."NOT(@CALL(Ipoint1))*".+...
	Decision	@CALL(Ipoint4t)

The instrumentation elements introduced by RapiCover need to be mapped to an equivalent FQL query using the features presented in Table 2. For this purpose, we replace their default implementation in RapiCover by synthesized substitutions which are optimized for efficient tracking by FShell. These mock implementations are synthesized for each query and injected into the program on-the-fly at analysis time. Standard FQL queries are then enough to examine these augmented models for the specified coverage goals. Table 3 shows explicitly how these goals can described using the FShell query syntax.

4   Evaluation

The FShell plugin for RVS has been tested on three industrial automotive use cases: an airbag control unit ("airbag"), a park control unit ("eshift"), a break-by-wire controller ("vtec") and a smaller message handler benchmark ("msg").[4]

4.1   Case Study: e-Shift Park Control Unit

To illustrate the characteristics of these benchmarks we describe the e-Shift Park Control Unit.[5] This system is in charge of the management of the mechanical park lock that blocks or unblocks the transmission to avoid unwanted movement of the vehicle when stopped. The park mode is enabled either by command of the driver via the gear lever (PRND: park/rear/neutral/drive) or automatically.

Figure 6 shows the architectural elements the e-Park system is communicating with. The vehicle control unit monitors the status of the vehicle via sensors and informs the driver, in particular, about the speed of the vehicle and the status of the gears via the dashboard. The e-Park Control Unit is responsible for taking control decisions when to actuate the mechanical park lock system.

Among many others, the following requirements have to be fulfilled:

1. Parking mode is engaged if vehicle speed is below 6 km/h and the driver presses parking button (P) and brake pedal.
2. If vehicle speed is above 6 km/h and the driver presses the parking button (P) and brake pedal then commands from the accelerator pedal are ignored; parking mode is activated as soon as speed decreases below 6 km/h.
3. If vehicle speed is below 6 km/h and the driver presses the driving button (D) and brake pedal, then forward driving mode is enabled.
4. If vehicle speed is above 6 km/h then backward driving mode (R) is inhibited.

As is typical for embedded software, the e-Park Control Unit software consists of tasks that — after initialization of the system on start-up — execute periodically in the control loop until system shutdown. A test vector hence consists of a sequence of input values (sensor values and messages received

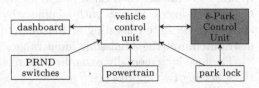

Fig. 6. e-Shift Park Control Unit

via the communication system) that may change in each control loop iteration. We call the number of iterations the *length* of the test vector.

To generate valid test vectors, a model of the vehicle is required. Otherwise, the test vector generator may produce results that are known not to occur in the

---

[4] The code for these benchmarks was provided by the respective companies under a GPL-like license and can be downloaded here: http://www.cprover.org/coverage-closure/nfm-package.zip.

[5] Provided by Centro Ricerche Fiat.

Table 4. Experimental setup of the two approaches that we compare.

	FShell plugin for RVS	random search + reduction
1.	Start with the initial test suite.	
2.	Compile and run the C source code with the current test suite, using RapiCover to generate a coverage report.	
3.	RapiCover provides FShell with a list of non-covered test goals.	
4.	FShell generates a test vector for these non-covered test goals.	Generate a random test vector, uniformly distributed over the admissible input ranges.
5.	FShell feeds back information about infeasible test goals and test vectors for feasible test goals.	·
6.	Automatically create C test cases based on these test vectors.	
7.	Re-compile and re-run the C code with this new test case, using RapiCover to verify that the generated test case does indeed cover the test goal.	
8.		If the coverage has increased then keep the test case; otherwise discard it.
9.	Repeat from step 3.	

running system, such as infinite vehicle velocity. For the case study this model consisted of assumptions about the input value ranges, such as "The speed of the car will not exceed 1000 km/h, or reduce below 0 km/h." These assumptions are part of the admissible operating conditions as stated in the requirements specification.

4.2 Experimental Setup

In order to evaluate the FShell plugin for RVS, we used four different industrial C source code case studies with a cumulative ~6700 LOC. We started out with an initial test suite consisting of 100 random test vectors of length 5 uniformly distributed over the admissible input ranges[6].

Then we incrementally extended this test suite by test vectors generated by the following two approaches:

1. FShell plugin for RVS following the process illustrated in Fig. 1.
2. A combination of test vector generation based on random search and greedy test suite reduction.

We compared the achieved coverage gain and resulting test suite sizes after running both approaches for 8 days, with the exception of the message handler,

---

[6] We chose length 5 because it seemed a good compromise between increasing coverage and keeping test execution times short for these case studies: on the e-Shift case study, adding 100 test vectors of length 5 increased coverage by 1.1 %; 100 test vectors of length 10 increased it by only 1.3 % while test execution times would double and only half as many test vectors could be explored.

Table 5. Evaluation results: comparing FShell plugin for RVS against test vectors generated by random search.

	airbag			eshift			vtec			msg		
Test Cases	Init	Rnd	FS	Init	Rnd	FS	Init	Rnd	FS	Init	Rnd	FS
Generated	100	35k	6	100	35k	6	100	16k	4	-	9k	1
New	-	0	6	-	13	6	-	2	4	-	0	1
Coverage (%)	Init	Rnd	FS	Init	Rnd	FS	Init	Rnd	FS	Init	Rnd	FS
Statement	41.6	41.6	**83.8**	52.2	53.0	**53.2**	76.3	77.3	**79.3**	87.9	87.9	**89.6**
Increase	-	0.0	**42.2**	-	0.8	**1.0**	-	1.0	**3.0**	-	0.0	**1.7**
MC/DC	16.0	16.0	**68.0**	31.2	34.5	**36.8**	40.0	48.0	**64.0**	53.8	53.8	**61.5**
Increase	-	0.0	**52.0**	-	3.3	**5.6**	-	8.0	**24.0**	-	0.0	**7.7**

which we only ran for 3 hours due to its smaller code size.[7] Table 4 describes our experimental setup.

The runtime of FShell is worst-case exponential in the loop bound of this main loop. Choosing a too high loop bound results in FShell taking prohibitively long to run, yet setting the loop bound too low results in some branches not being coverable. As mitigation, we started the experiment with a loop bound of 1, then we gradually increased the loop bound to cover those branches that we were not able cover in previous iterations. As explained in Sect. 2.1, step 6 in Table 4 is not automatic since it needs information from the requirements specification. For the sake of our comparison that does not care about the pass/fail status of the test, we skipped the manual addition of the expected test outcome.

4.3 Results

The results of our experiment are detailed in Table 5. They indicate that more than 99.99 % of the generated test vectors added by the random search are redundant and do not increase coverage. This confirms that these case studies represent particularly challenging cases for black-box test vector generation and that only very few test vectors in the input range lead to actual coverage increase.

The FShell plugin for RVS outperforms the random search strategy in all tested benchmarks. The difference between the two approaches becomes more pronounced for more complex benchmarks, which is expected. As an example, the random search is unable to generate any coverage for the complicated, multi-threaded airbag example, whereas the FShell plugin for RVS more than triples the initial coverage. On average our approach increased MC/DC coverage by 22.3 % and statement coverage by 11.9 %. By comparison, the random search only achieved an average 2.8 % and 0.5 % increase. The average test vector length generated by FShell plugin for RVS is 7.4.

---

[7] The msg benchmark achieved 100 loop unwindings in 3 hours, compared to 37, 6 and 58 unwindings for airbag, eshift and vtec in 8 days.

This evaluation thus underlines the benefit from our tool integration to support the coverage closure process on industrial case studies. The expected reduction in manual work needs to be investigated in a broader industrial evaluation involving verification engineers performing the entire coverage closure process.

5   Background and Applicability

There is much work existing for test case generation using Model Checking techniques [5], but a smaller amount targeted directly at the high criticality safety domain where the criterion and frameworks for test case generation are restricted. A useful survey relating to MC/DC can be found in [15]. In [6] Ghani and Clark present a search-based approach to test generation for Java—a language which is rarely used for safety-critical software, and particularly not for the most critical software. Their goal is to generate tests to ensure that the minimal set of truth tables for MC/DC were exercised, but without consideration of the validity of any of the test data by on-target coverage measurement. Additionally, we emphasize that our approach takes into account existing coverage that has already been achieved and complements the requirements based testing, rather than completely replacing it. Other work such as [9] looks at modification of the original source through mutation testing in order to assess effectiveness of the tests. This could be considered a useful adjunct to our methodology.

Lessons Learnt. In order to encourage wider adoption of this integrated tool, we need to consider where it would fit in users' workflow and verification processes, as well as meeting the practical requirements of the standard. As noted earlier, fully automated code coverage testing is not desirable as it misses the intent of the requirements based testing process. However, achieving full code coverage often requires a large amount of manual inspection of coverage results to examine what was missing. Hence providing the user with suggested test data is potentially very valuable and could improve productivity in one of the most time consuming and expensive parts of the safety certification process.

Another benefit of integrating test case generation and coverage measurement is test suite reduction. The coverage measurement tool returns for each test case a list of covered goals. Test suite reduction is hence the computation of a minimal set cover (an *NP*-complete problem). Approximate algorithms [14] may be used to achieve this in reasonable runtimes.

FShell uses a class of semantically exact, but computationally expensive, *NP*-complete algorithms relying on SAT solvers. Depending on the programs or problems posed to the solver the analysis may take long time to complete. Initial feedback on the tool showed that the concept was very well received by automotive engineers. Speed was considered an issue, however, keeping in mind that today's practice for full coverage testing may take several person months with an estimated cost of $100 per LOC,[8] there is great potential for cutting

---

[8] Atego. "ARINC 653 & Virtualization Solutions Architectures and Partitioning", Safety-Critical Tools Seminar, April 2012.

down time and cost spent in verification by running an automated tool in the background for a couple of days.

Initially, we sometimes failed to validate that a test vector that was generated to cover a test goal actually covers that test goal. E.g., one reason were imprecise decimal number representations in the test vector output. Using the exact hexadecimal representation for floating point constants fixed the problem. This highlights the value of bit-exact analysis as well as the importance of re-validating coverage using RapiCover in the process (Fig. 1).

Note also that this process itself is independent of the tools used which offers a high degree of flexibility. On the one hand, it is planned that in future RVS will support alternative backends in place of FShell. On the other hand, FShell can be combined – without changing the picture in Fig. 1 – with a mutation testing tool (in place of RapiCover) to generate test vectors to improve mutation coverage.

6   Conclusion

This paper has demonstrated the successful integration of the FShell tool with an industrial code coverage tool. Using the integrated tools we were able to increase MC/DC code coverage of four industrial automotive case studies by 22.3 % on average. When compared to a random black-box test vector generation strategy, our approach was on average able to generate 796 % more MC/DC coverage within the same amount of time. Our tool achieves this coverage gain with half as many test vectors, and these test vectors are much shorter than those generated by random search, leading to more compact test suites and faster test execution cycles. Moreover, the integration of the two tools simplifies test case generation and coverage measurement work flows into a unified process.

Future work will consider better integration with the debugging environment to inspect test vectors, and warning the user about potentially unrealistic environment assumptions such as ∞ for vehicle speed. In addition, better support should be provided for exporting the test vectors into the users' existing test suite and testing framework. Moreover, we would like to compare with other tools and further evaluate the coverage benefit from the exact floating point reasoning that we use in comparison to, e.g., rational approximations.

References

1. ISO26262 road vehicles – functional safety, Part 6: Product development at the software level, Annex B: Model-based development (2011)
2. Biere, A., Cimatti, A., Clarke, E., Zhu, Y.: Symbolic model checking without BDDs. In: Cleaveland, W.R. (ed.) TACAS 1999. LNCS, vol. 1579, p. 193. Springer, Heidelberg (1999)
3. Clarke, E., Kroening, D., Lerda, F.: A tool for checking ANSI-C programs. In: Jensen, K., Podelski, A. (eds.) TACAS 2004. LNCS, vol. 2988, pp. 168–176. Springer, Heidelberg (2004)

4. Dupuy, A., Leveson, N.: An empirical evaluation of the MC/DC coverage criterion on the HETE-2 satellite software. In: Digital Avionics Systems Conference, vol. 1, pp. 1B6/1–1B6/7 (2000)
5. Fraser, G., Wotawa, F., Ammann, P.: Testing with model checkers: a survey. Softw. Test., Verification Reliab. **19**(3), 215–261 (2009)
6. Ghani, K., Clark, J.A.: Automatic test data generation for multiple condition and MCDC coverage. In: ICSEA, pp. 152–157 (2009)
7. Holzer, A., Schallhart, C., Tautschnig, M., Veith, H.: FShell: systematic test case generation for dynamic analysis and measurement. In: Gupta, A., Malik, S. (eds.) CAV 2008. LNCS, vol. 5123, pp. 209–213. Springer, Heidelberg (2008)
8. Jia, Y., Harman, M.: An analysis and survey of the development of mutation testing. Trans. Software Eng. **37**(5), 649–678 (2011)
9. Kandl, S., Kirner, R.: Error detection rate of MC/DC for a case study from the automotive domain. In: Min, S.L., Pettit, R., Puschner, P., Ungerer, T. (eds.) SEUS 2010. LNCS, vol. 6399, pp. 131–142. Springer, Heidelberg (2010)
10. Kroening, D., Strichman, O.: Efficient computation of recurrence diameters. In: Zuck, L.D., Attie, P.C., Cortesi, A., Mukhopadhyay, S. (eds.) VMCAI 2003. LNCS, vol. 2575, pp. 298–309. Springer, Heidelberg (2002)
11. Rierson, L.: Developing Safety-Critical Software: A Practical Guide for Aviation Software and DO-178C Compliance. CRC Press, Boca Raton (2013). Chapter 14.3 Potential Risks of Model-Based Development and Verification
12. Schrammel, P., Melham, T., Kroening, D.: Chaining test cases for reactive system testing. In: Yenigün, H., Yilmaz, C., Ulrich, A. (eds.) ICTSS 2013. LNCS, vol. 8254, pp. 133–148. Springer, Heidelberg (2013)
13. Sheeran, M., Singh, S., Stålmarck, G.: Checking safety properties using induction and a SAT-solver. In: Johnson, S.D., Hunt Jr., W.A. (eds.) FMCAD 2000. LNCS, vol. 1954, pp. 108–125. Springer, Heidelberg (2000)
14. Tallam, S., Gupta, N.: A concept analysis inspired greedy algorithm for test suite minimization. In: PASTE, pp. 35–42 (2005)
15. Zamli, K.Z., Al-Sewari, A.A., Hassin, M.H.M.: On test case generation satisfying the MC/DC criterion. Int. J. Adv. Soft Comput. Appl. **5**(3) (2013)

Synthesizing Runtime Enforcer of Safety Properties Under Burst Error

Meng Wu, Haibo Zeng, and Chao Wang[✉]

Department of ECE, Virginia Tech, Blacksburg, VA 24061, USA
chaowang@vt.edu

Abstract. We propose a game-based method for synthesizing a runtime enforcer for a reactive system to ensure that a set of safety-critical properties always holds even if errors occur in the system due to design defect or environmental disturbance. The runtime enforcer does not modify the internals of the system or provide a redundant implementation; instead, it monitors the input and output of the system and corrects any erroneous output signal that may cause a safety violation. Our main contribution is a new algorithm for synthesizing a runtime enforcer that can respond to violations *instantaneously* and guarantee the safety of the system *under burst error*. This is in contrast to existing methods that either require significant delay before the enforcer can respond to violations or do not handle burst error. We have implemented our method in a synthesis tool and evaluated it on a set of temporal logic specifications. Our experiments show that the enforcer synthesized by our method can robustly handle a wide range of properties under burst error.

1 Introduction

A reactive system is a system that continuously responds to external events. In practice, reactive systems may have strict timing requirements that demand them to respond without any delay. Furthermore, they are often safety-critical in that a violation may lead to catastrophe. In this context, it is important to guarantee with certainty that the system satisfies a small set of safety properties even in the presence of design defect and environmental disturbance. However, traditional verification and fault-tolerance techniques cannot accomplish this task. In particular, fault-tolerance techniques are not effective in dealing with design defects whereas verification techniques are not effective in dealing with transient faults introduced by the environment. Furthermore, formal verification techniques such as model checking are limited in handling large designs and third-party IP cores without the source code.

In this paper, we propose a new method for synthesizing a runtime enforcer to make sure that a set of safety-critical properties are always satisfied even if the original reactive system occasionally makes mistakes. Unlike the replica in fault-tolerance techniques, our runtime enforcer is significantly cheaper in that it does not attempt to duplicate the functionality of the original system. Instead, it aims at preventing the violation of only a handful of safety properties whose violations

© Springer International Publishing Switzerland 2016
S. Rayadurgam and O. Tkachuk (Eds.): NFM 2016, LNCS 9690, pp. 65–81, 2016.
DOI: 10.1007/978-3-319-40648-0_6

may lead to catastrophe. Our approach also differs from classic methods for synthesizing a reactive system itself from the complete specification [14], which is known to be computationally expensive. In our approach, for example, it is perfectly acceptable for the system to violate some liveness properties, e.g., something good may never happen, as long as it guarantees that safety-critical violations never happen.

The overall flow of our synthesis method is shown in Fig. 1, which takes a safety specification φ^s of the reactive system $\mathcal{D}(I, O)$ as input, and returns another reactive system $\mathcal{S}(I, O, O')$ as output. Following Bloem et al. [3], we call $\mathcal{S}$ the shield. We use I and O to denote the set of input and output signals of the original system, respectively, and define the runtime enforcer $\mathcal{S}(I, O, O')$ as follows: It takes I and O

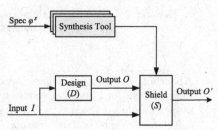

Fig. 1. Synthesizing the safety shield.

as input and returns a modified version of O as output to guarantee the combined system satisfies the safety specification; that is, $\varphi^s(I, O')$ holds even if $\varphi^s(I, O)$ is violated. Furthermore, the shield modifies O only when $\varphi^s(I, O)$ is violated, and even in that case, it tries to minimize the deviation between O and O'. This approach has several advantages. First, since $\mathcal{S}$ is a reactive system, it can correct the erroneous output in O in the same clock cycle. Second, since $\mathcal{S}$ is agnostic to the size and complexity of the system $\mathcal{D}$, it is cheaper and more scalable than fault-tolerance techniques. Finally, the approach works even if the design contains third-party IP cores.

Bloem et al. [3] introduced the notion of safety shield and the first algorithm for synthesizing the runtime enforcer, but the method does not robustly handle burst error. Specifically, the shield synthesized by their method minimizes the deviation between O and O' only if no two errors occur within the same k steps. If, for example, another error occurs before the end of this k-step recovery period, the shield would enter the fail-safe state and stop minimizing the deviation. In other words, the shield may generate O' arbitrarily to satisfy $\varphi^s(I, O')$ while ignoring the actual value of O. This often is not the desired behavior, e.g., when the shield enforces mutual-exclusion of a bus arbiter by hard-wiring all output signals to decline all requests.

Our new method, in contrast, can robustly handle burst error. Whenever the design $\mathcal{D}$ satisfies the specification φ^s, our shield ensures that $O' = O$ (no deviation). Whenever $\mathcal{D}$ violates φ^s, our shield takes the best recovery strategy among the set of all possible ones and, unlike the method by Bloem et al. [3], it never enters the fail-safe state. In order words, our method guarantees that the shield $\mathcal{S}$ keeps minimizing the deviation between O to O' even under burst error. We have implemented our new method in a software tool and evaluated it on a range of safety specifications. The experimental results show that the shield

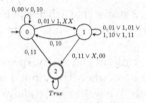

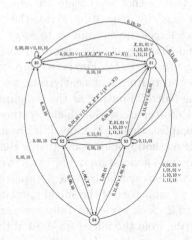

Fig. 2. Example safety specification φ^s.

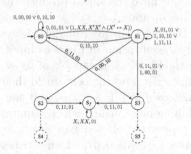

Fig. 3. The 2-stabilizing shield [3].   **Fig. 4.** Our new shield for burst error.

synthesized by our method can robustly handle burst error, whereas the shield synthesized by Bloem et al. [3] cannot.

To summarize, this paper makes the following contributions: (1) We propose a new method for synthesizing a runtime enforcer from a set of safety properties that can robustly handle burst error. (2) We implement the method in a software tool and evaluate it on a large set of benchmarks to demonstrate its effectiveness.

The remainder of this paper is organized as follows. First, we illustrate the main ideas of our new method using a motivating example in Sect. 2. Then, we establish the notation in Sect. 3 and present our method in Sect. 4. We develop a technique for improving the performance of our synthesis algorithm in Sect. 5. We describe our experimental results in Sect. 6. We review the related work in Sect. 7 and then give our conclusions in Sect. 8.

2   Motivation

In this section, we use an example to illustrate the main advantage of our shield synthesis method, which is the capability of handling burst error. Consider the automaton representation of a safety specification in Fig. 2, which has three states, one Boolean input signal, and two Boolean output signals. Here, the state 0 is the initial state and the state 2 is the unsafe state. Every edge in the figure represents a state transition. The edge label represents the values of the input and output signals, where the digit before the comma is for the input signal and the two digits after the comma are for the output signals. X stands for *don't care*, meaning that the digit can be either true (1) or false (0).

Among other things, the safety specification in Fig. 2 states that when the input value is 0, the two output values cannot be 11; furthermore, in state 1, the two output values cannot be 00.

Assume that the design $\mathcal{D}(i, o_1 o_2)$ occasionally violates the safety specification, e.g., by generating 11 for the output signals $o_1 o_2$ when the input i is 0, which forces the automaton to enter the unsafe state. We would like to have the shield $\mathcal{S}(i, o_1 o_2, o_1' o_2')$ to produce correct values for the modified output $o_1' o_2'$ as either 10, 01, or 00. Furthermore, whenever the design satisfies the specification or recovers from transient errors, we would like to have the shield produce the same (correct) output as the design; that is, $o_1' = o_1$ and $o_2' = o_2$.

Unfortunately, the shield synthesized by Bloem et al. [3] can not always accomplish this task. Indeed, if given the safety specification in Fig. 2 as input, their method would report that a 1-stabilizing shield, which is capable of recovering from a violation in one clock cycle, does not exist, and the best shield their method can synthesize is a 2-stabilizing shield, shown in Fig. 3 (to make it simple, we omit part of the shield unrelated to handling burst error), which requires up to 2 clock cycles to fully recover from a property violation. For example, starting from the initial state $S0$, if the shield sees $i, o_1 o_2 = 0, 01$, which satisfies φ^s, it will produce $o_1' o_2' = 01$ and go to the state $S1$. From $S1$, if the shield sees $i, o_1 o_2 = 0, 11$, which violates φ^s, it will produce $o_1' o_2' = 01$ and go to the state $S3$. At this moment, if the second violation $i, o_1 o_2 = 0, 11$ occurs, the shield will enter a *fail-safe* state S_f, where it stops minimizing the deviation between $o_1' o_2'$ and $o_1 o_2$.

Step	0	1	2	3	4	5	6	7	8	9
Input i	0	0	1	0	0	0	0	0	0	...
Output $o_1 o_2$	00	01	10	11	11	10	10	00	00	...
Shield output $o_1' o_2'$	00	01	10	01	01	01	01	01	01	...
State in Fig. 3	S0	S0	S1	S1	S3	S_f	S_f	S_f	S_f	...

Step	0	1	2	3	4	5	6	7	8	9
Input i	0	0	1	0	0	0	0	0	0	...
Design Output $o_1 o_2$	00	01	10	11	11	10	10	00	00	...
Shield output $o_1' o_2'$	00	01	10	01	01	10	10	00	00	...
State in Fig. 4	S0	S0	S1	S1	S3	S3	S0	S0	S0	...

Fig. 5. Simulation trace of 2-stabilizing shield.

Fig. 6. Simulation trace of our new shield.

Figure 5 shows the simulation trace where two consecutive errors occur in Steps 3 and 4, forcing the shield to enter the fail-safe state s_f where it no longer responds to the original output $o_1 o_2$. This is shown in Steps 5–8, where the original output no longer violates φ^s and yet the shield still modifies the values to 01.

In contrast, our new method would synthesize the shield shown in Fig. 4, which never enters any fail-safe state but instead keeps minimizing the deviation between $o_1' o_2'$ and $o_1 o_2$ even in the presence of burst error. As shown in the simulation trace in Fig. 6, when the two consecutive violations occur in Steps 3 and 4, our new shield will correct the output values to 01. Furthermore, immediately after the design recovers from the transient errors, the shield stops modifying the original output values. Therefore, in Steps 5–8, our shield maintains $o_1' o_2' = o_1 o_2$.

3 Preliminaries

In this section, we establish the notation used in the remainder of this paper.

The Reactive System. The reactive system to be protected by the shield is represented as a Mealy machine $\mathcal{D} = \langle S, s_0, \Sigma_I, \Sigma_O, \delta, \lambda \rangle$, where S is a finite set of states, $s_0 \in S$ is the initial state, Σ_I is the set of values of the input signals, Σ_O is the set of values of the output signals, δ is the transition function, and λ is the output function. More specifically, $\delta(s, \sigma_I)$ returns the unique next state $s' \in S$ for a given state $s \in S$ and a given input value $\sigma_I \in \Sigma_I$, while $\lambda(s, \sigma_I)$ returns the unique output value $\sigma_O \in \Sigma_O$.

The safety specification that we want to enforce is represented as a finite automaton $\varphi^s = \langle Q, q_0, \Sigma, \delta_\varphi, F_\varphi \rangle$, where Q is a finite set of states, $q_0 \in Q$ is the initial state, $\Sigma = \Sigma_I \times \Sigma_O$ is the input alphabet, δ_φ is the transition function, and $F_\varphi \subseteq Q$ is a set of unsafe (error) states. Let $\overline{\sigma} = \sigma_0 \sigma_1 \ldots$ be an input trace where for all $i = 0, 1, \ldots$ we have $\sigma_i \in \Sigma$. Let $\overline{q} = q_0 q_1 \ldots$ be the corresponding state sequence such that, for all $i = 0, 1, \ldots$, we have $q_{i+1} = \delta_\varphi(q_i, \sigma_i)$.

We assume the input trace $\overline{\sigma}$ of φ^s is generated by the reactive system $\mathcal{D}$. We say that $\overline{\sigma}$ satisfies φ^s if and only if the corresponding state sequence $\overline{q}$ visits only the safe states; that is, for all $i = 0, 1, \ldots$ we have $q_i \in (Q \setminus F_\varphi)$. We say that $\mathcal{D}$ satisfies φ^s if and only if all input traces generated by $\mathcal{D}$ satisfy φ^s. Let $L(\varphi^s)$ be the set of all input traces satisfying φ^s. Let $L(\mathcal{D})$ be the set of all input traces generated by $\mathcal{D}$. Then, $\mathcal{D}$ satisfies φ^s if and only if $L(\mathcal{D}) \subseteq L(\varphi^s)$.

The Safety Shield. Following Bloem et al. [3], we define the shield as another reactive system $\mathcal{S}$ such that, even if $\mathcal{D}$ violates φ^s, the combined system $(\mathcal{D} \circ \mathcal{S})$ still satisfies φ^s. We define the synchronous composition of $\mathcal{D}$ and $\mathcal{S}$ as follows:

Let the shield be $\mathcal{S} = \langle S', s_0', \Sigma, \Sigma_{O'}, \delta', \lambda' \rangle$, where S' is a finite set of states, $s_0' \in S'$ is the initial state, $\Sigma = \Sigma_I \times \Sigma_O$ is the input alphabet, $\Sigma_{O'}$, which is the set of values of O', is the output alphabet, $\delta' : S' \times \Sigma \to S'$ is the transition function, and $\lambda' : S' \times \Sigma \to \Sigma_{O'}$ is the output function.

The composition is $\mathcal{D} \circ \mathcal{S} = \langle S'', s_0'', \Sigma_I, \Sigma_{O'}, \delta'', \lambda'' \rangle$, where $S'' = (S \times S')$, $s_0'' = (s_0, s_0')$, Σ_I is the set of values of the input of $\mathcal{D}$, $\Sigma_{O'}$ is the set of values of the output of $\mathcal{S}$, δ'' is the transition function, and λ'' is the output function. Specifically, $\lambda''((s, s'), \sigma_I)$ is defined as $\lambda'(s', \sigma_I \cdot \lambda(s, \sigma_I))$, which first applies $\lambda(s, \sigma_I)$ to compute the output of $\mathcal{D}$ and then uses $\sigma_I \cdot \lambda(s, \sigma_I)$ as the new input to compute the final output of $\mathcal{S}$. Similarly, δ'' is a combined application of δ and λ from $\mathcal{D}$ and δ' from $\mathcal{S}$. That is, $\delta''((s, s'), \sigma_I) = (\delta(s, \sigma_I), \delta'(s', \sigma_I \cdot \lambda(s, \sigma_I)))$.

Let $L(\mathcal{D} \circ \mathcal{S})$ be the set of input traces generated by the composed system. Clearly, if $L(\mathcal{D}) \subseteq L(\varphi^s)$, the shield $\mathcal{S}$ should simply maintain $\sigma_O' = \sigma_O$. But if $L(\mathcal{D}) \nsubseteq L(\varphi^s)$, the shield $\mathcal{S}$ needs to modify the original output of $\mathcal{D}$ to eliminate the erroneous behaviors in $L(\mathcal{D}) \setminus L(\varphi^s)$.

In general, there are multiple ways for $\mathcal{S}$ to change the original output $\sigma_O \in \Sigma_O$ into $\sigma_O' \in \Sigma_{O'}$ to eliminate the erroneous behaviors, some of which are better than others in minimizing the deviation. Ideally, we would like the shield to do nothing when $\mathcal{D}$ satisfies φ^s; that is, $\sigma_O' = \sigma_O$. However, when $\mathcal{D}$ violates φ^s, the deviation is inevitable. Although the shield synthesis method by Bloem et al. [3] guarantees minimum deviation if no more than one error occurs in each k-step recovery period, under burst error, the shield would enter a *fail-safe* mode where it stops minimizing the deviation. This is undesirable because, even after the transient errors disappear, their shield would still keep modifying the output values.

4   The Synthesis Algorithm

In this section, we present our new shield synthesis algorithm for handling burst error.

4.1   The Overall Flow

Algorithm 1 shows the overall flow of our synthesis procedure. The input of the procedure consists of the safety specification $\varphi^s(I, O)$, and the set of signals in I, O, and O'. The output of the procedure is the safety shield $\mathcal{S}(I, O, O')$.

Algorithm 1. Synthesizing the shield $\mathcal{S}(I, O, O')$ from the safety specification $\varphi^s(I, O)$.

```
1:  SYNTHESIZE (specification φˢ, input I, output O, modified output O') {
2:      Q(I,O') ← GENCORRECTNESSMONITOR(φˢ)
3:      E(I,O,O') ← GENERRORAVOIDINGMONITOR(φˢ)
4:      G ← Q ∘ E         // create the safety game
5:      ρ ← COMPUTEWINNINGSTRAGETY(G)
6:      S(I,O,O') ← CONSTRUCTSHIELD(ρ)
7:      return S
8:  }
```

Starting from the safety specification φ^s, our synthesis procedure first constructs a correctness monitor $\mathcal{Q}(I, O')$. The correctness monitor $\mathcal{Q}$ ensures that the composed system, whose input is I and output is O', always satisfies the safety specification. That is, $\varphi^s(I, O')$ holds even if $\varphi^s(I, O)$ occasionally fails. Note that $\mathcal{Q}(I, O')$ alone may not be sufficient as a specification for synthesizing the desired shield $\mathcal{S}$, because it refers only to O' but not to O. For example, if we give $\mathcal{Q}$ to a classic reactive synthesis procedure, e.g., Pnueli and Rosner [14], it may produce a shield that ignores the original output O of the design and arbitrarily generates O' to satisfy $\varphi^s(I, O')$.

To minimize the deviation from O to O', we construct an error-avoiding monitor $\mathcal{E}(I, O, O')$ from φ^s. In this work, we use the Hamming distance between O and O' as the measurement of the deviation. Therefore, when the design $\mathcal{D}(I, O)$ satisfies $\varphi^s(I, O)$, the error-avoiding monitor ensures that $O' = O$. When $\mathcal{D}(I, O)$

violates $\varphi^s(I, O)$, however, we have to modify the output to avoid the violation of $\varphi^s(I, O')$; in such cases, we want to impose constraints in $\mathcal{E}$ so as to minimize the deviation from O to O'. The detailed algorithm for constructing $\mathcal{E}$ is presented in Sect. 4.2. Essentially, $\mathcal{E}(I, O, O')$ captures all possible ways of modifying O to O' to minimize the deviation. To pick the best possible modification strategy, we formulate the synthesis problem as a two-player safety game, where the shield corresponds to a winning strategy. Toward this end, we define a set of *unsafe* states of $\mathcal{E}$ as follows: they are the states where $\varphi^s(I, O)$ holds but $O' \neq O$, and they must be avoided by the shield while it modifies O to O'.

The two-player safety game is played in the game graph $\mathcal{G} = \mathcal{Q} \circ \mathcal{E}$, which is a synchronous composition of the correctness monitor $\mathcal{Q}$ and the error-avoiding monitor $\mathcal{E}$. Recall that $\mathcal{Q}$ is used to make sure that $\varphi^s(I, O')$ holds, and $\mathcal{E}$ is used to make sure that $O' = O$ whenever $\varphi^s(I, O)$ holds. Therefore, the set of *unsafe* states of $\mathcal{G}$ is defined as follows: they are the states that are unsafe in either $\mathcal{Q}$ or $\mathcal{E}$. Conversely, the *safe* states of $\mathcal{G}$ are those that simultaneously guarantee $\varphi^s(I, O')$ and minimum deviation from O to O'. The main difference between our new synthesis method and the method of Bloem et al. [3] is in the construction of this safety game: their method does not allow the second error to occur in O during the k-step recovery period of the first error, whereas our new method allows such error.

After solving the two-player safety game denoted as $\mathcal{G}(I, O, O')$, we obtain a winning strategy $\rho = (\delta_\rho, \lambda_\rho)$, which allows us to stay in the safe states of $\mathcal{G}$ by choosing proper values of O' regardless of the values of I and O. The winning strategy consists of two parts: δ_ρ is the transition function that takes a present state of $\mathcal{G}$ and values of I and O as input and returns a new state of $\mathcal{G}$, and λ_ρ is the output function that takes a present state of $\mathcal{G}$ and values of I and O as input and returns a new value for O'. Finally, we convert the winning strategy ρ into the shield $\mathcal{S}$, which is a reactive system that implements the transition function and output function in ρ.

4.2 Constructing the Safety Game

We first use an example to illustrate the construction of the safety game $\mathcal{G}$ from φ^s. Consider Fig. 7 (a), which shows the automaton representation of a safety property of the ARM bus arbiter [2]; the LTL formula is $\mathsf{G}(\neg R \to \mathsf{X}(\neg S))$, meaning that transmission cannot be *started* (S is the output) if the bus is not *ready* (R is the input signal). In Fig. 7 (a), the state 2 is unsafe. The first step of our synthesis procedure is to construct the correctness monitor $\mathcal{Q}(R, S')$, shown in Fig. 7 (b), which is a duplication of $\varphi^s(R, S)$ except for replacing the original output S with the modified output S'.

The next step is to construct the error-avoiding monitor $\mathcal{E}(R, S, S')$, which captures all possible ways of modifying S into S' to avoid reaching the unsafe state. This is where our method differs from Bloem et al. [3] the most. Specifically, Bloem et al. [3] assume that the second violation from the design will not occur during the k-step recovery period of the first violation. If there are more than one violations within k steps, it would enter a *fail-safe* state S_f, where it

Fig. 7. Example: (a) safety specification $\varphi^s(R, S)$ and (b) correctness monitor $\mathcal{Q}(R, S')$.

stops tracking the deviation from S to S'. Our method, in contrast, never enters the *fail-safe* state. It starts from the safety specification φ^s and replaces all transitions to the *unsafe* state with transitions to some safe states. This is achieved by modifying the value of the output signal S so that the transition matches some existing transition to a safe state. If there are multiple ways of modifying S to redirect the edges leading to unsafe states in φ^s, we simultaneously track all of these choices until the ambiguity is completely resolved. In other words, we keep correcting consecutive violations without ever giving up (entering S_f). This is done by modifying the error tracking automaton which is responsible for motoring the behavior of design: we conservatively assume the design will make mistakes at any time, so whenever there is a chance for the design to make mistakes, we generate a new abstract state to guess its correct behaviors.

Construction of $\mathcal{E}(I, O, O')$. Algorithm 2 shows the pseudocode for constructing the error-avoiding monitor $\mathcal{E}$. At the high level, $\mathcal{E} = \mathcal{U} \circ \mathcal{T}$, where $\mathcal{U}(I, O)$ is called the violation monitor and $\mathcal{T}(O, O')$ is called the deviation monitor.

- To construct the violation monitor $\mathcal{U}$, we start with a copy of the specification automaton φ^k, and then replace each existing edge to a failing state, denoted as $(s, l) \rightarrow t$, with an edge to a newly added abstract state s_g, denoted as $(s, l) \rightarrow s_g$. The abstract state s_g represents the set of possible safe states to which we may redirect the erroneous edge. That is, each safe state $s' \in s_g.states$ may be reached from s through $(s, l') \rightarrow t'$, where l, l' share common input label. Since each guessing state s_g represents a subset of the safe states in φ^s, the procedure for constructing $\mathcal{U}(I, O)$ from $\varphi^s(I, O)$ resembles the classic procedure for subset construction.
- To construct the deviation monitor $\mathcal{T}$, we start by creating two states A and B and treating values of O and O' as the input symbols. Whenever $O = O'$, the state transition goes to state A, and whenever $O \neq O'$, the state transition goes to B. Finally, we label A as the safe state and B as the unsafe state. Figure 10 shows the deviation monitor.

Consider the safety specification $\varphi^s(R, S)$ in Fig. 7 (a) again. To construct the violation monitor $\mathcal{U}(R, S)$, we first make a copy of the automaton φ^s, as shown in Line 2 of Algorithm 2. Then, starting from Line 3, we replace the edge to the unsafe state 2, denoted as $(1, S) \rightarrow 2$, with the edge to a guessing state, denoted as $(1, S) \rightarrow 2_g$, where the set of safe states in 2_g is $\{0, 1\}$. That is, if we modify the output value S to the new value $\neg S$, the transition from state 1 may

---

Algorithm 2. Generating error-avoiding monitor $\mathcal{E}$ from safety specification φ^s.

```
 1: GENERRORAVOIDINGMONITOR ( specification φˢ ) {
 2:     U ← copy of the specification automaton φˢ
 3:     while (∃ edge (s, l) → t in U where t is an unsafe state) {
 4:         Delete edge (s, l) → t from U
 5:         Add abstract state s_g and edge (s, l) → s_g into U     //{t'} ⊆ s_g.states
 6:         foreach (edge (s, l') → t' such that t' is safe, and l, l' share common input)
 7:             foreach (outgoing edge (t', l'') → t'')
 8:                 Add edge (s_g, l'') → t'' into U
 9:             U ← MERGEEDGESWITHSAMELABEL(U)
10:     }
11:     T ← the deviation monitor
12:     E ← U ∘ T
13:     return E
14: }
15: MERGEEDGESWITHSAMELABEL(monitor U) {
16:     while (∃ edges (s_g, l_1) → t_1 and (s_g, l_2) → t_2 in U where l_1 ∧ l_2 is not false) {
17:         Delete edges (s_g, l_1) → t_1 and (s_g, l_2) → t_2 from U
18:         if (l_1 ∧ ¬l_2 is not false)     Add edge (s_g, l_1 ∧ ¬l_2) → t_1 back to U
19:         if (l_2 ∧ ¬l_1 is not false)     Add edge (s_g, l_2 ∧ ¬l_1) → t_2 back to U
20:         Add abstract state s_m and edge (s_g, l_1 ∧ l_2) → s_m to U     //{t_1, t_2} ⊆ s_m.states
21:         foreach (outgoing edge of t_1 and t_2, denoted as (t_12, l') → t')
22:             Add edge (s_m, l') → t' into U
23:         if (t_1 or t_2 is unsafe)     return U
24:     }
25: }
```

---

go to either state 0 or state 1. This is shown in Fig. 8 (a). In Lines 6–8, for each outgoing edge of the states in $\{0, 1\}$, we add an outgoing edge from 2_g.

Next, we merge the outgoing edges with the same label in Line 9. This acts like a subset construction. For example we may first merge two edges with the label $R \wedge \neg S$, both of them lead to state 0. Then, we merge the two edges with the label $\neg R \wedge \neg S$. Then, consider the edge label $\neg R \wedge S$: starting from state $0 \in 2_g$, the next state is 1, and starting from state $1 \in 2_g$, the next state is 2. Therefore, the outgoing edge labeled $\neg R \wedge S$ goes to the abstract state 4_m, whose set of states is $\{1, 2\}$. Since 2 is an unsafe state, we return back to Line 3 in Algorithm 2 and replace it with other guessing states. More specifically, the state 2 is replaced with the state 1 and 4_m becomes 4_g. After adding all outgoing edges of 4_g, the resulting $\mathcal{U}$ is shown in Fig. 8 (a). Similarly, we merge the remaining outgoing edges of 2_g that are labeled $R \wedge S$ and create the abstract state 3_m, whose set of states is $\{0, 2\}$. Since 2 is an unsafe state, we go back to Line 3 and replace it again. This turns 3_m into 3_g and the resulting automaton is shown in Fig. 8 (b). At this moment, all error states (state 2) are eliminated and therefore $\mathcal{U}$ is fully constructed.

Unsafe States of $\mathcal{E} = \mathcal{U} \circ \mathcal{T}$. The error-avoiding monitor $\mathcal{E}$ is a synchronous composition of $\mathcal{U}$ and $\mathcal{T}$, where the unsafe states are defined as the union of the following sets:

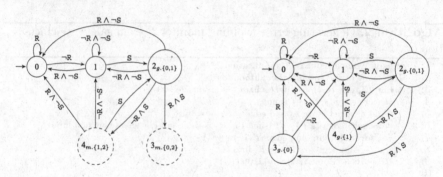

Fig. 8. Constructing the violation monitor $\mathcal{U}(R, S)$: Replacing edge $1 \to 2$ with $1 \to \{0, 1\}$.

- $\{(s, B) \mid s \text{ is a safe state in } \mathcal{U} \text{ coming from } \varphi^s\}$,
- $\{(s_m, B) \mid s_m \text{ results from merging edges and it contains no unsafe state}\}$, and
- $\{(s_g, A) \mid s_g \text{ results from replacing some unsafe states}\}$.

The reason is, when s is a safe state and s_m contains only safe states, the specification φ^s is not violated and therefore we must ensure $O' = O$ (state A in $\mathcal{T}$). In contrast, since s_g is created by replacing some originally unsafe states, the specification $\varphi^s(I, O)$ is violated, in which case $O' \neq O$ in order to avoid the violation of $\varphi^s(I, O')$. Figures 9, 10 and 11 show the resulting error-avoiding automaton. For brevity, only safe states and edges among these states are shown in Fig. 11. Note that $2_g B$, $3_g B$, $4_g B$ are there because they are created by replacing some unsafe states and $O' \neq O$ holds in the B states.

Figure 12 shows the game graph $\mathcal{G} = \mathcal{Q} \circ \mathcal{E}$ for the correctness monitor $\mathcal{Q}$ in Fig. 7 (b) and the error-avoiding monitor $\mathcal{E}$ in Fig. 11. For brevity, only the safe states in $\mathcal{G}$ and edges among these states are shown in Fig. 12. A safe state in $\mathcal{G}$ is a state $(g_\mathcal{Q}, g_\mathcal{E})$ where $g_\mathcal{Q}$ is safe in $\mathcal{Q}$ and $g_\mathcal{E}$ is safe in $\mathcal{E}$. The winning strategy of this safety game is denoted as $\rho = (\delta_\rho, \lambda_\rho)$, where δ_ρ is the transition function capturing a subset of the edges in Fig. 12, and λ_ρ is the output function determining the value of S' based on the current state and values of R and S. The shield $\mathcal{S}(R, S, S')$ is a reactive system that implements function δ_ρ and λ_ρ of ρ.

5   Solving the Safety Game

We compute the winning strategy $\rho = (\delta_\rho, \lambda_\rho)$ by solving the two-player safety game $\mathcal{G} = (G, g_0, \Sigma, \Sigma_{O'}, \delta, F)$, where G is a finite set of game states, $g_0 \in G$ is the initial state, $F \subseteq G$ are the final (unsafe) states, $\delta : G \times \Sigma \times \Sigma_{O'} \to G$ is a complete transition function. The two players of the game are the shield and the environment (including the design $\mathcal{D}$). In every game state $g \in G$, the environment first chooses an input letter $\sigma \in \Sigma$, and then the shield chooses some output letter $\sigma_O' \in \Sigma_{O'}$, leading to the next state $g' = \delta(g, \sigma, \sigma_O')$.

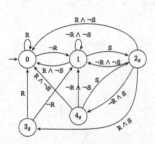

Fig. 9. Violation monitor $\mathcal{U}(R, S)$.

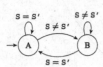

Fig. 10. Deviation monitor $\mathcal{T}(S, S')$.   **Fig. 11.** Error-avoiding monitor $\mathcal{E}(R, S, S')$.

The sequence $\overline{g} = g_0 g_1 \ldots$ of game states is called a *play*. We say that a play is *won* by the shield if and only if, for all $i = 0, 1, \ldots$ we have $g_i \in G \setminus F$.

5.1 Fix-Point Computation

In this work, we use the algorithm of Mazala [12] to solve the safety game. In this algorithm, we compute "attractors" for a subset of safe states $(G \setminus F)$ and final states (F), until reaching the fix-point. Specifically, we maintain two sets of states: $\mathcal{F}$ and the winning region $\mathcal{W}$. $\mathcal{F}$ is the set of states from which the shield will inevitably lose, while $\mathcal{W}$ is the set of states from which the shield has a strategy to win. We also define a function

$$MX(Z) = \{q \mid \exists \sigma \in \Sigma . \forall \sigma_{O'} \in \Sigma_{O'} . q' = \delta(q, \sigma, \sigma_{O'}) \wedge (q' \in Z)\}$$

That is, $MX(Z)$ is the set of states from which the environment can force the transition to a state in Z regardless of how the shield responds.

The fix-point computation starts with $\mathcal{W} = G \setminus F$ and $\mathcal{F} = F$. In each iteration, $\mathcal{W} = \mathcal{W} \setminus MX(\mathcal{F})$ and $\mathcal{F} = \mathcal{F} \cup MX(\mathcal{F})$. The computation stops when both $\mathcal{W}$ and $\mathcal{F}$ reach the fix-point.

5.2 Optimization

The computation of the winning strategy ρ in the safety game $\mathcal{G} = \mathcal{E} \circ \mathcal{Q}$ is time-consuming. In this section, we propose a new method for speeding up this computation. First, we note that a safe state in $\mathcal{G}$ must be safe in both $\mathcal{E}$ and $\mathcal{Q}$, meaning that a winning play in $\mathcal{G}$ must be winning in both of the subgames

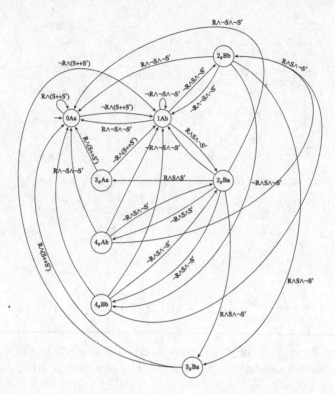

Fig. 12. The game graph $\mathcal{G}(R, S, S')$, which is the composition of $\mathcal{Q}(R, S')$ and $\mathcal{E}(R, S, S')$.

$\mathcal{E}$ and $\mathcal{Q}$. Therefore, instead of directly computing the winning region $\mathcal{W}$ of $\mathcal{G}$, which can be expensive due to the size of $\mathcal{G}$, we first compute the winning region $\mathcal{W}_1$ of the smaller subgame $\mathcal{G}_1 = \mathcal{E}$, then compute the winning region $\mathcal{W}_2$ of the smaller subgame $\mathcal{G}_2 = \mathcal{Q}$, and finally compute the winning region $\mathcal{W}$ of the game $\mathcal{G}$ by using $\mathcal{W}_1 \times \mathcal{W}_2$ as the starting point. Since a winning play in $\mathcal{G}$ is winning in both $\mathcal{G}_1$ and $\mathcal{G}_2$, we know $\mathcal{W} \subseteq \mathcal{W}_1 \times \mathcal{W}_2$.

Furthermore, due to the unique characteristics of the subgames $\mathcal{G}_1 = \mathcal{E}$ and $\mathcal{G}_2 = \mathcal{Q}$, in practice, $\mathcal{W}_1 \times \mathcal{W}_2$ is often close to the final fix-point $\mathcal{W}$. This is because both $\mathcal{E}(I, O, O')$ and $\mathcal{Q}(I, O')$ are derived from the specification automaton φ^s. Specifically, each state in $\mathcal{Q}$ is simply a copy of the corresponding state in φ^s, whereas each state in $\mathcal{E}$ is either a copy of a safe state s in φ^s, or a new abstract state s_g that replaces some unsafe states in φ^s, or a new abstract state s_m consisting of only safe states in φ^s. Since it is cheaper to compute $\mathcal{W}_1$ and $\mathcal{W}_2$, this optimization can significantly speed up the fix-point computation.

6   Experiments

We have implemented our new method in the same software tool that also implements the method of Bloem et al. [3]. The fix-point computation for solving safety games is implemented symbolically, using CUDD [19] as the BDD library, whereas the construction of the various monitors and the game graph are carried out explicitly. The tool takes the automaton representation of the safety specification φ^s as input and returns the Verilog program of the synthesized shield S as output.

We have evaluated our method on a range of safety specifications, including temporal logic properties from (1) the Toyota powertrain control verification benchmark [9], (2) an automotive design for engine and brake controls [13], (3) the traffic light controller example from the VIS model checker [4], (4) LTL property specification patterns from Dwyer et al. [6], and (5) parts of the ARM AMBA bus arbiter specification [2]. Specifically, properties from [9] are on the model of a fuel control system, specifying the performance requirements in various operation modes. Originally, they were represented in signal temporal logic (STL). We translated them to LTL by replacing the predicates over real variables with boolean variables. The properties for engine and brake control [13] are related to the safety of the brake overriding mechanism. The properties for traffic light controller [4] are for safety of a crossroads traffic light. The AMBA benchmark [2] includes combinations of various properties of an ARM bus arbiter. We also translate liveness properties in Dwyer et al. [6] to safety properties by adding a bound on the reaction time steps. For example, in the first columns of Table 1, the numbers besides F and U are the bound number, where F and U mean *Finally* and *Until* respectively. Details of these benchmarks can be found in the supplementary document on our tool repository website [20].

Table 1 shows the results of running our tool on these benchmarks and comparing it with the method of Bloem et al. [3]. Columns 1–2 show the benchmark name and the number of states of the safety specification φ^s. Columns 3–5 show the results of applying the k-stabilizing shield synthesis algorithm [3], including whether the resulting shield can handle burst error, the shield size in terms of the number of states, and the synthesis time in seconds. Similarly, Columns 6–8 show the results of applying our new synthesis algorithm. Note that the k-stabilizing shields do not guarantee to handle burst error, and as shown in Table 1, only some of them can actually handle burst error. Here, *"no (1-step)"* means the shield needs at least one more clock cycle to recover from the previous error before it can take on the next error, and *"no (2-step)"* means the shield needs at least two more clock cycles to recover. In contrast, the shield synthesized by our new method can recover instantaneously and therefore can always handle burst error.

In terms of the synthesis time, the result is mixed in that our new method is sometimes slower and sometimes faster than the existing method. There are two reasons for such results. On the one hand, our method is searching through a significantly larger game graph than the existing method in order to find the best winning strategy for handling burst error. On the other hand, our method

Table 1. Experimental results for comparing the two shield synthesis algorithms.

Property φ^s	Sates	K-Stabilizing Shield [3]			Burst-Error Shield (New)		
		Handle-Burst-Error	States in S	Time (s)	Handle-Burst-Error	States in S	Time (s)
Toyota powertrain [9]	23	yes	38	0.2	yes	38	0.3
Engine and brake ctrl [13]	5	yes	7	0.1	yes	7	0.1
Traffic light [4]	4	yes	7	0.1	yes	7	0.2
$F_{64}p$ [6]	67	yes	67	0.7	yes	67	0.5
$F_{256}p$	259	yes	259	46.9	yes	259	10.5
$F_{512}p$	515	yes	515	509.1	yes	515	54.4
$G(\neg q) \vee F_{64}(q \wedge F_{64}p)$ [6]	67	yes	67	0.7	yes	67	0.6
$G(\neg q) \vee F_{256}(q \wedge F_{256}p)$	259	yes	259	46.9	yes	259	10.7
$G(\neg q) \vee F_{512}(q \wedge F_{512}p)$	515	yes	515	517.7	yes	515	54.5
$G(q \wedge \neg r \rightarrow (\neg r \, U_4 \, (p \wedge \neg r)))$ [6]	6	yes	15	0.1	yes	145	0.1
$G(q \wedge \neg r \rightarrow (\neg r \, U_8 \, (p \wedge \neg r)))$	10	yes	109	0.2	yes	5,519	4.5
$G(q \wedge \neg r \rightarrow (\neg r \, U_{12} \, (p \wedge \neg r)))$	14	yes	753	6.3	yes	27,338	1,414.5
AMBA G1+2+3 [2]	12	yes	22	0.1	yes	22	0.1
AMBA G1+2+4 [2]	8	no (1-step)	61	6.3	yes	78	2.2
AMBA G1+3+4 [2]	15	no (1-step)	231	55.6	yes	640	97.6
AMBA G1+2+3+5 [2]	18	no (1-step)	370	191.8	yes	1,405	61.8
AMBA G1+2+4+5 [2]	12	no (1-step)	101	3,992.9	yes	253	472.9
AMBA G4+5+6 [2]	26	no (2-step)	252	117.9	yes	205	26.4
AMBA G5+6+10 [2]	31	no (2-step)	329	9.8	yes	396	31.4
AMBA G5+6+9e4+10 [2]	50	no (2-step)	455	17.6	yes	804	42.1
AMBA G5+6+9e8+10 [2]	68	no (2-step)	739	34.9	yes	1,349	86.8
AMBA G5+6+9e16+10 [2]	104	no (2-step)	1,293	74.7	yes	2,420	189.7
AMBA G5+6+9e64+10 [2]	320	no (2-step)	4,648	1,080.8	yes	9,174	2,182.5
AMBA G8+9e4+10 [2]	48	no (2-step)	204	7.0	yes	254	6.1
AMBA G8+9e8+10 [2]	84	no (2-step)	422	22.5	yes	685	33.7
AMBA G8+9e16+10 [2]	156	no (2-step)	830	83.7	yes	1,736	103.1
AMBA G8+9e64+10 [2]	588	no (2-step)	3,278	2,274.2	yes	7,859	2,271.5

utilizes the new optimization technique described in Sect. 5.2 for symbolically computing the winning region, which can significantly speed up the fix-point computation.

Table 2 shows the results of our synthesis algorithm with and without optimization. Columns 1–2 show the benchmark name and the size of the safety specification. Columns 3–4 show the size of the resulting shield and the synthesis time without using the optimization. Columns 5–6 show the shield size and the synthesis time with the optimization. In almost all cases, there is significant reduction in the synthesis time when the optimization is used. At the same time, there is slightly difference in the number of states in the resulting shield. This is because the game graph often contains multiple winning strategies, and currently our method for computing the winning strategy tends to pick an arbitrary one. Furthermore, since the shield is implemented in hardware, the difference in the number of bit-registers (flip-flops) needed to implement the two shields will be further reduced. For example, in the last benchmark, we have $\lceil log_2(3278) \rceil = 12$, whereas $\lceil log_2(7859) \rceil = 13$, meaning that the shield requires

Table 2. Experimental results for synthesizing the shield with and without optimization.

Property φ^s	States	Burst Error Shield Syn. (w/o Opt)		Burst Error Shield Syn. (w/ Opt)	
		States in S	Time (s)	States in S	Time (s)
Toyota powertrain [9]	23	38	0.3	38	0.3
Engine and brake ctrl [13]	5	7	0.1	7	0.1
Traffic light [4]	4	7	0.2	7	0.2
$F_{64}p$ [6]	67	67	0.7	67	0.5
$F_{256}p$	259	259	45.5	259	10.5
$F_{512}p$	515	5157	511.0	515	54.4
$G(\neg q) \vee F_{64}(q \wedge F_{64}p)$ [6]	67	67	0.8	67	0.6
$G(\neg q) \vee F_{256}(q \wedge F_{256}p)$	259	259	46.2	259	10.7
$G(\neg q) \vee F_{512}(q \wedge F_{512}p)$	515	515	668.1	515	54.5
$G(q \wedge \neg r \rightarrow (\neg r\ U_4\ (p \wedge \neg r)))$ [6]	6	98	0.1	145	0.1
$G(q \wedge \neg r \rightarrow (\neg r\ U_8\ (p \wedge \neg r)))$	10	4,002	3.9	5,519	4.5
$G(q \wedge \neg r \rightarrow (\neg r\ U_{12}\ (p \wedge \neg r)))$	14	95,357	1,506.9	27,338	1,414.5
AMBA G1+2+3 [2]	12	22	0.1	22	0.1
AMBA G1+2+4 [2]	8	69	2.3	78	2.2
AMBA G1+3+4 [2]	15	566	99.5	640	97.6
AMBA G1+2+3+5 [2]	18	1,256	58.4	1,405	61.8
AMBA G1+2+4+5 [2]	12	193	479.2	253	472.9
AMBA G4+5+6 [2]	26	206	26.3	205	26.4
AMBA G5+6+10 [2]	31	413	30.5	396	31.4
AMBA G5+6+9e4+10 [2]	50	796	40.4	804	42.1
AMBA G5+6+9e8+10 [2]	68	1,287	80.8	1,349	86.8
AMBA G5+6+9e16+10 [2]	104	2,334	194.2	2,420	189.7
AMBA G5+6+9e64+10 [2]	320	8,618	2,865.6	9,174	2,182.5
AMBA G8+9e4+10 [2]	48	233	5.6	254	6.13
AMBA G8+9e8+10 [2]	84	601	30.5	685	33.7
AMBA G8+9e16+10 [2]	156	1,344	111.0	1,736	103.1
AMBA G8+9e64+10 [2]	588	5,848	7,843	7,859	2,271.5

either 12 or 13 bit-registers. Nevertheless, for future work, we plan to investigate new ways of computing the winning strategy to further reduce the shield size.

7   Related Work

As we have already mentioned, our method for ensuring that the design $\mathcal{D}$ always satisfies the safety specification φ^s differs from both model checking [5,15], which checks whether $\mathcal{D} \models \varphi^s$ but does not enforce φ^s, and conventional reactive synthesis techniques [2,7,14,18], which synthesizes the design $\mathcal{D}$ from a complete specification. Since our method is agnostic to the size and complexity of $\mathcal{D}$, it can be significantly more scalable than reactive synthesis in practice. Our method differs from the existing shield synthesis method of Bloem et al. [3] in that it can robustly handle burst error.

Our shield is a reactive system that can respond to a safety violation instantaneously, e.g., in the same clock cycle where the violation occurs, and therefore differs from the many existing methods for enforcing temporal properties [8,10,17] that have to buffer the erroneous output before correcting them. Similarly, it differs from the methods [11,22] for enforcing temporal properties in concurrent software, which relies on delaying the execution of one or more threads to avoid unsafe states. It also differs from the method by Yu et al. [21], which aims at minimizing the edit-distance between two strings, but requires the entire input string to be available prior to generating the output string.

Renard et al. [16] proposed a runtime enforcement method for timed-automaton properties, but the method differs from ours as it assumes that the controllable input events can be delayed or suppressed, whereas our method relaxes such an assumption. Bauer et al. [1] and Falcone et al. [8] also studied what type of temporal logic properties can or cannot be monitored and enforced at run time. These works are orthogonal and complementary to ours. In this work, we focus on enforcing safety specification only. We leave the enforcement of liveness properties for future work.

8   Conclusions

We have presented a new method for synthesizing a runtime enforcer to ensure that a small set of safety-critical properties always hold in a reactive system. The shield responds to property violations instantaneously and robustly handles burst error. We have also presented an optimization technique for speeding up the symbolic fix-point computation for solving the underlying safety games. We have implemented our method in a software tool and evaluated it on a set of benchmarks. Our experimental results show that the new method is significantly more effective than existing methods for handling burst error.

References

1. Bauer, A., Leucker, M., Schallhart, C.: Runtime verification for LTL and TLTL. ACM Trans. Softw. Eng. Methodol. **20**(4), 14:1–14:64 (2011)
2. Bloem, R., Jobstmann, B., Piterman, N., Pnueli, A., Sa'ar, Y.: Synthesis of reactive(1) designs. J. Comput. Syst. Sci. **78**(3), 911–938 (2012)
3. Bloem, R., Könighofer, B., Könighofer, R., Wang, C.: Shield synthesis: Runtime enforcement for reactive systems. In: International Conference on Tools and Algorithms for Construction and Analysis of Systems, pp. 533–548 (2015)
4. Brayton, R.K., et al.: VIS: A system for verification and synthesis. In: International Conference on Computer Aided Verification, pp. 428–432 (1996)
5. Clarke, E.M., Emerson, E.A.: Design and synthesis of synchronization skeletons using branching time temporal logic. In: Grumberg, O., Veith, H. (eds.) 25MC Festschrift. LNCS, vol. 5000, pp. 196–215. Springer, Heidelberg (2008)
6. Dwyer, M.B., Avrunin, G.S., Corbett, J.C.: Patterns in property specifications for finite-state verification. In: International Conference on Software Engineering (1999)
7. Ehlers, R., Topcu, U.: Resilience to intermittent assumption violations in reactive synthesis. In: International Conference on Hybrid Systems: Computation and Control, pp. 203–212 (2014)

8. Falcone, Y., Fernandez, J.-C., Mounier, L.: What can you verify and enforce at runtime? J. Softw. Tools Technol. Transf. **14**(3), 349–382 (2012)
9. Jin, X., Deshmukh, J., Kapinski, J., Ueda, K., Butts, K.: Powertrain control verification benchmark. In: International Conference on Hybrid Systems: Computation and Control (2014)
10. Ligatti, J., Bauer, L., Walker, D.: Run-time enforcement of nonsafety policies. ACM Trans. Inf. Syst. Secur. **12**(3), 1–41 (2009)
11. Luo, Q., Roşu, G.: Enforcemop: a runtime property enforcement system for multi-threaded programs. In: International Symposium on Software Testing and Analysis, pp. 156–166 (2013)
12. Mazala, R.: Infinite games. In: Grädel, E., Thomas, W., Wilke, T. (eds.) Automata, Logics, and Infinite Games. LNCS, vol. 2500, pp. 23–38. Springer, Heidelberg (2002)
13. NHTSA. 49 CFR Part 571: Federal Motor Vehicle Safety Standards; Accelerator Control Systems. Department of Transportation (2012)
14. Pnueli, A., Rosner, R.: On the synthesis of a reactive module. In: ACM Symposium on Principles of Programming Languages, pp. 179–190 (1989)
15. Queille, J.P., Sifakis, J.: Specification and verification of concurrent systems in CESAR. In: Dezani-Ciancaglini, M., Montanari, U. (eds.) International Symposium on Programming. LNCS, vol. 137, pp. 337–351. Springer, Heidelberg (1982)
16. Renard, M., Falcone, Y., Rollet, A.: Optimal enforcement of (timed) properties with uncontrollable events (2016). https://hal.archives-ouvertes.fr/hal-01262444/
17. Schneider, F.B.: Enforceable security policies. ACM Trans. Inf. Syst. Secur. **3**, 30–50 (2000)
18. Sohail, S., Somenzi, F.: Safety first: A two-stage algorithm for the synthesis of reactive systems. J. Softw. Tools Technol. Transfer **15**(5–6), 433–454 (2013)
19. Somenzi, F.: CUDD: CU Decision Diagram Package. ftp://vlsi.colorado.edu/pub/
20. Wu, M.: iShield2 Synthesizer. https://bitbucket.org/mengwu/shield-synthesis/
21. Yu, F., Alkhalaf, M., Bultan, T.: Patching vulnerabilities with sanitization synthesis. In: International Conference on Software Engineering, pp. 251–260 (2011)
22. Zhang, L., Wang, C.: Runtime prevention of concurrency related type-state violations in multithreaded applications. In: International Symposium on Software Testing and Analysis, pp. 1–12 (2014)

Compositional Runtime Enforcement

Srinivas Pinisetty[1(✉)] and Stavros Tripakis[1,2]

[1] Aalto University, Espoo, Finland
{srinivas.pinisetty,stavros.tripakis}@aalto.fi
[2] University of California, Berkeley, USA

Abstract. Runtime enforcement is a methodology used to enforce that the output of a running system satisfies a desired property. Given a property, an enforcement monitor modifies an (untrusted) sequence of events into a sequence that complies to that property. In practice, we may have not one, but many properties to enforce. Moreover, new properties may arise as new capabilities are added to the system. It then becomes interesting to be able to build not a single, monolithic monitor that enforces all the properties, but rather several monitors, one for each property. The question is to what extent such monitors can be composed, and how. This is the topic of this paper. We study two monitor composition schemes, serial and parallel composition, and show that, while enforcement under these schemes is generally not compositional, it is for certain subclasses of regular properties.

1 Introduction

Runtime enforcement (RE) is a technique [5,11–14] to monitor the execution of a system at runtime and ensure its compliance against a set of formal requirements. An enforcement monitor (EM) is generally synthesized from a property expressed in a high-level formalism [5,11–14]. Similar to enforcement mechanisms in [13], we focus on online enforcement of regular properties defined as automata, where an EM is placed between an event emitter and an event receiver, operating at runtime. An EM takes as input a sequence of events σ (modeling an untrustworthy execution) and transforms it into a sequence of events o that complies with a given property φ that we want to enforce. The monitor is equipped with internal memory and is able to store some input events and release them later, after it receives some expected input.

For any complex system, we generally have several critical properties to enforce. Suppose that we want to enforce properties $\varphi_1, \varphi_2, \cdots \varphi_n$. An obvious approach is to take the conjunction of all these properties, $\varphi := \varphi_1 \wedge \cdots \wedge \varphi_n$, and synthesize an EM for the resulting property φ (illustrated in Fig. 1a). This *monolithic* approach has several drawbacks. First and foremost, is not *modular*. As the functionality of the system evolves, additional properties may be added to the set of properties we want to enforce. With a monolithic approach, a new EM needs to be constructed from scratch every time a new property is added. In addition to problems of *performance* and *scalability*, this also has implications to

© Springer International Publishing Switzerland 2016
S. Rayadurgam and O. Tkachuk (Eds.): NFM 2016, LNCS 9690, pp. 82–99, 2016.
DOI: 10.1007/978-3-319-40648-0_7

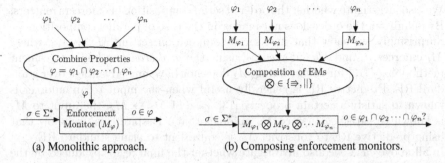

(a) Monolithic approach.   (b) Composing enforcement monitors.

Fig. 1. Monolithic and compositional runtime enforcement approaches.

system *security*. Indeed, in order to construct a monolithic EM for the conjunction $\varphi_1 \wedge \cdots \wedge \varphi_n$, *every* φ_i needs to be known. It may be the case, however, that some of these properties are unknown, or even secret. In that case, we would like to add new monitors that enforce new properties, without affecting the currently enforced properties, some of which may be unknown. We call this methodology *compositional runtime enforcement* (CRE).

CRE is particularly relevant in a security context. For instance, when an attack is detected, one may consider adding an additional property to the set of properties to be enforced. The additional property tries to prevent the detected attack. When a new property is added, it is natural to consider adding an additional layer on top of an existing one, i.e., a new enforcer on top of an existing one. This naturally leads to considering the composition of EMs. To continue this example, suppose that we already have an EM for some property φ_1, but φ_1 is secret and unknown. We are now given a new property φ_2, and we are asked to develop a system that enforces φ_2, without compromising φ_1. Therefore, the resulting system must enforce *both* φ_1 *and* φ_2. Since we don't know φ_1, we have no way of computing a monolithic EM for the conjunction $\varphi_1 \wedge \varphi_2$. Therefore, a compositional approach is necessary. We need to build an EM for φ_2, and somehow compose it with the existing EM for φ_1, so that the resulting system satisfies $\varphi_1 \wedge \varphi_2$.

How to compose two or more enforcement monitors? As illustrated in Fig. 1b, we consider *serial* and *parallel* composition of EMs, denoted by $\Rightarrow$ and $||$, respectively. Serial composition means that the output of one enforcer is fed as input to a next enforcer in a chain. Parallel composition means that all the EMs run in parallel and receive the same input, and that their outputs are *merged* somehow. Our results are as follows:

- We show that runtime enforcement is not compositional for general regular properties, neither w.r.t. serial nor parallel composition. This means that if EMs M_1 and M_2 enforce properties φ_1 and φ_2, respectively, neither $M_1 \Rightarrow M_2$ nor $M_1 || M_2$ generally enforce $\varphi_1 \wedge \varphi_2$.
- We show that compositionality holds for certain subclasses of regular properties, for instance when both φ_1 and φ_2 are safety (or co-safety) properties.

- We also investigate whether the order of serial composition of enforcers matters. By definition, the order does not matter in the case of parallel composition.
- Surprisingly, we show that in a serial composition setting $M_1 \Rrightarrow M_2$, where M_1 enforces φ_1 and M_2 enforces φ_2, using the *predictive* runtime enforcement methodology [13] for constructing M_2 does not have any advantage over standard RE. Predictive RE is generally useful when the input to an enforcer is known to satisfy a certain property [13]. case of $M_1 \Rrightarrow M_2$, the input to M_2 is known to satisfy φ_1 (since M_1 enforces that). Despite this, we show that using predictive RE to construct M_2 is equivalent to using standard RE.
- In all above cases we also investigate whether the final result produced by the composite enforcers is the same as what a monolithic enforcer would produce.

Outline. In Sect. 2 we introduce preliminaries and notation, and recall the runtime enforcement framework from previous work. In Sect. 3 we discuss the three enforcement approaches, namely, monolithic, using composition in series, and using composition in parallel. We show by example that RE is generally not compositional w.r.t. neither serial nor parallel composition. We also show that predictive RE does not help in a serial composition setting. In Sect. 4 we consider subclasses of regular properties, and show that the serial and parallel composition approaches work for these subclasses. Section 6 presents conclusions and future work.

2 Background

2.1 Preliminaries and Notation

Languages. A (finite) word over a finite alphabet Σ is a finite sequence $w = a_1 a_2 \cdots a_n$ of elements of Σ. The *length* of w is n and is noted $|w|$. The empty word over Σ is denoted by ϵ_Σ, or ϵ when clear from the context. The sets of *all words* and *all non-empty words* are denoted by Σ^* and Σ^+, respectively. A *language* or a *property* over Σ is any subset $\mathcal{L}$ of Σ^*.

The *concatenation* of two words w and w' is noted $w \cdot w'$. A word w' is a *prefix* of a word w, noted $w' \preccurlyeq w$, whenever there exists a word w'' such that $w = w' \cdot w''$; conversely w is said to be an *extension* of w'.

The set $\mathrm{pref}(w)$ denotes the *set of prefixes* of w and subsequently, $\mathrm{pref}(\mathcal{L}) \overset{\mathrm{def}}{=} \bigcup_{w \in \mathcal{L}} \mathrm{pref}(w)$ is the set of prefixes of words in $\mathcal{L}$. A language $\mathcal{L}$ is *prefix-closed* if $\mathrm{pref}(\mathcal{L}) = \mathcal{L}$ and *extension-closed* if $\mathcal{L} \cdot \Sigma^* = \mathcal{L}$.

Given an n-tuple of symbols $e = (e_1, \ldots, e_n)$, for $i \in [1, n]$, $\Pi_i(e)$ is the projection of e on its i-th element ($\Pi_i(e) \overset{\mathrm{def}}{=} e_i$).

Deterministic and Complete Automata. A *deterministic and complete automaton* $\mathcal{A} = (Q, q_0, \Sigma, \delta, F)$ is a tuple where, Q is the set of *locations*, $q_0 \in Q$ is the initial location, Σ is the alphabet, $\delta : Q \times \Sigma \to Q$ is the transition function and $F \subseteq Q$ is the set of accepting locations[1].

---

[1] In the rest of the paper the term automaton refers to a deterministic and complete automaton.

Function δ is extended to words by setting $\delta(q, \epsilon) = \epsilon$, and $\delta(q, a \cdot \sigma) = \delta(\delta(q, a), \sigma)$. A word σ is *accepted* by $\mathcal{A}$ *starting from location* q if $\delta(q, \sigma) \in F$, and σ is *accepted* by $\mathcal{A}$ if σ is accepted starting from the initial location q_0. The *language* of $\mathcal{A}$, denoted $\mathcal{L}(\mathcal{A})$, is is the set of all accepted words from location q_0.

Classification of Properties. A *regular property* is a language accepted by an automaton. In the sequel, we consider only regular properties and we refer to them as just properties. Safety (res. co-safety) properties are sub-classes of regular properties. Safety properties are the prefix-closed languages that can be accepted by an automaton. The set of safety properties is denoted as ρ_s. Co-safety properties are the extension-closed languages that can be accepted by an automaton. The set of co-safety properties is denoted as ρ_{cs}. We define another subset of regular properties $\rho = \rho_s \cup \rho_{cs}$. A regular property that belongs to this subset is either a safety or a co-safety property.

Thus, an automaton $\mathcal{A} = (Q, q_0, \Sigma, \delta, F)$ is a *safety* automaton if $\forall a \in \Sigma, q \notin F : \delta(q, a) \notin F$, and is a *co-safety* automaton if $\forall a \in \Sigma, q \in F : \delta(q, a) \in F$.

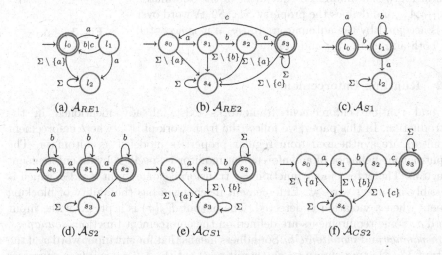

Fig. 2. Automata defining properties $RE1$, $RE2$, $S1$, $S2$, $CS1$ and $CS2$.

Example 1 (Properties Defined as Automata). Consider the following properties:

- $RE1$: Action a followed by b or c should alternate starting with an a.
- $RE2$: The first action should be an a, immediately followed by a b, then immediately followed by another a. This sequence can be repeated again with a c.
- $S1$: After a b occurs, it is forbidden to have an a.
- $S2$: We can have at most two a actions.
- $CS1$: The first two actions should be a followed by b.
- $CS2$: The first three actions should be a followed by b followed by c.

The set of actions $\Sigma = \{a, b, c\}$. The automata in Fig. 2 define these properties. Properties $RE1$ and $RE2$ are regular properties (that are neither safety nor co-safety), and are defined by automata in Fig. 2a and b respectively. Properties $S1$ and $S2$ are safety properties defined by safety automata in Fig. 2c and d respectively. Properties $CS1$ and $CS2$ are co-safety properties defined by co-safety automata in Fig. 2e and f respectively.

Intersection of Automata. Let $\mathcal{A} = (Q, q_0, \Sigma, \delta, F)$ and $\mathcal{A}' = (Q', q_0', \Sigma, \delta', F')$ be two automata over the same alphabet Σ. The *intersection* of $\mathcal{A}$ and $\mathcal{A}'$, denoted $\mathcal{A} \cap \mathcal{A}'$, is defined as $(Q \times Q', (q_0, q_0'), \Sigma, \delta \times \delta', F \times F')$, where $(\delta \times \delta')((q, q'), a) = (\delta(q, a), \delta'(q', a))$. We have $\mathcal{L}(\mathcal{A} \cap \mathcal{A}') = \mathcal{L}(\mathcal{A}) \cap \mathcal{L}(\mathcal{A}')$.

Example 2 (Intersection of Automata). Consider properties $S1$ and $S2$ from Example 1. Intersection of properties $S1$ and $S2$ informally mean that *"We can have at most two "a" actions before a 'b' action occurs."* The automaton in Fig. 3 is a minimized equivalent of the automaton $\mathcal{A}_{S1} \cap \mathcal{A}_{S2}$ and defines the property $S1 \cap S2$. A word over Σ is accepted by the automaton $\mathcal{A}_{S1 \cap S2}$ if it is accepted by both automata $\mathcal{A}_{S1}$ and $\mathcal{A}_{S2}$.

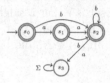

Fig. 3. $\mathcal{A}_{S1 \cap S2}$.

2.2   Runtime Enforcement

Several runtime enforcement frameworks exist, already mentioned in the introduction. In this paper, we follow the framework of [13], where enforcement monitors are synthesized from regular properties modeled as automata. The input-output behavior of an enforcement monitor is specified by an enforcement function. The enforcement function E_φ transforms some input word σ which is possibly incorrect w.r.t. φ. Enforcement mechanism has the ability of blocking events when a violation is detected. The output $E_\varphi(\sigma)$ is a prefix of the input word σ. Some requirements are defined on the enforcement function: *soundness*, *transparency* and *monotonicity*. Soundness means that for any input word σ, if the output $E_\varphi(\sigma)$ is not empty ($\neq \epsilon$), then it must satisfy φ. Transparency expresses how an enforcement mechanism is allowed to correct the input sequence: the output word is a prefix of the input, and if the input word satisfies the property, the output should be equal to the input. Monotonicity is related to online behavior of the enforcement mechanism, that it cannot undo what is already released as output during the incremental computation, and new events can be only appended to the tail of the output. Formal constraints are detailed in [13]. Let us see a definition of an enforcement function that incrementally builds the output.

Definition 1 (Enforcement Function). Given a property $\varphi \subseteq \Sigma^*$, the enforcement function is $E_\varphi : \Sigma^* \to \Sigma^*$, and is defined as $E_\varphi(\sigma) = \Pi_1\big(\text{store}_\varphi(\sigma)\big)$.

where:

- $\kappa_\varphi(\sigma) = (\sigma \in \varphi)$
- $\mathrm{store}_\varphi : \Sigma^* \to \Sigma^* \times \Sigma^*$ is defined as:

$$\mathrm{store}_\varphi(\epsilon) \quad = (\epsilon, \epsilon)$$
$$\mathrm{store}_\varphi(\sigma \cdot a) = \begin{cases} (\sigma_s \cdot \sigma_c \cdot a, \epsilon) & \text{if } \kappa_\varphi(\sigma_s \cdot \sigma_c \cdot a), \\ (\sigma_s, \sigma_c \cdot a) & \text{otherwise} \end{cases}$$

with $(\sigma_s, \sigma_c) = \mathrm{store}_\varphi(\sigma)$.

Function store_φ takes a word over Σ as input and returns a pair of words over Σ, and the first element of the output of function store_φ is the output of the enforcement function. The first element of the output of function store_φ is a prefix of the input that satisfies property φ; and the second element is a suffix of the input that the enforcer cannot output yet. Function store_φ is defined inductively (see [13] for detailed explanation).

Predictive Runtime Enforcement. In predictive RE setting [13], instead of considering Σ^* as the language of possible inputs, another property $\psi \subseteq \Sigma^*$ defines the set of possible sequences that the EM receives as input at runtime. ψ is considered to be an abstract model or knowledge of the system obtained using some static-analysis techniques.

In addition to soundness[2], transparency and monotonicity constraints, a predictive enforcement function should satisfy an additional constraint called *urgency*. Constraint urgency expresses that if the input received so far does not satisfy the property φ, it can still be released as output if all possible inputs that the EM will receive in the future will allow to satisfy φ. A predictive enforcement function takes words that belong to the input property ψ as input and outputs words that belong to φ. In addition to property φ, a predictive enforcement function also requires property ψ as input.

Definition 2 (Predictive Enforcement Function). Given $\varphi, \psi \subseteq \Sigma^*$, the predictive enforcement function is $E_{\psi \triangleright \varphi} : \Sigma^* \to \Sigma^*$, defined as $E_{\psi \triangleright \varphi}(\sigma) = \Pi_1\big(\mathrm{store}_{\psi \triangleright \varphi}(\sigma)\big)$.

The only difference in $\mathrm{store}_{\psi \triangleright \varphi}$ compared to store_φ (Definition 1) is in the condition that is checked upon receiving a new event a (to output events that were not released earlier (σ_c) followed by the received event a). In the non-predictive case function κ_φ is used for this purpose, which checks whether the input sequence received so far belongs to property φ. In the predictive case, it is replaced with the following function $\kappa_{\psi \triangleright \varphi}$.

$$\kappa_{\psi \triangleright \varphi}(\sigma) = (\forall \sigma_{\mathrm{con}} \in \Sigma^* : \sigma \cdot \sigma_{\mathrm{con}} \in \psi \implies \exists \sigma' \in \Sigma^* : \sigma' \preccurlyeq \sigma_{\mathrm{con}} \wedge \sigma \cdot \sigma' \in \varphi).$$

---

[2] In the predictive setting, soundness is restricted to input words that belong to ψ.

Function $\kappa_{\psi\triangleright\varphi}$ uses input property ψ to anticipate the future and release the received input earlier. It takes a word over Σ as input and returns a Boolean as output. If every possible continuation σ_{con} of the received input σ according to ψ allows to satisfy φ in the future, then it returns true. It returns false if the received input sequence does not satisfy φ, and there is a continuation σ_{con} of the received input σ that will not allow to satisfy φ (i.e., there is no prefix σ' of σ_{con} such that $\sigma \cdot \sigma' \in \varphi$).

Remark 1. In [13] we prove that the predictive enforcement function (Definition 2) satisfies soundness, transparency, monotonicity and urgency constraints. When $\psi = \Sigma^*$, we show that the urgency constraint reduces to one of the transparency constraints and the function $\kappa_{\psi\triangleright\varphi}(\sigma)$ can be simplified as $\kappa_{\psi\triangleright\varphi}(\sigma) = (\sigma \in \varphi)$. Thus, Definition 2 reduces to Definition 1 when $\psi = \Sigma^*$.

Algorithms and Implementation. Algorithms describing how to implement the enforcement functions are detailed in [13]. An implementation of these algorithms in Python is available for download at: https://github.com/SrinivasPinisetty/PredictiveRE.

3   Monolithic Vs. Compositional Runtime Enforcement Approaches

In this section we discuss three different approaches for enforcing multiple properties, namely, monolithic RE, and RE using serial or parallel composition of EMs. To simplify notation and explanations, we consider the enforcement of only two properties φ_1 and φ_2. The results generalize to any number of properties. Properties φ_1 and φ_2 are assumed to be regular properties defined by complete and deterministic automata $\mathcal{A}_{\varphi_1}$ and $\mathcal{A}_{\varphi_2}$ over some alphabet Σ.

3.1   Monolithic Approach

In the monolithic approach, properties are first combined using intersection and an EM for the resulting property is synthesized (See Fig. 1a). Specifically, given any two regular properties φ_1 and φ_2, to enforce both these properties, we first compute $\varphi = \varphi_1 \cap \varphi_2$ (by computing the product of the automata for φ_1 and φ_2). Then we synthesize an EM for φ using the approach described in Sect. 2.2. For any input word σ, $E_\varphi(\sigma)$ is sound and transparent with respect to $\varphi_1 \cap \varphi_2$. Since $E_\varphi(\sigma)$ satisfies $\varphi_1 \cap \varphi_2$, $E_\varphi(\sigma)$ obviously satisfies both φ_1 and φ_2. Regarding transparency, if the input satisfies only φ_1 (or only φ_2), then the output will not be equal to the input. The output will be equal to the input only if the input satisfies $\varphi_1 \cap \varphi_2$ (i.e., the input satisfies both φ_1 and φ_2).

Remark 2 (Maximality). From [13] we know that for any given regular property φ, for any sequence $\sigma \in \Sigma^*$, if $E_\varphi(\sigma) \neq \epsilon$ then it is the maximal prefix of σ that satisfies φ. Thus, for any given regular properties φ_1 and φ_2, for any input word $\sigma \in \Sigma^*$, if $E_{\varphi_1 \cap \varphi_2}(\sigma) \neq \epsilon$, it is the maximal prefix of σ that satisfies both properties φ_1 and φ_2 (i.e., maximal prefix that belongs to $\varphi_1 \cap \varphi_2$).

Table 1. Counterexamples to compositionality of the serial approach.

σ	$E_{RE1}(\sigma)$	$E_{RE2}(E_{RE1}(\sigma))$	$E_{RE2}(\sigma)$	$E_{RE1}(E_{RE2}(\sigma))$
a	ϵ	ϵ	ϵ	ϵ
ab	ab	ϵ	ϵ	ϵ
aba	ab	ϵ	aba	$ab \notin RE1 \cap RE2$
$abac$	$abac$	$aba \notin RE1 \cap RE2$	aba	$ab \notin RE1 \cap RE2$

Example 3. Consider the property $S1 \cap S2$ defined by the automaton in Fig. 3, where $\Sigma = \{a, b\}$. Consider input sequence $\sigma = abbb$. The output of the EM $E_{S1 \cap S2}(abbb) = abbb$. Notice that the word $abbb$ is accepted by the automaton $\mathcal{A}_{S1 \cap S2}$, and it is also accepted by automata $\mathcal{A}_{S1}$ and $\mathcal{A}_{S2}$. Consider another input sequence $\sigma = aaabb$. The output of the EM will be aa which is the maximal prefix of σ accepted by $\mathcal{A}_{S1 \cap S2}$. Notice that the input word $aaabb$ is accepted by $\mathcal{A}_{S1}$, but is not accepted by $\mathcal{A}_{S2}$.

3.2 Serial Composition of Enforcement Monitors

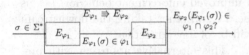

Fig. 4. Serial composition.

Given two properties φ_1 and φ_2, we can synthesize EMs E_{φ_1} and E_{φ_2} for each of them, and then compose them in series, as illustrated in Fig. 4. In this type of serial composition the output of E_{φ_1} is fed as input to E_{φ_2}. As a result we obtain a new EM, denoted $E_{\varphi_1} \Rrightarrow E_{\varphi_2}$. In this section we investigate whether $E_{\varphi_1} \Rrightarrow E_{\varphi_2}$ generally enforces $\varphi_1 \cap \varphi_2$. We are also interested to see whether the final output that we obtain using the serial composition approach is equal to the output we would obtain using the monolithic approach.

Let us now formally define serial composition of two EMs.

Definition 3 (Serial Composition of Enforcement Monitors). Let $E_{\varphi_1} : \Sigma^* \to \Sigma^*$ be the enforcer for a property $\varphi_1 \subseteq \Sigma^*$, and $E_{\varphi_2} : \Sigma^* \to \Sigma^*$ be the enforcer for a property $\varphi_2 \subseteq \Sigma^*$. Their serial composition is a new enforcer $E_{\varphi_1} \Rrightarrow E_{\varphi_2} : \Sigma^* \to \Sigma^*$ defined as follows: $\forall \sigma \in \Sigma^*, (E_{\varphi_1} \Rrightarrow E_{\varphi_2})(\sigma) = E_{\varphi_2}(E_{\varphi_1}(\sigma))$.

Example 4 (Composing Enforcers in Series does Not Generally Enforce Both Properties). Let the automaton in Fig. 2a define property φ_1, and the automaton in Fig. 2b define property φ_2. Table 1 shows the outputs $E_{RE1}(\sigma)$, $E_{RE2}(E_{RE1}(\sigma))$, $E_{RE2}(\sigma)$, and $E_{RE1}(E_{RE2}(\sigma))$, when the input sequence $\sigma = abac$ is processed incrementally. We notice that generally $E_{RE2}(E_{RE1}(\sigma)) \neq E_{RE1}(E_{RE2}(\sigma))$, which implies that $E_{\varphi_1} \Rrightarrow E_{\varphi_2}$ and $E_{\varphi_2} \Rrightarrow E_{\varphi_1}$ generally differ. Also notice that $E_{RE1}(E_{RE2}(abac))$ is ab which does not satisfy $RE1 \cap RE2$, and $E_{RE2}(E_{RE1}(abac))$ is aba which also does not satisfy $RE1 \cap RE2$.

What the above example shows is that, independently of the order used, the serial approach is generally non-compositional. In particular, given regular properties φ_1, φ_2, and input sequence $\sigma \in \Sigma^*$, neither $E_{\varphi_1}(E_{\varphi_2}(\sigma))$ nor $E_{\varphi_2}(E_{\varphi_1}(\sigma))$ generally satisfy $\varphi_1 \cap \varphi_2$. This is despite the fact that $E_{\varphi_1}(\sigma)$ is guaranteed to satisfy φ_1 and $E_{\varphi_2}(\sigma)$ is guaranteed to satisfy φ_2. As we shall see later in Sect. 4, the serial approach is compositional for certain subclasses of regular properties.

3.3 Predictive Runtime Enforcement in Serial Composition (does Not Help)

Let us now consider the predictive RE mechanism in a serial composition setting. Predictive RE mechanism makes use of knowledge of the system allowing to output some events immediately instead of delaying or blocking them [13]. In predictive RE, instead of letting the input sequence σ range over Σ^*, we let it range over a given property $\psi \subseteq \Sigma^*$ where ψ captures a model or some knowledge that we have about the system.

When we consider serial composition of enforcers $E_{\varphi_1} \Rrightarrow E_{\varphi_2}$, we know that every input received by E_{φ_2} belongs to φ_1. This is because every input received by E_{φ_2} is an output generated by E_{φ_1}, and the latter is guaranteed to enforce φ_1. Thus, it makes sense to use the predictive method to generate the downstream enforcer, hoping that this will result in improved enforcement behavior. Let us now see whether this is indeed the case, i.e., whether taking the downstream enforcer to be $E_{\varphi_1 \triangleright \varphi_2}$ instead of E_{φ_2}, will be of any advantage.[3]

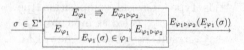

Fig. 5. Serial composition with prediction.

This alternative approach with prediction is illustrated in Fig. 5. We consider serial composition where the downstream EM (i.e., the EM for φ_2) is the predictive EM $E_{\varphi_1 \triangleright \varphi_2}$. The input that $E_{\varphi_1 \triangleright \varphi_2}$ receives is $E_{\varphi_1}(\sigma)$, which is guaranteed to belong to φ_1.

One generally expects that in some cases, considering predictive RE for the second EM in serial composition allows to output some events earlier, and there may be some situations where $E_{\varphi_1 \triangleright \varphi_2}(E_{\varphi_1}(\sigma)) \neq E_{\varphi_2}(E_{\varphi_1}(\sigma))$ (in fact $E_{\varphi_1 \triangleright \varphi_2}(E_{\varphi_1}(\sigma))$ to be longer compared to $E_{\varphi_2}(E_{\varphi_1}(\sigma))$). Surprisingly, we found that this is not the case. For any given regular properties φ_1 and φ_2, we show that considering predictive enforcement for the second EM in serial composition has no advantage and the output for any input sequence will be equal to the output that we obtain using standard EM.

According to the definition of predictive enforcer (Definition 2), given properties $\psi, \varphi \subseteq \Sigma^*$, where ψ is the property defining the input and φ is the property we want to enforce, at runtime though the received input sequence σ_o does not satisfy the property φ, it is still immediately released as output if for every possible extension σ_{con} of σ_o such that $\sigma_o \cdot \sigma_{con} \in \psi$, there is a prefix $\sigma' \preccurlyeq \sigma_{con}$ such that $\sigma_o \cdot \sigma'$ satisfies φ.

---

[3] Note that in order to compute $E_{\varphi_1 \triangleright \varphi_2}$ both φ_1 and φ_2 need to be known.

Table 2. Comparing predictive RE, and serial composition with/without prediction.

σ_o	$E_\psi(\sigma_o)$	$E_{\psi \triangleright \varphi}(E_\psi(\sigma_o))$	$E_\varphi(E_\psi(\sigma_o))$	$E_{\psi \triangleright \varphi}(\sigma_o)$
r	ϵ	ϵ	ϵ	r
ra	ϵ	ϵ	ϵ	ra
$rag \in \psi$	rga	rga	rga	rga
$ragr$	rga	rga	rga	$rgar$
$ragra$	rga	rga	rga	$rgara$
$ragrag \in \psi$	$ragrag$	$ragrag$	$ragrag$	$ragrag$

As illustrated in Example 5, during some steps at runtime, the received input may not belong to the input property ψ (but we know that it will be eventually in the future according to ψ). According to the definition of $\kappa_{\psi \triangleright \varphi}$, predicting future input sequences helps only at those moments when the received input σ_o does not belong to ψ, and it also does not belong to φ (the property we want to enforce), but if every extension of σ_o according to ψ allows to satisfy φ, then σ_o is output immediately since according to ψ we will receive some more events in the future that will certainly allow to satisfy φ.

Consequently, in the serial composition approach, where we consider the enforcer for the second property φ_2 as predictive enforcer and the input property for it to be φ_1, in serial composition $E_{\varphi_1} \Rightarrow E_{\varphi_1 \triangleright \varphi_2}$, first notice that E_{φ_1} (standard non-predictive enforcer for φ_1) will only output sequences that belong to φ_1. When the observed input does not satisfy φ_1, then E_{φ_1} will block and wait for more events to be received. So, what the second enforcer $E_{\varphi_1 \triangleright \varphi_2}$ receives as input will always belong to φ_1. Thus, knowledge of φ_1 for the second enforcer in serial composition is not useful in any case.

Example 5 Consider two properties ψ and φ defined by the automata in Fig. 6, where the set of actions $\Sigma = \{r, a, g\}$. Let us consider input sequence $\sigma = ragrag \in \psi$. Table 2 illustrates the output at each step when the input word σ is processed incrementally. At each step, the observation of the input is a prefix of σ (denoted as σ_o). In the third column ($E_{\psi \triangleright \varphi}(E_\psi(\sigma_o))$), we consider serial composition of the enforcer for ψ and $E_{\psi \triangleright \varphi}$ (thus, $E_\psi(\sigma_o)$ is fed as input to $E_{\psi \triangleright \varphi}$). In the fifth column ($E_{\psi \triangleright \varphi}(\sigma_o)$), ψ is considered as a model of the system, and the observed input σ_o is fed as input to $E_{\psi \triangleright \varphi}$.

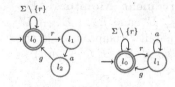

Fig. 6. $\mathcal{A}_\psi$ (left), $\mathcal{A}_\varphi$ (right).

We can clearly notice that from where the predictive enforcer $E_{\psi \triangleright \varphi}$ receives the input also matters. If $E_{\psi \triangleright \varphi}$ receives the input event after event from some system (event emitter), where ψ is a model of the system, then prediction indeed helps to release events earlier as illustrated in this example (column $E_{\psi \triangleright \varphi}(\sigma_o)$ in Table 2) and other examples in [13]. If $E_{\psi \triangleright \varphi}$ receives the input from a standard enforcer for

ψ (column $E_{\psi \triangleright \varphi}(E_\psi(\sigma_o))$ in Table 2) which is the case in serial composition, knowledge of ψ for the second enforcer is not useful. In this particular example, we can also notice that $E_{\psi \triangleright \varphi}(E_\psi(\sigma_o)) = E_\varphi(E_\psi(\sigma_o))$.

Theorem 1 (Serial Composition with Prediction does Not Help). *For any two regular properties $\varphi_1 \subseteq \Sigma^*$ and $\varphi_2 \subseteq \Sigma^*$, $\forall \sigma \in \Sigma^*$, $E_{\varphi_1 \triangleright \varphi_2}(E_{\varphi_1}(\sigma)) = E_{\varphi_2}(E_{\varphi_1}(\sigma))$.*

We prove that given any two regular properties φ_1 and φ_2, in the serial composition approach, considering predictive enforcement for the second enforcer (when we do not have a model of the system and when the first enforcer is a standard non-predictive one) has no advantage, and for any input, the output will be equal to the output we obtain using standard non-predictive enforcer for φ_2.

We thus conclude that if we do not have a model or knowledge of the system, and if the first enforcer in non-predictive, using predictive RE for second enforcer (though we know that the input words it receives belongs to φ_1) is not useful. When we have a property describing possible input sequences that the enforcement mechanism receives from a system, and if first enforcer is a predictive enforcer, then using predictive RE for the second enforcer in serial composition is useful.

3.4   Parallel Composition of Enforcement Monitors

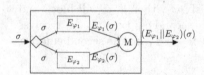

Fig. 7. Parallel composition.

We now introduce the parallel composition of two EMs E_{φ_1} and E_{φ_2}, denoted $E_{\varphi_1} || E_{\varphi_2}$, and check whether it enforces $\varphi_1 \cap \varphi_2$. As illustrated in Fig. 7, in the parallel composition approach, the input sequence σ is fed into both E_{φ_1} and E_{φ_2} simultaneously. The enforcement monitors E_{φ_1} and E_{φ_2} run in parallel. Then their outputs $E_{\varphi_1}(\sigma)$ and $E_{\varphi_2}(\sigma)$ are somehow *merged* (block denoted M in the figure) in order to obtain the output of the composite enforcer $E_{\varphi_1} || E_{\varphi_2}$.

In our case, the merge block outputs the maximal common prefix of its inputs. Formally, we define the *merge* of two words $\sigma_1, \sigma_2 \in \Sigma^*$ as $merge(\sigma_1, \sigma_2) = max_{\preccurlyeq} \{ \sigma \in \Sigma^* | \sigma \preccurlyeq \sigma_1 \wedge \sigma \preccurlyeq \sigma_2 \}$.

Definition 4 (Parallel Composition of Enforcement Monitors). Let $E_{\varphi_1} : \Sigma^* \to \Sigma^*$ be the enforcer for a property $\varphi_1 \subseteq \Sigma^*$, and $E_{\varphi_2} : \Sigma^* \to \Sigma^*$ be the enforcer for a property $\varphi_2 \subseteq \Sigma^*$. Their parallel composition is the enforcer $E_{\varphi_1} || E_{\varphi_2} : \Sigma^* \to \Sigma^*$ defined as follows: $\forall \sigma \in \Sigma^*, (E_{\varphi_1} || E_{\varphi_2})(\sigma) = merge(E_{\varphi_1}(\sigma), E_{\varphi_2}(\sigma))$.

Example 6 (Composing Enforcers in Parallel does Not Generally Enforce Both Properties). Consider two regular properties $RE1$ and $CS2$, defined by automata in Figs. 2a and f. Table 3 illustrates the outputs of E_{RE1}, E_{CS2}, and

$E_{RE1}||E_{CS2}$ when the input sequence abc is processed incrementally. Notice that $(E_{RE1}||E_{CS2})(abc)$ is ab which does not satisfy $RE1 \cap CS2$.

For some regular properties φ_1, φ_2, for some input sequence $\sigma \in \Sigma^*$, $(E_{\varphi_1}||E_{\varphi_2})(\sigma)$ may not satisfy $\varphi_1 \cap \varphi_2$. Thus, when we want to enforce two regular properties φ_1 and φ_2, we cannot use parallel composition since the final output may not belong to $\varphi_1 \cap \varphi_2$ as illustrated in our example. As we shall see later in Sect. 4, parallel composition is compositional for certain subclasses of regular properties.

Remark 3 (Merge). Our *merge* function is independent of the properties and also of the enforcers. This is intentional, as we want to achieve maximal modularity. We are currently exploring alternative merge operations which are compositional for all regular properties, yet exhibit the same degree of modularity. A potential such alternative is a merge which outputs the maximal prefix of the input streams that it receives only when new "chunks" are added to both input streams. We plan to formalize and study further the compositionality properties of this alternative merge operator in future work.

4   Compositionality for Subclasses of Regular Properties

In Sect. 3, we saw that the serial and parallel approaches are not compositional for all regular properties. In this section we consider subclasses of regular properties, and in particular, safety or co-safety properties, and investigate compositionality for these subclasses.

Table 3. Counterexample to compositionality of the parallel approach.

σ	$E_{RE1}(\sigma)$	$E_{CS2}(\sigma)$	$(E_{RE1}||E_{CS2})(\sigma)$
a	ϵ	ϵ	ϵ
ab	ab	ϵ	ϵ
abc	ab	abc	$ab \notin RE1 \cap CS2$

Safety and Co-Safety Properties. Given two properties φ_1 and φ_2 such that one is a safety property and the other is a co-safety property, for some input words, the output of serial and parallel composition of EMs E_{φ_1} and E_{φ_2} may not satisfy $\varphi_1 \cap \varphi_2$. Moreover, the output obtained using serial and parallel composition approaches may not be equal to the output obtained using the monolithic approach. For serial composition, the order of composition of enforcers also matters. We illustrate this via Example 7.

Table 4. Composing enforcers of a safety and a co-safety property.

σ	$E_{S1}(\sigma)$	$E_{CS2}(\sigma)$	$E_{S1 \cap CS2}(\sigma)$	$E_{CS2}(E_{S1}(\sigma))$	$E_{S1}(E_{CS2}(\sigma))$	$(E_{S1}||E_{CS2})(\sigma)$
ϵ	ϵ	ϵ	ϵ	ϵ	ϵ	ϵ
a	a	ϵ	ϵ	ϵ	ϵ	ϵ
ab	ab	ϵ	ϵ	ϵ	ϵ	ϵ
abc	ab	abc	ϵ	ϵ	ab	ab

Example 7 (Composing Enforcers of a Safety and a Co-Safety Property does Not Generally Enforce Both Properties). Consider the safety automaton in Fig. 2c and the co-safety automaton in Fig. 2f defining properties $S1$ and $CS2$ respectively. Table 4 presents $E_{S1}(\sigma)$, $E_{CS2}(\sigma)$, $E_{S1 \cap CS2}(\sigma)$, $E_{CS2}(E_{S1}(\sigma))$, $E_{S1}(E_{CS2}(\sigma))$ and $(E_{S1} \| E_{CS2})(\sigma)$ when the input sequence $\sigma = abc$ is processed incrementally. We can notice that in the last step, upon receiving abc, $E_{S1}(E_{CS2}(\sigma))$ and $(E_{S1} \| E_{CS2})(\sigma)$ is ab which does not satisfy $CS2$ and thus also does not satisfy $S1 \cap CS2$.

Composing in Series Enforcers of a Safety Property and a Regular Property. In Sect. 3 we already saw that for two regular properties serial composition may not work. Via Example 7 we also saw that when one property is a safety property and the other property is a co-safety property, then serial composition approach may not work. However, in Example 7, we can also notice that at every step $E_{CS2}(E_{S1}(\sigma))$ satisfies $S1 \cap CS2$.

In fact, we show that given two properties φ_1 and φ_2, if one of them is identified to be a *safety* property (say φ_1), then serial composition approach works by fixing the order of composition. Property φ_1 should be considered as the first (upstream) property in serial composition. The second (downstream) property φ_2 can be any regular property.

Since φ_1 is a safety property, for any input word σ, all the prefixes of $E_{\varphi_1}(\sigma)$ satisfies φ_1. Thus when $E_{\varphi_1}(\sigma)$ is fed as input to E_{φ_2} (where φ_2 is any regular property), its output will be the maximal prefix of $E_{\varphi_1}(\sigma)$ that satisfies φ_2, which will be the maximal prefix of σ satisfying both properties φ_1 and φ_2.

Theorem 2 (Serial Composition of a Safety and a Regular Property).
Given a safety property $\varphi_1 \subseteq \Sigma^*$, and a regular property $\varphi_2 \subseteq \Sigma^*$, $\forall \sigma \in \Sigma^*$,
$E_{\varphi_2}(E_{\varphi_1}(\sigma)) = E_{\varphi_1 \cap \varphi_2}(\sigma).$

Let us now see whether serial or parallel composition works when both properties φ_1 and φ_2 are safety (or both co-safety).

Serial Composition (Safety Properties). When both φ_1 and φ_2 are safety properties, it is straightforward from Theorem 2 that serial composition approach works and the order of composition of enforcers also does not matter. To understand further, consider $E_{\varphi_1} \Rightarrow E_{\varphi_2}$. For any word σ, $E_{\varphi_1}(\sigma)$ is the maximal prefix of σ satisfying φ_1. Since φ_1 is prefix-closed, any prefix of $E_{\varphi_1}(\sigma)$ satisfies φ_1. $E_{\varphi_2}(E_{\varphi_1}(\sigma))$ will be the maximal prefix of $E_{\varphi_1}(\sigma)$ satisfying φ_2, which also satisfies φ_1. Similarly, we can also easily notice that $E_{\varphi_2} \Rightarrow E_{\varphi_1}$ will also satisfy both φ_1 and φ_2 since both are safety properties.

Corollary 1. *Given any two safety properties φ_1 and φ_2, $\forall \sigma \in \Sigma^*$, $E_{\varphi_1}(E_{\varphi_2}(\sigma)) = E_{\varphi_2}(E_{\varphi_1}(\sigma)) = E_{\varphi_1 \cap \varphi_2}(\sigma).$*

Corollary 1 is a direct consequence of Theorem 2. When both φ_1 and φ_2 are safety properties, for any input word, the output we obtain by composing enforcers E_{φ_1} and E_{φ_2} in series will be equal to the output obtained using the monolithic approach and thus satisfies $\varphi_1 \cap \varphi_2$ (if it is $\neq \epsilon$).

Parallel Composition (Safety Properties). When both φ_1 and φ_2 are safety properties, then parallel composition also works. Since both φ_1 and φ_2 are prefix-closed, any prefix of $E_{\varphi_1}(\sigma)$ satisfies φ_1, and any prefix of $E_{\varphi_2}(\sigma)$ satisfies φ_2. $(E_{\varphi_1}\|E_{\varphi_2})(\sigma)$ is the maximal common prefix of both these words which also satisfies both φ_1 and φ_2.

Theorem 3 (Parallel Composition of Safety Properties). *Given any two safety properties φ_1 and φ_2, $\forall \sigma \in \Sigma^*$, $(E_{\varphi_1}\|E_{\varphi_2})(\sigma) = E_{\varphi_1 \cap \varphi_2}(\sigma)$.*

Theorem 3 shows that when both φ_1 and φ_2 are safety properties, for any input word, the output we obtain by composing enforcers E_{φ_1} and E_{φ_2} in parallel will be equal to the output obtained using the monolithic approach and thus satisfies $\varphi_1 \cap \varphi_2$ (if it is $\neq \epsilon$).

Table 5. Composing enforcers of two safety properties.

σ	$E_{S1}(\sigma)$	$E_{S2}(\sigma)$	$E_{S1 \cap S2}(\sigma)$	$E_{S2}(E_{S1}(\sigma))$	$E_{S1}(E_{S2}(\sigma))$	$(E_{S2}\|E_{S1})(\sigma)$
a	a	a	a	a	a	a
aa	aa	aa	aa	aa	aa	aa
aaa	aaa	aa	aa	aa	aa	aa
$aaab$	$aaab$	aa	aa	aa	aa	aa

Example 8 (Composing Enforcers of Two Safety Properties). Let us consider properties $S1$ and $S2$ defined by automata in Fig. 2c and d. Table 5 illustrates the output of different methods for enforcing $S1 \cap S2$ when the input sequence $aaab$ is processed incrementally. We can notice that at every step, all the methods result in the same output which satisfies the property $S1 \cap S2$.

Co-Safety Properties. When both φ_1 and φ_2 are co-safety properties, then both serial and parallel composition work. Regarding serial composition, consider $E_{\varphi_1} \Rrightarrow E_{\varphi_2}$. For any input word $\sigma \in \Sigma^*$, since φ_1 is extension-closed, if $\sigma \notin \varphi_1$, then $E_{\varphi_1}(\sigma) = \epsilon$ and thus $E_{\varphi_2}(E_{\varphi_1}(\sigma)) = \epsilon$ (irrespective of whether $\sigma \in \varphi_2$ or not). If $\sigma \in \varphi_1$, then $E_{\varphi_1}(\sigma) = \sigma$. In this case, if $\sigma \in \varphi_2$, then $E_{\varphi_2}(E_{\varphi_1}(\sigma)) = \sigma$ which is the maximal prefix of σ satisfying both φ_1 and φ_2. But if $\sigma \notin \varphi_2$, then since φ_2 is extension-closed, there is no prefix of $E_{\varphi_1}(\sigma)$ (which is σ) that satisfies φ_2, and the output will be ϵ.

Regarding parallel composition, for any input word σ if $\sigma \notin \varphi_1$ and $\sigma \notin \varphi_2$, then $E_{\varphi_1}(\sigma)$ and $E_{\varphi_2}(\sigma)$ will be ϵ (since the properties are extension-closed) and thus $(E_{\varphi_1}\|E_{\varphi_2})(\sigma)$ will also be ϵ. If σ satisfies only one property among φ_1 and φ_2, then the output of one of the enforcers will be ϵ, and thus the final output (which is the maximal common prefix of both the outputs) will be ϵ. Finally, if σ satisfies both φ_1 and φ_2 then $E_{\varphi_1}(\sigma)$ and $E_{\varphi_2}(\sigma)$ will be σ, the final output will thus be σ in this case.

Table 6. Composing enforcers of two co-safety properties.

σ	$E_{CS1}(\sigma)$	$E_{CS2}(\sigma)$	$E_{CS1 \cap CS2}(\sigma)$	$E_{CS2}(E_{CS1}(\sigma))$	$E_{CS1}(E_{CS2}(\sigma))$	$(E_{CS1}\|E_{CS2})(\sigma)$
a	ϵ	ϵ	ϵ	ϵ	ϵ	ϵ
ab	ab	ϵ	ϵ	ϵ	ϵ	ϵ
abc	abc	abc	abc	abc	abc	abc
$abca$	$abca$	$abca$	$abca$	$abca$	$abca$	$abca$

Example 9 (Composing Enforcers of Two Co-Safety Properties). Consider two co-safety properties $CS1$ and $CS2$ defined by automata in Fig. 2e and f. From Table 6, when the input sequence abc is processed incrementally, we can notice that at every step, the output of all the three methods (monolithic, serial and parallel composition) are equal and belongs to $CS1 \cap CS2$ (if $\neq \epsilon$).

Theorem 4 (Serial and Parallel Composition of Co-Safety Properties).
Given any two co-safety properties φ_1 and φ_2, $\forall \sigma \in \Sigma^*$,

1. $E_{\varphi_1}(E_{\varphi_2}(\sigma)) = E_{\varphi_2}(E_{\varphi_1}(\sigma)) = E_{\varphi_1 \cap \varphi_2}(\sigma)$,
2. $(E_{\varphi_1}\|E_{\varphi_2})(\sigma) = E_{\varphi_1 \cap \varphi_2}(\sigma)$.

Theorem 4 shows that when both φ_1 and φ_2 are co-safety properties, for any input word, the output we obtain by composing enforcers E_{φ_1} and E_{φ_2} in series (or parallel) will be equal to the output obtained using the monolithic approach and thus satisfies $\varphi_1 \cap \varphi_2$ (if it is $\neq \epsilon$).

Monolithic, Serial and Parallel Composition Approaches. From Theorems 2, 3 and 4 (also illustrated by our examples), we conclude that for safety (or co-safety) properties, all the three approaches are equivalent with respect to the input-output behavior. For any input word σ, we obtain the same output using any of these three approaches, which is the maximal prefix of σ that satisfies all the properties (if the output is $\neq \epsilon$).

Corollary 2. *Given two safety (co-safety) properties φ_1 and φ_2, for any input sequence $\sigma \in \Sigma^*$ the output of the enforcer that we obtain for enforcing $\varphi_1 \cap \varphi_2$ using any of the methods (composing properties and synthesising a single EM, serial composition of enforcers, and parallel composition of enforcers) will be equal.*

$$\forall \sigma \in \Sigma^*, E_{\varphi_1 \cap \varphi_2}(\sigma) = E_{\varphi_2}(E_{\varphi_1}(\sigma)) = E_{\varphi_2}(E_{\varphi_1}(\sigma)) = (E_{\varphi_1}\|E_{\varphi_2})(\sigma).$$

5   Related Work

Compositionality is essential for the design, analysis and verification of large and complex systems, and has been extensively studied in various settings such as test generation [7], model-checking [3,8] and reactive synthesis [9].

In the area of runtime monitoring, [10] deals with composition of monitors for runtime verification. Composition of two monitors raises an alarm whenever one of them does so, and the authors discuss about different ways to organize monitors (based on how information flows between them). In [4] authors integrate runtime verification in to the BIP (Behavior, Interaction and Priority) framework, which is a component-based framework that allows to build complex systems by coordinating the behavior of atomic components described as labeled transition systems (LTS). However, it does consider sub-properties, and composition of monitors, and deals with integrating verification monitor for a property in to the BIP framework.

Runtime enforcement was initiated by security automata proposed by Schneider [14] that focus on safety properties, and blocks the execution when an illegal sequence of actions (not compliant with the property) is recognized. Several enforcement models have been proposed later which also allow a monitor to correct the input sequence by suppressing and (or) inserting events [11]. Bloem et al. [2] presented a framework to synthesize enforcement monitors for reactive systems, called *shields*, from a set of safety properties. In all these approaches, system is considered as a black-box. Recently, predictive RE framework presented in [13] makes use of a-priori knowledge of the system for providing better quality-of-service. All these approaches focus mainly on synthesis of an EM for a given property but do not handle compositionality of EMs. If enforcing a set of properties is considered, is is done using the monolithic approach.

The framework in [5] deals with producing a monitor from a property defined as a Street automaton. Enforcers in [5] are finite state machines with auxiliary memory, and can be composed by a product-automaton type of construction. This resembles our parallel composition of enforcers, but with a different merge operation which is less modular as product of automata requires the "internals" (e.g., state-space) of both enforcers to be known. Also, serial composition is not discussed in [5].

Polymer [1] is a programming language supporting definition and composition of runtime security policies for Java applications. Policies in Polymer specify runtime constraints on un-trusted Java programs. Polymer allows composition of smaller sub-policy modules.

6   Conclusion

When we want to enforce multiple properties on a system, an obvious solution is to use a monolithic approach, where the properties are first combined into one single property φ, and a single enforcer is synthesized for φ. The drawback of this approach is that it is not modular. In this paper, we study the compositionality of runtime enforcement, with the goal of developing modular approaches which address scalability, reuse, and security concerns.

On the negative side, we showed that enforcement of regular properties is generally non-compositional, w.r.t. both serial and parallel composition. On the positive side, we identified special cases (subclasses of regular properties, such as safety or co-safety properties) for which enforcement is compositional. We also showed that using the predictive RE method to compute the downstream enforcer in a serial composition setting does not improve quality-of-service. This is a surprising result, since predictive RE generally results in enforcers which anticipate their input to reduce delays in their output [13].

In addition to the benefits listed above, the compositional approach presented in this paper allows for easier fault *localization* compared to the monolithic approach (e.g., identifying which sub-property is causing the problem, when it is impossible to correct a given input stream). We plan to investigate such localization in future work. Future work also includes studying compositionality in the context of runtime enforcement for real-time systems. (Monolithic) RE for real-time systems has been studied in [6,12]. We intend to study serial and parallel composition schemes in these timed settings.

In our earlier work [13] we described a prototype implementation of enforcer synthesis algorithms, now also available at https://github.com/Srinivas Pinisetty/PredictiveRE. This prototype can be used straightaway to synthesize enforcers for each individual property in our compositional schemes. Then it remains to provide implementations of auxiliary operators such as *merge*. We plan to do so, and therefore have a complete implementation of the compositional RTE framework presented here. We also plan to evaluate our approach on case studies, for instance in the context of security [14].

Acknowledgement. This work was partially supported by the Academy of Finland and the U.S. National Science Foundation (awards #1329759 and #1139138).

References

1. Bauer, L., Ligatti, J., Walker, D.: Composing expressive runtime security policies. ACM Trans. Softw. Eng. Methodol. **18**(3), 9 (2009)
2. Bloem, R., Könighofer, B., Könighofer, R., Wang, C.: Shield synthesis: runtime enforcement for reactive systems. In: Baier, C., Tinelli, C. (eds.) TACAS 2015. LNCS, vol. 9035, pp. 533–548. Springer, Heidelberg (2015)
3. Clarke, E., Long, D., McMillan, K.: Compositional model checking. In: 1989 Fourth Annual Symposium on Logic in Computer Science, LICS 1989, Proceedings., pp. 353–362 (1989)
4. Falcone, Y., Jaber, M., Nguyen, T.H., Bozga, M., Bensalem, S.: Runtime verification of component-based systems in the BIP framework with formally-proved sound and complete instrumentation. Softw. Syst. Model. **14**(1), 173–199 (2015)
5. Falcone, Y., Mounier, L., Fernandez, J.C., Richier, J.L.: Runtime enforcement monitors: composition, synthesis, and enforcement abilities. FMSD **38**(3), 223–262 (2011)
6. Falcone, Y., Jéron, T., Marchand, H., Pinisetty, S.: Runtime enforcement of regular timed properties by suppressing and delaying events. Sci. Comput. Program. **123**, 2–41 (2016)
7. Godefroid, P.: Compositional dynamic test generation. In: Proceedings of the 34th Annual ACM SIGPLAN-SIGACT. pp. 47–54. POPL, ACM, New York, USA (2007)

8. Grumberg, O., Long, D.E.: Model checking and modular verification. ACM Trans. Program. Lang. Syst. **16**(3), 843–871 (1994)
9. Kugler, H., Segall, I.: Compositional synthesis of reactive systems from live sequence chart specifications. In: Kowalewski, S., Philippou, A. (eds.) TACAS 2009. LNCS, vol. 5505, pp. 77–91. Springer, Heidelberg (2009)
10. Levy, J., Saïdi, H., Uribe, T.E.: Combining monitors for runtime system verification. Electron. Notes Theor. Comput. Sci. **70**(4), 112–127 (2002). runtime Verification
11. Ligatti, J., Bauer, L., Walker, D.: Run-time enforcement of non safety policies. ACM Trans. Inf. Syst. Secur. **12**(3), 19:1–19:41 (2009)
12. Pinisetty, S., Falcone, Y., Jéron, T., Marchand, H., Rollet, A., Nguena Timo, O.: Runtime enforcement of timed properties revisited. FMSD **45**(3), 381–422 (2014)
13. Pinisetty, S., Preoteasa, V., Tripakis, S., Jéron, T., Falcone, Y., Marchand, H.: Predictive runtime enforcement. In: Symposium on Applied Computing (SAC-SVT). ACM (2016)
14. Schneider, F.B.: Enforceable security policies. ACM Trans. Inf. Syst. Secur. **3**(1), 30–50 (2000)

Improving an Industrial Test Generation Tool Using SMT Solver

Hao Ren[1], Devesh Bhatt[2(✉)], and Jan Hvozdovic[3]

[1] Department of Electrical and Computer Engineering, Iowa State University,
Ames, IA 50014, USA
[2] Honeywell Aerospace Advanced Technology, 1985 Douglas Dr N,
Golden Valley, MN 55422, USA
devesh.bhatt@honeywell.com
[3] Honeywell spol. s.r.o. - Aerospace Engineering, 100 Turanka,
627 00 Brno, Czech Republic

Abstract. We present an SMT solving based test generation approach
for MATLAB Simulink designs, implemented in the HiLiTE tool developed by Honeywell for verification of avionic systems. The test requirements for a Simulink model are represented by a set of behavioral equivalence classes for each block in the model, in terms of its input(s) and
output. A unique feature of our approach is that the equivalence class
definitions, as well as the upstream subgraph of a block under test, are
translated as constraints into SMT expressions. An SMT solver is called
at the back-end of HiLiTE to find a satisfiable solution that is further
augmented into an end-to-end test case at the model level.

1 Introduction

As the industry practices engage model-based design increasingly, model-based
verification and testing [1] techniques emerge to keep up with the trends. In
avionics area, comprehensive testing methods and tools are required to assure
that safety-critical systems like flight controls are certified to the guidelines
established by standard processes such as the DO-178C [2].

At Honeywell, researchers have developed the *Honeywell Integrated Lifecycle
Tools & Environment (HiLiTE)* suite of tools for the automated verification
of avionics applications developed using MATLAB Simulink/Stateflow. HiLiTE
performs automatic test generation [3] on Simulink models based upon the low-
level requirements (LLRs) expressed by the model elements. The tests are then
applied to the executable object code generated from the model to verify that the
code complies with the LLRs in the design model. HiLiTE has been qualified as a
DO-178C verification tool and deployed in several avionics product certifications
to deliver significant cost savings in the verification effort.

This paper presents an SMT solving technique to extend the earlier
heuristics-based test case generation approaches implemented in HiLiTE, providing improved performance on models with complex constraints or non-linear

This research was supported in part by NASA Contract NNA13AC55C.

© The Author(s) 2016

S. Rayadurgam and O. Tkachuk (Eds.): NFM 2016, LNCS 9690, pp. 100–106, 2016.
DOI: 10.1007/978-3-319-40648-0_8

arithmetic computations. SMT solving is the decision procedure of determining whether a formula in first-order-logic is satisfiable and finding a concrete solution if it is. SMT Solvers, such as Z3 [4], Yices [5], etc., have rapidly matured over the last 5 years and have been used in various areas including automated test case generation [6,7]. In our SMT solving based approach, each LLR equivalence class for a block type is represented by a set of constraints, applied on block-level input(s) and expected output. Meanwhile, test space is also constrained by the subgraph environment that the block under test (BUT) is embedded in. The collection of constraints can be formulated as an SMT problem and expressed in a standard format by HiLiTE in an automatic fashion. SMT solver is then called to generate the satisfiable solution once for all ports in the related subgraph. The solution is merged back to the entire graph for a complete model-level input-to-output test case. With the integration of heuristics and SMT solving techniques, HiLiTE has been successfully used to generate requirement-based test cases for a great range of large-scale complex constrained avionics models.

Section 2 describes the HiLiTE normal test case generation approach and the need for improvements. Section 3 describes the formalized language of equivalence classes of block's behaviors and SMT solving based test case generation approach. Finally, the conclusion and future work are discussed in Sect. 4.

2 HiLiTE Test Generation Approach

HiLiTE generates specific tests at the model level to exercise the equivalence classes of the behavior of each block embedded in the model. In the original HiLiTE tool, each equivalence class of a block's behavior is represented by a set of *test case templates*, each of which uses heuristics to select a specific combination of values for the block under test (BUT) input(s) and output that satisfy this equivalence class. Backward and forward propagation search through the computations of other blocks in the model generates a test vector in terms of model inputs and outputs to ensure controllability of the BUT inputs and observability of the expected BUT output. Figure 1 shows a Simulink model extracted from a complex industrial model to illustrate this.

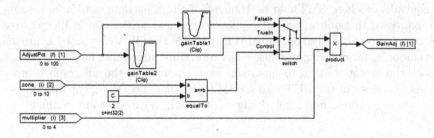

Fig. 1. Test case generation for product block.

When the **product** block is the BUT, the test case template (Fig. 2) assigns the two inputs with non-zero values 2 and 4 respectively. After the backward and forward propagation search, the generated test vectors are given in Fig. 2 where blue column heading denotes model input and green denotes model output.

Test Case Name	Test Case Description	Test Requirements Covered	No. of Time Steps	Normal Range	Block Under Test Ports			Step Description
					Input[1]	Input[2]	Output	
				min →	0.44	0	0	
				max →	2	4	8	
Product Operation (Using OpMax)	Test product operation ,Avoid 0 and 1 at the input.	Functional: Non Zero Output	1		2	4	8	Set all inputs to maximun value,avoid 0 and 1 at input

Test Case Name	Time Steps	signal name → zone	2	multiplier	equalTo.O1	AdjustPct	gainTable2.O1	switch.O1	GainAdj
		range		Input[2]				Input[1]	Output
		min → 0	2	0	0	0	0.44	0.44	0
		max → 10	2	4	1	100	2	2	8
Product Operation (Using OpMax)	1	2	2	4	1	0.000000E+	2	2	8

Fig. 2. Test case template (top) and test vector for the **product** block in Fig. 1.

When the **switch** block is the BUT, the equivalence class requires different values at its data inputs (**FalseIn**, **TrueIn**) to verify unique impact of an input on the block's output. One test case template assigns 44 to **FalseIn** and 46 to **TrueIn**, but this leads to a conflict at the model input **AdjustPct** after backward computation through the two look-up tables since their data points are in the same range. HiLiTE then further tries several alternative templates based on heuristics, yet all result in search failure. The root cause is that HiLiTE templates heuristics in the equivalence class domain prematurely pick block's local input values, while this problem involves taking into account constraints imposed by the look-up table blocks driven by the same input **AdjustPct**.

3   Applying SMT Solving in Test Case Generation

Test generation difficulties such as those noted above can be addressed by an approach that solves computational constraints of the upstream subgraph of BUT in conjunction with the constraints on BUT inputs imposed by the behavior equivalence class. SMT can be thought of the constraint satisfaction problem expressed in Boolean formulas, linear/nonlinear arithmetic in integer/real domain, bit-vectors and so on. In HiLiTE, we added SMT solving based approach that embodies formulating test case generation constraints from both equivalence classes, constraints related to upstream source ports and the subgraph computations upstream of the BUT into an SMT problem. Therefore, constraints can be solved together to find a satisfying solution which excludes any conflicts.

3.1   Formal Specification of Equivalence Classes of Block Behaviors

An equivalence class of a block behavior, which represents a test requirement, is now expressed in HiLiTE with formalized rules on the block's input and output

Table 1. Equivalence class definitions for switch block.

Equiv. Class Name	Equiv. Class Definition for each input and output			
	TrueIn	FalseIn	Control	Output
Verify TRUE Input	Exists	NEQ(FalseIn, TrueIn)	EQ(Control, 1)	Valid
Verify FALSE Input	Exists	NEQ(FalseIn, TrueIn)	EQ(Control, 0)	Valid

ports. These rules are expressed in a language as shown in Table 1 for switch block with rule names in blue. Each rule is automatically translated, based upon formal definitions, into SMT logic formula in a straightforward way. For example, "Exists" for port TrueIn is evaluated to "true" if any value is present, "NEQ(FalseIn, TrueIn)" of port FalseIn is interpreted as "FalseIn $\neq$ TrueIn", and "Equal(Control, 1)" of port Control is interpreted as "Control = true" since Control has a Boolean type. The overall SMT logic formula for an equivalence class is the conjunction of individual formulas translated from equivalence class rules for each block port. E.g., the equivalence class "Verify TRUE Input" corresponds to "(FalseIn $\neq$ TrueIn)$\wedge$(Control = true)".

3.2 SMT Logic Formula for the Blocks' Computation

SMT logic formula for a block captures the block's mathematical computation for each time step; block formulas are stitched together to yield a subgraph formula. Let m be the number of time steps tried in test case generation. Examples:

- **Sum:** $\bigwedge_{j=0}^{m-1}(\text{Out}_j = \Sigma_{i=1}^{n}\text{In\_i}_j)$.
- **Comparator:** $\bigwedge_{j=0}^{m-1}(\text{Out}_j = \text{In\_1}_j \sim \text{In\_2}_j)$, $\sim \in \{=, \neq, >, <, \geq, \leq\}$.
- **Switch:** $\bigwedge_{j=0}^{m-1}(((!\text{In\_3}_j) \wedge (\text{Out}_j = \text{In\_1}_j)) \vee (\text{In\_3}_j \wedge (\text{Out}_j = \text{In\_2}_j)))$.
- **1D Look-up Table:** $\bigwedge_{j=0}^{m-1}((\bigvee_{i=1}^{n}((\text{In}_j \in Range_i)\wedge(\text{Out}_j = f_i(\text{In}_j)))))$, where f_i is a linear function of In_j given the value of In_j in $Range_i$.
- **UnitDelay:** $(\text{Out}_0 = initial\_constant) \wedge \bigwedge_{j=1}^{m-1}(\text{Out}_j = \text{In}_{j-1})$.

Note: support for time-dependent blocks (e.g., UnitDelay) also allows us to explore feedback loops in the model for bounded number of steps.

3.3 Formulated SMT Problem

HiLiTE explores the upstream subgraph of the BUT to ensure all constraints imposed by the subgraph computations on the test case generation are included. The subgraph exploration uses depth-first search, starting from the inputs of the BUT identified in its equivalence class, all the way back to the model inputs. Once the SMT-available subgraph is obtained, HiLiTE loops through each block in it to collect its SMT logic formulas. SMT logic formulas are further translated into expressions in SMT-LIB 2.0 standard format, recognized by popular SMT solvers like Z3, with actual port names as variables. Additionally, to specify the block connections, each input in the formula is replaced by its source block output. For instance, the SMT expression for the *switch* block in Fig. 1 is *(assert (and (not (= gainTable 1.O1 gainTable 2.O1)) (= equalTo.O1 true)))*. Finally, the variables in the SMT expressions are substituted by a short form y_i_j (time step subscript $\_j$ is omitted if there are no time-dependent blocks), where each block is assigned with a unique index i as shown in Fig. 3.

Breakpoints	Column	(1)
Row		..
(1)	0	2
(2)	10	2
(3)	15	1.28
(4)	20	0.62
(5)	25	0.47
(6)	30	0.46
(7)	35	0.44
(8)	40	0.63
(9)	45	0.67
(10)	50	1.01

```
;; y_0 is the output port "Output" of block "AdjustPct".
(declare-const y_0 Real)
;; y_1 is the output port "Out" of block "gainTable1".
(declare-const y_1 Real).
(assert (or (and (<= y_0 0) (= y_1 2))(and (>= y_0 50) (= y_1 2))(and (>= y_0 0) (<= y_0 10) (= y_
y_0 0)) (- 10 0))))) (and (>= y_0 10) (<= y_0 15) (= y_1 (+ 2 (/ (* (- 1.28 2) (- y_0 10)) (- 15 10))))) (-
(<= y_0 20) (= y_1 (+ 1.28 (/ (* (- 0.62 1.28) (- y_0 15)) (- 20 15))))) (and (>= y_0 20) (<= y_0 25) (-
0.47 0.62) (- y_0 20)) (- 25 20))))) (and (>= y_0 25) (<= y_0 30) (= y_1 (+ 0.47 (/ (* (- 0.46 0.47) (-
25))))) (and (>= y_0 30) (<= y_0 35) (= y_1 (+ 0.46 (/ (* (- 0.44 0.46) (- y_0 30)) (- 35 30))))) (and (
40) (= y_1 (+ 0.44 (/ (* (- 0.63 0.44) (- y_0 35)) (- 40 35))))) (and (>= y_0 40) (<= y_0 45) (= y_1 (+
0.63) (- y_0 40)) (- 45 40))))) (and (>= y_0 45) (<= y_0 50) (= y_1 (+ 0.67 (/ (* (- 1.01 0.67) (- y_0 45)) (- 50 45)))))))

■ ■ ■
;; The ports "equalTo.O1, TAV_VGM_MAP1.O1, TAV_VGM_MAP4.O1" are asserted to satisfy the following:
(assert (and (= y_2 true) (not (= y_1 y_5))))    ◄——From switch block equivalence class
(set-option :pp-decimal true)
(check-sat)
(get-model)
```

Look Up Table Data Points and Interpolation equations

Fig. 3. Input file for SMT solver Z3 of test generation for `switch` block in Fig. 1.

The SMT logic formula is built initially with the number of time steps m determined by the equivalence class of the BUT: if the result of SMT solving is "unsat", the formula is then updated with $m \leftarrow m + 1$. The process is repeated until either SMT solver returns "sat" or a pre-defined time step limit is reached. In the worst case, m may become very large before a value at some point (such as the output of a timer/integrator/counter) of the model is accumulated to satisfy the constraints, in which case SMT solver may break down or return "unknown". To bypass blocks causing over-sized formulas, and certain mathematical blocks (e.g., `sin`) not supported by SMT solving, HiLiTE identifies those blocks, records them as *pending*, and explores the neighbor paths, resulting in an incomplete subgraph. The pending blocks and their upstream blocks are excluded from the solution returned by SMT solver. HiLiTE normal method then picks up from here to further propagate the pending values. An improvement can be done if the backward search goes through a switch block, only one data input of which has pending block(s) on its upstream. The values on the branch with pending block(s) do not matter if we force the switch block to disable that branch. This is done by modifying the SMT logic formula of that switch block. Suppose port In_1 of block `switch` is to be disabled, then the SMT logic formula becomes $\bigwedge_{j=0}^{m-1}(\text{In\_3}_j \wedge (\text{Out}_j = \text{In\_2}_j))$.

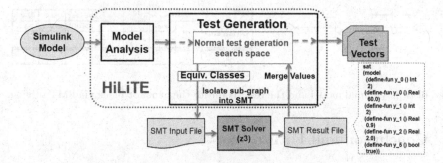

Fig. 4. Architecture of SMT solving in test case generation.

3.4 Tool Architecture

The SMT solving based test case generation is implemented by HiLiTE as a fully automated process shown in Fig. 4. Test cases needing SMT solving based approach are identified by the complexity of relationships detected during model analysis. For these, the test generation module formulates a collection of SMT expressions and writes them into a .smt2 file as described in Sect. 3. The SMT solver is called as a back-end, generating a solution which is then merged into test generation search space. HiLiTE normal method takes over from here to propagate the `switch` block output through the forward path to the model output `GainAdj` via the intervening `product` block, using a non-zero value for the second input of `product` block to ensure observability. This process results in valid test cases (Fig. 5) for the `switch` block in Fig. 2.

signal name →			zone	2	multiplier	equalTo.O1	AdjustPct	gainTable1.O1	gainTable2.O1	switch.O1	GainAdj
Test Case Name	Time Steps	range					Control		FalseIn	TrueIn	Out	
		min →	0	2	0	0	0	0.44	0.44	0.44	0
		max →	10	2	4	1	100	2	2	2	8
True Input Max Value to Output	1		0	2	2	0	60	0.9	2	0.9	1.8
False Input Min Value to Output	1		2	2	2	1	60	0.9	2	2	4

Fig. 5. Test vector generated for the `switch` block in Fig. 2 via SMT solving.

3.5 Nonlinear Applications

Modern SMT solvers are capable of solving a great range of non-linear problems used be computational intractable. Figure 6 shows a simple two-variable 2nd-order polynomial model. Z3 returns an answer for this case (as shown in Fig. 6) as in many other nonlinear problems.

Fig. 6. A polynomial model and the test vector for the `product` block via SMT solving.

4 Conclusion and Future Work

We extended the HiLiTE test generation capability with an SMT solving based approach for solving certain complex constrained problems. The improved tool combines HiLiTE normal search method and SMT solving, and has been successfully applied on many large-scale industrial models. HiLiTE is also being extended to derive invariant bounds on the number of time steps (e.g., for a timer) that will help bound the array size. We are also applying SMT solving to support such invariant generation, in which each condition-guarded path that captures a certain pattern of model behavior can be validated by SMT solving.

Open Access. This chapter is distributed under the terms of the Creative Commons Attribution 4.0 International License (http://creativecommons.org/licenses/by/4.0/), which permits use, duplication, adaptation, distribution and reproduction in any medium or format, as long as you give appropriate credit to the original author(s) and the source, a link is provided to the Creative Commons license and any changes made are indicated.

The images or other third party material in this chapter are included in the work's Creative Commons license, unless indicated otherwise in the credit line; if such material is not included in the work's Creative Commons license and the respective action is not permitted by statutory regulation, users will need to obtain permission from the license holder to duplicate, adapt or reproduce the material.

References

1. Bhatt, D., Madl, G., Oglesby, D.: System Architecture Driven Software Design Analysis Methodology and Toolset. In: SAE International (2012)
2. RTCA DO-178C, Software Considerations in Airborne Systems and Equipment Certification, RTCA Inc. (2011)
3. Bhatt, D., Madl, G., Oglesby, D., Schloegel, K.: Towards scalable verification of commercial avionics software. In: Proceedings of the AIAA Infotech @ Aerospace Conference, April 2010
4. Z3Prover. https://github.com/Z3Prover/z3/wiki/
5. The Yices SMT Solver. http://yices.csl.sri.com/
6. Beyer, D., Chlipala, A.J., Henzinger, T.A., Jhala, R., Majumdar, R.: Generating Tests from Counterexamples. In: ICSE (2004)
7. Peleska, J., Vorobev, E., Lapschies, F.: Automated test case generation with SMT-solving and abstract interpretation. In: Bobaru, M., Havelund, K., Holzmann, G.J., Joshi, R. (eds.) NFM 2011. LNCS, vol. 6617, pp. 298–312. Springer, Heidelberg (2011)

The comKorat Tool: Unified Combinatorial and Constraint-Based Generation of Structurally Complex Tests

Hua Zhong[1]([⊠]), Lingming Zhang[2], and Sarfraz Khurshid[1]

[1] Department of Electrical and Computer Engineering,
The University of Texas at Austin, Austin 78712, USA
{hzhong,khurshid}@utexas.edu
[2] Department of Computer Science, The University of Texas at Dallas,
Richardson 75080, USA
lingming.zhang@utdallas.edu

Abstract. This tool paper presents comKorat, which unifies constraint-based generation of structurally complex tests with combinatorial testing. Constraint-based test generation is an effective approach for generating structurally complex inputs for systematic testing. While this approach can typically generate large numbers of tests, it has limited scalability – tests generated are usually only up to a small bound on input size. Combinatorial test generation, e.g., pair-wise testing, is a more scalable approach but is challenging to apply on commercial software systems that require complex input structures that cannot be formed by using arbitrary combinations. The comKorat tool integrates Korat and ACTS test generators to generate test suites for large scale commercial systems. This paper presents a case-study of applying comKorat on a software application developed at Yahoo!. The experimental results show that comKorat outperforms existing solution in execution time and finds a total of 23 previously unknown bugs in the application.

1 Introduction

In this tool paper, we present comKorat, which combines *constriant-based* test generation [2] and *combinatorial* testing [3] – two approaches for automated test generation [1] – and applies them in synergy to benefit from their strengths. Specifically, comKorat builds on the Korat [2] test generator, which generates non-equivalent input structures using imperative constraints, and the ACTS [4] combinatorial testing tool, which generates combinatorial tests to populate the structures generated by Korat.

A key strength of constraint-based test generation, is that it can systematically generate such complex inputs [2]. While this approach is very effective for testing some programs, scaling it to commercial software applications is challenging for two reasons. One, the underlying search spaces are usually too large to be explored exhaustively. Two, systematic generation will likely create an enormous number of test inputs, which are impractical to run.

© Springer International Publishing Switzerland 2016
S. Rayadurgam and O. Tkachuk (Eds.): NFM 2016, LNCS 9690, pp. 107–113, 2016.
DOI: 10.1007/978-3-319-40648-0_9

A key strength of combinatorial testing is its effectiveness at reducing test input combinations [3–5]. It usually enables a significant reduction in the number of test cases without compromising much functional coverage. For example, to test a program with 10 binary parameters, an exhaustive suite has 2^{10} tests, whereas the pair-wise setting would use just 6. However, combinatorial testing cannot be directly applied to create diverse suites of structurally complex tests.

This tool paper makes the following contributions [6]:

- **Tool.** We present the comKorat tool for integrating constraint-based test generation with combinatorial testing.
- **Case-Study.** We present a case study on a commercial software application developed at Yahoo!. The results show that comKorat can substantially reduce the search space and the number of structurally complex tests generated. comKorat generated tests detected 23 previously unknown defects.

2 Motivating Example

The benchmark system we tested with comKorat is a backend system within the Yahoo! search engine. This system demands the test generation algorithm to explore a generic tree data structure (master tree) and return a set of subtrees from the master tree (Fig. 1). These subtrees serve as test inputs to the system.

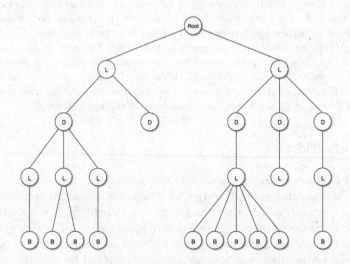

Fig. 1. A sample master tree

A typical master tree has 4 types of nodes: a Root, a set of L nodes, a set of D nodes, and a set of B nodes. The master tree has a few constraints: (1) a B node can only be a leaf node in the master tree; (2) the parent of a B node is an L node; the parent of a D node is an L node; and the parent of an L node is either the Root or a D node; (3) the children of Root are L nodes. A valid test

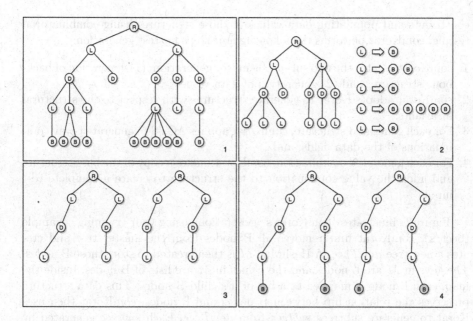

Fig. 2. comKorat's workflow on the master tree example. (1) a master tree. (2) a *newTree* and HashMap M with L nodes as key and lists of B nodes as value. (3) comKorat generated subtrees. (4) complete test case trees with ACTS generated B nodes combinations.

case is a subtree of the master tree and there are also some constraints on the test cases: (1) all test case trees have the same root as the master tree; (2) a test case tree must contain two or more B nodes and it cannot contain two B nodes from the same parent; (3) all leaf nodes in a test case tree are B nodes; (4) if two B nodes have two different D nodes as their ancestors and those two D nodes share the same parent, these two B nodes are in "conflict" with each other and thus cannot be in the same test case; (5) a parameter *size* is introduced to limit the number of B nodes(leaves) in a test case. When *size* is equal to 3, it means all generated subtrees have up to 3 B nodes. The ideal test suite should cover all possible combinations of B nodes. A naive implementation of such a test suite could exhaustively enumerates all possible subtrees in the master tree to cover the above combinations. However, most of the exhaustively generated subtrees will violate some of the structural constraints described above and will become invalid inputs to the system.

We developed comKorat to resolve the above issues.

3   The comKorat Tool

Given constraints that describe desired tests, comKorat divides the test generation problem into generating back-bone structure by solving structural constraints and populating data values in those structures using combinatorial testing. comKorat performs the following four steps for test generation:

1. comKorat creates the two sub-problems for generation: (1) generation of back-bone structure, and (2) generation of data values;
2. comKorat adopts Korat to generate structures with respect to the structural invariants;
3. For each generated structure, comKorat applies ACTS to generate t-way combinations of the data fields; and
4. For each generated combination, comKorat makes a copy of the base structure and adds the value combination to the structure to create a complete test input.

Figure 2 illustrates comKorat's generation using our running example (Sect. 2). comKorat first removes all B nodes from the master tree and creates a new tree *newTree*. A HashMap *M* is then created to store those B nodes. The keys in *M* are L nodes and the values in *M* are lists of B nodes. Inside the map, each L node is mapped to a list of it's child B nodes. This data structure preserves the relationship between B nodes and L nodes. comKorat then uses Korat to generate subtrees *subtree* from *newTree*. Each *subtree* generated by Korat contains two or more leaf L nodes. In the next step, comKorat uses these L nodes to retrieve a set of B node lists *listSet* from *M*. Finally, comKorat adopts ACTS to generate combinatorial tests using *listSet*. We use the generated B nodes to grow *subtree* to a complete test case tree and add the test case to the test suite. comKorat uses a t-way combinatorial method to cover the B nodes combinations. comKorat can also uses a smaller *size* parameter to reduce the number of tests generated by Korat, while retaining a t-way combination coverage of B nodes.

4   Case Study

The case study discussed in this paper are performed on a Mac machine with a 2.5 GHz Intel Core i7 processor and 16 GB 1600 MHz DDR3 RAM running JVM 1.8.0-45 on OS X Yosemite 10.10.1.

4.1   Result Analysis

Table 1 presents the test generation result of comKorat. Empirical investigations suggest 90 % of the problems can be triggered by the interaction of three or fewer parameters in commercial web applications [4]. We also found out that our comKorat technique which exercises high degree interaction combinations (4-way or above) will either generate an enormous large number of tests or timeout during test generation. Therefore, we tried 2 to 4 way combinatorial generation.

comKorat can generate all tests even for very large state spaces because separation of structure generation and value generation allows Korat to explore

Table 1. comKorat's performance. *size* is the parameter used to limit the maximum number of B nodes in a test case. Time is the elapsed real time in seconds for the 2-way generation.

Benchmark	Size	Time (s)	Struc. gen.	Candi. expl.	Combinatorial tests		
					2-way	3-way	4-way
Yahoo! prod.	3	2.53	31	71	16970	32114	32114
	4	4.29	458	2521	260214	500312	826404
	5	10.94	4298	66221	2210309	4883621	10383222

Table 2. Performance comparison. Performance of comKorat (use 2-way combination) and Korat are compared.

		comKorat			Korat	
Benchmark	Size	Struc. gen	Test gen. (2-way)	Total time	Struc. gen	Total time
Yahoo! prod.	3	31	16970	2.53s	32114	3.43s
	4	458	260214	4.29s	826404	17.72s
	5	4298	2210309	10.94s	27653142	986.63s

only a tiny fraction of the input space. Shown in Column 5 of Table 1, comKorat only needs to check a small number of candidates during it's structure generation stage. The number of structures generated by Korat is also very small, and ACTS is brought in to search rest of the space to reduce the number of generated tests. Without ACTS, Korat would generate infeasibly many tests.

Table 2 compares the performance between comKorat and Korat. We compare the total number of structures/tests and the time to generate them for a range of parameter values. From Table 2, we can see that comKorat significantly reduced the number of tests. During our experiment, we found out that it is not feasible to execute Korat generated tests directly as these large test suites will cause the execution framework to timeout. However, the performance of Korat is quite robust, e.g., Korat generated 387175 tests in less than 20 s. For our study, comKorat largely reduced the execution time and allowed the system to explore subtrees with up to 5 B nodes (size=5) in less than 11 s.

Table 3 compares the performance between comKorat generated suite with existing test suite. comKorat also reveals new defects from the program. After the comparison, we can find that automated test generation using comKorat not only removes the laborious human effort, but also reduces human bias and thus can have higher fault detection rate.

4.2 Qualitative Analysis

To further understand the performance of comKorat, we manually select some interesting defects found by the tool to analyze why comKorat outperforms the existing solution and why it is infeasible to use only Korat or ACTS to generate

Table 3. Performance comparison between existing test suites and comKorat.

Benchmark	comKorat			Existing solution	
	# Tests	# New defects	Time	# Tests	Time
Yahoo! prod.	260214 (*size*=4)	23	4.29 s	5815 (*size*=2)	146.30 s

those tests. We also select one user reported issue and analyze why comKorat failed to produce an input to uncover this defect.

Defect 1. In comKorat generated suites, 3 test case trees caused backend system to return empty responses for the given inputs. These B nodes combinations (*size*=3) caused backend system unable to locate information in data store to rank a particular search result and the system times out searching for the information. As we introduced in above sections, existing solution can not generate t-way combinations on test case trees and failed to uncover the issue.

Defect 2. During our study, we found one end user reported defect which comKorat failed to discover. The root cause is the same as the above defect, but the difference is that it is caused by a combination of 5 B nodes. Although comKorat has the ability to generate 5 way combinations, the generated test suite is too large and we are unable to execute all of them in practice.

In summary, comKorat is able to generate t-way combination tests for structurally complex test inputs. comKorat outperforms existing solutions in test generation time and fault detection. Given a small number of t ($t \leq 4$), comKorat can generate effective test suites for commercial software while significantly reducing the number of tests. However, it is still difficult to use comKorat to enable extremely thorough testing of applications with manageable numbers of test cases, and we plan to further explore this direction in our future work.

5   Conclusions

This tool paper presents the comKorat test generator for creating structurally complex test inputs. comKorat integrates the strengths of two approaches for test generation: constraint-based generation and combinatorial generation, which are traditionally employed separately. Specifically, comKorat builds on Korat and ACTS to embody a synergistic approach. We applied comKorat for testing a commercial application developed at Yahoo!. The experimental results show that it is feasible to automate generation of test cases for such applications, even when the search space for inputs is very large. Furthermore, comKorat detected 23 previously unknown bugs in the studied application.

Acknowledgment. Part of this work was completed when the first author worked at Yahoo!. Lingming Zhang was funded in part by UT Dallas start-up fund and Google Faculty Research Award. Sarfraz Khurshid was funded in part by National Science Foundation (Grant No. CCF-0845628).

References

1. Anand, S., Burke, E.K., Chen, T.Y., Clark, J., Cohen, M.B., Grieskamp, W., Harman, M., Harrold, M.J., Mcminn, P.: An orchestrated survey on automated software test case generation. J. Syst. Softw. **86**(8), 1978–2001 (2013)
2. Boyapati, C., Khurshid, S., Marinov, D.: Korat: automated testing based on java predicates. In: ISSTA, pp. 123–133 (2002)
3. Cohen, D., Dalal, S., Fredman, M.L., Patton, G.: The AETG system: an approach to testing based on combinatorial design. TSE **23**(7), 437–444 (1997)
4. Kuhn, R., Kacker, R., Lei, Y., Hunter, J.: Combinatorial software testing. IEEE Comput. **42**(8), 94–96 (2009)
5. Richard Kuhn, D., Okum, V.: Pseudo-exhaustive testing for software. In: SEW (2006)
6. Zhong, H.: Pairwise-Korat: Automated Testing Using Korat in an Industrial Setting. Master's Report, The University of Texas at Austin, USA (2015)

Code Generation and Synthesis

Automated Synthesis of Safe Autonomous Vehicle Control Under Perception Uncertainty

Susmit Jha[✉] and Vasumathi Raman

United Technology Research Center, Berkeley, USA
{jhask,ramanv}@utrc.utc.com

Abstract. Autonomous vehicles have found wide-ranging adoption in aerospace, terrestrial as well as marine use. These systems often operate in uncertain environments and in the presence of noisy sensors, and use machine learning and statistical sensor fusion algorithms to form an internal model of the world that is inherently probabilistic. Autonomous vehicles need to operate using this uncertain world-model, and hence, their correctness cannot be deterministically specified. Even once probabilistic correctness is specified, proving that an autonomous vehicle will operate correctly is a challenging problem. In this paper, we address these challenges by proposing a *correct-by-synthesis* approach to autonomous vehicle control. We propose a probabilistic extension of temporal logic, named Chance Constrained Temporal Logic (C2TL), that can be used to specify correctness requirements in presence of uncertainty. We present a novel automated synthesis technique that compiles C2TL specification into mixed integer constraints, and uses second-order (quadratic) cone programming to synthesize optimal control of autonomous vehicles subject to the C2TL specification. We demonstrate the effectiveness of the proposed approach on a diverse set of illustrative examples.

1 Introduction

Intelligent systems with varying degrees of autonomy, from recommendation systems [34] to fully autonomous aerial vehicles [23], have been widely adopted for controlling ground, air and under-water vehicles. These systems are increasingly deployed in safety-critical applications, both in military domains such as aerospace missions, search and rescue, and surveillance, as well as in civilian infrastructure like factories and farms. Their increasing prevalence makes it vital to be able to ensure the correctness of their operation in an efficient and reliable manner. Currently, these systems are often designed manually, and their certification relies on tests and extensive requirements on the design process. These are complex systems with tightly-coupled components that implement control, perception and logical decision making, and proving the correctness of manual designs is challenging [26,33]. The difficulty of this task is further amplified by the uncertain environment in which these systems operate, and the inherent probabilistic nature of the statistical techniques used to observe the environment. In this paper, we address this challenge by defining a new specification

© Springer International Publishing Switzerland 2016
S. Rayadurgam and O. Tkachuk (Eds.): NFM 2016, LNCS 9690, pp. 117–132, 2016.
DOI: 10.1007/978-3-319-40648-0_10

language, Chance Constrained Temporal Logic (C2TL), that extends linear temporal logic to capture uncertainty in environment and perception. We present a novel approach to designing autonomous control algorithms that are guaranteed to satisfy C2TL properties.

An autonomous control system can be conceptually divided into two key subsystems: a perception pipeline to observe the world, and a control pipeline comprising high-level reasoning and low-level motion planning. Both these subsystems are well-studied in the control and robotics literatures, but the quantification of uncertainty in perception [14] and control under uncertainty [4] remain challenging. The traditional approach to the design of autonomous systems decouples perception uncertainty and control by using probabilistic thresholds in perception, and building a conservative world model: the control is designed with respect to this conservative model. This decoupling leads to overly conservative control in practice, and also makes it difficult to establish formal guarantees and prove safety of these systems. For example, it is clear that any qualitative Boolean property would be violated with non-zero probability in a setting with perception uncertainty modeled using Gaussian noise. Chance constraints [31] provide a natural way to specify probabilistic correctness properties, but have so far only be shown useful for specifying invariant-like properties. On the other hand, temporal logics such as signal temporal logic (STL) [15] and linear temporal logic (LTL) [27] have emerged as effective specification languages for verifying and synthesizing automated control subject to complex specifications, including history-dependent and timing requirements.

C2TL extends temporal logic with chance constraints, thus providing an effective specification language for the autonomous control of systems operating under uncertainty. We show that C2TL formulae can be compiled into mixed integer constraints; thus, C2TL strikes the right balance between expressiveness and ease of reasoning. Quadratic cone programming can be used to automatically synthesize optimal control satisfying the C2TL specifications.

We make the following contributions:

1. We define *Chance Constrained Temporal Logic* (C2TL) and demonstrate its use to specify correctness of autonomous vehicle system control.
2. We formulate the problem of synthesizing autonomous vehicle control subject to C2TL specifications while optimizing a quadratic cost function; we reduce this problem to a second order (quadratic) cone program that can be solved using scalable tools such as CVXOPT [3].
3. We demonstrate the effectiveness of our approach on a diverse set of examples.

2   Background and Related Work

Projects such as the Defense Advanced Research Projects Agency (DARPA) Urban Challenge [32] and the VisLab Intercontinental Autonomous Challenge [10] have been instrumental in spurring the development and maturation of autonomous vehicle technology. One key area where autonomous systems still struggle is in dealing with uncertainty, arising from stochastic environments or noisy perception. Most autonomous systems learn about their environment using sensors such as cameras and LIDAR units to infer the environment state, which is maintained in the form of probabilistic beliefs. Uncertainty in these probabilistic beliefs arise from two sources [13,20,21,25]. First, the environment states are often dynamic and change over time. Second, the information gathered from sensors is often not sufficient to exactly infer the environment state. As an example, consider a popular perception technique like *simultaneous localization and mapping* [5](SLAM), which is used for determining the current position of an autonomous vehicle. The estimated position of the vehicle and the coordinates of other entities in the map are often assumed to have Gaussian noise. Aside from localization and mapping, another critical perception challenge for autonomous vehicles is obstacle detection and tracking [9,22]. Camera and laser range finders are used to locally detect and avoid obstacles during navigation for a previously constructed map. This is particularly useful in the presence of dynamic objects whose locations are not fixed in the environment map. The uncertainty in the parametric models representing the obstacles is usually also modeled using Gaussian random variables. The proposed C2TL specifications incorporate these Gaussian models of uncertainty in perception by allowing the predicates in the formulae to be chance constraints [31] over Gaussian random variables.

The control of stochastic systems has been extensively investigated, beginning with the work of Pontryagin [28] and Bellman [7], and extending to more recent literature [11,17,29,30]. Its applications include optimal guidance for spacecrafts [2] and flight-controllers [6]. The focus has been on the safety problem, where the goal is to determine a control policy that maximizes the probability of remaining within a safe set during a finite time horizon [1]. This safe control problem is usually reformulated as a stochastic optimal control problem with multiplicative costs over a controlled Markov chain. In contrast, our goal is to satisfy a probabilistic temporal logic specification while optimizing over a given cost metric. This can be naturally modeled using chance constrained programs [12,24], used for uncertainty modeling in various engineering fields [19,37]. For a detailed recent survey of the literature on chance constrained programming approaches, the interested reader is directed to [31]. Here we extend these approaches to temporal logic specifications. Another dimension along which we extend existing stochastic control techniques [36] is in our consideration of nonconvex feasible spaces, which is critical for autonomous vehicles operating in environments with obstacles.

Recent work has developed scalable, optimization-based methods for the automatic synthesis of controllers from temporal logic specifications with deterministic constraints [16]. Signal temporal logic (STL) [15] has been proposed for controller synthesis, because it combines dense time modalities with numerical predicates over continuous state variables. C2TL extends STL to specify probabilistic temporal properties, by allowing predicates to be *chance constraints* over continuous state variables rather than just real-valued functions. The uncertainty is restricted to probabilistic predicates, and temporal operators are not probabilistic; this is in contrast to other probabilistic extensions of temporal logics [18]. We show that C2TL can be used to specify correctness requirements for an autonomous vehicle under perception uncertainty. We also present a reduction from C2TL constraints to mixed integer constraints which are linear in the state variables. Thus, C2TL provides a balance between expressiveness of the specification language and efficiency of automated synthesis.

3   Automated Synthesis of Autonomous Vehicle Control

We first define *Chance Constrained Temporal Logic* (C2TL), and then illustrate how the correctness of autonomous vehicle control can be specified using C2TL. We then describe how C2TL specifications can be compiled into deterministic mixed integer conic constraints. We then formulate the problem of synthesizing the correct control of autonomous systems as a second order cone programming problem. The cost being optimized is quadratic and optimization is done with respect to conic constraints that are bilinear in the state variables and perception coefficients.

Notation: The correctness property is specified over the system state variables $X = \{x_1, x_2, \ldots, x_n\}$, which can represent the position of the vehicle, its velocity, acceleration, orientation, angular velocities and other relevant parameters. The domain of X is denoted $Dom(X)$, and is usually a subset of $\mathbb{R}^n$. The state of the system at time t is denoted by $\mathbf{x}_t \in Dom(X)$.

In this work, half-planes form the basic unit of representation of knowledge acquired through perception. This is motivated by the observation that perception algorithms often employ half-plane learning techniques such as Bayesian linear regression and classifiers. For example, an obstacle can be perceived as an intersection of half-planes which represent the convex hull of the obstacle. Half-planes are represented as $\phi_{lin} : \mathbf{a}_i\mathbf{x}_t + b_i \leq 0$ or $\mathbf{a}_i\mathbf{x}_t + b_i < 0$, where the coefficients $\mathbf{a}_i, b_i$ are inferred by perception algorithms. Due to uncertainty in perception, the coefficients are not deterministically known: rather, we only know the probability distribution over the coefficients. Let $Dom(\mathbf{a}_i), Dom(b_i)$ denote the domain of the coefficients, and $p(\mathbf{a}_i), p(b_i)$ denote the respective probability density functions. So, the constraints from perception are not tautological, but instead hold with an associated probability, that is, $Pr(\mathbf{a}_i\mathbf{x}_t + b_i \leq 0) \geq 1 - \delta$ or $Pr(\mathbf{a}_i\mathbf{x}_t + b_i < 0) \geq 1 - '\delta$.

We denote the control inputs of the autonomous system, which are the values to be synthesized, by U; the value at each time instant t is $\mathbf{u}_t$. A trace of system states and control values is denoted by $\tau : \mathbb{R}_{\geq 0} \to X \times U$ where $\tau(t) = (\mathbf{x}_t, \mathbf{u}_t)$.

3.1   Chance Constrained Temporal Logic

We now define chance constrained temporal logic as a probabilistic extension of signal temporal logic, motivated by two key observations:

- For specifications applied to autonomous systems, temporal aspects of correctness arise from mission requirements such as reaching specific positions in sequence while staying away from particular regions. These temporal aspects of mission requirements do not usually have any associated uncertainty.
- Perception gathers information about a particular instant of time, and uncertainty in perception is hence reflected only in the predicates computed on the system states at a given time, and not on the temporal operators.

We therefore introduce chance constraints at the atomic predicate level of our logic. The syntax definition of C2TL is as follows:

$$\phi_{det} := \phi_{lin} \mid \phi_{lin} \wedge \phi_{lin} \mid \neg\phi_{lin}$$
$$\phi_{cc} := [Pr(\phi_{det}) \geq 1 - \delta] \mid \neg\phi_{cc} \mid \sim\phi_{cc} \mid \phi_{cc} \wedge \phi_{cc} \mid \phi_{cc} \vee \phi_{cc} \mid \phi_{cc}U_{[a,b]}\phi_{cc},$$

where:

- *linear predicate* ϕ_{lin} over the variables $v \subseteq X \cup U$ is of the form

$$\phi_{lin}(v) : \mathbf{a}_i v + b_i \leq 0 \quad \text{or} \quad \mathbf{a}_i v + b_i < 0$$

- *deterministic predicate* ϕ_{det} is a Boolean combination of linear predicates.
- *chance-constraint* [12] is a probabilistic extension of deterministic predicates and is of the form $Pr(\phi_{det}) \geq 1 - \delta$. where $0 \leq \delta \leq 1$ represents uncertainty about whether the inequality holds.
- The coefficients $\mathbf{a}_i, b_i$ of the chance constraints are random variables with Gaussian probability distributions, rather than constants.

The set of coefficients that satisfy a deterministic predicate ϕ_{det} over variables v is denoted by $R(\phi_{det}, v)$. So, the probability of satisfying ϕ_{det} when the coefficients are probabilistic is given by $p_c(\phi_{det}, v) = \int_{c \in R(\phi_{det}, v)} p(c)dc$ where $c = (\mathbf{a}, b)$. C2TL admits the standard *globally* (G), *eventually* (F) and *until* (U) operators of temporal logic; here we restrict discussion to the *until* (U) operator, which can be used to represent all of the others. The subscripts of the operators denote the time interval associated with the property, as in STL.

The satisfaction of a C2TL formula over a trace τ at time t is defined recursively as follows:

$$\tau(t) \models \phi_{lin} \qquad\qquad \Leftrightarrow \qquad \phi_{lin}(\tau(t))$$
$$\tau(t) \models \neg\phi_{lin}^1 \wedge \phi_{lin}^2 \qquad \Leftrightarrow \qquad \phi_{lin}^1(\tau(t)) \wedge \phi_{lin}^2(\tau(t))$$
$$\tau(t) \models \neg\phi_{lin} \qquad\qquad \Leftrightarrow \qquad \neg\phi_{lin}(\tau(t))$$
$$\tau(t) \models [Pr(\phi_{det}) \geq 1 - \delta] \quad \Leftrightarrow \qquad p_c(\phi_{det}, \tau(t)) \geq 1 - \delta$$
$$\tau(t) \models \neg[Pr(\phi_{det}) \geq 1 - \delta] \quad \Leftrightarrow \qquad p_c(\phi_{det}, \tau(t)) < 1 - \delta$$
$$\tau(t) \models \sim[Pr(\phi_{det}) \geq 1 - \delta] \quad \Leftrightarrow \qquad \tau(t) \models [Pr(\neg\phi_{det}) \geq 1 - \delta]$$
$$\tau(t) \models \phi_{cc}^1 \wedge \phi_{cc}^2 \qquad\qquad \Leftrightarrow \qquad \tau(t) \models \phi_{cc}^1 \wedge \tau(t) \models \phi_{cc}^2$$
$$\tau(t) \models \phi_{cc}^1 \vee \phi_{cc}^2 \qquad\qquad \Leftrightarrow \qquad \tau(t) \models \phi_{cc}^1 \vee \tau(t) \models \phi_{cc}^2$$
$$\tau(t) \models \phi_{cc}^1 U_{[a,b]}\phi_{cc}^2 \qquad \Leftrightarrow \qquad \exists t_1\, t + a \leq t_1 \leq t + b \wedge \tau(t_1) \models \phi_{cc}^2$$
$$\wedge\, (\forall t_2\, t \leq t_2 \leq t_1 \Rightarrow \tau(t_2) \models \phi_{cc}^1)$$

As a special case, when $\delta = 0$, chance constraints become deterministic. Chance constraints have two kinds of negations: *logical* negation denoted by $\neg$ and *probabilistic* negation denoted by $\sim$. Consider a deterministic formula ϕ_{det} and its logical negation $\neg\phi_{det}$, and corresponding chance constraints $\phi_{cc} \equiv Pr(\phi_{det}) \geq 1-\delta$ and the probabilistic negation $\sim\phi_{cc} \equiv Pr(\neg\phi_{det}) \geq 1 - \delta$. If $\delta = 0.8$, then $\phi_{cc} \equiv Pr(\phi_{det}) \geq 0.2$, that is, $Pr(\neg\phi_{det}) < 0.8$. This is consistent with $\sim\phi_{cc} \equiv Pr(\neg\phi_{det}) \geq 0.2$. Thus, it is possible for both ϕ_{cc} and its probabilistic negation $\sim\phi_{cc}$ to simultaneously be true.

The following theorem relates probabilistic negation and logical negation when $\delta < 0.5$. This case is relevant because it corresponds to "likely" chance constraints, where the probability of violation is less than 0.5. In practice, most useful constraints obtained from perception have significantly high confidence and δ is very small.

Theorem 1. *If $\delta < 0.5$, probabilistic negation is equivalent to logical negation, that is, $\neg\phi_{cc} \equiv \sim\phi_{cc}$.*

Proof. $\neg\phi_{cc} \equiv \neg[Pr(\phi_{det}) \geq 1-\delta] \equiv \neg[Pr(\neg\phi_{det}) < \delta]$. Now, $\delta < 0.5 \equiv \delta < 1-\delta$. Thus, $\neg\phi_{cc} \equiv \neg[Pr(\neg\phi_{det}) < \delta < 1 - \delta]$, that is, $\neg\phi_{cc} \equiv \neg[Pr(\neg\phi_{det}) < 1 - \delta]$ when $\delta < 0.5$. Further, $\neg[Pr(\neg\phi_{det}) < 1 - \delta] \equiv [Pr(\neg\phi_{det}) \geq 1 - \delta] \equiv \sim\phi_{cc}$. Hence, $\neg\phi_{cc} \equiv \sim\phi_{cc}$ if $\delta < 0.5$. □

3.2 C2TL Specification for Autonomous Vehicle Control

We now describe how the correctness properties of an autonomous system can be specified using C2TL.

Obstacles: Any obstacle can be approximated by a union of a finite number of convex polytopes. The planes forming the convex polytopes are only probabilistically known, due to perception uncertainty. A convex polytope is a conjunction of half-planes (linear constraints), and can be represented as $\bigwedge_i(\mathbf{a}_i\mathbf{x}_t + b_i > 0)$, where the coefficients $\mathbf{a}_i \sim \mathcal{N}(\mathbf{a}_i^\mu, \mathbf{a}_i^\Sigma)$ are assumed to be Gaussian variables whose mean and variance are estimated by the perception pipeline. Since the coefficients are Gaussian, collision with obstacles cannot be ruled out deterministically. Let δ_{obs} be the user-specified threshold for the maximum allowable probability of collision with obstacles. This collision avoidance property is specified in C2TL as: $Pr(\bigvee_i \mathbf{a}_i\mathbf{x}_t + b_i \leq 0) \geq 1 - \delta_{obs}$. The property of avoiding multiple obstacles j is specified as: $Pr(\bigwedge_j \bigvee_i \mathbf{a}_{ij}\mathbf{x}_t + b_{ij} \leq 0) \geq 1 - \delta_{obs}$.

We assume that the map consists of static and dynamic obstacles as well as real or virtual walls that restrict the vehicle to be within a bounded region, but outside of obstacle areas. Let $\mathbf{a}_{ij}$ be the coefficients of the obstacles and $\mathbf{w}_{ij}$ be the coefficients of the perceived walls. The unobstructed map with uncertainty can thus be represented using a formula $\phi_{map} :=$

$$[Pr(\bigwedge_j \bigvee_i \mathbf{a}_{ij}\mathbf{x}_t + b_{ij} \leq 0) \geq 1 - \delta_{obs}] \wedge [Pr(\bigwedge_j \bigvee_i \mathbf{w}_{ij}\mathbf{x}_t + b_{ij} \leq 0) \geq 1 - \delta_{wall}]$$

where $\mathbf{a}_{ij} \sim \mathcal{N}(\mathbf{a}_{ij}^{\mu}, \mathbf{a}_{ij}^{\Sigma})$ represents the uncertain perception of obstacles, and $\mathbf{w}_{ij} \sim \mathcal{N}(\mathbf{w}_{ij}^{\mu}, \mathbf{w}_{ij}^{\Sigma})$ represents the uncertain perception of walls (which in practice includes uncertainty in self-localization). Similar constraints can be added for other parameters of an autonomous system such as constraints on speed or acceleration based on the system's current region in the map.

Mission: Apart from the safe navigation requirement represented by the global property $G(\phi_{map})$, a second set of useful specifications on autonomous vehicles corresponds to mission requirements. For example, the vehicle must reach its final destination within some time-bound t_{max}. Because of uncertainty in perception, we can not guarantee this property deterministically. Given a user-specified probability threshold $\delta_{mission}$ of failing to achieve the mission goals, the goal of reaching the destination is specified as $F_{[0,t_{max}]}(Pr(\mathbf{x} = \mathbf{x}_{dest}) \geq 1 - \delta_{mission})$. Other examples include the requirement that an autonomous car wait at a stop sign until all cross-traffic arriving at the intersection before it has passed, and that an aircraft flies straight without turning till it reaches the safe velocity range for turning. These properties can be specified using *until* properties, $\phi_1 U_{[0,t]} \phi_2$. We denote the set of mission constraints by $\phi_{mission}$.

The overall specification for the safe control of autonomous system is thus $\phi_{map} \wedge \phi_{mission}$: that is, the system achieves the temporal specification of mission goals while remaining safe with respect to the map. We note that the focus of this paper is on autonomous vehicles, but C2TL can also be used to specify behavior of other autonomous systems such as robotic manipulators, and the techniques presented in this paper extend beyond this application domain.

3.3   C2TL to Conservative Linear Constraints

In this section, we present a translation of C2TL constraints over Gaussian random variables to deterministic linear constraints. The constraints are linear with respect to system (state) variables and conic overall due to uncertain coefficients. The first part of the translation deals with temporal logic formulae and Boolean combinations of elementary chance constraints. The second part of translation focuses on elementary chance constraints, and reduces those to deterministic constraints linear in the state variables.

We focus on chance constraints with violation probability threshold less than 0.5^1. Similar to the STL encoding provided in [16], we introduce Boolean, that is, $\{0, 1\}$ integer variables $m_t^{\phi_{cc}}$ for each chance constraint ϕ_{cc} and time t. These Boolean variables are related in the same way as for the STL encoding.

---

[1] As discussed in Sect. 3.1, probabilistic negation is not the same as logical negation when violation probability (δ) can be 0.5 or more, and hence, we will need two $\{0, 1\}$ integer variables to represent the truth value of each chance constraint, to account for four cases depending on the truth value of the chance constraint and its probabilistic negation. For likely (violation probability $\delta < 0.5$) chance constraints, one $\{0, 1\}$ integer variable is sufficient by Theorem 1.

- Negation: $m_t^{\neg\phi_{cc}} = 1 - m_t^{\phi_{cc}}$
- Conjunction: $m_t^{\phi_{cc}^1 \wedge \phi_{cc}^2} = \min(m_t^{\phi_{cc}^1}, m_t^{\phi_{cc}^2})$
- Disjunction: $m_t^{\phi_{cc}^1 \vee \phi_{cc}^2} = \max(m_t^{\phi_{cc}^1}, m_t^{\phi_{cc}^2})$
- Until: $m_t^{\phi_{cc}^1 U_{[a,b]} \phi_{cc}^2} = \max_{t' \in [t+a, t+b]}(\min(m_{t'}^{\phi_{cc}^2}, \min_{t'' \in [t,t']}(m_{t''}^{\phi_{cc}^1})))$

The next challenge is in translating the probabilistic chance constraints over Gaussian variables to deterministic mixed integer constraints that are linear in the state variables. We consider chance constraints of the form:

$$\phi_{cc}^{elem} \equiv Pr(\bigwedge_j \bigvee_i^{N_j} \mathbf{a}_{ij}\mathbf{x}_t + b_{ij} \leq 0) \geq 1 - \delta_{tm}.$$

In the rest of the section, we show how we can conservatively over-approximate ϕ_{cc}^{elem} using mixed integer constraints which are satisfiable only if ϕ_{cc}^{elem} is satisfiable. We first note that $\phi_{cc}^{elem} \equiv :$

$$Pr(\bigwedge_{i,j} \mathbf{a}_{ij}\mathbf{x}_t + b_{ij} - Mz_{ij} \leq 0) \geq 1 - \delta_{tm} \wedge \bigwedge_j \left(\sum_i z_{ij} < N_j \wedge z_{ij} \in \{0,1\} \right),$$

where M is a sufficiently large positive number. This transformation uses the big-M reduction common in non-convex optimization, see [8] for examples. The above equivalence holds because at least one z_{ij} is 0 for each j since $\sum_i z_{ij} < N_j$ and $z_{ij} \in \{0,1\}$, and thus, at least one of the constraints in $\bigvee_i^{N_j} \mathbf{a}_{ij}\mathbf{x}_t + b_{ij} \leq 0$ must be true for each j.

Next, we use Boole's inequality to decompose the conjunction in the probabilistic chance constraint as follows.

$$Pr(\bigwedge_{i,j} \mathbf{a}_{ij}\mathbf{x}_t + b_{ij} - Mz_{ij} \leq 0) \geq 1 - \delta_{tm} \Leftrightarrow Pr(\bigvee_{i,j} \mathbf{a}_{ij}\mathbf{x}_t + b_{ij} - Mz_{ij} > 0) < \delta_{tm}.$$

Further, $Pr(\bigvee_{i,j} \mathbf{a}_{ij}\mathbf{x}_t + b_{ij} - Mz_{ij} > 0) < \sum_{i,j} Pr(\mathbf{a}_{ij}\mathbf{x}_t + b_{ij} - Mz_{ij} > 0)$

since the probability of union of events is less than the sum of the individual probabilities of the occurrence of each event.

Next, we introduce new variables $0 \leq \epsilon_{ij} \leq 1$ with $\sum_{i,j} \epsilon_{ij} < \delta_{tm}$, and conservatively approximate the chance constraint as:

$$Pr(\bigwedge_j \bigvee_i^{N_j} \mathbf{a}_{ij}\mathbf{x}_t + b_{ij} \leq 0) \geq 1 - \delta_{tm} \Leftarrow \bigwedge_{i,j} Pr(\mathbf{a}_{ij}\mathbf{x}_t + b_{ij} - Mz_j \leq 0) \geq 1 - \epsilon_{ij}$$

$$\wedge \bigwedge_{ij} 0 \leq \epsilon_{ij} \leq 1 \wedge \sum_{ij} \epsilon_{ij} < \delta_{tm} \wedge \sum_j z_j < N_j \wedge \bigwedge_j z_j \in \{0,1\}$$

With $N = \sum_j N_j$, we choose $\epsilon_{ij} = \delta_{tm}/N$, which corresponds to uniform risk allocation among the probabilistic constraints above. However, more efficient risk allocation techniques [38] can also be used. Since $\mathbf{a}_{ij}$ is a Gaussian random variable, the linear combination of Gaussian variables $\mathbf{a}_{ij}\mathbf{x}_t + b_{ij} - Mz_j$ is also Gaussian. Further, the uniform risk allocation ensures that the violation probability bounds are constant. So, $Pr(\mathbf{a}_{ij}\mathbf{x}_t + b_{ij} - Mz_j \leq 0) \geq 1 - \epsilon_{ij}$ can be translated to a deterministic constraint $\mathbf{a}_{ij}\mathbf{x}_t + b_{ij} - Mz_j \leq \mathtt{ErfInv}(\epsilon_{ij})$ where $\mathtt{ErfInv}$ is the Gaussian inverse error function computed using the table for Gaussian distributions, as discussed in [36]. Consequently, the probabilistic chance constraints are reduced to a set of deterministic constraints. This completes the translation of C2TL constraints to a set of deterministic mixed integer linear constraints over the system variables.

The following theorem summarizes the conservative nature of the above translation. Given the control specification for an autonomous vehicle ψ^{C2TL}, the above translation generates ψ^{MILP} which conservatively approximates ψ^{C2TL}.

Theorem 2. *Given C2TL constraints ψ^{C2TL}, the translation presented above will generate a set of mixed integer constraints ψ^{MILP} such that $\psi^{C2TL} \Rightarrow \psi^{MILP}$.*

There are two sources of conservativeness of ψ^{MILP}:

- We use the sum of the probabilities of chance constraints to upper-bound the probability of their disjunction. If the constraints are completely independent of each other, the sum of their individual probabilities is exactly the probability of their disjunction. The approximation is small if the constraints are mostly independent, which is often the case for specifying autonomous vehicle systems, since obstacles usually do not overlap.
- We use a uniform risk allocation of the violation probability bounds for each individual constraint. This can be further improved using more effective risk allocation techniques [38].

Thus, the translation of C2TL constraints to mixed integer constraints is conservative, but the approximation introduced is expected to be tight for C2TL specifications used for automated vehicle control.

3.4 Optimal Autonomous Vehicle Control

The goal of synthesizing optimal control for autonomous vehicles is to automatically generate the control inputs $\mathbf{u}$. The control inputs applied at time k are denoted by $\mathbf{u}_k$. Often, the dynamical system can be approximated by *linearizing the system* around the current point of operation and using *model predictive* or *receding horizon control*. A detailed discussion on model predictive control for signal temporal logic can be found in [16]. We employ a similar approach here.

A finite parametrization of a linear system assuming piecewise constant control inputs yields the following difference equation:

$$\mathbf{x}_{k+1} = A_k\mathbf{x}_k + B_k\mathbf{u}_k,$$

where $\mathbf{x}_k \in \mathcal{R}^{n_x}$ is the system state in n_x dimensions, $\mathbf{u}_k \in \mathcal{R}^{n_u}$ denotes the n_u control inputs, and A_k, B_k are coefficients representing linear system dynamics around the state $\mathbf{x}_k$. We consider the control problem over a bounded time horizon T, that is, $0 \leq k \leq T$.

Further, the control inputs $\mathbf{u}_k$ at all time steps k are required to be in a convex feasible region $\mathcal{F}_u$, that is,

$$\mathcal{F}_u \equiv \bigwedge_{i=1}^{N_g} (g_i^T \mathbf{u} \leq c_i); \quad \bigwedge_k \mathbf{u}_k \in \mathcal{F}_u$$

where the convex region $\mathcal{F}_u$ is represented as intersection of N_g half-planes.

The state variables are required to satisfy the autonomous vehicle correctness specification ψ_{ap}^{C2TL}, that is, $\mathbf{x}_k \models \psi_{ap}^{C2TL}$ for all k. We can conservatively approximate the autonomous vehicle correctness specification by ψ_{ap}^{MILP} as discussed earlier, that is, $\mathbf{x}_k \models \psi_{ap}^{MILP} \Rightarrow \mathbf{x}_k \models \psi_{ap}^{C2TL}$

In addition to correctness specification, the synthesized vehicle control is also expected to minimize a user-specified cost function $J(\mathbf{x}, \mathbf{u})$. We restrict the cost function J to be quadratic in order to ensure that solving the control synthesis problem is computationally efficient. Quadratic functions can capture cost metrics of the form $\sum_i \mathbf{u}_k^\dagger U^\dagger U \mathbf{u}_k + \mathbf{x}_k^\dagger S^\dagger S \mathbf{x}_k$ with appropriate scaling vectors U and S, where $\dagger$ denotes the transpose of a matrix. These can represent metrics such as fuel consumption as well as metrics on the vehicle path.

Problem 1 (Autonomous Vehicle Control)

$\arg\min_{\mathbf{u}} J(\mathbf{x}, \mathbf{u})$

s.t. $\mathbf{x}_{k+1} = \mathbb{A}_k \mathbf{x}_k + \mathbb{B}_k \mathbf{u}_k, k = 1 \ldots T, \mathbf{u}_k \in \mathcal{F}_u, \mathbf{x}_k \models \psi_{ap}^{C2TL}$

Problem 2 (Conservative Autonomous Control)

$\arg\min_{\mathbf{u}} J(\mathbf{x}, \mathbf{u})$

s.t. $\mathbf{x}_{k+1} = \mathbb{A}_k \mathbf{x}_k + \mathbb{B}_k \mathbf{u}_k, k = 1 \ldots T, \mathbf{u}_k \in \mathcal{F}_u, \mathbf{x}_k \models \psi_{ap}^{MILP}$

Recall that every solution to Problem 2 also solves Problem 1. Moreover, for a bounded time horizon T and a quadratic cost function, since all the constraints are linear in system variables and conic due to the presence of uncertain coefficients, the conservative autonomous control problem can be solved using scalable second order (quadratic) cone programming tools such as CVXOPT [3]. The following theorem summarizes the correctness guarantee:

Theorem 3. *The solution to Problem 2 is sound with respect to Problem 1: if control inputs are synthesized for the conservative problem, they are guaranteed to satisfy the specified correctness property ψ_{ap}^{C2TL}.*

This theorem follows from Theorem 2 because $\mathbf{x}_k \models \psi_{ap}^{C2TL} \Leftarrow \mathbf{x}_k \models \psi_{ap}^{MILP}$. Note, however, that the proposed synthesis method (i.e. solving the more efficiently solvable conservative problem using second order cone programming) is incomplete for the autonomous control problem due to the conservative approximation of C2TL constraints ($\psi_{ap}^{C2TL} \Leftarrow \psi_{ap}^{MILP}$).

The incompleteness relates to degree of conservative approximation introduced in the translation of C2TL constraints to MILP constraints.

4   Case Studies

We now experimentally demonstrate the effectiveness of our approach. All experiments were done on a Intel Core-i7 2.9 GHz x 8 machine with 16 GB memory. Where applicable, we use a baseline comprised of a modified LQG-based motion planning algorithm [35] and a Monte Carlo sampling-based search algorithm to find an optimal trajectory over the uncertain world model. Our technique is more general than sampling-based approaches because we can enforce temporal logic specifications beyond reachability goals common in classical motion planning. Additionally, the uncertainty in our problem lies within the perceived world model rather than the system evolution.

Navigation in an Uncertain Map: The first case-study considers the problem of navigation in an uncertain map from [39]. Parameter values and other details of the map can be found in [39]. A point mass with two modes – moving forward and turning – is expected to navigate safely in the map shown in Fig. 1. The walls in the map and the obstacle in the center are modeled using probabilistic constraints that incorporate the uncertainty in perception. The uncertain walls

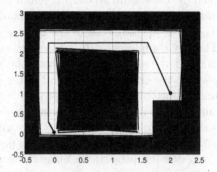

Fig. 1. Navigation in an uncertain map

are illustrated in the map by sampling values of the coefficients and drawing the corresponding walls. The probabilistic safety requirement in this case is a global property requiring that the vehicle avoid the walls and obstacles with a very high probability. The objective function being optimized is quadratic in the final state as well as the control inputs:

$$f(\mathbf{x}, \mathbf{u}) = 50(\mathbf{x}_N - \mathbf{x}_{dest})^T(\mathbf{x}_N - \mathbf{x}_{dest}) + 0.001 \sum_i \mathbf{u}_i^T \mathbf{u}_i,$$

where $\mathbf{x}_{dest}$ is the destination state $(2, 1)$. Observe that although the cost function drives the optimization to minimize the path length, the generated path goes around the obstacle, taking the longer path. This is because the shorter path would violate the C2TL safety constraints due to the uncertainty in the location of the obstacles and walls. This is illustrated in Fig. 1.

When compared to the approach in [39], the method proposed in this paper takes 4.1 s instead of 25.2 s to compute a sequence of control inputs. Monte Carlo simulation was used to estimate the probability of constraint violation. For each simulation, the location of the walls and the obstacles was determinized by sampling from the corresponding Gaussian distribution. We then checked whether the automatically generated path intersected with the walls or obstacles, violating the safety requirement. When the violation probability in the C2TL specification was set to 0.001, Monte Carlo trials did not find a single instance out of

10000 simulations in which the property was violated. We increased the violation probability to 0.01, and found 8 out of 10000 simulations that violated the
probability; i.e., the estimated violation probability was 0.0008. This demonstrates how the proposed approach conservatively approximates the specified
probabilistic constraint, generating a motion plan that satisfies the probabilistic
safety property.

Lane Change: The second case-study is on the synthesis of control for an
autonomous vehicle such as a car, trying to pass a tractor-trailer in an adjacent
lane, as described in [40]. The trailer can probabilistically switch into the passing
car's lane. If the car is ahead of the trailer when the trailer initiates a lane change,
then the car should accelerate, and if the car is behind the trailer when the trailer
initiates the lane change, the car should decelerate. If the trailer switches lanes
when it is just adjacent to the car, the car has no action to prevent an accident.
Thus, a completely safe course of action is not possible for the autonomous
car and it can only try to keep the risk below a user-specified threshold by
passing the trailer quickly and not staying in the unsafe region for long. The
uncertainty arises due to a probabilistic model of when the trailer will switch
lanes, based on the car's observations of its behavior. This case-study assumes
a static jump Markov model of this uncertainty, as shown in Fig. 3 of [40]. The
safety specification requires that the passing car is either decelerating and behind
the trailer until the trailer make the lane switch, or the trailer remains in its lane
until the passing the car is accelerating and ahead of the trailer. We also require
the separation between the car and trailer to be above a safe limit with a high
probability. The threshold of violing the specification was set to 0.015. The cost
function was the time spent behind the trailer but not in the same lane. Autopilot
generation took 5.8 s, and Monte Carlo simulations of the generated autopilot
showed that the actual threshold of violation is 0.0004.

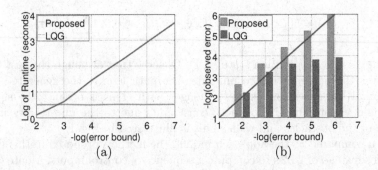

Fig. 2. (a) Runtime Comparison, (b) Accuracy Comparison. (Color figure online)

In order to compare with LQG-based sampling techniques, we change the
cost function to incorporate temporal logic requirements by penalizing the car for
coming close to trailer, and rewarding it for either passing the trailer or traveling

behind it in the same lane if the trailer changed lanes. In Fig. 2(a), we compare runtime of the synthesis technique for each specified violation probability. While our proposed technique's runtime is not very sensitive to the violation probability, the runtime of the sampling-based approach increases sharply due to the increase in the number of required simulation runs. In Fig. 2(b), we present the violation probability observed in Monte Carlo simulations when both approaches are given the same runtime, by restricting the number of simulation runs. All bars above the diagonal line satisfy the probabilistic constraint, while bars below it do not (note the negative log scale on y-axis as well as x-axis). No violations were found for our proposed technique for error bounds 10^{-6} and lower. Thus, the proposed method always satisfies the specification, whereas sampling fails to do so for smaller error bounds.

Passing a Vehicle Using Oncoming Traffic Lane: The third case-study is from recent work by Xu et al. [41]. In this case-study, a vehicle's lane is blocked and it needs to move into the lane of oncoming traffic to go around the obstacle. The perception pipeline on the vehicle estimates the position and the speed of oncoming traffic before deciding to get into the oncoming traffic lane. The dynamics and parameters are described in [41], and we discuss only the results here. Due to uncertainty in perception, we can not deterministically guarantee safe maneuvering of the vehicle, but we require that the probability of collision with oncoming traffic or with the obstacle in the vehicle's lane is below a threshold of ϵ. The uncertainty in perception of the speed of the oncoming traffic is represented by the standard deviation sd of the random variable representing the speed. We modify the cost function from the original case-study, because we use C2TL constraints to specify the safety conditions. The cost function measures the time taken to re-enter the lane after crossing the obstacle.

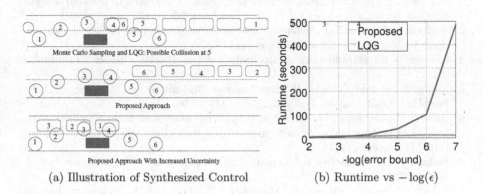

(a) Illustration of Synthesized Control   (b) Runtime vs $-\log(\epsilon)$

Fig. 3. Left: Positions of the autonomous vehicle (circle) and oncoming traffic (rectangle) at different (1–6) time steps are shown. The red rectangle is the obstacle. Right: Runtime comparison for different violation probability bounds. (Color figure online)

We illustrate the qualitative nature of the synthesized control in Fig. 3(a). For violation probability $\epsilon = 0.0001$, the control synthesized by the sampling-based technique in time comparable to our approach (4 s) is not probabilistically safe. The control synthesized using the proposed technique relies on speeding up and getting around the obstacle before the oncoming traffic. When we increase the standard deviation in the perception of the speed of the oncoming traffic by 10X, the control synthesized by our approach picks a less optimum, higher-cost solution in order to meet the safety violation probability requirement, which slows the vehicle and waits for the oncoming traffic to pass before going around the obstacle. Figure 3(b) shows that the runtime of the sampling-based approach increases rapidly with a decrease in ϵ, while it does not change significantly for our technique.

5   Conclusion

In this paper, we present a formal approach to synthesizing autonomous vehicle control in presence of perception uncertainty. Chance constrained temporal logic (C2TL) is proposed to capture correctness specifications in the presence of uncertainty. The autonomous vehicle control synthesized by our technique is guaranteed to satisfy the probabilistic specifications, as demonstrated in several case studies.

References

1. Abate, A., Prandini, M., Lygeros, J., Sastry, S.: Probabilistic reachability and safety for controlled discrete time stochastic hybrid systems. Automatica **44**(11), 2724–2734 (2008)
2. Acikmese, B., Acikmese, S.R.: Convex programming approach to powered descent guidance for mars landing. J. Guid. Control Dyn. **30**(5), 1353–1366 (2007)
3. Andersen, M.S., Dahl, J., Vandenberghe, L.: Cvxopt: a python package for convex optimization, version 1.1.6. (2013). cvxopt.org
4. Åström, K.J.: Introduction to stochastic control theory. Courier Corporation (2012)
5. Bailey, T., Durrant-Whyte, H.: Simultaneous localization and mapping (SLAM): Part II. J. Guid. Control Dyn. **13**(3), 108–117 (2006)
6. Barr, N.M., Gangsaas, D., Schaeffer, D.R.: Wind models for flight simulator certification of landing and approach guidance and control systems. Technical report, DTIC Document (1974)
7. Bellman, R.: Introduction to the mathematical theory of control processes, vol. 2. IMA (1971)
8. Belotti, P., Lee, J., Liberti, L., Margot, F., Wachter, A.: Branching and bounds tightening techniques for non-convex MINLP. Optim. Meth. Softw. **24**, 597–634 (2009)
9. Bernini, N., Bertozzi, M., Castangia, L., Patander, M., Sabbatelli, M.: Real-time obstacle detection using stereo vision for autonomous ground vehicles: a survey. In: ITSC, pp. 873–878. IEEE (2014)

10. Broggi, A.: Autonomous vehicles control in the vislab intercontinental autonomous challenge. J. Guid. Control Dyn. **36**(1), 161–171 (2012)
11. Cassandras, C.G., Lygeros, J.: Stochastic hybrid systems, vol. 24. CRC Press (2006)
12. Charnes, A., Cooper, W.W., Symonds, G.H.: Cost horizons and certainty equivalents: An approach to stochastic programming of heating oil. J. Guid. Control Dyn. **4**(3), 235–263 (1958)
13. De Nijs, R., Ramos, S., Roig, G., Boix, X., Gool, L.V., Kuhnlenz, K.: On-line semantic perception using uncertainty. In: IROS, pp. 4185–4191. IEEE (2012)
14. Devroye, L., Györfi, L., Lugosi, G.: A Probabilistic Theory of Pattern Recognition, vol. 31. Springer Science & Business Media, New York (2013)
15. Donzé, A., Maler, O.: Robust satisfaction of temporal logic over real-valued signals. In: Chatterjee, K., Henzinger, T.A. (eds.) FORMATS 2010. LNCS, vol. 6246, pp. 92–106. Springer, Heidelberg (2010)
16. Raman, V., et al.: Model predictive control with signal temporal logic specifications. In: CDC, pp. 81–87, December 2014
17. Koutsoukos, X.D., Riley, D.: Computational methods for reachability analysis of stochastic hybrid systems. In: Hespanha, J.P., Tiwari, A. (eds.) HSCC 2006. LNCS, vol. 3927, pp. 377–391. Springer, Heidelberg (2006)
18. Kwiatkowska, M., Norman, G., Parker, D.: PRISM: probabilistic symbolic model checker. In: Field, T., Harrison, P.G., Bradley, J., Harder, U. (eds.) TOOLS 2002. LNCS, vol. 2324, p. 200. Springer, Heidelberg (2002)
19. Li, P., Arellano-Garcia, H., Wozny, G.: Chance constrained programming approach to process optimization under uncertainty. Comput. Chem. Eng. **32**(1–2), 25–45 (2008)
20. Martinet, P., Laugier, C., Nunes, U.: Special issue on perception and navigation for autonomous vehicles (2014)
21. Mathys, C.D., et al.: Uncertainty in perception and the hierarchical gaussian filter. Front. Hum. Neurosci. **8**(825) (2014)
22. McGee, T.G., Sengupta, R., Hedrick, K.: Obstacle detection for small autonomous aircraft using sky segmentation. In: ICRA 2005, pp. 4679–4684. IEEE (2005)
23. Meier, L., Tanskanen, P., Fraundorfer, F., Pollefeys, M.: PIXHAWK: a system for autonomous flight using onboard computer vision. In: ICRA, pp. 2992–2997. IEEE (2011)
24. Miller, B.L., Wagner, H.M.: Chance constrained programming with joint constraints. J. Guid. Control Dyn. **13**(6), 930–945 (1965)
25. Nassar, M.R., et al.: An approximately bayesian delta-rule model explains the dynamics of belief updating in a changing environment. J. Guid. Control Dyn. **30**(37), 12366–12378 (2010)
26. Patchett, C., Jump, M., Fisher, M.: Safety and certification of unmanned air systems. Eng. Technol. Ref. **1**(1) (2015)
27. Pnueli, A.: The temporal logic of programs. In: Providence, pp. 46–57 (1977)
28. Pontryagin, L.S.: Optimal control processes. Usp. Mat. Nauk **14**(3), 3–20 (1959)
29. Prajna, S., Jadbabaie, A., Pappas, G.J.: A framework for worst-case, stochastic safety verification using barrier certificates. IEEE Trans. Autom. Control **52**(8), 1415–1428 (2007)
30. Prandini, M., Hu, J.: Stochastic reachability: theory and numerical approximation. J. Guid. Control Dyn. **24**, 107–138 (2006)
31. Prékopa, A.: Stochastic Programming, vol. 324. Springer, Netherlands (2013)
32. Rouff, C., Hinchey, M.: Experience from the DARPA urban challenge. Springer Science & Business Media, London (2011)

33. Rushby, J.: New challenges in certification for aircraft software. In: EMSOFT, pp. 211–218. ACM (2011)
34. Terwilliger, B.A., Ison, D.C., Vincenzi, D.A., Liu, D.: Advancement and application of unmanned aerial system Human-Machine-Interface (HMI) technology. In: Yamamoto, S. (ed.) HCI 2014, Part II. LNCS, vol. 8522, pp. 273–283. Springer, Heidelberg (2014)
35. Van Den Berg, J., Abbeel, P., Goldberg, K.: LQG-MP: optimized path planning for robots with motion uncertainty and imperfect state information. J. Guid. Control Dyn. **30**(7), 895–913 (2011)
36. Vitus, M.: Stochastic Control Via Chance Constrained Optimization and its Application to Unmanned Aerial Vehicles. PhD thesis, Stanford University (2012)
37. Vitus, M.P., Tomlin, C.J.: Closed-loop belief space planning for linear, Gaussian systems. In: ICRA, pp. 2152–2159. IEEE (2011)
38. Vitus, M.P., Tomlin, C.J.: On feedback design and risk allocation in chance constrained control. J. Guid. Control Dyn. **2011**, 734–739 (2011)
39. Vitus, M.P., Tomlin, C.J.: A hybrid method for chance constrained control in uncertain environments. In: CDC, pp. 2177–2182, December 2012
40. Vitus, M.P., Tomlin, C.J.: A probabilistic approach to planning and control in autonomous urban driving. In: CDC, pp. 2459–2464 (2013)
41. Xu, W., Pan, J., Wei, J., Dolan, J.M.: Motion planning under uncertainty for on-road autonomous driving. In: ICRA, pp. 2507–2512. IEEE (2014)

Obfuscator Synthesis for Privacy and Utility

Yi-Chin Wu[1,2]([✉]), Vasumathi Raman[3], Stéphane Lafortune[2],
and Sanjit A. Seshia[1]

[1] UC Berkeley, Berkeley, USA
yichin.wu@berkeley.edu, sseshia@eecs.berkeley.edu
[2] University of Michigan, Ann Arbor, USA
stephane@umich.edu
[3] United Technologies Research Center, Berkeley, USA
ramanv@utrc.utc.com

Abstract. We consider the problem of synthesizing an obfuscation policy that enforces privacy while preserving utility with formal guarantees. Specifically, we consider plants modeled as finite automata with predefined secret behaviors. A given plant generates event strings for some useful computation, but meanwhile wants to hide its secret behaviors from any outside observer. We formally capture the privacy and utility specifications using the automaton model of the plant. To enforce both specifications, we propose an obfuscation mechanism where an edit function "edits" the plant's output in a reactive manner. We develop algorithmic procedures that synthesize a correct-by-construction edit function satisfying both privacy and utility specifications. To address the state explosion problem, we encode the synthesis algorithm symbolically using Binary Decision Diagrams. We present EdiSyn, an implementation of our algorithms, along with experimental results demonstrating its performance on illustrative examples. This is the first work, to our knowledge, to successfully synthesize controllers satisfying both privacy and utility requirements.

1 Introduction

Many systems transmit information to the outside world during their operation. For example, location-based services require devices such as smartphones to transmit location information to other devices or to servers in the cloud. Similarly, in defense and aerospace applications, a network of drones may need to broadcast location information to a variety of agents, including other drones, ground personnel, and remote base stations. These settings often involve nodes that are resource-constrained or connected in ad-hoc, dynamically-changing networks. Some of the transmitted information may reveal secrets about the system

This work was supported in part by TerraSwarm, one of six centers of STARnet, a Semiconductor Research Corporation program sponsored by MARCO and DARPA, and in part by the National Science Foundation under grants CCF-1138860 and CCF-1139138 (NSF Expeditions in Computing project ExCAPE: Expeditions in Computer Augmented Program Engineering) and CNS-1421122.

© Springer International Publishing Switzerland 2016
S. Rayadurgam and O. Tkachuk (Eds.): NFM 2016, LNCS 9690, pp. 133–149, 2016.
DOI: 10.1007/978-3-319-40648-0_11

or its users; therefore, privacy is an important design consideration. At the same time, the agents to which this information is being sent must have enough information to provide relevant services or perform other actions. Thus, the transmission of information from the system to the outside world needs to balance the contrasting requirements of privacy and utility.

Consider the following illustrative example:

Example 1. We consider a user Alice moving in a building. Information about Alice's location needs to be sent to a server and other agents in order to perform some useful actions; e.g., adjusting the heating system based on Alice's location and other occupancy levels in the building, or directing her to the closest coffee machine. Suppose also that there are some "secret" locations, and that Alice does not want others to know when or whether she visits these locations. An example could be a room containing highly sensitive data, such that the mere act of being able to visit it discloses compromising information that Alice wishes to protect (i.e., there are only a handful of people who can visit this room, and their identity is to be kept secret). However, Alice also wants the server to be able to compute some information that is useful based on her location, because otherwise Alice is always cold and uncaffeinated.

Suppose that an "event generator" (e.g., on Alice's phone) generates events based on her movements, and broadcasts these events to other agents. Suppose further that the quality of the service that requires tracking Alice's reported location degrades based on the Euclidean distance from her true location. How can one generate an output event stream that does not reveal whether Alice visited a secret location while also providing sufficient accuracy for determining her location for the relevant services?

Following the terminology used in supervisory control of discrete event systems [9], we refer to the combination of the event generator and the process it is based on (Alice, in our example) as the *plant*. Our goal is to introduce an element of decision-making into the event generator so that it can modify the events to be output before relaying them in order to meet both the privacy and utility requirements. We refer to this decision-making as an *obfuscation policy*.

In this paper, we present a formalization of this problem, along with an algorithm to synthesize an obfuscation policy. We are given a plant modeled as a finite automaton, with formally specified secret behaviors and a specification of utility. The plant must generate event strings that provide sufficient utility while hiding its secret behaviors from an outside observer. The privacy and utility specifications are captured as automata-theoretic requirements on the model of the plant. To enforce both specifications, we propose an obfuscation mechanism whereby the plant *edits* its output in a reactive manner, such that all resulting output strings provably satisfy the specifications. The presented algorithm synthesizes a correct-by-construction edit function that maps true executions of the plant to ones that achieve the privacy and utility specifications.

The paper is structured as follows. We first define the obfuscation problem in Sect. 2. In Sect. 3 we describe our algorithm for automatically editing reported values. The treatment in this section is "explicit", i.e., in terms of graph operations on discrete game structures. To address the state explosion problem, we encode the synthesis algorithm symbolically using Binary Decision Diagrams (BDDs) [1], as described in Sect. 4. We then demonstrate our approach empirically in Sect. 5, using EdiSyn, an open source Python toolkit we developed for this purpose. We conclude after a discussion about related work and future directions.

2 Preliminaries and Problem Statement

2.1 Preliminaries

A Nondeterministic Finite Automaton (NFA) is a tuple $G = (Q, \Sigma, \delta, Q_0)$ with a finite set of states Q, a finite set of events Σ, a state transition function $\delta : Q \times \Sigma \to 2^Q$, and a set of initial states $Q_0 \subseteq Q$. An NFA G is called a Deterministic Finite Automaton (DFA) when $|Q_0| = 1$ and $|\delta(q, e)| \leq 1$ for every state $q \in Q$ and event $e \in \Sigma$. More explicitly, for a DFA as $G = (Q, \Sigma, \delta, q_0)$, the single initial state is $q_0 \in Q$ and the transition function is $\delta : Q \times \Sigma \to Q$, which deterministically defines the next state given the current state and the event.

Given an NFA transition function $\delta : Q \times \Sigma \to 2^Q$, we extend it to $\delta^* : Q \times \Sigma^* \to 2^Q$ recursively as follows: $\delta^*(q, \varepsilon) = \{q\}$, $\delta^*(q, e) = \delta(q, e)$, $\delta^*(q, e_1 e_2 \cdots e_n) = \cup_{q' \in \delta^*(q, e_1)} \delta^*(q', e_2 \cdots e_n)$, where Σ^* is the set of finite strings of events and ε denotes the empty string. The *language* generated by G is the set of strings defined by $\mathcal{L}(G) := \{t \in \Sigma^* : \exists q_0 \in Q_0 \text{ s.t. } \delta^*(q_0, t) \neq \emptyset\}$. A DFA transition function $\delta : Q \times \Sigma \to Q$ is extended to $\delta^* : Q \times \Sigma^* \to Q$ in a similar manner. Also, the language of a DFA is defined similarly. Given string t, we use $t' \preccurlyeq t$ to denote that string t' is a prefix of t, and use $t^{1:k}$ to denote the length-k prefix of t. Finally, $|t|$ denotes the length of t.

In this paper, the system of interest, called the *plant*, is modeled as a DFA $G = (Q, \Sigma, \delta, q_0)$. In our model, the state of the plant cannot be observed directly. However, upon each transition, an event is emitted and can be observed by an outside observer. Hence, an outside observer can infer the state of the plant based on the observation of the string of events emitted upon transitions.

2.2 Threat Model

We consider a scenario where the plant G has a set of *secret states* $Q_S \subset Q$ that need to be kept hidden from the outside observer. The observer of the plant's output strings is a passive-but-curious adversary that has a copy of G, and can see all strings output by the plant; the observer can mimic transitions in its copy of G based on the output strings. We assume that the observer is also a legitimate recipient in the sense that the plant emits strings in order to deliver some information to the observer. However, the plant also wants to hide from the observer whether it is ever in a secret state.

In the following, we will call a string $t \in \mathcal{L}(G)$ a *secret string* if $\delta^*(q_0, t) \in Q_S$ and a *public string* otherwise.

Example 2. Alice and Bob are trying to arrange a secret meeting to exchange a top secret package in a $m \times n$ grid world. We model the generator of Alice and Bob's movements as a plant $G = (Q, \Sigma, \delta, q_0)$ with secret states Q_S, where

- The set of states is $Q = Loc^2 \cup \{init\}$ where $Loc = \{1, \cdots, m \times n\}$ contains the set of all locations on the grid word.
- The set of events is $\Sigma = \{a_{ij}b_{kl} : i, j, k, l \in Loc\}$, where $a_{ij}b_{kl}$ specifies Alice's movement from i to j and Bob's movement from k to l.
- The transition function δ is defined such that, for both Alice and Bob, only moving to neighboring locations or staying at the current location is allowed.
- The set of secret states is $Q_S = \{(i, k) \in Loc : i = k\}$, where Alice and Bob are in the same location.

We show in Fig. 1 the 2×2 grid world and a partial plant automaton of G representing the generator of Alice and Bob's movements. The full model of G contains 17 states and 144 events. Because of space limitations, we do not draw all the states and transitions, and only show a partial plant automaton of G. State $init$ is introduced to model the initial moment when no locations from Alice and Bob have been reported. For each state $(i, j) \in Loc^2$, there is a transition from $init$ to (i, j) with event label $a_{ii}b_{jj}$. For each state (i, j), there is a transition from (i, j) to (k, l) with event label $a_{ik}b_{jl}$ as long as k is a neighboring location of i and l is a neighboring location of j. The red states in G are secret where Alice and Bob meet in the same location.

Let the quality of the service degrade with the L_1 distance from Alice's and Bob's true locations. That is, the quality loss from state (i, j) to state (k, l) is $||(i_x, i_y, j_x, j_y) - (k_x, k_y, l_x, l_y)||_1 = |i_x - k_x| + |i_y - k_y| + |j_x - l_x| + |j_y - l_y|$, where i_x and i_y are the x-coordinate and y-coordinate of location i, and similarly for locations j, k, l. Hence, in reporting the locations of Alice and Bob, we would like to maintain the L_1-distance between the real and the reported locations within some allowable range. This could be because we want an external observer to be able to track the progress of Alice and Bob towards their goal of meeting, while not knowing exactly when or where they meet.

2.3   Edit Functions

To defend against attacks as described in the previous section, we propose to add an interface at the output of the plant that hides secret strings while preserving the utility of the original string. The interface *edits* the plant's original string t as it is produced ("online"), such that the resulting string $\tilde{t}$ after editing never reveals the secret, and yet preserves the utility of t within an allowable range. As this interface is a function that maps each plant output event to another event or string, we refer to it as an *edit function*.

We permit edit functions $f_e : \Sigma^* \times \Sigma \to \Sigma^*$ that map an output event to another event or string with *one* replacement, deletion, or insertion operation. Given past output string t, $f_e(t, e) = o$ means that the plant's output event e is edited to o. Note that $o \in \Sigma^*$ in general because we allow event insertion as

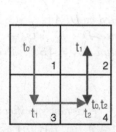

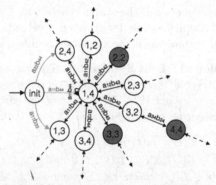

(a) The 2×2 grid world and samples traces of Alice (red) and Bob (blue). Alice and Bob meet at time t_2.

(b) A partial plant automaton of G modeling the generator of Alice and Bob's movements. The secret states are colored in red.

Fig. 1. The 2×2 grid world and a partial plant automaton G representing the generator of Alice and Bob's movements. (Color figure online)

well as deletion. If event e is deleted, then the output is $o = \epsilon$; on the other hand, if a string t_I is inserted before e, then the output is $o = t_I e$. Every edit function is *causal*: it can only edit the current output event e and not any previous output. For convenience of notation, we also define a *string-based* edit function $\hat{f}_e : \Sigma^* \to \Sigma^*$ recursively from f_e such that $\hat{f}_e(\varepsilon) = \varepsilon$ and $\hat{f}_e(te) = \hat{f}_e(t) f_e(t, e)$. Note that, in general, $\hat{f}_e$ is a partial function, and $\hat{f}_e(t)$ may only be defined for selected $t \in \Sigma^*$. Also, since an edit function is causal, its string-based version is *prefix-preserving*: $\forall t_1, t_2 \in \Sigma^*, t_1 \preccurlyeq t_2 \Rightarrow f_e(t_1) \preccurlyeq f_e(t_2)$. An edit function of the above form can be implemented by a deterministic, potentially infinite-state automaton, which we call the *edit automaton*, and denote by $\mathcal{EA} = (S, \Sigma, Trans, s_0)$. The elements of the $\mathcal{EA}$ tuple are the set of states S, the set of events Σ, the transition relation $Trans \subseteq S \times \Sigma \times \Sigma^* \times S$, and the initial state s_0. Each transition in $Trans$ is a tuple (s, e, o, s') of the starting state s, the input event e, the output string o, and the target state s'. Given an edit function f_e, there is a corresponding transition relation $Trans$ with $(s, e, o, s') \in Trans$ iff $f_e(t, e) = o$ and s is the state reached on input string t. The transition relation for f_e is deterministic: $\forall s \in S, \forall e \in \Sigma, |\{s' : (s, e, o, s') \in Trans, o \in \Sigma^*\}| = 1$.

Throughout the paper, we use "edit" to collectively refer to any replacement, deletion, and insertion operation. We will call the output string from the plant as the *original string* t, and call the string after editing as the *obfuscated string* $\tilde{t}$.

2.4 Problem Formulation

Our goal is to synthesize an edit function f_e that hides the plant's secret strings while preserving the utility of the original strings within some allowable range. We capture the *utility* of each original string t by the final state that is reached by t in the plant DFA, and define the utility loss in mapping t to $\tilde{t}$ by the utility difference between the states reached by t and $\tilde{t}$. Without loss of generality, we model the utility loss by an integer-valued distance metric $D : Q \times Q \to \mathbb{N}$. The formal statement of the synthesis problem is as follows:

Problem 1 (Edit Synthesis). *Given a plant modeled as DFA $G = (Q, \Sigma, \delta, q_0)$ with a set of secret states $Q_S \subset Q$, utility distance $D : Q \times Q \to \mathbb{N}$, and accuracy budget $W \in \mathbb{N}$, construct an edit automaton $\mathcal{EA} = (S, \Sigma, Trans, s_0)$ implementing an edit function f_e such that:*

(1) $\forall t \in \mathcal{L}(G)$, $\hat{f}_e(t)$ is defined

(2) $\forall t \in \mathcal{L}(G), \delta^*(q_0, \hat{f}_e(t)) \neq \emptyset$ and $\delta^*(q_0, \hat{f}_e(t)) \notin Q_S$ (privacy specification)

(3) $\forall te \in \mathcal{L}(G)$ where $t \in \Sigma^*$ and $e \in \Sigma$, $D\big(\delta^*(q_0, te), \delta^*(q_0, \hat{f}_e(t)o)\big) \leq W$ and $D\big(\delta^*(q_0, t), \delta^*(q_0, \hat{f}_e(t)o^{1:k})\big) \leq W$ where $o = f_e(t, e)$, for $k = 1, \dots, |o| - 1$ (utility specification)

Remark 1. Note that the privacy specification is a safety property on the output of the edit function.

3   Edit Synthesis Algorithm

We solve Problem 1 by formulating it as a safety game between the edit function and the plant. Such game formulations are common for program synthesis, where the program is modeled as a protagonist playing against the adversarial environment, with the goal of satisfying a given specification. For the edit synthesis problem, the edit function is the "program" to be synthesized, and the plant is the environment that provides inputs to the edit function: adversarialism here means that the plant can evolve arbitrarily, and the edit function must satisfy the specification under all possible evolutions.

3.1   Edit Patterns Satisfying the Specifications

To construct the game, we first want to easily determine whether an edit pattern satisfies the privacy and utility specifications. One challenge is that determining whether an edit pattern satisfies the privacy and utility specifications requires examining not only the obfuscated string, but also its distance from the original string. Fortunately, we can construct an NFA that recognizes all valid edit patterns.

Lemma 1. *There exists an NFA $\mathcal{PA}$, with state space $O(|Q|^2)$, that recognizes all edit patterns satisfying the privacy specification in Problem 1.*

Proof Sketch. Given G, we first build the "edit-pattern"NFA $G_e = (Q, \Sigma \cup \{\varepsilon\}, \delta_e, q_0)$ that recognizes all edit patterns, by adding transitions to G. Transition function δ_e is defined with respect to decomposition $\delta_e := \delta \cup \delta_r \cup \delta_i$. More concretely, consider the plant G in Fig. 1(b). The corresponding G_e is built as shown in Fig. 2(a), such that (i) all original transitions exist, as depicted by the (black) solid arrows; (ii) the replacement transitions δ_r are defined by adding a replacement transition for every event in parallel with the original transition, as depicted by the (red) dashed arrows; and (ii) the insertion transitions δ_i are defined by adding a self loop for every event at every state, as depicted by the (blue) dotted arrows. No replacement or insertion transition is added if an original transition for the given event already exists. Deletion is subsumed by replacement, as deleting an event is the same as replacing the event by the empty string ε. We then construct in Fig. 2(b) the "public-behavior" DFA $G_p = (Q, \Sigma, \delta_p, q_0)$ from G, by pruning away all secret states. Finally, to find all edit patterns satisfying the privacy specification, we compose G_e and G_p and build the product automaton $\mathcal{PA}$. Specifically, the composition synchronizes δ and δ_p (the original transitions), δ_r and δ_p (the replacement transitions), and δ_i and δ_p (the insertion transitions), thereby preserving the edit choices. In sum, since G_e recognizes all edit patterns and G_p recognizes all public behaviors, $\mathcal{PA}$ recognizes each edit pattern for which no obfuscated string ever visits secret states. □

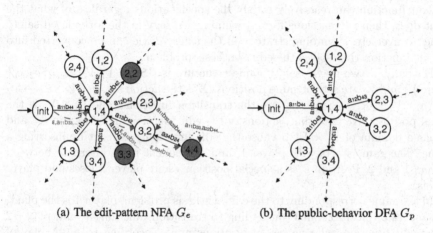

(a) The edit-pattern NFA G_e (b) The public-behavior DFA G_p

Fig. 2. Partial automata of the edit-pattern NFA G_e and the public-behavior DFA G_p for the plant G in Fig. 1(b). In G_e, the solid black arrows depict the original transitions, the dotted blue arrows depict the insertion transitions, and the dashed red arrows depict the replacement transitions. (Color figure online)

Note that, as an interface at the output of the plant, the edit function does not change the plant's original dynamics. This feature is captured in our construction of G_e: neither insertion nor replacement transition changes the real plant state in G_e. Consider an edit pattern with $t, \tilde{t}$, and edit operations. We can uniquely determine a path because each edit transition function is deterministic. Given an edit pattern from t to $\tilde{t}$, by the construction of $\mathcal{PA}$, the ending state of the trace of this edit pattern in $\mathcal{PA}$ is a state pair (q_e, q_p) where $q_e = \delta^*(q_0, t)$ is the plant's real state and $q_p = \delta^*(q_0, \tilde{t})$ is the state perceived by the outside observer based on $\tilde{t}$. Hence, with $\mathcal{PA}$ capturing the pair $(q_e, q_p) = (\delta^*(q_0, t), \delta^*(q_0, \tilde{t}))$ for every t, we can now build from $\mathcal{PA}$ an NFA that recognizes all edit patterns satisfying both the privacy and the utility specifications.

Lemma 2. *There exists an NFA $\mathcal{A}$, with state space $O(|Q|^2)$, that recognizes all edit patterns satisfying the privacy and the utility specifications in Problem 1.*

Proof. Consider $\mathcal{PA}$ from Lemma 1 that recognizes all edit patterns satisfying the privacy specification. Because the distance function D is defined with respect to state pairs, we can determine if the given edit pattern violates the utility specification based on the reached state pair in $\mathcal{PA}$. That is, we can build $\mathcal{A}$ from $\mathcal{PA}$ by pruning all (q_e, q_p) where $D(q_e, q_p) > W$.   □

3.2   Safety Game Formulation

The edit synthesis problem is formulated as a safety game between the edit function and the plant. In the safety game, the outputs of the plant are the inputs to the edit function, and the edit function must react to its inputs (i.e., the plant's outputs) and satisfy both the privacy and the utility specifications. If the edit function can reactively satisfy the specifications regardless of what the plant does, then its reactions form a winning strategy in the formulated safety game. Conversely, a winning strategy in the safety game can be converted into an edit function that solves the edit synthesis problem.

Formally, a two-player safety game structure is $\mathcal{GS} = (V_1, V_2, \Sigma, \rho_1, \rho_2, v_0)$ where V_1 and V_2 are sets of game positions, Σ is the action set, $\rho_1 : V_1 \times \Sigma \to V_2$ and $\rho_2 : V_2 \times \Sigma^* \to (V_1 \cup \bot)$ are the transition functions, and $v_0 \in V_1$ is the initial position. We note that, actions of the edit function are strings in Σ^* and ρ_2 has a domain of $V_2 \times \Sigma^*$ because the edit function can react by inserting a string. The game starts with player 1, and subsequent plays alternate between players 1 and 2. Position $\bot$ is a special position where player 2 loses and player 1 wins.

In the game corresponding to the edit synthesis problem, player 1 is the plant, who moves on positions in V_1 according to transition function ρ_1, and player 2 is the edit function, who moves on positions in V_2 according to ρ_2. A play of $\mathcal{GS}$ is a sequence of positions $v_0 v_1 v_2 \cdots \in (V_1 V_2)^*$ that starts from the initial position. Given a play, the edit function wins if $\bot$ is never visited, and the plant wins otherwise.

Consider the automaton $\mathcal{A} = (Q^2, \Sigma \cup \{\varepsilon\}, \delta_A, q_{A,0})$ in Lemma 2. Recall from Lemma 1 that the transition function of G_e is decomposed, and the synchronous composition used to obtain $\mathcal{PA}$ distinguishes edit choices. Hence, δ_A can also be decomposed into the original transition function $\delta_{A,o}$, the replacement transition function $\delta_{A,r}$, and the insertion transition function $\delta_{A,i}$. We build the safety game structure $\mathcal{GS} = (V_1, V_2, \Sigma, \rho_1, \rho_2, v_0)$ between the edit function and the plant from $\mathcal{A}$ as follows.

- $V_1 = Q^2 \cup \{\bot\}, V_2 = Q^2 \times \Sigma$
- $\rho_1 : V_1 \times \Sigma \to V_2$ is defined such that $\forall (q_e, q_p) \in V_1, \forall e \in \Sigma$,
  $\rho_1((q_e, q_p), e) = ((q_e, q_p), e)$ if $\delta(q_e, e) \neq \emptyset$
- $\rho_2 : V_2 \times \Sigma^* \to V_1$ is defined such that $\forall ((q_e, q_p), e) \in V_2, \forall o \in \Sigma^*$, we have the following four cases:

(i) $\rho_2\big(((q_e, q_p), e), o\big) = \delta_{A,o}((q_e, q_p), e)$ if $o = e$ and $\delta_{A,o}((q_e, q_p), e) \neq \emptyset$

(ii) $\rho_2\big(((q_e, q_p), e), o\big) = \delta_{A,r}((q_e, q_p), o) = (q_e', q_p')$ if $o \in (\Sigma \setminus \{e\}) \cup \{\varepsilon\}$, $\delta_{A,r}((q_e, q_p), o) \neq \emptyset$, and $q_e' = \delta(q_e, e)$

(iii) $\rho_2\big(((q_e, q_p), e), o\big) = \delta_{A,o}\big(\delta_{A,i}^*((q_e, q_p), t_I), e\big)$ if $o = t_I e$, $t_I \in \Sigma^*$, and $\delta_{A,o}\big(\delta_{A,i}^*((q_e, q_p), t_I), e\big) \neq \emptyset$

(iv) $\rho_2\big(((q_e, q_p), e), o\big) = \perp$ if none of cases (i)–(iii) holds

  – $v_0 = q_{A,0} = (q_0, q_0)$

Transition functions ρ_1 and ρ_2 define all possible actions of the plant and the edit function, respectively. Specifically, ρ_1 captures the plant dynamics and is determined by the plant's transition function δ. On the other hand, ρ_2 defines all edit actions. Cases (i)–(iii) are edit actions defined in $\mathcal{A}$, which by Lemma 2 satisfy both the private and the utility specifications. In particular, the edit function outputs the original event from the plant in case (i), replace or delete the plant's original output event in case (ii), insert events before the plant's original output event in case (iii). In case (iv), the edit action cannot satisfy the specifications and leads to the losing position $\perp$. For every plant's output event, the edit function reacts with *one* edit operation.

4 Symbolic Encoding of Edit Synthesis

So far we have assumed that the plant automaton model in the edit synthesis problem is given explicitly, i.e., as an explicit list of states and transitions. However, in practice, such explicit representations lead to what is known as the state explosion problem: a system with n variables that take k possible values requires at least k^n states to model, and thus these models quickly become impractical. In order to mitigate the state explosion problem, we represent the plant model symbolically using sets of states and sets of transitions, both represented compactly as implicit solutions to logical equations. We can then analyze the state space symbolically using Binary Decision Diagrams (BDDs) [1]. By using BDDs to reason about propositional formulas representing the state space, we avoid building the state graph explicitly.

In this section, we present our encoding of the given plant automaton symbolically using propositional formulae. We will explain how the safety game can be constructed symbolically, as well as how to extract a winning edit strategy from the symbolic encoding of the safety game.

4.1 Symbolic Automata

Given an explicit DFA $G = (Q, \Sigma, \delta, Q_0)$, we encode G symbolically as $(B^Q, B^\Sigma, \Delta_\delta, \overline{b^{q_0}})$, where $B^Q = \{y_1^q, \cdots, y_n^q\}$ is the set of Boolean variables that encode the states, $B^\Sigma = \{y_1^e, \cdots, y_m^e\}$ is the set of Boolean variables encoding the events, $\Delta_\delta : B^Q \times B^\Sigma \times B^{Q'} \to \{0, 1\}$ is the propositional formula representing the transition function δ, and $\overline{b^{q_0}}$ is the Boolean encoding of the initial state. The *primed set* $B^{Q'} = \{y_1^{q'}, \cdots, y_n^{q'}\}$ is the Boolean variables that encode the target states in transitions. Given Boolean variable set $\{y_1, \cdots, y_n\}$, we use $\bar{y}$ to denote the variable tuple $(y_1, \cdots, y_n)$. We will write $\chi(\bar{b})$ if a function χ over variables $\bar{y}$ is evaluated with the Boolean vector $\bar{b} = (b_1, \cdots, b_n)$. For a function χ of variables $\bar{y}$, we use $\chi\{\bar{y} \leftarrow \bar{z}\}$ to denote the new function obtained from χ with the variable y_i renamed to z_i.

With a slight abuse of notation, we write $\overline{b^q} \in Q$ if $\overline{b^q}$ is the Boolean encoding of a state in Q and use $\overline{b^q}$ directly to refer to the given state; similar notation applies for events and primed states. We use Δ to denote the propositional formulae for transition functions. Propositional formula Δ_δ is defined such that $\Delta_\delta(\overline{b^q}, \overline{b^\Sigma}, \overline{b^{q'}}) = 1$ iff $\overline{b^{q'}} \in \delta(\overline{b^q}, \overline{b^\Sigma})$.

To symbolically solve the edit synthesis problem, it remains for us to encode the privacy and utility specifications. We encode the secret state set Q_S as a Boolean function $\chi_{Q_S} : B^Q \rightarrow \{0,1\}$ such that $\chi_{Q_s}(\overline{b^q}) = 1$ iff state $\overline{b^q} \in Q_S$. Given the utility distance function D and the accuracy budget W, we construct a propositional function $\Delta_{D_W} : B^Q \times B^{Q'} \rightarrow \{0,1\}$ such that $\Delta_{D_W}(\overline{b^q}, \overline{b^{q'}}) = 1$ iff $D(\overline{b^q}, \overline{b^{q'}}) \leq W$; i.e., the accuracy loss in obfuscating state $\overline{b^q}$ to state $\overline{b^{q'}}$ is bounded by the given budget.

4.2   Symbolic Game Structure

We are now ready to solve the edit synthesis problem symbolically. Consider the plant modeled as a symbolic automaton $G = (B^Q, B^\Sigma, \Delta_\delta, \overline{b^{q_0}})$, the symbolic encoding of secret states χ_{Q_S}, and the propositional formula for the utility specification Δ_{D_W}. We follow the procedures in Sect. 3, first building symbolic intermediate automata G_e, G_p, $\mathcal{PA}$, and $\mathcal{A}$ and then build the symbolic game structure.

First, we construct the symbolic edit-pattern NFA $G_e = (B^e, B^\Sigma, \Delta_{\delta_e}, \overline{b^{e_0}})$ where:

- $B^e = \{y_1^q, \cdots, y_n^q\}$ are the Boolean variables for the *original* plant states.
- $\Delta_{\delta_e} = \Delta_\delta \vee \Delta_{\delta_r} \vee \Delta_{\delta_i}$ where
  - Δ_δ defines the original transitions.
  - $\Delta_{\delta_r} = (\exists \overline{y^\Sigma}.\Delta_\delta) \wedge \neg\Delta_\delta$ defines the replacement transitions.
  - $\Delta_{\delta_i} = (\overline{y^q} \Leftrightarrow \overline{y^{q'}}) \wedge \neg\Delta_\delta$ defines the insertion transitions.
- $\overline{b^{e_0}} = \overline{b^{q_0}}$

We can similarly build the symbolic public-behavior DFA $G_p = (B^p, B^\Sigma, \Delta_{\delta_p}, \overline{b^{p_0}})$, where B^p are the Boolean variables for the *fake* states and Δ_{δ_p} prunes all secret states. Next, we build the product automaton $\mathcal{PA}$ from G_e and G_p, and then prune the state pairs that violate the utility specification to obtain $\mathcal{A} = (B^A, B^\Sigma, \Delta_{\delta_A}, \overline{b^{A_0}})$. Here $\Delta_{\delta_A} = \Delta_{\delta_e} \wedge \Delta_{\delta_p} \wedge \chi_{D_W}\{\overline{y^{q'}} \leftarrow \overline{y^p}\} = \Delta_{\delta_{A,o}} \vee \Delta_{\delta_{A,r}} \vee \Delta_{\delta_{A,i}}$ is decomposed into the original transitions $\Delta_{\delta_{A,o}}$, the replacement transitions $\Delta_{\delta_{A,r}}$, and the insertion transitions $\Delta_{\delta_{A,i}}$ for technical convenience later. Symbolic automaton $\mathcal{A}$ recognizes all edit patterns satisfying the privacy and utility specifications.

Finally, we build the symbolic game structure $\mathcal{GS} = (B^V, B^I, B^O, \Delta_{\rho_1},$ $\Delta_{\rho_2}, \overline{b^{v_0}})$. Let $\overline{y^A} = (y_1^q, \cdots, y_n^q, y_1^p, \cdots, y_n^p)$, we will use $\overline{y_{\Downarrow q}^A}$ to denote the projection of of $\overline{y^A}$ onto variables y_i^q. That is, $\overline{y_{\Downarrow q}^A} = (y_1^q, \cdots, y_n^q)$. Similarly, $\overline{y_{\Downarrow p}^A} = (y_1^p, \cdots, y_n^p)$.

- $B^V = B^A$ are the Boolean variables encoding the game positions.
- $B^I = B^\Sigma$ are the Boolean variables for the plant's actions. Superscript I means they are input variables to the edit function.
- $B^O = \{y_1^O, \cdots, y_m^O\}$ are the Boolean variables for the edit function's actions. Superscript O means they are output variables of the edit function.
- $\Delta_{\rho_1} : B^V \times B^I \to \{0, 1\}$ such that $\Delta_{\rho_1}(\overline{y^A}, \overline{y^\Sigma}, \overline{y^{A'}}) = \Delta_\delta(\overline{y_{\Downarrow q}^A}, \overline{y^\Sigma}, \overline{y_{\Downarrow q}^{A'}})$
- $\Delta_{\rho_2} : B^V \times B^I \times B^O \times B^{V'} \to \{0, 1\}$ that is decomposed into $\Delta_{\rho_2, or} \vee \Delta_{\rho_2, i}$
  - $\Delta_{\rho_2, or}(\overline{y^A}, \overline{y^\Sigma}, \overline{y^O}, \overline{y^{A'}}) =$
    $\left(\Delta_\delta(\overline{y_{\Downarrow q}^A}, \overline{y^\Sigma}, \overline{y_{\Downarrow q}^{A'}}) \wedge \Delta_{\delta_{A,o}}(\overline{y^A}, \overline{y^\Sigma}, \overline{y^{A'}})\{\overline{y^\Sigma} \leftarrow \overline{y^O}\} \right) \vee$
    $\left(\Delta_\delta(\overline{y_{\Downarrow q}^A}, \overline{y^\Sigma}, \overline{y_{\Downarrow q}^{A'}}) \wedge \Delta_{\delta_{A,r}}(\overline{y^A}, \overline{y^\Sigma}, \overline{y^{A'}})\{\overline{y^\Sigma} \leftarrow \overline{y^O}\} \right)$
  - $\Delta_{\rho_2, i}(\overline{y^A}, \overline{y^\Sigma}, \overline{y^O}, \overline{y^{A'}}) =$
    $\exists \overline{y^{A''}}. \left(\overline{y^{A''}} \in Reach_i(\overline{y^A}) \wedge \Delta_{\delta_{A,o}}(\overline{y^{A''}}, \overline{y^\Sigma}, \overline{y^{A'}}) \right)$, where
    * $Post_i(Z) = \{\overline{y^{A'}} \mid \exists \overline{y^\Sigma} \exists \overline{y^A}.(\overline{y^A} \in Z) \wedge \Delta_{\delta_{A,i}}(\overline{y^A}, \overline{y^\Sigma}, \overline{y^{A'}})\}$
    * $Reach_i(\overline{y^A}) = \mu Z. Post_i(\overline{y^A}) \vee Post_i(Z)$
- $\overline{b^{v_0}} = \overline{b^{A_0}}$

Observe that Δ_{ρ_2} is decomposed into two parts, one containing the original and the replacement actions $\Delta_{\rho_2, or}$, and another containing only the insertion actions $\Delta_{\rho_2, i}$. We make this partition because the outputs for insertion actions are in general strings whose lengths are not known in advance. To symbolically encode all such output strings, we would need to introduce a potentially unbounded number of Boolean variables corresponding to all possible events and intermediate states on allowed output strings. To avoid this, we only encode in the game construction whether it is possible for the edit function to react with an insertion action. That is, a transition $(\overline{b^V}, \overline{b^I}, \overline{b^O}, \overline{b^{V'}}) \models \Delta_{\rho_2, i}$ if it is possible to move from position $\overline{b^V}$ to position $\overline{b^{V'}}$ with insertion. Here, the output $\overline{b^O}$ is unconstrained as it is not used: the actual insertion string will be computed explicitly in the synthesis algorithm in Sect. 4.3. We use μ-calculus [3,6] to formulate the problem of determining whether it is possible to apply insertion actions. The μ-calculus formula $\mu Z. Post_i(\overline{y^A}) \vee Post_i(Z)$ is the least fixed point that computes all positions that are reachable from $\overline{y^A}$ via a non-zero length insertion string.

When computing $\Delta_{\rho_2, i}(\overline{y^A}, \overline{y^\Sigma}, \overline{y^O}, \overline{y^{A'}})$, the intermediate steps of the fixpoint computation $Reach_i(\overline{y^A})$ encode the insertions themselves, and are stored in a data structure ins to be used later to extract the edit function. Informally, we store in $ins_{\overline{y^A}, \overline{y^\Sigma}}[i]$ the set of positions reachable from $\overline{y^A}$ via an insertion string of length i followed by an input event $\overline{y^\Sigma}$.

4.3   Synthesis

With the game structure $\mathcal{GS}$, we now compute the set of winning positions for the edit function and synthesize a winning edit strategy in Algorithm 1. We characterize the set of winning positions $\mathcal{W}$ using a μ-calculus formula. Specifically, in step 2, the μ-calculus formula $\nu Z.Pre(Z)$ is the greatest fixed point containing all positions where the edit function can continuously react to the plant with a winning edit action. If $\mathcal{W}$ does not contain the initial position $\overline{b}^{v_0}$, then Algorithm 1 returns that the edit synthesis problem is not feasible; i.e., Problem 1 has no solution. Otherwise, there exists a winning edit strategy and we synthesize, starting from step 4, a winning edit automaton $\mathcal{EA}$ by breadth-first search on the winning positions. The initial state of $\mathcal{EA}$ is the initial position $\overline{b}^{v_0}$ of $\mathcal{GS}$. Steps 6–18 compute concrete winning actions and construct the corresponding explicit edit automaton. χ_s is the set of explored positions in $\mathcal{GS}$. In each iteration, we take newly-reached positions $\chi_{s,diff}$ and compute in step 9 the one-step winning actions act from $\chi_{s,diff}$, using function $\texttt{Winning\_Actions}$. With act being computed, in the inner while loop, we extract concrete transitions in act. In step 12, function $\texttt{Extract\_One}$ extracts one concrete transition. Then, in step 18, we subtract from act all transitions with the same game position $\overline{b}^V$ and plant output event $\overline{b}^I$, as an edit action for that position and event has already been found. This inner while loop terminates until act is empty. In each iteration, if the extracted transition is an insertion action, then we compute the output string for the insertion action using function $\texttt{Compute\_Insert\_Out}$. Otherwise, the output is the event $\overline{b}^O$ in the extracted transition.

Function $\texttt{Compute\_Insertion}$ returns a string o of legal insertion events leading from position $\overline{b}^V$ to $\overline{b}^{V'}$ on input $\overline{b}^I$, and we describe it here informally. Recall the data structure ins stored during the fixpoint computation that defines $\Delta_{\rho_2,i}$ in Sect. 4.2. Since $(\overline{b}^V, \overline{b}^I, \overline{b}^O, \overline{b}^{V'}) \models \Delta_{\rho_2,i}$, we have $\overline{b}^{V'} \in ins_{\overline{b}^V, \overline{b}^I}[i]$ for some $i \geq 0$. Informally, $\overline{b}^{V'}$ is reachable from $\overline{b}^V$ via an insertion string of length i followed by $\overline{b}^I$. Note that we will want to find a *shortest* such i, for which $\overline{b}^{V'} \in ins_{\overline{b}^V, \overline{b}^I}[i]$ but $\overline{b}^{V'} \notin ins_{\overline{b}^V, \overline{b}^I}[i-1]$. Now, we can reconstruct a path of insertions from $\overline{b}^V$ to $\overline{b}^{V'}$ by working backwards from $ins_{\overline{b}^V, \overline{b}^I}[i]$ as follows. Set $o_i = \overline{b}^I$. At each iteration, we extract an insertion action o_{i-1} that leads from $ins_{\overline{b}^V, \overline{b}^I}[i-1]$ to $ins_{\overline{b}^V, \overline{b}^I}[i]$. We repeat this until we arrive at $ins_{\overline{b}^V, \overline{b}^I}[0] = \overline{b}^V$. The resulting $o = o_0 o_1 ... o_i$ is the output after insertion.

Theorem 1. *Given a plant G with a set of secret states Q_S, utility distance D, and accuracy budget W, Algorithm 1 returns a finite edit automaton $\mathcal{EA} = (S, Trans, s_0)$ that solves Problem 1, if one exists, and declares infeasibility otherwise.*

Proof. Recall that the game structure $\mathcal{GS}$ is constructed from G_e that recognizes all edit patterns. Hence, the symbolic $\mathcal{GS}$ enumerates all edit strategies in a finite structure that satisfy the privacy and utility specifications before potentially reaching a losing position. Because the winning set $\mathcal{W}$ is a set of positions where the edit function can *continuously* react to the plant with an edit action satisfying

---

Algorithm 1. Edit function synthesis

---

input : $G = (Q, \Sigma, \delta, q_0)$, $Q_S \subset Q$, $D : Q \times Q \to \mathbb{N}$, $W \in \mathbb{N}$
output: $\mathcal{EA} = (S, Trans, s_0)$

1   Construct $\mathcal{GS} = (B^V, B^I, B^O, \Delta_{\rho_1}, \Delta_{\rho_2}, \overline{b^{v_0}})$ per Sect. 4.2
2   Compute winning set $\mathcal{W} = \nu Z.Pre(Z)$ where
$Pre(Z) =$
$$\{\overline{y^A} \mid \forall \overline{y^\Sigma} \; \forall \overline{y^{A'}_{\Downarrow q}} \; \exists \overline{y^{A'}_{\Downarrow p}} \; \exists \overline{y^O}. \left[\Delta_{\rho_1}(\overline{y^A}, \overline{y^\Sigma}, \overline{y^{A'}}) \Rightarrow \overline{y^{A'}} \in Z \wedge \Delta_{\rho_2}(\overline{y^A}, \overline{y^\Sigma}, \overline{y^O}, \overline{y^{A'}}) \right] \}$$
3   **if** $\mathcal{W} \wedge \overline{b^{v_0}} = $ **False then**
    $\llcorner$ **return** Infeasible
4   $s_0 := \overline{b^{v_0}}, S \leftarrow \{s_0\}$
5   $\chi_s \leftarrow \overline{b^{v_0}}, \chi_{s,old} \leftarrow$ **False**
6   **while** $\chi_s \neq \chi_{s,old}$ **do**
7      $\chi_{s,diff} \leftarrow \chi_s \wedge \neg \chi_{s,old}$
8      $\chi_{s,old} \leftarrow \chi_s$
9      $act \leftarrow$ **Winning_Actions**$(\chi_{s,diff}, \Delta_{\rho_1}, \Delta_{\rho_2}, \mathcal{W})$
10     $\chi_s \leftarrow \chi_{s,old} \vee act_{\Downarrow A}\{\overline{y^{A'}} \leftarrow \overline{y^A}\}$
11   **while** $act \neq$ **False do**
12       $(\overline{b^V}, \overline{b^I}, \overline{b^O}, \overline{b^{V'}}) \leftarrow$ **Extract_One**(act)
13       $S \leftarrow S \cup \{\overline{b^{V'}}\}$
14   **if** $(\overline{b^V}, \overline{b^I}, \overline{b^O}, \overline{b^{V'}}) \models \Delta_{\rho_2,i}$ **then**
15        $\mid$ $o \leftarrow$ **Compute_Insertion**$((\overline{b^V}, \overline{b^I}, \overline{b^O}, \overline{b^{V'}}))$
        else
16        $\llcorner$ $o \leftarrow \overline{b^O}$
17       $Trans \leftarrow Trans \cup \{(\overline{b^V}, \overline{b^I}, o, \overline{b^{V'}})\}$
18       $act \leftarrow act \wedge \neg(\overline{b^V} \wedge \overline{b^I})$

19 **return** $(S, Trans, s_0)$

---

the specifications, we can synthesize an edit automaton that solves Problem 1 iff the initial game position is winning. A winning edit strategy can in general require memory: it can choose different edit actions based on the history. But because the game is a safety game, we can convert any such strategy to a winning memoryless strategy by repeatedly selecting the same edit action every time it visits the same game position. In fact, Algorithm 1 considers only memoryless edit strategies. Therefore, the synthesized edit automaton is guaranteed to be finite.

4.4 Complexity

Computing the winning set $\mathcal{W}$, which is expressed as a μ-calculus formula of alternation depth 1, can be solved with effort $O(N)$ where N is the number of states the game structure $\mathcal{GS}$, which is $O(n^2)$ if n is the number of states in the plant G. Here effort is measured in symbolic steps, i.e., in the number of preimage computations in the fixpoint in step 1 of the Algorithm. Extracting an edit function also takes $O(N)$, and hence Algorithm 1 has complexity $= O(N) = O(n^2)$. However, constructing the game structure $\mathcal{GS}$ has additional complexity $O(N^2) = O(n^4)$ because of the least fixpoint computation for every state in the game structure when computing $\Delta_{\rho_2,i}$. In all, Algorithm 1 has complexity of $O(n^4)$.

5 Case Studies and Experiments

We demonstrate our approach empirically using EdiSyn, an open source Python toolkit we developed for this purpose[1]. EdiSyn implements the synthesis algorithm based on Binary Decision Diagrams (BDDs), and relies on the CUDD BDD library [11] and DD [5], an open source Python binding to CUDD. We ran EdiSyn with Example 2 introduced in Sect. 2.2. The utility distance is defined based on the L_1 distance, as defined in Sect. 2.2. Finally, we let the accuracy budget be 2.

We shown in Fig. 3 the real and the obfuscated moving traces of Alice and Bob. t_i's denote the time points where their locations are reported. The left figure depicts the real moving traces. At time t_2, Alice and Bob meet at location $(2,2)$, which corresponds to a secret state. The right figure depicts the traces output from the edit function. The edit function obfuscates their traces such that Alice and Bob are never reported to be in the same location. Furthermore, the distance between the original and the obfuscated locations always remain within 2.

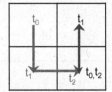 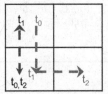

Fig. 3. Left: The original moving traces of Alice (in blue) and Bob (in red). Right: The obfuscated moving traces output from the synthesized edit function. (Color figure online)

We also ran EdiSyn with examples in the same settings but increasing grid sizes. Grid$_{k \times k}$ is the example where Alice and Bob move in the $k \times k$ grid world and want to hide their secret meetings. The accuracy budget is set to 2 in all examples. The results of this experiment are summarized in Table 1. For each grid example, Table 1 shows the number of plant variables (i.e., the number of states plus the number of events), the computation time of the symbolic implementation, the peak number of BDD nodes, and the memory used during the synthesis computation. The experiment was performed on an Intel Core i5 (2.4 GHz, 4 GB) machine running Mac OS X 10.10.5 Yosemite. While we also

---

[1] EdiSyn is available at https://bitbucket.org/yichinwu/edisyn.

implemented the explicit (non-symbolic) algorithm, the explicit implementation threw outOfMemory errors on all of the grid examples.

These are preliminary results based on a simple, unoptimized implementation. In addition to optimizing the implementation in terms of memory usage and efficiency of operations, comparison of various variable ordering strategies for the BDDs and reuse of intermediate stages of the fixpoint computations while constructing the game structure are also acknowledged as worthy of further exploration. Finally, observe that the synthesis algorithm is computed offline. Once an edit function is synthesized, it can be used to efficiently edit the plant's output online.

Table 1. Scalability test for the grid world example, with a timeout of 60 minutes.

Example	Variables	Synthesis time (min)	Peak nodes	Memory (MB)
Grid$_{2\times2}$	161	0.05	21274	30.8
Grid$_{3\times3}$	1171	2.90	261446	151.3
Grid$_{4\times4}$	4353	42.37	1103200	637.7
Grid$_{5\times5}$	11651	Timeout	N/A	N/A

6   Related Work

This work combines perspectives and techniques from computer security and formal synthesis. Our threat model and problem formulation are inspired by the definition of differential privacy [2], where the consumers of data include both legitimate receivers and adversaries, and the goal is to provide privacy while preserving utility with respect to the desired data analytics. Informally, ϵ-differential privacy guarantees that the resulting output is insensitive (up to a factor dependent on ϵ) to the modification, deletion or addition of any single record in the original dataset. Utility of a differentially private mechanism is evaluated using query-dependent measures of the deviation between results obtained from the original dataset obtained by applying the mechanism to the original dataset. The edit functions in this work can be viewed as a discrete logic counterpart of differentially private mechanisms; privacy and accuracy here are captured by logical conditions on the edited executions of the plant in comparison with the real executions. Additionally, most traditional approaches to providing privacy rely on cryptographic primitives; however, such schemes require an infrastructure to create and distribute secret keys. In the settings we consider, especially those involving ad-hoc and dynamic networks, and resource-constrained devices, a non-cryptographic solution such as ours may be preferred.

There has been some previous work on the synthesis of artifacts enforcing privacy requirements in the discrete logic setting. Specifically, synthesis for a privacy notion called opacity has been explored by researchers in discrete event systems; see e.g., [4,10,12]. The edit mechanism in this paper is related to but more powerful than the insertion mechanism developed in [12]. The most distinguishing feature of this work is the threat model. All existing works on synthesis for opacity consider an threat model where every outside observer of the system is malicious. In contrast, the malicious outside observer in this paper is also endowed with some legitimate observational needs. As a consequence of this different threat model, none of the above works addresses questions of the preserving utility of observations. To the best of our knowledge, this paper is the first attempt to formulate the synthesis problem for both privacy and utility. Our work is also distinguished by the presentation of a symbolic encoding of the solution. We encode the synthesis problems symbolically using Binary Decision Diagrams, and are thereby better equipped to address the state explosion problem.

In addition to the field of discrete event systems, we draw inspiration from recent work in robotics that considers the design of discrete filters satisfying privacy and utility constraints provided as pairwise distinguishability (and indistinguishability) requirements on states [8]. Our work is most similar in spirit to this effort, but our privacy and utility constraints are specified as automata theoretic winning conditions instead of pairwise requirements on states. In [8], the requirements are satisfied via graph colorings: states that must be indistinguishable have the same color and ones to be distinguished are colored differently. Our edit mechanism is more general, in that it also allows inserting fictitious events.

Finally, the idea of editing event labels on automaton transitions is also employed in [7], where the authors considered a selfish environment that edits the inputs to the plant automaton. However, the focus in [7] is on deciding whether the plant is resilient to such a selfish environment rather than on synthesizing an edit strategy with privacy and utility objectives.

7   Conclusion and Future Work

We have defined the problem of synthesizing an obfuscation policy that enforces privacy specifications while preserving utility. The specifications in this work were captured as automata-theoretic requirements on a finite state model of the plant's outputs. Our method allows plants to generate and broadcast event strings for some useful computation, while simultaneously hiding certain secret behaviors from an outside observer. To enforce the privacy and utility specifications, we automatically synthesized an edit function that reacts to the plant's outputs and transforms them in a way that meets both requirements. Our synthesis algorithm was encoded symbolically, improving the efficiency of obtaining a solution. This is, to our knowledge, the first work to consider synthesis for both privacy and utility specifications.

In this work, we considered simple privacy and utility specifications: in fact, our privacy requirement is a safety guarantee. In the future, we will explore the use of more complicated specifications to express these desirables. For example, temporal logics are expressive tools for stating requirements. Formulating privacy and utility as temporal logic formulae would allow a much richer set of specifications. Also, so far our utility specification has taken the form of an accuracy budget constraining the distance between the real and released states. In the future, we will tackle an optimization problem that asks the question, what is the smallest budget for which the problem in this paper becomes feasible?

References

1. Bryant, R.E.: Graph-based algorithms for Boolean function manipulation. IEEE Trans. Comput. **C-35**(8), 677–691 (1986)
2. Dwork, C.: Differential privacy. In: International Conference on Automata, Languages and Programming, pp. 1–12 (2006)
3. Emerson, E.A.: Model checking and the mu-calculus. DIMACS Ser. Discrete Math. **31**, 185–214 (1997)
4. Falcone, Y., Marchand, H.: Runtime enforcement of K-step opacity. In: 52nd IEEE Conference on Decision and Control (2013)
5. Filippidis, I.: https://github.com/johnyf/dd
6. Kozen, D.: Results on the propositional μ-calculus. Theor. Comput. Sci. **27**(3), 333–354 (1983)
7. Kupferman, O., Tamir, T.: Coping with selfish on-going behaviors. In: Clarke, E.M., Voronkov, A. (eds.) LPAR-16 2010. LNCS, vol. 6355, pp. 501–516. Springer, Heidelberg (2010)
8. O'Kane, J.M., Shell, D.A.: Automatic design of discreet discrete filters. In: IEEE International Conference on Robotics and Automation (ICRA), pp. 353–360 (2015)
9. Ramadge, P.J., Wonham, W.M.: Supervisory control of a class of discrete event processes. SIAM J. Control Optim. **25**(1), 206–230 (1987)
10. Saboori, A., Hadjicostis, C.N.: Opacity-enforcing supervisory strategies via state estimator constructions. IEEE Trans. Autom. Control **57**(5), 1155–1165 (2012)
11. Somenzi, F.: CUDD: CU decision diagram package release 2.3.0. University of Colorado at Boulder (1998)
12. Wu, Y.-C., Lafortune, S.: Synthesis of insertion functions for enforcement of opacity security properties. Automatica **50**(5), 1336–1348 (2014)

Code Generation Using a Formal Model
of Reference Counting

Gaspard Férey[1(✉)] and Natarajan Shankar[2]

[1] École Polytechnique, Palaiseau, France
gaspard.ferey@polytechnique.edu
[2] Computer Science Laboratory, SRI International, Menlo Park, CA 94025, USA
shankar@csl.sri.com

Abstract. Reference counting is a popular technique for memory management. It tracks the number of active references to a data object during the execution of a program. Reference counting allows the memory used by a data object to be freed when there are no active references to it. We develop the metatheory of reference counting by presenting an abstract model for a functional language with arrays. The model is captured by an intermediate language and its operational semantics, defined both with and without reference counting. These two semantics are shown to correspond by means of a bisimulation. The reference counting implementation allows singly referenced data objects to be updated in place, i.e., without copying. The main motivation for our model of reference counting is in soundly translating programs from a high-level functional language, in our case, an executable fragment of the PVS specification language, to efficient code with a compact footprint in a small subset of a low-level imperative language like C.

1 Introduction

We present an abstract formal model of reference counting [4] in the context of a simple intermediate language with an applicative semantics. We demonstrate the soundness of an operational semantics with reference counting and in-place updates for this model by establishing a bisimulation between it and the idealized version. The intermediate language is used to generate efficient imperative code with a small footprint in the C programming language from executable PVS specifications. We present some performance comparisons against code written directly in C.

The background for this work is the translation of programs in a high-level specification language, in our case PVS [10], to a low-level language such as C

This work was supported by NSF Grant CSR-EHCS(CPS)-0834810, NASA Cooperative Agreement NNA10DE73C, and by DARPA under agreement number FA8750-12-C-0284 and FA8750-16-C-0043. The views and conclusions contained herein are those of the authors and should not be interpreted as necessarily representing the official policies or endorsements, either expressed or implied, of NSF, NASA, DARPA or the U.S. Government.

© Springer International Publishing Switzerland 2016
S. Rayadurgam and O. Tkachuk (Eds.): NFM 2016, LNCS 9690, pp. 150–165, 2016.
DOI: 10.1007/978-3-319-40648-0_12

using a code generator called PVS2C. Our formal model of reference counting can also be used in other contexts, including other source and target languages, in specific applications requiring memory management, and as a semantic framework for static analysis. Strong typechecking in PVS ensures that the intermediate language programs generated from it do not trigger runtime errors including type errors, out-of-bounds array accesses, null dereferences, or division by zero. The only way they can fail is by exhausting stack or heap space.

To keep things simple, we restrict ourselves to arrays as the only aggregate data structure accessed through references, since other data structures can be handled similarly. The intermediate language contains constants, variables, let-bindings, conditionals, function application, new array constructors, and updates. In PVS2C, the intermediate language has a type system to allow bitwidths to be computed for numeric values, but we use an untyped intermediate language here to present the theory in its most general form. The syntax of the intermediate language is *flattened* in a manner similar to the A-normal form [6] so that compound expressions can only appear in the binding or body of a let-expression or on the branches of a conditional expression. This allows the order of evaluation to be fixed and simplifies the tracking of reference counts.

The idealized operational semantics for the intermediate language, given by means of a small-step relation using evaluation contexts [5], implements array updates nondestructively, i.e., by copying. We then augment the semantics with a reference count that accurately tracks the number of active references during evaluation. The semantics depends on a preprocessing step to eliminate redundant let-bindings and to mark the final occurrence of each variable within its scope. This allows the reference count for a reference to be decremented as soon as a variable containing that reference is no longer active. The eager release of references is critical since it allows the maximal safe use of in-place updates. We then prove various metatheorems about the reference counting operational semantics, including the main invariant that captures the meaning of the reference count. The operational semantics automatically discards data objects with a zero reference count and admits in-place updates of references with a reference count of one. The use of evaluation contexts yields a simple proof for the correctness of the operational semantics based on reference counting.

The formal model of reference counting allows a high-level language like PVS with an applicative semantics to be implemented efficiently by means of a low-level language like C without the need for an independent garbage collector. Indeed, it is quite challenging to implement correct garbage collectors directly for languages like C that admit explicit pointers, pointer arithmetic, and typecasts [1]. Also, the use of a garbage collector does not help to identify opportunities for safe in-place updates as reference counting does. Our reference counting semantics correctly handles nested updates which pose challenges for static update analysis employed in the existing PVS code generator [11]. Reference counting fails when there are reference cycles [9], but such cycles are inadmissible in both the source language PVS and in the intermediate language.

Our abstract model of reference counting is for an applicative language, such as the functional subset of PVS. The reference counting semantics is *exact*, as is demonstrated in Theorem 9. Our main result is captured in Theorem 10 which establishes the correspondence between the idealized operational semantics of the intermediate language and one based on reference counting and in-place updates. The intermediate representation with the latter semantics can then be translated to one of several implementation languages. The target language we have used is C. Reference counting makes it easy to map executable operations from a high-level representation like PVS to a low-level programming language like C. We are currently working toward formally verifying the claims in this paper using PVS, as a step toward establishing the semantic correspondence between the generated C code and the source PVS definitions. The target C code generated is suitable for compilation with the formally verified CompCert compiler [8].

Reference counting is one of the oldest ideas in modern computing and there is a large body of literature devoted to it. Much of the work on reference counting is in the context of garbage collection [12]. Several popular programming language, e.g., C++ (through smart pointers), D, Perl, PHP, Python, Smalltalk, and Swift, support reference counting as a mechanism for memory management that either avoids or reduces the need for garbage collection. Though reference counting is a popular technique, both in language implementations and in application software, there are very few abstract treatments of it in the literature. Hudak [7] presents a denotational semantics for reference counting where each occurrence of a variable is counted as a separate reference. Our model for reference counting does not count occurrences. Hudak's semantic definition is primarily used for abstract interpretation to compute useful approximations of the reference counts. Chirimar et al. [2] describe an operational semantics for a computational interpretation of linear logic based on reference counting. Their model uses the primitives: `share`, to distribute a reference; `dispose`, to release a reference; `store`, creates a new shareable object (with reference counting) and `fetch` accesses the value of a shareable reference. Since linearly typed variables can be used exactly once along a branch of the computation, contents of shareable variables, i.e., those of nonlinear type, have to be explicitly copied and disposed. To our knowledge, none of the above models has been used in code generation. Our approach is based on the more general case of an untyped intermediate language with no explicit constructs for memory management. Reference counting is directly embedded into the operational semantics of this language to support memory management and safe in-place updates. The theory underlying the operational semantics covers any typed or untyped pure applicative functional language with a fixed evaluation order.

2   Executing PVS Specifications

The PVS specification language is based on classical simply typed higher-order logic augmented with predicate subtypes, dependent types, and algebraic and

```
swap : THEORY

  BEGIN

  nat32: TYPE = upto(4294967295)

  numrows: MACRO nat32 = 10
  numcols: MACRO nat32 = 15

  rows: TYPE = below(numrows)
  cols: TYPE = below(numcols)

  nestedArray: TYPE = [rows -> [cols -> nat32]]

  A: VAR nestedArray

  swap(A, (i, j : rows)): nestedArray =
    A WITH [(i) := A(j),
            (j) := A(i)]

  innerSwap(A, (i, j : rows)): nestedArray =
     A WITH [(i)(j) := A(j)(i), (j)(i) := A(i)(j)]

  mkNestedArray: nestedArray =
    (LET x = (LAMBDA (k: cols): k) WITH [(numcols - 1) := 0]
      IN (LAMBDA (i: rows): x))

  END swap
```

Fig. 1. PVS theory using nested arrays

coalgebraic datatypes. Here, we restrict our attention to a simple first-order fragment of PVS. A PVS theory, as shown in Fig. 1, is a list of declarations of constants, types, and formulas (axioms, lemmas, theorems). The types include basic ones like bool and number, where the latter also has subtypes such as the integers int the non-negative integers nat, the rational numbers rat, and the real numbers real. A subtype of the elements of a type T satisfying a predicate p can be defined as $\{x : T \mid p(x)\}$. For example, various subranges of integers can be written this way, and a specific example of this is the type below(k) defined as $\{x : \text{nat} \mid x < k\}$. For this presentation, the only number type used is nat32, the type of unsigned 32-bit integers. An array type is any map from below(k) to a range type, either nat32 or another array type as with the nestedArray type shown in Fig. 1. Even though arrays are just functions in PVS, we treat them as first-order entities for the present purpose. We also restrict ourselves to PVS expressions consisting of constants, variables, function applications (including array accesses), conditionals, let-expressions, updates, and lambda abstraction (used solely to construct arrays). The code generator also handles records, tuples, and algebraic datatypes.

3   The Intermediate Language and Its Operational Semantics

We use a simple intermediate language based on A-normal form [6] to formalize reference counting. We assume a set Θ of explicit reference constants excluding the empty reference `nil` and disjoint from the numeric constants. By convention, the metavariables x, y, z range over variables, k ranges over numerals, c ranges over numeric constants, u, v range over values (constants and explicit references), w ranges over atomic expressions (i.e., variables and values), i and j range over the natural numbers, a ranges over arrays, r ranges over reference constants drawn from Θ, f ranges over function symbols, and $d, e, g,$ and h range over expressions. The language contains the following constructs.

1. Variables: x, y, z, etc.
2. Constants: Non-negative (machine) integers 0, 1, 2, etc., up to the maximum representable, and explicit references from Θ.
3. Let: **let** $x = e$ **in** h
4. Apply: $f(x_1, .., x_n)$, where f is an n-ary operation.
5. Conditional: **if** x **then** e **else** g.
7. Update: $x[y := z]$
8. New Array: **newInt**(k) and **newRef**(k): Both operations create a fresh array reference r of size k (a constant) with each $r[i]$ initialized to 0 for **newInt** and `nil` for **newRef**, for $0 \leq i < k$.
9. Array access: $x[y]$

The evaluation is carried out relative to a fixed *program* Δ where $\Delta(f)$ is a definition of the form $f(y_1, \ldots, y_n) = e$ where $y_i \not\equiv y_j$ for $i \neq j$, and $vars(e) \subseteq \{y_1, \ldots, y_n\}$. Expressions can also contain primitive operations like $+$ and $-$ whose arguments and results must be non-references. The `swap` operation from the PVS theory in Fig. 1 is represented in the intermediate language as shown below.

$$\mathtt{swap}(x, y, z)$$
$$= \mathbf{let}\ y_1 = x[y]\ \mathbf{in\ let}\ z_1 = x[z]\ \mathbf{in\ let}\ x_1 = x[y := z_1]\ \mathbf{in}\ x_1[z := y_1]$$

The expression grammar is extended to include explicit reference constants. The initial expression being evaluated should be *pure*, i.e., not contain such occurrences, but they can appear during evaluation, e.g., as the value of **newInt**(k) or **newRef**(k)). We also add an expression form **pop**(e) that is used during evaluation to record the need to pop the stack to terminate the scope of a let-binding. A value v now is either a variable, a constant, or an explicit reference. Let $S(x)$ represent the topmost binding for x in stack S, and $S(v)$ is just v itself.

The operational semantics employs an evaluation *context* $E\{\}$ which is a kind of expression that contains exactly one occurrence of the *hole* `{}` as a subexpression.[1] The result of filling the hole in the evaluation context $E\{\}$ with an expression g is represented as $E\{g\}$. An expression e is evaluated by first decomposing it as $E\{g\}$ where g is a *redex*. The redex g is *reduced* to the *residue* g' in a single evaluation step, so that a single step of evaluation applied to e

---

[1] Braces are used instead of square brackets to represent holes to avoid confusion with array accesses and updates.

yields $E\{g'\}$ along with modifications to the store R and stack S. Evaluation contexts can be defined by the grammar

$$K := \{\} \mid \mathbf{let}\ x = K\ \mathbf{in}\ g \mid \mathbf{pop}(K)$$

From this definition, it follows that evaluation contexts are of one of the forms

1. $\{\}$
2. $\mathbf{let}\ x = \{\}\ \mathbf{in}\ g$
3. $\mathbf{pop}(\{\})$
4. The composition $E_1\{E_2\{\}\}$ of two evaluation contexts $E_1\{\}$ and $E_2\{\}$.

It also follows that any free variable occurrences in g are also free in $E\{g\}$.

The small-step operational semantics is given in terms of an *evaluation state* that is a triple $\langle e, R, S \rangle$ consisting of

1. An expression e
2. A store R which is a partial map from nonempty references $dom(R) \subseteq \Theta$, to arrays, and
3. A stack S binding variables to values.

We define some purely mathematical operations that are used in the definition of the operational semantics of the intermediate language. For an array a of size k, the operation $update(a, i, v)$ for $i < k$ defines an array a' such that for any $j < k$, $a'(j) = a(j)$ if $i \neq j$, and $a(j) = v$, otherwise. The operation $pop(S)$ pops the stack by dropping the top element, and $push(x, v, S)$ is the stack obtained by pushing the binding of x to v on the top of S. Let $\overline{x}$ represent a sequence $x_1, \ldots, x_n$ of variables and $\overline{v}$ represent a sequence of $v_1, \ldots, v_n$ of values. We overload $S(\overline{x})$ to represent the sequence $S(x_1), \ldots, S(x_n)$, and $push(\overline{x}, \overline{v}, S)$ to represent $push(x_n, v_n, \ldots push(x_1, v_1, S) \ldots)$ when $\overline{x}$ and $\overline{v}$ have the same length. We assume that any intermediate expressions have been preprocessed to replace $\mathbf{let}\ x = e\ \mathbf{in}\ g$ by g, when x does not occur free in g, and $\mathbf{let}\ x = y\ \mathbf{in}\ g$ by $g[x \mapsto y]$, the result of substituting y for the free occurrences of x in g. The operation $R\{r \mapsto a\}$ updates or extends the store R so that it maps r to a, and behaves like R, otherwise.

The reduction rules are given below by the relation $\langle e, R, S \rangle \longrightarrow \langle e', R', S' \rangle$. In each of these rules, the left-hand side is a triple $\langle e, R, S \rangle$, where e is redex.

1. $\langle \mathbf{let}\ x = v\ \mathbf{in}\ g, R, S \rangle \longrightarrow \langle \mathbf{pop}(g), R, push(x, v, S) \rangle$.
2. $\langle f(x_1, \ldots, x_n), R, S \rangle \longrightarrow \langle v, R, S \rangle$, for a primitive operation f, where $f(S(x_1), \ldots, S(x_n))$ evaluates to v. The values $v, S(x_1), \ldots, S(x_n)$, must all be non-references.
3. $\langle f(x_1, \ldots, x_n), R, S \rangle \longrightarrow \langle \mathbf{pop}^n(e), R, push(\overline{y}, S(\overline{x}), S) \rangle$, where $\Delta(f) = (f(y_1, \ldots, y_n) = e)$.
4. $\langle \mathbf{if}\ v\ \mathbf{then}\ e\ \mathbf{else}\ g, R, S \rangle \longrightarrow \begin{cases} \langle e, R, S \rangle, & \text{if } S(v) \neq 0 \\ \langle g, R, S \rangle, & \text{if } S(v) = 0 \end{cases}$
5. $\langle x[y := z], R, S \rangle \longrightarrow \langle r, R\{r \mapsto update(R(u), v, w)\}, S \rangle$, where r is fresh, $u = S(x)$, $v = S(y)$, $w = S(z)$.

6. $\langle \mathbf{newInt}(w), R, S \rangle \longrightarrow \langle r, R', S \rangle$, where $k = S(w)$, $R' = R\{r \mapsto a\}$, $a[i] = 0$ for i from 0 to $k - 1$, r is fresh.
7. $\langle \mathbf{newRef}(w), R, S \rangle \longrightarrow \langle r, R', S \rangle$, where $k = S(w)$, $R' = R\{r \mapsto a\}$, $a[i] =$ nil for i from 0 to $k - 1$, r is fresh.
8. $\langle x[y], R, S \rangle \longrightarrow \langle R(S(x))[S(y)], R, S \rangle$.
9. $\langle \mathbf{pop}(v), R, S \rangle \longrightarrow \langle v, R, pop(S) \rangle$.
10. $\langle \mathbf{pop}(x), R, S \rangle \longrightarrow \langle S(x), R, pop(S) \rangle$.

The small step semantics operates on an evaluation state $\langle e, R, S \rangle$ consisting of an expression e, a store R and a stack S. The evaluation starts in an initial state with the original program e which contains no free variables, explicit references, nor occurrences of the **pop** operation, along with an empty store and stack: $\langle e, \emptyset, \emptyset \rangle$. In each evaluation step, we have $\langle e, R, S \rangle \Longrightarrow \langle e', R', S' \rangle$, if e can be decomposed into an evaluation context $E\{e_1\}$, where e_1 is a redex such that $\langle e_1, R, S \rangle \longrightarrow \langle e_1', R', S' \rangle$, and $e' \equiv E\{e_1'\}$. If the evaluation encounters a state $\langle e, R, S \rangle$ that is not reducible according to one of the rules above and where e is not a value, then $\langle e, R, S \rangle \Longrightarrow \bot$, where $\bot$ is an error state. A state $\langle e, R, S \rangle$ is *well-formed* if e is a well-formed expression, all the free variables in e are defined in S, all the references in e, R, and S are defined in R, i.e., appear in the domain $dom(R)$ of R, and any explicit reference r in e occurs in a hole so that $e = E\{r\}$ for some context E that contains no explicit references. Theorem 1 below ensures that there is at most one explicit reference in e.

Figure 2 shows an example evaluation with the copying semantics of the expression **let** $z = \{+(y, 1)\}$ **in** $\mathrm{swap}(x, y, z)$ (with the context demarcated) in a state with reference r mapped to the array $[0, 1]$ in store R and x bound to r and y bound to 0 in the stack S.

$$\langle \mathbf{let}\ z = \{+(y,1)\}\ \mathbf{in}\ \mathrm{swap}(x,y,z), \{r \mapsto [0,1]\}, (y \mapsto 0, x \mapsto r) \rangle$$
$$\Longrightarrow \langle \{\mathbf{let}\ z = 1\ \mathbf{in}\ \mathrm{swap}(x,y,z)\}, \{r \mapsto [0,1]\}, (y \mapsto 0, x \mapsto r) \rangle$$
$$\Longrightarrow \langle \mathbf{pop}(\{\mathrm{swap}(x,y,z)\}), \{r \mapsto [0,1]\}, (z \mapsto 1, \ldots) \rangle$$
$$\Longrightarrow \langle \ldots \mathbf{let}\ y_1 = \{u[v]\}\ \mathbf{in}\ \ldots, \{r \mapsto [0,1]\}, (w \mapsto 1, v \mapsto 0, u \mapsto r, \ldots) \rangle$$
$$\Longrightarrow \langle \ldots \{\mathbf{let}\ y_1 = 0\ \mathbf{in}\ \ldots\}, \{r \mapsto [0,1]\}, (w \mapsto 1, v \mapsto 0, u \mapsto r, \ldots) \rangle$$
$$\Longrightarrow \langle \ldots \mathbf{let}\ z_1 = \{u[w]\}\ \mathbf{in}\ \ldots, \{r \mapsto [0,1]\}, (y_1 \mapsto 0, \ldots) \rangle$$
$$\Longrightarrow \langle \ldots \{\mathbf{let}\ z_1 = 1\ \mathbf{in}\ \ldots\}, \{r \mapsto [0,1]\}, (y_1 \mapsto 0, \ldots) \rangle$$
$$\Longrightarrow \langle \ldots \mathbf{let}\ x_1 = \{u[v := z_1]\}\ \mathbf{in}\ \ldots, \{r \mapsto [0,1]\}, (z_1 \mapsto 1, \ldots) \rangle$$
$$\Longrightarrow \langle \ldots \{\mathbf{let}\ x_1 = r'\ \mathbf{in}\ x_1[w := y_1]\}, \{r' \mapsto [1,1], \ldots\}, (z_1 \mapsto 1, \ldots) \rangle$$
$$\Longrightarrow \langle \ldots \{x_1[w := y_1]\}, \{r' \mapsto [1,1], \ldots\}, (x_1 \mapsto r', \ldots) \rangle$$
$$\Longrightarrow \langle \ldots \{r''\}, \{r'' \mapsto [1,0], \ldots\}, (x_1 \mapsto r', \ldots) \rangle$$
$$\overset{*}{\Longrightarrow} \langle r'', \{r'' \mapsto [1,0], \ldots\}, (y \mapsto 0, x \mapsto r) \rangle$$

Fig. 2. Example evaluation with copying semantics

In the above operational semantics, each update step introduces a new array that is a *copy* of the given array modified at the updated index. The binding between the references and these arrays is maintained by the store R. There is no garbage collection since nothing ever gets discarded from the store. We state a few simple theorems about the idealized operational semantics given above.[2]

Theorem 1. *For any well-formed expression e, either e is a value or there is exactly one way to decompose an expression e as $E\{g\}$ where E is an evaluation context E and g is a redex.*

Each evaluation step preserves the well-formedness of the state, and in particular, any occurrence of an explicit reference must be the residue of the most recently reduced redex by one of the rules 5–10, or it appeared in e as $E\{\text{let } x = r \text{ in } g\}$ for some reference-free E, and the resulting residue does not contain any references.

Theorem 2. *If $\langle e, R, S \rangle$ is a well-formed state and $\langle e, R, S \rangle \implies \langle e', R', S' \rangle$, then $\langle e', R', S' \rangle$ is also a well-formed state.*

One important invariant is that for any state $\langle e, R, S \rangle$, there is at most one occurrence of a reference in e, namely as the residue of the most recently reduced redex.

Theorem 3. *In any evaluation state $\langle e, R, S \rangle$, if an explicit reference r occurs in e, then e is of the form $E\{r\}$ where E contains no explicit references.*

Another useful invariant is that the **pop** operation can only occur in an evaluation context.

Theorem 4. *For any expression e in an evaluation state $\langle e, R, S \rangle$, if it contains a sub-expression $\mathbf{pop}(g)$, then $e \equiv E\{\mathbf{pop}(g)\}$ for some evaluation context E.*

It follows from this theorem that all the occurrences of **pop** are linearly nested since they must all contain, not necessarily strictly, the current redex. The maximal depth of nesting corresponds to the depth of the stack. It follows from this that the execution of the **pop** step will never try to pop an empty stack. Furthermore, when the evaluation of a closed expression, i.e., one with no free variables, has been completed, the stack is empty.

Next, we present the operational semantics for the intermediate language with reference counting, and establish its equivalence with the semantics presented in this section.

4   Operational Semantics with Reference Counting

The operational semantics given above is enhanced by adding a component C to the state to maintain reference counts for each reference in $dom(R)$. Before augmenting the operational semantics with reference counting, we introduce some useful operations.

$$\mathtt{swap}(x, y, z)$$
$$= \mathbf{let}\ y_1 = x[y]\ \mathbf{in}\ \mathbf{let}\ z_1 = x[z]\ \mathbf{in}\ \mathbf{let}\ x_1 = \underline{x}[\underline{y} := \underline{z_1}]\ \mathbf{in}\ \underline{x_1}[\underline{z} := \underline{y_1}]$$

---

[2] All proofs have been omitted due to lack of space.

$$mark(x, X) = \begin{cases} x, \text{ if } x \in X \\ \underline{x}, \text{ otherwise} \end{cases}$$

$$mark(c, X) = c$$

$$mark(\textbf{let } x = e \textbf{ in } g, X) = \textbf{let } x = mark(e, X \cup vars(g)) \textbf{ in } mark(g, X - \{x\})$$

$$mark(\textbf{if } x \textbf{ then } e \textbf{ else } g, X) = \textbf{if } x' \text{ then } mark(e, X) \textbf{ else } mark(g, X), \text{ where}$$
$$x' = mark(x, X \cup vars(e) \cup vars(g))$$

$$mark(x[y := z], X) = x'[y' := z'], \text{ where}$$
$$x' = mark(x, X \cup \{y, z\}),$$
$$y' = mark(y, X \cup \{z\}),$$
$$z' = mark(z, X)$$

$$mark(x[y], X) = mark(x, X \cup \{y\})[mark(y, X)]$$

$$mark(f(x_1, \ldots, x_n), X) = f(y_1, \ldots, y_n),$$
$$\text{where } y_i \equiv mark(x_i, X \cup \{x_{i+1}, \ldots, x_n\})$$

$$mark(\textbf{pop}(e), X) = \textbf{pop}(mark(e, X))$$

$$mark(e, X) = e, \text{ otherwise.}$$

Fig. 3. Marking the last variable occurrence along each evaluation branch

The first operation *marks* the occurrences of a variable in an expression that are evaluated last so that we can identify variables that are no longer live in the evaluation. The operation $mark(e, X)$ shown in Fig. 3 marks variables in the expression e given that the variables in X are *live*, i.e., possibly used in the evaluation following e.

In the definitions Δ, we replace each occurrence of $f(y_1, \ldots, y_n) = e$ by $f(y_1, \ldots, y_n) = mark(e, \emptyset)$. For example, the swap operation can be defined as

$$\textbf{swap}(x, y, z)$$
$$= \textbf{let } y_1 = x[y] \textbf{ in let } z_1 = x[z] \textbf{ in let } x_1 = \underline{x}[y := \underline{z_1}] \textbf{ in } \underline{x_1}[\underline{z} := \underline{y_1}]$$

Let $mvars(e)$ be the subset of marked variables in e from $vars(e)$. Theorem 5 establishes that a marked variable in an expression is not live in the context.

Theorem 5. *If $e = E\{g\}$ then for any $x \in vars(e)$, x is marked in g, i.e., $x \in mvars(g)$, iff x does not occur in $vars(E)$.*

The new component C of the evaluation state maps each non-nil reference r to $C(r)$ its reference count. Unlike R, C is a total function: if r is not in the domain of R, i.e., $dom(R)$, then $C(r) = 0$. References are counted with respect to e, R, and S, and the count $C(r)$ for each reference r reflects the sum of the occurrences of r including

1. The single reference r that might occur directly in e,
2. References nested within R such that $R(r')(i) = r$ for some r' and i, and
3. References bound within S such that $S(x) = r$ for some x.

We define $refCount(\langle e, R, S \rangle, r)$ as

$$refCount(e, r) + refCount(R, r) + refCount(S, r), \text{ where}$$

1. $refCount(R, r)$ is the number of references to r nested in R.
2. $refCount(e, r)$ is the number of references to r in e, either 0 or 1.
3. $refCount(S, r)$ is the cardinality of $\{r | r = S(x), \text{ for some } x\}$.

Next, we define two operations that increment and decrement reference counts in C:

1. $inc(C, r)$ defines a C' such that for each r', $C'(r') = C(r)$ if $r' \neq r$, and $C'(r) = C(r) + 1$, otherwise.
2. $inc(C, c) = C$.
3. $dec(C, r)$ defines a C' such that for each r', $C'(r') = C(r')$ if $r' \neq r$ or $C(r) = 0$, and $C'(r) = C(r) - 1$, otherwise.
4. $dec(C, c) = C$.

Let $size(a)$ be the size of the array a. We define three decrement operations on reference counts: *release*, *releaseVar*, and *releaseVars*. The operation $release(R, C, r)$ is defined to release a single reference to r from the store R. It does this by checking the reference count $C(r)$. If $C(r) > 1$, then the reference count is reduced by one. If $C(r) = 1$, then the array $R(r)$ is freed by recursively releasing each reference in $R(r)$ and replacing it by `nil`, and then dropping r from $dom(R)$. The recursive definition for *release* is terminating since the cumulative reference count decreases by at least one with each recursive call.

$release(R, C, r) = \langle R, dec(C, r) \rangle$, if $C(r) > 1$

$release(R, C, r) = \langle update(R_n, r, \perp), update(C_n, r, 0) \rangle$, if $C(r) = 1$, where

$\qquad \langle R_0, C_0 \rangle = \langle R, C \rangle$

$\qquad \langle R_{i+1}, C_{i+1} \rangle = \begin{cases} release(R'_i, C_i, r'), \text{ for } r' = R(r)(i) \text{ and} \\ \qquad R'_i = update(R_i, r, update(R_i(r), i, \texttt{nil})) \\ \langle R_i, C_i \rangle, \text{ otherwise} \end{cases}$

$\qquad$ for $i < n = size(R(r))$

The key property of the *release* operation is that the change to the count $C(r')$ for some reference r' reflects the difference in the actual reference counts.

Theorem 6. *For store R and reference r, if*

1. $C(r) > 0$
2. $C(r') \neq 0 \iff r' \in dom(R)$, *for each r' and*
3. $C(r') \geq refCount(R, r') + refCount(r, r')$ *for each r',*

and $\langle R', C' \rangle = release(R, C, r)$, then for each r' we have

1. $C'(r') \neq 0 \iff r' \in dom(R')$
2. $C(r') - C'(r') = refCount(R, r') - refCount(R', r') + refCount(r, r')$
3. $C'(r') \geq refCount(R', r')$.

The operation $releaseVar(R, S, C, x)$ invokes $release(R, C, S(x))$ to decrement the count for the reference $S(x)$, while setting $S(x)$ to nil.

$$releaseVar(R, S, C, x) = \langle R', S', C' \rangle, \text{ where}$$

$$\langle R', C' \rangle = \begin{cases} release(R, C, r), & \text{for } r = S(x) \\ \langle R, C \rangle, & \text{otherwise} \end{cases}$$

$$S' = \begin{cases} update(S, x, \text{nil}), & \text{for } r = S(x) \\ S, & \text{otherwise} \end{cases}$$

$$releaseVars(R, S, C, \{x\} \uplus X) = releaseVars(R', S', C', X), \text{ where}$$

$$\langle R', S', C' \rangle = releaseVar(R, S, C, x)$$

$$releaseVars(R, S, C, \emptyset) = \langle R, S, C \rangle$$

Note that $releaseVar(R, S, C, x)$ is just $\langle R, S, C \rangle$ when $S(x)$ is not a reference. The key property of the $releaseVar$ operation is captured by the following theorem.

Theorem 7. *For $r = S(x)$ and $\langle R', S', C' \rangle = releaseVar(R, S, C, x)$, if for each reference r', $C(r') = refCount(S, r') + refCount(R, r')$ and $C(r') > 0 \iff r' \in dom(R)$, then for each reference r'*

1. $S' = update(S, x, \text{nil})$
2. $C'(r') \neq 0 \iff r' \in dom(R')$
3. $C(r') - C'(r') = refCount(R, r') - refCount(R', r') + refCount(S(x), r')$

The operation $incr(C, R, r)$ is defined to return a C' such that for each $r' \in dom(R)$, $C'(r') = C(r') + n$, when r' occurs n times in $R(r)$. We also use the notation $[i : 0..(k - 1) \mid c]$ to represent a k-element array initialized to c.

The reduction rules for redexes are enumerated below. The reader should check that the accounting behind the reference count in C reflects the sum of occurrences of each reference in e, R, and S.

1. $\langle \textbf{let } x = v \textbf{ in } g, R, S, C \rangle \xrightarrow{+} \langle \textbf{pop}(g), R, S', C \rangle$, where $S' = push(x, v, S)$. Note that C is unchanged.
2. $\langle f(x_1, \ldots, x_n), R, S, C \rangle \longrightarrow \langle v, R, S, C \rangle$ for primitive f, where $f(S(x_1), \ldots, S(x_n))$ evaluates to v.
3. $\langle f(x_1, \ldots, x_n), R, S, C \rangle \xrightarrow{+} \langle \textbf{pop}^n(e), R', S'', C'' \rangle$, where
   $\Delta(f) = (f(y_1, \ldots, y_n) = e)$, $\overline{u} = S(\overline{x})$, $S' = push(\overline{y}, \overline{u}, S)$,
   $C' = C_n$, where $C_0 = C$, $C_{i+1} = inc(C_i, u_{i+1})$, for $1 \leq i < n$,
   $\langle R', S'', C'' \rangle = releaseVars(R, S', C', X)$, where
   $X = mvars(f(x_1, \ldots, x_n)) \cup (\{y_1, \ldots, y_n\} \setminus vars(e))$.
4. $\langle \textbf{if } x \textbf{ then } e \textbf{ else } g, R, S, C \rangle \xrightarrow{+} \begin{cases} \langle e, R', S', C' \rangle, & \text{if } S(x) \neq 0 \\ \langle g, R'', S'', C'' \rangle, & \text{if } S(x) = 0 \end{cases}$
   where $X' = mvars(x) \bigcup (mvars(g) - mvars(e))$,

$\langle R', S', C' \rangle = releaseVars(R, S, C, X')$,
$X'' = mvars(x) \bigcup (mvars(e) - mvars(g))$, and
$\langle R'', S'', C'' \rangle = releaseVars(R, S, C, X'')$.

5. $\langle x[y := z], R, S, C \rangle \xrightarrow{+} \langle r', R'', S', C''' \rangle$, where
$r = S(x)$, $c = S(y)$, $v = S(z)$,
$C(r) > 1$ or x is unmarked, r' is fresh,
$R' = R\{r' \mapsto update(R(r), c, v)\}$, $C' = C\{r' \mapsto 1\}$, $C'' = incr(C', R', r')$,
$\langle R'', S', C''' \rangle = releaseVars(R', S, C'', mvars(z))$,

6. $\langle x[y := z], R, S, C \rangle \xrightarrow{+} \langle r, R''', S', C'' \rangle$, where
$r = S(x)$, $c = S(y)$, $v = S(z)$,
$C(r) = 1$ and x is marked,
$R' = update(R, r, update(R(r), u, v))$, $C' = inc(inc(C, v), r)$,
$\langle R'', C'' \rangle = release(R', C', R(r)[c])$, $S' = update(S, x, \text{nil})$,
$\langle R''', S', C'' \rangle = releaseVars(R'', S, C', X)$, where $X = mvars(x[y := z])$.

7. $\langle x[y], R, S, C \rangle \xrightarrow{+} \langle v, R', S', C'' \rangle$, where
$r = S(x)$, $u = S(y)$, $v = R(r)[u]$, $C' = inc(C, v)$, and
$\langle R', S', C'' \rangle = releaseVar(R, S, C', x)$, if x is marked, and
$\langle R', S', C'' \rangle = \langle R, S, C' \rangle$, otherwise.

8. $\langle \textbf{newInt}(w), S, R, C \rangle \xrightarrow{+} \langle r, S, R', C' \rangle$, where
$k = S(w)$, $R' = R\{r \mapsto [i : 0..k - 1 \mid 0]\}$, r fresh, and $C' = C\{r \mapsto 1\}$.

9. $\langle \textbf{newRef}(w), S, R, C \rangle \xrightarrow{+} \langle r, S, R', C' \rangle$, where
$k = S(w)$, $R' = R\{r \mapsto [i : 0..k - 1 \mid \text{nil}]\}$, r fresh, and $C' = C\{r \mapsto 1\}$.

10. $\langle \textbf{pop}(v), S, R, C \rangle \xrightarrow{+} \langle v, pop(S), R, C \rangle$.

11. $\langle \textbf{pop}(x), S, R, C \rangle \xrightarrow{+} \langle S(x), pop(S), R, C' \rangle$, where $C' = C$ if x is marked, and $C' = inc(C, S(x))$, otherwise.

The evaluation relation $\langle e, R, S, C \rangle \xRightarrow{+} \langle r', R', S', C' \rangle$ holds when e can be decomposed as $E\{g\}$, where $\langle g, R, S, C \rangle \xrightarrow{+} \langle g', R', S', C' \rangle$ and $e' \equiv E\{g\}$. Note that the evaluation relation employs destructive, in-place array updates in the reduction rule 6, and frees unused memory through the use of *release* and *releaseVars*. An example evaluation using reference counts (indicated by the superscript to the reference in the store) is shown in Fig. 4.

Theorem 8 notes that marking is preserved under evaluation, where $unmark(e)$ represents the result of replacing each marked $\underline{x}$ with x. Theorem 9 captures the main invariant about the accuracy of the reference counts.

Theorem 8. *Each evaluation step preserves the consistency of the marking, i.e., $e = mark(unmark(e), \emptyset)$, of the evaluation state $\langle e, R, S, C \rangle$.*

Theorem 9. *The following invariants are preserved for any evaluation step $\langle e, R, S, C \rangle \xrightarrow{+} \langle e', R', S', C' \rangle$:*

1. *The triple $\langle e, R, S \rangle$ is well-formed.*
2. *If for some variable $x \in dom(S)$, $x \notin vars(e)$, then $S(x) = c$ for some c or $S(x) = \text{nil}$.*

$$\langle \mathtt{let}\ z = \{+(y, 1)\}\ \mathtt{in}\ \mathtt{swap}(\underline{x}, y, z), \{r^1 \mapsto [0, 1]\}, (y \mapsto 0, x \mapsto r)\rangle$$
$$\stackrel{+}{\Longrightarrow} \langle\{\mathtt{let}\ z = 1\ \mathtt{in}\ \mathtt{swap}(\underline{x}, y, z)\}, \{r^1 \mapsto [0, 1]\}, (y \mapsto 0, x \mapsto r)\rangle$$
$$\stackrel{+}{\Longrightarrow} \langle \mathtt{pop}(\{\mathtt{swap}(\underline{x}, y, z)\}), \{r^1 \mapsto [0, 1]\}, (z \mapsto 1, \ldots)\rangle$$
$$\stackrel{+}{\Longrightarrow} \langle \ldots \mathtt{let}\ y_1 = \{u[v]\}\ \mathtt{in}\ \ldots, \{r^1 \mapsto [0, 1]\}, (w \mapsto 1, v \mapsto 0, u \mapsto r, \ldots, x \mapsto \mathtt{nil}, \ldots)\rangle$$
$$\stackrel{+}{\Longrightarrow} \langle \ldots \{\mathtt{let}\ y_1 = 0\ \mathtt{in}\ \ldots\}, \{r^1 \mapsto [0, 1]\}, (w \mapsto 1, v \mapsto 0, u \mapsto r, \ldots)\rangle$$
$$\stackrel{+}{\Longrightarrow} \langle \ldots \mathtt{let}\ z_1 = \{u[w]\}\ \mathtt{in}\ \ldots, \{r^1 \mapsto [0, 1]\}, (y_1 \mapsto 0, \ldots)\rangle$$
$$\stackrel{+}{\Longrightarrow} \langle \ldots \{\mathtt{let}\ z_1 = 1\ \mathtt{in}\ \ldots\}, \{r^1 \mapsto [0, 1]\}, (y_1 \mapsto 0, \ldots)\rangle$$
$$\stackrel{+}{\Longrightarrow} \langle \ldots \mathtt{let}\ x_1 = \{\underline{u}[v := z_1]\}\ \mathtt{in}\ \ldots, \{r^1 \mapsto [0, 1]\}, (z_1 \mapsto 1, \ldots, u \mapsto \mathtt{nil}, \ldots)\rangle$$
$$\stackrel{+}{\Longrightarrow} \langle \ldots \{\mathtt{let}\ x_1 = r\ \mathtt{in}\ \underline{x_1}[w := y_1]\}, \{r^1 \mapsto [1, 1]\}, (z_1 \mapsto 1, \ldots)\rangle$$
$$\stackrel{+}{\Longrightarrow} \langle \ldots \{\underline{x_1}[w := y_1]\}, \{r^1 \mapsto [1, 1]\}, (x_1 \mapsto r, \ldots)\rangle$$
$$\stackrel{+}{\Longrightarrow} \langle \ldots \{r\}, \{r^1 \mapsto [1, 0]\}, (x_1 \mapsto \mathtt{nil}, \ldots)\rangle$$
$$\stackrel{*}{\Longrightarrow} \langle r, \{r^1 \mapsto [1, 0]\}, (y \mapsto 0, x \mapsto \mathtt{nil})\rangle$$

Fig. 4. Example evaluation with reference counting

3. *The reference count* $C(r)$ *is* $refCount(\langle e, R, S\rangle, r)$ *for each* r, *and* $C(r) > 0 \iff r \in dom(R)$.

With this invariant, we can establish a bisimulation between the basic evaluation step and the reference counting one. This bisimulation ρ between $\langle e_1, R_1, S_1\rangle$ and $\langle e_2, R_2, S_2, C_2\rangle$ is basically defined by an injection from the references in R_2 to those in R_1. We define ρ as holding when there exists an injection π from $dom(R_2)$ to $dom(R_1)$ such that

1. $e_1 = \pi(e_2)$, where $\pi(e_2)$ is the result of replacing each reference r in e_2 with $\pi(r)$.
2. $R_1(\pi(r)) = \pi(R_2(r))$, for each $r \in dom(R_2)$, where $\pi(R_2(r))$ is the result of replacing each element r' in $R(r)$ with $\pi(r')$.
3. $S_1(x) = \pi(S_2(x))$, for each $x \in dom(S_2)$.

Theorem 10. *The relation* ρ *defines a bisimulation between* $\Longrightarrow$ *and* $\stackrel{+}{\Longrightarrow}$.

We can thus conclude from Theorem 10 that the evaluation relation $\stackrel{+}{\Longrightarrow}$ returns the same value (if numeric) as the evaluation relation $\Longrightarrow$, when these are applied to the initial states $\langle e, \emptyset, \emptyset, \emptyset\rangle$ and $\langle e, \emptyset, \emptyset\rangle$, respectively.

5   Observations

The PVS2C code generator that implements the reference counting semantics can be described briefly as follows. For each array type in the intermediate representation, the code generator defines a **struct** type with a **count** field

Matrix size	100	1000	10000	100000
Hand-written C	0m0.002s	0m0.013s	0m1.398s	6m26.415s
C generated from PVS	0m0.002s	0m0.013s	0m2.363s	12m58.976s

Fig. 5. Comparing the performance of hand-written C code with the generated C code

(for the reference count[3]) and an `elems` field (for the array). Each such type also has operations for *creating* a new data object, *copying* an existing data object while updating the reference counts of any embedded references, *updating* a data object either by copying or by an in-place update as required, and an operation for *releasing* a reference to a data object and possibly freeing it by first decrementing the reference counts of any embedded references. The **let**-expressions in the intermediate representation are transformed to assignment statements. The array construction operations are implemented by creating a new data object and initializing it. Conditional expressions are implemented by C conditional statements, and similarly for function applications.

The PVS2C code generator has been applied to a small number of examples covering arrays, records, and lists. Our preliminary experiments indicate that the overhead of reference counting is quite manageable and the performance is quite competitive with hand-written C programs. As a stress-test for reference counting, we defined a matrix transpose operation in PVS and generated C code from it. This matrix is represented as an array of nested arrays, one to each row in the matrix. In the initial matrix, all the rows contain exactly the same reference with a reference count of N. As the transposition proceeds, copies are made until each row corresponds to a unique array reference that is updated in place. The table in Fig. 5 compares the performance of the generated C code against the matrix transpose procedure written directly in C for $N \times N$ matrices with N ranging from 100 (a 40 KB matrix) to 100,000 (a 40 GB matrix). Both versions were compiled with the Clang compiler with the `-O fast` flag on a MacBook Air with a 1.7 GHz Intel Core i7 processor and 8 GB of memory.

PVS itself does not generate any cyclic data structures, and it is impossible to construct cyclic structures in the intermediate language. The only way to construct a cyclic structure is through the evaluation of $x[y := z]$ as a destructive update since a non-destructive update returns a fresh reference. For the evaluation of $x[y := z]$ to be destructive, the variable x must be marked and the reference count $C(S(x))$ must one. In this case, the reference $S(x)$ cannot be accessible from z, since this would imply $C(S(x)) > 1$.

6   Conclusions

Wide-spectrum specification languages can be used to capture abstract models of software and hardware systems together with any relevant background

---

[3] We do not check the count for possible overflow since it would take an extraordinarily long computation to cause a 64-bit counter to overflow [3].

mathematical theories. These models can be refined to a level of concreteness where they are actually executable. By generating code in a practical programming language, we can leverage the comprehensive libraries and advanced compiler technologies that accompany these languages. The generation of code from specifications must be trusted to preserve the semantics of the source language. This is particularly critical for a language like PVS where the generation of proof obligations during typechecking ensures the absence of any runtime execution errors (modulo resource bounds). This property has to be preserved in the generated code. We have described a workflow that generates code for definitions in an executable fragment of the PVS specification language. We have presented a formal model of reference counting that can be used to justify the correctness of the transformation from PVS to C (and other languages). The proof of the correctness of reference counting and the correspondence between the idealized and reference counting operational semantics are both straightforward. The generated code is itself in a small fragment of the C programming language whose semantics can be succinctly formalized. The C fragment is easily supported by formally verified compilers such as CompCert [8]. The use of reference counting makes the generated code efficient and self-contained. The theory we have presented also extends to closures and polymorphism, two features that have yet to be implemented in PVS2C. The project we have described is itself a small step in the larger vision of providing a single coherent development environment for specifications, background theories, and software.

Acknowledgments. An earlier version of the intermediate language used here was developed by the second author in collaboration with Basile Clement (École Normal Supérieure, Paris) and Simon Halfon (École Normal Supérieure, Cachan). We thank them for many illuminating conversations on topics related to this paper. We thank Greg Morrisett (Cornell University), Sam Owre (SRI), Bruno Dutertre (SRI), Andrew Tolmach (Portland State University), Jean-Christophe Filliâtre (LRI Université Paris-Sud), John Launchbury (DARPA I20), Robin Larrieu (École Polytechnique), and the anonymous referees for their helpful suggestions and useful feedback.

References

1. Boehm, H.-J., Weiser, M.: Garbage collection in an uncooperative environment. Softw.: Pract. Exp. **18**(9), 807–820 (1988)
2. Chirimar, J., Gunter, C.A., Riecke, J.G.: Reference counting as a computational interpretation of linear logic. J. Funct. Program. **6**(2), 195–244 (1996)
3. Clochard, M., Filliâtre, J.-C., Paskevich, A.: How to avoid proving the absence of integer overflows. In: Gurfinkel, A., et al. (eds.) VSTTE 2015. LNCS, vol. 9593, pp. 94–109. Springer, Heidelberg (2016). doi:10.1007/978-3-319-29613-5_6
4. George, E.: Collins: a method for overlapping and erasure of lists. Commun. ACM **3**(12), 655–657 (1960)
5. Felleisen, N.: On the expressive power of programming languages. In: Jones, N. (ed.) ESOP 1990. LNCS, vol. 432, pp. 35–75. Springer, Heidelberg (1990)

6. Flanagan, C., Sabry, A., Duba, B.F., Felleisen, M.: The essence of compiling with continuations (with retrospective). In: McKinley, K.S. (ed.) Best of PLDI, pp. 502–514. ACM (1993)
7. Hudak, P.: A semantic model of reference counting and its abstraction (detailed summary). In: Proceedings of 1986 ACM Conference on LISP and Functional Programming, pp. 351–363. ACM, August 1986
8. Leroy, X.: Formal verification of a realistic compiler. Commun. ACM **52**(7), 107–115 (2009)
9. Harold, J.: McBeth: On the reference counter method. Commun. ACM **6**(9), 575 (1963)
10. Owre, S., Rushby, J., Shankar, N., von Henke, F.: Formal verification for fault-tolerant architectures: prolegomena to the design of PVS. IEEE Trans. Softw. Eng. **21**(2), 107–125 (1995). PVS home page: http://pvs.csl.sri.com
11. Shankar, N.: Static analysis for safe destructive updates in a functional language. In: Pettorossi, A. (ed.) LOPSTR 2001. LNCS, vol. 2372, pp. 1–24. Springer, Heidelberg (2002)
12. Wilson, P.R.: Uniprocessor garbage collection techniques. In: Proceedings of International Workshop on Memory Management, IWMM 1992, St. Malo, France, pp. 1–42, 17–19 September 1992

EventB2Java: A Code Generator for Event-B

Néstor Cataño and Víctor Rivera[✉]

Innopolis University, Tatarstan, Russia
{n.catano,v.rivera}@innopolis.ru

Abstract. Event-B is a formal specification language and a methodology used to build software systems. Formal specifications are more useful when they can be executed. An executable formal specification provides insight on the behaviour of the system being modelled *w.r.t* an expected behaviour. This paper presents a tool that generates executable implementations of Event-B models. The tool is implemented as a plug-in of the Rodin platform, an Eclipse IDE that provides a set of tools to work with Event-B models. Our tool has extensively been used for generating code for Event-B models of Android applications, reactive systems, Smart Cards, searching algorithms, among others. The first author regularly uses EventB2Java in teaching to help master students of Software Engineering to get a better grasp of the behaviour of a model in Event-B and to detect inconsistencies in the model.

Keywords: Code generation · Event-B · EventB2Java · Java · JML · Rodin

1 Introduction

Event-B [2] is a formal method technique to describe and analyse the behaviour of reactive systems. Event-B language is based on predicate logic and set theory. It includes a full-fledged battery of operations over sets and relations for modeling software systems. Event-B represents software systems as discrete transition systems. It represents system components as a succession of states connected through a series of transitions called events. States are composed of constants and variables, and Events are composed of guards and actions. Event guards are written in predicate logic, and event actions are encoded as assignments.

Software development with Event-B follows the *Parachute* strategy [2]. It starts with an initial and very abstract model in Event-B. As the paratrooper descends, more details become clearer to her, and thus she is able to add more details to the initial model. How can the paratrooper make sure that what she modelled in Event-B faithfully reflects what she saw when she was descending? EventB2Java gives a key answer to that question. The EventB2Java tool is a Java code generator for Event-B. It generates Java implementations of Event-B models. Therefore, the *paratrooper* can generate a Java code for her Event-B models, run them in Java, and check whether the running code meets her

© Springer International Publishing Switzerland 2016
S. Rayadurgam and O. Tkachuk (Eds.): NFM 2016, LNCS 9690, pp. 166–171, 2016.
DOI: 10.1007/978-3-319-40648-0_13

expectations. That is, she can validate whether the behaviour of the running code matches the behaviour she expects from the system.

This paper presents the EventB2Java tool that generates Java executable implementations of Event-B models.

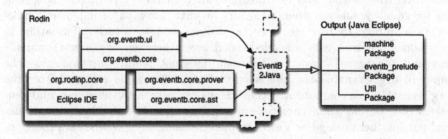

Fig. 1. Structure of the EventB2Java tool

2 Implementation of EventB2Java

The EventB2Java tool[1] implements the rules presented in [13]. It is implemented as a plug-in of Rodin [3]. Left part of Fig. 1 shows the main components of Rodin as sub-packages and classes of the `org` package. The figure also shows the relation among those components and the EventB2Java plug-in through solid arrows. Rodin is built on top of Eclipse. The `org.rodinp.core` component implements the core functionality of Rodin, e.g. it includes a database for manipulating Event-B models, and classes for storing components such as proofs and proof obligations. The `org.eventb.core` package implements all the database elements needed for writing models in Event-B. It further includes a static checker, a proof obligation generator and a prover. The `org.eventb.-core.ast` component includes a library for manipulating mathematical formulas in the form of Abstract Syntax Trees (ASTs). This component provides an abstract Visitor class for parsing mathematical formulas. The Sequent Prover (`org.eventb.core.seqprover`) component contains a library for proving sequents. The Event-B User Interface (`org.eventb.ui`) component contains the Graphic User Interfaces that permit users to feed Event-B models into Rodin and discharge proof obligations. EventB2Java uses Rodin's `org.eventb.ui` component to manipulate context menus so as to enable users to select the type of code implementation that is intended (sequential or multi-threaded). The relationship between `org.eventb.ui` and EventB2Java is depicted in Fig. 1 with a double-headed arrow. `org.eventb.ui` passes EventB2Java a user request, and this feeds back the generated code for the request.

---

[1] The EventB2Java tool is hosted at http://poporo.uma.pt/EventB2Java/.

Event-B models are written in predicate logic. The `org.eventb.core.ast` component encodes Event-B's mathematical language as ASTs. This component provides various services such as parsing a formula (computing its AST from a string of characters), pretty-printing it, constructing new formulas directly using the API library, type-checking formulas (inferring the types of the expressions occurring within and decorating them with their types), testing formulas for equality, among others. The `org.eventb.core.ast` component implements a library to traverse trees (a Visitor) and to attach information to tree nodes. Figure 1 uses a single-headed arrow between `org.eventb.core.-ast` and the EventB2Java tool since it does not modify any formula. The input to `org.eventb.core.ast` is part of the information collected from the `org.eventb.core` component. EventB2Java extends the Visitor class and generates code in one pass. After collecting information of contexts and machines and parsing them using the Visitor implementation, the EventB2Java tool generates an Eclipse Java project, which includes a `machine` package that contains the translation of the machines and contexts, and a main class with information about carrier sets, constants, and variables from the Event-B model. This package also contains the translation of each machine event. EventB2Java can produce both multi-threaded and sequential implementations of Event-B models. For supporting multi-threaded Java implementations, EventB2Java extends the standard Java `Thread` class by properly overriding the `run()` method.

Event-B relies on five mathematical languages (see Chap. 9 of [2]): (*i.*) a Propositional Language, (*ii.*) a Predicate Language, (*iii.*) an Equality Language, (*iv.*) a Set-Theoretic Language, and (*v.*) a Boolean and Arithmetic Language. The `eventb_prelude` package of EventB2Java includes classes with implementations of each respective language (some constructs are supported natively by Java, for instance negation in Event-B ($\neg$) is represented as ! in Java). These classes are: `BOOL`, `INT`, `NAT`, `NAT1`, `Enumerated`, `Pair`, `BSet`, `BRelation`, and `ID`, implementing, respectively, booleans, integers, natural numbers with and without 0, the enumerated type, pairs of elements, sets, relations, and the identity relation. Finally, EventB2Java includes a `Util` class with methods such as `SomeVal` that returns an arbitrary value within a set, and `SomeSet` that returns an arbitrary subset of a set. The former is used to assign a variable or a constant an arbitrary value.

3   Experience Using EventB2Java

EventB2Java has extensively been used to generate Java code for diverse Event-B models of systems and programs of various types. Statistics about some of these models are shown in Fig. 2, where "**LOC**" stands for Lines of Code in Event-B, and "**# Mch**" and "**# Evt** " are the number of machines and events of each model, respectively[2]. For instance, the Event-B model for Social-Event Planner contains 1326 lines of code in Event-B, it is composed of 9 machine

---

[2] Event-B models and respective Java code generated by EventB2Java can be reached at http://poporo.uma.pt/EventB2Java/EventB2Java_studies.html.

Event-B Model	LOC	# Mch	# Evt
Social-Event Planner [12]	1326	9	35
MIO [4]	586	7	21
Heating Controller [7]	458	15	32
State Machine [15]	86	2	5
Binary Search [1]	101	3	3
Linear Search [1]	54	2	2
Minimum Element [1]	64	2	3
Reversing Array [1]	64	2	2
Sorting Array [1]	137	3	4
Square Root Number [1]	84	3	2

Fig. 2. Statistics of the Event-B models

refinements and 35 events. The Social-Event Planner [12] is an Android application of a planner for social events in which a user can create a social event and invite a list of people to join it. The Android app was developed following the MVC design pattern. The Model part is written in Event-B and EventB2Java was used to generate code of the core functionality of the planner. MIO [4] is an Event-B model of a massive transportation system that includes articulated buses following the main corridor routes of a city. The Heating Controller [7] is an Event-B model of a heating controller that provides an interface to adjust and display a target temperature, and to sense and display the current temperature, among other functionality. The State Machine [15] is an Event-B model of state machines. The rest of the examples are sequential program developments written by Abrial in [1]. Linear and Binary Search are the Event-B models of the respective searching algorithms. Minimum Element is an Event-B model for finding the minimum element of an array of integers. Reversing and Sorting Array are Event-B models for reversing and sorting an array respectively. Square Root Number is an Event-B model for calculating the square root of a number. The reader is encouraged to consult [14] for a full discussion on these examples.

3.1   Use of EventB2Java for Teaching

The first author has regularly used EventB2Java in several Formal Methods and SE courses. In Fall 2015, he introduced Event-B and EventB2Java to students of the MSIT-SE (Master of Science in Information Technology - Software Engineering) at Carnegie Mellon University (CMU), Pittsburgh, USA. This course is a mandatory course for master students. He used a social networking example in Event-B [5] to motivate students and to introduce refinement calculus techniques, and used EventB2Java to generate code. He has previously used EventB2Java for teaching similar master courses at the University of Madeira, Portugal, and universities EAFIT, Andes, and PUJ, in Colombia.

EventB2Java generates JML [8] annotations in addition to Java code. JML and Java use less intimidating mathematical notations than Event-B, and so less expertise is required by students or engineers to use tools that provide support to JML and Java. It seems thus reasonable that students can take full advantage of the most appropriate software methodology and tools when developing their software. EventB2Java bridges software development in Event-B with software development with Java and JML, by using Design-by-Contract techniques [10].

4   Related Work

In [9], Méry and Singh present the EB2ALL tool-set that includes the EB2C, EB2C++, EB2J, and EB2C# plug-ins, which translate Event-B machines into C, C++, Java, and C$^\sharp$ respectively. Unlike EventB2Java, EB2ALL provides support for a small part of Event-B's syntax, and users are required to write a final Event-B implementation refinement in the syntax supported by the tool. In [11], Ostroumov and Tsiopoulos present the EHDL prototype tool that generates VHDL code from Event-B models. The tool supports a reduced part of Event-B's syntax and users are demanded to extend the Event-B model before it can be translated. In [16], Wright defines a B2C extension to the Rodin platform that translates Event-B models into C code. Also, the Code Generation tool [6] generates concurrent Java and Ada programs for a *tasking* extension of Event-B. As part of the process of generating code with the Code Generation tool, users have to decompose the Event-B model by employing the Machine Decomposition plug-in. The decomposed models are refined and non-deterministic assignments are eliminated. Finally, users are requested to model the flow of the execution of events in the tasking extension. Unlike all these tools, our tool does not require user's intervention, while it works on the proper syntax of the Event-B model.

5   Conclusion

EventB2Java generates Java implementations of Event-B models written at any level of abstraction. It largely supports Event-B's syntax and it's fully integrated to Rodin, but it has some limitations. Code generation of values that adhere to a non-deterministic assignment is not automated. One could use `SomeVal` (see Sect. 2) to generate an arbitrary value and then a constraint solver to check if the value adheres to machine axioms, but this is still future work. EventB2Java generates JML software contracts in addition to Java code. This is useful for programmers who want to customise the generated Java code and want to check if their customisations are correct.

The second author uses the Event-B tool regularly to generate code of Android apps in his courses of Software Engineering and the Android laboratory of Programming Usable Interfaces lectured at Carnegie Mellon University (CMU), the University of Madeira (UMa), the Pontificia Universidad Javeriana (PUJ), and the EAFIT University. His students are always motivated by the possibility of being able to run mathematical Event-B models in Java automatically.

References

1. Abrial, J.-R.: Sequential Program Development: Teaching Resources (2009). http://deploy-eprints.ecs.soton.ac.uk/122/1/sld.ch15%2Cseq.pdf. Accessed 2015
2. Abrial, J.-R.: Modeling in Event-B: System and Software Design. Cambridge University Press, New York (2010)
3. Abrial, J.-R., Butler, M., Hallerstede, S., Hoang, T.S., Mehta, F., Voisin, L.: Rodin: an open toolset for modelling and reasoning in Event-B. Softw. Tools Technol. Transf. **12**(6), 447–466 (2010)
4. Catano, N., Rueda, C.: Teaching formal methods for the unconquered territory. In: Gibbons, J., Oliveira, J.N. (eds.) TFM 2009. LNCS, vol. 5846, pp. 2–19. Springer, Heidelberg (2009)
5. Catano, N., Rueda, C.: Matelas: a predicate calculus common formal definition for social networking. In: Frappier, M., Glässer, U., Khurshid, S., Laleau, R., Reeves, S. (eds.) ABZ 2010. LNCS, vol. 5977, pp. 259–272. Springer, Heidelberg (2010)
6. Edmunds, A., Butler, M.: Tool support for Event-B code generation. In: Workshop on Tool Building in Formal Methods, Québec, Canada. John Wiley and Sons (2010)
7. Edmunds, A., Rezazedeh, A.: Development of a Heating Controller System (2011). http://wiki.event-b.org/index.php/Development_of_a_Heating_Controller_System. Accessed Mar 2015
8. Leavens, G., Baker, A., Ruby, C.: Preliminary design of JML: a behavioral interface specification language for Java. ACM Spec. Interest Group Softw. Eng. **31**(3), 1–38 (2006)
9. Méry, D., Singh, N.: Automatic code generation from Event-B models. In: Symposium on Information and Communication Technology, Hanoi, Vietnam. ACM (2011)
10. Meyer, B.: Object-Oriented Software Construction, 2nd edn. Prentice-Hall Inc, Upper Saddle River (1997)
11. Ostroumov, S., Tsiopoulos, L.: VHDL code generation from formal Event-B models. In: Euromicro Conference on Digital System Design, pp. 127–134 (2011)
12. Víctor, R., Cataño, N.: The Social-Event Planner (2012). http://poporo.uma.pt/favas/Social-Event_Planner.html. Accessed 2015
13. Rivera, V., Cataño, N.: Translating Event-B to JML-specified Java programs. In: 29th ACM SAC, Gyeongju, South Korea, 24–28 March 2014
14. Rivera, V., Cataño, N., Wahls, T., Rueda, C.: Code generation for Event-B. Int. J. Softw. Tools Technol. Transf. (STTT), pp. 1–22 (2015)
15. State-Machines and Code Generation (2012). http://wiki.event-b.org/index.php/State-Machines_and_Code_Generation. Accessed Aug 2013
16. Wright, S.: Automatic generation of C from Event-B. In: Workshop on Integration of Model-based Formal Methods and Tools, Nantes, France. Springer-Verlag (2009)

Applications of Formal Methods

A Formally Verified Checker of the Safe Distance Traffic Rules for Autonomous Vehicles

Albert Rizaldi$^{(\boxtimes)}$, Fabian Immler, and Matthias Althoff

Institut für Informatik, Technische Universität München, Munich, Germany
{rizaldi,immler,althoff}@in.tum.de

Abstract. One barrier in introducing autonomous vehicle technology is the liability issue when these vehicles are involved in an accident. To overcome this, autonomous vehicle manufacturers should ensure that their vehicles always comply with traffic rules. This paper focusses on the safe distance traffic rule from the Vienna Convention on Road Traffic. Ensuring autonomous vehicles to comply with this safe distance rule is problematic because the Vienna Convention does not clearly define how large a safe distance is. We provide a formally proved prescriptive definition of how large this safe distance must be, and correct checkers for the compliance of this traffic rule. The prescriptive definition is obtained by: (1) identifying all possible relative positions of stopping (braking) distances; (2) selecting those positions from which a collision freedom can be deduced; and (3) reformulating these relative positions such that lower bounds of the safe distance can be obtained. These lower bounds are then the prescriptive definition of the safe distance, and we combine them into a checker which we prove to be sound and complete. Not only does our work serve as a specification for autonomous vehicle manufacturers, but it could also be used to determine who is liable in court cases and for online verification of autonomous vehicles' trajectory planner.

1 Introduction

Liability is an important but rarely studied area in autonomous vehicle technology. For example, who should be held liable when a collision involving an autonomous vehicle occurs? In our previous paper [23], we proposed to solve this issue by formalising vehicles' behaviours and traffic rules in higher-order logic (HOL). This formalisation allows us to check formally whether an autonomous vehicle complies with traffic rules. If autonomous vehicles always comply with traffic rules, then they should not be held liable for any accident.

One of the most important traffic rules is to maintain a safe distance between a vehicle and the vehicle in front of it. This notion of safe distance is crucial for traffic simulation, automatic cruise controller (ACC), and safe intersections. Traffic simulation [1] relies on this notion to update the speed and acceleration of each vehicle such that a collision will not occur in the simulation, even when

A. Rizaldi and F. Immler—Supported by the DFG Graduiertenkolleg 1480 (PUMA)

© Springer International Publishing Switzerland 2016

S. Rayadurgam and O. Tkachuk (Eds.): NFM 2016, LNCS 9690, pp. 175–190, 2016.
DOI: 10.1007/978-3-319-40648-0_14

the front vehicle brakes abruptly. ACC [26] and safe intersection systems [14,16] rely on this notion to control the engine and brake module such that a rear-end collision can be avoided.

The Vienna Convention on Road Traffic defines a 'safe distance' as the distance such that *a collision between vehicles can be avoided if the vehicle in front performs an emergency brake* [24]. Note that this rule states the requirement for safe distance descriptively; there is no prescriptive expression against which a distance can be compared. This makes the process of formally checking the compliance of an autonomous vehicle's behaviour with the safe distance rule problematic.

We follow our previous design decision [23] to use Isabelle/HOL [18] for three reasons. Firstly, it has rich libraries of formalised real analysis which is required to turn the descriptive definition of safe distance into the prescriptive one. Secondly, it allows us to generate code, which we use to evaluate a real data set. Finally, as a theorem prover, Isabelle checks every reasoning step formally and, hence, one only has to trust how we specify the notion of safe distance. Our contributions are as follows:[1]

- We formalise a descriptive notion of safe distance from the Vienna Convention on Road Traffic (Sect. 2).
- We turn this formalised descriptive definition of safe distance into a prescriptive one through logical analysis (Sect. 3).
- We generate executable and formally verified checkers in SML for validating the safe distance rule (Sect. 4).
- We evaluate the US Highway 101 data set from the Next Generation SIMulation (NGSIM) project as benchmark for our checkers (Sect. 5).
- We argue that our prescriptive definition of *safe distance* generalises all definitions of safe distance in the literature (Sect. 6).

We conclude and outline the possible extension of our work in Sect. 7.

2   Formalising Safe Distance from the Vienna Convention

Figure 1 illustrates the scenario for the safe distance problem as defined in the Vienna Convention on Road Traffic. The scenario consists of two vehicles: the *ego* vehicle and the closest vehicle in front of it—which we term *other* vehicle[2]. This scenario is uniquely characterised by six constants: $s_{0,e}, v_e, a_e \in \mathbb{R}$ from the ego vehicle and $s_{0,o}, v_o, a_o \in \mathbb{R}$ from the other vehicle. Constants s_0, v, a denote the initial position, initial speed, and maximum deceleration value, respectively, of a vehicle. Note that $s_{0,e}$ denotes the *frontmost* position of the ego vehicle, while $s_{0,o}$ denotes the *rearmost* position of the other vehicle. Additionally, we also make the following assumptions:

---

[1] Our formalisation is available at http://home.in.tum.de/~immler/safedistance/index.html

[2] NGSIM has identified the other vehicle for each ego vehicle in the US-101 Highway data set.

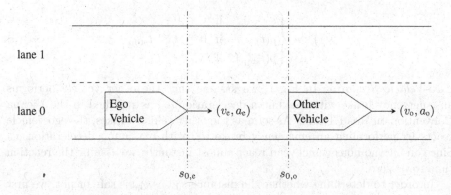

Fig. 1. Scenario for safe distance problem.

Assumption 1. *The values of v_e and v_o are non-negative:* $0 \leq v_e \wedge 0 \leq v_o$.

Assumption 2. *The values of a_e and a_o are negative:* $a_e < 0 \wedge a_o < 0$.

Assumption 3. *The other vehicle is located in front of the ego vehicle:* $s_{0,e} < s_{0,o}$.

Continuous Dynamics. As specified by the Vienna Convention on Road Traffic, the ego vehicle needs to avoid collision with the other vehicle when both vehicles are braking. To do so, the ego vehicle needs to *predict* its own braking movement and that of the other vehicle over time. We formalise the prediction of this braking movement p with a second-order ordinary differential equation (ODE)[3] $p''(t) = a$ and initial value conditions $p(0) = s_0$ and $p'(0) = v$. The closed-form solution to this ODE is as follows:

$$p(t) := s_0 + vt + \frac{1}{2}at^2 \ . \tag{1}$$

Hybrid Dynamics. Since Eq. (1) is a quadratic equation, it has the shape of a parabola when $a \neq 0$. This implies that a vehicle would move backward after it stops. Hence, Eq. (1) is only valid for the interval $[0, t_{\text{stop}}]$ where t_{stop} is the stopping time. The stopping time t_{stop} is the time when the first derivative of p is zero, that is, $p'(t_{\text{stop}}) = 0$. Substituting t with t_{stop} in the derivative of Eq. (1) results into the following expression for t_{stop}:

$$t_{\text{stop}} := -\frac{v}{a} \ . \tag{2}$$

Thus, we can extend the movement p of Eq. (1) by introducing discrete jumps (the deceleration makes a jump from $a < 0$ to $a = 0$) into the overall movement s as follows.

---

[3] We use Lagrange's notation f' and f'' to denote the first and the second derivative of f.

$$s(t) := \begin{cases} s_0 & \text{if } t \leq 0 \\ p(t) & \text{if } 0 \leq t \leq t_{\text{stop}} \\ p(t_{\text{stop}}) & \text{if } t_{\text{stop}} \leq t \end{cases} \tag{3}$$

Two-Vehicle Scenario. In Fig. 1, we assume that the other vehicle performs an emergency brake with maximum deceleration a_o, as specified in the Vienna Convention on Road Traffic. As soon as the other vehicle brakes, the ego vehicle reacts by performing an emergency brake too with maximum deceleration a_e. Since an autonomous vehicle can react almost instantly, we assume the reaction time to be zero.

In order to determine whether the distance $s_{0,o} - s_{0,e}$ is safe or not, we first use Eq. (3) to predict the movement of the ego vehicle $s_e(t)$ and the other vehicle $s_o(t)$ over time. Then, a collision will occur if we can find future time t such that $s_e(t) = s_o(t)$. To generalise this predicate, we define *collision* over a set of real numbers $T \subseteq \mathbb{R}$ as follows:

$$collision(T) := (\exists t \in T.\ s_e(t) = s_o(t)). \tag{4}$$

Equations (1) to (3), assumptions 1 to 3, and the definition in (4) above are our formalisation of the safe distance rule from the Vienna Convention on Road Traffic. The remaining results presented in this paper are deduced from there. The deductions are also formally checked by Isabelle theorem prover.

3   Logical Analysis of the Safe Distance Problem

This section analyses the safe distance problem by performing two case distinctions based on stopping times and stopping distances. The first case distinction (Sect. 3.1) is more suitable for *checking* whether there will be a collision or not. The second case distinction (Sect. 3.2) meanwhile is about eliminating the existential quantifier in Eq. (4) and rearranging the resulting formula such that one can obtain lower bounds for the initial distance $s_{0,o} - s_{0,e}$ that is still safe. In principle, after resolving the discrete jumps, this quantifier elimination for real arithmetic could be achieved by automatic procedures as implemented in modern computer algebra systems (CASs). There is even a proof-producing procedure implemented in the HOL-Light theorem prover [17]. However, our seven-variable formula appears to be too complex for HOL-Light's quantifier elimination procedure. Therefore, manually finding this lower bound with an interactive theorem prover is necessary. This makes our results more robust against changes in the formalisation and more readable compared to those from CASs'.

3.1   Case Distinction Based on Stopping Times

To check for collisions, we need to find the solution of Eq. (4). However, finding the solution is problematic due to the occurrences of the if-construct in the definition of the overall movement in Eq. (3). Therefore, we perform case distinction based on two stopping times conditions: $0 \leq t \leq t_{\text{stop}}$ and $t_{\text{stop}} < t$ for

Table 1. Four cases of stopping times and the corresponding equations of $s_e(t) = s_o(t)$.

	$0 \leq t \leq t_{\text{stop,e}}$	$t_{\text{stop,e}} < t$
$0 \leq t \leq t_{\text{stop,o}}$	(a) $p_e(t) = p_o(t)$	(b) $p_e(t_{\text{stop,e}}) = p_o(t)$
$t_{\text{stop,o}} < t$	(c) $p_e(t) = p_o(t_{\text{stop,o}})$	(d) $p_e(t_{\text{stop,e}}) = p_o(t_{\text{stop,o}})$

both vehicles. This produces four cases in total (see Table 1). Each case is the equation where $s_e(t) = s_o(t)$ with functions $s_e(t)$ and $s_o(t)$ are substituted as in Eq. (3), depending on which stopping time condition holds. Since each case is a pure quadratic equation, we can use a decision procedure for finding roots of univariate polynomials for each case. A checker based on such a decision procedure is described in Sect. 4.1.

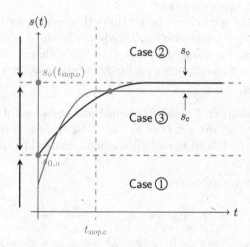

Fig. 2. Three cases obtained from case distinction based on stopping distances.

3.2 Case Distinction Based on Stopping Distances

Figure 2 illustrates the case distinction based on stopping distances. It plots an example of overall movement for the other vehicle $s_o(t)$ and divides this movement into three regions (cases) where a stopping distance of the ego vehicle $s_{\text{stop,e}} := s_e(t_{\text{stop,e}})$ could be located:

①. $s_{\text{stop,e}} < s_{0,o}$;

②. $s_{\text{stop,o}} \leq s_{\text{stop,e}}$.

③. $s_{0,o} \leq s_{\text{stop,e}} < s_{\text{stop,o}}$.

These stopping distances can be obtained by substituting t_{stop} in Eq. (2) to s in Eq. (3) for the ego and the other vehicle as follows:

$$s_{\text{stop,e}} = s_{0,\text{e}} - \frac{v_{\text{e}}^2}{2 \cdot a_{\text{e}}} \quad \text{and} \quad s_{\text{stop,o}} = s_{0,\text{o}} - \frac{v_{\text{o}}^2}{2 \cdot a_{\text{o}}} \ . \tag{5}$$

For any case in which collision freedom can be deduced, we rearrange the terms and the deduction into the following pattern:

$$s_{0,\text{o}} - s_{0,\text{e}} > \textit{safe-distance}\,(a_{\text{e}}, v_{\text{e}}, a_{\text{o}}, v_{\text{o}}) \implies \textit{precondition}\,(a_{\text{e}}, v_{\text{e}}, a_{\text{o}}, v_{\text{o}}) \implies$$
$$\neg\,\textit{collision}\,[0; \infty) \ . \tag{6}$$

This pattern has the interpretation that if the initial distance $s_{0,\text{o}} - s_{0,\text{e}}$ is bigger than the expression $\textit{safe-distance}\,(a_{\text{e}}, v_{\text{e}}, a_{\text{o}}, v_{\text{o}})$ and the $\textit{precondition}\,(a_{\text{e}}, v_{\text{e}}, a_{\text{o}}, v_{\text{o}})$ holds, too, then we can guarantee that there will be no collision. We claim that the expression $\textit{safe-distance}\,(a_{\text{e}}, v_{\text{e}}, a_{\text{o}}, v_{\text{o}})$ defines the notion of safe distance *prescriptively*; one can easily check whether a collision exists by comparing the initial distance with this expression.

In the rest of this section, we prove three theorems—one for each of these three cases—which determine whether there is a collision or not. As an overview, collision freedom can be deduced in case ① while collision can be deduced in case ②. In case ③, collision depends on further conditions than just the premise $s_{0,\text{o}} \leq s_{\text{stop,e}} < s_{\text{stop,o}}$.

Background Formalisation. Consider the quadratic equations of the form $p(x) := ax^2 + bx + c$ with the discriminant $D := b^2 - 4ac$. The analysis of the movement can be carried out with the following well-known mathematical facts about quadratic forms.

– Solution of quadratic equation:

$$D \geq 0 \implies x_{1,2} := \frac{-b \pm \sqrt{D}}{2a} \tag{7}$$

$$a \neq 0 \implies p(x) = 0 \iff (D \geq 0 \wedge (x = x_1 \vee x = x_2)) \tag{8}$$

– Condition for convexity:

$$x < y < z \ \wedge \ p(x) > p(y) \leq p(z) \implies a > 0 \tag{9}$$

– Monotonicity:

$$(t \leq u \implies s(t) \leq s(u)) \wedge (t < u \wedge u \leq t_{\text{stop}} \implies s(t) < s(u)) \tag{10}$$

– Maximum at the stopping time:

$$p(t) \leq p(t_{\text{stop}}) \ \wedge \ s(t) \leq s(t_{\text{stop}}) \tag{11}$$

Because these are all basic, well-known facts, one can expect that the overhead of using a theorem prover be kept within limits. Indeed, all of the facts in Eqs. (7) to (11) can be proved automatically with one of Isabelle's automatic provers: the sum-of-squares methods (ported from Harrison [11]) or rewriting of arithmetic expressions combined with classical reasoning.

Theorems. We start with the first theorem for case ① which states that this case implies collision freedom. Intuitively speaking, there will be no collision in this case because the ego vehicle is located so far that it stops before the initial position of the other vehicle.

Theorem 1 (Obvious collision freedom in case ①)

$$s_{\text{stop,e}} < s_{0,o} \implies \neg\, collision\,[0; \infty) \tag{12}$$

Proof. This is true because $s_e(t) < s_o(t)$ holds for every time $t \geq 0$: $s_e(t) \leq s_e(t_{\text{stop,e}}) = s_{\text{stop,e}} < s_{0,o} = s_o(0) \leq s_o(t)$ due to transitivity, the assumption, and monotonicity of s in Eq. (10), and the maximum at the stopping time in Eq. (11). □

Since this case implies absence of collision, we can unfold the definition of $s_{\text{stop,e}}$ in Eq. (5) and rearrange Theorem 1 according to the pattern in Eq. (6) into the following safe distance expression:

$$safe\text{-}distance_1 := -\frac{v_e^2}{2 \cdot a_e} \tag{13}$$

For case ②, we first give the following lemma which provides a sufficient condition for a collision in a bounded interval. It follows directly from the continuity of s and an application of the intermediate value theorem for $s_o - s_e$ between 0 and t.

Lemma 1 (Upper bounds on collision time)

$$(s_e(t) \geq s_o(t) \implies collision\,[0; t]) \wedge (s_e(t) > s_o(t) \implies collision\,[0; t))$$

Then, the following theorem states that case ② necessarily implies a collision.

Theorem 2 (Obvious Collision in Case ②)

$$s_{\text{stop,e}} \geq s_{\text{stop,o}} \implies collision\,[0; \infty)$$

Proof. Since by definition $s_{\text{stop,e}} = s_e(t_{\text{stop,e}})$ and $s_{\text{stop,o}} = s_o(t_{\text{stop,o}})$, setting $t := \max\{t_{\text{stop,e}}, t_{\text{stop,o}}\}$ in Lemma 1 above proves that this case implies a collision. □

Since case ② implies collision, no safe distance expression is produced from the logical analysis of case ②.

We now consider case ③, where the ego vehicle stops behind the other vehicle. There can still be a collision, i.e. the movement of the ego vehicle can intersect the movement of the other vehicle and still stop behind the other vehicle (see Fig. 2). The following lemma states that a collision (if any) in case ③ must occur while *both* cars are still moving. This lemma therefore allows us to reduce the reasoning to the continuous part p of the movement s.

Lemma 2 (Collision within stopping times in case ③)

$s_{0,o} \leq s_{stop,e} < s_{stop,o} \implies$

$$collision\,[0; \infty) \iff collision\,(0; \min\{t_{stop,e}, t_{stop,o}\}) \tag{14}$$

Proof. The "$\Longleftarrow$"-part is obvious and we only prove the "$\Longrightarrow$"-part. If a collision happens at time t while one of the vehicles has already stopped, then it must be the ego vehicle which has stopped ($t_{stop,e} < t$). Also, we have $s_e(t_{stop,e}) > s_o(t_{stop,e})$ because according to Eq. (10), s_o is strictly increasing in $[t_{stop,e}; t]$ (see Fig. 2). Then, Lemma 1 yields a suitable witness for an earlier collision $t' < t_{stop,e}$. The whole proof takes just about 80 lines in the formalisation. □

Then, the following theorem characterises the conditions for ensuring a collision in case ③.

Theorem 3 Conditional collision in case ③)

$s_{0,o} \leq s_{stop,e} < s_{stop,o} \implies collision\,[0; \infty) \iff$

$$a_o > a_e \,\wedge\, v_o < v_e \,\wedge\, s_{0,o} - s_{0,e} \leq \frac{(v_o - v_e)^2}{2 \cdot (a_o - a_e)} \,\wedge\, t_{stop,e} < t_{stop,o} \tag{15}$$

Proof. *("$\Longleftarrow$".)* Case ③ and Eqs. (7), (8), and (15) yield a root of $p_o - p_e$, which is contained in the interval $(0; \min\{t_{stop,e}, t_{stop,o}\})$. The root is therefore also a root of $s_o - s_e$ and therefore witnesses *collision* $[0; \infty)$.

Only if ("$\Longrightarrow$")-part of the conclusion. From *collision* $[0; \infty)$, we obtain a root t with $s_o(t) - s_e(t) = 0$. Then, Lemma 2 allows us to deduce $p_o(t) - p_e(t) = 0$ and condition (9) for convexity (for $p_o - p_e$ at times $0 < t < \min\{t_{stop,e}, t_{stop,o}\}$) yields $a_o > a_e$. This gives, together with the fact that the discriminant of $p_o - p_e$ is nonnegative according to Eq. (8), the remaining conjuncts of Eq. (15) after some arithmetic manipulations and reasoning. The whole proof takes about 130 lines in the formalisation. □

In order to unify this theorem with the pattern in (6), we negate the logical equivalence in (15) and rearrange the theorem as follows.

$$s_{0,o} - s_{0,e} > \frac{v_o^2}{2 \cdot a_o} - \frac{v_e^2}{2 \cdot a_e} \implies s_{0,o} - s_{0,e} > \frac{(v_o - v_e)^2}{2 \cdot (a_o - a_e)} \implies s_{0,o} \leq s_{stop,e} \implies$$

$$(a_o > a_e \,\wedge\, v_o < v_e \,\wedge\, t_{stop,e} < t_{stop,o}) \implies \neg\, collision\,[0; \infty) \tag{16}$$

This reformulation fits the pattern in (6) and now we have two possible safe distance expressions and one for precondition:

$$safe\text{-}distance_2 := \frac{v_o^2}{2 \cdot a_o} - \frac{v_e^2}{2 \cdot a_e} \qquad safe\text{-}distance_3 := \frac{(v_o - v_e)^2}{2 \cdot (a_o - a_e)},$$

$$precondition := s_{0,o} \leq s_{stop,e} \,\wedge\, (a_o > a_e \,\wedge\, v_o < v_e \,\wedge\, t_{stop,e} < t_{stop,o}) \tag{17}$$

To choose between these two expressions, we use the following lemma which determines their relative position.

Lemma 3 (Relative position of safe distance expressions)

$$a_o > a_e \implies \textit{safe-distance}_2 \leq \textit{safe-distance}_3$$

Proof. We prove this lemma by multiplying both sides with the multiplier $2 \cdot (a_0 - a_e)$ which is positive. Then, we reason backwards by performing arithmetical reasoning which eventually leads to $0 \leq (t_{\text{stop,e}} - t_{\text{stop,o}})^2$ which is always true. $\square$

With this lemma, we choose *safe-distance*$_3$ when the *precondition* holds. Otherwise, it must be the case that $\neg\,(a_o > a_e \,\wedge\, v_o < v_e \,\wedge\, t_{\text{stop,e}} < t_{\text{stop,o}})$—since we assume case ③. Then, Theorem 3 ensures that *safe-distance*$_2$ is indeed a prescriptive definition of safe distance.

Overall Definition. To sum up our logical analysis, *safe-distance*$_1$ always holds as a prescriptive definition of the safe distance. Expression *safe-distance*$_3$ holds when it is case ③ and *precondition* holds, while *safe-distance*$_2$ is valid when it is still case ③ but *precondition* does not hold.

4 Designing Sound Checkers for the Safe Distance Rule

We use the analyses from Sect. 3 to guide the design of sound and complete abstract checkers in Sect. 4.1; these checkers are defined in terms of real numbers and other non-executable constructs. We then show how to turn them into executable checkers by using exact rational arithmetic, symbolic decision procedures, or interval arithmetic in Sect. 4.2.

4.1 Abstract Checkers

We design two checkers here: a descriptive and a prescriptive version. Both checkers are derived from the case distinction in Sects. 3.1 and 3.2, respectively.

Descriptive Checker. From the case distinction based on stopping times in Sec. 3.1, we conclude that the problem of detecting collision is reduced into the problem of finding solutions for each entry in Table 1 in the corresponding time interval. This is formalised with the predicate *has-root-in*, defined as $f(t)$ *has-root-in* $T \longleftrightarrow \exists t \in T.\ f(t) = 0$. A checker based on this approach can then be defined as follows.

$$\textit{checker}_d := \neg \left(\begin{array}{ll} p_e(t) - p_o(t) \ \textit{has-root-in}\ [0; \min\{t_{\text{stop,e}}, t_{\text{stop,o}}\}] & \vee \\ p_e(t_{\text{stop,e}}) - p_o(t) \ \textit{has-root-in}\ [t_{\text{stop,e}}; t_{\text{stop,o}}] & \vee \\ p_o(t_{\text{stop,o}}) - p_e(t) \ \textit{has-root-in}\ [t_{\text{stop,o}}; t_{\text{stop,e}}] & \vee \\ p_e(t_{\text{stop,e}}) - p_o(t_{\text{stop,o}}) \ \textit{has-root-in}\ [\max\{t_{\text{stop,e}}, t_{\text{stop,e}}\}; \infty) & \end{array}\right)$$

The following theorem ensures that the checker is both sound and complete. It follows immediately from the definitions of braking movement p, stopping time t_{stop}, predicate *has-root-in*, and predicate *collision*:

Theorem 4 (Correctness of abstract descriptive checker)

$$\textit{checker}_d \iff \neg\textit{collision}\,[0; \infty)$$

Prescriptive Checker. From the case distinction based on stopping distances in Sect. 3.2, we have defined three expressions of safe distances. Each expression has associated preconditions for which the expression is valid. We can design the prescriptive checker from these expressions as follows:

$$checker_\mathrm{p} := \textbf{let } dist = s_{0,\mathrm{o}} - s_{0,\mathrm{e}} \textbf{ in}$$
$$\quad \textbf{if } \underline{dist > safe\text{-}distance_1} \textbf{ then } \textit{True}$$
$$\quad \textbf{else if } a_0 > a_\mathrm{e} \wedge v_\mathrm{o} < v_\mathrm{e} \wedge t_{\mathrm{stop,e}} < t_{\mathrm{stop,o}} \textbf{ then } \underline{dist > safe\text{-}distance_3}$$
$$\quad \textbf{else } \underline{dist > safe\text{-}distance_2}$$

The following theorem states that the prescriptive checker is also sound and complete.

Theorem 5 (Correctness of abstract prescriptive checker)

$$checker_\mathrm{p} \iff \neg collision\,[0;\infty)$$

Proof. The soundness follows from the Theorems 1, 2, and 3 in Sect. 3 while the completeness comes from the fact that case ①, ②, and ③ cover all possible cases. ☐

4.2 Executable Checkers

A fragment of HOL can be seen as a functional programming language. When we talk about *executable* specifications, we talk about specifications within that fragment. In principle, such specifications could be evaluated inside Isabelle's kernel. For a more efficient evaluation, Isabelle/HOL comes with a code generator [10], which translates executable specifications to code for (functional) programming languages like SML, OCaml, Scala, or Haskell. We will generated the code for SML to evaluate the US-101 Highway data set in Sect. 5.

The aforementioned checkers $checker_\mathrm{d}$ and $checker_\mathrm{p}$ are formally proved correct, but are not executable, because they involve e.g., real numbers or quantifiers over real numbers (via *has-root-in*). We therefore refine them towards executable formulations. To this end, Isabelle provides a variety of techniques, and we explore the use of the following:

1. *Exact arithmetic on rational numbers.*
   Exact arithmetic on rational numbers can be directly used for $checker_\mathrm{p}$ if all parameters are rational numbers. It requires, however, the manual work of formalising the analysis presented in Sect. 3.2.
2. *Decision procedure for finding roots of univariate polynomials.*
   By contrast, using a decision procedure based on Sturm sequences for *has-root-in* in $checker_\mathrm{d}$ requires almost no manual reasoning. However, it has to be used as a black-box method and might not be easy to extend, if it is required.
3. *Interval arithmetic.*
   With interval arithmetic, one can include uncertainties into parameters of the model and could even address non-polynomial problems. Numerical uncertainties can, however, cause the checkers to be incomplete.

Exact Rational Arithmetic. All the operations occurring in *checker*$_p$ could be executed on rational numbers. Under the assumption that all the parameters are rational numbers, *checker*$_p$ can be executed using the standard approach of *data-refinement* [9] for real numbers in Isabelle/HOL. That is, the code generator is instructed to represent real numbers as a data type with a constructor *Ratreal* : $\mathbb{Q} \to \mathbb{R}$. Then, operations on the rational subset of the real numbers are defined by pattern matching on the constructor, and performing the corresponding operation on rational numbers. For example, addition $+_\mathbb{R}$ on *Ratreal*-constructed real numbers can be implemented with addition $+_\mathbb{Q}$ on rational numbers: *Ratreal*$(p) +_\mathbb{R}$ *Ratreal*$(q) =$ *Ratreal*$(p +_\mathbb{Q} q)$. Therefore, as long as the input is given as rational numbers, code generation for *checker*$_p$ works without further manual setup. Correctness follows from Theorem 5.

Sturm Sequences. A different approach can be followed by looking at the prescriptive formulation *checker*$_d$. To evaluate *has-root-in*, we can resort to a decision procedure based on *Sturm sequences* which been formalised in Isabelle [5]. The interface to this decision procedure is an executable function *count-roots*(p, I), which returns the number of roots of a given univariate polynomial p in a given interval I. It satisfies the proposition p *has-root-in* $T \longleftarrow (\textit{count-roots}(p, I) > 0)$ and can therefore be used as an executable specification for the occurrences of *has-root-in* in *checker*$_d$. Correctness follows from Theorem 4.

Interval Arithmetic. The previous two approaches both assume that the parameters are given as exact rational numbers. One could argue that this is an unrealistic assumption, because real-world data cannot be measured exactly. For this checker, we therefore allow intervals of parameters. Isabelle's *approximation* [12] method allows us to interpret *checker*$_p$ (a formula with inequalities over real numbers) as an expression in interval arithmetic. The resulting checker *checker*$_i$ takes a Cartesian product of intervals as enclosure for the parameters as input.

Theorem 6 (Correctness of Checker)
If $(s_e, v_e, a_e, s_o, v_o, a_o) \in S_e \times V_e \times A_e \times S_o \times V_o \times A_o$, then

$$\textit{checker}_i\,(S_e, V_e, A_e, S_o, V_o, A_o) \implies \neg\textit{collision}[0; \infty)$$

Proof. The theorem follows directly from the correctness of *approximation*. □

Note that we lose completeness in this approach; the checker could fail to prove collision-freedom because of imprecision in the approximate calculations. Such imprecision occurs because of, e.g., finite precision calculations or case distinctions that cannot be resolved. It might be that in a case distinction $a < b \vee a \geq b$, none of the two disjuncts can be proved (consider e.g. $a \in [0; 1], b \in [0; 1]$) with just interval arithmetic. Tracking dependencies between input variables or interval constraint propagation approaches could alleviate this problem.

5   Data Analysis of the Safe Distance Problem

The traffic data used in this evaluation are obtained from the Next Generation SIMulation (NGSIM) project of the U.S. Department of Transportation Federal Highway Administration (FHWA). We specifically focus on the data set for the US Highway 101 (US-101). The length of the study area is about 640 m with five lanes in total and the data was collected for 45 min. For every identified car, the data set provides information such as the position, speed, acceleration, length of the vehicle, and distance to the other vehicle with a time resolution of 0.1 s.

The US-101 data set does not provide any information about the maximum deceleration of the vehicles. The maximum deceleration value can be obtain from the values of tyre friction on dry condition. We take these values from the domain of traffic collision reconstruction [6] which has been used by lawyers in court [3]. The tyre friction values for automobile and motorcycle are $\mu_{motor} = 0.75$ and $\mu_{auto} = 0.8$, respectively. As for truck and bus, we take the value from [19], i.e., $\mu_{truck} = 0.7$. By assuming $g = 9.8\,\mathrm{m\,s^{-2}}$, these tyre friction values correspond to maximum deceleration values of $a_{motor} = -7.35\,\mathrm{m\,s^{-2}}$, $a_{auto} = -7.84\,\mathrm{m\,s^{-2}}$, and $a_{truck} = -6.86\,\mathrm{m\,s^{-2}}$.

Table 2. Number of detected safe distance situations and time performance of each checker (for $N = 3,915,006$ data points).

Checker	u	Safe dist. (%)	Time
Descriptive$_{Sturm}$	-	99.74 %	1068.32 s
Prescriptive$_{exact}$	-	99.74 %	168.93 s
Prescriptive$_{interval}$	7	99.05 %	352.73 s
Prescriptive$_{interval}$	5	97.48 %	323.56 s
Prescriptive$_{interval}$	3	90.92 %	324.23 s

We evaluate three executable checkers: (1) the exact rational arithmetic-based prescriptive checker, (2) the Sturm sequences-based descriptive checker, and (3) the interval arithmetic-based prescriptive checker. Interval arithmetic-based checker is parameterised with uncertainty u which represents the measurement error in the data. This parameter, however, does not represent the error due to floating-point computation which is handled internally by the *approximation* decision procedure in this interval arithmetic-based checker. Each time this checker evaluates an arithmetic expression, the interval of each evaluated subexpression is enlarged accordingly so as to include the error due to fixed precision of floating-point numbers.

Two aspects are measured for each checker: the number of detected safe distance situations and the CPU time for checking the whole data set. The measurement is performed with an Intel i5-4330M 2.80 GHz processor and 12 GB of RAM. We draw four conclusions from the results in Table 2:

1. Both prescriptive$_{\text{exact}}$ and descriptive$_{\text{Sturm}}$ checkers detect the same number of safe distance situations. This is not surprising since we have formally proved the correctness of both checkers and they use exact arithmetic.
2. Interval arithmetic-based checkers detect fewer safe distance situations than the other checkers do. This shows that this checker is more conservative and incomplete.
3. The number of safe distance scenario detected decreases as the uncertainty parameter u decreases. This is because the uncertainty parameter u corresponds to the uncertainty value of 2^{-u} and, hence, a decrease of uncertainty parameter u is equivalent to an increase of the uncertainty value.
4. The prescriptive checker has a better time performance than the descriptive checker. This is understandable because the descriptive checker is based on a more general decision procedure (Sturm sequences), and the prescriptive checker is heavily tuned for this safe distance problem.
5. The prescriptive$_{\text{exact}}$ checker detects safe distance situations approximately *two* times faster than those prescriptive$_{\text{interval}}$ checkers. This is because the critical factor in the time performance of these two types of checkers lies in the computation of *dist* in *checker*$_{\text{p}}$. Subtracting an interval by another interval essentially consists of *two* exact arithmetic subtractions — one each for the lower bound and upper bound.

Two caveats regarding the results from Table 2 are worth mentioning here. First, when the prescriptive$_{\text{exact}}$ and descriptive$_{\text{Sturm}}$ checker return *False*, they do not detect a collision but a guaranteed-to-happen collision if the ego and the other vehicles brake with full deceleration. Second, when the prescriptive$_{\text{interval}}$ checkers return *False*, no conclusion can be drawn concerning the potential collision due to violating safe distance rule (see Theorem 6). This inconclusive answer is because either the uncertainty u for the data is too large or the precision for the floating-point approximation is too limited.

6   Related Work

In this section, we compare our formalisation with results from the domain of transportation engineering and formal verification. One notable difference between our work with the others is that we ignore the reaction time for the ego vehicle. Hence, when comparing our work with others, those parameters are set to zero. In general, all related works discussed here except the work by Goodloe et al. [8] are incomplete, and those in the domain of transportation engineering (discussed here) are not formally proved.

In the domain of traffic engineering, there are two areas which are related to our work: traffic simulation and collision warning. Mazda and PATHS algorithms [1]—for collision warning—and Gipps's model [7]—for traffic simulation—formulate the notion of safe distance which exactly match our second definition of safe distance in Eq. (17). Qu et al. [22] analyse the safe distance problem by applying a technique from molecular dynamics. Unlike the case distinction in our work, they have three cases which depend on the relationship between v_e and v_o. Their notion of safe distance for case $v_e > v_o$ and $v_e = v_o$ matches exactly with our second definition of safe distance in Eq. (17). However, their notion of safe distance when $v_e < v_o$ does not match with any of our definitions of safe distance due to different assumptions. A more detailed analysis for the safe distance problem is given by Chen et al. [4]. If we consider their single lane scenario only, their definitions of safe distance for stationary and decelerating case exactly match our first and second definition of safe distance in Eqs. (13) and (17), respectively.

The related work described up until now always assume that the maximum deceleration for all vehicles is the same. Therefore, none of the works described previously matches our third definition of safe distance. Wilson [25] performs case distinction based on the stopping times and graphically identifies the region called "envelope of opportunity" for each case. This envelope of opportunity divides the plot between the reaction time and the deceleration of the ego vehicle into safe and unsafe region. The envelope of opportunity for $t_{stop,e} > t_{stop,o}$ and $t_{stop,e} < t_{stop,o}$ match our second and third definition of safe distance in Eq. (17), respectively.

Loos et al. [15] verify ACC formally in KeYmaera where, in their model of ACC, they axiomatise that a safe distance is formalised as the second safe distance definition in Eq. (17). This safe distance definition is then modified to take into account all possible impacts of control decisions for the future of reaction time, and then setting it as an invariant for the controller. They then use the proof calculus for the quantified differential dynamic logic ($Qd\mathcal{L}$) [21] to prove that the controller maintains this invariant, which in turn implies the axiomatised safe distance in Eq. (17) by transitivity. Our work completes theirs by proving that this axiomatised safe distance is indeed safe. However, their controller is safe on the assumption that all vehicles have the same braking performance.

Although Goodloe et al. [8] formally verify programs for aerospace applications, namely airborne conflict detection and resolution (CD&R), their approach is in general very similar to ours. Their objective is to verify whether a checker correctly determines that two aircraft maintain a minimum separation distance. Similar to our work, they also define an abstract checker, prove its soundness and completeness in PVS theorem prover, derive a concrete checker in C, and prove that the refinement from abstract to concrete checker is correct in Frama-C. Our work differs in the step to convert from abstract to concrete checker. Thanks to the code generation facility in Isabelle, we can generate the concrete checker *automatically* in SML.

7   Conclusion and Future Work

We have formalised descriptive and prescriptive versions of the safe distance traffic rule from the Vienna Convention on Road Traffic. For each version, we have also derived two corresponding abstract checkers, which operate on real numbers, and proved their soundness and completeness. The prescriptive checker is refined further into a concrete checker in SML which operates on rational numbers. Interval arithmetic is used here to ensure that it preserves the soundness property despite the error due to the limited precision of floating-point numbers. We then use these two checkers together with the Sturm sequences-based checker to evaluate the US-101 Highway data set from NGSIM.

Our work serves as an example of how one can use theorem provers, especially Isabelle, to turn a vague requirement from a legal text into a more precise and concrete specification. Isabelle, as a framework, also provides us with a unified platform to prove theorems, to design a checker, to prove the soundness of the checker, and to generate the (functional) code automatically. From the evaluation of the data set, we found that at least 90% of the time, each traffic participant—if we assume them to be autonomous vehicles—obeys the safe distance rule. *Our work advances the state-of-the-art by providing a unique combination of formally proved and complete safe distance definitions which generalise all definitions in the literature, formally proved checkers without strict assumptions on braking performance, and real data evaluation.*

We wish to extend this work by considering the reaction time of the ego vehicle. It might also be interesting to see how our third definition of safe distance can be incorporated into the controller in [15] when considering vehicles with different braking performance. To make the reasoning easier, we would like to have more automation for real arithmetic in Isabelle/HOL. We assume that the verification could be more organised by following a dedicated calculus for hybrid systems [20], which could be embedded in Isabelle/HOL. Our checker could also be extended with reachability analysis [2,13] in order to verify a continuous trace. Lastly, aligned with our previous work in formalisation of traffic rules [23], we wish to increase the number of formalised traffic rules such that the liability issue can be deduced automatically with our checkers.

References

1. Aghabayk, K., Sarvi, M., Young, W.: A state-of-the-art review of car-following models with particular considerations of heavy vehicles. Transport Rev. **35**(1), 82–105 (2015)
2. Althoff, M., Dolan, J.: Online verification of automated road vehicles using reachability analysis. IEEE Trans. Robot. **30**(4), 903–918 (2014)
3. American Prosecutors Research Institute: Crash Reconstruction Basics for Prosecutors: Targeting Hardcore Impaired Drivers. Author (2003)
4. Chen, C., Liu, L., Du, X., Pei, Q., Zhao, X.: Improving driving safety based on safe distance design in vehicular sensor networks. Int. J. Distrib. Sens. Netw. **2012**(469067), 13 (2012)
5. Eberl, M.: A decision procedure for univariate real polynomials in Isabelle/HOL. In: Proceedings of the 2015 Conference on Certified Programs and Proofs. CPP 2015, Mumbai, India, pp. 75–83. ACM, New York (2015). http://doi.acm.org/10.1145/2676724.2693166
6. Fricke, L.: Traffic Accident Reconstruction. The Traffic Accident Investigation Manual, vol. 2, Northwestern University Center for Public Safety (1990)
7. Gipps, P.: A behavioural car-following model for computer simulation. Transp. Res. B Methodological **15**(2), 105–111 (1981)

8. Goodloe, A.E., Muñoz, C., Kirchner, F., Correnson, L.: Verification of numerical programs: from real numbers to floating point numbers. In: Brat, G., Rungta, N., Venet, A. (eds.) NFM 2013. LNCS, vol. 7871, pp. 441–446. Springer, Heidelberg (2013)

9. Haftmann, F., Krauss, A., Kunčar, O., Nipkow, T.: Data refinement in Isabelle/HOL. In: Blazy, S., Paulin-Mohring, C., Pichardie, D. (eds.) ITP 2013. LNCS, vol. 7998, pp. 100–115. Springer, Heidelberg (2013)

10. Haftmann, F., Nipkow, T.: Code generation via higher-order rewrite systems. In: Blume, M., Kobayashi, N., Vidal, G. (eds.) FLOPS 2010. LNCS, vol. 6009, pp. 103–117. Springer, Heidelberg (2010)

11. Harrison, J.: Verifying nonlinear real formulas via sums of squares. In: Schneider, K., Brandt, J. (eds.) TPHOLs 2007. LNCS, vol. 4732, pp. 102–118. Springer, Heidelberg (2007)

12. Hölzl, J.: Proving inequalities over reals with computation in Isabelle/HOL. In: Proceedings of the ACM SIGSAM International Workshop on Programming Languages for Mechanized Mathematics Systems. pp. 38–45 (2009)

13. Immler, F.: Verified reachability analysis of continuous systems. In: Baier, C., Tinelli, C. (eds.) TACAS 2015. LNCS, vol. 9035, pp. 37–51. Springer, Heidelberg (2015)

14. Kowshik, H., Caveney, D., Kumar, P.: Provable systemwide safety in intelligent intersections. IEEE Trans. Veh. Technol. 60(3), 804–818 (2011)

15. Loos, S.M., Platzer, A., Nistor, L.: Adaptive cruise control: hybrid, distributed, and now formally verified. In: Butler, M., Schulte, W. (eds.) FM 2011. LNCS, vol. 6664, pp. 42–56. Springer, Heidelberg (2011)

16. Loos, S., Platzer, A.: Safe intersections: at the crossing of hybrid systems and verification. In: IEEE Conference on Intelligent Transportations Systems. pp. 1181–1186, October 2011

17. McLaughlin, S., Harrison, J.V.: A proof-producing decision procedure for real arithmetic. In: Nieuwenhuis, R. (ed.) CADE 2005. LNCS (LNAI), vol. 3632, pp. 295–314. Springer, Heidelberg (2005)

18. Nipkow, T., Paulson, L.C., Wenzel, M.: Isabelle/HOL - A Proof Assistant for Higher-Order Logic. LNCS, vol. 2283. Springer, Heidelberg (2002)

19. Olsen, R.A.: Pedestrian injury issues in litigation. In: Karwowski, W., Noy, Y.I. (eds.) Handbook of Human Factors in Litigation, pp. 15-1–15-23. CRC Press, Boca Raton (2004)

20. Platzer, A.: Logical Analysis of Hybrid Systems. Springer, Heidelberg (2010)

21. Platzer, A.: A complete axiomatization of quantified differential dynamic logic for distributed hybrid systems. Logical Methods Comput. Sci. 8(4), 1–44 (2012)

22. Qu, D., Chen, X., Yang, W., Bian, X.: Modeling of car-following required safe distance based on molecular dynamics. Math. Probl. Eng. 2014(604023), 7 (2014)

23. Rizaldi, A., Althoff, M.: Formalising traffic rules for accountability of autonomous vehicles. In: IEEE Conference on Intelligent Transportation Systems. pp. 1658–1665 (2015)

24. Vanholme, B., Gruyer, D., Lusetti, B., Glaser, S., Mammar, S.: Highly automated driving on highways based on legal safety. IEEE Trans. Intell. Transp. Syst. 14(1), 333–347 (2013)

25. Wilson, B.H.: How soon to brake and how hard to brake: unified analysis of the envelope of opportunity for rear-end collision warnings. In: Enhanced Safety of Vehicles. vol. 47 (2001)

26. Xiao, L., Gao, F.: A comprehensive review of the development of adaptive cruise control systems. Veh. Syst. Dyn. 48(10), 1167–1192 (2010)

Probabilistic Formal Verification of the SATS Concept of Operation

Muhammad Usama Sardar[1(✉)], Nida Afaq[1], Khaza Anuarul Hoque[2],
Taylor T. Johnson[2], and Osman Hasan[1]

[1] School of Electrical Engineering and Computer Science (SEECS),
National University of Sciences and Technology (NUST), Islamabad, Pakistan
{usama.sardar,nida.afaq,osman.hasan}@seecs.nust.edu.pk
[2] Department of Computer Science and Engineering (CSE),
University of Texas at Arlington, Arlington, USA
{khaza.hoque,taylor.johnson}@uta.edu

Abstract. The objective of NASA's Small Aircraft Transportation System (SATS) Concept of Operations (ConOps) is to facilitate High Volume Operation (HVO) of advanced small aircraft operating in non-towered non-radar airports. Given the safety-critical nature of SATS, its analysis accuracy is extremely important. However, the commonly used analysis techniques, like simulation and traditional model checking, do not ascertain a complete verification of SATS due to the wide range of possibilities involved in SATS or the inability to capture the randomized and unpredictable aspects of the SATS ConOps environment in their models. To overcome these limitations, we propose to formulate the SATS ConOps as a fully synchronous and probabilistic model, i.e., SATS-SMA, that supports simultaneously moving aircraft. The distinguishing features of our work include the preservation of safety of aircraft while improving throughput at the airport. Important insights related to take-off and landing operations during the Instrument Meteorological Conditions (IMC) are also presented.

Keywords: Formal verification · Probabilistic analysis · Model checking · SATS · SATS Concept of Operations · Aircraft safety · Aircraft separation · Landing and departure operations

1 Introduction

Small Aircraft Transportation System (SATS) [13], developed by NASA, provides access to more communities with less time delays by leveraging upon the recent advances in navigation and communication technologies. When a number of aircraft are in different parts of the airport, aircraft safety has to be ensured through timely separation and sequencing. Traditionally, non-towered non-radar airports rely on procedural separation during Instrument Meteorological Conditions (IMC), i.e., allowing only one aircraft to get access to the airport airspace

© Springer International Publishing Switzerland 2016
S. Rayadurgam and O. Tkachuk (Eds.): NFM 2016, LNCS 9690, pp. 191–205, 2016.
DOI: 10.1007/978-3-319-40648-0_15

at a given time, which significantly decreases the potential airport through-put [23]. The main objective of SATS is to facilitate high volume operations (HVO) of advanced small aircraft at such airports with minimum infrastructure and low cost. Some representative SATS aircraft are Very Light Jet (VLJ) air-craft, an advanced technology Single-Engine (SE), piston-powered aircraft and an advanced technology Multi-Engine (ME), piston-powered aircraft [33].

Conventionally, SATS HVO simulations have been performed using com-puter programs in which aircraft modules were operated manually by pilots. These simulations develop the human-in-the-loop scenarios to check the effect of SATS procedures in the operational environment, on the pilot's responses in terms of work load and situational awareness [12,16,31,32]. In [12], off-nominal situations were also simulated, in addition to the nominal situations, to check the resulting effect on the pilot's state of mind. Proof-of-concept simulation studies were performed in the Air Traffic Control (ATC) simulation pilot lab at Federal Aviation Administration William J. Hughes Technical Center (FAATC) [30]. These simulations validated that the ATC can accept the SATS procedures, are able to control SATS traffic into and out of the Self Controlled Area (SCA), and support high volume operations. The simulations with pilots were used only for validation purposes and confirmed that SATS procedures are manageable by the airport management module (AMM). AMM's performance during high arrival rates of aircraft into the SCA has also been studied and found to have less delays as compared to one-in-one-out method [27]. Recently, an algorithm has been developed to optimize SATS landing sequence for multiple aircraft in [4], to make it conflict-free and with less delays, using Microsoft VC++ 6.0 simulation environment. However, these piloted simulation methods lack exhaustiveness [14] in terms of coverage of all the possible states as a rigorous piloted simulation of all possible scenarios requires a large number of tests, which in turn demands a significant amount of computational power and time. This leads to another major challenge of simulation-based verification of the SATS Concept of Opera-tions (ConOps), i.e., selection of test vectors. A random selection of test vectors cannot offer a guarantee of correctness of the SATS ConOps since it might miss the meaningful portion of the design space. Moreover, it may not be possible to consider or even foresee all corner cases. Consequently, simulation-based verifi-cation of the SATS ConOps is incomplete with respect to error detection, i.e., all errors in a system cannot be guaranteed to be detected, which is a severe limitation considering the safety-critical nature of passenger aircraft.

In order to have a complete analysis, automatic parameterized verification of hybrid automata [19,20] was recently employed to verify properties of the SATS ConOps using model checking principles, while considering position of the air-craft as a continuous variable modeled either as a timer [19] or as a rectangular differential inclusion [20]. While this methodology allows for verification regard-less of the number of aircraft, a limitation of this work is that the methodology requires the user to specify inductive invariants sufficient to establish safety. While the process of finding inductive invariants sufficient to establish safety of the SATS ConOps has been successfully automated through an extension of invisible invariants [3], this is an incomplete (heuristic) method that, in general, may fail to find such inductive invariants [21]. The analysis and formal verification of the timing constraints of SATS was done in [10] using Linear Real-Time Logic (LRTL). The higher-order-logic theorem prover PVS [26] has also been used for the safety verification of the SATS ConOps [9,13,23,29]. In particular, it has been formally verified that SATS rules and procedures can provide minimum required spacing between two and more aircraft. A hybrid modeling technique was also developed in PVS using the PVS tool Besc [25].

In the above-mentioned methods of validation and verification of SATS, only the procedures and transition rules are considered. With these considerations, any model with appropriate conditions can validate that the procedures are enough for the assurance of safe separation between the aircraft. The missed approach transition is dependent on many random factors, for instance, low visibility. In conventional airports, it is mainly caused by the bad weather, increased air-borne traffic density, and ground traffic and its delays [15]. It is also required upon the execution of a rejected landing because of objects, such as men, equipment or animals, on the runway [1]. Due to such uncertainties involved, it is necessary to incorporate the probabilistic considerations of the system into the validation methods and safety verifications of SATS. Hence, we propose to use probabilistic model checking [5,11] for the verification of the SATS ConOps. This paper presents a fully synchronous Discrete-Time Markov Chain (DTMC) model of the SATS ConOps and the verification of the safety properties of SATS, including the landing and take-off procedures, using the probabilistic model checker PRISM [22]. PRISM has been extensively used to formally model and analyze a wide variety of systems, including communication and multimedia protocols, randomised distributed algorithms, security protocols, biological systems and many others, that exhibit random or probabilistic behaviour [2].

The rest of the paper is organized as follows: Sect. 2 describes the SATS operational concept to facilitate the understanding of the rest of the paper. Section 3 explains the main challenges that we faced in modeling the considered, fully synchronous, system in PRISM and the assumptions used in our DTMC model. In this section, our modeling methodology is also explained through discussion about each module, transition rules and procedures. Section 4 presents the probabilistic verification results of the SATS ConOps and the novel observations made. Finally, Sect. 5 concludes this paper by drawing conclusions and mentioning some directions of future work.

2   SATS ConOps

The ConOps for SATS is primarily a set of rules and procedures based on an area surrounding the airport, called the SCA, a centralized automated system, called the AMM, data communication between AMM and aircraft and state data broadcast from the aircraft [7,8]. The SCA is typically taken as a region with 12–15 NM radius and 3000 ft above the ground [8,9]. It is arranged in a T structure, consisting of base, intermediate and final zones. It is divided into a number of segments and fixes which are the latitude/longitude points in space. The fixes are initial arrival fixes (IAFs), intermediate fix (IF), final approach fix (FAF) and departure fixes (DFs), as shown in Fig. 1. The IAFs serve two purposes, i.e., holding fix, when an aircraft enters the SCA, and missed approach holding fix (MAHF), which is required when an aircraft misses landing, and flies back to the IAF via missed approach path.

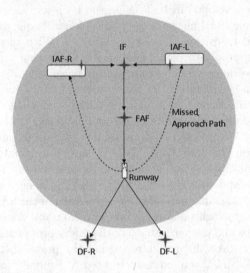

Fig. 1. Top view of the SCA [13]

There are two types of entries into the SCA: vertical entry and lateral entry [9,25], as depicted in Fig. 2. Vertical entry is always made from the 3000 ft holding fix at the left (above IAF-L) or right (above IAF-R). Thereafter, the aircraft descends to the respective 2000 ft holding fix when it becomes available. Next, under certain conditions, the aircraft moves to the base segment (IAF to IF). On the other hand, in a lateral entry, the aircraft flies from the point of entry to the base segment directly or through the 2000 ft holding fix. Once the aircraft is in the base segment or 2000 ft holding fix, there is no dependency on its type of entry. After base segment, the aircraft goes through the IF, FAF, and finally reaches the runway. This procedure is primarily composed of a series of transitions through different segments of the SCA that are conducted by the aircraft if sufficient separation from the other aircraft is available and all conditions for the given transitions hold. If an aircraft misses its landing, due to any reason, it has to follow the missed approach path to move to the IAF corresponding to its MAHF assignment, as shown in Fig. 1.

The AMM has the responsibility to grant permissions to the aircraft for entering the SCA [7,31]. While granting the permission, the AMM assigns a landing sequence and a MAHF to the aircraft. These landing sequence numbers encode the leader information and also identify whether an aircraft is the first

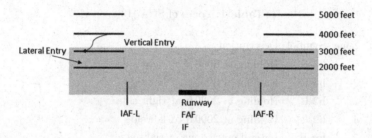

Fig. 2. Side view of the SCA [13]

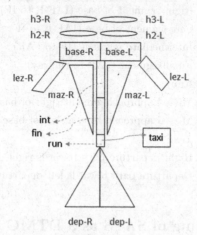

Fig. 3. Zones of the SCA [13]

aircraft in a specific zone of SCA. The aircraft entering later thus follows the leader during the transitions. The MAHF assignment is in terms of 'side', which can assume values of right or left. If the entering aircraft is the first one in sequence, then its MAHF will be in the same side from which it is entering. Whereas, the next aircraft, with sequence other than 1, will have the MAHF that is opposite to that of its leader.

Departure fixes are outside the SCA and under the ATC control. An aircraft ready to depart requests ATC for clearance. After clearance, the departure operation starts at the runway and it moves to the departure fix corresponding to its MAHF assignment. A safe distance of 10 or 5 NM has to be maintained from the aircraft flying to the same or opposite departure fixes, respectively [13].

The SCA can be divided into different zones, illustrated in Fig. 3 and presented in Table 1. These zones represent the state of the aircraft. The complete information about the aircraft will thus include the sequence and MAHF assigned by AMM and the current location/zone of aircraft. The safety verification is based on the number of aircraft in a zone and their separation from other aircraft in other zones [23].

Table 1. Zones of SCA [13]

Zone	Symbol	Description
1	h3-R	Holding at 3000 ft at right side
2	h3-L	Holding at 3000 ft at left side
3	h2-R	Holding at 2000 ft at right side
4	h2-L	Holding at 2000 ft at left side
5	lez-R	Lateral entry zone at right side
6	lez-L	Lateral entry zone at left side
7	base-R	Right segment of base (IAF-R to IF)
8	base-L	Left segment of base (IAF-L to IF)
9	int	Intermediate segment (IF to FAF)
10	fin	Final segment (FAF to runway)
11	run	Runway
12	maz-R	Missed approach zone at right of base
13	maz-L	Missed approach zone at left of base
14	taxi	Taxi
15	dep-R	Right departure path towards right departure fix
16	dep-L	Departure path towards left departure fix

3   Formal Modeling of SATS as a DTMC in PRISM

In this section, we first describe our refinements to the SATS ConOps. Then the main challenges encountered in modeling the system in PRISM are presented. This is followed by the description of how these challenges were tackled in our model.

3.1   Refinements to Original SATS

The proposed model of the SATS ConOps in the PRISM language overcomes some of the limitations of the non-deterministic, asynchronous transition system presented by Dowek et. al [13]. Before presenting the details of our model, we find it appropriate to point out the discrepancies in the existing algorithm and our proposed solution.

1. In a non-deterministic model, if two or more rules are enabled simultaneously, any one of them is allowed to be executed. In other words, only one non-deterministic action happens at a time. This means that in such a model, at each time step, *only one* aircraft will move to the next zone while all other aircraft hold in the same zone, even if the conditions are satisfied for all aircraft to move to their respective next zones. Thus, one aircraft could change zones several times while another remains idle [13]. Hence, such a model is unrealistic [23], as it fails to depict the real scenario.

2. The lowest available altitude determination (Rule 12) [13] is a simultaneous transition, potentially involving 2 aircraft, when the holding pattern at 3000 ft is occupied but 2000 ft is available. In this case, the transition determines 3000 ft as the lowest available altitude and forces the aircraft holding at 3000 ft to descend to the holding pattern at 2000 ft. This is a weakness of the model because simultaneous transition is not possible in a fully non-deterministic model.

Our proposed solution for both the above limitations is to build a fully synchronous model that allows simultaneously moving aircraft. Hence, at each time step, all aircraft satisfying conditions to move to their respective next zones are allowed to proceed concurrently. Moreover, this model also facilitates the simultaneous transition in the lowest available altitude determination.

3.2   Modelling Challenges of SATS in PRISM

Parallel Composition of Modules. Parallel composition of modules in PRISM may seem to be the best option for developing the interleaved model of concurrency of aircraft in the SCA, where each module represents an aircraft. However, there are critical limitations in such a model, as discussed in Sect. 3.1. When multiple commands (belonging to any of the modules) are enabled at the same time, the choice between which command is executed by PRISM is *non-deterministic* in case of Markov decision process (MDP) and *probabilistic* in case of DTMC [2]. Specifically in the case of a DTMC, PRISM selects the command for execution uniformly at random. For instance, if there are 4 aircraft in the SCA and guards are satisfied for one command in each module, then there is a probability of 0.25 for each aircraft to move forward to the next zone. But only one of them is selected to move at a time.

Synchronization. PRISM supports synchronized transitions using synchronization labels. In this case, commands can be labelled with actions, which can be used to force two or more modules to make transitions simultaneously. By default, all modules are combined using the standard CSP parallel composition, i.e., modules synchronize over all their common actions [2]. However, in SATS application, the aircraft can be in any of the 16 zones and thus only a *specific scenario* can be modelled using synchronization labels. For instance, if there are two aircraft and the command for the first aircraft to be in the third zone is synchronized with the command for the second aircraft to be in the first zone, then they will make the transition simultaneously, if available, but it models a special case out of the many possibilities. They will no longer be synchronized in some future time step when the first aircraft is, for instance, in the seventh zone while the second aircraft is in the first zone.

Global variables with Synchronization. Global variables seem useful in modelling the state of the aircraft in the SCA as, unlike local variables, they are modifiable from any module. However, an important restriction on the use of global variables in PRISM is the fact that global variables cannot be updated on a synchronized command [2]. PRISM detects this and reports an error if an attempt is made to do so.

Probabilistic Updates. In order to correctly model the semantics of the communication between aircraft and AMM, both aircraft and AMM should have separate modules in PRISM. Unfortunately, there is no direct way of changing a variable in a different module for *only one* probabilistic update of a command in the *same* time step. However, such probabilistic updates are frequently required. For instance, when an aircraft is in the final zone and it can move to the runway or missed approach path with certain probabilities. In case a pilot chooses the missed approach path, a new sequence number is to be assigned to the aircraft by the AMM while in case of transition to runway, there is no change in the sequence number. A possible solution could be to change the model such that the relevant variable is part of the same module as the probabilistic update but it will not represent the actual scenario of the communication between aircraft and the AMM.

Therefore, the challenge is to achieve a synchronization such that all aircraft move together whenever the guard conditions are satisfied, while incorporating probabilistic updates from the AMM in the model.

3.3   Modeling SATS in PRISM

In our formal model [28], we formulate the SATS ConOps as a DTMC in the PRISM model checker using an abstract timing model. Both sides of the approach are symmetric [13,29] and there can be at most two aircraft on each side of the SCA [13,23]. Therefore, we have assumed two aircraft in the right side of the SCA in this work for the purpose of simplicity. Our model ensures that after a landing aircraft has landed safely, it unloads passengers of the current flight in the taxi state. Then, it loads passengers of the next flight and is ready for departure. After departure, it reaches its destination and the next time it becomes a landing aircraft for the SCA. Hence, the process of landing and departure continues.

Model of Concurrency. In order to cope with the challenges, described in Sect. 3.2, we modeled the SATS ConOps as fully synchronously parallel automata, as in [17], where each transition is labeled with the same synchronization label, and therefore at each time step, at least one transition of each module is active. Hence, in such a fully synchronous model, both aircraft move concurrently to the next respective zones whenever the conditions are satisfied. In order to use the same synchronization label t with all commands in all modules, we ensure that *at least* one condition is true for each module for each reachable state in our model.

Model of SATS Transition Rules and Procedures. The modules `aircraft1` and `aircraft2` in our formal model [28], corresponding to each aircraft, implement the rules of ConOps, i.e., under what conditions the aircraft moves from one zone to the next. The modules are symmetric except that priority is assigned to `aircraft1` in case of simultaneous entry. Due to our proposed fully synchronous model, aircraft can enter inside the SCA individually or simultaneously with another aircraft. The state variables `zone1` and `zone2` represent the current zone of `aircraft1` and `aircraft2`, respectively. They are modelled as integer variables with values in the range 0–16, and the encoding is listed in Table 1. One additional zone is to be included into the model, which is the 'fly zone', for an aircraft outside the SCA. We encode it with a value of zero. In our model, we used formulas for compact representation of the conditions and to avoid repetition. For instance, `z1_total` represents the total number of aircraft in zone 1 and `z7_total_R` represents number of aircraft in zone 7 with an MAHF assignment of right, as shown in the following lines of the code in PRISM language:

$$formula\ z1\_total = (zone1 = 1?1 : 0) + (zone2 = 1?1 : 0);$$

$$formula\ z7\_total\_R = (zone1 = 7\ \&\ mahf1 = true?1 : 0)$$
$$+ (zone2 = 7\ \&\ mahf2 = true?1 : 0);$$

Model of the AMM. The AMM is the sequencer of the SCA. It typically resides at airport ground and communicates with the aircraft via a data link [8]. We model AMM as a separate module $\overline{AMM}$ in PRISM to represent this communication with the aircraft. It has two state variables, i.e., `seq` and `mahf` for each aircraft. For a landing aircraft, `seq` represents the relative landing sequence number, such that the aircraft with landing sequence n is the leader of the aircraft with landing sequence $n+1$, i.e., an aircraft with sequence number 1 is leader of the aircraft with sequence number 2. It is modelled as an integer variable with values in the range 0–10. When an aircraft enters the SCA, `seq` is assigned a new value calculated by the formula `nextseq`. This value is calculated based on the number of the aircraft already in the landing zones of the SCA. In case of simultaneous entry by both aircraft, different sequence numbers are assigned to both the aircraft, with priority to `aircraft1`. A new sequence number is also assigned when an aircraft initiates a missed approach path and the sequence numbers of all other aircraft in the landing zones of the SCA are decremented by one. Moreover, when an aircraft enters runway, the sequence numbers of all other aircraft in the SCA are again decremented by one. When an aircraft moves to the taxi state, its sequence number becomes 0. For a departing aircraft, `seq` represents the distance of the aircraft from runway in nautical miles. It is incremented by one in each time step when it is in one of the departure zones, until it becomes 10, where it is assumed to have left the SCA. The MAHF of an aircraft, represented by `mahf`, is a boolean variable with `true` representing right MAHF, and `false` representing left MAHF. It is assigned whenever an aircraft enters the SCA. Moreover, it is re-assigned when an aircraft executes a missed path approach. We consider MAHF of only right side for simplicity of the model in this paper.

Timing Model. We use an abstract timing model in our formalization of the SATS ConOps. We assume that each aircraft stays in a zone for at least one time step. So, an aircraft must transition to the next zone after one time unit if the conditions for transition are satisfied. When the guard conditions are not fulfilled, it stays in the zone until the conditions become true.

Randomness in Model. Since there is no direct way of changing a variable in a different module for only one probabilistic update of a command in the *same* time step, we introduce an additional chooser module for each probabilistic decision. For instance, consider an aircraft in the final zone. Now it can either choose the missed approach path with a probability p_map or it can continue landing and transit to the runway with probability 1-p_map. In case of the missed approach path, a new sequence number and MAHF is to be assigned to the aircraft. However, there is no change in its sequence number and MAHF if it proceeds to runway. We propose to use the chooser module, choose_p_map which contains a single state variable p_map_state of type integer and with two possible values: 0 and 1. When the probability p_map is selected, p_map_state is set to 1, otherwise it is 0. This is achieved by using the following command in PRISM:

$$[t] \; Guard \rightarrow p\_map : (p\_map\_state' = 1) + (1 - p\_map) : (p\_map\_state' = 0);$$

It is important to note that instead of setting true as a guard, we use the conditions of transition to final zone, i.e., one step back condition as the guard [28]. This way, the command does not execute on each time step. p_map_state is updated when the aircraft enters the final zone and is ready to be used when checking conditions for the next transition to runway or missed approach zone in the next time step.

The value of p_map_state is now used in such a way that the guard condition of p_map_state=1 checks whether p_map is selected. For instance, in the AMM module, the following command ensures that seq1 and mahf1 are updated as soon as it makes the transition to zone 12:

$$[t] \; Guard \; \& \; p\_map\_state = 1 \rightarrow (seq1' = nextseq) \; \& \; (mahf1' = nextmahf1);$$

4   Verification Results

4.1   Safety Properties

Based on our model, explained in Sect. 3, safe separation is not maintained when two aircraft reside simultaneously in the specific zones. These zones include the approach, final approach, missed approach, runway and departure zones. Hence, we label this state danger as follows:

$$label \ \text{``}danger\text{''} = ((zone1 = 7 \& zone2 = 7) \mid (zone1 = 9 \& zone2 = 9)$$
$$\mid (zone1 = 10 \& zone2 = 10) \mid (zone1 = 11 \& zone2 = 11)$$
$$\mid (zone1 = 12 \& zone2 = 12) \mid (zone1 = 15 \& zone2 = 15));$$

Safety in all Paths: $P =? \ [F \ \text{``}danger\text{''}]$;

We analyze safety in our model using the above property, which computes the value of the probability that danger is satisfied in the future by the paths from the initial state. PRISM shows a result of 0, which confirms that no path leads to a collision from the initial state.

Safety in all Reachable States: $filter \ (forall, P <= 0 \ [F \ \text{``}danger\text{''}])$;

In order to confirm that the probability of occurrence of danger remains 0 for all *reachable* states, we formalize the property using filters as above. The property verifies to be true in PRISM and thus guarantees the safety in our model.

4.2   Analysis of Landing and Departure Operations

Expected Time for Landing: $R =? \ [F \ \text{``}landings1\text{''}]$; We utilize the *reachability* reward [2] in PRISM to find the *expected* time taken for the landing of an aircraft in our model. In this case, a reward of unity is awarded to each state of the model and the rewards are accumulated along a path until a certain point is reached. We define this point as the state in which the aircraft is in the taxi state, for instance, for aircraft1:

$$label \ \text{``}landings1\text{''} = (zone1 = 14);$$

Since very limited information is available on the probability of executing a missed approach path p_map for SATS, we leverage upon the PRISM's parametric model checking functionality to perform the sensitivity analysis on the values of p_map from 0.001 to 0.9. The results are shown in Fig. 4, which depict the exponential increase in the expected time taken for landing with p_map. Since aircraft1 is assigned priority in case of simultaneous entry, the values for this aircraft are slightly smaller as compared to those of aircraft2. The overall expected time for any aircraft to land is also shown.

Expected Number of Departures in a Fixed Time: $R =? \ [C <= T]$; We leverage upon the *cumulative* reward properties [2] to find the *expected* number of departures of the aircraft in a fixed time in our model. In this case, a reward of unity is awarded to each transition of departure and the rewards are accumulated until T time steps have elapsed. Figure 5 shows the results of an experiment with T set to 10,00,000 which is large enough for the purpose of comparative analysis. Since aircraft1 is assigned priority in case of simultaneous departure,

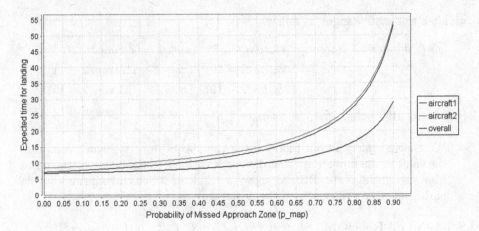

Fig. 4. Expected time for landing vs. Probability of the Missed Approach Zone (Colour figure online)

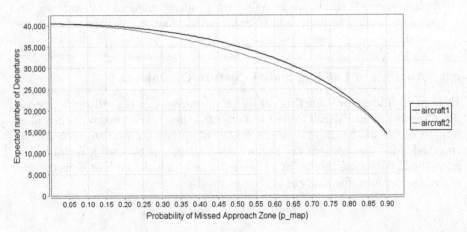

Fig. 5. Expected departures vs. Probability of the Missed Approach Transition (Color figure online)

the expected number of departures for this aircraft are slightly larger as compared to those of `aircraft2`.

Comparison of SATS and SATS-SMA. Reproduction of the corresponding non-deterministic model [13] in PRISM shows that the expected number of landing or departure operations are much greater in our proposed SATS-SMA than the corresponding non-deterministic model. For instance, with no aircraft executing a missed approach path, i.e., `p_map` of 0, the *expected* operations in the original non-deterministic asynchronous model and our refined SATS-SMA are 51280 and 81081, respectively, i.e., around 1.6 times greater throughput. The reason is that original SATS allows only one aircraft to move at a time while we allow all aircraft satisfying the conditions to move simultaneously to the respective next zones.

The key advantages of this work include the increase in the throughput, while maintaining aircraft safety, through simultaneous operations. The work also provides important quantitative landing and departure insights of the SATS ConOps. Our PRISM code and properties file is available for download [28], and thus can be benefited by researchers and verification engineers for further developments and analysis of the SATS ConOps.

5 Conclusion

Given the random and unpredictable nature of entry of aircraft into the SCA and transitions between the zones, we propose to use a probabilistic model checker, PRISM, to analyze the SATS ConOps in this paper. A fully synchronous DTMC model of SATS is proposed and is verified to increase the expected throughput of the airport as compared to the traditional non-deterministic, asynchronous model. Moreover, the successful modeling and verification of the transition procedures for two aircraft moving concurrently, has verified the safety of aircraft in terms of safe separation in all zones including take-off and landing. The landing and departure operations of SATS are analyzed with respect to the probability associated with the missed approach transition.

An important direction of future work is to improve the timing model by incorporating zone distances and abstract aircraft kinematics [25]. A more detailed analysis can be carried out by removing the simplifying assumptions of 2 aircraft and right side MAHF. Similarly, detailed comparison of non-SATS (one-in/one-out), SATS and SATS-SMA is an interesting direction for future research. Furthermore, we also plan to conduct the probabilistic analysis of the SATS ConOps under off-nominal conditions [6,12,24], such as equipment malfunction and emergency situations, using the parametric model checking functionality of PRISM, like it was utilized for the analysis of probability of missed approach in this paper. Moreover, Continuous-Time Markov Chains (CTMCs) of the SATS ConOps can also be developed to verify some time-related properties, where Erlang distribution can be used to model discrete time delays [18].

Acknowledgments. We would like to express our profound gratitude and heartfelt thanks to Dr. Cesar A. Munoz from NASA Langley Research Center for the valuable insights related to SATS and their model. We are also enormously pleased to precise our intense gratefulness and deepest gratitude to Dr. Matthias Gudemann for his helpful tips on modeling the system in PRISM. K. A. Hoque and T. T. Johnson are supported in part by the National Science Foundation (NSF) via grant number CNS 1464311, the Air Force Research Laboratory (AFRL) via contract number FA8750-15-1-0105, and the Air Force Office of Scientific Research (AFOSR) via contract number FA9550-15-1-0258. Any opinions, findings, and conclusions or recommendations expressed in this publication are those of the authors and do not necessarily reflect the views of AFRL, AFOSR, or NSF.

References

1. Instrument Procedures Handbook. U.S. Department of Transportation, Federal Aviation Administration (2015)
2. PRISM - Probabilistic Symbolic Model Checker (2016). http://www.prismmodelchecker.org
3. Arons, T., Pnueli, A., Ruah, S., Xu, Y., Zuck, L.D.: Parameterized verification with automatically computed inductive assertions. In: Berry, G., Comon, H., Finkel, A. (eds.) CAV 2001. LNCS, vol. 2102, pp. 221–234. Springer, Heidelberg (2001)
4. Bai, C., Zhang, X.: Aircraft landing scheduling in the small aircraft transportation system. In: International Conference on Computational and Information Sciences, pp. 1019–1022. IEEE (2011)
5. Baier, C., Katoen, J.P., et al.: Principles of model checking, vol. 26202649. MIT Press, Cambridge (2008)
6. Baxley, B., Williams, D., Consiglio, M., Adams, C., Abbott, T.: The small aircraft transportation system (SATS), higher volume operations (HVO) off-nominal operations. In: Aviation, Technology, Integration, and Operations Conference. American Institute of Aeronautics and Astronautics (2005)
7. Baxley, B., Williams, D., Consiglio, M., Adams, C., Abbott, T.: Small aircraft transportation system, higher volume operations concept and research summary. J. Aircr. **45**(6), 1825–1834 (2008)
8. Carreño, V.: Concept for multiple operations at non-tower non-radar airports during instrument meteorological conditions. In: Digital Avionics Systems Conference, vol. 1, pp. 5.B.1–5.1-9. IEEE (2003)
9. Carreño, V., Muñoz, C.: Safety verification of the small aircraft transportation system concept of operations. In: Aviation, Technology, Integration, and Operations Conference. American Institute of Aeronautics and Astronautics (2005)
10. Cheng, A., Niktab, H., Walston, M.: Timing analysis of small aircraft transportation system (SATS). In: Conference on Embedded and Real-Time Computing Systems and Applications, pp. 58–67. IEEE (2012)
11. Clarke Jr., E.M., Grumberg, O., Peled, D.A.: Model Checking. MIT Press, Cambridge (1999)
12. Consiglio, M., Conway, S., Adams, C., Syed, H.: SATS HVO procedures for priority landings and mixed VFR/IFR operations. In: Digital Avionics Systems Conference, vol. 2, pp. 13.B.2-1–13.B.2-8. IEEE (2005)
13. Dowek, G., Munoz, C., Carreño, V.A.: Abstract model of the SATS concept of operations: Initial results and recommendations. Technical report NASA/TM-2004-213006, NASA Langley Research Center (2004)
14. Fedeli, A., Fummi, F., Pravadelli, G.: Properties incompleteness evaluation by functional verification. IEEE Trans. Comput. **56**(4), 528–544 (2007)
15. Gariel, M., Spieser, K., Frazzoli, E.: On the statistics and predictability of go-arounds. In: Conference on Intelligent Data Understanding (2011)
16. Greco, A., Magyarits, S., Doucett, S.: Air traffic control studies of small aircraft transportation system operations. In: Digital Avionics Systems Conference, vol. 2, pp. 13.A.4-1–13.A.4-12. IEEE (2005)
17. Güdemann, M., Ortmeier, F.: A framework for qualitative and quantitative formal model-based safety analysis. In: Symposium on High-Assurance Systems Engineering, pp. 132–141. IEEE (2010)

18. Hoque, K.A., Mohamed, O.A., Savaria, Y.: Towards an accurate reliability, availability and maintainability analysis approach for satellite systems based on probabilistic model checking. In: Design, Automation Test in Europe Conference Exhibition, pp. 1635–1640. IEEE (2015)
19. Johnson, T.T., Mitra, S.: Parameterized verification of distributed cyber-physical systems: an aircraft landing protocol case study. In: International Conference on Cyber-Physical Systems, pp. 161–170. IEEE (2012)
20. Johnson, T.T., Mitra, S.: A small model theorem for rectangular hybrid automata networks. In: Giese, H., Rosu, G. (eds.) FORTE 2012 and FMOODS 2012. LNCS, vol. 7273, pp. 18–34. Springer, Heidelberg (2012)
21. Johnson, T.T., Mitra, S.: Invariant synthesis for verification of parameterized cyber-physical systems with applications to aerospace systems. In: Infotech at Aerospace Conference. American Institute of Aeronautics and Astronautics (2013)
22. Kwiatkowska, M., Norman, G., Parker, D.: PRISM 4.0: verification of probabilistic real-time systems. In: Gopalakrishnan, G., Qadeer, S. (eds.) CAV 2011. LNCS, vol. 6806, pp. 585–591. Springer, Heidelberg (2011)
23. Muñoz, C., Dowek, G., Carreño, V.: Modeling and verification of an air traffic concept of operations. Softw. Eng. Notes **29**(4), 175–182 (2004)
24. Muñoz, C., Carreño, V.A., Dowek, G.: Formal analysis of the operational concept for the small aircraft transportation system. In: Butler, M., Jones, C.B., Romanovsky, A., Troubitsyna, E. (eds.) Rigorous Development of Complex Fault-Tolerant Systems. LNCS, vol. 4157, pp. 306–325. Springer, Heidelberg (2006)
25. Muñoz, C., Dowek, G.: Hybrid verification of an air traffic operational concept. In: IEEE ISoLA Workshop on Leveraging Applications of Formal Methods, Verification, and Validation (2005)
26. Owre, S., Rushby, J.M., Shankar, N.: PVS: a prototype verification system. In: Kapur, D. (ed.) CADE 1992. LNCS, vol. 607, pp. 748–752. Springer, Heidelberg (1992)
27. Peters, M.: Capacity analysis of the NASA Langley airport management module. In: Digital Avionics Systems Conference, vol. 1, pp. 4.D.6–41–12. IEEE (2005)
28. Sardar, M.U., Hoque, K.A.: Probabilistic formal verification of the SATS concept of operation (2016). http://save.seecs.nust.edu.pk/projects/SATS
29. Umeno, S., Lynch, N.A.: Proving safety properties of an aircraft landing protocol using I/O automata and the PVS theorem prover: a case study. In: Misra, J., Nipkow, T., Sekerinski, E. (eds.) FM 2006. LNCS, vol. 4085, pp. 64–80. Springer, Heidelberg (2006)
30. Viken, S.A., Brooks, F.M.: Demonstration of four operating capabilities to enable a small aircraft transportation system. In: Digital Avionics Systems Conference, vol. 2, pp. 13.A.1-1–13.A.1-16. IEEE (2005)
31. Williams, D.M.: Point-to-point! validation of the small aircraft transportation system higher volume operations concept. In: International Congress of Aeronautical Sciences (2006)
32. Williams, D., Consiglio, M., Murdoch, J., Adams, C.: Flight technical error analysis of the SATS higher volume operations simulation and flight experiments. In: Digital Avionics Systems Conference, vol. 2, pp. 13.B.1-1–13.B.1-12. IEEE (2005)
33. Xu, Y., Baik, H., Trani, A.: A preliminary assessment of airport noise and emission impacts induced by small aircraft transportation system operations. In: Aviation Technology, Integration and Operations Conference. American Institute of Aeronautics and Astronautics (2006)

Formal Translation of IEC 61131-3 Function Block Diagrams to PVS with Nuclear Application

Josh Newell[1]([⊠]), Linna Pang[1], David Tremaine[1], Alan Wassyng[2],
and Mark Lawford[2]

[1] Systemware Innovation Corporation, Toronto M4P 1E4, Canada
{jnewell,lpang,tremaine}@swi.com
[2] McMaster Centre for Software Certification, McMaster University,
Hamilton L8S 4K1, Canada
{wassyng,lawford}@mcmaster.ca

Abstract. The trip computers for the two reactor shutdown systems of
the Ontario Power Generation (OPG) Darlington Nuclear Power Generating Station (DNGS) are being refurbished due to hardware obsoles-
cence. For one of the systems, the general purpose computer originally
used is being replaced by a programmable logic controller (PLC). The
trip computer application software has been rewritten using function
block diagrams (FBDs), a commonly used PLC programming language
defined in the IEC 61131-3 standard. The replacement project's quality assurance program requires that formal verification be performed to
compare the FBDs against a formal software requirements specification
(SRS) written using tabular expressions (TEs). The PVS theorem proving tool is used in the formal verification. Custom tools developed for
OPG are used to translate TEs and FBDs into PVS code. In this paper,
we present a method to rigorously translate the graphical FBD language
to a mathematical model in PVS using an abstract syntax to represent
the FBD constructs. We use an example from the replacement project
to demonstrate the use of the model to translate a FBD module into a
PVS specification.

Keywords: Safety critical systems · IEC 61131-3 · Function block
diagrams · Formal specification · PVS · Tabular expressions

1 Introduction

Many industrial, safety-critical control systems leverage programmable technologies for their flexibility and scalability. The use of programmable technologies
for safety-critical design is now commonplace in nuclear, aerospace and automotive applications, and formal methods can play an important role in ensuring
that those applications are safe. In the aviation domain, DO-178C [2] advocates
the use of formal methods to create mathematical models for the specification

© Springer International Publishing Switzerland 2016
S. Rayadurgam and O. Tkachuk (Eds.): NFM 2016, LNCS 9690, pp. 206–220, 2016.
DOI: 10.1007/978-3-319-40648-0_16

and analysis of system behaviour. In the nuclear industry, IEEE 7-4.3.2 [1] lists acceptance criteria for mission- or safety- critical systems that practitioners need to comply with. In the context of formal methods, two important criteria are: (1) the software requirements are both precise and complete; and (2) the software implementation is correct with respect to specified behaviour. In the Canadian nuclear industry, CE-1001-STD [7] governs the software engineering of safety critical applications. It prescribes not only the formal specification of requirements and design, but also the formal proof of correctness of implementation against requirements. Traditionally, CE-1001-STD has been applied to general purpose computer languages. It is now being applied to the application-oriented language paradigm of programmable logic controllers (PLCs). PLCs provide a higher level of abstraction for the programmer via a set of built-in hierarchical function blocks (FBs) that can be safety certified for use in critical applications.

The Ontario Power Generation (OPG) Darlington Nuclear Generating Station (DNGS) in Ontario, Canada uses two diverse, computerised special safety systems for emergency shutdown of the reactor. These are referred to as Shutdown System One and Two (i.e., SDS1 and SDS2). They were completed in the early 1990s and are based on an arrangement of real-time general purpose computers. Each SDS has three redundant trip computers (TCs) in a 2-out-of-3 voting configuration. The TCs are categorized as safety critical and were engineered in compliance with CE-1001-STD, which defines a comprehensive set of development, verification and validation processes. Formal requirements and design specification were developed and documented using tabular expressions (TEs) [13]. In addition to various review and overlapping testing processes, formal proof of correctness was performed using a theorem prover Prototype Verification System PVS [9].

Currently, SDS1 and SDS2 are being refurbished to extend the nuclear plant's life and both hardware platforms are being replaced. A safety-certified PLC compliant with IEC 61131-3 [4] was selected for the SDS1 TC replacement. As with the original project, the software requirements are specified using TEs, but the software design is now specified in a function block diagram (FBD) language using built-in IEC 61131-3 FBs provided by a PLC vendor[1,2]. Using the PLC platform, the detailed design automatically generates executable code. PVS is used to formally verify the design against the requirements.

PVS provides an integrated environment with mechanized support for the syntax and semantics of TEs and (higher-order) predicates. Based on [10], an approach was developed for the replacement project to support the formal verification of FBDs. The process is as follows: (1) the trip computer design, described in a collection of FBDs, is translated into PVS; (2) the requirements described in tabular expressions are translated into PVS; and (3) formal proofs for systematic design verification are automated using PVS.

---

[1] A small portion of the software design is written using structured text (ST), but that is not relevant to the subject of this paper.

[2] The use of IEC 61131-3 compliant built-in FBs eased formal specification and subsequent verification of their behavior; one of many PLC qualification activities.

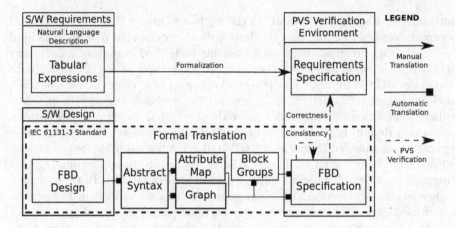

Fig. 1. Framework diagram

Step (1) of the process is the subject of this paper and is based on our experience in the replacement project. An abstract syntax is created to represent the constructs of a FBD and rigorous translation rules are defined for the general translation of FBDs into PVS specifications.

Figure 1 summarizes the overall verification process and contributions. As shown on the left, the requirements are documented using tabular expressions. The design is written in a FBD language that is complaint with IEC 61131-3. In the center of the diagram, we highlight our main contributions within a dashed rectangle. We define an abstract syntax for FBDs using a FBD design as input. With values from the abstract syntax as input, we define an attribute map and labelled directed graph to represent relationships in the FBD. Given an attribute map and graph, we define an additional data structure, block groups, to reduce the complexity of PVS translation. Shown on the right side of Fig. 1, the requirements are formalized in PVS whereas the FBD specification is produced from our methodology. Based on [10], our technique also produces the consistency theorems[3] for FBDs, which are verified manually in PVS. The correctness theorems are manually specified and verified in PVS. The future automation of consistency and correctness proofs is discussed in Sect. 8.

2   Preliminaries

2.1   Tabular Expressions

Tabular expressions [13] (a.k.a., function tables) are a proven and effective approach for describing conditionals and relations, and thus are ideal for documenting many system requirements. They are arguably easier to comprehend and to

---

[3] A FBD design is consistent if for every input there exists an output that satisfies the internal relationships. Otherwise, a FBD design trivially satisfies any requirement.

maintain than conventional mathematical expressions. Formal semantics for tabular expressions have been well-developed in [6] and are useful for inspections, testing and verification [17,18]. Tabular expressions were used on the original SDS1 project and continue to be used on the replacement project for specifying software requirements. As an example of a tabular expression (Fig. 2), we consider the *c_PressParmTrip* requirement that will be used as a running example. The function calculates the parameter trip value using the process variable *m_Presssure* compared against the setpoint value *k_PressSP*[4]. We present the detailed discussion in Sect. 6.1.

| | Result |
Condition	c_ PressParmTrip
m_ Pressure $\leq$ k_ PressSP - k_ DeadBand	e_ not_ tripped
k_ PressSP - k_ DeadBand $<$ m_ Pressure $<$ k_ PressSP	No Change
k_ PressSP $\leq$ m_ Pressure	e_ tripped

assume: *0 < k_ DeadBand << k_ PressSP*

Fig. 2. Tabular expression of *c_PressParmTrip*

2.2 IEC 61131-3 FBDs

To unify the syntax and semantics of PLC programming languages, the International Electrotechnical Committee (IEC) first published IEC 61131-3 in 1993, with its latest version being published in 2013 [4]. The DNGS SDS1 trip computer uses built-in IEC 61131-3 FBs as the basis of the formal software design. The methodology outlined in [10,11], used as a basis for this paper, provides an approach for formally verifying built-in IEC 61131-3 FBs. It also generalizes the approach for verifying generic FBDs using tabular expressions (Sect. 2.1) and PVS. Figure 3 presents an example FBD design (seeded with an error) for the requirement described in Fig. 2, which is further discussed in Sect. 6.2.

2.3 PVS Grammar

The PVS specification language [9] is based on classical higher-order logic equipped with dependent and subtyping mechanisms. PVS has a powerful interactive prover to perform sequent-style deductions. It is used in both academia and industry to analyze formal software specifications. We rely on the syntax and semantic mechanisms implemented in PVS to perform systematic design verification on SDS1. To provide a formal translation to PVS, we select a subset of the PVS grammar as a target language for FBD specifications.

---

[4] The prefixes in this section refer to monitored variables (m_....), controlled variables (c_....), enumerations (e_....), and constants (k_....).

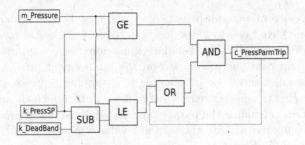

Fig. 3. FBD design for $c\_PressParmTrip$[5]

3   FBD Abstract Syntax

We propose an abstract mathematical model to represent various FBD components. We consider FBDs as a named collection of variables and networks. In practice, a FBD may consist of several networks used to specify the dataflow and transitions between variables and internal FBs. We allow for negated statements as well as feedback connections to support typical programming practices. In addition, the variable set includes interface properties and a named instance for each internal FB[6].

Using basic mathematical constructs, we define recursive and terminal components of a FBD. We use the following notations: "$\times$" for Cartesian product, "$+$" for disjoint union, "$\{\}$" for set, "$\langle\rangle$" for sequence, "$:$" for type definition and "$\rightarrow$" for function. We begin by defining the following types: I_{ident} is an identifier type that has decidable equality; $K_{conn} : type = \{direct, feedback\}$ is an enumerated type for direct and feedback connections; $C_{class} : type = \{input, output, extern, local, wire\}$ is an enumerated type containing five tokens for FBD variable classification; and $I_{init} : type = I_{ident} + \epsilon$ is an initial value that is either a value represented by an identifier or is empty.

$$F_{fbd} = F_{ident} \times W_{vars} \times \{N_{ntwk}\} \tag{1}$$

$$W_{vars} = \{D_{decl}\} \tag{2}$$

$$D_{decl} = R_{var} + (B_{ident} \times H_{ident} \times \{R_{var}\}) \tag{3}$$

$$R_{var} = V_{ident} \times T_{ident} \times C_{class} \times I_{init} \tag{4}$$

$$N_{ntwk} = N_{ident} \times \{S_{stm}\} \tag{5}$$

$$S_{stm} = U_{velm} \times K_{conn} \times U_{velm} \tag{6}$$

$$U_{velm} = Q_{svar} + Z_{neg} \tag{7}$$

$$Q_{svar} = V_{ident} + (B_{ident} \times P_{ident}) \tag{8}$$

$$Z_{neg} = Q_{svar} \tag{9}$$

---

[5] There are five internal FBs: subtraction (SUB), less than or equal to (LE), greater than or equal to (GE), logical disjunction (OR) and logical conjunction (AND).

[6] Concrete examples are available to assist the reader with the translation rules (Sects. 3 and 4) at http://www.swi.com/research/NFM2016.

The abstract syntax is a recursive data structure, defined by Eqs. (1)–(9), with an entry value of F_{fbd}. A F_{fbd} consists of an identifier accompanied by a variable collection and a set of networks. The variable collection W_{vars} is defined by a set of declarations; D_{decl} is either a variable declaration or a block declaration. A variable declaration R_{var} consists of a variable identifier, a type identifier, and a classification. The second variant of D_{decl} is a block declaration consisting of a block identifier and a block name, and a set of variable declarations that describes the interface of the block. The variable names for the interface are referred to as interface variable identifiers P_{ident}. A network N_{ntwk} contains an identifer for the network and a set of statements. A statement consists of a two variable elements and a connector. A variable element U_{velm} consists of two variants, Q_{svar} and Z_{neg}. Z_{neg} is a recursive reference to Q_{svar} and represents a negated interface connection. Q_{svar} has two variants. The first represents a FBD variable identifier and the second is a block identifier and an interface variable identifier. Statements represent the connections between variables and blocks.

The graph models connections between FBD variables and FBs. Variable-to-variable statements do not satisfy this condition. Representing block-to-block statements is syntatic sugar. These statements are rewritten as block-to-variable and a variable-to-block statements before producing the graph. The variable introduced is refered to as an interconnector, which is necessary for the PVS formalization. Lastly, the classification property for interface variables are exclusively *input* or *output* values.

4   Graph Model

In this section we summarize our formalization technique using the abstract syntax, previously defined, as input. We make use of an attribute map, and labelled directed graph to represent interconnections in a FBD network. The labels of the graph contain indices that are used to retrieve properties for blocks, variables and connections from the attribute map. Given the abstract syntax, we use W_{vars} and N_{ntwk} to construct the attribute map and N_{ntwk} to construct the graph. We chose to use variable identifiers I_{ident} to construct the indices.

4.1   Attribute Map

The attribute map is an associative structure that relates indicies to properties for FBD variables and interface variables. It is created to separate attributes from identifiers. The map is used in conjunction with the graph to retrieve properties for nodes and edges in a FBD network.

$$M_{map} = \langle (I_{idf} \rightarrow A_{varf}) + (I_{idi} \rightarrow A_{vari}) \rangle \tag{10}$$

$$I_{idf} = V_{ident} \tag{11}$$

$$I_{idi} = B_{ident} \times P_{ident} \tag{12}$$

$$A_{varf} = T_{ident} \times V_{class} \times I_{init} \tag{13}$$

$$A_{vari} = I_{ident} \times T_{ident} \times P_{class} \tag{14}$$

The attribute map, defined by Eqs. (10)–(14), is a sequence of functions from indices to attributes as described by M_{map}. The map has two possible function variants. The first function is the mapping between the index of a FBD variable to its attributes A_{varf}: FBD variable type, classification and initial value. The second index is a block identifier and one of its interface variables. The second function maps an index I_{idi} to the attributes A_{vari}: block name, interface variable type, and interface variable classication. For a given FBD network, a map is defined to store each FBD, interface and interconnector variable.

4.2   Graph Model

A directed graph is mathematically defined as a pair of nodes $\mathbb{N}$, and edges E. Formally, a graph is defined by Eqs. (15) and (16). From the abstract syntax, we construct a graph for each FBD network.

$$G = (\mathbb{N}, E) \tag{15}$$

$$E \subseteq \mathbb{N} \times \mathbb{N} \tag{16}$$

$$L_{node} = V_{ident} + B_{ident} \tag{17}$$

$$L_{edge} = P_{ident} \times \mathbb{B} \times \mathbb{B} \tag{18}$$

A labelled graph consists of a node and edge labelling function (i.e., l_{node} : $\mathbb{N} \rightarrow L_{node}$ and $l_{edge} : E \rightarrow L_{edge}$) that is used to map nodes and edges with their respective labels. We select labels, for the node and edge respectively, as described by Eqs. (17) and (18). L_{node} is either a variable identifier (i.e., I_{ident}) or a block identifier. L_{edge} contains an interface variable identifier, a boolean flag identifying the edge as a feedback and a boolean flag identifying the negation of a interface connection.

4.3   Block Groups

Given an attribute map and graph for a FBD network, we define an additional data structure that reduces the complexity of our PVS translation by restructuring the data to a format similar to the target expression. The block group data structure, defined by Eqs. (19)–(22), is motivated by the PVS predicate expression for composite FBDs. In a composite FBD, the predicate for each internal block consists of the internal block name and its associated arguments.

Block groups require two structures defined by B_{io} and B_{group} that depend on the secondary structures K_{blk} and I_{arg}. K_{blk} consists of a block identifier and block name. I_{arg} associates a FBD variable identifier to an interface variable identifier, with boolean flags for feedback and negation. FB arguments are ordered using the interface variable element index from an attribute map.

$$K_{blk} = B_{ident} \times H_{ident} \tag{19}$$

$$I_{arg} = V_{ident} \times I_{ident} \times \mathbb{B} \times \mathbb{B} \tag{20}$$

$$B_{io} = K_{blk} \times I_{arg} \tag{21}$$

$$B_{group} = K_{blk} \times \langle I_{arg} \rangle \tag{22}$$

$$f_{io} : M_{map} \rightarrow G \rightarrow \mathbb{N} \rightarrow \{B_{io}\} \tag{23}$$

$$f_{group} : M_{map} \rightarrow \{B_{io}\} \rightarrow \langle B_{group} \rangle \tag{24}$$

We present two functions that describe the process for constructing block group values in Eqs. (23) and (24). These functions implement the logic to group and order various elements. Function f_{io} constructs B_{io} values from an attribute map, graph and block node. The attribute map is required to retrieve properties for nodes and edges in the graph. Values constructed from variable nodes are not valid. B_{io} consists of granular inputs or outputs for a block. Function f_{group} constructs B_{group} values from a set of B_{io} values by extracting inputs or outputs and grouping the block identifier and block name. The resulting B_{group} set is ordered using M_{map}, as are individual I_{arg} sequences.

5 PVS Translation

We summarize our contributions for translating our mathematical model to PVS expressions. Based on [11], the resulting expression is a predicate with input and output arguments existentially quantified over all its internal FBs.

5.1 Identifying Predicate Arguments

The graph maps interconnections between variables and blocks. From this relationship, we determine whether variables behave as inputs or outputs in a given FBD network. It is possible the determination differs from the classification property in the attribute map since the classification does not represent the use of a variable in a given network. For example, if a *local* variable is set at the end of network 1 and used as input in network 2, then it is consistent with its use as an output of network 1 and an input of network 2. Thus, it is not sufficent to rely on the classification value of *local* from the attribute map.

From graph theory, the degree of a node is the number of incident edges to and from a node. Since the graph is directed, we are able to determine the input degree (i.e., deg^+) and output degree (i.e., deg^-) of a node based on the position of the node in the ordered product of an edge. To find input variables, the graph is searched for all nodes that have an input degree of zero, and nodes that satisfy the variable predicate P_{var} (i.e., nodes that are FBD variables and not blocks). This is precisely described by inference rule (25), which is implemented by our translation process.

$$\frac{n : \mathbb{N} \quad P_{var}(n) \quad deg^+(n) = 0}{P_{input}(n)} \tag{25}$$

$$\frac{\forall(e:E):\neg P_{fback}(e) \quad n:\mathbb{N} \quad P_{var}(n) \quad deg^-(n)=0}{P_{output}(n)} \tag{26}$$

An output variable is defined as a terminal node in a dataflow. If an output variable is used as feedback in a FBD, then it will have an edge with a feedback property set to TRUE, thus the output degree will be non-zero. These edges represent inputs from the previous cycle and satisfy the predicate P_{fback}. To correctly identify output variables, feedback edges are excluded, which causes the output degree to become zero for terminal nodes. This is precisely described by inference rule (26). Using rules (25) and (26) we construct the predicate arguments and resolve the type for each using the attribute map. This information also allows us to construct the expression used in the consistency theorem from [11].

5.2 Identifying Existential Variables

The next step of the predicate formalization is the existential quantification of all interconnections between internal blocks. The determination of interconnectors is performed using a similar search predicate from inference rule (26). Feedback edges are excluded to avoid identifying output variables as interconnectors. As a result, the input and output degree of a node should not be zero (i.e., each node has at least one input and one output). This is precisely described by inference rule (27), which is implemented by our translation process.

$$\frac{\forall(e:E):\neg P_{fback}(e) \quad n:\mathbb{N} \quad P_{var}(n) \quad deg^-(n)\neq 0 \quad deg^+(n)\neq 0}{P_{internal}(n)} \tag{27}$$

Using rule (27), we construct the existential quantification over all internal blocks using the attribute map to resolve types. This is the initial component necessary to specify the predicate expression for a composite FBD.

5.3 Function Block Composition

The last step of the composite FBD formalization is a PVS expression consisting of all internal FBs composed by logical conjunction. To define this, we consider several functional structures interpreted with PVS syntactic types.

A fold is a higher order function that takes a binary function as input to reduce a recursive data structure to a terminal value. We define a function f_{expr} in Eq. (28) that translates a block grouping (i.e., B_{group}) to a PVS application expression[7]. Considering f_{group}, an ordered list of $Expr$ elements is produced using the function defined by the function f_{exprl} from Eq. (29).

---

[7] The application expression consists of the block name applied with ordered arguments. An example of a PVS application expression is *MOVE(input, output)* where *MOVE* is the block name, and *input* and *output* are the arguments.

$$f_{expr} : B_{group} \rightarrow Expr \tag{28}$$

$$f_{exprl} = \text{map}(f_{expr}, f_{group}) \tag{29}$$

$$M_{expr} = (Expr, f_{and}) \tag{30}$$

$$f_{and} : Expr \rightarrow Expr \rightarrow Expr \tag{31}$$

$$f_{pexpr} = \text{fold}(f_{and}, f_{exprl}) \tag{32}$$

To specify a binary function for the fold, we define a monoid in Eq. (30), with a signature defined in Eq. (31). The definition of f_{and} constructs an "$Expr$ AND $Expr$" value from the two $Expr$ inputs. Each $Expr$ input is a PVS application expression for a given composite block. Using the ordered list of $Expr$ elements, and the binary function from the monoid M_{expr}, the completed conjunctive expression is defined by the function f_{pexpr} in Eq. (32).

6   Nuclear Industry Case Study

The DNGS SDS1 TCs monitor a diverse set of nuclear and secondary parameters that cover all critical design basis accident scenarios. In the case of anomalous behavior, the TCs respond via control logic to signal a reactor trip. Signals from three redundant SDS1 TCs are connected to 2-out-of-3 voting logic that ultimately initiates a reactor trip[8]. The SDS1 TC software requirements are formalized using TEs and the software is designed using FBDs. First, we present a simplified example of verifying a parameter trip requirement. Second, we demonstrate the application of our formal translation rules and discuss the verification results from applying PVS.

6.1   Parameter Trip Setpoint Requirements

In this example, we consider the requirements of a generalized parameter trip. The special safety system is designed to provide coverage of a pressure input $m\_Pressure$. The TE (Fig. 2, Sect. 2.1) specifies that $c\_PressParmTrip$ generates a trip response, if the pressure input ($m\_Pressure$) is above or equal to the setpoint ($k\_PressSP$). It will not generate a trip response, if the pressure input is below or equal to the setpoint minus the deadband value. The deadband value is assumed to be positive (or else the tabular expression is ill-formed), and much smaller in value than the absolute value of the setpoint (or else it affects behaviour rather than simply reducing noise). The value of $c\_PressParmTrip$ does not change at all if the pressure input is in the deadband region. Note that, since the function value may be left unchanged, an initial value must be provided. In keeping with the safety priority of the system, the initial value in this case would be e_tripped.

---

[8] SDS2 uses diverse technologies to cause a reactor trip if SDS1 were to fail.

6.2   Design and Formal Translation

An example design (Fig. 3, Sect. 2.2) uses several built-in IEC 61131-3 FBs to specify the functional behaviour and uses a feedback connection for the hysteresis effect. It is important to note that the target PLC treats "de-energised" ("FALSE" = 0) as the safe state, therefore $c\_PressParmTrip = FALSE$ is equivalent to $c\_PressParmTrip = e\_tripped$.

For this example, we use the prototype translator to demonstrate our translation rules. Mapping this diagram to an abstract syntax is performed by preparing an ASCII input file and using a simple parser. We have implemented a function to modify block-to-block connections by introducing an additional "wire" variable. These variables are added to an attribute map and are used in the labels of a graph, as illustrated in Fig. 4.

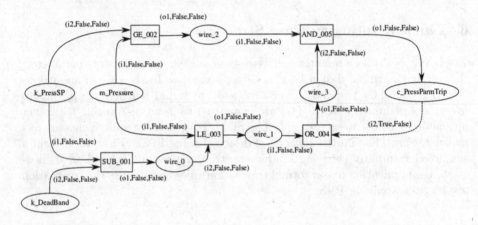

Fig. 4. Labelled directed graph for $c\_PressParmTrip$

The translation rules are further applied and the resulting PVS code is illustrated in Fig. 5. Using the input and output identification rules from Eqs. (25) and (26), inputs and outputs of the graph in Fig. 4 are respectively: $k\_PressSP$, $k\_DeadBand$, $m\_Pressure$, and $c\_PressParmTrip$. The existential identification rule from Eq. (27) yields the internal variables: $wire\_0$, $wire\_1$, $wire\_2$, and $wire\_4$. Lastly, the conjunction of internal blocks SUB, GE, LE, OR[9] and AND completes the expression as shown[10].

6.3   Verification

CE-1001-STD [7] specifies a set of complementary and overlapping verification processes, one of them being systematic design verification (SDV). The objective of SDV is to verify that all functions in the design are equivalent to their

---

[9] The underscore (....) is used for generated names that conflict with PVS keywords.
[10] The FBD is formalized over a discrete time series of equally distributed samplings, i.e., ticks. The *pre* operator returns the previous time sample.

```
c_PressParmTrip ( k_PressSP  : [ tick → DINT ] ,
                  k_DeadBand : [ tick → DINT ] ,
                  m_Pressure : [ tick → DINT ] ,
                  c_PressParmTrip : [ tick → BOOL ] )
                ( t : tick ) : bool =
  if init ( t ) then
  c_PressParmTrip ( t ) = false
  else
  exists ( wire0 : [ tick → DINT ] ,
           wire1 : [ tick → BOOL ] ,
           wire2 : [ tick → BOOL ] ,
           wire3 : [ tick → BOOL ] ) :
  AND_ ( wire2 ,
         wire3 ,
         c_PressParmTrip )( t ) and
  GE ( m_Pressure ,
       k_PressSP ,
       wire2 )( t ) and
  LE ( m_Pressure ,
       wire0 ,
       wire1 )( t ) and
  OR_ ( wire1 ,
        lambda ( t : noninit_elem ) :
        c_PressParmTrip ( pre ( t ) ) ,
        wire3 )( t ) and
  SUB ( k_PressSP ,
        k_DeadBand ,
        wire0 )( t )
  endif
```

Fig. 5. Generated PVS for *c_PressParmTrip*

corresponding functions in the requirements using mathematical techniques or rigorous argument. SDV uses a specialization of the four variable model [12] to confirm the satisfaction of Eq. (33).

$$OUT \circ SOF \circ IN \vdash REQ \tag{33}$$

For the purposes of our example, *REQ* is the TE from Fig. 2 plus other supporting information (not shown) that defines the monitored and controlled variables, the constants, and the enumerated types. *SOF* is the FBD from Fig. 3 plus other supporting information (not shown) that defines the input and output variables and constants used. *IN* and *OUT* are functions that translate monitored variables to input variables and output variables to controlled variables, respectively (an example of such a translation for *c_PressParmTrip* is shown in Sect. 6.2). Our verification was performed in PVS using *cond* expressions to specify the requirements [18]. We then created a PVS specification containing a theorem in the form of Eq. (33). By running PVS, we discovered an unprovable sequent that prevented us from discharging the proof. Upon investigation, we recognize the design failed to add a negation to the first input of the AND block. This is a clear demonstration of how formal verification detects subtle design flaws that could potentially result in unintended behaviour.

The application of the approach[11] for SDV on the DNGS SDS1 TC replacement project helped identify design pattern inconsistencies that led to an improved FBD-based design approach, uncovered inconsistencies in TEs that led to a more precise requirements specification, and identified an omitted conversion in the FBD for performing an average power calculation. PVS was used to verify all FBDs in the design, which accounted for 80 % of the overall SDV effort. Our approach was used to automatically discharge 70 % of the proof obligations. The most complicated FBD, a module with 20 FBs and 39 variables, and modules with real-time properties, required user interaction with PVS to discharge the proof.

7   Related Work

IEC 61131-3 provides definitions for five PLC languages[12] and various research work has produced formalization and verification of PLC programs. In terms of the formal verification of PLC programs written in these languages, there are typically two main approaches to prove or disprove the correctness of a design with respect to a certain formal requirements specification or required property: model checking and theorem proving.

In the case of model checking, [8] provides the formal verification of a safety procedure in a nuclear power plant (NPP) in which a verified Coloured Petri Net (CPN) model is derived by reinterpretation from the FBD description. [15] transforms FBD descriptions to its logically equivalent Uppaal models that perform the verification of safety applications in the industrial automation domain. [5] translates ST and FBD into a synchronized data-flow language SIGNAL to compile and reason about the verification of specifications. In the case of theorem proving, [3] uses Coq to check the correctness of SFC programs, which is automatically generated from a graphical front-end. [16] formalizes PLC programs using higher-order logic and uses HOL to discharge safety properties. Also, [14] presents an algebraic approach to verify PLC programs.

In the case of model checking, there is difficulty scaling up to industrial-size applications. In theorem proving, complex formalisms can be handled, but the process of proofs is not fully automated and adds additional overhead to industrial scale applications. Thus, the strengths and weaknesses for model checking and theorem proving are complementary. To balance this issue, our technique has been successfully used in an on-going nuclear industrial application, and it is

---

[11] The approach was qualified using a combination of trial use, inspection and acceptance testing.

[12] Function block diagram (FBD), structured text (ST), instruction list (IL), ladder diagram (LD) and sequential function chart (SFC).

novel in that: (1) we translate a FBD design to a formal PVS model; and (2) the resulting PVS model can be verified against TE-based requirements input to PVS.

8   Conclusion and Future Work

In this paper, we have extended the work presented in [10] with an industrial-scaled methodology for the systematic translation of FBD designs compliant with IEC 61131-3 into the PVS formal specification language. The approach was developed for OPG and is in current use as part of the verification of the DNGS SDS1 TCs. In combination with PVS, this work has proven effective in uncovering subtle inconsistencies in applying design patterns, inconsistencies in the requirements documented using TEs, and non-conformance between a FBD design and its requirements.

As on-going and future work, we first aim to improve our translation rules using PVS to provide more precision for potential tool designers. Secondly, we are currently formalizing proof scripts to increase the level of automation, which has potential application in other industrial domains, e.g., aerospace. Lastly, we plan to extend our formalization technique to other IEC 61131-3 compliant programming languages, e.g., Structured Text (ST).

Acknowledgements. We would like to thank OPG for their permitting us to describe the work related to the DNGS TC replacement project. The methodology and tools described herein are the property of OPG. Particularly we thank Ivan Dimitrov, Section Manager, Safety Related Computers, Computers and Control Design, and Mike Viola, SDS Replacement Project Manager, for their valued oversight and assistance. We would also like to thank Lucian Patcas for his thorough review.

References

1. IEEE 7–4.3.2: Standard for Digital Computers in Safety Systems of Nuclear Power Generating Stations (Revision of IEEE Std 7–4.3.2-2003). The Institute of Electrical and Electronics Engineers (IEEE) (2010)
2. DO-178C: Software Considerations in Airborne Systems and Equipment Certification. Special Committee 205 of RTCA (2011)
3. Blech, J.O., Biha, S.O.: On formal reasoning on the semantics of PLC using Coq. CoRR abs/1301.3047 (2013)
4. IEC: 61131–3 Ed. 3.0 en: 2013: Programmable Controllers – Part 3: Programming Languages. International Electrotechnical Commission (2013)
5. Jimenez-Fraustro, F., Rutten, E.: A synchronous model of IEC 61131 PLC languages in SIGNAL. In: Euromicro Conference On Real-Time Systems, pp. 135–142 (2001)
6. Jin, Y., Parnas, D.L.: Defining the meaning of tabular mathematical expressions. Sci. Comput. Program. **75**(11), 980–1000 (2010)

7. Joannou, P., Harauz, J., Viola, M., Cirjanic, R., Chan, D., Whittall, R., Tremaine, D., Moum, G.: Standard for Software Engineering of Safety Critical Software. CANDU Computer Systems Engineering Centre of Excellence Standard CE-1001-STD Rev. 3 (2014)

8. Németh, E., Bartha, T.: Formal verification of safety functions by reinterpretation of functional block based specifications. In: Cofer, D., Fantechi, A. (eds.) FMICS 2008. LNCS, vol. 5596, pp. 199–214. Springer, Heidelberg (2009)

9. Owre, S., Rushby, J.M., Shankar, N.: PVS: A prototype verification system. In: Kapur, D. (ed.) CADE 1992. LNCS, vol. 607, pp. 748–752. Springer, Heidelberg (1992)

10. Pang, L.: An Engineering Methodology for the Formal Verification of Function Block Based Systems. Ph.D. thesis. McMaster University, Department of Computing and Software (2015)

11. Pang, L., Wang, C., Lawford, M., Wassyng, A.: Formal verification of function blocks applied to IEC 61131-3. Sci. Comput. Program. **113**, 149–190 (2015)

12. Parnas, D.L., Madey, J.: Functional documents for computer systems. Sci. Comput. Program. **25**(1), 41–61 (1995)

13. Parnas, D.L., Madey, J., Iglewski, M.: Precise documentation of well-structured programs. IEEE Trans. Software Eng. **20**, 948–976 (1994)

14. Roussel, J.M., Faure, J.: An algebraic approach for PLC programs verification. In: 6th International Workshop on Discrete Event Systems, pp. 303–308 (2002)

15. Soliman, D., Thramboulidis, K., Frey, G.: Transformation of function block diagrams to Uppaal timed automata for the verification of safety applications. Annu. Rev. Control **36**, 338–345 (2012)

16. Völker, N., Krämer, B.J.: Automated verification of function block-based industrial control systems. Sci. Comput. Program. **42**(1), 101–113 (2002)

17. Wassyng, A., Janicki, R.: Tabular expressions in software engineering. In: International Conference on Software & System Engineering and their Applications, vol. 4, pp. 1–46 (2003)

18. Wassyng, A., Lawford, M.: Lessons learned from a successful implementation of formal methods in an industrial project. In: Araki, K., Gnesi, S., Mandrioli, D. (eds.) FME 2003. LNCS, vol. 2805, pp. 133–153. Springer, Heidelberg (2003)

Formal Analysis of Extended Well-Clear Boundaries for Unmanned Aircraft

César Muñoz$^{(\boxtimes)}$ and Anthony Narkawicz

NASA Langley Research Center, Hampton, VA 23681-2199, USA
{cesar.a.munoz,anthony.narkawicz}@nasa.gov

Abstract. This paper concerns the application of formal methods to the definition of a detect and avoid concept for unmanned aircraft systems (UAS). In particular, it illustrates how formal analysis was used to explain and correct unexpected behaviors of the logic that issues alerts when two aircraft are predicted not to be well clear from one another. As a result of this analysis, a recommendation was proposed to, and subsequently adopted by, the US standards organization that defines the minimum operational requirements for the UAS detect and avoid concept.

1 Introduction

One of the major challenges to the integration of Unmanned Aircraft Systems (UAS) into the NAS (National Aerospace System) is the lack of an on-board pilot to comply with US and international legal requirements [5,8]. In manned aircraft operations, on-board pilots have the responsibility for not "operating an aircraft so close to another aircraft as to create a collision hazard", "to see and avoid other aircraft", and when complying with the particular rules addressing right-of-way, on-board pilots "may not pass over, under, or ahead [of the right-of-way aircraft] unless well clear". To address the safety challenge and establish parallel requirements for UAS, the final report of the Federal Aviation Administration (FAA) Sense and Avoid (SAA) Workshop [3] defined the concept of *sense and avoid* as "the capability of a UAS to remain well clear from and avoid collisions with other airborne traffic." This concept, which is now called *detect and avoid*, has been proposed as a means of compliance with the preceding legal requirements.

In 2013, the RTCA organization established the Special Committee (SC) 228 to provide technical guidance to the FAA for defining minimum operational performance standards for the UAS detect and avoid concept, based on a quantitative definition of the well-clear boundary. The well-clear boundary adopted by RTCA SC-228 is defined by a Boolean formula based on the Resolution Advisory (RA) detection logic of the second generation of the Traffic Alerting and Collision Avoidance System (TCAS II) [2]. To accommodate sensor uncertainty and other conditions, the detect and avoid concept considered by RTCA SC-228

© Copyright 2016 U.S. Government, as represented by the Administrator of the National Aeronautics and Space Administration. No copyright is claimed in the United States under Title 17, U.S. Code. All Other Rights Reserved.

S. Rayadurgam and O. Tkachuk (Eds.): NFM 2016, LNCS 9690, pp. 221–226, 2016.
DOI: 10.1007/978-3-319-40648-0_17

allows for the use of extended well-clear boundaries in the logic that issues alerts when aircraft are predicted to lose well-clear status. This paper presents a formalization of extended well-clear boundaries and the verification of their main properties. In particular, it presents a novel result that explains and corrects a potentially unsafe property of extended well-clear boundaries when their threshold parameters are not properly set. The formal analysis presented in this paper resulted in a recommendation to RTCA SC-228 that has been adopted in the current draft of the Minimum Operational Requirements Standards (MOPS) for UAS.

The mathematical development in this paper has been conducted in the Prototype Verification System (PVS) [7]. For readability, this paper uses mathematical notation instead of concrete PVS syntax. For further information on this formal development, the reader is referred to the directory `WellClear` in the NASA PVS Library[1].

2   Well-Clear Boundary and Its Extensions

This paper considers two aircraft, called *ownship* and *intruder*, whose states are given by position and velocity vectors in a local East, North, Up (ENU) Cartesian coordinate system. Since it is notationally convenient, horizontal and vertical components of a three-dimensional vector are represented by a two-dimensional vector and a scalar, respectively, and these components are presented in a relative coordinate system where the intruder is at the origin and the ownship moves relative to the intruder.

The set of relative aircraft states that are in well-clear violation, i.e., inside the well-clear boundary, is defined as follows.

$$WCV(\mathbf{s}, s_z, \mathbf{v}, v_z) \equiv HWCV(\mathbf{s}, \mathbf{v}) \wedge VWCV(s_z, v_z), \tag{1}$$

where $\mathbf{s}, \mathbf{v} \in \mathbb{R}^2$ are the respective relative horizontal position and velocity vectors of the aircraft, and $s_z, v_z \in \mathbb{R}$ are the respective relative vertical positions and velocities. Informally, a well-clear violation, characterized by the predicate WCV, occurs when the aircraft are in horizontal violation, characterized by the predicate $HWCV$, and in vertical violation, characterized by the predicate $VWCV$. The horizontal and vertical violation predicates are defined as follows.

$$HWCV(\mathbf{s}, \mathbf{v}) \equiv \|\mathbf{s}\| \leq \texttt{DMOD} \vee (HMDF(\mathbf{s}, \mathbf{v}) \wedge 0 \leq \tau_{\mathrm{mod}}(\mathbf{s}, \mathbf{v}) \leq \texttt{TAUMOD}), \tag{2}$$

$$VWCV(s_z, v_z) \equiv |s_z| \leq \texttt{ZTHR} \vee 0 \leq t_{\mathrm{coa}}(s_z, v_z) \leq \texttt{TCOA}, \tag{3}$$

where `TAUMOD` and `DMOD` are horizontal time and distance thresholds, respectively, and `TCOA` and `ZTHR` are vertical time and distance thresholds, respectively. The predicate $HMDF$ is called the *horizontal miss-distance filter* and is defined as $HMDF(\mathbf{s}, \mathbf{v}) \equiv d_{\mathrm{cpa}}(\mathbf{s}, \mathbf{v}) \leq \texttt{HMD}$, where `HMD` is the horizontal miss-distance threshold and is usually set to the same value as `DMOD`. The distance function

---

[1] https://github.com/nasa/pvslib.

d_{cpa} computes the projected horizontal distance of the aircraft at their closest point of approach, assuming constant relative horizontal velocity, $\mathbf{v}$, and is formally defined as $d_{\text{cpa}}(\mathbf{s}, \mathbf{v}) \equiv \|\mathbf{s} + t_{\text{cpa}}(\mathbf{s}, \mathbf{v})\mathbf{v}\|$. The time function t_{cpa} is the time to closest point of approach, which is defined as $t_{\text{cpa}}(\mathbf{s}, \mathbf{v}) \equiv -\frac{\mathbf{s} \cdot \mathbf{v}}{\mathbf{v}^2}$, when $\|\mathbf{v}\| \neq 0$, and 0 otherwise. The time function τ_{mod}, called *modified tau*, was introduced in the TCAS II RA logic [4]. In the vector notation used in this paper, modified tau is defined as $\tau_{\text{mod}}(\mathbf{s}, \mathbf{v}) \equiv \frac{\text{DMOD}^2 - \mathbf{s}^2}{\mathbf{s} \cdot \mathbf{v}}$, when $\mathbf{s} \cdot \mathbf{v} < 0$, and -1 otherwise. The time function t_{coa} computes the time to co-altitude assuming constant relative vertical speed v_z. It is defined as $t_{\text{coa}}(s_z, v_z) \equiv -\frac{s_z}{v_z}$, when $s_z v_z < 0$, and -1 otherwise. The conditions $\mathbf{s} \cdot \mathbf{v} < 0$ and $s_z v_z < 0$ hold when the aircraft are horizontally converging and vertically converging, respectively.

For arbitrary values of DMOD, ZTHR, TAUMOD, and TCOA, with HMD = DMOD, Formula (1) satisfies several operational requirements [6]. The values of these thresholds recommended by the UAS SARP [2] and adopted by the RTCA SC-228 are DMOD = HMD = 4000ft, ZTHR = 450ft, TAUMOD = 35s, and TCOA = 0s. These values were chosen using a collision-risk analysis and acceptability metrics aimed to defining a well-clear boundary that is large enough to avoid safety concerns for controllers and see-and-avoid pilots, but small enough to avoid disruptions to traffic flow [1]. Furthermore, the detect and avoid concept considered by RTCA SC-228 only applies to certain types of UAS and in classes of airspace that are usually below 10,000 ft, that is, Class D, Class E, and perhaps Class G airspace.

The well-clear boundary defined by Formula (1) assumes perfect aircraft state information. To accomodate for uncertainty in the position and velocity information, the RTCA SC-228 requirements for the well-clear alerting logic allows for the use of a larger set of threshold values within some ranges. An *extended well-clear boundary* is characterized by a predicate WCV^* defined by Formula (1), but using parameters DMOD* $\geq$ DMOD, HMD* $\geq$ HMD, ZTHR* $\geq$ ZTHR, TAUMOD* $\geq$ TAUMOD, and TCOA* $\geq$ TCOA. The following property, which is proven in PVS, guarantees that the well-clear boundary, instantiated with standard threshold values, is safely included in any of its extensions.

Theorem 1 (Extension). *WCV is included in WCV^*, i.e., for all relative states $\mathbf{s}, s_z, \mathbf{v}, v_z$, $WCV(\mathbf{s}, s_z, \mathbf{v}, v_z) \implies WCV^*(\mathbf{s}, s_z, \mathbf{v}, v_z)$.*

3 An Unexpected Result When HMD* > DMOD*

In flight simulations at NASA, an unexpected behavior was observed in the alerting logic. In some converging, non-maneuvering encounters (i.e., aircraft flying converging straight line trajectories), alerts due to predicted violation of an extended well-clear boundary suddenly disappear before the closest-point of approach. This behavior was originally blamed on a possible coding error. To understand the actual explanation of this behavior, it is necessary to review the origins of the τ_{mod} function and the horizontal-miss distance filter in the TCAS II RA detection logic.

The definition of the UAS well-clear boundary in Sect. 2 closely follows the detection logic of the TCAS II RA algorithm[2]. However, while Formula (1) assumes state information in vector form, which is readily available through modern global positioning systems such as GPS, the family of TCAS devices assumes that aircraft are equipped with active transponders, which provide less precise aircraft state information. Earlier versions of the TCAS alerting logic used a simpler variant of Formula (2): $\|\mathbf{s}\| \leq \mathtt{DMOD} \vee 0 \leq \tau(\mathbf{s}, \mathbf{v}) \leq \mathtt{TAUMOD}$, where τ is defined as range over closure rate or, in vector form, $-\frac{\mathbf{s}^2}{\mathbf{s} \cdot \mathbf{v}}$ when $\mathbf{s} \cdot \mathbf{v} < 0$ and -1 otherwise.

Two problems may arise with use of the simpler variant of Formula (2). The first problem involves encounters with low closure rates. It holds that τ tends to positive infinity as the aircraft reach the closest point of approach, which is attained when the closure rate is 0, i.e., when $\mathbf{s} \cdot \mathbf{v} = 0$. TCAS II addresses this problem by using a modified version of τ, i.e., τ_{mod}. Both τ_{mod} and τ are approximations of time to closest point of approach, t_{cpa}. Indeed, it has been formally proven that for horizontally converging trajectories whose initial states are outside $\mathtt{DMOD}$, i.e., $\mathbf{s} \cdot \mathbf{v} < 0$, $\|\mathbf{s}\| > \mathtt{DMOD}$, and $d_{\mathrm{cpa}}(\mathbf{s}, \mathbf{v}) \leq \mathtt{DMOD}$, $\tau_{\mathrm{mod}}(\mathbf{s}, \mathbf{v}) \leq t_{\mathrm{cpa}}(\mathbf{s}, \mathbf{v}) \leq \tau(\mathbf{s}, \mathbf{v})$ [6]. In contrast to t_{cpa}, the computations of τ and τ_{mod} can be done without directional information. The second problem involves high closure rates with large miss distances, which creates a high rate of false RA alerts. TCAS II addresses this problem by employing a horizontal miss distance filter [4]. The idea behind the filter is to stop RA issuances when the projected future distance at the closest point of approach will be greater than a given distance $\mathtt{HMD}$. In TCAS II, the value $\mathtt{HMD}$ is set to be equal to $\mathtt{DMOD}$. The actual horizontal miss-distance filter in TCAS II employs a sophisticated parabolic range tracker to provide projected range, range rate, and range acceleration. Depending on the quality of the range rate estimate computed by the tracker and other conditions, the TCAS II RA system may disable the use of the horizontal miss distance filter. This is in contrast to the well-clear boundary definition where the horizontal miss-distance filter is never disabled. This may cause situations where aircraft are inside the TCAS II RA boundary, but not inside the well-clear boundary. Hence, in the case of the UAS detect and avoid concept, it is tempting to mitigate this problem by using an alerting logic with an extended well-clear boundary where $\mathtt{HMD}^* > \mathtt{DMOD}^*$.

One key property that can affect the properties of an extended well-clear boundary is whether τ_{mod}, as a function of time for a straight line relative trajectory, i.e., $\tau_{\mathrm{mod}} : t \to \tau_{\mathrm{mod}}(\mathbf{s} + t\mathbf{v}, \mathbf{v})$, is monotonically decreasing before closest point of approach. The following lemma, which is proven in PVS, provides a necessary and sufficient condition for the function τ_{mod} to be monotonically decreasing for straight line trajectories.

Lemma 1. *The function τ_{mod} is monotonically decreasing for straight line trajectories if and only if $\|\mathbf{s} + t\mathbf{v}\| \leq DMOD^*$ for some time t.*

---

[2] The TCAS II RA logic uses $\mathtt{TAUMOD}$ instead of $\mathtt{TCOA}$ in the vertical dimension.

Consider an extended well-clear boundary where $\mathtt{HMD}^* \leq \mathtt{DMOD}^*$. Note that this is actually the case in the current version of the TCAS II RA logic, where $\mathtt{HMD}^*$ is equal to $\mathtt{DMOD}^*$. If there is an alert, then there must be some t where $\|\mathbf{s}+t\mathbf{v}\| \leq \mathtt{HMD}^* \leq \mathtt{DMOD}^*$. By Lemma 1, this means that τ_{mod} is *always decreasing*. Its graph is shaped as in Fig. 1. In this case, the following theorem, which is proven in PVS, holds.

Theorem 2 (Convergence). *An extended well-clear boundary where $\mathtt{HMD}^* \leq \mathtt{DMOD}^*$ is convergent, i.e., for all relative states $\mathbf{s}, s_z, \mathbf{v}, v_z$, with $\mathbf{s}\cdot\mathbf{v} \leq 0$, $s_z v_z \leq 0$, and either $v_z = 0$ or $s_z \neq 0$, if $WCV^*(\mathbf{s}, s_z, \mathbf{v}, v_z)$ then for all $0 \leq t \leq t^*$, $WCV^*(\mathbf{s}+t\mathbf{v}, s_z + tv_z, \mathbf{v}, v_z)$, where t^* is $t_{cpa}(\mathbf{s}, \mathbf{v})$ if $v_z = 0$, $t_{coa}(s_z, v_z)$ if $\mathbf{v} = 0$, and, in any other case, $\min(t_{cpa}(\mathbf{s}, \mathbf{v}), t_{coa}(s_z, v_z))$.*

The convergence property guarantees that, in a non-maneuvering encounter, a violation of an extended well-clear boundary, where $\mathtt{HMD}^* \leq \mathtt{DMOD}^*$, never disappears before closest point of approach.

On the other hand, when $\mathtt{HMD}^* > \mathtt{DMOD}^*$, there are cases where $\|\mathbf{s} + t\mathbf{v}\| > \mathtt{DMOD}^*$ for every possible value of t but where $\|\mathbf{s} + t\mathbf{v}\| < \mathtt{HMD}^*$ for some t. Thus, there is some time region where τ_{mod} is increasing. In fact, just before closest point of approach, the numerator of τ_{mod} is negative and its denominator is both negative and *approaching negative infinity*. This case is illustrated in Fig. 2. This observation leads to the following theorem, which is also proven in PVS.

Theorem 3. *If $\mathtt{HMD}^* > \mathtt{DMOD}^*$, then there exist relative vectors $\mathbf{s}, \mathbf{v}$ such that $d_{cpa}(\mathbf{s}, \mathbf{v}) < \mathtt{HMD}^*$, $\mathbf{s} \cdot \mathbf{v} < 0$, and $d_{cpa}(\mathbf{s}, \mathbf{v}) > \mathtt{DMOD}^*$. In these situations, the value of $\tau_{\mathrm{mod}}(t)$ tends to positive infinity as the aircraft reach the closest point of approach.*

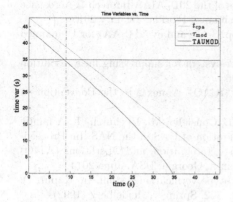

Fig. 1. Case $\mathtt{HMD}^* \leq \mathtt{DMOD}^*$

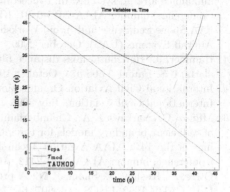

Fig. 2. Case $\mathtt{HMD}^* > \mathtt{DMOD}^*$

From an operational point of view, a negative consequence of Theorem 3 is that in a non-maneuvering encounter where $\mathtt{HMD}^* > \mathtt{DMOD}^*$, a violation of an extended well-clear boundary may disappear before the aircraft have reached the closest point of approach. In this case, an alerting logic that protects against such an extended well-clear boundary may unexpectedly stop issuing alerts before the aircraft reach the closest point of approach.

4   Conclusion

This paper reported on the application of formal methods, in particular interactive theorem proving in PVS, to the analysis of extended well-clear boundaries based on the TCAS II alerting logic. In particular, it has been formally proven that an extended well-clear boundary is convergent if $\mathtt{HMD}^* \leq \mathtt{DMOD}^*$. Furthermore, the analysis explains why, when $\mathtt{HMD}^* > \mathtt{DMOD}^*$, an alerting logic that protects against such an extended boundary may stop issuing alerts before the aircraft reach the closest point of approach. To the knowledge of the authors, there has been no prior report and explanation of this result. As result of this analysis, the authors recommended to RTCA SC-228 that when an extended well-clear boundary is used by a detect and avoid algorithm, the value of $\mathtt{HMD}^*$ is set to $\mathtt{DMOD}^*$ (the case $\mathtt{HMD}^* < \mathtt{DMOD}^*$ is not operationally interesting). This recommendation has been accepted and is part of the current draft of the RTCA SC-228 MOPS for UAS.

References

1. Consiglio, M., Chamberlain, J., Muñoz, C., Hoffler, K.: Concept of integration for UAS operations in the NAS. In: Proceedings of 28th International Congress of the Aeronautical Sciences, ICAS 2012, Brisbane, Australia (2012)
2. Cook, S.P., Brooks, D., Cole, R., Hackenberg, D., Raska, V.: Defining well clear for unmanned aircraft systems. In: Proceedings of the 2015 AIAA Infotech @ Aerospace Conference, number AIAA-2015-0481, Kissimmee, Florida, January 2015
3. FAA Sponsored Sense and Avoid Workshop. Sense and avoid (SAA) for Unmanned Aircraft Systems (UAS), October 2009
4. Hammer, J.: Horizontal miss distance filter system for suppressing false resolution alerts, U.S. Patent 5,566,074, October 1996
5. International Civil Aviation Organization (ICAO). Annex 2 to the Convention on International Civil Aviation, July 2005
6. Muñoz, C., Narkawicz, A., Chamberlain, J., Consiglio, M., Upchurch, J.: A family of well-clear boundary models for the integration of UAS in the NAS. In: Proceedings of the 14th AIAA Aviation Technology, Integration, and Operations (ATIO) Conference, number AIAA-2014-2412, Atlanta, Georgia, USA, June 2014
7. Owre, S., Rushby, J., Shankar, N.: A prototype verification system. In: Kapur, D. (ed.) CADE 1992. LNCS, vol. 607, pp. 748–752. Springer, Heidelberg (1992)
8. US Code of Federal Regulations. Title 14 Aeronautics and Space; Part 91 General operating and fight rules (1967)

Formal Validation and Verification Framework for Model-Based and Adaptive Control Systems

Sergio Guarro[1(✉)], Umit Ozguner[2], Tunc Aldemir[2], Matt Knudson[3], Arda Kurt[2], Michael Yau[1], Mohammad Hejase[2], and Steve Kwon[2]

[1] ASCA, Inc., Redondo Beach, CA, USA
{sergio.guarro,mike.yau}@ascainc.com
[2] Ohio State University, Columbus, OH, USA
{ozguner.1,aldemir.1,kurt.12,hejase.1,
kwon.317}@osu.edu
[3] NASA Ames Research Center, Moffett Field, CA, USA
matt.knudson@nasa.gov

Abstract. This paper presents the interim results of a three-year NASA project for the development of a comprehensive framework for the validation and verification (V&V) of model-based control systems and adaptive control systems (MBCSs/ACSs), with focus on Unmanned Aircraft Systems (UAS) applications. The framework applies a formal V&V methodology based on a combination of logic-dynamic model constructs and associated analysis processes, to support the generation of a documentable assurance case for a UAS control system, and to demonstrate its compliance with applicable aviation system certification standards.

Keywords: Validation and verification · Safety case · Model based control system · Adaptive control system · Unmanned aircraft system

1 Introduction

As part of the NASA System-Wide Safety and Assurance Technologies (SSAT) Project, the Ames Research Center (ARC) is sponsoring research directed at developing advanced V&V techniques for model based control systems (MBCSs) and adaptive control systems (ACSs), including system applications for use in UASs. Within these activities, the research presented in this paper seeks to develop a practically oriented and risk-informed MBCS/ACS V&V approach, and characterize it in relation to the current certification process for aeronautic control systems and software [1]. The concept being developed utilizes time-dependent multi-valued discrete logic models, and fits within the framework of an assurance case. The concept is being tested using case studies of progressively increasing complexity.

Section 2 provides a brief overview of the assurance case framework and the underlying time-dependent multi-valued logic models. Section 3 presents the development of the case studies, Sect. 4 discusses the demonstration of the multi-valued

© Springer International Publishing Switzerland 2016
S. Rayadurgam and O. Tkachuk (Eds.): NFM 2016, LNCS 9690, pp. 227–233, 2016.
DOI: 10.1007/978-3-319-40648-0_18

logic tools, Sect. 5 describes the ongoing and future work, Sect. 6 provides a summary and conclusions.

2 Validation and Verification Framework Concept

The V&V framework fits within the Goal Structure Notation (GSN) "safety case" architecture developed by researchers at the NASA Ames Research Center (ARC) [2]. In this framework, compliance with overall safety goals is demonstrated by identifying and addressing the significant hazard and risk scenarios arising from all aspects of UAS operation, each decomposed in progressively greater levels of detail. "Interim" safety cases are constructed in the early design phases with specification information, and refined into final form as design/implementation details become available. The preliminary concept for constructing a Risk Informed Safety Case (RISC) under the GSN framework is shown in Fig. 1. Hazards and risk scenarios associated with each UAS operational-phase and function are systematically identified in top-down fashion. Proof of their control or mitigation to compliance level is then prioritized and provided using the time-dependent multi-valued logic tools Dynamic Flowgraph Methodology (DFM) and Markov Cell-to-Cell Mapping Technique (CCMT), as discussed in Sect. 4. DFM and Markov CCMT models can be constructed to a level of detail consistent with stage of system design development and corresponding data availability. Accordingly, the V&V framework can be applied for early or detailed design validation, or for system verification.

A significant subset of the system and software V&V activities discussed in the DO-178C certification standard [1] can be accomplished with the DFM/Markov CCMT-supported safety case framework. This subset of software verification activities includes: (1) validation of high-level requirements, (2) validation of low-level requirements, (3) verification of software source code, (4) software testing, and (5) verification of test coverage. These findings have been fully documented in the project annual report submitted to NASA [3].

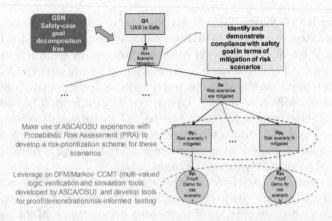

Fig. 1. Risk informed safety case development within the GSN framework

3 Case Study Design Specification and Development

The feasibility of the V&V framework concept is being demonstrated using UAS case studies that include simulators of "next generation" UASs and associated MBCSs, executing representative missions in progressive level of complexity. A simulator is made up of several components with tasks assigned to each of them:

- A ground control station defines mission scenarios and handles data logging and visualization.
- A model-based flight executive issues set-points for the autopilot and responds to scenario contexts and conditions, including possible hazards and threats.
- An autopilot works at achieving the set-points and risk-response maneuvers generated by the flight executive while maintaining UAS stability.
- A Flight Dynamics Model emulates the real behavior of a UAS.

The flight executive was designed and developed using a top down approach, decomposing the mission management from the overall "successful mission execution" objective, down to a sequential set of clearly defined tasks for the flight executive to achieve under pre-identified conditions, which also include risk-prioritized off-nominal and hazard scenarios. A system functional hierarchy (SFH) of goals and tasks, reflecting the main phases of the mission – e.g., Take-Off, Waypoint Following, and Landing – was formulated and designed using the procedure described by [4], to arrange the mission decision making and scenario-resolution process into a hierarchical tree. A Finite State Machine (FSM) was then constructed using the end nodes of the functional hierarchy. The FSM defines a mission in terms of the transitions between mission phases and corresponding flight maneuvers the UAS may go through, and identifies the functions of the flight executive that controls such transitions and chooses the corresponding flight maneuvers at the higher level. At a lower level, an autopilot consisting of multiple closed-loop controllers uses the set-points and controller parameters generated by the flight executive to carry out maneuvers and control UAS states.

In the first year of research, a 2-dimensional (2-D) simulator was designed and constructed to demonstrate the feasibility of the design validation portion of the V&V concept. A nonlinear longitudinal model was used to represent the 2-D simplified UAS behavior. The 2-D equations of motion are mainly based on the ones in [5], with the addition of the ground effects that occur in the Take Off and Landing phases. The development of a more realistic and higher fidelity 3-D simulator has also been partially completed. These simulators are also documented in [3].

4 Demonstration of Formal Multi-valued Logic Tools

As discussed earlier in Sect. 2, time-dependent multi-valued logic tools, namely DFM and Markov CCMT, are used to produce evidence in support of a "safety case". The following steps for implementing this MBCS Logic-Dynamic Model V&V framework were formulated, as also illustrated by Fig. 2:

1. Define the nominal system functional hierarchy (SFH) of the control system,
2. Translate the SFH into a FSM model (without off-nominal response actions),
3. Augment the FSM model with off-nominal contingency and emergency actions corresponding to a prioritized list of significant hazard and risk scenarios.
4. Develop an event tree model with pivotal events that include all the nominal, as well as the pre-identified contingency and emergency actions,
5. Expand the pivotal events with DFM and Markov models for detailed analysis,
6. Analyze the DFM and Markov models to produce evidence of control action coverage of the prioritized risk scenarios that have been identified.

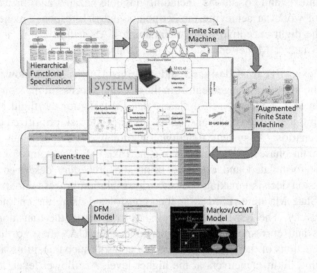

Fig. 2. MBCS logic-dynamic model framework process steps

4.1 Dynamic Flowgraph Methodology Modeling and Analysis

DFM were developed in the mid-90 s and refined over time, and currently are implemented in a software tool [6]. They are visually constructed in digraph form, with nodes representing variables and parameters within a given system, and edges representing, deterministic and/or probabilistically, the time-dependent cause-effect and physical relations among such parameters. The basic combination of DFM elements that represents a system physical or control relation can be expressed mathematically in the form given below:

$$\lfloor V^{out} @t = 0 \rfloor \Leftarrow \left\{ \lfloor V_1^{in} @t = -x_1 \rfloor, \ldots, \lfloor V_N^{in} @t = -x_N \rfloor \right\}, \tag{1}$$

where: $\lfloor V^{out} @t = 0 \rfloor$ is the state of an "output parameter" at the current time t = 0 and $\lfloor V_i^{in} @t = -x_j \rfloor$ is the state of the i-th "input parameter" an integer j number of discrete time steps before the current time.

In the early-design validation demonstration, DFM models of the 2-D UAS and control simulator implementation of the FSM mission sequence phases, including hazard and risk scenarios within the assumed control system "design envelope," were constructed and analyzed (Step 5 of V&V process summarized above). As an example, one of these models represented the UAS during the "accelerate to take off velocity" segment of the Take Off phase, and was analyzed via the automated DFM deductive-inductive engine to prove correctness of the UAS control system behavior under nominal and risk-scenario response conditions.

The validation of system design is supported by DFM analyses in two complementary modes, to prove that:

1. As-designed behavior is accomplished by UAS control system actions in nominal conditions and in response to "recoverable failures" and off-nominal conditions within the system design envelope.
2. Undesirable behavior cannot be caused by UAS control system actions, but only by failures and off-nominal conditions within the system design envelope.

For example, DFM analyses validated the correctness of the flight control software design specification addressing an engine thrust loss during the takeoff run, i.e., a reduction of thrust and application of brakes commanded by the control executive to abort the takeoff and bring the UAS to an off-nominal runway stop.

4.2   Markov/Cell-to-Cell Mapping Technique Modeling and Analysis

The Markov/Cell-to-Cell-Mapping (CCMT) technique [7] represents system evolution in time through a series of discrete-time transitions among computational cells V_j that partition the system state space in a manner similar to finite difference or finite element methods. System state is defined in terms of the system location in the partitioned state space, corresponding to specific hardware/software/firmware configurations and time-dependent evolution. The cells V_j can be regarded as accounting for the uncertainty in the location of the system state at a given point in time. System transition among V_j is represented in terms of probabilities determined from a model describing the dynamic behavior of the system and the system hardware/firmware/software states.

Similar to the DFM demonstration summarized above, a Markov/CCMT model was constructed per V&V Step 5, to represent in further detail the behavior of the UAS during takeoff acceleration. This model used a 6-parameter vector to represent the process variables (such as velocity, position, etc.) and a 4-state parameter to represent the engine states. The model was interfaced with the 2-D simulator (Sect. 3) to determine the transition probabilities in the UAS dynamic behavior. An automated scenario backtracking process was implemented to identify conditions in preceding time steps that lead to any undesirable outcomes, and prove that such conditions do not include control system erroneous specs or faults.

5 Ongoing and Future Work

In the second year of research, the case study is being expanded into a full 3-dimension (3-D), 6-degrees-of-freedom definition, to test the scalability of the design validation concept and the implementation of the system verification portion of the V&V framework. The 3-D includes system dynamics based on general nonlinear equations of motion [8]. A version of this simulator can alternatively interface with the commercial grade JSBSim software integrated with Simulink for higher fidelity dynamics.

In parallel, as the 3-D versions of the UAS simulator become available, the DFM and Markov/CCMT analyses are being expanded and coupled with the latter to fully demonstrate via a systematic set of inductive/deductive analysis test cases, the logic-dynamic V&V framework capability to validate the design specifications and verify the fully simulated system behavior.

In project final year, the V&V process will be adapted and demonstrated for application to UAS adaptive control systems (ACSs).

6 Summary and Conclusions

With the present and future foreseeable growth in the use of model-based and adaptive control paradigms, tools and methods are needed to support demonstration of compliance of control system designs developed according to these paradigms with certification processes such as DO-178C. The V&V framework presented here addresses this need by linking a logic set of design V&V processes and models within the GSN safety case architecture. Preliminary design validation case-study tests indicate the feasibility of this approach. Full design validation and scalability evaluation are currently being executed.

Acknowledgements. The presented work is sponsored by a 3-year project funded by the NASA Ames Research Center. The authors would like to thank the sponsor for this support.

References

1. RTCA: DO-178C, Software Considerations in Airborne Systems and Equipment Certification (2011)
2. Denney, E., Pai, G., Whiteside, I.: Formal foundations for hierarchical safety cases. In: Proceedings of the 16th IEEE International Symposium on High Assurance Systems Engineering (2015)
3. ASCA, Inc.: Development of Framework for the Validation and Verification of Model-Based and Adaptive Control System, Interim Annual Report for Year 1 (2015)
4. Ozguner, U.: Coordination of hierarchical systems. In: Proceedings of the 5th IEEE International Symposium on Intelligent Control, vol. 1, pp. 2–7 (1990)
5. Espinoza, T., Dzul, A., Llama, M.: Linear and nonlinear controllers applied to fixed-wing UAV. Int. J. Adv. Robot. Syst. **10**, 33 (2013)

6. Guarro, S., Yau, M., Dixon, S.: Applications of the dynamic flowgraph methodology to dynamic modeling and analysis. In: Proceedings of the 11th International Conference on Probabilistic Safety Assessment and Management (PSAM 11) (2012)
7. U.S. Nuclear Regulatory Commission: A Benchmark Implementation of Two Dynamic Methodologies for the Reliability Modeling of Digital Instrumentation and Control Systems, NUREG/CR-6985, Washington, D.C. (2009)
8. Fossen, T.I.: Mathematical models for control of aircraft and satellites, Department of Engineering Cybernetics Norwegian University of Science and Technology (2011)

Techniques for Automated Verification

Verifying Relative Safety, Accuracy, and Termination for Program Approximations

Shaobo He[1]([✉]), Shuvendu K. Lahiri[2], and Zvonimir Rakamarić[1]

[1] University of Utah, Salt Lake City, UT, USA
{shaobo,zvonimir}@cs.utah.edu
[2] Microsoft Research, Redmond, WA, USA
shuvendu@microsoft.com

Abstract. Approximate computing is an emerging area for trading off the accuracy of an application for improved performance, lower energy costs, and tolerance to unreliable hardware. However, developers must ensure that the leveraged approximations do not introduce significant, intolerable divergence from the reference implementation, as specified by several established robustness criteria. In this work, we show the application of automated differential verification towards verifying relative safety, accuracy, and termination criteria for a class of program approximations. We use mutual summaries to express *relative* specifications for approximations, and SMT-based invariant inference to automate the verification of such specifications. We perform a detailed feasibility study showing promise of applying automated verification to the domain of approximate computing in a cost-effective manner.

1 Introduction

Continuous improvements in per-transistor speed and energy efficiency are fading, while we face increasingly important concerns of power and energy consumption, along with ambitious performance goals. The emerging area of *approximate computing* aims at lowering the computational effort (e.g., energy and runtime) of an application through controlled (small) deviations from the intended results [15,32,34,35]. These studies illustrate a large class of applications (e.g., machine learning, web search, multimedia, sensor data processing) that can tolerate small approximations without significantly compromising quality. Low-level approximation mechanisms include, for example, approximating digital logic elements, arithmetic, or sensor readings; high-level mechanisms include approximating loop computations, generating multiple approximate candidate implementations, or leveraging neural networks.

There is a growing need to develop *formal* and *automated* techniques that allow approximate computing trade-offs to be explored by developers. Prior research has ranged from the use of type systems [35], to static analyses [6], and interactive theorem provers [5] to study the effects of approximations while also providing various correctness guarantees. While these techniques have significantly increased the potential to employ approximate computing in practice,

© Springer International Publishing Switzerland 2016
S. Rayadurgam and O. Tkachuk (Eds.): NFM 2016, LNCS 9690, pp. 237–254, 2016.
DOI: 10.1007/978-3-319-40648-0_19

a drawback is that they often either lack the required level of precision or degree of automation.

In this work, we describe the application of SMT-based (Satisfiability Modulo Theories [2]) automated *differential program verifiers* [3,13] for specifying and verifying properties of approximations. Such verifiers (e.g., SymDiff [17,18]) leverage SMT solvers to check assertions and semi-automatically infer intermediate program invariants over a pair of programs. We describe three broad classes of approximation robustness criteria that are amenable to SMT-based automated checking: *relative safety*, *relative accuracy*, and *relative termination*. Relative safety criteria ensure that approximations preserve a set of generic (program agnostic) properties. For example, *relative assertion safety* [5,18] ensures that the approximation does not introduce any new assertion failures over the base program (e.g., it is desirable to ensure that an approximation does not introduce an array out of bound access). Similarly, *relative control flow safety* ensures that the approximation does not influence the control flow of a program [35]. Relative accuracy criteria specify the acceptable difference between precise and approximate outputs for specific approximations [5]. In addition to these established criteria, we propose the concept of relative termination [8,13] as another important (program-agnostic) criterion for ensuring robustness of approximations. Intuitively, relative termination ensures that the approximation (such as loop perforation) does not change a terminating execution to a non-terminating one. We illustrate these on a few concrete examples next.

1.1   Motivating Examples

Relative Assertion Safety. Figure 1 describes two implementations of a string copy procedure: Strcpy is the precise version and StrcpyApprox is the approximate one. The approximate version implements a variant of *loop perforation* (a well-known approximation technique [22]) that only copies every other element from src to dst. The changes are highlighted using the underlined statements. The original program scans the src array until a designated end marker (0 in this example) is encountered, and copies the elements to the dst array. The approximation

```
var src:[int]int, srcLen:int;          procedure StrcpyApprox() {
var dst:[int]int, dstLen:int;            var i:int; var j:int;
                                         i := 0; j := 0;
procedure Strcpy() {
  var i:int;                             while(src[i] != 0) {
  i := 0;                                  assert i<srcLen && j<dstLen;
                                           dst[j] := src[i];
  while(src[i] != 0) {                     i := i + 1; j := j + 1;
    assert i<srcLen && i<dstLen;          if (src[i] == 0) { break; }
    dst[i] := src[i];                      i := i + 1;
    i := i + 1;                          }
  }                                      dst[j] := 0;
  dst[i] := 0;                         }
}
```

Fig. 1. Approximating string copy.

introduces a fresh index variable j for indexing dst and increments i twice every iteration (unless the loop exit condition is true).

The memory safety of the program is ensured by a set of implicit assertions that guard for out-of-bound access of the arrays (e.g., **assert** i < srcLen before the access src[i]) — we only show a subset of assertions in the example. The bounds srcLen and dstLen are additional parameters to represent the bounds of the arrays. It is not hard to see that the base program Strcpy satisfies memory safety under some non-trivial preconditions. For example, a caller needs to ensure that src contains 0 within its bounds, and that the dst array has enough capacity to copy src. In addition, the client needs to ensure that the value of srcLen (resp. dstLen) is within the runtime bounds of the src (resp. dst) array — such bounds are not readily available for low-level languages such as C. In other words, the proof of (absolute) array bound safety of Strcpy requires access to additional runtime state for bounds, non-trivial preconditions, and loop invariants for the loop.

On the contrary, it is relatively simple to establish that the approximate version StrcpyApprox is *relative assertion safe* with respect to Strcpy. We provide an *almost* automatic proof using a differential verifier[1], without access to additional runtime states or preconditions (Sect. 5). The intuition is that the approximation StrcpyApprox does not access any *additional* indices that could not be accessed in Strcpy. At the same time, the complexity of the example (loop exit condition depends on array content) and approximation (introducing a **break** statement) makes it difficult for any existing static-analysis-based approaches (e.g., [22,35]) to ensure the safety of the approximation.

Relative Termination. Just like preserving assertions, preserving terminating executions is an important criteria for almost any approximation. In other words, if an input leads to a terminating execution on the precise program, one needs to ensure that the approximation does introduce a non-terminating behavior. Consider again procedure StrcpyApprox from Fig. 1, and let us assume unbounded integers (i and j) and unbounded arrays (src and dst). Let us also assume that assertion failure does not terminate the program. In such a case, the base version Strcpy only terminates for those inputs where src has 0 as its element — other inputs may cause non-termination. It is desirable to ensure that StrcpyApprox at least terminates on all such inputs. For example, if the line i := i + 1 is (mistakenly) replaced with i := i - 1, the verifier should reject the approximation.

Similar to the proof of (absolute) assertion safety for Strcpy, a proof of (absolute) termination would require (i) a non-trivial existentially quantified precondition about the existence of 0 and (ii) a ranking function relating i with the first index containing 0, among other ingredients. We show that we are able to avoid these complexities by reasoning about relative termination [13], instead of establishing each program terminates in isolation.

---

[1] We required the user to provide a simple additional predicate and unroll the first loop once.

```
var str:[int]int, x:int, y:int;          tmp := str[i];
procedure ReplaceChar() {                 havoc tmp;
  call Helper(0);                         str[i] := tmp==x ? y : tmp;
}                                         call Helper(i+1);
procedure Helper(i:int) {               }
  var tmp:int;                          }
  if (str[i] != 0) {
```

Fig. 2. Replacing a character in a string.

Control Flow Safety. The program in Fig. 2 replaces a given character x with y in a character array str. The procedure Helper iterates over indices of the array until the termination character (0 in this case) is reached. Consider the approximation of the variable tmp indicated by the underlined statement — this models a case where the variable tmp is stored in an *unreliable memory* that may trade off cost for accuracy [24]. Approximating statements that impact control flow often leads to serious problems such as unacceptably high corruptions in output data and program crashes. Hence, preservation of control flow has been identified as a natural and useful relaxed specification for approximations [35]. Since tmp flows into str that controls the conditional, a standard dataflow-based analysis would mark the approximation as unsafe.

However, observe that the fragment of the array that stores the value in tmp in fact never participates in the conditional. Our approach leverages differential verification to check for control flow safety, which allows for precise analysis (Sect. 3.2). Interestingly, we formalize the concept that an approximation does not affect control as a pair of incomparable relative properties: (i) a relative safety property that all pairs of terminating executions follow same control flow sequence (Sect. 3.2), and (ii) a relative termination property that the sets of terminating executions are identical in the two programs.

1.2   Our Approach and Contributions

In this paper, we perform a *feasibility study* of using a differential verifier (Sect. 2) for expressing and verifying various relative specifications related to approximations (Sect. 3). We are the first to propose and demonstrate the idea of *relative termination* to the problem of verifying approximations. We leverage and extend the SymDiff infrastructure [13,17,18] to express and verify these specifications. We describe some of the extensions needed to improve the automation for the benchmarks we considered (Sect. 4). Overall, our verifier requires less than 1 manually supplied predicate on average to verify the safety of the approximations (Sect. 5). This is due to the fact that most proofs require relatively simple 2-program relational properties, as opposed to complex program-specific invariants. Our results give us confidence to apply the prototype on original source code written in languages such as C and Java, to serve as an independent validator for approximations introduced by approximate compilers (i.e., translation validation [23] for approximate compilers such as ACCEPT [35]).

2   Background

2.1   Programs

A program $P \in Programs$ consists of a set of procedures in $Procedures$ and a
set of global variables. Each procedure $p \in Procedures$ contains a list of input
and output parameters, local variables, and a *body*. A body for a procedure
p is an acyclic control flow graph with a set of nodes $Nodes_p$ and $Edges_p \subseteq
Nodes_p \times Nodes_p$, with an entry node $n_p^e \in Nodes_p$ and an exit node $n_p^x \in Nodes_p$.
Each node $n \in Nodes_p$ in the control flow graph contains one of the following
statements in $Stmts$:

$$s, t \in Stmts ::= \textbf{skip} \mid \textbf{assume } e \mid \textbf{assert } e \mid \textbf{havoc } x \mid$$
$$x := e \mid \textbf{call } x_1, \ldots x_k := q(e_1, \ldots, e_n)$$

where x, x_i represent program variables and $e, e_i \in Exprs$ are *expressions*. The
precise set of types of variables and the expression language are left unspecified.
Types include Booleans and integers, while expressions are built up using constants, interpreted (e.g. arithmetic and relational operations) or uninterpreted
functions. Arrays are modeled using interpreted functions *select* and *update* from
the logical theory of arrays [2].

We only sketch the semantics for the statements here — the semantics of
programs is built up using semantics of statements over control flow graphs and
is fairly standard [1]. A *state* $\sigma \in \Sigma$ is an assignment of values to variables in
scope. To model assertions, we introduce a ghost Boolean global variable OK,
and model **assert** e as an assignment $OK := OK \wedge e$. A state $\sigma \in \Sigma$ for which
OK evaluates to **false** under σ is termed as an *error state*. Each statement
$s \in Stmts$ defines a transition relation $\|s\| \subseteq \Sigma \times \Sigma$, where **skip** represents the
identity relation and $(\sigma, \sigma) \in \|\textbf{assume } e\|$ if σ evaluates the Boolean expression
e to **true**. Moreover, $(\sigma, \sigma') \in \|x := e\|$ if σ' is obtained by updating the value of
variable x with the valuation of e in σ. Similarly, $(\sigma, \sigma') \in \|\textbf{havoc } x\|$ if σ' and
σ agree on the value of all variables except x. The semantics of a call statement
is standard — it pushes the caller state on a *call stack*, executes the callee q with
values of e_i as inputs, and upon termination pops the call stack and updates x_i
variables with values of outputs of q. We denote a node n containing a call to q
as a callsite of q. Conditional statements are encoded using **assume** and **skip**
statements on the control flow graph [1]; loops are encoded using tail-recursive
procedures.

An *execution* is a sequence $\langle (n_0, \sigma_0), \ldots, (n_i, \sigma_i), \ldots \rangle$ where either (i)
$(n_i, n_{i+1}) \in Edges_p$ (for some p) and $(\sigma_i, \sigma_{i+1}) \in \|s_i\|$ where s_i is a non-call
statement at n_i, or (ii) n_i is a callsite of q, n_{i+1} equals n_q^e (the entry node of q),
and σ_{i+1} is the input state of q obtained from the caller state σ_i, or (iii) n_i is n_q^x
(the exit node of q), n_{i+1} is the unique successor of the corresponding callsite of
q, and σ_{i+1} is the caller state (after the call) obtained from the output state σ_i.
For each procedure p, we define its input-output transition relation $\mathscr{T}_p$ as the
set of pairs (σ, σ') such that there is an execution of p starting in input state σ
(with an empty call stack) and terminating in output state σ' (with an empty

call stack). For the rest of the paper, we assume that we are given two versions $P_1, P_2 \in Programs$ of a program with disjoint sets of procedures and globals. We distinguish components of the two versions using subscripts 1 and 2 respectively.

2.2 Mutual Summary Specifications

Given two procedures $p_1 \in P_1$ and $p_2 \in P_2$, we define a *2-program input-output expression* as an expression over inputs and outputs of p_1 and p_2. The inputs can refer to the input parameters and globals (within an **old**(e) subexpression where the construct **old** evaluates the subexpression at procedure entry), and outputs can refer to the output parameters and globals. For example, if g_i refers to global variables, x_i (resp. y_i) refers to input (resp. output) parameters of a pair of procedures p_1, p_2, the expression $\neg (\mathbf{old}(g_1 \leq g_2) \wedge x_1 \leq x_2 \wedge g_1 + y_1 > g_2 + y_2)$ is a 2-program input-output expression relating inputs and outputs of p_1 and p_2. Given such a 2-program input-output expression e, and two pairs of input-output states $(\sigma_1, \sigma_1') \in \mathscr{T}_{p_1}$ and $(\sigma_2, \sigma_2') \in \mathscr{T}_{p_2}$, the value of e is obtained by evaluating the inputs (resp. outputs) of f_i under σ_i (resp. σ_i').

Definition 1 (Mutual Summary [13]). *Given two procedures $p_1 \in P_1$ and $p_2 \in P_2$, a 2-program input-output Boolean expression e is a mutual summary for p_1, p_2 if the value of e evaluates to* **true** *for every pair of input-output states in $\mathscr{T}_{p_1} \times \mathscr{T}_{p_2}$.*

We use mutual summaries to express relative safety and accuracy specifications over two programs. Intuitively, a mutual summary is a summary (or postcondition) for the product procedure over the pair of procedures p_1, p_2.

2.3 Relative Termination Specifications

Given two procedures $p_1 \in P_1$ and $p_2 \in P_2$, we define a *2-program input expression* as an expression over inputs of p_1 and p_2. Such expressions do not contain **old**(e) since they may only refer to the input globals. The expression $(g_1 \leq g_2 \wedge x_1 = x_2)$ is an example of a 2-program input expression relating inputs of two procedures.

Definition 2 (Relative Termination Conditions [13]). *Given two procedures $p_1 \in P_1$ and $p_2 \in P_2$, a 2-program input Boolean expression e is a relative termination condition for p_1, p_2 if for each pair of input states σ_1, σ_2 of p_1, p_2 that evaluates e to* **true**, *if σ_1 has at least one terminating execution for p_1, then so does σ_2 for p_2.*

Note that for inputs satisfying the relative termination condition, the procedure p_2 terminates at least as often as the procedure p_1. This is helpful for specifying intermediate relationships between recursive procedure pairs when p_2 terminates in fewer iterations than p_1 under the same input.

3   Preserving Safety, Accuracy, and Termination

In this section, we first show that mutual summary specifications can be used to capture both relative safety (assertion Sect. 3.1 and control flow Sect. 3.2) and relative accuracy (Sect. 3.3) for approximations. Finally, we describe the use of relative termination specifications for describing approximations (Sect. 3.4).

3.1   Preserving Assertion Safety

Recall from Sect. 1.1 that we informally describe relative assertion safety as a robustness criterion that assertions in approximate programs should fail less often than their counterparts in precise programs. We formalize this as follows:

> A procedure $p_2 \in P_2$ has a differential error with respect to a procedure $p_1 \in P_1$ if there exists a common input state σ such that $(\sigma, \sigma_1) \in \mathscr{T}_{p_1}$ and σ_1 is not an error state, and there exists $(\sigma, \sigma_2) \in \mathscr{T}_{p_2}$ such that σ_2 is an error state. *Relative assertion safety* of p_2 with respect to p_1 holds if there are no differential errors in p_2 with respect to p_1.

Recall that assertions are desugared using a ghost variable OK (Sect. 2.1). Relative assertion safety is then encoded as the following mutual summary specification for p_1 and p_2: $\big(\mathbf{old}(\bigwedge_{x \in X} x_1 = x_2)\big) \Rightarrow (OK_1 \Rightarrow OK_2)$, where X denotes the set of input parameters and globals of p — each variable $x \in X$ is named x_1 (resp. x_2) in program P_1 (resp. P_2).

3.2   Preserving Control Flow Safety

Preserving control flow safety has been identified as an important robustness criterion for approximations (Sect. 1.1). Next, we show that we can use mutual summaries to capture that the approximation does not affect control flow (modulo termination). We first define an automatic program instrumentation for tracking control flow. Let a *basic block* be the maximal sequence of statements that do not contain any conditional statements. We also assume that each such basic block has a unique identifier associated with it. To track the sequence of basic blocks visited along any execution, we augment the state of a program by introducing an integer-valued global variable *cflow*. Then, we instrument every basic block of the program with a statement of the form $cflow := trackCF(cflow, blockID)$, where $trackCF$ is an uninterpreted function defined as $trackCF(int, int)$ $returns$ int, and $blockID$ is the unique integer identifier of the current basic block.

Let $p_1 \in P_1$ and $p_2 \in P_2$ be the two versions of a procedure p in the original and the approximate program. We denote with X the set of input parameters and globals of p — each variable $x \in X$ is named x_1 (resp. x_2) in program P_1 (resp. P_2). Then the mutual summary $\big(\mathbf{old}(\bigwedge_{x \in X} x_1 = x_2)\big) \Rightarrow (cflow_1 = cflow_2)$ states that if the two procedures start out in the same state, the values of the *cflow* variables are equal on termination. If p_1 and p_2 satisfy this mutual summary specification, then the following holds:

For any pair of executions $(\sigma, \sigma_1) \in \mathcal{T}_{p_1}$ and $(\sigma, \sigma_2) \in \mathcal{T}_{p_2}$ starting at the same input state σ, the sequences of basic blocks in the two executions are identical.

Note that the specification only ensures that every pair of terminating executions from σ follow the same control flow. It does not preclude p_2 to not terminate on the input state σ. We address this issue using relative termination specifications that further ensure that (for deterministic programs) if p_1 terminates on σ, then so does p_2.

3.3   Preserving Accuracy

The accuracy criterion ensures that approximations do not cause unacceptable divergence of outputs between two program versions. For example, a write operation to approximate memory may introduce a small error into the written value [24]. Such errors can be amplified by a program (e.g., through multiplication by a large constant), and lead to significant and unintended output difference between the original and approximate program. Hence, the accuracy criterion is used to capture the acceptable quantitative gap between precise and approximate outputs. Mutual summaries naturally express such specifications by relating the inputs and outputs of a procedure pair.

Figure 3 gives the *Swish++* open-source search engine example taken from a recent approximate computing work by Carbin et al. [5]. The example is a simple model that abstracts many implementation details. It takes as input a threshold for the maximum number of results to display max_r and the total number of search results N, and returns the actual number of results to display num_r bounded by max_r and N. The approximation nondeterministically changes the threshold to a possibly smaller number, without suppressing the top 10 results. This allows the search engine to trade-off the number of search results to display under heavy server load, since users are typically interested in the top few results. The predicate *RelaxedEq* denotes the relationship between the original and the approximate value. We express and prove the accuracy criterion (akin to *acceptability property* [5,28]) as the mutual summary $\mathbf{old}(max\_r_1 = max\_r_2 \wedge N_1 = N_2) \Rightarrow RelaxedEq(num\_r_1, num\_r_2)$.

```
function RelaxedEq(x:int, y:int) returns (bool) {
  (x <= 10 && x == y) || (x > 10 && y >= 10 && x >= y)
}
procedure Swish(max_r:int, N:int) returns (num_r:int) {
  var old_max_r:int;
  old_max_r := max_r; havoc max_r; assume RelaxedEq(old_max_r, max_r);
  num_r := 0;
  while (num_r < max_r && num_r < N) num_r := num_r + 1;
  return;
}
```

Fig. 3. Swish++ open-source search engine example.

3.4   Preserving Termination

We use relative termination conditions (Sect. 2.3) to specify that the approximate program terminates at least as often as the base program, and we note the following. The relative termination conditions for a procedure pair may not always be simple equalities over input states. For the pair of **Helper** procedures in Fig. 2, the relative termination condition satisfied by the two versions is $i_1 = i_2 \land (\forall j :: j \geq i_1 \Rightarrow src_1[j] = src_2[j])$, since the recursive calls may not preserve the segment of the array before i. In the presence of a **havoc** statement in p_2 (Fig. 2), the specification only guarantees that p_2 has at least one terminating execution on a common input to p_1. To address this, we perform a standard trick of modeling a **havoc** x statement as a read from a global stream of unconstrained values [17]. This can be done using a global array a and a counter c into the array, and replacing **havoc** x with $x := a[c + +]$. With this, the array becomes a part of the input and the *internal* non-determinism is converted into an input non-determinism. For the transformed program the relative termination specification ensures that none of the terminating executions in p_1 fails to terminate in p_2.

4   Verifying Relative Specifications

In this section, we describe how we leverage and extend SymDiff [13,17,18], a differential verifier for procedural programs that employs SMT-based checking and automatic invariant inference. Although SymDiff already provided many building blocks, we extended it to improve the automation of checking mutual summaries and relative termination conditions. Previously, to verify the relative specifications on the (top-level) entry procedures, the user had to fully annotate all intermediate mutual summaries and relative specification conditions for every pair of procedures [13]; SymDiff only provided a verifier for fully annotated pairs of procedures. We improve the automation in three main directions:

1. We leverage a product program construction for procedural programs that allows inferring relative specifications using off-the-shelf invariant inference tools [18]. This product construction was already present in SymDiff but was customized for checking a specific form of relative specifications (namely, relative assertion safety).
2. We use inferred preconditions for the product program as candidate relative termination conditions for intermediate procedure pairs.
3. We augment the specific invariant inference scheme used in SymDiff over the product program to allow for the user to supply additional predicates.

We informally elaborate on these ideas next. The details of the product construction [18] and checking relative termination conditions [13] are beyond the scope of this paper.

4.1 Procedural Product Programs

We recollect a particular product construction for procedural programs as implemented in SymDiff [18]. The product construction is novel in several ways. First, it can handle procedures (including recursion) in P_1 and P_2 unlike most other product constructions that are intraprocedural [3]. Second, the product program can be fed to any off-the-shelf invariant inference engine to infer mutual summaries over P_1 and P_2.

Given P_1 and P_2, the product program $P_{1\times2}$ consists of procedures in P_1, P_2 and a set of product procedures described below. The set of globals of $P_{1\times2}$ is the disjoint union of globals of P_1 and P_2. For a pair of procedures $p_1 \in P_1$ and $p_2 \in P_2$, we introduce a product procedure $p_{1\times2}$ whose input (resp. output) parameters are the disjoint union of input (resp. output) parameters of p_1 and p_2. The body of $p_{1\times2}$ is a sequential composition of bodies of p_1 and p_2 followed by a series of *replay* blocks. We informally sketch these replay blocks using an example. Let q_1 be a call within p_1 body and q_2 be a call within p_2 body. For any path in $p_{1\times2}$ where q_1 and q_2 are executed with inputs i_1, i_2 resp. and produce outputs o_1, o_2 resp. (where both inputs and outputs include global mutable state), we constrain (o_1, o_2) to be the output of executing $q_{1\times2}$ over inputs (i_1, i_2) in the product program. To perform the replay, each call site in p_1 and p_2 is instrumented to record the inputs and outputs, and global state is set/reset in the replay code.

The resultant product program (which is just another program in *Programs*) has the following property (this paper is the first to formalize this connection):

> For any product procedure $p_{1\times2} \in P_{1\times2}$, if a 2-program 2-state expression e is satisfied by every $(\sigma_{1\times2}, \sigma'_{1\times2}) \in \mathscr{T}_{p_{1\times2}}$, then e is a mutual summary specification for (p_1, p_2).

In other words, if an expression e (over the two program states) is a valid summary (or postcondition) for $p_{1\times2}$, it is a valid mutual summary for the pair of procedures p_1 and p_2. This provides a sound rule for proving mutual summaries over P_1 and P_2: we can express a mutual summary over p_1 and p_2 (e.g., any of the specifications in Sect. 3) as a specification over the product procedure $p_{1\times2}$, and verify $P_{1\times2}$ using any off-the-shelf program verifier.

4.2 Invariant Inference

To verify a mutual summary, we annotate the resultant product program $P_{1\times2}$ with a summary of the top-level procedures, and let a program verifier infer intermediate specifications (preconditions and postconditions of intermediate $q_{1\times2}$ procedures). It was noted in earlier work that most specifications on product procedures tend to be relational or 2-program (e.g., $i_1 \leq i_2$), which requires exploiting the structural similarity between P_1 and P_2. Running an invariant inference engine as is (e.g., Duality [20]) results in generation of single-program invariants and fails to infer relational 2-program specifications. Therefore, SymDiff exploits the mapping between parameters and globals to automatically add candidate relational predicates such as $i_1 \bowtie i_2$, where $\bowtie \in \{\leq, \geq, <, >, \Leftarrow, \Rightarrow, =\}$, for copies of a variable i in two programs. Relational specifications can be generated by composing these predicates using predicate abstraction [12] or Houdini [10]. SymDiff leverages Houdini (that only infers subsets of these predicates) since it is typically fast and predictable, and has been shown to scale to very large programs [38]. We also added a facility for a user to augment the set of automatically generated predicates. Our study shows that such a mechanism was useful in several cases to provide domain-specific guesses for the required predicates.

4.3 Inferring Relative Termination Conditions

The product program $P_{1\times2}$ is not suitable for proving termination related properties as it is meant for proving relative safety properties (on pairs of terminating executions). We therefore fall back to the technique proposed for checking relative termination conditions [13]. We briefly sketch the technique before highlighting the inference extension we have implemented.

Given P_1 and P_2, we construct a product program $P_{1\otimes2}$ by creating product procedures $p_{1\otimes2}$ for two versions of each procedure p. Let us assume that we have a relative termination condition $RT_{p_{1\otimes2}}$ for the procedure $p_{1\otimes2}$. Recall that $RT_{p_{1\otimes2}}$ is an expression over inputs of p_1 and p_2 (Sect. 2.3). For each procedure p (in either version), we create an uninterpreted relation R_p containing all the input-output state pairs of p (i.e., overapproximates $\mathscr{T}_p$). We add a background axiom encoding the assumption that if there exists $(\sigma_1, \sigma_1') \in R_{p_1}$ and $(\sigma_1, \sigma_2) \in RT_{p_{1\otimes2}}$, then there exists σ_2' such that $(\sigma_2, \sigma_2') \in R_{p_2}$:

$$\forall \sigma_1, \sigma_1', \sigma_2 :: \big(R_{p_1}(\sigma_1, \sigma_1') \wedge RT_{p_{1\otimes2}}(\sigma_1, \sigma_2)\big) \Rightarrow (\exists \sigma_2' :: R_{p_2}(\sigma_2, \sigma_2')).$$

Each procedure $p_{1\otimes2}$ starts by assuming the relative termination condition, followed by the body of p_1 and p_2, all composed sequentially. Before any call (to say q_2) inside p_2's body, we add the assertion **assert** $\exists \sigma_2' :: R_{q_2}(\sigma_2, \sigma_2')$, where σ_2 is the state of the input to the call to q_2 and σ_2' is the output state of q_2. Since R_{q_2} is uninterpreted, the only way to prove this assertion is to use an axiom like above (just instantiated for procedure q), which requires R_{q_1} and $RT_{q_{1\otimes2}}$ to hold. Intuitively, such an assertion before every call (which is the only way to cause non-termination in the absence of loops) when combined with the introduced axioms ensures that a call to q_2 must be preceded by a call to q_1 in the path inside $p_{1\otimes2}$ — in other words, q_2 is called less often than q_1 on any execution. If all such assertions hold for the given $RT_{q_{1\otimes2}}$ for all procedures $q \in P$, then the relative termination of the entry level procedures is established.

Although the relative termination condition for the top-level procedures is often simple (equality of the input states), intermediate procedures may only satisfy weaker relationships. For example, sometimes a relationship such as $i_1 \leq i_2$ holds for a loop index i to indicate that the second procedure terminates earlier. Also, recall the non-trivial specification for the intermediate *Helper* procedure in Sect. 3.4 where only segments of arrays are equal. Clearly, manually specifying all the RT can be quite cumbersome in the presence of multiple procedures.

We leverage the product program $P_{1 \times 2}$ used earlier to heuristically guess possible RT expressions. We have observed that the inferred preconditions to a product procedure $p_{1 \times 2}$ often represent sound relationships between inputs of p_1 and p_2 in any execution. One can, however, construct examples where the inferred precondition is not sound for relationship between inputs to p_1 and p_2 — e.g., due to non-termination or fewer call-sites of a procedure in the new version. We heuristically install a precondition to $p_{1 \times 2}$ (from $P_{1 \times 2}$) as $RT_{p_{1 \otimes 2}}$ (in $P_{1 \otimes 2}$) and try verifying $P_{1 \otimes 2}$. If verification succeeds, we have established the relative termination property. In the case study, we show that this heuristic suffices for all but one of our benchmarks.

5   Case Study

In this section, we describe our feasibility study of using differential program verification techniques for automatic verification of several classes of program approximations.

Benchmarks. Table 1 lists our benchmarks and presents the results of verifying them using our framework. We used the following benchmarks in our experiments:

- Case studies taken from previous work by Carbin et al. [5]: *LU Decomposition*, *Water*, and *Swish++*. We provide the same guarantees as this previous work, and in addition we prove relative termination for a modified version of *Swish++*.
- Array and string operations: *Replace Character*, *Array Operations*, *Array Search*, *String Hash*, *String Copy*, *Selection Sort*, and *Bubble Sort*.
- Loop approximation examples: *Cube Root*, *Gradient Descent*, *Loop Perforation*, and *Pointer Perforation*.
- Image processing programs taken from the ACCEPT benchmark suite [33]: *ReadCell* (extracts information from the header of an image file), *Sobel* (implements a Sobel image filter), and *JPEG Quantization* (quantization stage of a JPEG encoder).

We only prove important criteria for every benchmark since some either do not hold or are trivial to prove. All experiments were performed on a 2.3 GHz Intel i7-3610QM machine with 8 GB RAM and running Microsoft Windows. They are reproducible using a custom Apt platform profile at https://www.aptlab.net/p/fmr/approx-nfm2016.

Discussion. As experimental results show, we successfully used our approach to verify a variety of approximation robustness criteria. Verification of most benchmarks terminates in under one minute, which indicates that our technique has potential to scale to larger examples. Only two manual steps were occasionally needed to complete the proof. First, in several benchmarks we had to unroll once

Table 1. Experimental results. LOC is the number of lines of Boogie code in approximate programs; Criterion is the verified property; #Preds is the number of predicates automatically generated by SymDiff; #Man is the number of manually provided predicates; Time is the total runtime in seconds, including inference.

Benchmark	LOC	Criterion	#Preds	#Man	Time(s)
Cube Root	7	Relative Termination	12	0	6.5
Loop Perforation	11	Relative Termination	10	0	4.8
Gradient Descent	17	Relative Termination	22	0	6.4
String Hash	19	Assertion Safety	25	0	7.8
		Relative Termination	19	0	4.9
Swish++	22	Accuracy	14	2	6.5
		Relative Termination	14	0	4.8
Water	27	Assertion Safety	32	0	5.8
Pointer Perforation	28	Relative Termination	26	0	5.1
Replace Character	31	Assertion Safety	15	0	7.7
		Control Flow Safety	15	0	7.9
		Termination	5	0	5.1
String Copy	32	Assertion Safety	20	2	7.7
		Relative Termination	14	0	6.5
LU Decomposition	33	Accuracy	32	2	5.7
Array Search	33	Relative Termination	30	0	7.1
Array Operations	43	Control Flow Safety	44	0	8.2
Sobel	49	Relative Termination	190	1	5.3
Selection Sort	57	Control Flow Safety	81	0	8.5
ReadCell	60	Assertion Safety	37	1	14.0
		Control Flow Safety	37	1	14.0
Bubble Sort	67	Control Flow Safety	59	0	8.2
JPEG Quantization	96	Accuracy	19	3	6.3

tail-recursive procedures extracted from loops (e.g., *String Copy*, *String Hash*). (This can be automated by trying in parallel all combinations of unrollings: unroll first procedure, unroll second procedure, unroll both.) Second, we had to provide additional predicates for the benchmarks with non-zero #Man field in Table 1. The need for manual predicates can be broken down into roughly two categories: (i) simple non-relational predicates such as $j_2 \leq i_2$ (e.g., *String Copy*), and (ii) non-trivial relational predicates that require arithmetic such as RelaxedEq (e.g., *Swish++* in Fig. 3, *LU*). These predicates are mainly used for proving domain-specific relative accuracy properties, and reusing the predicate RelaxedEq often suffices for the proof. Our study shows that our Houdini-based inference techniques successfully generated most of the required specifications automatically, indicating that relative specifications do not heavily depend on complex program-specific invariants.

5.1 Experience

We describe next in more detail our experience verifying some of the listed benchmarks.

Replace Character and Sorting. Recall the *Replace Character* example from Fig. 2, where we wish to verify that the approximation maintains control flow safety. The main challenge of this verification task is to capture the fact that control flow depends on only a fragment of the array, which is identical in the two programs. We capture this property by defining a quantified predicate template $ArrayEqAfter(str_1, str_2, i_1) \doteq \forall j : \mathbf{int} :: j \geq i_1 \Rightarrow str_1[j] = str_2[j]$. The proof of control flow safety for the selection sort example also leverages this predicate (see our technical report [14]). The selection sort algorithm sorts an array by pushing the maximum element of the $[c \ldots n-1]$ subarray to the position c after every iteration. Once an element has been pushed to the front, it does not play a part in determining future control flow behavior. Therefore, approximating such end elements does not influence the control flow of the algorithm. In addition to selection sort, we also verified control flow safety for a version of bubble sort containing a similar approximation. Unlike selection sort where the leftmost index is approximated, the approximation in bubble sort requires introducing an additional instruction to havoc the rightmost array element of each iteration. A similar predicate $ArrayEqBefore$, specifying that the two arrays are equal before some index, captures that fact that the subarray before each iteration is precise and thus facilitates the proof. Our experience shows that $ArrayEqAfter$ and $ArrayEqBefore$ are needed for most examples with arrays, and hence we automatically instantiate them using our inference engine.

JPEG Quantization. This is a JPEG encoder quantization stage taken from the ACCEPT benchmark suite [33] (see our technical report [14]). In the benchmark, each element is computed by ultimately dividing it by 2^{15}. Hence, it is suitable for an approximation that allocates data in approximate memory since the error introduced to the stored value (denoted by the predicate `RelaxedEq`) is masked or reduced after division by 2^{15}. The following expresses the desired relative accuracy specification:

$$\mathbf{old}(data_1 = data_2) \Rightarrow (\forall\, i : \mathbf{int} :: (i \geq 0 \wedge i \leq 63) \Rightarrow RelaxedEq(Temp_1[i], Temp_2[i], 2))$$

The most involved manually provided predicate $RelaxedAfter(Temp_1, Temp_2, i)$ is similar to $ArrayEqAfter$. It is based on the observation that after each iteration of the loop, all corresponding elements of the arrays $Temp_1$ and $Temp_2$ after index i should satisfy $RelaxedEq$ with the error bound of 2.

String Examples. To prove relative assertion safety for the example from Fig. 1, we had to manually unroll the loop in Strcpy once and provide two atomic predicates. Such loop unrolling helps SymDiff to infer the equality between i_1 and i_2, which indicates that the *src* arrays are accessed in the same way and thus implies relative assertion safety. The manual predicates needed for this example relate indices of array *dst*, and have the form $j_2 \leq i_2$. With these predicates, relative assertion safety is established for array *dst* since dst_2 is accessed less often than dst_1. In addition, we proved relative termination of StrcpyApprox with respect to Strcpy. This required a simple relative termination condition automatically inferred by SymDiff, $src_1 = src_2 \wedge i_1 = i_2$, since we unrolled the loop in *Strcpy* once. Such bounded loop unrolling often facilitates the verification of relative termination since it allows for the proof to be discharged using a simpler relative termination condition.

Simple Cube Root Calculation. We implemented a benchmark that calculates the integer approximation r of the cube root of x by performing a simple iterative search guarded with the nonlinear condition r * r * r <= x (see our technical report [14]). We further approximate this computation by performing loop perforation, which speeds up the search at the expense of losing precision, and potentially leads to non-termination. Automatically proving program termination is especially hard when loop conditions contain nonlinear arithmetic, which complicates generation of adequate ranking functions. We easily proved relative termination of this benchmark using the simple relative termination condition $r_1 \leq r_2$ that is automatically inferred.

6   Related Work

A number of complementary approaches have been recently proposed to reason about approximations. These approaches can be roughly categorized (with over-laps) into (i) language based, (ii) static analysis, and (iii) dynamic approaches. Language based approaches propose language constructs and annotations to make approximations explicit in a program. EnerJ [35] introduces approximate types and ensures that such values do not impact precise computations, including conditional statements. ACCEPT [33] automatically searches for code regions that can be approximated based on type annotation and static compiler analysis pass. FlexJava [25] allows users to annotate scoped variables (e.g., return values), and then it automatically infers safe-to-approximate variables and operations using a simple taint analysis. Our work can be used to improve the precision of these analyses, as shown in Sect. 1.1.

Carbin et al. [5] develop a special-purpose language and constructs for introducing approximations and relaxed specifications (based on *relational Hoare logic* [3]), and prove correctness of transformations using the general purpose Coq theorem prover [7]. Each proof for their three benchmarks required roughly 330 lines of proof scripts according to the authors. We provide the same guarantees for these three benchmarks almost completely automatically (see Sect. 5), thereby showing that mutual summaries and SMT-based verification can significantly improve the automation for most transformations covered by this approach.

Rely [6] is a programming language that allows users to verify probabilistic quantitative reliability guarantees of programs running on unreliable hardware using an associated static analysis. Chisel [21] is a synthesis framework that generates optimal programs for execution on approximate hardware that satisfy given accuracy and reliability specifications. Unlike our approach, Chisel can only establish relative specifications for syntactically equivalent program versions and it ensures control flow equivalence using a simple dependence analysis. On the other hand, Chisel can reason about probabilities, which our approach currently does not support. ExPAX [26] generates a set of safe-to-approximate operations based on a dataflow taint analysis, and then computes allowed approximation for each operation to minimize energy consumption while satisfying reliability constraints. DECAF [4] combines static type inference, dynamic tracking, and runtime check to give probabilistic guarantee on the quality of approximate programs.

Among dynamic approaches, fault injection at the source or intermediate representation level has been used to profile the sensitivity of output quality to approximations. Fault injectors such as KULFI [36] and LLFI [37] approximate instructions at runtime. Though such tools achieve high levels of accuracy, they provide no formal coverage guarantees. Offline dynamic analysis techniques compute information on dataflow and correlation difference (e.g., [29,30]). The former may be imprecise as it is based on static dataflow analysis, while the latter again offers no formal guarantees. Although there are optimizations for selective instruction perturbation, such as statistical methods [31], the reasoning is only for a subset of all the possible executions of the program.

Finally, our work is related to previous approaches to translation validation [23,27] and regression verification [9,11], which leverage SMT solvers to discharge equivalence properties. In contrast, our mutual summaries and product construction allow for richer relaxed specifications other than equivalence, interprocedural reasoning [13,18], and leveraging off-the-shelf verifiers and inference engines.

7   Conclusions and Future Work

In this paper, we have described the application of automated SMT-based differential verification for providing formal guarantees of approximations. The structural similarity between original and approximate programs are leveraged to automate most intermediate relative specifications. Our extensions to SymDiff allowed us to verify a variety of criteria that ensure robustness of approximate programs, including relative control flow safety, assertion safety, accuracy, and termination. We are also first to propose relative termination as an important robustness criterion. Our feasibility study shows that the techniques we developed can be effectively used to automatically prove program approximations. We are currently working on automating predicate generation, using more expressive inference engines such as interpolants [19] and indexed predicate abstraction [16] to infer remaining specifications.

Acknowledgments. We thank Adrian Sampson for his feedback and for helping out with benchmark selection, and Akash Lal for helping out with Houdini. This work was supported in part by NSF award CCF 1255776 and SRC contract 2013-TJ-2426.

References

1. Barnett, M., Chang, B.-Y.E., DeLine, R., Jacobs, B., M. Leino, K.R.: Boogie: a modular reusable verifier for object-oriented programs. In: Boer, F.S., Bonsangue, M.M., Graf, S., Roever, W.-P. (eds.) FMCO 2005. LNCS, vol. 4111, pp. 364–387. Springer, Heidelberg (2006)
2. Barrett, C., Sebastiani, R., Seshia, S., Tinelli, C.: Satisfiability modulo theories. In: Handbook of Satisfiability (2009)
3. Benton, N.: Simple relational correctness proofs for static analyses and program transformations. In: POPL (2004)
4. Boston, B., Sampson, A., Grossman, D., Ceze, L.: Probability type inference for flexible approximate programming. In: OOPSLA (2015)
5. Carbin, M., Kim, D., Misailovic, S., Rinard, M.C.: Proving acceptability properties of relaxed nondeterministic approximate programs. In: PLDI (2012)
6. Carbin, M., Misailovic, S., Rinard, M.C.: Verifying quantitative reliability for programs that execute on unreliable hardware. In: OOPSLA (2013)
7. The Coq proof assistant. http://coq.inria.fr
8. Elenbogen, D., Katz, S., Strichman, O.: Proving mutual termination. FMSD **47**(2), 204–229 (2015)
9. Felsing, D., Grebing, S., Klebanov, V., Rümmer, P., Ulbrich, M.: Automating regression verification. In: ASE (2014)
10. Flanagan, C., Leino, K.R.M.: Houdini, an annotation assistant for ESC/Java. In: Oliveira, J.N., Zave, P. (eds.) FME 2001. LNCS, vol. 2021, p. 500. Springer, Heidelberg (2001)
11. Godlin, B., Strichman, O.: Regression verification. In: DAC (2009)
12. Graf, S., Saïdi, H.: Construction of abstract state graphs with PVS. In: Grumberg, O. (ed.) CAV 1997. LNCS, vol. 1254, pp. 72–83. Springer, Heidelberg (1997)
13. Hawblitzel, C., Kawaguchi, M., Lahiri, S.K., Rebêlo, H.: Towards modularly comparing programs using automated theorem provers. In: Bonacina, M.P. (ed.) CADE 2013. LNCS, vol. 7898, pp. 282–299. Springer, Heidelberg (2013)
14. He, S., Lahiri, S.K., Rakamarić, Z.: Verifying relative safety, accuracy, and termination for program approximations. Tech. rep., Microsoft Research (2016)
15. Kugler, L.: Is "good enough" computing good enough? Commun. ACM **58**(5), 12–14 (2015)
16. Lahiri, S.K., Bryant, R.E.: Predicate abstraction with indexed predicates. ACM Trans. Comput. Log. **9**(1) (2007)
17. Lahiri, S.K., Hawblitzel, C., Kawaguchi, M., Rebêlo, H.: SYMDIFF: a language-agnostic semantic diff tool for imperative programs. In: Madhusudan, P., Seshia, S.A. (eds.) CAV 2012. LNCS, vol. 7358, pp. 712–717. Springer, Heidelberg (2012)
18. Lahiri, S.K., McMillan, K.L., Sharma, R., Hawblitzel, C.: Differential assertion checking. In: ESEC/FSE (2013)
19. McMillan, K.L.: An interpolating theorem prover. In: Jensen, K., Podelski, A. (eds.) TACAS 2004. LNCS, vol. 2988, pp. 16–30. Springer, Heidelberg (2004)
20. McMillan, K.L.: Lazy annotation revisited. In: Biere, A., Bloem, R. (eds.) CAV 2014. LNCS, vol. 8559, pp. 243–259. Springer, Heidelberg (2014)

21. Misailovic, S., Carbin, M., Achour, S., Qi, Z., Rinard, M.C.: Chisel: Reliability-and accuracy-aware optimization of approximate computational kernels. SIGPLAN Not. **49**, 309–328 (2014)
22. Misailovic, S., Sidiroglou, S., Hoffmann, H., Rinard, M.: Quality of service profiling. In: ICSE (2010)
23. Necula, G.C.: Translation validation for an optimizing compiler. In: PLDI (2000)
24. Nelson, J., Sampson, A., Ceze, L.: Dense approximate storage in phase-change memory. In: Ideas and Perspectives session at ASPLOS (2001)
25. Park, J., Esmaeilzadeh, H., Zhang, X., Naik, M., Harris, W.: FlexJava: language support for safe and modular approximate programming. In: ESEC/FSE (2015)
26. Park, J., Ni, K., Zhang, X., Esmaeilzadeh, H., Naik, M.: Expectation-oriented framework for automating approximate programming. In: WACAS (2014)
27. Pnueli, A., Siegel, M.D., Singerman, E.: Translation validation. In: Steffen, B. (ed.) TACAS 1998. LNCS, vol. 1384, pp. 151–166. Springer, Heidelberg (1998)
28. Rinard, M.: Acceptability-oriented computing. In: OOPSLA (2003)
29. Ringenburg, M.F., Sampson, A., Ackerman, I., Ceze, L., Grossman, D.: Dynamic analysis of approximate program quality. Tech. Rep. UW-CSE-14-03-01, University of Washington
30. Ringenburg, M.F., Sampson, A., Ceze, L., Grossman, D.: Profiling and autotuning for energy-aware approximate programming. In: WACAS (2014)
31. Roy, P., Ray, R., Wang, C., Wong, W.F.: ASAC: Automatic sensitivity analysis for approximate computing. In: LCTES (2014)
32. Sampson, A.: Hardware and Software for Approximate Computing. Ph.D. thesis (2015)
33. Sampson, A., Baixo, A., Ransford, B., Moreau, T., Yip, J., Ceze, L., Oskin, M.: ACCEPT: a programmer-guided compiler framework for practical approximate computing. Tech. Rep. UW-CSE-15-01-01, University of Washington
34. Sampson, A., Bornholt, J., Ceze, L.: Hardware-software co-design: not just a cliché. In: SNAPL (2015)
35. Sampson, A., Dietl, W., Fortuna, E., Gnanapragasam, D., Ceze, L., Grossman, D.: EnerJ: approximate data types for safe and general low-power computation. In: PLDI (2011)
36. Sharma, V.C., Haran, A., Rakamarić, Z., Gopalakrishnan, G.: Towards formal approaches to system resilience. In: PRDC (2013)
37. Thomas, A., Pattabiraman, K.: LLFI: an intermediate code level fault injector for soft computing applications. In: SELSE (2013)
38. Vanegue, J., Lahiri, S.K.: Towards practical reactive security audit using extended static checkers. In: S&P (2013)

Bandwidth and Wavefront Reduction for Static Variable Ordering in Symbolic Reachability Analysis

Jeroen Meijer$^{(\boxtimes)}$ and Jaco van de Pol

Formal Methods and Tools, University of Twente, Enschede, The Netherlands
{j.j.g.meijer,j.c.vandepol}@utwente.nl

Abstract. We investigate the use of bandwidth and wavefront reduction algorithms to determine a static BDD variable ordering. The aim is to reduce the size of BDDs arising in symbolic reachability. Previous work showed that minimizing the (weighted) event span of the variable dependency graph yields small BDDs. The bandwidth and wavefront of symmetric matrices are well studied metrics, used in sparse matrix solvers, and many bandwidth and wavefront reduction algorithms are readily available in libraries like Boost and ViennaCL.

In this paper, we transform the dependency matrix to a symmetric matrix and apply various bandwidth and wavefront reduction algorithms, measuring their influence on the (weighted) event span. We show that Sloan's algorithm, executed on the total graph of the dependency matrix, yields a variable order with minimal event span. We demonstrate this on a large benchmark of Petri nets, DVE, PROMELA, B, and mCRL2 models. As a result, good static variable orders can now be determined in milliseconds by using standard sparse matrix solvers.

Keywords: Bandwidth · Profile · Wavefront · Event span · Symbolic reachability · Sparse matrix · Event locality · Decision diagram · Petri net

1 Introduction

Reachability analysis is an approach for investigating properties of reachable states of computer programs. Some type of computer programs allow efficient storage of its set of reachable states by means of decision diagrams, this technique is known as symbolic reachability analysis. Storing sets of states symbolically entails storing sets of integer vectors as binary formulas in for example Binary Decision Diagrams (BDDs) [4]. One major issue with this approach is the ordering of variables in Decision Diagrams (DDs) representing the formula. Improving variable ordering is known to be NP-complete [3]. DD variable ordering has been extensively studied [1,12,26,28]. Dynamic reordering modifies variable orders during computations, while static variable ordering precomputes a total order based on some structure of the input. In the latter case, several metrics have been proposed that lead to small DDs [25]. However, to the best of our knowledge, there is no

© Springer International Publishing Switzerland 2016
S. Rayadurgam and O. Tkachuk (Eds.): NFM 2016, LNCS 9690, pp. 255–271, 2016.
DOI: 10.1007/978-3-319-40648-0_20

systematic research on good algorithms to obtain orders with low values for such metrics. An existing algorithm for static variable ordering is Noack's algorithm [22], but Noack's algorithm is only applicable to Petri nets. The only existing algorithm that can compete with our proposed ones is FORCE [1]. We will show that four well known algorithms used in sparse matrix solvers can drastically and very quickly improve variable orders for any modeling language, just like FORCE can[1]. A novel contribution in this paper is a systematic benchmark for Noack, FORCE and our proposed bandwidth and wavefront reduction algorithms executed on many specifications written in different languages.

Static variable ordering exploits the notion of event locality. Events, such as program statements or transitions in Petri nets are often local, i.e. they touch only a few variables or places and ordering these local variables near each other tends to significantly reduce the memory footprint of the DDs. An appropriate metric for indicating the quality of the variable order is Event Span (ES), by Siminiceanu et al. [28]. The event span metric is used to measure the total distance between the minimum variable and maximum variable of all events. Additionally Siminiceanu et al. introduce an extension of ES, called Weighted Event Span (WES). The weight of every event signifies the location of a span, i.e. whether the span changes the top or bottom of the DD. It is known that operations changing the bottom of the DD are cheaper [6], which is beneficial for the saturation strategy in particular.

The quality of the variable order can be visualized using matrices. Such an approach is taken in [21], where a dependency matrix has rows as transitions and columns as variables. A nonzero entry indicates that a transition depends on a variable. These dependency matrices tend to be sparse, hinting that traditional sparse matrix algorithms can be applied to these matrices.

A subcategory of sparse matrix algorithms are bandwidth reduction algorithms. One key example of a bandwidth reduction algorithm is by Cuthill and McKee developed in 1969 [10]. The goal of these algorithms is very similar to ES reduction algorithms. The bandwidth measures the distance of nonzeros from the diagonal of the matrix. Bandwidth is related to event span, because of the triangle inequality, which states that event span is always smaller than twice the bandwidth.

Another popular algorithm is Sloan's [29] algorithm, which optimizes total bandwidth (also called profile), and wavefront. The graph algorithm has a very low time complexity $\mathcal{O}(\log \hat{D} \cdot |E|)$, where $\hat{D}$ is the maximum degree, and E the set of edges in the adjacency graph. This results in runtimes of mere seconds when applied to matrices with a million rows and columns – or transitions and variables. Conveniently, Sloan's algorithm is freely available in Boost's graph library. Every model checker written in C/C++ or Python can be linked to Boost without much effort.

While bandwidth and wavefront reduction algorithms have proven themselves during the past decades, they only work on symmetric matrices. A dependency matrix is asymmetric because clearly, transitions (rows) and variables (columns)

---

[1] We restrict ourselves to languages that induce a disjunctive transition relation.

are different objects and there exists no natural total order on the union of both. Reid et al. [24] discuss several methods of symmetrizing asymmetric matrices. With visualizations and experimental data we show that indeed, adding the inverse set of edges, and simply assigning some total order, that preserves the partial order on transitions and variables works well.

We extensively benchmark the Cuthill McKee, Gibbs Poole Stockmeyer, King and Sloan nodal ordering algorithms implemented in Boost and ViennaCL [27]. The benchmark consists of 785 model specifications, written in PNML, DVE, mCRL2, PROMELA and B. The model checker LTSMIN [14] is already capable of handling all five input languages. By linking Boost and ViennaCL to LTSMIN we can execute the nodal ordering algorithms and measure their influence on bandwidth, wavefront and (weighted) event span.

The rest of the paper is structured as follows. In Sect. 2 we introduce symbolic reachability analysis and explain what the role of the dependency matrix is. Next, Sect. 3 explains the nodal ordering algorithms and why these can not be directly applied to the dependency matrix. The solution is given in Sect. 4; it involves symmetrizing the dependency matrix; permuting the matrix and de-symmetrizing the matrix. An experimental evaluation is given in Sect. 5 and we conclude our findings in Sect. 6.

2   Symbolic Reachability Analysis

Reachability analysis involves analyzing whether or not a system can enter a particular state. Consider Fig. 1, which is an example of a Petri net. A Petri net is a bipartite graph, where vertices represent places (circles) or transitions (squares). Places contain a non-negative number of tokens (dots). The edges in the graph are called arcs. For each place, an outgoing arc means that tokens will be consumed and an incoming arc means that tokens will be produced. In Fig. 1, after transition t_1 fires, p_4 will have no token, while both p_2 and p_5 get one token. A

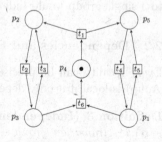

Fig. 1. A Petri net

reachability question is whether or not p_1 will eventually have a token, which it will, after firing t_1 followed by t_4. Petri nets model many kinds of systems, like distributed protocols, control and data flow in concurrent software, business processes, or even biological systems.

2.1   Transition Systems

A state of a Petri net is a marking, and firing a transition produces a new marking of a Petri net. Other specification languages also describe transition systems; we generalize the concept as follows.

Definition 1 (Transition System). *A Transition System (TS) is a tuple* $(S, \rightarrow, \iota)$, *where S is a set of states,* $\rightarrow \subseteq S \times S$ *is a transition relation and*

$\iota \in S$ is the initial state. Furthermore let $\rightarrow^*$ be the reflexive an transitive closure of $\rightarrow$, then the set of reachable states is $R = \{s \in S \mid \iota \rightarrow^* s\}$.

Computing the set of reachable states R is very time- and memory-consuming. Many techniques exist to alleviate this problem. In this paper, we focus on symbolic reachability analysis. Storing the set of reachable states symbolically involves using Boolean expressions to describe this set. Symbolic reachability analysis works well when there is a high locality of events. To precisely describe event locality, we introduce a more fine-grained view of a transition system.

Definition 2 (Partitioned Transition System). *A Partitioned Transition System (PTS) is a tuple* $\mathcal{P} = ((S_1, \ldots, S_N), (\rightarrow_1, \ldots, \rightarrow_M), (\iota_1, \ldots, \iota_N))$, *where the sets of values* $S_1, \ldots, S_N$ *define the set of states* $S_\mathcal{P} = S_1 \times \cdots \times S_N$. *The transition groups* $\rightarrow_i \subseteq S_\mathcal{P} \times S_\mathcal{P}$, $\forall 1 \leq i \leq M$, *define the transition relation* $\rightarrow_\mathcal{P} = \bigcup_{i=1}^{M} \rightarrow_i$. *The initial state is* $\iota = (\iota_1, \ldots, \iota_N) \in S_\mathcal{P}$. *The defined TS of* $\mathcal{P}$ *is* $(S_\mathcal{P}, \rightarrow_\mathcal{P}, \iota)$. *For convenience, we write* $s \rightarrow_i t$ *when* $(s, t) \in \rightarrow_i$, $\forall 1 \leq i \leq M$.

Thus, a state $(s_1, \ldots, s_N) \in S_\mathcal{P}$ is a tuple of length N. An element s_j in such a tuple is a value for *state slot j*. The PTS induced by Fig. 1 has the set of natural numbers as its values $S_j = \mathbb{N}$, as it represents the number of tokens in a place. The number of state slots is 5; every place gets a state slot. The number of transition groups is 6; every transition gets its own transition group. The initial state is the marking shown. Note that assigning all transitions of the Petri net to a single group would hide event locality.

2.2 Dependencies and Event Locality

Event locality can be precisely described with a PTS. An event (or transition group) is local if it only depends on a few state slots.

Definition 3 (Independence). *Given a PTS* $\mathcal{P} = ((S_1, \ldots, S_N), (\rightarrow_1, \ldots, \rightarrow_M), \iota)$, *transition group* $\rightarrow_i$ *is independent on values* S_j *iff* $\forall (s_1, \ldots, s_N)$, $(t_1, \ldots, t_N) \in S_\mathcal{P}$, *whenever* $(s_1, \ldots, s_j, \ldots, s_N) \rightarrow_i (t_1, \ldots, t_j, \ldots, t_N)$, *then:*

1. $s_j = t_j$, *and*   (not modified)
2. $\forall r_j \in S_j \cdot (s_1, \ldots, r_j, \ldots, s_N) \rightarrow_i (t_1, \ldots, r_j, \ldots, t_N)$ (irrelevant).

Condition 1 says that a transition group must not modify a state slot to be independent. Condition 2 says that a transition in group i should be enabled regardless of the value at state slot j. In practice, we work with a syntactic overapproximation of the dependency relation. We have recently shown [21] that distinguishing read and write dependencies is beneficial for symbolic model checking, but this distinction has not yet been exploited in the current paper.

In order to illustrate dependencies we introduce the notion of ordered graphs and adjacency matrices. The dependency relation is described as edges between vertices that represent transition groups and state slots.

Definition 4 (Order). *Given a set V, an order on V is a (reflexive, antisymmetric and transitive) relation $O \subseteq V \times V$. We write $a \leq b = (a, b) \in O$. If $\forall a, b \in V : (a, b) \in O \vee (b, a) \in O$ then O is total, otherwise O is partial.*

Definition 5 (Graph). *A graph is a pair $G = (V, E)$, where V is a set of vertices and $E \subseteq V \times V$ is a set of edges. If E is symmetric, then G is undirected, else G is directed. An order on the vertices of G is denoted $O \subseteq V \times V$. We subscript a vertex $(v_i \in V)$ to denote its position in an order: $i = |\{u \mid (u, v_i) \in O\}|$.*

Definition 6 (Dependency Graph). *Given a PTS $\mathcal{P} = ((S_1, \ldots, S_N), (\rightarrow_1, \ldots, \rightarrow_M), \iota)$, a dependency graph is a partially ordered, directed, bipartite graph on rows and columns, $D = (\{r_1, \ldots, r_M\} \cup \{c_1, \ldots, c_N\}, E)$, such that the edges form an over-approximation of the dependency relation in Definition 3:*

$$E \supseteq \{(r_i, c_j) \mid \rightarrow_i \text{ is not independent on } S_j\}.$$ *Furthermore, the vertices of D are partially ordered, but both parts of its vertices are totally ordered. The dependency matrix $\boldsymbol{D} \in \{0, 1\}^{M \times N}$, such that $\boldsymbol{D}_{ij} = 1 \iff (r_i, c_j) \in E$ is the bi-adjacency matrix of the dependency graph.*

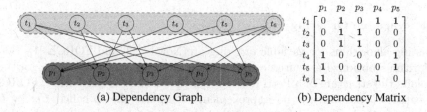

	p_1	p_2	p_3	p_4	p_5
t_1	0	1	0	1	1
t_2	0	1	1	0	0
t_3	0	1	1	0	0
t_4	1	0	0	0	1
t_5	1	0	0	0	1
t_6	1	0	1	1	0

(a) Dependency Graph   (b) Dependency Matrix

Fig. 2. Representation of dependencies

The *dependency graph* of the Petri net in Fig. 1, with a partial alphanumeric order $(t_1 < t_2 < t_3 < t_4 < t_5 < t_6 \cup p_1 < p_2 < p_3 < p_4 < p_5)$ is shown in Fig. 2a. The locality of events can be seen clearly in the matrix in Fig. 2b, for example transition group t_1 does not depend on state slots p_1 and p_3 in any way.

2.3 Symbolic Algorithms

The most basic algorithm to compute the set of reachable states in Definition 1 is a breadth first algorithm that repeatedly applies a symbolic representation of a transition group to a set of states until a fixed point ($=R$) is reached, beginning from the initial state. More advanced algorithms also exist, such as *chaining* (which updates the set of states each time a subrelation is applied) and *saturation* [6] (which saturates an increasing part at the bottom of the decision diagram). Decision Diagrams (DDs) are used to represent both the set of reachable states and the transition groups.

Figure 3 shows the set of reachable states of the Petri net in Fig. 1 in a particular kind of DD, namely List Decision Diagrams (LDDs) [2], with different variable orders.

Every path from the top left node to the `True` node represents a reachable state. The value in a node indicates the number of tokens. One can see that Fig. 3a, whose variable order is computed using Cuthill McKee, has fewer nodes than Fig. 3a with the default alphanumeric variable order. Thus storing the decision diagram in Fig. 3b requires less memory. Improving the variable ordering of decision diagrams is a classic NP-Complete [3] problem.

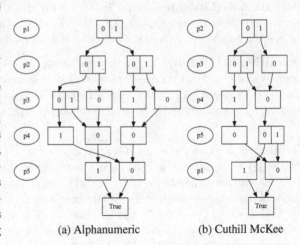

(a) Alphanumeric   (b) Cuthill McKee

Fig. 3. Reachable states as LDD with different orders

2.4 Variable Ordering

Existing algorithms for variable ordering are Noack [22] and FORCE [1]. Both algorithms optimize a heuristic called *span*, or *event span*. Noack's algorithm exploits the structure of a Petri net to order places close to each other. FORCE repeatedly (until there is no improvement) computes the so called *Center Of Gravity* (COG) of transition groups, to place state slots close to each other. Span is an important metric for symbolic reachability, because it tells how close related variables are ordered near each other. Ordering related variables near each other results in smaller DDs. Span is defined on the dependency matrix and measures the distance between the leftmost and rightmost nonzero column (representing a state slot) of row i (representing a transition group).

Definition 7 (Span). *Given an ordered graph* $G = (V, E)$, *the* vertex span *is a function* $s_G \colon V \to \mathbb{N}$, *such that*

$$s_G(v_i) := \begin{cases} 0, & \text{if } \nexists v_j \in V . (v_i, v_j) \in E, \\ \max_{(v_i,v_j)\in E} j - \min_{(v_i,v_j)\in E} j + 1, & \text{otherwise.} \end{cases}$$

The span *or* event span *of a graph is* $ES_G = \sum_{v \in V} s_G(v)$.

For example, let D be the graph in Fig. 2, the vertex span for t_1 is $s_D(t_1) = 4$, $s_D(p_1) = 0$, the event span is $ES_D = 22$.

We also introduce a version of span that assigns weights to rows of a matrix, that signify the location of spans in rows, following [28]. Siminiceanu et al. have shown that it is important that spans in rows appear as far right as possible so that when a transition relation (of a row) is applied, the bottom of a decision diagram is changed rather than the top. Indeed, the leftmost column corresponds with the top of the decision diagram, and the rightmost with the bottom of the DD. Changing the bottom of the DD is apparently cheaper than changing the top.

Definition 8 (Weighted Span). *Given an ordered graph $G = (V, E)$, and $C = \{v \in V \mid \exists u \,.\, (u, v) \in E\}$, the weighted span or weighted event span of a graph is $WES_G = \sum_{v_i \in V} s_G(v_i) \cdot \frac{|C| - m(v_i)}{|C|/2}$, where $m(v_i) = 0$ if $\nexists v_j \in V \,.\, (v_i, v_j) \in E$ and $m(v_i) = \min_{(v_i, v_j) \in E} j$ otherwise. Normalization yields $NWES_G = WES_G / (|C| \cdot |V - C|)$.*

If WES is measured on the dependency graph, then C is (w.l.o.g.) precisely the set of vertices that represent state slots, and $m(v_i)$ gives the leftmost nonzero column number of row i in the dependency matrix. For example, let D be the graph in Fig. 2, the weighted event span is $WES_D = 32$, and $NWES_D = 1.1$. Normalization of WES allows us to compare matrices of different sizes with each other.

Optimizing (weighted) event span is well known [28] to work well for symbolic reachability analysis, but like improving variable orders it is also NP-Complete. We will show that algorithms that have been around for decades and are used in sparse matrix solvers are actually very capable at reducing (weighted) span.

3   Nodal Ordering for Sparse Matrix Solvers

Sparse matrix solvers solve a system of linear equations, and this system can be put in a symmetric matrix. As a preprocessing step it is necessary to order these equations in a particular way to limit memory and time usage during solving. Metrics that indicate the memory and time usage are bandwidth and wavefront respectively. Bandwidth measures the distance of nonzeros to the diagonal of a matrix. The wavefront of a row i measures the number of nonzeros in all rows smaller or equal to i. In this section we show how to apply nodal ordering algorithms on symmetric matrices to reduce bandwidth and wavefront. This immediately raises an issue, since the dependency matrix in the previous section is asymmetric. We will address this in the next section. As an example algorithm we explain Cuthill McKee [10], a simple but effective algorithm, developed in 1969.

3.1   Graph Metrics

The bandwidth of a row in a matrix measures the distance of nonzeros in that row to the diagonal. Our conjecture is that bandwidth is important for symbolic reachability, because it tells how close related variables are ordered near the diagonal. We will substantiate this claim in the next sections. The difference between bandwidth and span reduction is that instead of moving a cluster of nonzeros towards an arbitrary column, nonzeros are always moved towards the diagonal. Bandwidth is formalized as follows.

Definition 9 (Bandwidth). *Given an ordered graph $G = (V, E)$, the* vertex bandwidth *[29] is a function $b_G: V \to \mathbb{N}$, such that*

$$b_G(v_i) := \begin{cases} 0, & if \nexists v_j \in V.\ (v_i, v_j) \in E, \\ \max_{(v_i, v_j) \in E} |i - j|, & otherwise. \end{cases}$$

The bandwidth *of a graph is the maximum bandwidth of all vertices $B_G = \max_{v \in V} b_G(v)$. The* profile *of a graph is the sum of all bandwidths $P_G = \sum_{v \in V} b_G(v)$.*

For the dependency graph D of Fig. 2, we have $b_D(t_1) = 4, B_D = 5$ and $P_D = 18$. The *wavefront* of a vertex v is the number of adjacent vertices of all vertices smaller or equal to v. Our conjecture is that wavefront is important for symbolic reachability analysis because the lower the wavefront is, the more nonzeros are located near the bottom right of the matrix, similar to the WES-metrics. The rightmost column corresponds to the bottom variable of the DD, so repeatedly applying the transition relations at the bottom rows in the matrix will correspond to saturating the bottom of the DD. This means that when the wavefront is low, less transitions will be fired at the top of the DD during saturation. Wavefront is formalized as follows.

Definition 10 (Wavefront). *Given an ordered graph $G = (V, E)$, function $adj: 2^V \to 2^V$, is defined such that $adj(X) := \{y \mid (x, y) \in E \wedge x \in X\} \setminus X$, giving the adjacency set of a set X. The* vertex frontwidth *or* vertex wavefront *[29] is a function $f_G: V \to \mathbb{N}$, such that $f_G(v_i) := |\{v_i\} \cup adj(\{v_1, \dots, v_i\})|$. The* average wavefront *of G is $F_G = \sum_{v \in V} f_G(v)/|V|$.*

For the dependency graph D of Fig. 2, $f_D(t_2) = 6$, $f_D(p_1) = 1$ and $F_D = 5.5$.

3.2   Nodal Ordering

Nodal ordering is a method of applying a permutation to the order of vertices in a graph. We will illustrate this with an algorithm by Cuthill and McKee. The way to apply permutations is however identical for all algorithms in this paper.

Definition 11 (Graph Permutation). *Given an ordered graph $G = (V, E)$ with order O, a permutation is a bijective function $\pi_G: V \to V$. The permuted order O^π is:*

$$a \leq_\pi b = (a, b) \in O^\pi \iff \pi(a) \leq \pi(b) = (\pi(a), \pi(b)) \in O.$$

Cuthill McKee is a nodal ordering algorithm for bandwidth reduction. The input to the algorithm is a totally ordered undirected graph. Cuthill McKee is a simple breadth first graph traversal that visits neighbors of vertices in increasing order of degree. If there are vertices with the same degree, an arbitrary vertex may be chosen. The order in which vertices are visited is equivalent to the permutation it produces. The resulting permutation can be directly applied to the input graph.

The reason why Cuthill McKee does not work on asymmetric matrices can be seen in Fig. 2a; the vertices $p_1, \dots, p_5$ do not have outgoing edges, meaning that not all vertices will be visited. The solution to this problem is presented in Sect. 4. The solution involves adding extra edges.

In total we benchmark with six different implementations of nodal ordering algorithms, implemented in Boost and ViennaCL. The implementations are summarized in Fig. 4. There are three categories of algorithms, those that reduce only bandwidth, reduce both bandwidth and profile, and those that reduce profile and wavefront. In both Boost and ViennaCL the Cuthill McKee algorithm is implemented.

Our results confirm that the Cuthill McKee implementations differ in both tools. The Gibbs Poole Stockmeyer (GPS) algorithm is only implemented in ViennaCL and the time complexity of algorithms in ViennaCL is not precisely known, but should be in the order of similar BFS algorithms.

Algorithm	Package	Time complexity	Reducing type
Cuthill McKee	Boost	$\mathcal{O}(\hat{D} \cdot \log \hat{D} \cdot |V|)$	bandwidth
King [17]		$\mathcal{O}(\hat{D}^2 \cdot \log \hat{D} \cdot |E|)$	bandwidth, profile
Sloan [29]		$\mathcal{O}(\log \hat{D} \cdot |E|)$	profile, wavefront
Cuthill McKee	ViennaCL	unknown	bandwidth
adv. Cuthill McKee		unknown	bandwidth
GPS [11]		unknown	bandwidth, profile

Notation: $\hat{D}$ is the maximum degree over all vertices

Fig. 4. List of nodal ordering algorithms

4   Problem and Solution

The main problem with applying nodal ordering algorithms to the dependency graph is that the dependency graph is a directed graph, while nodal ordering algorithms only work on undirected graphs. In other words, the adjacency matrix of such a graph is asymmetric and nodal ordering algorithms only work on symmetric matrices. In this section we show how to symmetrize asymmetric matrices, how bandwidth relates to span and how to de-symmetrize matrices.

4.1   Representations of Dependencies

Symmetrization [24] of a directed graph is defined as follows.

Definition 12 (Symmetrization). *Given an asymmetrix matrix* $A \in \{0,1\}^{M \times N}$, *its symmetrized matrix is* $\hat{A} = \begin{bmatrix} \mathbf{0}^{M \times M} & A \\ A^T & \mathbf{0}^{N \times N} \end{bmatrix}$, *where* $\mathbf{0}^{X \times X}$ *is a square matrix of size X with only 0 entries and A^T is the transpose of A.*

On the graph level, this means that we add the inverse set of edges and assign a total order, i.e. let $A = (V, E)$ be the bi-adjacency graph of A with order O, and $\hat{A}$ the adjacency graph of $\hat{A}$ with order $\hat{O}$, then $\hat{A} = (V, E \cup E^{-1})$ and the vertices of $\hat{A}$ are totally ordered, but constrained to $O \subseteq \hat{O}$.

Figure 5 shows the symmetrized graph $\hat{D}$ of graph D in Fig. 2, the associated metrics are $B_{\hat{D}} = 10$, $P_{\hat{D}} = 87$ and $F_{\hat{D}} = 4.3$. Note that the total order we chose is $t_1 < t_2 < t_3 < t_4 < t_5 < t_6 < p_1 < p_2 < p_3 < p_4 < p_5$.

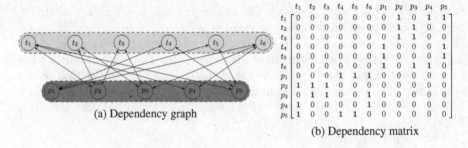

(a) Dependency graph

	t_1	t_2	t_3	t_4	t_5	t_6	p_1	p_2	p_3	p_4	p_5
t_1	0	0	0	0	0	0	0	1	0	1	1
t_2	0	0	0	0	0	0	0	1	1	0	0
t_3	0	0	0	0	0	0	0	1	1	0	0
t_4	0	0	0	0	0	0	1	0	0	0	1
t_5	0	0	0	0	0	0	1	0	0	0	1
t_6	0	0	0	0	0	0	1	0	1	1	0
p_1	0	0	0	1	1	1	0	0	0	0	0
p_2	1	1	1	0	0	0	0	0	0	0	0
p_3	0	1	1	0	0	1	0	0	0	0	0
p_4	1	0	0	0	0	1	0	0	0	0	0
p_5	1	0	0	1	1	0	0	0	0	0	0

(b) Dependency matrix

Fig. 5. Symmetrized versions of the dependencies

Nodal ordering algorithms can be run on any symmetric matrix. It is thus also possible, but optional, to create a total graph of the symmetric dependency matrix. Kaveh [16] hints that some nodal ordering algorithms produce even better permutations on the total graph. Making a graph total involves transforming edges to vertices and connecting incident edges.

Definition 13 (Total Graph). *Given a graph* $G = (V, E)$, *a total graph of* G *is* $G_T = (V_T, E_T)$, *where* $V_T = V \cup E$ *is a set of vertices and* $E_T = E \cup \{(a, (a, b)), ((a, b), a) \mid (a, b) \in E\} \cup \{((a, c), (c, b)) \mid \{(a, c), (c, b)\} \subseteq E\} \subseteq V_T \times V_T$ *is the set of edges, i.e. we add all possible vertex-edge edges, edge-vertex edges and edge-edge edges.*

For example, let $\hat{D}$ be the directed graph in Fig. 5 and $\hat{D}_T$ its *total graph*, if we order the new vertices in $\hat{D}_T$ in lexicographic order we have $B_{\hat{D}_T} = 19$, $P_{\hat{D}_T} = 395$ and $F_{\hat{D}_T} = 11$. We now have two type of graphs to represent the dependencies on which nodal ordering algorithms can be run.

We can apply Cuthill McKee to reduce bandwidth as follows. The dependency graph $\hat{D}$ in Fig. 5 has multiple vertices with equal degree. When vertices have equal degree, we pick the smallest vertex. As a starting vertex we thus pick t_2. Then Cuthill McKee visits vertices in the order $t_2 < p_2 < p_3 < t_3 < t_1 < t_6 < p_4 < p_5 < p_1 < t_4 < t_5$.

Figure 6 shows the permuted symmetrized dependency matrix. Its associated metrics are $B_{\hat{D}^\pi} = 3$, $P_{\hat{D}^\pi} = 40$, $F_{\hat{D}^\pi} = 3.2$. This is a reduction in bandwidth of 7. If we permute the total graph with Cuthill McKee in Boost we get $B_{\hat{D}_T^\pi} = 7$, $P_{\hat{D}_T^\pi} = 165$ and $F_{\hat{D}_T^\pi} = 5.0$. With the total graph we have a reduction in bandwidth of 12.

Why reducing bandwidth may also reduce span is because span is limited by twice the bandwidth, plus the diagonal.

	t_2	p_2	p_3	t_3	t_1	t_6	p_4	p_5	p_1	t_4	t_5
t_2	0	1	1	0	0	0	0	0	0	0	0
p_2	1	0	0	1	1	0	0	0	0	0	0
p_3	1	0	0	1	0	1	0	0	0	0	0
t_3	0	1	1	0	0	0	0	0	0	0	0
t_1	0	1	0	0	0	0	1	1	0	0	0
t_6	0	0	1	0	0	0	1	0	1	0	0
p_4	0	0	0	0	0	1	0	0	1	0	0
p_5	0	0	0	0	1	0	0	0	0	1	1
p_1	0	0	0	0	0	1	0	0	0	1	1
t_4	0	0	0	0	0	0	1	1	0	0	0
t_5	0	0	0	0	0	0	1	1	0	0	0

Fig. 6. Permuted matrix

Theorem 1 (Bandwidth Limits Span). *Given an ordered graph* $G = (V, E)$, *we have* $\forall v \in V \colon s_G(v) \le 2 \cdot b_G(v) + 1.$[2]

Proposition 1 (Span and Symmetrization). *Give a graph* $G = (V, E)$, *and its symmetrized graph* $\hat{G}$, *we have* $ES_{\hat{G}} = ES_G + ES_H$, *where* $H = (V, E^{-1})$.

If G represents the dependency relation, these results tell that the profile $P_{\hat{G}}$ limits the event span ES_G. Thus reducing the value $P_{\hat{G}}$ should also reduce the value ES_G.

4.2   De-symmetrization of Permuted Matrices

The question that remains now is how to de-symmetrize the dependency matrix in Fig. 6. This is essential, because if we would simply use the permuted total order we can incorrectly swap columns with rows and vice versa. De-symmetrization works as follows. Consider a PTS $\mathcal{P} = ((S_1, \ldots, S_N),$ $(\rightarrow_1, \ldots, \rightarrow_M), \iota)$, with a symmetrized dependency graph $\hat{D} = (R \cup C, E)$ and a permuted total order $\hat{O}^\pi$, where R represents the transition groups $1, \ldots, M$ and C represents the state slots $1, \ldots, N$. The de-symmetrized matrix, or directed graph is $D = (R \cup C, E \cap (R \times C))$. Its permuted partial order is $O^\pi = (\hat{O}^\pi \cap (R \times R)) \cup (\hat{O}^\pi \cap (C \times C))$. If a nodal ordering algorithm is run on the total graph of the dependency graph with order O_T^π, the approach to obtain the partial order is identical (i.e. $O^\pi = (\hat{O}_T^\pi \cap (R \times R)) \cup (\hat{O}_T^\pi \cap (C \times C)))$.

Figure 7 shows the de-symmetrization of the dependency matrix in Fig. 6. Let D^π be the de-symmetrized graph, the event span metrics are $ES_{D^\pi} = 16$ and $WES_{D^\pi} = 19$. The partial order for D^π is $t_2 < t_3 < t_1 < t_6 < t_4 < t_5 \cup p_2 < p_3 <$ $p_4 < p_5 < p_1$. We thus have a reduction in event span of 6 (compared to the value computed in Theorem 7), and a reduction in weighted event span from 32 to 19. If we permute the total graph with Cuthill McKee in Boost we also get $ES_{D^\pi} = 16$ and $WES_{D^\pi} = 19$.

$$
\begin{array}{c}
\begin{array}{ccccc}
p_2 & p_3 & p_4 & p_5 & p_1
\end{array} \\
\begin{array}{c}
2 \\ 3 \\ 1 \\ 6 \\ 4 \\ 5
\end{array}
\left[
\begin{array}{ccccc}
1 & 1 & 0 & 0 & 0 \\
1 & 1 & 0 & 0 & 0 \\
1 & 0 & 1 & 1 & 0 \\
0 & 1 & 1 & 0 & 1 \\
0 & 0 & 0 & 1 & 1 \\
0 & 0 & 0 & 1 & 1
\end{array}
\right]
\end{array}
$$

Fig. 7. Asymmetric matrix

Figure 8a and b visualize some dependency matrices from real world examples, after applying some nodal reordering algorithms from Fig. 4. Their NWES metrics are shown as well. The first two matrices are of a model with 20 dining philosophers, one of the best results achieved in our benchmarks. Even on instances with 5000 philosophers (*25.000 variables*) we get very small weighted event span, and the permutation is computed within milliseconds. The matrices from the `database10UNFOLD.pnml` show the more typical structure of dependency matrices, e.g. the *band* produced by the GPS algorithm is clearly visible. In Fig. 8b one can see the difference between Sloan and GPS; Sloan does not try to reduce bandwidth, only profile. In our experiments we also see that Sloan is more capable at reducing WES than GPS.

---

[2] Theorem 1 can be easily proven with the triangle inequality theorem.

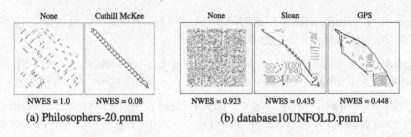

Fig. 8. Example de-symmetrized matrices

We have set up a large number of experiments, in order to answer several relevant questions: First, which algorithm and which type of symmetric graph is best for reducing WES? Second, how well does this result compare to Noack and FORCE, which are currently considered state of the art? Third, does the choice of best algorithm/graph depend on the chosen specification language? Fourth, can we quantify the performance of the best algorithm/graph?

5   Experiments

To show the applicability of nodal ordering algorithms to variable ordering, we benchmark with five different modeling formalisms[3]. There are 47 B specifications, collected through the B community [19]. We have 264 DVE specifications from the BEEM [23] database. From the examples directory in the mCRL2 [9] distribution we collected 142 specifications. There are 314 Petri nets from the 2015 model checking contest [18]. Also, we have a collection of 18 PROMELA models. For two reasons, we could not always use complete sets of specifications, such as for the PNML language, where the complete set consists of 361 Petri nets. First, some total graph representations of the dependencies are too large to compute an ordering for within our time limit of one hour. Second, the implementation of Sloan in Boost crashes when run on a graph that has disconnected components. In our benchmarks we thus vary over a total of 785 specifications, two graph representations, and 9 ordering algorithms. The 9 algorithms consists of those in Fig. 4, 2 variations of Noack's [22] algorithm, and FORCE [1].

Our benchmark generates a lot of data; to concisely present this data we use graphics instead of tables. To show which combination of algorithm and graph performs best we compute Mean Standard Scores (MSSs) and show scatter plots that allow us to quantify the performance of the best algorithm/graph. Figure 9 shows the MSSs for all five languages, plus the MSS for all languages combined.

The MSS for a combination of algorithm and graph is defined as follows. Let A be the set of combinations of algorithms and graph representations, i.e. the values on the x-axes in Fig. 9. We use some abbreviations: CMB = Cuthill McKee in Boost, aCM = advanced Cuthill McKee, K = King, GPS = Gibbs Poole Stockmeyer, and CMV = Cuthill McKee in ViennaCL. Let S be the

---

[3] Reproduction instructions at: https://github.com/utwente-fmt/BW-NFM2016

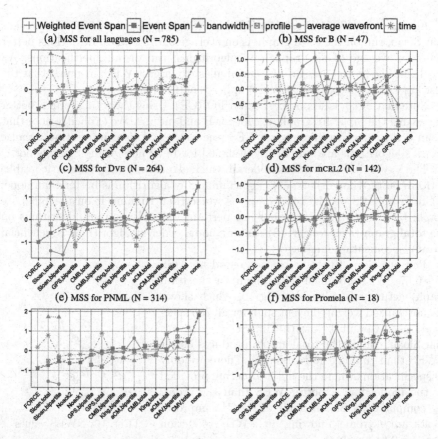

Fig. 9. Mean Standard Scores for WES, indicating the best algorithm (Color figure online)

set of specifications, e.g. a Petri net with 20 dining philosophers. The used set S appears in the titles of Fig. 9a to f: $|S| = N$. Given a combination of an algorithm and graph $a \in A$, the MSS for a metric m, such as event span, is $MSS_a = \sum_{s \in S} \frac{m(s,a) - \mu_{a' \in A} m(s,a')}{\sigma_{a' \in A} m(s,a')} / |S|$, where $m(s,a)$ denotes the value of the metric for a combination of an algorithm and a graph of a specification s, and $\mu_{a' \in A} m(s,a')$ and $\sigma_{a' \in A} m(s,a')$ denote the mean and standard deviation for s over all combinations of algorithms and graphs. The values of MSS_a appear on the y-axes.[4]

---

[4] There are three side notes. First, μ and σ for bandwidth, profile and wavefront are computed per graph type, because the bipartite and total graph have different sizes. Second, Noack1 and Noack2 can only be computed directly on Petri nets (PNML, Fig. 9e), so bandwidth, profile and wavefront are unknown. Third, when FORCE is executed or without reordering, bandwidth, profile and wavefront are not reported. The reason is that our symmetrization approach typically produces high values for those metrics. Event span does not have this problem.

An example MSS in Fig. 9a for WES is $MSS_{(Sloan,total)} = -0.57$. This means that Sloan, run on the total graph, is on average 0.57 standard deviations better than the average of all graphs and algorithms, run on all specifications. All graphs in Fig. 9a to f are sorted from smallest to largest WES, meaning that the best algorithm (according to WES) appears on the left.

Note that Sloan is second best (after FORCE). Using the total graph is better than using the bipartite graph, except for B and mCRL2. We explicitly note that Sloan beats Noack in minimizing WES (see Fig. 9e). This is interesting because Noack's algorithms are specifically designed for Petri nets, while Sloan is not.

The results in Fig. 9 tell us in detail which algorithms and symmetric graphs perform better than others, e.g.: (1) running any algorithm is better than none; (2) running GPS on the total graph is worse than running it on the bipartite graph; (3) King's algorithm does not perform well; (4) running algorithms on the total graph takes longer; (5) running nodal ordering algorithms is beneficial for any specification language.

The question still remains, how good an MSS of -0.57 (WES obtained with Sloan on the total graph) actually is. Consider Fig. 10, which shows the normalized weighted event span for all 785 specifications. A point below the line $x = y$ means that Sloan, run on the total graph, produces better NWES than running no reordering. There are only 69 specifications where the initial ordering provided by the model had a better WES than the ordering computed by Sloan. Some of the 716 improvements are extreme, showing an NWES reduction from ~ 1.0 to nearly 0.

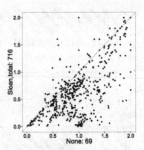

Fig. 10. NWES values

6   Conclusion

We have shown that bandwidth and wavefront reduction algorithms are clearly applicable to symbolic reachability analysis for many specification formalisms. We demonstrated how they perform relative to each other and to other state-of-the-art algorithms. The best nodal ordering algorithm for variable reordering is Sloan; for all five tested specification languages Sloan is the clear winner when it comes to reduction of weighted event span. Furthermore Sloan's algorithm beats Noack's algorithms that are specifically designed for Petri nets, but FORCE performs even better on WES.

There are two branches of possibilities for future work. The first is to confirm the applicability to other model checkers, such as SmArT [7], MARCIE [13] and ITS-Tools [30]. These tools employ advanced saturation algorithms, which can be used to confirm whether bandwidth and wavefront reduction is useful in other model checkers as well. Our approach works for disjunctive partitioning schemes. A remaining question is, whether our method also works for conjunctive [5] partitioning schemes, such as in NuSMV [8]. Furthermore bandwidth and wavefront reduction should be applicable to SAT/SMT solving, since also the FORCE algorithm is used in both symbolic reachability and SAT/SMT solving. The hypergraph used by FORCE is equivalent to our dependency graph: a hyperedge is equivalent to a vertex (including its edges) that represents a transition group.

The second branch of related work is to consider other graph representations and other bandwidth and wavefront reduction algorithms. Kaveh [16] discusses many different graph transformations of the dependency graph on which nodal ordering algorithms can be run. We have only investigated the total graph. Reid et al. [24] provide two more methods of symmetrizing an asymmetric matrix A, namely $A + A^T$ and $A \cdot A^T$. Additionally the authors provide a modified Cuthill McKee algorithm that can be run on an asymmetric matrix directly, available in the HSL library. A survey [20] covers the state of the art in bandwidth reduction, including metaheuristic algorithms, of which many have been developed in the past decade. Recently, advances have been made in parallelizing [15] nodal ordering algorithms. Running nodal ordering algorithms on the total graph is considerably slower than on the default dependency graph, so running parallel algorithms on the total graph would provide a welcome speedup.

Figure 9 showed that FORCE produces better WES than Sloan. Future work includes performing extensive benchmarks to see how well saturation algorithms actually perform with the variable orders computed by the presented nodal ordering algorithms. We have done some preliminary experiments with a saturation-like algorithm in LTSMIN, mainly to illustrate how Sloan affects WES, *peak nodes*, and reachability time. The peak nodes indicate the highest number of DD nodes to store the visited set during the whole computation, often much higher than the DD-size at the end of reachability. So peak nodes indicate the limiting factor in terms of memory usage. Keeping the number of peak nodes low is the main motivation to perform static variable ordering.

Figure 11 shows the Mean Standard Score (MSS) for peak nodes, WES and reachability time. The MSS values are sorted from smallest peak nodes to largest, showing the best algorithm on the left. We ran a benchmark on all 106 PNML models for which the saturation algorithm completed within 30 min. For peak nodes

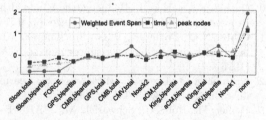

Fig. 11. Saturation results (N = 106) (Color figure online)

and time, the best algorithm is Sloan, not FORCE. The difference in MSS between Sloan/total and FORCE for peak nodes is 0.13. Also, Noack appears even further to the right than in Fig. 9e. This suggests that Sloan has interesting properties, besides showing that bandwidth reduction is a good alternative to span reduction. We conjecture that Sloan is a good algorithm for full saturation since it also reduces wavefront. Moreover, nodal ordering algorithms also compute an order on the transition groups, unlike FORCE and Noack. It would be interesting to see how chaining and saturation benefit from the computed order on transition groups.

References

1. Aloul, F.A., Markov, I.L., Sakallah, K.A.: FORCE: a fast and easy-to-implement variable-ordering heuristic. In: 13th ACM, VLSI, pp. 116–119. ACM (2003)
2. Blom, S., van de Pol, J.: Symbolic reachability for process algebras with recursive data types. In: Fitzgerald, J.S., Haxthausen, A.E., Yenigun, H. (eds.) ICTAC 2008. LNCS, vol. 5160, pp. 81–95. Springer, Heidelberg (2008)
3. Bollig, B., Wegener, I.: Improving the variable ordering of OBDDs is NP-complete. IEEE Trans. Comput. **45**(9), 993–1002 (1996)
4. Bryant, R.E.: Graph-based algorithms for boolean function manipulation. IEEE Trans. Comput. **35**(8), 677–691 (1986)
5. Burch, J.R., Clarke, E.M., Long, D.E.: Symbolic model checking with partitioned transition relations. In: VLSI 1991 (1991)
6. Ciardo, G., Marmorstein, R.M., Siminiceanu, R.: The saturation algorithm for symbolic state-space exploration. STTT **8**(1), 4–25 (2006)
7. Ciardo, G., Miner, A.S., Wan, M.: Advanced features in SMART: the stochastic model checking analyzer for reliability and timing. SIGMETRICS PER **36**(4), 58–63 (2009)
8. Cimatti, A., Clarke, E., Giunchiglia, E., Giunchiglia, F., Pistore, M., Roveri, M., Sebastiani, R., Tacchella, A.: NuSMV 2: an opensource tool for symbolic model checking. In: Brinksma, E., Larsen, K.G. (eds.) CAV 2002. LNCS, vol. 2404, p. 359. Springer, Heidelberg (2002)
9. Cranen, S., Groote, J.F., Keiren, J.J.A., Stappers, F.P.M., de Vink, E.P., Wesselink, W., Willemse, T.A.C.: An overview of the mCRL2 toolset and its recent advances. In: Piterman, N., Smolka, S.A. (eds.) TACAS 2013 (ETAPS 2013). LNCS, vol. 7795, pp. 199–213. Springer, Heidelberg (2013)
10. Cuthill, E., McKee, J.: Reducing the bandwidth of sparse symmetric matrices. In: Proceedings 24th National Conference, pp. 157–172. ACM (1969)
11. Gibbs, N.E., Poole Jr., W.G., Stockmeyer, P.K.: An algorithm for reducing the bandwidth and profile of a sparse matrix. SIAM J. Num. Anal. **13**(2), 236–250 (1976)
12. Grumberg, O., Livne, S., Markovitch, S.: Learning to order BDD variables in verification. JAIR **18**, 83–116 (2003)
13. Heiner, M., Rohr, C., Schwarick, M.: MARCIE – model checking and reachability analysis done efficiently. In: Colom, J.-M., Desel, J. (eds.) PETRI NETS 2013. LNCS, vol. 7927, pp. 389–399. Springer, Heidelberg (2013)
14. Kant, G., Laarman, A., Meijer, J., van de Pol, J., Blom, S., van Dijk, T.: LTSmin: high-performance language-independent model checking. In: Baier, C., Tinelli, C. (eds.) TACAS 2015. LNCS, vol. 9035, pp. 692–707. Springer, Heidelberg (2015)
15. Karantasis, K.I., et al.: Parallelization of reordering algorithms for bandwidth and wavefront reduction. In: ICHPC 2014, pp. 921–932. IEEE (2014)
16. Kaveh, A.: Ordering for Optimal Patterns of Structural Matrices. Wiley, New York (2006). pp. 191–271
17. King, I.P.: An automatic reordering scheme for simultaneous equations derived from network systems. Int. J. Numer. Meth. Eng. **2**(4), 523–533 (1970)

18. Kordon, F., et al.: Complete Results for the 2015 Edition of the Model Checking Contest (2015). http://mcc.lip6.fr/2015/results.php
19. Leuschel, M., Butler, M.J.: ProB: an automated analysis toolset for the B method. STTT **10**(2), 185–203 (2008)
20. Mafteiu-Scai, L.O.: The bandwidths of a matrix. A survey of algorithms. Ann. West Univ. Timisoara-Math. **52**(2), 183–223 (2014)
21. Meijer, J., Kant, G., Blom, S., van de Pol, J.: Read, write and copy dependencies for symbolic model checking. In: Yahav, E. (ed.) HVC 2014. LNCS, vol. 8855, pp. 204–219. Springer, Heidelberg (2014)
22. Noack, A.: A ZBDD package for efficient model checking of Petri nets. Forschungsbericht, Branderburgische Technische Uinversität Cottbus (1999)
23. Pelánek, R.: BEEM: benchmarks for explicit model checkers. In: Bošnački, D., Edelkamp, S. (eds.) SPIN 2007. LNCS, vol. 4595, pp. 263–267. Springer, Heidelberg (2007)
24. Reid, J.K., Scott, J.A.: Reducing the total bandwidth of a sparse unsymmetric matrix. SIAM J. Matrix Anal. Appl. **28**(3), 805–821 (2006)
25. Rice, M., Kulhari, S.: A survey of static variable ordering heuristics for efficient BDD/MDD construction. Technical report, University of California (2008)
26. Rudell, R.: Dynamic variable ordering for ordered binary decision diagrams. In: ICCAD1993. IEEE (1993)
27. Rupp, K., Rudolf, F., Weinbub, J.: ViennaCL - a high level linear algebra library for GPUs and multi-core CPUs. In: GPUScA 2010, pp. 51–56 (2010)
28. Siminiceanu, R.I., Ciardo, G.: New metrics for static variable ordering in decision diagrams. In: Hermanns, H., Palsberg, J. (eds.) TACAS 2006. LNCS, vol. 3920, pp. 90–104. Springer, Heidelberg (2006)
29. Sloan, S.W.: A FORTRAN program for profile and wavefront reduction. Int. J. Numer. Meth. Eng. **28**(11), 2651–2679 (1989)
30. Thierry-Mieg, Y.: Symbolic model-checking using ITS-tools. In: Baier, C., Tinelli, C. (eds.) TACAS 2015. LNCS, vol. 9035, pp. 231–237. Springer, Heidelberg (2015)

Gray-Box Learning of Serial Compositions
of Mealy Machines

Andreas Abel$^{(\boxtimes)}$ and Jan Reineke

Department of Computer Science, Saarland University, Saarbücken, Germany
{abel,reineke}@cs.uni-saarland.de

Abstract. We study the following *gray-box learning* problem: Given the serial composition of two Mealy machines A and B, where A is known and B is unknown, the goal is to learn a model of B using only output and equivalence queries on the composed machine.

We introduce an algorithm that solves this problem, using at most $|B|$ equivalence queries, independently of the size of A. We discuss its efficient implementation and evaluate the algorithm on existing benchmark sets as well as randomly-generated machines.

1 Introduction

Tools to analyze software or hardware systems, such as static analyzers or model checkers, require accurate system models as input. Third-party components, however, are rarely specified at the level of detail required by such tools.

One approach to automatically obtain formal models of systems is active learning. Here, one commonly assumes an oracle, or teacher, that admits two kinds of queries about the system: output queries return the result of the system for a specific input; equivalence queries check whether a conjectured model is consistent with the system to be learned and return a counterexample if not. Based on this setup, Angluin introduced the L^* algorithm [2] for learning deterministic finite automata. L^* has since been extended to other modeling formalisms, such as Mealy machines [19], register automata [11], or symbolic automata [16]. It is also at the heart of several model checking approaches, including [4,8,20].

As the system is treated as a black box, no information about the internal structure of the system can be taken into account by most existing learning algorithms. In practice, however, systems are often composed of sub-components, for some of which models might be available, but it is not possible to access the known and the unknown parts separately from the outside. Partial information about the inner workings of a system may be inferred from manuals or conjectured from similar, yet better documented systems. This scenario is depicted in Fig. 1.

While it is in theory possible to learn a model of the entire system using existing black-box approaches, this is often not viable in practice because the state space is too large. A problem, which has received little attention in the literature so far, is how to use the available information about the system to focus the learning algorithm on those parts that are unknown. This problem could be termed *gray-box learning*.

© Springer International Publishing Switzerland 2016
S. Rayadurgam and O. Tkachuk (Eds.): NFM 2016, LNCS 9690, pp. 272–287, 2016.
DOI: 10.1007/978-3-319-40648-0_21

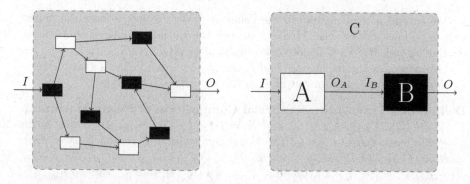

Fig. 1. Mealy machine network   **Fig. 2.** Serial composition

In this paper, as a first step toward solving this problem, we study one specific instance: We assume that the system C is the serial composition of two Mealy machines A and B, and that we have a model for the left machine (A) and want to learn the right machine (B). We further assume that we can perform output and equivalence queries only on C as a whole. This scenario is shown in Fig. 2.

While output queries can often be realized cheaply by measurements on the actual system, equivalence queries can usually only be approximated by a large number of such measurements. Our primary focus is thus to minimize the number of equivalence queries. We introduce an algorithm to exactly learn B in the context of A that performs at most $|B|$ equivalence queries, where $|B|$ denotes the number of states of B. We also discuss a more practical variant of this algorithm that requires a polynomial number of equivalence queries in the size of B.

We evaluate several variants of our approach on compositions of randomly-generated machines against an implementation of the classic L^* algorithm in LearnLib [13]. Furthermore, we also compare the performance of our approach with the tool BICA [17] on a set of standard benchmarks for minimizing incompletely specified Mealy machines. We show that our approach requires significantly fewer output and equivalence queries on most benchmarks.

2   Problem Statement

In this section, we first formally define several concepts used throughout this paper. Then, we give a precise description of the problem that we address.

2.1   Basic Notions

Definition 1 (Mealy Machine). *A Mealy machine M is a tuple (Q, I, O, δ, q_r), where $Q \neq \emptyset$ is a finite set of states, $I \neq \emptyset$ is a finite set of input symbols, $O \neq \emptyset$ is a finite set of output symbols, $\delta : Q \times I \to Q \times O$ is the transition function, and $q_r \in Q$ is the initial (reset) state.*

We extend δ to sequences in the usual way. We use ϵ to denote the empty sequence. Further, we use $M(x)$ to denote the output sequence of M when reading x, and $M_L(x)$ to denote last output of M when reading x.

Given two Mealy machines A and B, we can compose them to a serial Mealy machine C by using the output of A as the input for B. Formally:

Definition 2 ((Synchronous) Serial Composition of Mealy Machines).
Let $A = (Q_A, I_A, O_A, \delta_A, q_{r,A})$ and $B = (Q_B, I_B, O_B, \delta_B, q_{r,B})$ be two Mealy machines such that $O_A \subseteq I_B$. The serial composition of A and B is a Mealy machine $C = (Q, I, O, \delta, q_r)$, where $Q := Q_A \times Q_B$, $I := I_A$, $O := O_B$, $\delta((q_A, q_B), i) := ((q'_A, q'_B), o)$, where $(q'_A, o_A) := \delta_A(q_A, i)$, and $(q'_B, o) := \delta_B(q_B, o_A)$, and $q_r = (q_{r,A}, q_{r,B})$.

Given a composition of two Mealy machines A and B, we define a machine B' to be right-equivalent to B in the context of A if the composition of A and B describes a machine that is equivalent to the composition of A and B'. Formally:

Definition 3 (Right-equivalence). *Let A, B, and B' be Mealy machines. Then, B' is right-equivalent to B in the context of A iff $\forall x \in I^* : B(A(x)) = B'(A(x))$.*

2.2   The Gray-Box Learning Problem

In this paper, we address the following problem. We assume that we have a serial composition C of two Mealy machines A and B. Further, we assume that we have a model of A, but B is unknown. While we do not have a model of C, we assume that we can determine the output of C on any input by an *output query*, and we can test whether a machine is equivalent to C by an *equivalence query*.

Using existing techniques, like Angluin's L^* algorithm [2], one could consider C to be a black box and learn a model of C. Such an approach would in the worst case employ a polynomial number of output and equivalence queries in the size of C, which can be up to $|A| \cdot |B|$.

Instead, our goal is to exploit the knowledge we have about A, and to learn a model of a minimum-size machine B', such that B' is right-equivalent to B in the context of A. In particular, as we consider equivalence queries to be more expensive than output queries, we want the number of equivalence queries to be polynomial in the number of states of B', independently of the size of A.

3   Preliminaries

Existing active learning approaches for Mealy machines (and related machine types) are usually based on a Myhill-Nerode-like equivalence relation that partitions the set of input words into classes such that the words that are in the same class cannot be distinguished with respect to different suffixes:

Definition 4 (Equivalence of input words). *Given a function $F : I^* \to O$, two words $x, y \in I^*$ are equivalent, $x \sim y$, iff $\forall z \in I^* : F(x \cdot z) = F(y \cdot z)$.*

F can be modeled by a Mealy machine iff this relation has finitely many equivalence classes. One can then construct a minimum-size Mealy machine whose states are the equivalence classes of this relation. Existing approaches compute the equivalence relation in a co-inductive fashion. In the beginning, they consider all words to be equivalent. Then, in each round this hypothesis is refined by identifying at least one new equivalence class, until the equivalence relation is fully determined.

If we consider the machine B in the serial composition with A, then it is possible that not all input sequences for B can be produced by A. Let $tr(A) = \{A(x) \mid x \in I^*\}$ be the set of output sequences that A can produce. For each output sequence $x \in tr(A)$ there might be multiple input sequences that produce this output. Let $A^{-1} : tr(A) \rightarrow I^*$ be a function such that $A^{-1}(x)$ returns one of these input sequences. In the following, it will not be important which of the possibly multiple sequences is actually returned.

We have that every right-equivalent Mealy machine B' for B in the context of A has to agree with the partial function $F_P : I_B^* \rightharpoonup O$ such that $\forall x \in tr(A) : F_P(x) = B_L(x)$. Note that while we do not have immediate access to B, we can use output queries on C to access B, as for all $x \in tr(A)$, $B_L(x) = C_L(A^{-1}(x))$.

Similarly to Definition 4, we define two words to be *right-compatible* in the context of A iff they cannot be distinguished with respect to different suffixes.

Definition 5 (Right-compatibility). *Two words* $x, y \in I_B^*$ *are right-compatible in the context of* A, $x \sim_A y$, *iff* $\forall z \in I_B^* : (xz \notin tr(A) \vee yz \notin tr(A) \vee B_L(xz) = B_L(yz))$. *Otherwise,* x *and* y *are incompatible,* $x \nsim_A y$.

However, right-compatibility is, unlike equivalence, not transitive. Thus it is not an equivalence relation, which means we cannot directly use the construction sketched above to build a minimum-size machine.

To see this, consider a Mealy machine A and two output symbols $a, b \in O_A$ with $\forall z \in I_B^* : az, bz \in tr(A) \wedge B_L(az) = 0 \wedge B_L(bz) = 1$ and $\forall z \in I_B^* : cz \notin tr(A)$. So B always outputs 0 if the first output of A was a, it always outputs 1 if the first output of A was b, and A never outputs c as the first output.

This means that $a \sim_A c$ and $b \sim_A c$, but $a \nsim_A b$. For this example, we can build a machine with three states that is right-equivalent to B. From the start state, a transition with c can go to any state. This also shows that there can be multiple machines with the minimum number of states that are right-equivalent to B.

4   Approach

Equivalence queries are typically assumed to be more expensive than output queries. Many existing active learning techniques therefore focus on keeping the number of required equivalence queries low.

At a high level, Angluin's L^* algorithm for instance, can be described as follows. In each round, the algorithm first performs a sequence of output queries in a systematic way, until there is exactly one machine of minimum size that is consistent with the results from all output queries performed so far. Only then, the algorithm performs an equivalence query. If this query returns a counterexample, this implies that the correct machine must have at least one additional state. Thus, Angluin's algorithm performs at most n equivalence queries, where n is the size of the minimal correct machine.

Unlike in Angluin's setting, in general no unique machine of minimum size that is consistent with a set of observations exists. The basic idea behind our approach is to perform output queries until *all* machines of minimum size that are consistent with these queries are right-equivalent in the context of A. We then perform an equivalence query for one of these machines. If this query results in a counterexample, this counterexample witnesses that all of these machines are incorrect, and thus, the correct machine must have at least one additional state.

One challenge is to find a suitable sequence of output queries that is guaranteed to reduce the number of machines that are consistent with all queries performed so far. The basic idea is to iteratively construct all machines of minimum size that agree with all of the previous queries. We can then check whether each pair of these machines is right-equivalent. If they are not, we use a distinguishing sequence as a counterexample, without performing an equivalence query.

However, applying this approach naively would not be viable in many cases because there can be an exponential number of machines of the same size that are consistent with a set of observations, in particular in the beginning, when only a small number of queries have been performed. Thus, we identify a number of necessary conditions for candidate machines to be right-equivalent which can be efficiently determined on observation tables. Some of these conditions correspond to notions from Angluin's algorithm, such as consistency and closedness, while others, like input-completeness, are special to our particular setting.

In the rest of this section, we describe our proposed algorithm in detail and introduce the necessary theoretical concepts. In particular, we describe in detail which output queries our algorithm performs to systematically reduce the number of machines that are consistent with the observations made so far. In the following, we assume that the reader is familiar with Angluin's L^* algorithm [2].

4.1   Observation Tables

The main data structure used in our approach is an *observation table*. The rows of the table are indexed by a set of prefixes, the columns by a set of suffixes, and the entries of the table store the last output symbol of an output query for the concatenation of the corresponding prefix and suffix. If this concatenation is not a possible output sequence of the left machine A, we do not perform an output query, but store $\bot$ in this cell instead. In contrast to most previous definitions, our observation tables *do not* consist of two explicitly distinguished parts.

Definition 6 (Observation Table). *An observation table $T = (S, E, Q)$ consists of a finite non-empty prefix-closed set of prefixes $S \subseteq tr(A)$, a finite suffix-closed set of suffixes $E \subseteq I_B^*$ (such that $I_B \subseteq E$, and $\epsilon \notin E$), and a function $Q : (S, E) \to O_B$ such that $Q(x, e) = C_L(A^{-1}(xe))$ iff $xe \in tr(A)$ and $Q(x, e) = \bot$ otherwise.*

For a set $R \subseteq S$ and $a \in I_B$, let $Succ_T(R, a) := \{xa \mid x \in R \land xa \in S\}$, i.e., $Succ_T(R, a)$ is the set of successor rows for elements of R that are in the table.

In the following, we will use the term *row* both for the prefixes and for the entries of a row, when it is clear what is meant from the context.

We call two rows compatible if all columns that are not $\perp$ in both rows are the same.

Definition 7 (Compatibility). *The rows for two prefixes $x, y \in S$ are compatible iff $\forall e \in E : Q(x, e) = \perp \lor Q(y, e) = \perp \lor Q(x, e) = Q(y, e)$.*

We call an observation table consistent if whenever two rows are compatible, their successors are also compatible.

Definition 8 (Consistency). *An observation table T is consistent iff for all prefixes $x, y \in S$ such that the rows for x and y are compatible, for all $a \in I_B$ all rows in $Succ_T(\{x, y\}, a)$ are compatible.*

If there is a suffix $e \in E$ that shows that the successors of x and y under an input a are not compatible, then ae is a suffix that shows that the rows for x and y are also not compatible. Thus, we can add ae to E to resolve this inconsistency.

We define a partition of the set of rows as follows.

Definition 9 (Partition). *A partition for observation table $T = (S, E, Q)$ is a partition $P = \{P_1, ..., P_k\}$ of S, such that*

- *for all $x, y \in P_i$: the rows for x and y are compatible,*
- *for each P_i, and for all $a \in I_B$, there is a P_j, such that: $Succ_T(P_i, a) \subseteq P_j$.*

Note that if $Succ_T(P_i, a) \neq \emptyset$ then there is only one such P_j since all classes of the partition are disjoint.

We will later show how we can use partitions to build candidate machines that are consistent with the observations made so far. The words in the same class of a partition will then lead to the same states in these candidate machines.

We call a partition closed if for each class of the partition and each input symbol a, the observation table contains a successor row (under a) for at least one word of this class, if we know from the observations made so far that such a successor must exist. Our inference algorithm uses closedness as a way to determine which additional rows should be added to the table.

Definition 10 (Closedness for Partitions). *Let $P = \{P_1, ..., P_k\}$ be a partition for $T = (S, E, Q)$. P is closed if for all $P_i \in P$: if there is some $x \in P_i$ and some sequence $az \in E$ with $a \in I_B$ and $z \in I_B^*$ such that $Q(x, az) \neq \perp$, then there must be some $y \in P_i$ for which $Q(y, az) \neq \perp$, and $ya \in S$.*

Given an observation table T, let $\Pi(T, n)$ be the set of all partitions of size n. Let $\Pi_{min}(T)$ be the set of partitions of minimum size for an observation table T, i.e., $\Pi_{min}(T) = \Pi(T, m)$ where $m = min\{n \mid \Pi(T, n) \neq \emptyset\}$.

Definition 11 (Closedness). *An observation table $T = (S, E, Q)$ is closed if all minimum-size partitions $P \in \Pi_{min}(T)$ are closed.*

Definition 12 (Partial Closedness). *An observation table T is partially closed (p-closed) iff for all prefixes $x \in S$ and all sequences $az \in E$ such that $Q(x, az) \neq \bot$, there is a prefix $y \in S$ such that the rows for x and y are compatible, $Q(y, az) \neq \bot$ and $ya \in S$.*

If a table is not p-closed, then no partition can be closed.

Definition 13 (Agreement). *A Mealy machine M agrees with an observation table $T = (S, E, Q)$ if for all $x \in S$ and $e \in E$, $Q(x, e) = \bot \vee Q(x, e) = M_L(xe)$.*

For any closed partition $P = \{P_1, ..., P_k\}$ in $\Pi_{min}(T)$, we can build the following Mealy machine $M_P = (Q, I, O, \delta, q_r)$ with $k + 1$ states: $Q := P \cup \{error\}$, $I := I_B$, $O := O_B \cup \bot$, $\delta(P_i, a) := (error, \bot)$ if $Succ_T(P_i, a) = \emptyset$, otherwise: $\delta(P_i, a) := (P_j, b)$ such that for some $x \in P_i$: $Q(x, a) = b \neq \bot$ and $Succ_T(P_i, a) \subseteq P_j$, and $q_r := P_i$ such that $\epsilon \in P_i$.

This machine enters a special error state if there is a class of the partition, for which the successor class is not defined.

In the following, we will use the notation $\pi_i(t)$ to denote the i-th component of a tuple t, e.g., $\pi_2(q_r, a) = a$.

Lemma 1. *Let P be a closed partition of an observation table $T = (S, E, Q)$, and $M_P = (Q, I, O, \delta, q_r)$ the Mealy machine constructed as described above. Then for all words $x \in S$, $x \in \pi_1(\delta^*(q_r, x))$.*

Theorem 1. *For a closed partition P of an observation table T, the machine M_P agrees with T.*

Definition 14. *Let $\gamma(M_P)$ be the set of machines with k states that can be obtained from M_P by removing the error state and replacing the transitions to the error state by transitions with arbitrary outputs and successor states.*

Theorem 2. *Let T be a closed observation table. Then every minimum-size machine M that agrees with T is isomorphic to an element of $\gamma(M_P)$ for some $P \in \Pi_{min}(T)$.*

Theorem 3. *If for a closed partition P the error state is not reachable in a composition of A with M_P, then all machines in $\gamma(M_P)$ are right-equivalent.[1]*

If the error state is reachable, we can use an input sequence that leads to the error state to extend the observation table.

Definition 15 (Input-Completeness). *An observation table $T = (S, E, Q)$ is input-complete if for all minimum-size partitions $P \in \Pi_{min}(T)$, the error state is not reachable in a composition of A with M_P.*

Definition 16 (Uniqueness). *An observation table $T = (S, E, Q)$ is unique if for all pairs of minimum-size partitions $P, P' \in \Pi_{min}(T)$, the machines M_P and $M_{P'}$ are right-equivalent in the context of A.*

---

[1] The proofs for the theorems in this section are available at http://embedded.cs.uni-saarland.de/GrayBoxLearning/details.pdf.

It follows that all machines of minimum-size size that agree with a consistent, closed, input-complete, and unique observation table are right-equivalent, and they can be obtained from the partitions.

Algorithm 1. Main algorithm

Input: Machine A, OutputQuery OQ, EquivalenceQuery EQ
begin
  ObservationTable OT ← empty table
  addRow([ϵ])
  curSize ← 1
  while *(true)* **do**
    while *(¬consistent ∨ ¬p-closed)* **do**
      makeConsistent()   `// consistency`
      makePClosed()   `// p-closedness`
    set partitions ← ∅
    prevMachine ← ⊥
    while *(true)* **do**
      partition ← findNextPartition(partitions, curSize)
      if *(partition = ⊥)* **then**
        if *(prevMachine = ⊥)* **then**
          curSize ← curSize+1
          continue
        else
          counterexample ← EQ(prevMachine)
          if *(counterexample = ⊥)* **then**
            removeErrorState(prevMachine)
            return *prevMachine*
          else
            handleCounterexample(counterexample)
            break
      if *(¬isClosed(partition))* **then**
        closePartition()   `// closedness`
        break
      machine ← getMachineForPartition(partition)
      errorPath ← getPathToErrorStateInComposition(A,machine)
      if *(errorPath ≠ ⊥)* **then**
        handleCounterexample(errorPath) `// input-completeness`
        break
      if *(prevMachine ≠ ⊥)* **then**
        distInput ← checkRightEquivalence(A, machine, prevMachine)
        if *(distInput ≠ ⊥)* **then**
          handleCounterexample(distInput)   `// uniqueness`
          break
      partitions ← partitions ∪ {partition}
      prevMachine ← machine

4.2 Inference Algorithm

At a high level, our algorithm works as shown in Algorithm 1. In each iteration of the main loop, we first make sure that the observation table is consistent and p-closed (by adding additional rows and columns if necessary). Then, we successively determine the partitions of minimum size for the observation table. Whenever we find a partition that is not closed, we add new rows to the table such that the partition becomes closed, and we continue with the next iteration of the main loop. If we find a closed partition, we check whether the error state is reachable in a composition of the corresponding machine with A. If we find a sequence that leads to the error state, this means that the table is not input-complete. Thus, we add this sequence (and its prefixes) to the observation table and continue with the next iteration of the main loop. If we find more than one closed and input-complete partition in the same iteration of the main loop, we check whether the machines for these two partitions are right-equivalent in the context of A. If we find a distinguishing sequence, we extend the observation table accordingly, and continue with the next iteration of the main loop. If finally the table is consistent, closed, input-complete, and unique, we perform an equivalence query for the last machine we found (which is right-equivalent to all machines of minimum size that agree with the table). If the equivalence query is successful, we are done, otherwise, we get a counterexample that we add to the table.

5   Implementation

In this section, we describe how our algorithm can be implemented. We also propose some improvements that make the algorithm more usable in practice.

5.1   Computing the Partitions

We reduce the problem of finding the partitions for a given size n, which is an NP-complete problem, to a boolean satisfiability (SAT) problem. Related reductions were used by [1] for minimizing incompletely-specified Mealy machines, and by [10] for finding DFAs that agree with a set of positive and negative input samples.

For space reasons, we will omit the details of our reduction approach. They are available at embedded.cs.uni-saarland.de/GrayBoxLearning/details.pdf.

5.2   Reachability of the Error State

If the error state is reachable with an input a from a state in the composition of the hypothesis machine with the left machine A, this means for no prefix p in the observation table that leads to this state, the input pa is a possible output of the left machine, however, there is another possible output sequence that leads to the same state that has a corresponding successor. We can thus use this sequence as a counterexample.

A straightforward way to check the reachability would be to build the composition, and then to perform a breadth-first search on the composition. A necessary condition for the reachability of the error state in the composition is that the error state is reachable in the hypothesis machine. We have observed that in practice, if the error state is reachable in the hypothesis machine, then in many cases, it is also reachable in the composition. Thus, we use the following approach to find a corresponding sequence quickly: We first determine for each state of the hypothesis machine the distance of the shortest path to the error state. We then use this distance to guide the search in a modified breadth-first search in the composed machine.

5.3   Checking if Two Machines Are Right-Equivalent

A straightforward way to check whether two hypothesis machines B and B' are equivalent in the context of A would be to compose both with A, and then check the two compositions for equivalence, for example using Hopcroft-Karp's near-linear algorithm. However, this can be computationally expensive when A is large compared to B and B', as it requires building the composition twice.

Therefore, we take the following alternative approach. We build a new machine D that outputs 1 iff the outputs of B and B' differ on (a prefix of) the corresponding input, and 0 otherwise. While the size of D can be quadratic in the size of B, we have observed that, after minimization, in practice the sizes are smaller or comparable to B. To check whether B and B' are right-equivalent we can then just check whether the composition of A with the minimized version of D can output 1, using the search algorithm described in the previous section.

5.4   Performing Additional Equivalence Queries

While evaluating our approach on the benchmarks from Sect. 6.2, we came across several benchmarks, for which the number of right-equivalent machines is very large. We propose the following modification of our algorithm that uses some additional equivalence queries to achieve better performance in practice. For each value of *curSize*, we perform the n-th equivalence query after computing 2^n partitions, rather than first enumerating all right-equivalent machines.

The number of Mealy machines of size n with input alphabet I and output alphabet O that compute different functions is bounded by $(n \cdot |O|)^{n \cdot |I|}$. So the number of equivalence queries performed for machines of size i is at most $\log_2(i \cdot |O|)^{i \cdot |I|} = i \cdot |I| \cdot \log_2(i \cdot |O|)$. For $n = |B|$, the modified algorithm performs at most $\sum_{i=1}^{n} i \cdot |I| \cdot \log_2(i \cdot |O|) \in \mathcal{O}(n^3 \cdot |I| \cdot \log_2 |O|)$ many equivalence queries.

5.5   Handling Counterexamples

Like in the original version of Angluin's L^* algorithm, we handle counterexamples by adding all prefixes of the counterexamples as rows to the table. Since, in general, the length of a counterexample can depend on $|C|$, the number of rows that are added (and hence the number of output queries that need to be performed to determine their entries) is not independent of $|A|$.

Rivest and Schapire [18] described an improved approach to handle counterexamples that needs to perform only a logarithmic number of membership queries (in the length of the counterexample). However, it is not possible to directly adapt this method to our setting, since it requires that there is always a suffix of the counterexample that is a distinguishing suffix for two compatible rows. It is future work to develop more advanced methods to deal with counterexamples in our setting.

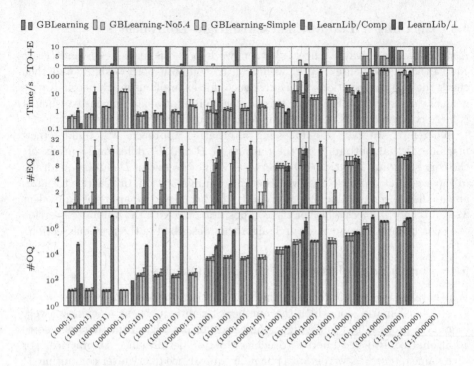

Fig. 3. Evaluation on randomly-generated machines (Color figure online)

6   Evaluation

6.1   Randomly-Generated Machines

In this section, we compare several variants of our approach (that differ, in particular, with respect to the number of equivalence queries they perform) with the Mealy machine version of Angluin's L^* algorithm. We use a set of randomly generated compositional Mealy machines with between $1,000$ and $1,000,000$ states, and an input and output alphabet of size 4.

The results are shown in Fig. 3. *GBLearning* ("Gray-box Learning") is an implementation of the approach described in the previous sections. *GBLearning-No5.4* is a variant of our approach that does not perform the additional equivalence queries described in Sect. 5.4. *GBLearning-Simple* is another variant of our approach that does neither check whether the error state is reachable, nor whether different machines that are consistent with the observation table are right-equivalent. Instead, it immediately performs an equivalence query upon finding a closed partition. Thus, the number of equivalence queries of this variant is *not* independent of the size of the right machine.

We compare these implementations with two variants of Angluin's L^* algorithm, as implemented in LearnLib [13] (*ExtensibleLStarMealy*). *LearnLib/Comp* treats the system as a black box, and learns the composition. Furthermore, we modified LearnLib (*LearnLib/*⊥) such that it uses L^* on the right machine; impossible inputs are assumed to result in a special output symbol (⊥). Equivalence queries are performed by first composing the hypothesis for the right machine with the left machine. Note that this variant does not learn a minimum-size machine; in fact, the learned machine might even be larger than the composition.

The columns of Fig. 3 show the sizes of the randomly-generated machines in the form ($|Q_A|$; $|Q_B|$). The rows show the number of output queries (#OQ), equivalence queries (#EQ), and the execution time in seconds (averages, minima and maxima for the successful runs of 10 different randomly-generated machines of the same size). The row $TO+E$ shows on how many of the 10 runs a timeout (5 min), or an error occurred. For *LearnLib/Comp* we observed one error, and for *LearnLib/*⊥ three errors due to an exception ("incompatible output symbols"). All other entries in this row were timeouts. We used the jar-Release of LearnLib in version 0.9.1-ase2013-tutorial-r1. Both our tool and LearnLib use a query cache to avoid performing the same output query multiple times.

We observe that *LearnLib/*⊥ was only successful when A had 10 or fewer states, or when B had just one state. It performed slightly better than *LearnLib/Comp* in only a few cases where $|Q_A| = 1$ or $|Q_B| = 1$. *LearnLib/Comp* was successful on almost all benchmarks with up to 100,000 states; however, it could not solve any benchmark with more states.

The implementations of our tool could also handle composed machines of larger sizes, in particular when B is relatively small. *GBLearning* and *GBLearning-No5.4* were successful on all benchmarks where B had up to 1,000 states, on several where B had 10,000 states, and on two where B had 100,000 states.

For those machines that our implementations and *LearnLib/Comp* could handle, the number of required output queries was much smaller for our implementations if $|Q_A| > 1$. In this case, there was no significant difference in the number of output queries between the different variants of our approach. Also, for $|Q_A| > 1$, the number of output queries depends mainly on $|Q_B|$ for all three variants.

For *GBLearning* and *GBLearning-No5.4*, the number of equivalence queries was mostly 1 or 2 even for relatively large unknown machines; however, randomly-generated machines might not be representative in this regard. *GBLearning-Simple* needed significantly more equivalence queries than these two variants for $|Q_B| > 1$, but significantly fewer than *LearnLib/Comp* for $|Q_A| > 10$.

6.2 Benchmarks for the Minimization of Incomplete Mealy Machines

We now compare the same variants of our implementation with BICA [17]. BICA is a tool that uses a modification of Anguin's L^* algorithm for minimizing incompletely specified Mealy machines, a known NP-complete problem. If we choose as the left machine A of the composition a machine such that $tr(A)$ corresponds exactly to the specified inputs of the right machine, the minimization of incompletely specified Mealy machines can be considered to be a special case of our approach.

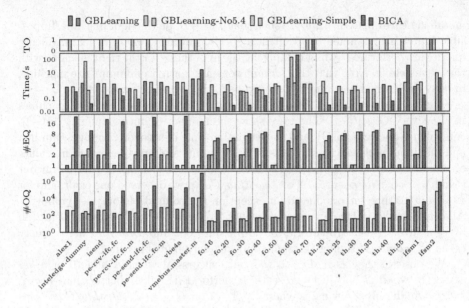

Fig. 4. Minimization benchmarks (Color figure online)

We use the same set of benchmarks that was used by the authors of BICA to evaluate their approach, but we excluded those benchmarks for which some output bits are not specified, as this is currently not supported by our implementation. We use BICA in version 5.0.3. We added code to count the number of output and equivalence queries.

The results are shown in Fig. 4. All variants of our approach require significantly fewer output queries than BICA; this might in part be due to the use of a query cache in our implementations. Both *GBLearning* and *GBLearning-No5.4* require significantly fewer equivalence queries than BICA; however, *GBLearning-No5.4* did not terminate on several of them within a timeout of 5 min. *GBLearning-Simple* could solve all benchmarks; the number of equivalence queries was comparable to *GBLearning* for about one third of the benchmarks, on the remaining benchmarks it was comparable to BICA. However, the objective of the algorithm used by BICA was not mainly to minimize the number of queries, since output and in particular equivalence queries are very cheap in the present scenario, as the machines to be minimized are readily available, and equivalence queries can be performed by automata constructions. Instead, the focus of their approach was to minimize the execution time. In such a case, minimizing the number of equivalence queries as we do, by checking right-compatibility of many different candidates, is not beneficial in terms of runtime. In fact, BICA was faster on many of the benchmarks.

7   Related Work

The concept of actively learning DFAs using membership and equivalence queries was introduced by Angluin in [2]. Angluin developed a polynomial-time learning algorithm, called L^*, for fully-specified DFAs. Rivest and Schapire [18] later improved this algorithm and proposed a modification that does not require the system to have a reset state.

Multiple studies [6,7,12,15,17] considered scenarios in which the teacher is unable to answer some output queries. In contrast to our setting, where the input language is a known regular language, these approaches assume that no information about the unspecified inputs is available a priori, so that whether a particular input is specified can only be determined by performing an output query. In this scenario, the best bound Leucker and Neider [15] could give for the number of required equivalence queries is $n^{\mathcal{O}(n)}$. Hsu and Lee [12] claimed that their approach is able learn a minimum-size model for an incompletely specified FSM in polynomial time. However, this approach is incorrect; it does in general not find a minimum-size machine [14].

The term "gray-box" has been used in relation with Angluin's algorithm before, but in different contexts. Babic et al. [3] describe an approach to learn an input-output relation for a program. They propose a symbolic version of L^* that is allowed to inspect the internal symbolic state of the program. Henkler et al. [9] consider real-time statecharts that have an additional interface for retrieving the current internal state. Elkind et al. introduce grey-box checking [5]. A grey-box system consists of completely-specified (white boxes) and unknown components (black boxes). The goal of grey-box checking is then to check whether the system satisfies a property, given e.g. by an LTL formula. The main problem studied by Elkind et al. is to learn a model of the entire system given the knowledge about the white boxes, which can then be used to model check the property. In contrast to our setting, they consider finite automata that synchronize on common letters in their alphabet, whereas we consider Mealy machines with explicit inputs and outputs. Furthermore, they only use output queries; equivalence queries are realized via a large number of output queries.

8   Discussion and Future Work

We have introduced an algorithm for gray-box learning of serial compositions of Mealy machines. Experimental results confirm that taking into account prior knowledge about a system to be learned often yields significant performance gains.

There are plenty of open problems left for future work: In this paper, we have considered the serial composition of two Mealy machines. In future work, we would like to extend our approach to arbitrary composition topologies.

While we can precisely bound the number of equivalence queries, we lack such knowledge about the number of output queries. More generally, we would like to better understand the computational complexity of the problem at hand.

In our experimental evaluation, we realized equivalence queries by automata-theoretic constructions, as we had precise knowledge of the system to be learned.

In real application scenarios, such knowledge is not available. In those cases, it would be interesting to systematically perform measurements in a way that focuses on the unknown parts.

References

1. Abel, A., Reineke, J.: MeMin: SAT-based exact minimization of incompletely specified mealy machines. In: ICCAD 2015. IEEE Press (2015)
2. Angluin, D.: Learning regular sets from queries and counter examples. Inf. Comput. **75**(2), 87–106 (1987)
3. Babic, D., Botincan, M., Song, D.: Symbolic grey-box learning of input-output relations. Technical Report UCB/EECS-2012-59. University of California, Berkeley (2012)
4. Cobleigh, J.M., Giannakopoulou, D., Păsăreanu, C.S.: Learning assumptions for compositional verification. In: Garavel, H., Hatcliff, J. (eds.) TACAS 2003. LNCS, vol. 2619, pp. 331–346. Springer, Heidelberg (2003)
5. Elkind, E., Genest, B., Peled, D.A., Qu, H.: Grey-box checking. In: Najm, E., Pradat-Peyre, J.-F., Donzeau-Gouge, V.V. (eds.) FORTE 2006. LNCS, vol. 4229, pp. 420–435. Springer, Heidelberg (2006)
6. Grinchtein, O., Leucker, M.: Learning finite-state machines from inexperienced teachers. In: Sakakibara, Y., Kobayashi, S., Sato, K., Nishino, T., Tomita, E. (eds.) ICGI 2006. LNCS (LNAI), vol. 4201, pp. 344–345. Springer, Heidelberg (2006)
7. Grinchtein, O., Leucker, M., Piterman, N.: Inferring network invariants automatically. In: Furbach, U., Shankar, N. (eds.) IJCAR 2006. LNCS (LNAI), vol. 4130, pp. 483–497. Springer, Heidelberg (2006)
8. Groce, A., Peled, D.A., Yannakakis, M.: Adaptive model checking. In: Katoen, J.-P., Stevens, P. (eds.) TACAS 2002. LNCS, vol. 2280, pp. 357–370. Springer, Heidelberg (2002)
9. Henkler, S., et al.: Legacy component integration by the Fujaba real-time tool suite. In: Proceedings of the 32nd ACM/IEEE International Conference on Software Engineering, ICSE 2010, vol. 2. pp. 267–270. ACM, New York (2010)
10. Heule, M.J.H., Verwer, S.: Exact DFA identification using SAT solvers. In: Sempere, J.M., García, P. (eds.) ICGI 2010. LNCS, vol. 6339, pp. 66–79. Springer, Heidelberg (2010)
11. Howar, F., Steffen, B., Jonsson, B., Cassel, S.: Inferring canonical register automata. In: Kuncak, V., Rybalchenko, A. (eds.) VMCAI 2012. LNCS, vol. 7148, pp. 251–266. Springer, Heidelberg (2012)
12. Hsu, Y., Lee, D.: Machine learning for implanted malicious code detection with incompletely specified system implementations. In: IEEE International Conference on Network Protocols, Washington, DC, USA, pp. 31–36 (2011)
13. Isberner, M., Howar, F., Steffen, B.: The open-source LearnLib. In: Kroening, D., Păsăreanu, C.S. (eds.) CAV 2015. LNCS, vol. 9206, pp. 487–495. Springer, Heidelberg (2015)
14. Lee, D.: Personal communication, January 2015
15. Leucker, M., Neider, D.: Learning minimal deterministic automata from inexperienced teachers. In: Margaria, T., Steffen, B. (eds.) ISoLA 2012, Part I. LNCS, vol. 7609, pp. 524–538. Springer, Heidelberg (2012)
16. Maler, O., Mens, I.-E.: Learning regular languages over large alphabets. In: Ábrahám, E., Havelund, K. (eds.) TACAS 2014 (ETAPS). LNCS, vol. 8413, pp. 485–499. Springer, Heidelberg (2014)

17. Pena, J., Oliveira, A.: A new algorithm for exact reduction of incompletely speci-
    fied finite state machines. IEEE Trans. Comput. Aided Des. Integr. Circuits Syst.
    18(11), 1619–1632 (1999)
18. Rivest, R.L., Schapire, R.E.: Inference of finite automata using homing sequences.
    Inf. Comput. **103**(2), 299–347 (1993)
19. Shahbaz, M., Groz, R.: Inferring mealy machines. In: Cavalcanti, A., Dams, D.R.
    (eds.) FM 2009. LNCS, vol. 5850, pp. 207–222. Springer, Heidelberg (2009)
20. Vardhan, A., Sen, K., Viswanathan, M., Agha, G.: Using language inference to
    verify omega-regular properties. In: Halbwachs, N., Zuck, L.D. (eds.) TACAS 2005.
    LNCS, vol. 3440, pp. 45–60. Springer, Heidelberg (2005)

Theorem Proving and Proofs

Specification and Proof of High-Level Functional Properties of Bit-Level Programs

Clément Fumex[1,2,3], Claire Dross[3], Jens Gerlach[4], and Claude Marché[1,2(✉)]

[1] Inria, Université Paris-Saclay, 91893 Palaiseau, France
Claude.Marche@inria.fr
[2] LRI, CNRS & Univ. Paris-Sud, 91405 Orsay, France
[3] AdaCore, 75009 Paris, France
[4] Fraunhofer FOKUS, Berlin, Germany

Abstract. In a computer program, basic functionalities may be implemented using bit-wise operations. To formally specify the expected behavior of such a low-level program, it is desirable that the specification should be at a more abstract level. Formally proving that low-level code conforms to a higher-level specification is challenging, because of the gap between the different levels of abstraction. We address this challenge by designing a rich formal theory of fixed-sized bit vectors, which on the one hand allows a user to write abstract specifications close to the human—or mathematical—level of thinking, while on the other hand permits a close connection to decision procedures and tools for bit vectors, as they exist in the context of the Satisfiability Modulo Theory framework. This approach is implemented in the Why3 environment for deductive program verification, and also in its front-end environment SPARK for the development of safety-critical Ada programs. We report on several case studies used to validate our approach.

1 Introduction

It is quite common in computer programs that some basic functionality is implemented, for efficiency reasons, using bit-wise operations. There is even a famous book, *Hacker's delight* [24], which is dedicated only to this kind of smart and efficient code.

An extreme example is the following 2-line C program (a so-called "signature program" designed by Marcel van Kervinc, http://www.iwriteiam.nl/SigProgC.html).

```
t(a,b,c){int d=0,e=a&~b&~c,f=1;if(a)for(f=0;d=(e-=d)&-e;f+=t(a-d,(b+d)*2,(
c+d)/2));return f;}main(q){scanf("%d",&q);printf("%d\n",t(~(~0<<q),0,0));}
```

It reads an integer n and prints another integer $f(n)$. Assuming n is smaller than the machine word size in bits (say 32), then $f(n)$ appears to be the number of

Work partly supported by the Joint Laboratory ProofInUse (ANR-13-LAB3-0007, http://www.spark-2014.org/proofinuse) of the French national research organization.

© Springer International Publishing Switzerland 2016

S. Rayadurgam and O. Tkachuk (Eds.): NFM 2016, LNCS 9690, pp. 291–306, 2016.
DOI: 10.1007/978-3-319-40648-0_22

solutions to the *n-queens problem*: the number of ways of placing n queens on a $n \times n$ chessboard so that they do not threaten each other. Even more remarkable, this program implements the most efficient algorithm known so far to solve this problem.

Solving the n-queens problem was used in the past as a challenge for *deductive program verification*. The challenge is to attach to such code a formal specification, expressing its expected behavior at an abstract mathematical level (*i.e.* expressing that it really computes the number of solutions to the n-queens problem), and to prove formally that the code respects this specification. The solutions presented by Filliâtre [15], and other authors for a simplified version computing only the first solution [18], considered more abstract implementations, that do not operate directly on bits.

Deductive program verification typically proceeds by generating, from both the code and the formal specification, a set of logic formulas. These are called *verification conditions* because if one proves they are all tautologies, then the program is guaranteed to respect its specification. In program verification environments like Dafny [19] and Why3 [7], verification conditions are discharged using theorem provers, in particular those of the *Satisfiability Modulo Theories* (SMT) family such as Alt-Ergo [6], CVC4 [3], and Z3 [22]. The SMT approach is very promising for one who seeks to verify programs operating at the level of bits, because, in this context, theories for fixed-size bit vectors have been investigated for quite a long time and efficient decision procedures are known [4,10,12]. The SMT-LIB international initiative (http://smtlib.cs.uiowa.edu/) aims at providing standard languages and descriptions of theories for interacting with SMT solvers. SMT-LIB provides a fairly rich standard theory for fixed-size bit vectors, and decision procedures for this theory are implemented in several SMT solvers, including CVC4 and Z3.

Our objective is to add support for bit-wise operations in Why3 and its front-end SPARK2014 [21] that deals with safety-critical Ada programs. In particular, we want to exploit the bit vector decision procedures provided by SMT solvers. However, in such a context, bit-wise operations are mixed with other objects occurring in programs and specifications, such as unbounded integers, arrays, and records. We need to rely on other theories supported by SMT solvers, and also on their support for quantified axioms. Exploiting an SMT solver when several theories are mixed together with quantified axioms requires special care. This paper reports on our design choices and on some experiments we made. We start in Sect. 2 by illustrating our approach on a short (although non-trivial) example. In Sect. 3 we describe the theories for bit vectors we designed for use in Why3. In Sect. 4 we present how our Why3 theories are exploited in the SPARK2014 front-end. In Sect. 5 we illustrate our approach on a case study originating from industrial code. Our developments are distributed in SPARK Pro 16.0 and will be in the release 0.87 of Why3. More details and more case studies (including the 2-line n-queens program) are discussed in a technical report [14] and the files for the case studies are available on Toccata's Web gallery of verified programs (http://toccata.lri.fr/gallery/bitwise.en.html).

2 Illustrative Example

We want to specify, at an abstract level, programs that directly manipulate bits. Our approach is to exploit in parallel the theory of bit vectors supported by SMT-solvers, and their support for arithmetic and quantifiers. We provide a theory that allows the use of both on the same program. In order to do so, the intended methodology to use this theory is to specify programs at an abstract level, closer to the human mind, *e.g.* with mathematical integers, while at the same time exploiting the bit vector theories of SMT solvers, by providing explicit hints for provers (typically under the form of extra assertions in the code) when it is necessary to help them to make the appropriate bridge between the bit vector level and the abstract level.

Let us consider an example from the Esterel compiler [5]. Each instruction returns an integer code between 1 and a fixed N. Parallel execution returns the maximum of the codes of its branches. A static analysis approximates programs by considering the set $\overline{P}$ of all possible return codes of P. Hence $\overline{P\|Q} = \{max(p,q)|p \in \overline{P}, q \in \overline{Q}\}$. Sets of return codes are implemented as bit vectors, a 1 at position i in $\overline{P}$ meaning that $i \in \overline{P}$. It was suggested by Gonthier that $\overline{P\|Q}$ can be computed as $(\overline{P|Q})\&(\overline{P|} - \overline{P})\&(\overline{Q|} - \overline{Q})$.

We want to formally specify this behavior at an abstract level, not using any low-level operation like a bit-wise 'and'. Let us consider the case where $N = 32$.

Formal Specification. Fig. 1 presents how this code is formally specified in our setting (see [14] for details on Why3's syntax). The **use** declarations import the theory of 32-bit bit vectors we designed and the theory of finite set of integers from the Why3 library. From the former theory we use the type t of bit vectors, and the operator nth: nth x n is the n-th bit of x as a Boolean.

We want to relate a bit vector to its abstract view as a set of integers. We introduce a record type s with a field bv : t, and a ghost field mdl : set int a set of integers. A *type invariant* specifies that for each a :

```
use import bv.BV32
use import set.FSetInt

type s = { bv : t; ghost mdl: set int; }
invariant { forall i: int.
    (0 ≤ i < size ∧ nth self.bv i)
  ↔ mem i self.mdl }

let maxUnion (a b : s) : s
  requires { not is_empty a.mdl
           ∧ not is_empty b.mdl }
  ensures { forall x. mem x result.mdl ↔
      exists y z. mem y a.mdl ∧ mem z b.mdl
          ∧ x = max y z }
  = ...
```

Fig. 1. maxUnion: formal specification

s the elements of a.mdl are the indexes of the 1-bits in a.bv. The precondition requires of maxUnion that the inputs are not zeros. The postcondition formalizes the former informal specification. The important point is that the formal

```
let aboveMin (a : s) : s
  requires { not is_empty a.mdl }
  ensures { result.mdl = interval (min_elt a.mdl) 32 }
= let ghost p = min_elt a.mdl in
  let ghost p_bv = of_int p in
  assert { eq_sub_bv a.bv zeros zeros p_bv };
  let res = bw_or a.bv (neg a.bv) in                      (* a | -a *)
  assert { eq_sub_bv res zeros zeros p_bv };
  assert { eq_sub_bv res ones p_bv (sub (of_int 32) p_bv) };
  { bv = res; mdl = interval p 32 }


let union (a b: s) : s                          (* operator a|b *)
  ensures  { result.mdl = union b.mdl a.mdl }
= { bv = bw_or a.bv b.bv; mdl = union b.mdl a.mdl }


let intersection (a b : s) : s                  (* operator a&b *)
  ensures { result.mdl = inter a.mdl b.mdl }
= { bv = bw_and a.bv b.bv; mdl = inter a.mdl b.mdl }


let maxUnion (a b : s) : s
  requires { not is_empty a.mdl ∧ not is_empty b.mdl }
  ensures {
    forall x. mem x result.mdl ↔ exists y z. mem y a.mdl ∧ mem z b.mdl ∧ x = max y z }
= let res = intersection (union a b) (intersection (aboveMin a) (aboveMin b)) in
  assert { forall x. mem x res.mdl →
    let (y,z) = if mem x a.mdl then (x,min_elt b.mdl) else (min_elt a.mdl,x)
    in mem y a.mdl ∧ mem z b.mdl ∧ x = max y z };
  res
```

Fig. 2. maxUnion: annotated code

specification is at an abstract mathematical level which is quite far from the code in the body of the function. Proving that the code satisfies the specification is thus a difficult task.

Proof. The code of maxUnion is split in three sub-functions shown in Fig. 2. It makes use of additional operations:

- of_int x: integer x converted to a bit vector
- eq_sub_bv x y i l: means that the bits of a and b between positions i and $i + l - 1$ are equal
- bw_or, bw_and, neg, sub: bit-wise and arithmetic operators on bit vectors
- min_elt a: the minimal element of a
- interval i j: the set $\{i \dots j - 1\}$

We emphasize that the code of aboveMin contains three assertions involving only bit vectors and bit-wise operators. This form of intermediate assertion is an example of a general strategy that we explain in Sect. 3.3.

The proof results are displayed in Fig. 3. A red background indicates an unsuccessful proof, (10 m) meaning that the timeout of 10 min is reached, (6G) meaning that the memory limit of 6 GB is reached. We stress that we use CVC4 and Z3 in two different modes. The default mode exploits their native support for bit vectors, whereas the other mode, nicknamed 'noBV' for 'no bit vectors', does not. The two VCs, 2 and 3 for aboveMin, are proved using the native bit vector support. On the contrary VCs 1 and 4 for aboveMin and the VCs for

Proof obligations	Alt-Ergo (1.01)	CVC4 (1.4)	CVC4 (1.4 noBV)	Z3 (4.4.2)	Z3 (4.4.2 noBV)
VC for union	0.20	506.10	0.11	(10m)	(6G)
VC for intersection	0.18	505.55	0.10	(10m)	(6G)
VC for aboveMin 1. assertion	0.28	(10m)	0.16	(10m)	(6G)
2. assertion	(10m)	0.42	(10m)	1.09	(6G)
3. assertion	(10m)	0.86	(10m)	(10m)	(6G)
4. type invariant	0.64	(10m)	0.31	(10m)	(6G)
5. postcondition	0.02	0.03	0.05	0.01	0.00
VC for aboveMin 1. precondition	0.01	0.05	0.07	0.01	0.01
2. precondition	0.02	0.05	0.08	0.01	0.01
3. assertion	0.45	0.25	0.22	0.48	(6G)
4. postcondition	1.70	0.26	0.27	(10m)	(6G)
5. postcondition	(10m)	0.06	0.15	(6G)	(6G)
	0.43	0.31	0.26	466.08	(6G)

Fig. 3. maxUnion: proof results

union and intersection are proved only in the mode not using native support. This need for two modes for one prover shows up in all the case studies that we considered [14]. We detail the design of these two modes in Sect. 3.3.

3   The Why3 Bit Vector Theory

Our theory of bit vectors is generic with respect to the size of bit vectors. It is then instantiated for size 8, 16, 32 and 64. In Why3, such an instance is possible through the so-called *cloning* feature: when a theory has one or more components that are declared abstract (a type, a function symbol) then one can *clone* that theory while giving some instance to some or all of these abstract components. This results in a new theory containing a copy of the original theory, with all declarations appropriately instantiated.

In the following, we only describe a representative part of the theory. We refer to the report [14] for its full description as well as a discussion of its consistency and soundness, which is established through realizations in the Coq proof assistant and in Isabelle/HOL as well.

3.1   Bit-Wise Operators

The first part of the theory is shown in Fig. 4. It starts with the declaration of the (positive) parameter size, representing the number of bits of all bit vectors. The type of bit vectors is introduced as an abstract type t equipped with one uninterpreted function nth. The intended meaning is that (nth b n) gives the n-th bit of b, as a Boolean. Note the convention that bit 0 is the least significant

```
(* core of the bit vector theory *)
constant size : int
axiom size_pos : size > 0
type t
function nth t int : bool
axiom nth_out_of_range:
   forall x:t, n:int. (n < 0 ∨ n ≥ size) → nth x n = False
constant zeros : t
axiom zeros_spec: forall n:int. nth zeros n = False
constant ones : t
axiom ones_spec: forall n:int. 0 ≤ n < size → nth ones n = True

(* bit-wise Boolean operators, shifts *)
function bw_and t t : t                        (* bit-wise 'and' of two bit vectors *)
axiom bw_and_spec: forall v1 v2:t, n:int. 0 ≤ n < size →
   nth (bw_and v1 v2) n = andb (nth v1 n) (nth v2 n)
(* ... similar declarations and axioms for bw_or, bw_xor, bw_not ... *)
function lsr t int : t                          (* logical shift right    *)
function asr t int : t                          (* arithmetic shift right *)
function lsl t int : t                          (* logical shift left     *)
axiom lsr_spec_low: forall b:t,n s:int. 0 ≤ s → 0 ≤ n → n+s < size →
   nth (lsr b s) n = nth b (n+s)
axiom lsr_spec_high: forall b:t,n s:int. 0 ≤ s → 0 ≤ n → n+s ≥ size →
   nth (lsr b s) n = False
(* ... similar axioms for lsr and asr ... *)
```

Fig. 4. Generic theory for bit vectors: core, bit-wise Boolean operators and shifts

bit, and (nth b n) returns False when n is out of the range $0 \ldots \texttt{size} - 1$. We introduce two constants zeros and ones for the bit vectors that have all bits not set or set, respectively. These are axiomatized using nth.

The bit-wise operators 'and', 'or', 'xor' and 'not' come next. Their behavior is axiomatized with the help of the nth operator as seen in Fig. 4. Shift operators are also axiomatized using the nth operator. Notice that the second argument of shift operators is an integer and not a bit vector.

3.2 Conversion To and From Integers

The second part of our theory, presented in Fig. 5, deals with conversion between bit vectors and integers. For lack of space, we only describe here the interpretation of bit vectors as non-negative integers, that interprets $b_{n-1} \cdots b_1 b_0$ as $\sum_{i=0}^{n-1} b_i \times 2^i$. We start by defining the maximum representable integer, and its successor: 2 to the power of size. Then we introduce two abstract functions for the conversions. These are not fully specified from nth; it would be a very involved axiomatization that is unlikely to be useful for automated provers. Instead, we provide a few useful axioms on those functions, regarding constants size, zeros and ones, and relation to equality.

```
constant two_power_size : int = pow2 size
constant max_int : int = two_power_size - 1
function to_uint t : int                (* conversion to an unsigned integer *)
function of_int int : t                 (* conversion from any integer
                                           (taken modulo two_power_size)    *)
constant size_bv : t = of_int size      (* bit vectors size, as a bit vector *)
axiom Of_int_zeros : zeros = of_int 0
axiom Of_int_ones: ones = of_int max_int
axiom to_uint_extensionality : forall v,v':t. to_uint v = to_uint v' → v = v'
predicate uint_in_range (i : int) = 0 ≤ i ≤ max_int
axiom to_uint_bounds : forall v:t. uint_in_range (to_uint v)
axiom to_uint_of_int : forall i:int. uint_in_range i → to_uint (of_int i) = i

predicate ult (x y:t) = to_uint x < to_uint y        (* unsigned 'less than' *)
(* ... similar def for ule, ugt, uge ... *)
function add t t : t                                          (* addition *)
axiom add_spec: forall x y:t.
  to_uint (add x y) = mod (to_uint x + to_uint y) two_power_size
lemma add_bounded: forall x y:t. to_uint x + to_uint y < two_power_size →
  to_uint (add x y) = to_uint x + to_uint y
(* ... similar declarations for sub, neg, mul, udiv, urem ... *)
```

Fig. 5. Bit Vector theory: conversions and arithmetic

Arithmetic operations do not need to distinguish between signed and unsigned variants, except for division and remainder. Their behavior is axiomatized via to_uint to express that computation is done modulo 2^{size}. Derived lemmas like add_bounded are added to help provers.

3.3   Strategy for Isolating Bit-Level Reasoning

The set of operators that we defined so far is expressive enough to formally specify programs. In order to discharge VCs a first idea would be to map each symbol of our theory to the corresponding symbol in the SMT-LIB theory, provided such a symbol exists, whilst keeping the other symbols uninterpreted and keeping all the axioms. However, we observed that this is not sufficient in practice: provers do not work well on VCs mixing bit-wise operators and conversions with integers (provers with native support for bit vectors have a hard time mixing bit vectors and integers, provers without it have a hard time to reason on bit-wise operators with the axioms only). Our approach to overcome this issue is two-fold. First, we provide a means for the user to isolate pure bit vector VCs from other VCs. Second, we provide to provers two alternative translations of our bit vector theory, to target specifically either provers with native support, or provers without it. The proof strategy used for the Rightmost Bit trick example (Fig. 3) exploits this approach.

```
function nth_bv t t : bool                    (* same as nth with bv arguments *)
axiom nth_bv_def:
  forall x i:t. nth_bv x i = not (bw_and (lsr_bv x i) (of_int 1) = zeros)
axiom Nth_bv_is_nth: forall x i:t. nth_bv x i = nth x (to_uint i)
axiom Nth_is_nth_bv: forall x:t, i:int. uint_in_range i →
  nth_bv x (of_int i) = nth x i
function lsr_bv t t : t                        (* same as lsr with bv arguments *)
axiom lsr_bv_is_lsr: forall x n:t. lsr_bv x n = lsr x (to_uint n)
axiom to_uint_lsr: forall v n:t.
  to_uint (lsr_bv v n) = div (to_uint v) (pow2 ( to_uint n ))
(* ... similar def and axioms for lsl_bv and asr_bv ... *)

predicate eq_sub (a b:t) (i n:int) =          (* a[i..i+n-1] = b[i..i+n-1] *)
  forall j:int. i ≤ j < i + n → nth a j = nth b j
predicate eq_sub_bv (a b:t) (i n:t) =     (* same as eq_sub with bv arguments *)
  let mask = lsl_bv (sub (lsl_bv (of_int 1) n) (of_int 1)) i (* ((1<<n)-1)<<i *)
  in bw_and b mask = bw_and a mask              (* a & mask = b & mask *)
axiom eq_sub_equiv: forall a b i n:t.
  eq_sub a b (to_uint i) (to_uint n) ↔ eq_sub_bv a b i n
```

Fig. 6. Additional operators in the bit vector theory

Bit-Level Operator Variant. The theory is augmented with the additional operators presented in Fig. 6. We provide pure bit vector alternatives for nth and shifts. We also introduce the eq_sub operator and its bit-level variant eq_sub_bv.

The Two Drivers. Why3's *driver* mechanism allows us to tell for each object (type, function symbol) of the Why3 theory what is the syntax for the corresponding object of the target prover. Figure 7 summarizes the two driver variants for the instance of the theory with size=32. The second column is the mapping for provers with native bit vector support, the third column is for the other provers as well as for the noBV variants of CVC4 and Z3. The driver for provers with native support maps the type t to the corresponding type in SMT-LIB. Each operator is mapped to the corresponding symbol in the SMT-LIB theory, if it exists, and is kept uninterpreted otherwise. The axioms that link the uninterpreted operators with the native ones are kept as-is. The remaining axioms are removed. There are two exceptions: nth_bv and eq_sub_bv are not in the SMT-LIB theory. Therefore, we keep the axioms that define them in term of pure bit-level operators. The driver for provers without native support keeps all symbols uninterpreted. All the axioms are kept except the ones that define the bit-wise operators, in order to prevent the provers from trying to prove bit-level properties.

object	prover with native BV support	prover without native BV support
type t	(_ BitVec 32)	abstract
nth	uninterpreted	uninterpreted
zeros	#x00000000	uninterpreted
ones	#xFFFFFFFF	uninterpreted
bw_and	bvand	uninterpreted
axioms {zeros,ones,bw _and} _spec	removed	kept
add	bvadd	uninterpreted
axiom add_spec	removed	removed
lemma add_bounded	removed	kept
lsr	uninterpreted	uninterpreted
axioms lsr _spec _{low,high}	removed	kept
to _uint	bv2nat	kept
axiom to _uint _extensionality	removed	kept
of _int	nat2bv	kept
nth _bv	uninterpreted	uninterpreted
axiom nth _bv_def	kept	removed
axiom nth _bv_is _nth	kept	kept
lsr _bv	bvlshr	uninterpreted
axiom lsr _bv_is _lsr	kept	kept
eq_sub	uninterpreted	uninterpreted
eq_sub _bv	uninterpreted	uninterpreted
axiom eq_sub _bv_def	kept	removed

Fig. 7. Mapping to SMT-LIB, for the case `size=32`

4   Adding Support for Bit Vectors in SPARK2014

Ada 2012 is the latest version of the Ada language [1], a programming language targeting real-time embedded software that requires a high level of safety, security, and reliability. This version adds new features for specifying the behavior of programs, such as subprogram contracts and type invariants. SPARK is a subset of Ada targeting formal verification [11,21]. Its restrictions ensure that the behavior of a SPARK program is unambiguously defined. The SPARK language and toolset for static verification has been applied for many years in on-board aircraft systems, control systems, cryptographic systems, and rail systems. It provides dedicated features that are not part of Ada 2012. Essential constructs for formal verification (*e.g.* loop invariants) have also been introduced. To formally prove a SPARK 2014 program, GNATprove uses the language WhyML as an intermediate. The SPARK program is translated into a WhyML program which can then be verified using the Why3 tool.

Modular Integer Types. Ada's very rich type system allows us to define various kinds of integer types. There are mostly of two kinds, namely *signed* and *modular* integer types. Modular integer types are defined by specifying a modulus, and are the types on which bit-wise operations apply. For example

```
type BV8 is mod 2**8;
```

defines a type BV8 that contains unsigned integers between 0 and $2^8 - 1$. Overflows never occur when computing with it: computations use modular arithmetic semantics. The package `Interfaces` from Ada's standard library introduces predefined names `Unsigned_8`, `Unsigned_16`, `Unsigned_32` and `Unsigned_64`, respectively for the modular types modulo 2^8, 2^{16}, 2^{32} and 2^{64}. Bit-wise Boolean operations are written as infix operators `and`, `or`, `xor`, `not`. Ada provides, in its standard library, functions `Shift_Left`, `Shift_Right`, and `Shift_Right_Arithmetic`. These are defined only when the first argument is a modular type for the standard bit sizes 8, 16, 32, and 64. The second argument of these operations is not of modular type but of type `Natural`, that is the signed integer type of only non negative values defined in Ada's standard library.

Handling of Modular Types in SPARK 2014. GNATprove translates each Ada variable, resp. each expression, into a Why3 variable, resp. expression, of some adequate type [17]. Variables and expressions of some modular type are translated into variables and expressions of some bit vector type of the Why3 theory described in the previous section. Their size is either 8, 16, 32, or 64, the smallest of those that can represent all the values of the original Ada type. To simplify the presentation below, we consider only the four predefined modular types `Unsigned_8`, `Unsigned_16`, `Unsigned_32` and `Unsigned_64` corresponding to 8, 16, 32, and 64-bits integers. The translation of the Boolean bit-wise operations is directly the equivalent introduced in our Why3 theory. The translation of shifts is just slightly more complex because their second argument in Ada is a signed type and not a modular type. For instance, we translate `Shift_Left(X,Y)` as `(lsl_bv X (if Y < size then (of_int Y) else size_bv))`.

5   The "Bitwalker" Case Study, Using SPARK2014

The original C version of the BitWalker was provided by Siemens in the context of the ITEA 2 project OpenETCS. The version presented here was rewritten by Fraunhofer FOKUS to simplify the formal verification with Frama-C/WP [16]. The formal specification relies on a theory of bit vectors designed in the Coq proof assistant, and a significant part of the proofs were done interactively within Coq.

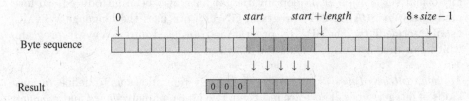

Fig. 8. Schematic view of the Peek function (on 8-bit instead of 64-bit)

```
// sets the bit at index [left] in [value] to the value of [flag]
static inline uint64_t PokeBit64(uint64_t value, uint32_t left, int flag) {
  uint64_t mask = ((uint64_t) 1u) << (63 - left);
  return (flag == 0) ? (value & ~mask) : (value | mask);
}


// return the 64-bit value extracted from the byte sequence [addr],
// from index [start] to index [start+length-1]
uint64_t Peek(uint32_t start, uint32_t length, uint8_t* addr, uint32_t size) {
  if (start + length > 8 * size) return 0;
  uint64_t retval = 0;
  for (uint32_t i = 0; i < length; i++) {
    int flag = PeekBit8Array(addr, size, start + i);
    retval = PokeBit64(retval, 64u - length + i, flag);
  }
  return retval;
}
```

Fig. 9. The BitWalker, C version, the Peek function

Bitwalker is about interacting with a stream of bytes. One of the two main functions, Peek, copies a value from the byte stream to a 64-bit unsigned integer. The expected behavior of Peek, illustrated in Fig. 8, can be expressed at a high-level by saying that the integer value of the result is the value read in the byte stream starting from the bit number start and reading length bits. The most significant bits of the result, of index larger or equal to length, must be all zero. Figure 9 presents the C source code of Peek as well as one of its main auxiliary function, PokeBit64. The code of Peek does not make use of low-level bit-wise operators, but calls instead auxiliary functions. On the contrary, the code of low-level auxiliary functions PeekBit8 and PokeBit64 make use of bit-wise operators, so there is a need at some point to relate those bit-wise operations with more high-level arithmetic notions. In the following, we propose a SPARK program equivalent to the C code of Fig. 9, with appropriate formal specifications.

Specification and Verification of PokeBit64. The function PokeBit64 writes a bit in an Unsigned_64 value at the given position Left. In order to specify this we need to: first write that the mentioned bit is correctly set after the function is called, and then not to forget that all other bits remain unchanged. Its SPARK specification is given in Fig. 10. A first difference between the C and SPARK version appears in the types: in C, the first two parameters are unsigned types and the third parameter is an integer. In Ada, since the function manipulates the first parameter's bits, it has to be of modular type. However, the parameter Left represents a position: it is not intended to be manipulated at the level of its bits and we do not want a modular arithmetic semantics, hence we set its type to Natural. This is consistent with the typing of shifts in Ada as described in Sect. 4. The last parameter, as it represents the state of a bit, is naturally given the type `Boolean`. Note the use of function `Nth` which refers to the Why3 operator `nth`. While the SPARK language does not have this function built in, we use the SPARK feature *external axiomatization* to lift it, as well as some others, to the level of SPARK language [14].

```
function PokeBit64(Value: Unsigned_64; Left: Natural; Flag: Boolean)
        return Unsigned_64
with Pre => Left < 64,
     Post => (Flag = Nth (PokeBit64'Result, 63 - Left)) and
        (for all I in Natural range 0 .. 63 =>
         (if I /= 63 - Left then Nth (PokeBit64'Result, I) = Nth (Value, I)));
```

Fig. 10. Specifications of auxiliary functions for `Peek`

The verification of `PokeBit64` is not straightforward: we are in the case of a mix of bit vectors and integers. Following the proof strategy of Sect. 3.3 we introduce assertions to separate the part dischargeable by provers with native bit vector support from the rest. The code, with the assertions used to prove the specification, is given in Fig. 11. The third and last assertions reformulate the postcondition for CVC4 and Z3 at the bit level. The three other assertions deal with conversions between modulars and integers, and are proved by other provers.

```
1  function PokeBit64(Value: Unsigned_64; Left: Natural;
2                     Flag: Boolean) return Unsigned_64 is
3   Left_Bv: constant Unsigned_64 := Unsigned_64(Left);
4  begin
5   pragma Assert (Left_Bv < 64);
6   pragma Assert (63-Left_Bv = Unsigned_64(63-Left));
7   declare
8    Mask: constant Unsigned_64 := Shift_Left(1,63-Left);
9    R: constant Unsigned_64 :=  (if Flag then
10              (Value or Mask) else (Value and (not Mask)));
11   begin
12    pragma Assert (for all I in Unsigned_64 range 0..63 =>
13      (if I /= 63 - Left_Bv then
14         Nth_Bv (R, I) = Nth_Bv (Value, I)));
15    pragma Assert (for all I in Natural range 0 .. 63 =>
16      (0 <= Unsigned_64(I) and then Unsigned_64(I) <= 63));
17    pragma Assert (Flag = Nth_Bv (R, 63 - Left_Bv));
18    return R;
19   end;
20  end PokeBit64;
```

Proof obligations	Alt-Ergo (1.01)	CVC4 (1.4)	CVC4 (1.4 noBV)	Z3 (4.4.2)	Z3 (4.4.2 noBV)
1. assertion	0.05	(10m)	0.08	0.33	7.95
2. precondition	0.03	0.11	0.08	0.03	0.14
3. assertion	0.29	(10m)	0.07	0.14	(6G)
4. precondition	0.04	0.14	0.05	0.02	0.11
5. range check	0.03	0.05	0.04	0.01	0.01
6. range check	0.03	0.04	0.04	0.01	0.00
7. assertion	(10m)	0.44	(10m)	0.21	(6G)
8. assertion	0.36	(10m)	0.10	0.23	(6G)
9. range check	0.06	0.03	0.04	0.01	0.00
10. assertion	(10m)	0.15	(10m)	0.10	(6G)
11. precondition	0.08	0.04	0.02	0.01	0.01
12. range check	0.04	0.04	0.04	0.00	0.01
13. range check	0.05	0.03	0.04	0.01	0.00
14. range check	0.04	0.03	0.04	0.01	0.00
15. postcondition	(10m)	0.23	0.11	(10m)	(6G)

Fig. 11. PokeBit64: annotated code and proof results

Specification and Proof of Bitwalker `Peek`. The SPARK specification of the main function `Peek` is given in Fig. 12. As for `PokeBit64` there is a difference in the types: in Ada, `Start` and `Length` are naturals, by extension to what was said on

```
1   type Byte_Sequence is                          1   function Peek (Start, Length : Natural;
2     array (Natural range ≠) of Unsigned_8;       2       Addr : Byte_Sequence) return Unsigned_64 is
3                                                   3   begin
4   function Nth8_Stream (Stream : Byte_Sequence;   4     if Start + Length > 8 * Addr'Length then
5           Pos : Natural) return Boolean is        5       return 0;
6     (Nth (Stream (Pos / 8), 7 - (Pos rem 8)))     6     end if;
7   with Pre => Stream'First = 0 and then           7     declare
8           (Pos / 8 ≤ Stream'Last), Ghost;         8       Retval : Unsigned_64 := 0;
9                                                   9       Flag   : Boolean;
10  function Peek (Start, Length : Natural;        10     begin
11      Addr : Byte_Sequence) return Unsigned_64   11       for I in 0 .. Length - 1 loop
12  with                                           12         pragma Loop_Invariant
13    Pre => Addr'First = 0 and then               13         (for all J in Length - I .. Length - 1 =>
14    Length ≤ 64 and then                         14           Nth8_Stream(Addr, Start+Length-J-1) =
15    Start + Length ≤ Natural'Last and then       15           Nth(Retval, J));
16    8 * Addr'Length ≤ Natural'Last,              16         pragma Loop_Invariant
17    Contract_Cases => (                          17         (for all J in Length .. 63 =>
18      Start + Length > 8 * Addr'Length =>        18           not Nth (Retval, J));
19        Peek'Result = 0,                         19         Flag := PeekBit8Array(Addr, Start + I);
20      Start + Length ≤ 8 * Addr'Length =>        20         Retval := PokeBit64(Retval,64-Length+I,Flag);
21        (for all I in 0 .. Length - 1 =>         21       end loop;
22          Nth8_Stream (Addr, Start+Length-I-1) = 22       return Retval;
23          Nth (Peek'Result, I))                  23     end;
24        and then                                 24   end Peek;
25        (for all I in Length .. 63 =>
26          not Nth (Peek'Result, I)));
```

Fig. 12. Ada specification and body of Peek function

PokeBit64 type. Note also the absence of the parameter size: it corresponds to Addr'Length in Ada. The precondition starts on line 13, by specifying that the first index of our byte sequence is 0, as in the C code. We then bound Length, the number of bits to copy, by 64. The last two preconditions are here to avoid any arithmetic overflow with Start, Length, and the size of Addr. The postcondition starts on line 17, and is made of two disjoint cases. First, if the last bit to copy is out of the bounds of the byte sequence the default value 0 is returned. In the other case, we specify two things: that the i-th bit of the result, for $0 \leq i <$ Length is equal to the bit of the sequence at position Start $+$ Length $- i - 1$, as shown in Fig. 8. The n-th bit of a ByteSequence is specified by the auxiliary function Nth8_Stream given on line 3 of Fig. 12. Finally we specify that the other bits of the result are set to zero.

The Ada code of Peek is very close to the original C code of Fig. 9. We only add two loop invariants (lines 12–18) that are directly derived from the post-conditions. These invariants are the expected ones in presence of such a loop. Note that, following our reasoning on type assignment, Start and Length are Naturals, whereas the contents of the array Addr are 8-bit modular types, and the result of Peek is a 64-bit modular. As expected, since there is no bit-level code in Peek, there is no need for bit-level assertions and the proof does not need the provers with native bit vector support.

6   Conclusions

We designed a rich formal theory including arbitrary fixed-size bit vectors, a large set of bit-wise operations, and a large set of operations involving both bit vectors and unbounded integers. Thanks to the driver mechanism of Why3, proof obligations that make use of this theory can be discharged either by SMT solvers with bit vector support (CVC4, Z3) or by solvers that handle this theory as an axiomatic first-order theory (Alt-Ergo, and CVC4 and Z3 in non native support mode). We presented several case studies illustrating how one can specify and prove bit-level code correct with respect to a high-level specification. We emphasize that it is important for the user to understand well the respective capabilities of the provers, (do they support bit vector theories or not) and to respect a refinement-like methodology when writing annotations: to prove that bit-level code satisfies a high-level postcondition, one may need to provide a hint in the form of an assertion rephrasing the postcondition at the bit-level, and help the provers with assertions to enforce them to convert bit vectors to integers when required. Fortunately, as shown by proof of `Peek` in BitWalker, our approach allows a good modularity principle: as soon as low-level code is given a high-level specification, the procedures calling such code do not need to be aware that the low-level code operates at the bit level. The support of Ada's modular types via bit vectors is included since 2015 in SPARK releases. The first feedback from AdaCore's customers is very positive: many proof obligations that were not checked automatically before are now proved by CVC4 or Z3.

About SPARK Interpretation of Signed Integers. We chose to map Ada's signed integer types to mathematical unbounded integers. Another choice would be to map them to bit vectors and use the signed arithmetic operators provided by SMT-LIB. We tried this alternative and noticed regressions in the rate of automatically proved VCs: on the SPARK test suite the support for unbounded integer arithmetic in SMT solvers is better than the support for arithmetic operators of BV theory.

Related Tools and Experiments. Stefan Berghofer (Secunet, Germany) is using the support for bit vectors in SPARK, on the big number package of libsparkcrypto (https://bitbucket.org/sberghofer/libsparkcrypto/). He uses Isabelle/HOL to interactively discharge the VCs that cannot be proved automatically. The BitWalker case study was initially written in C and specified using the ACSL specification language of Frama-C. For that purpose a theory of bit vectors of unbounded size was designed using the Coq proof assistant, and the proofs were done with a significant amount of interaction within Coq. Thanks to the mapping of our bit vector theory to SMT-LIB we were able to prove Bit-Walker fully automatically. The source language, C or Ada, is not important, although the choice between signed versus unsigned types in the source makes a difference: in Ada their semantics are significantly different. The Boogie [2] verifier and its front-ends VCC [13] and Dafny [19] also use the built-in bit vector support of Z3, to model machine words. We are not aware of any work, in this context, about the problem of mixing bit vectors with high-level specifications.

Future Work. The need to use two different drivers for the same prover is somehow unsatisfactory. The decision of using the native support for bit vectors in provers could be made by an automatic analysis of the goal. A possible alternative would be to provide appropriate constructs in the specification language so that the user could indicate the intended level of abstraction in her code. For instance, in our solution to the n-queens example [14], it would have been convenient to express with a source annotation that we want to interpret a machine word into the set of positions of its bits set to 1.

There is some need to apply the same approach to floating-point numbers, in order to exploit decision procedures for floating-point arithmetic that are now available in SMT solvers [9] (http://www.cprover.org/SMT-LIB-Float/). In the past, floating-point programs were specified in terms of real numbers [8] and proved by specific solvers. As we did for bit vectors and integers, it is therefore desirable to design a theory that would allow the combination of floating-point numbers with real numbers and at the same time would make use of SMT-LIB support for floating-point arithmetic. Last but not least, there are some programs that operate on floating-point numbers at the bit-level [20]. Proving such code would be a hard challenge [23].

Acknowledgments. Thanks to Stefan Gerken from Siemens for providing the original implementation of the BitWalker. Thanks to Stefan Berghofer for providing us with an Isabelle/HOL realization of Why3's bit vector theory. Thanks to Jean-Christophe Filliâtre, Stuart Matthews, Yannick Moy and Mário Pereira for their comments on preliminary versions of this paper.

References

1. Barnes, J.: Programming in Ada 2012. Cambridge University Press, Cambridge (2014)
2. Barnett, M., Chang, B.-Y.E., DeLine, R., Jacobs, B., M. Leino, K.R.: Boogie: a modular reusable verifier for object-oriented programs. In: de Boer, F.S., Bonsangue, M.M., Graf, S., de Roever, W.-P. (eds.) FMCO 2005. LNCS, vol. 4111, pp. 364–387. Springer, Heidelberg (2006)
3. Barrett, C., Conway, C.L., Deters, M., Hadarean, L., Jovanović, D., King, T., Reynolds, A., Tinelli, C.: CVC4. In: Gopalakrishnan, G., Qadeer, S. (eds.) CAV 2011. LNCS, vol. 6806, pp. 171–177. Springer, Heidelberg (2011)
4. Barrett, C.W., Dill, D.L., Levitt, J.R.: A decision procedure for bit-vector arithmetic. In: Design Automation Conference. pp. 522–527. ACM (1998)
5. Berry, G.: The foundations of esterel. In: Plotkin, G., Stirling, C., Tofte, M. (eds.) Proof, Language, and Interaction, Essays in Honour of Robin Milner, pp. 425–454. The MIT Press, Cambridge (2000)
6. Bobot, F., Conchon, S., Contejean, E., Iguernelala, M., Lescuyer, S., Mebsout, A.: The Alt-Ergo automated theorem prover (2008). http://alt-ergo.lri.fr/

7. Bobot, F., Filliâtre, J.C., Marché, C., Paskevich, A.: Let's verify this with Why3. Int. J. Softw. Tools Technol. Transf. **17**(6), 709–727 (2015)

8. Boldo, S., Marché, C.: Formal verification of numerical programs: from C annotated programs to mechanical proofs. Math. Comput. Sci. **5**, 377–393 (2011)

9. Brain, M., Tinelli, C., Ruemmer, P., Wahl, T.: An automatable formal semantics for IEEE-754 floating-point arithmetic. In: ARITH. pp. 160–167 (2015)

10. Bryant, R.E., Kroening, D., Ouaknine, J., Seshia, S.A., Strichman, O., Brady, B.A.: An abstraction-based decision procedure for bit-vector arithmetic. Int. J. Softw. Tools Technol. Transf. **11**(2), 95–104 (2009)

11. Chapman, R., Schanda, F.: Are we there yet? 20 years of industrial theorem proving with SPARK. In: Klein, G., Gamboa, R. (eds.) ITP 2014. LNCS, vol. 8558, pp. 17–26. Springer, Heidelberg (2014)

12. Cyrluk, D., Rueß, H., Möller, O.: An efficient decision procedure for the theory of fixed-sized bit-vectors. In: Grumberg, O. (ed.) Computer Aided Verification. LNCS, vol. 1254, pp. 60–71. Springer, Heidelberg (1997)

13. Dahlweid, M., Moskal, M., Santen, T., Tobies, S., Schulte, W.: VCC: contract-based modular verification of concurrent C. In: ICSE. pp. 429–430. IEEE Computer Society Press (2009)

14. Dross, C., Fumex, C., Gerlach, J., Marché, C.: High-level functional properties of bit-level programs: Formal specifications and automated proofs. Research Report 8821, Inria (2015)

15. Filliâtre, J.-C.: Verifying two lines of C with Why3: an exercise in program verification. In: Joshi, R., Müller, P., Podelski, A. (eds.) VSTTE 2012. LNCS, vol. 7152, pp. 83–97. Springer, Heidelberg (2012)

16. Gerlach, J.: Validation and verification of implementation/code. Technical report D4.3.2, OpenETCS (2015). https://github.com/openETCS/governance/wiki/State-of-Deliverables

17. Kanig, J., Schonberg, E., Dross, C.: Hi-Lite: the convergence of compiler technology and program verification. In: HILT. pp. 27–34. ACM Press (2012)

18. Klebanov, V., Müller, P., Shankar, N., Leavens, G.T., Wüstholz, V., Alkassar, E., Arthan, R., Bronish, D., Chapman, R., Cohen, E., Hillebrand, M., Jacobs, B., Leino, K.R.M., Monahan, R., Piessens, F., Polikarpova, N., Ridge, T., Smans, J., Tobies, S., Tuerk, T., Ulbrich, M., Weiß, B.: The 1st verified software competition: experience report. In: Butler, M., Schulte, W. (eds.) FM 2011. LNCS, vol. 6664, pp. 154–168. Springer, Heidelberg (2011)

19. Leino, K.R.M., Wüstholz, V.: The Dafny integrated development environment. F-IDE. EPTCS **149**, 3–15 (2014)

20. Lomont, C.: Fast inverse square root. Technical report, Indiana: Purdue University (2003). http://www.lomont.org/Math/Papers/2003/InvSqrt.pdf

21. McCormick, J.W., Chapin, P.C.: Building High Integrity Applications with SPARK. Cambridge University Press, Cambridge (2015)

22. de Moura, L., Bjørner, N.S.: Z3: an efficient SMT solver. In: Ramakrishnan, C.R., Rehof, J. (eds.) TACAS 2008. LNCS, vol. 4963, pp. 337–340. Springer, Heidelberg (2008)

23. Nguyen, T.M.T.: Taking architecture and compiler into account in formal proofs of numerical programs. Thèse de doctorat, Université Paris-Sud (2012)

24. Warren, H.S.: Hackers's Delight. Addison-Wesley, Boston (2003)

Formal Verification of an Executable LTL Model Checker with Partial Order Reduction

Julian Brunner$^{(\boxtimes)}$ and Peter Lammich

Technische Universität München, Munich, Germany
{brunnerj,lammich}@in.tum.de

Abstract. We present a formally verified and executable on-the-fly LTL model checker that uses ample set partial order reduction. The verification is done using the proof assistant Isabelle/HOL and covers everything from the abstract correctness proof down to the generated SML code. Building on Doron Peled's paper "Combining Partial Order Reductions with On-the-Fly Model-Checking", we formally prove abstract correctness of ample set partial order reduction. This theorem is independent of the actual reduction algorithm. We then verify a reduction algorithm for a simple but expressive fragment of PROMELA. We use static partial order reduction, which allows separating the partial order reduction and the model checking algorithms regarding both the correctness proof and the implementation. Thus, the CAVA model checker that we verified in previous work can be used as a back end with only minimal changes. Finally, we generate executable SML code using a stepwise refinement approach. We test our model checker on some examples, observing the effectiveness of the partial order reduction algorithm.

1 Introduction

Partial order reduction [25] is an important optimization for model checkers, enabling them to deal better with models involving concurrency. It allows the model checker to consider only a subset of all possible interleavings of concurrently executing operations by identifying equivalences between them. Unfortunately, partial order reduction is notoriously complex and can easily affect the correctness of the model checker. For instance, [25] describes a partial order reduction algorithm and claims that it can simply be used with on-the-fly nested depth-first search. It was found out later that this compromises correctness due to the reduction possibly differing between the inner and the outer search [8]. Moreover, while formalizing the algorithm in [25], we discovered that its correctness proof uses an invalid lemma (see Sect. 2.2).

There is also the issue of implementation correctness, which is usually addressed via testing in the context of model checking algorithms. Since testing is necessarily incomplete, it may lead to incorrect implementations due to missed corner cases. Furthermore, when using models of realistic size, determining the correct outcome for a given test input requires the use of a model checker.

Research supported by DFG grant CAVA (Computer Aided Verification of Automata).

© Springer International Publishing Switzerland 2016
S. Rayadurgam and O. Tkachuk (Eds.): NFM 2016, LNCS 9690, pp. 307–321, 2016.
DOI: 10.1007/978-3-319-40648-0_23

Thus, although in widespread use, neither the correctness of partial order reduction algorithms, nor the correctness of their implementations can be taken for granted. This is especially problematic since the trust in the correctness of a single model checker is used to justify the confidence in the correctness of the many models that it checks. In order to meet the very strict correctness requirements of model checking algorithms, we implement and formally verify a partial order reduction algorithm.

In previous work [5], we have presented the CAVA model checker, a fully verified and executable LTL model checker à la SPIN. The verification was done with the proof assistant Isabelle/HOL [24] and covers everything from the correctness of the algorithms down to the implementation. Due to its LCF-like architecture, Isabelle/HOL is more trustworthy than a large unverified implementation like SPIN (see Sect. 3.1). This paper now adds the following contributions:

1. Formalization of a fragment of the modeling language PROMELA
2. Formalization of the static analysis required for partial order reduction
3. Formal abstract correctness proof for ample set partial order reduction
4. Verified implementation and integration into the CAVA model checker
5. Development of reusable libraries for automata and trace theory

This results in what we believe to be the first formally verified and executable implementation of a partial order reduction algorithm, addressing both of the issues mentioned earlier. The verification is carried out completely in Isabelle/HOL, such that the correctness of the model checker only depends on the correctness of Isabelle/HOL. This integration avoids logical gaps that may arise when manually composing the results of different verification tools. Most importantly, we now have a formally verified reference implementation that can deal with many formerly infeasible models, improving its usefulness for testing other model checkers.

To the best of our knowledge, there has been only one other attempt at formalizing partial order reduction [4]. However, it does not cover the reduction algorithm and is restricted to a specific fairness assumption (see Sect. 2).

The rest of this paper is organized as follows. In Sect. 2, we cover theoretical aspects of partial order reduction and elaborate on our choice of algorithm. In Sect. 3, we report on our Isabelle/HOL formalization. In Sect. 4, we compare the performance of our model checker to that of SPIN. Finally, in Sect. 5, we give conclusions and future research directions.

2   Theory

Figure 1 illustrates the basics of partial order reduction. In regular model checking, the system automaton 'S' is derived from the system and used as input for the model checker together with the formula 'φ'. The model checker then determines if the system automaton satisfies the property expressed by the formula ($\mathcal{L}\ S \subseteq \mathcal{L}\ \varphi$). When using partial order reduction, a reduction algorithm obtains a reduced system automaton 'R' from the system instead, which fulfills certain *reduction conditions.* These conditions imply stuttering equivalence between the language of the system automaton and that of the reduced system automaton ($\mathcal{L}\, S \approx \mathcal{L}\, R$). Since properties expressed by next-free LTL formulae are stuttering-invariant [26], using the reduced system automaton instead of the system automaton when model checking yields the same result ($\mathcal{L}\, S \subseteq \mathcal{L}\, \varphi \iff \mathcal{L}\, R \subseteq \mathcal{L}\, \varphi$).

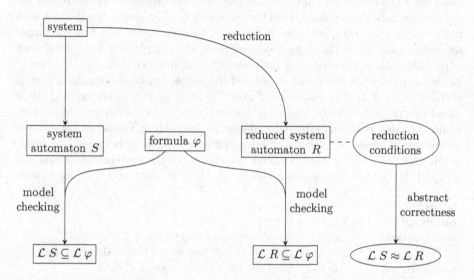

Fig. 1. Partial Order Reduction Overview. A reduction algorithm obtains the reduced system automaton 'R', which is then used as an input of the model checker instead of the system automaton 'S'. The reduction algorithm guarantees that the reduced system automaton fulfills certain reduction conditions, from which one can prove stuttering equivalence between the two languages. This implies that the result of the model checker is not affected by the reduction.

Note that this is a very abstract description of partial order reduction. In actual implementations, the reduced system automaton may be represented implicitly, and the reduction algorithm may be merged with the model checking algorithm. However, this view allows us to identify the three major tasks involved in developing a verified implementation of partial order reduction:

1. Reduction algorithm correctness: The automaton produced by the reduction algorithm fulfills the reduction conditions.
2. Abstract correctness: If an automaton fulfills the reduction conditions, its language is stuttering equivalent to that of the system automaton.
3. Implementation and verification of the reduction algorithm.

Unlike our formalization, [4] only covers the second task. This means there is no input language, no static analysis, no reduction algorithm, no implementation, and no executable model checker. Furthermore, it only covers the case where a certain fairness assumption is met, which simplifies the abstract correctness proof. In absence of other formalization attempts, we believe that our work is a significant contribution over the existing body of research.

2.1 Reduction Conditions

Both the reduction algorithm and the abstract correctness are built around the reduction conditions, making them the main object of interest when dealing with partial order reduction. We chose to implement an algorithm based on the ample set method and chose the reduction conditions accordingly. Let 'en q' be the set of enabled actions at state 'q' of the system automaton (*enabled set*). Let 'ren q' be the set of enabled actions at state 'q' of the reduced system automaton (*ample set*) Let 'ex a q' be the successor of state 'q' after executing action 'a' ('ex' is called *execution function*). This way, '(en, ex)' represents the system automaton, while '(ren, ex)' represents the reduced system automaton. The set of finite words executable at state 'q' of the system automaton 'words q' is defined in terms of 'en' and 'ex'. For a more detailed description of the system definitions, see Sect. 3.4. With these prerequisites, we define the following reduction conditions:

subset	$\forall q.\ \text{ren}\ q \subseteq \text{en}\ q$
nonempty	$\forall q.\ \text{ren}\ q \subset \text{en}\ q \implies \text{ren}\ q \neq \{\}$
independent	$\exists\ \text{independence relation}\ I.\ \forall q\,w.\ \text{ren}\ q \subset \text{en}\ q \implies$
	$w \in \text{words}\ q \implies \text{ren}\ q \cap \text{set}\ w = \{\} \implies I\,(\text{ren}\ q)\,(\text{set}\ w)$
wellfounded	$\exists\ \text{well-founded relation}\ R.\ \forall q\,a.\ \text{ren}\ q \subset \text{en}\ q \implies$
	$a \in \text{ren}\ q \implies R\,(\text{ex}\ a\ q)\,q$
invisible	$\forall q.\ \text{ren}\ q \subset \text{en}\ q \implies \text{ren}\ q \subseteq \text{invisible}$

Condition **subset** states that the reduced system automaton is a subautomaton of the system automaton and is usually not stated explicitly in the literature. Condition **nonempty** states that the reduction algorithm must not omit all of the actions at any state. Condition **independent** requires that all the actions that are executed after reaching some state but before an action from the ample set at this state are *independent* of all the actions in this ample set. Condition **wellfounded** requires that every cycle in the system automaton contains at least one state where no reduction is performed. Condition **invisible** states that when a proper reduction takes place, the ample set cannot contain any actions that are *visible* to the formula. Conditions **nonempty**, **independent**, and **wellfounded** correspond to conditions C0, C1, and C2 in [4, pages 268, 269], while condition **invisible** corresponds to condition C3' in [25, page 50]. Note that even though the reduction conditions are similar, our formalization is not based on [4].

2.2 Reduction Algorithm

These conditions are very abstract, so there are still many choices to be made with respect to the actual reduction algorithm. We originally planned to verify dynamic partial order reduction with on-the-fly model checking [25], but soon encountered difficulties. Dynamic partial order reduction detects cycles during the emptiness check in order to ensure condition **wellfounded**. This tight integration with the emptiness check has led to bugs in the past [8]. When used with on-the-fly model checking, this integration also extends to the product construction, effectively turning the whole system into one monolithic algorithm. It also introduces a mismatch since an algorithm that conceptually works on a system automaton is now used with a product automaton, requiring complicated reasoning. And indeed, during our effort of formalizing the proof given in [25], we discovered a counterexample for one of the lemmata used in this proof. This counterexample is based on the fact that, when exploring the product automaton, different instances of the system automaton appearing in the product automaton may be reduced differently. A more detailed description can be found in [3, Sect. 8.4]. Note that this, while refuting the lemma, does not necessarily invalidate the correctness theorem, only the proof thereof. However, despite investing a significant amount of time, we were unable to find an alternative proof as it seems that the reasoning required is more complex than anticipated in the original paper.

We chose to implement a static partial order reduction [9] algorithm instead, which avoids these problems of the dynamic approach. It ensures condition **wellfounded** by performing some static analysis initially, identifying a set of *sticky* edges which breaks every cycle in the control flow graph. Static partial order reduction is much more modular, making it possible to verify the reduction algorithm independently of the product construction and the emptiness check. This way, we were able to simply add the reduction algorithm as a preprocessing step to the existing CAVA model checker, enabling reuse of existing optimizations.

The reduction algorithm itself is similar to the one used in SPIN [7]. The basic idea is to take the set of enabled actions of each process in the state as a candidate for an ample set. For each candidate, an over-approximation of the reduction conditions is tested. If no candidate satisfies the conditions, the state is fully expanded, that is, no reduction is performed.

For instance, our approximation checks that, in order to be used as an ample set, the actions of a process must be independent of all actions of other processes. Moreover, it is checked that no additional action of this process can be enabled as a consequence of executing actions of other processes. Thus, only independent actions of other processes can be executed before an action of the ample set, which implies condition **independent**.

3   Formalization

Our formalization contains all three of the tasks outlined in Sect. 2. The implementation was integrated into the CAVA model checker, which was published previously [5,6]. Since then, various features have been added to this model checker. For instance, it now supports using PROMELA as an input language [22]. Furthermore, the library for automata has been updated [13] and a new framework for depth-first search algorithms has been formalized [16]. Also, an alternative algorithm for deciding language emptiness of Büchi automata based on Gabow's strongly-connected components algorithm has been implemented [10]. However, the focus of this paper is on the implementation and verification of the partial order reduction algorithm.

In this section, we give some technical background regarding the tools that were used as well as a high-level overview of the formalization. We also describe certain noteworthy aspects of the formalization in isolated detail. The full formalization is available at https://cava.in.tum.de/CAVA_POR.

3.1 Isabelle/HOL

Isabelle/HOL [23, 24] is a proof assistant based on Higher-Order Logic (HOL), which can be thought of as a combination of functional programming and logic. Formalizations done in Isabelle/HOL are trustworthy for two reasons. Firstly, Isabelle's LCF architecture guarantees that all proofs are checked using a very small logical core which is rarely modified but tested extensively over time. This reduces the trusted code base to a minimum. Secondly, bugs in the core rarely lead to accidentally proving false propositions. Bugs that have large effects are easily caught, while the limited applicability of bugs with small effects is unlikely to coincide with a logical mistake in the large-scale structure of the proof.

Isabelle/HOL notation resembles standard mathematical notation with just a few differences. For instance, as in functional programming, functions are usually curried in HOL. This means that instead of '$f :: A \times B \to C$' with application syntax '$f(x,y)$', we have '$f :: A \to B \to C$' with application syntax '$f\ x\ y$'.

3.2 Refinement Framework

When developing formally verified algorithms, there is a trade-off between the efficiency of the algorithm and the efficiency of the proof: For complex algorithms, a direct proof of an efficient implementation tends to get unmanageable, as implementation details obfuscate the main ideas of the proof. A standard approach to this problem is stepwise refinement [1], which modularizes the correctness proof: One starts with an abstract version of the algorithm and then refines it in correctness preserving steps to the concrete, efficient version. A refinement step may reduce the nondeterminism of a program, replace abstract mathematical specifications by concrete algorithms, and replace abstract datatypes by their implementations. For example, selection of an arbitrary element from a set may be refined to getting the head of a list. This approach separates the correctness proof of the algorithm, which focuses on the main algorithmic ideas, from the correctness proof of the implementation, where the proof of each refinement step focuses on a specific implementation detail, not caring about the overall correctness property.

In Isabelle/HOL, stepwise refinement is supported by the Refinement Framework [12, 17] and the Isabelle Collection Framework [11, 15]. The former framework implements a refinement calculus [1] based on a nondeterminism monad [27], and the latter provides a library of verified efficient data structures. Both frameworks come with tool support to simplify their usage for algorithm development and to automate canonical tasks such as verification condition generation.

3.3 Basics

The most basic concept needed for nearly all parts of the formalization is that of *sequences*. With HOL being very similar to functional programming languages like SML or Haskell, the standard library already includes extensive support for *finite sequences* via the type 'α list = Nil | Cons α (α list)'. For *infinite sequences*, the type 'α word' is used, which is simply a type synonym for '$\mathbb{N} \to \alpha$'.

We also use the library Coinductive [18] which formalizes lazy lists using codatatypes [2]. It provides the type 'α llist', which models both finite and infinite sequences. This is useful for selecting subsequences of infinite lists that can be either finite or infinite. Reasoning about selections and indices of lazy lists required us to significantly extend the library Coinductive.

Another important component needed for partial order reduction is stuttering equivalence and the proof that next-free LTL formulae can only express stuttering-invariant properties. The library Stuttering Equivalence [20] is used for both.

3.4 Systems

Model checkers usually represent systems using the type '(state $\times$ state) set'. Reasoning about partial order reduction requires transitions to be labeled with actions, suggesting the type '(state $\times$ action $\times$ state) set'. However, this type allows multiple successor states to be reached given a state and an action, making the type a bad fit for the deterministic action model of partial order reduction. This leads to unnecessary wellformedness conditions, inaccessible successor states, and overspecified path predicates. We thus chose the following representation of the system automaton which was already referred to in Sect. 2.1:

$$\text{en} :: \text{state} \to \text{action set} \tag{1a}$$
$$\text{ex} :: \text{action} \to \text{state} \to \text{state} \tag{1b}$$
$$\text{init} :: \text{state set} \tag{1c}$$

Here, 'en' is the set of enabled actions at a state (*enabled set*), 'ex' is the function that, given an action, maps each state to its successor state (*execution function*), and 'init' is the *set of initial states*.

This representation allows paths to be introduced in a straightforward way via the inductively defined set 'words :: state $\to$ action list set':

$$[] \in \text{words } p \tag{2a}$$
$$a \in \text{en } p \implies w \in \text{words (ex } a\ p) \implies a \# w \in \text{words } p \tag{2b}$$

Inductive definitions in Isabelle/HOL specify the smallest sets that satisfy the given rules. Equivalently, they specify the sets containing those elements whose membership can be derived using the given rules. These rules can be declared as safe introduction rules, so that whenever Isabelle/HOL encounters proof obligations of the form '[] ∈ words p' or '$a \# w \in$ words p', it can automatically split them into simpler goals or discharge them completely.

We prove an additional rule for the append operator on lists:

$$u \in \text{words } p \implies v \in \text{words (fold ex } u\ p) \implies u @ v \in \text{words } p \qquad (3)$$

Note how 'fold' lifts the execution function 'ex :: action → state → state' from single actions to sequences of actions 'fold ex :: action list → state → state'. Also note how this rule generalizes rule 2b.

Together, rules 2a, 2b, and 3 form a set of introduction rules that break down most goals automatically. For instance, the goal '$u @ a \# v \in$ words p' gets transformed into three subgoals:

$$u \in \text{words } p \qquad (4a)$$

$$a \in \text{en (fold ex } u\ p) \qquad (4b)$$

$$v \in \text{words (ex } a \text{ (fold ex } u\ p)) \qquad (4c)$$

This automates proofs significantly, in some cases shortening proofs comprised of 50 to 100 lines to one-liners. We have proven many more rules about this system formalization, making it a useful addition to the CAVA automata library.

3.5   Trace Theory

Partial order reduction introduces the concept of *independent* actions, which can be executed in any order without changing the result or enabling or disabling each other. Trace theory [19] lifts this notion of commutable items to that of *equivalent* sequences, which is needed in the abstract correctness proof.

Finite sequences are equivalent if they differ by a finite number of commutations of independent actions. This concept is then extended to infinite sequences [25, page 41]. This definition by case distinction makes lazy lists difficult to use, so we decided to work with separate types and definitions for finite and infinite sequences.

Formalizing the necessary parts of trace theory took significant effort due to the large number of theorems. There are also some theorems that look simple but are difficult to prove, for instance:

$$w_1 \equiv_I w_2 \iff u @ w_1 @ v \equiv_I u @ w_2 @ v \qquad (5)$$

The left to right direction can be proven via rule induction on the transitive structure of '$\equiv_I$'. Doing the same for the right to left direction results in an unprovable induction step. It was necessary to prove the following lemmata:

$$w_1 \equiv_I w_2 \implies \text{remove1 } c\ w_1 \equiv_I \text{remove1 } c\ w_2 \qquad (6a)$$

$$u @ w_1 \equiv_I u @ w_2 \implies w_1 \equiv_I w_2 \qquad (6b)$$

$$w_1 \equiv_I w_2 \implies \text{rev } w_1 \equiv_I \text{rev } w_2 \qquad (6c)$$

Here, 'remove1 c w' removes the first occurrence of 'c' from the sequence 'w', and 'rev w' reverses the sequence 'w'. Lemma 6a uses 'remove1' to avoid the fact that rule induction does not work with modified assumptions. We use Lemma 6a to prove Lemma 6b via reverse induction on the sequence 'u'. Lemma 6c is proven via rule induction and with Lemma 6b, it completes the proof of Theorem 5.

We also had to define some concepts specific to partial order reduction. For instance, the predicate specifying that the first occurrence of a symbol in a sequence is independent of all symbols before it. In the end, the formalization of the relevant aspects of trace theory required about as much proof text as the formalization of the abstract correctness proof itself.

3.6   Abstract Correctness

Assume that 'S' is a system automaton and 'R' is a reduced system automaton such that the reduction conditions introduced in Sect. 2.1 hold. Then, the abstract correctness theorem states that the languages of 'S' and 'R' are stuttering equivalent:

$$\mathcal{L}\,S \approx \mathcal{L}\,R \tag{7}$$

The proof of this theorem required about 1000 lines of formal proof text and dozens of lemmata. Its structure is similar to that of the informal proof [25] and we will thus not repeat it here.

However, we present the formalization of a Lemma [25, Theorem 3.11] in detail and highlight the differences between the formal and the informal proof:

> **lemma** reduction_word:
>> **assumes** "$q \in$ reachable"   "$v \in$ words$_S$ q"
>> **obtains** u w
>> **where**
>>> "$w \in$ words$_R$ q"
>>> "$v \equiv_I u$"   "$u \preceq_I w$"
>>> "lproject visible (inf_llist u) = lproject visible (inf_llist w)"

Note that we do not present the formal definitions of all the constants used in this theorem. Informally, the theorem states that, given an infinite sequence 'v' in the system automaton, it is possible to find a corresponding sequence 'w' in the reduced system automaton. The theorem also implies the existence of an intermediate sequence 'u', which is needed since 'w' may contain actions that are not in 'v'.

The proof consists of two parts. In the first part, we construct an arbitrarily long but finite sequence in the reduced system automaton by transcribing longer and longer prefixes of the infinite sequence in the system automaton. In order to do so, we inductively define a predicate that describes a valid state during this construction process where a prefix of the sequence in the system automaton has already been processed. This predicate specifies that the state of the construction where both the sequence in the system automaton and the one in the reduced system automaton are empty is valid. It also specifies how one can extend a valid construction state by adding a step in the system automaton and a sequence of corresponding steps in the reduced system automaton. At each point of the construction, we can then prove that some invariants hold and that the construction can be extended. Proving these invariants and the extension property required a lot of effort as the informal proof only provided a rough sketch of the argument. The formal proof constitutes both a certificate of the theorem's correctness as well as a detailed documentation of the reasoning used to prove it.

The second part of the proof consists of using the first part to show that there exists an infinite sequence with the required properties in the reduced system automaton. While this step is almost completely skipped in the informal proof, the formal one forces us to consider it rigorously. For instance, the first part supplies a theorem which guarantees that for any number of steps that were already taken, another step can be taken, extending the sequence in the process. Intuitively, such a theorem can be applied "infinitely often" to obtain an infinite sequence, but this is not logically sound. Performing a step like this in a formal proof requires precise reasoning and in our case the use of Hilbert's epsilon operator. We believe that this is not a flaw of formal logic or the particular instance we are using. Instead, we think that situations like this point to areas where it became customary to use sloppy reasoning in informal proofs, possibly leading to mistakes or overlooked side conditions. For instance, it is often not made clear in which way variables depend on each other or what guarantees that an infinite sequence can actually be constructed from a set of finite sequences. Formal proofs point out required side conditions like the fact that the infinite concatenation of these finite sequences needs to be infinite. It also brought attention to the fact that many concepts need to be defined on both finite and infinite sequences and that they need to correspond to each other in a specific way.

As mentioned in Sects. 3.3, 3.4, and 3.5, a large amount of foundational work was required in order to formally prove the abstract correctness theorem.

3.7 The SM Language

In order to implement an executable reduction algorithm, we require a concrete modeling language. We use a simple fragment of PROMELA that is expressive enough to model interesting examples. We call this fragment the *SM language*.

A program in this language consists of a set of processes, each of which is described using a guarded command language. Each process has a set of local variables and communication between processes is modeled via global variables. A configuration of the system consists of a valuation of the global variables and a list of process configurations, where a process configuration consists of a command and a valuation of the local variables. The main PROMELA feature not supported by SM is channels, which can be emulated by global variables.

We specify a structural operational semantics that establishes a control flow graph where the nodes are commands and the edges are labeled with *local actions*. A local action can be a guarded assignment, a test, or the skip action.

Each local action is assigned an enabledness check and an effect function on the local and global variables.

The system semantics describes a step relation between configurations by nondeterministically picking a process from a configuration, following an edge in the control flow graph from the process' command that is labeled with an enabled local action, and applying the effect of the local action to the local and global state. To ensure that all runs of the system are infinite, we apply a stuttering extension, that is, if there is no process with an enabled action, the system may take a step that does not change the configuration.

Since we want to use the SM language in an LTL model checker, we need to define *atomic propositions* and their connection to the system states. In our case, atomic propositions are simply expressions in the SM language that contain only global variables. Then, we define the *interpretation function* to map each state to the set of expressions that evaluate to true in this state.

We define the language of a program as the set of infinite sequences of sets of atomic propositions that correspond to infinite runs of the program:

$$\mathcal{L} :: \text{program} \rightarrow \text{exp set word set} \tag{8}$$

We define a *global action* to consist of a process id and a control flow graph edge. The process id is the position of the associated process in the list of all processes. A global action is enabled if the associated process exists, the control flow graph edge is consistent with the current command of the associated process, and the corresponding local action is enabled. Execution of a global action transforms the state of the associated process and the global variables according to the corresponding local action.

3.8   Reduction Algorithm

Next, we define a function that selects an ample set for a configuration. Similar to SPIN, candidates for ample sets are the sets of enabled actions of each process. We make a rather crude approximation and allow a nonempty set of enabled actions of a process as an ample set, if (1) there is no statically enabled action of the process that reads or writes global variables, and (2) none of the enabled actions corresponds to a sticky edge in the control flow graph. Here, (1) is a simple way of guaranteeing condition **independent** (see Sect. 2.1), and (2) is the condition imposed by static partial order reduction (see Sect. 2.2).

We implemented and verified an algorithm based on depth-first search which computes the set of sticky edges before the actual model checking phase. This algorithm starts with the set of edges labeled with actions containing global variables and extends it to a feedback arc set on the control flow graphs of the processes. For this task, we used the Depth-First Search Framework [16], which simplifies the implementation and verification of efficient DFS-based algorithms.

We define the reduced system automaton based on this ample function and prove that all of the reduction conditions from Sect. 2.1 are fulfilled. This allows us to invoke the abstract correctness theorem to obtain stuttering equivalence between the language of the system automaton and that of the reduced system automaton. Together with the assumption that the formula is next-free, this implies that using the reduced system automaton for model checking instead of the system automaton does not change the result.

3.9 Integration

We refine the ample function, the execution function, and the interpretation function to efficiently executable implementations. Among other steps, this includes compilation of the model to a more efficient representation. Finally, instantiating the generic infrastructure of the CAVA model checker yields an executable LTL model checker 'cava' which uses the reduced system automaton. Obtaining the main theorem of our development is then merely a matter of combining the correctness theorem of the CAVA model checker with that of abstract partial order reduction:

$$\textbf{case } \text{cava } S \, \varphi \textbf{ of } \text{SAT} \Rightarrow \mathcal{L} \, S \subseteq \mathcal{L} \, \varphi \mid \text{UNSAT} \Rightarrow \mathcal{L} \, S \nsubseteq \mathcal{L} \, \varphi \qquad (9)$$

This theorem states that the function 'cava' decides whether or not the sequences of atomic propositions admitted by runs of the program satisfy the LTL formula. The meaning of this statement only depends on the abstract semantics of the SM language (term '$\mathcal{L} \, S$') and the abstract semantics of LTL formulae (term '$\mathcal{L} \, \varphi$'). All other parts of the formalization, including partial order reduction, LTL model checking, and refinement towards efficiently executable definitions, are covered by this machine-checked correctness theorem. Note that we also formalized a version of the model checker that provides a counterexample in case the program does not satisfy the formula.

Finally, Isabelle/HOL can generate Standard ML code from the definition of the function 'cava'. This code then constitutes a formally verified and executable LTL model checker. A snapshot of this formalization can be found at https:// cava.in.tum.de/CAVA_POR.

We conclude with some statistics about the formalization, which took about 15 man-months and resulted in about 13 k lines of theory text being added to the model checker. This includes both definitions and proofs and splits up into 6 k lines for abstract partial order reduction and 7k lines for the SM language and the associated program analysis. The size of the whole codebase of the model checker and its libraries is about 140 k lines of theory text.

4 Evaluation

We perform some basic sanity checks using two systems that admit no reduction and complete sequentialization, respectively. As a practical example, we implement a distributed mutual exclusion algorithm called MULOG [21] using the supported PROMELA fragment. The property used for testing states that at most one process can be in the critical section at any point in time. We perform

Example	Processes	States SPIN	States SPIN*	States CAVA	States CAVA*
MULOG	1	27	27	52	52
MULOG	2	2,674	2,004	5,538	4,284
MULOG	3	2,376,180	1,171,578	5,205,376	2,779,218

Fig. 2. Reduction effectiveness. Shown are the number of states that were explored during model checking using both the CAVA and the SPIN model checkers. The starred variants indicate where partial order reduction was used.

model checking using both the CAVA and the SPIN model checkers, both with and without partial order reduction. Figure 2 shows the reduction effectiveness for this algorithm.

Both the CAVA and the SPIN model checker show a significant reduction in the number of states. The reduction factors are comparable (roughly 1.3 for two processes and roughly 2 for three processes). The SPIN model checker explores fewer states in total (roughly factor 2) and has shorter execution times (roughly factor 400) than the CAVA model checker.

We would like to emphasize that in this paper, it is not our goal to compete with SPIN in absolute terms. Instead, our focus is on providing a verified and executable reference implementation of partial order reduction. The SPIN model checker employs various other optimizations and compilation to C code, while the CAVA model checker interprets the semantics of the modeling language. Thus, little insight can be gained by directly comparing execution time and memory consumption. Incorporating these optimizations is orthogonal to partial order reduction and we consider this subject of further research. Due to the modular architecture of the CAVA model checker, doing so will not make this contribution obsolete. At this point, it will also be possible to perform a more comprehensive evaluation with multiple example algorithms.

5   Conclusion

Formal verification is sometimes downplayed as "careful documentation of known theorems" or "filling in obvious details in proofs". In practice, formal verification usually involves extensive modeling as well as abstraction, generalization, and simplification of the theory. What may seem like trivial completion of the informal proof often involves bridging large gaps and proving omitted corner cases.

In this project, we discovered an issue with the correctness proof given in [25] (see Sect. 2.2). This demonstrates both the need for and the usefulness of formal verification. More importantly, we developed a formally verified and executable LTL model checker with partial order reduction. As the verification is machine-checked and covers everything from the abstract algorithm to the generated SML code, this is a very strong correctness guarantee. Our model checker is fast enough to serve as a reference implementation for other model checkers on models of realistic size. This constitutes a much-needed source of trust given the widespread use of partial order reduction together with its history of issues. The formalization can further serve as a detailed description of the theory of partial order reduction and its correctness proof, which is useful since nontrivial gaps were bridged in the proof. We also developed a significant amount of foundational theories that can be reused in other projects dealing with similar concepts. Finally, our work demonstrates that large systems can now be verified using proof assistants via modularization and reuse of existing theories.

Future work consists of extending the SM language to make it more practical, with the ultimate goal of supporting most or all of the features of PROMELA. It is also possible to find smaller sets of sticky actions by incorporating heuristics about variable increments/decrements [9]. Another way to improve reduction consists of using additional static analysis to find larger independence relations. Finally, there is still room for improvement concerning the implementation, especially via the use of imperative data structures [14].

References

1. Back, R.J., von Wright, J.: Refinement Calculus: A Systematic Introduction. Graduate Texts in Computer Science. Springer, Heidelberg (1998)
2. Blanchette, J.C., Hölzl, J., Lochbihler, A., Panny, L., Popescu, A., Traytel, D.: Truly modular (co)datatypes for Isabelle/HOL. In: Klein, G., Gamboa, R. (eds.) ITP 2014. LNCS, vol. 8558, pp. 93–110. Springer, Heidelberg (2014)
3. Brunner, J.: Implementation and Verification of Partial Order Reduction for On-The-Fly Model Checking. MA thesis. Technische Universität München, 83 p., 15 July 2014. http://www21.in.tum.de/brunnerj/documents/ivporotfmc.pdf
4. Chou, C.T., Peled, D.: Formal verification of a partial-order reduction technique for model checking. In: Margaria, T., Steffen, B. (eds.) TACAS 1996. LNCS, vol. 1055, pp. 241–257. Springer, Heidelberg (1996)
5. Esparza, J., Lammich, P., Neumann, R., Nipkow, T., Schimpf, A., Smaus, J.-G.: A fully verified executable LTL model checker. In: Sharygina, N., Veith, H. (eds.) CAV 2013. LNCS, vol. 8044, pp. 463–478. Springer, Heidelberg (2013)
6. Esparza, J., Lammich, P., Neumann, R., Nipkow, T., Schimpf, A., Smaus, J.G.: A fully verified executable LTL model checker. Archive of Formal Proofs, May 2014. http://afp.sf.net/entries/CAVA_LTL_Modelchecker.shtml, formal proof development
7. Holzmann, G.J.: The SPIN Model Checker. Primer and Reference Manual. Addison-Wesley Professional, Reading (2003)
8. Holzmann, G.J., Peled, D., Yannakakis, M.: On nested depth first search. In: SPIN Workshop, vol. 32, pp. 81–89 (1996)
9. Kurshan, R.P., Levin, V., Minea, M., Peled, D.A., Yenigün, H.: Static partial order reduction. In: Steffen, B. (ed.) TACAS 1998. LNCS, vol. 1384, pp. 345–357. Springer, Heidelberg (1998)
10. Lammich, P.: Verified efficient implementation of Gabow's strongly connected component algorithm. In: Klein, G., Gamboa, R. (eds.) ITP 2014. LNCS, vol. 8558, pp. 325–340. Springer, Heidelberg (2014)
11. Lammich, P.: Collections framework. Archive of Formal Proofs, November 2009. http://afp.sf.net/entries/Collections.shtml, formal proof development

12. Lammich, P.: Refinement for monadic programs. Archive of Formal Proofs, January 2012. http://afp.sf.net/entries/Refine_Monadic.shtml, formal proof development
13. Lammich, P.: The CAVA automata library. Archive of Formal Proofs, May 2014. http://afp.sf.net/entries/CAVA_Automata.shtml, formal proof development
14. Lammich, P.: Refinement to Imperative/HOL. In: Urban, C., Zhang, X. (eds.) ITP 2015. LNCS, vol. 9236, pp. 253–269. Springer, Switzerland (2015)
15. Lammich, P., Lochbihler, A.: The Isabelle collections framework. In: Kaufmann, M., Paulson, L.C. (eds.) ITP 2010. LNCS, vol. 6172, pp. 339–354. Springer, Heidelberg (2010)
16. Lammich, P., Neumann, R.: A Framework for Verifying Depth-First Search Algorithms. In: CPP, pp. 137–146. ACM, 13 January 2015
17. Lammich, P., Tuerk, T.: Applying data refinement for monadic programs to Hopcroft's algorithm. In: Beringer, L., Felty, A. (eds.) ITP 2012. LNCS, vol. 7406, pp. 166–182. Springer, Heidelberg (2012)
18. Lochbihler, A.: Coinductive. Archive of Formal Proofs, February 2010. http://afp. sf.net/entries/Coinductive.shtml, formal proof development
19. Mazurkiewicz, A.: Trace theory. In: Reisig, W., Brauer, W., Rozenberg, G. (eds.) APN 1986. LNCS, vol. 255, pp. 278–324. Springer, Heidelberg (1987)
20. Merz, S.: Stuttering equivalence. Archive of Formal Proofs, May 2012. http://afp. sf.net/entries/Stuttering_Equivalence.shtml, formal proof development
21. Naimi, M., Trehel, M., Arnold, A.: A log (n) distributed mutual exclusion algorithm based on path reversal. J. Parallel Distrib. Comput. 34(1), 1–13 (1996)
22. Neumann, R.: Using Promela in a fully verified executable LTL model checker. In: Giannakopoulou, D., Kroening, D. (eds.) VSTTE 2014. LNCS, vol. 8471, pp. 105–114. Springer, Heidelberg (2014)
23. Nipkow, T., Paulson, L.C., Wenzel, M. (eds.): Isabelle/HOL. LNCS, vol. 2283. Springer, Heidelberg (2002)
24. Paulson, L., Nipkow, T., Wenzel, M.: Isabelle (2014). http://isabelle.in.tum.de
25. Peled, D.: Combining partial order reductions with on-the-fly model-checking. Formal Meth. Syst. Des. 8(1), 39–64 (1996)
26. Peled, D., Wilke, T.: Stutter-invariant temporal properties are expressible without the next-time operator. Inf. Process. Lett. 63(5), 243–246 (1997)
27. Wadler, P.: Comprehending monads. Math. Struct. Comput. Sci. 2, 461–493 (1992)

A Modular Way to Reason About Iteration

Jean-Christophe Filliâtre[1,2] and Mário Pereira[1,2(✉)]

[1] Laboratoire de Recherche en Informatique,
University of Paris-Sud, CNRS, 91405 Orsay, France
`Mario.Parreira-Pereira@lri.fr`
[2] INRIA Saclay – Île-de-France, 91893 Orsay, France

Abstract. In this paper we present an approach to specify programs performing iterations. The idea is to specify iteration in terms of the finite sequence of the elements enumerated so far, and only those. In particular, we are able to deal with non-deterministic and possibly infinite iteration. We show how to cope with the issue of an iteration no longer being consistent with mutable data.

We validate our proposal using the deductive verification tool Why3 and two iteration paradigms, namely cursors and higher-order iterators. For each paradigm, we verify several implementations of iterators and client code. This is done in a modular way, *i.e.*, the client code only relies on the specification of the iteration.

1 Introduction

Iteration is a central concept in programming. It can be as simple as a while loop or a recursive function, but it can also appear as a more complex artifact, such as a cursor, a higher-order iterator, a generator, or a lazy list. When it comes to verifying the correctness of a program, we need tools to reason about iteration. Typically, we provide a suitable loop invariant for a while loop and a contract for a recursive function. In this paper, we consider the problem of verifying programs where iteration is performed by other means, such as cursors or higher-order iterators. In particular, we are interested in answering the following challenges:

- Iteration is not necessarily the traversal of a data structure. It can be, for instance, the result of an algorithm, such as the enumeration of all prime numbers.
- Iteration is not necessarily finite, as in the aforementioned case of prime numbers.
- Iteration is not necessarily deterministic. The simplest example is that of a symbol generator. From the client point of view, the only required property is that the next element is distinct from the previous ones. Another example is the traversal of a set where elements are presented in some unspecified order. When the iteration is deterministic, however, we want to be able to specify it.

M. Pereira—This research was partly supported by the Portuguese Foundation for Sciences and Technology (grant FCT-SFRH/BD/99432/2014) and by the French National Research Organization (project VOCAL ANR-15-CE25-008).

© Springer International Publishing Switzerland 2016
S. Rayadurgam and O. Tkachuk (Eds.): NFM 2016, LNCS 9690, pp. 322–336, 2016.
DOI: 10.1007/978-3-319-40648-0_24

- When iteration depends on mutable data, client code may put iteration in some inconsistent state. In Java, for instance, this problem is solved by maintaining version numbers and by raising an exception in the case of a concurrent modification. In our case, we wish instead to be able to prove, statically, that there is no concurrent modification.
- When a data structure is abstract (for example, a set for which we do not know the implementation) we still want to be able to specify an iteration over its elements and to verify a program using such an iteration. Even when we have access to the implementation of the iteration, we are still interested in performing verification in a modular way with an abstraction barrier. It means verifying the client code independently of a particular implementation for the iteration.

In this paper we propose a way to specify iteration that fulfills all the above-mentioned requirements. We validate our work using the deductive verification tool Why3 [1], but the idea is broader and could be implemented in any other deductive verification tool. Our contribution is twofold:

- An approach to *specify* an iteration process, independently of how it is implemented (cursor, higher-order function, etc.);
- A methodology to *verify* implementations and use of cursors and higher-order iteration functions.

This paper is organized as follows. Section 2 introduces our proposal to specify an iteration. Section 3 gives a brief overview of Why3. Then we consider cursors in Sect. 4 and higher-order iterators in Sect. 5. We discuss related work in Sect. 6 before concluding. The Why3 developments from this paper can be found at the following address: http://www.lri.fr/~mpereira/iteration/.

2   Specifying Iteration

We present in this section our proposal to formally specify an iteration. We use several examples to illustrate this approach, including cases of non-deterministic and infinite iteration.

The idea is to specify the iteration in terms of the finite sequence v of the elements enumerated so far, and only those. More precisely, such a specification is composed of two predicates: the first predicate, called *enumerated*, characterizes the elements of v; the second predicate, called *completed*, indicates whether the iteration is completed. In the following, $\|v\|$ denotes the length of v, $v[i]$ denotes the i-th element of v (assuming a 0-based indexation), and $x \in v$ means that x occurs in v.

Consider for instance the iteration over an array a, from left to right. The first predicate, *enumerated*, is as follows:

$$enumerated(v, a) \triangleq \forall i.\ 0 \leq i < \|v\| \implies v[i] = a[i]$$

In other words, the sequence v is a prefix of the array a. The second predicate, *completed*, simply compares the length of v with that of a:

$$completed(v, a) \triangleq \|v\| = length(a)$$

Let us now consider the iteration over the elements of a finite set s, in a non-deterministic way. Such an iteration can be specified as follows:

$$enumerated(v, s) \triangleq distinct(v) \wedge \forall x.\ x \in v \implies x \in s$$
$$completed(v, s) \triangleq \|v\| = card(s)$$

The condition $distinct(v)$ means that the sequence v contains no duplicate elements, to account for the fact that no element is visited twice (s is a set, not a multiset). We also require the elements of v to be elements of s. Since we do not require any additional property, we have a non-deterministic iteration. The iteration is completed whenever the length of v is equal to the cardinal of s.

Let us now assume that we want to specify instead a *deterministic* iteration over the elements of s. One way to do this is to introduce some oracle function *elements* that returns a sequence containing the elements of s in the order they will be visited. Then *enumerated* merely says that we have already visited a prefix of this sequence, that is,

$$enumerated(v, s) \triangleq prefix(v, elements(s))$$

with a natural definition for *prefix*:

$$prefix(s_1, s_2) \triangleq \|s_1\| \leq \|s_2\| \wedge \forall i.\ 0 \leq i < \|s_1\| \implies s_1[i] = s_2[i]$$

With this specification, the behavior of the enumeration is determined from the beginning. For instance, if the elements of s are totally ordered, then $elements(s)$ could be the sorted sequence of the elements of s.

Let us switch now to examples of iteration that are not traversals of a data structure. Consider for instance an iteration obtained by the repeated application of a function f starting with some initial value x_0, that is, the infinite sequence

$$x_0,\ f(x_0),\ f(f(x_0)),\ f(f(f(x_0))),\ \ldots$$

On way to specify it is as follows:

$$enumerated(v, x_0, f) \triangleq \forall i.\ 0 \leq i < \|v\| \implies v[i] = f^i(x_0)$$

assuming f^i is defined as the ith functional power of f. Besides, to account for the fact that this iteration never halts, we simply define

$$completed(v, x_0, f) \triangleq false$$

The next example is the specification of a scanner for a possibly infinite channel c. The elements of v are characters and a special character EOF marks the end of the channel. The specification looks like:

$$enumerated(v, c) \triangleq \cdots \wedge \forall i.\ 0 \leq i < \|v\| - 1 \implies v[i] \neq \text{EOF}$$
$$completed(v, c) \triangleq \|v\| > 0 \wedge v[\|v\| - 1] = \text{EOF}$$

```
type seq 'a
function length (seq 'a) : int
axiom length_nonnegative: forall s: seq 'a. 0 ≤ length s
constant empty: seq 'a
axiom empty_length: length empty = 0
function ([]) (seq 'a) int : 'a
function snoc (seq 'a) 'a : seq 'a
axiom snoc_length: forall s: seq 'a, x: 'a. length (snoc s x) = 1 + length s
axiom snoc_get:
  forall s: seq 'a, x: 'a, i: int. 0 ≤ i ≤ length s  →
  (snoc s x)[i] = if i< length s then s[i] else x
```

Fig. 1. Sequence theory (excerpt).

This specification covers both the case of a finite channel, with a terminal EOF, and the case of an infinite channel, where EOF never shows up.

Our last example is that of a *symbol generator*, that is, a program that generates fresh symbols on demand. Its output is an infinite iteration of distinct symbols, that is

$$enumerated(v) \triangleq distinct(v)$$
$$completed(v) \triangleq false$$

In this case, *enumerated* does not depend on any information other than the sequence v itself.

3   Why3 in a Nutshell

Our goal is to apply the idea of specifying an iteration using the predicates *enumerated* and *completed* in the context of deductive program verification. To this end, we used the Why3 tool to explore this approach. However, this proposal is general and is not tied to Why3. Any other deductive verification tool could be used. In this section, we briefly describe the Why3 platform, its organization and principal features.

The Why3 platform proposes a set of tools allowing the user to implement, formally specify, and prove programs. The use of Why3 is oriented towards automatic proofs, as it supports many external automatic theorem provers. Why3 can also interact with interactive proof assistants, such as Coq, Isabelle, or PVS, when a proof obligation cannot be automatically discharged.

Why3 comes with a programming language, WhyML [9], an ML dialect with some restrictions in order to make automatic proof simpler. This language offers some features commonly found in functional languages, like pattern-matching, algebraic types and polymorphism, but also imperative constructions, like records with mutable fields and exceptions. Programs written in WhyML can be annotated with contracts, that is, pre- and postconditions. The code itself can be annotated, for instance, to express loop invariants or to justify termination of loops and recursive functions. It is also possible to add intermediate assertions in the code to ease automatic proofs. The WhyML language allows to write ghost code [8], which is used only for specification and proof purposes and can be removed with no observable modification in the program's execution. The system uses the annotations to generate proof obligations thanks to a weakest precondition calculus.

The logic used to write formal specifications is an extension of first-order logic with rank-1 polymorphic types, algebraic types, (co-)inductive predicates and recursive definitions [7], as well as a limited form of higher-order logic [4]. This logic is used to write theories for the purpose of modeling the behavior of programs. Such theories are most of the time axiomatic. Figure 1 represents a fragment from the sequence theory provided by the Why3 standard library. We can find there the polymorphic type of finite sequences (seq 'a), a constant representing the empty sequence (empty), function symbols (length for the sequence length, $\cdot[\cdot]$ to access the i-th element, and snoc to add an element at the end of a sequence), together with axioms defining these symbols. Why3 standard library is formed of many logic theories of this kind, in particular for integer and floating point arithmetic, sets, and dictionaries.

The entire standard library, numerous verified examples, as well as a more detailed presentation of Why3 and WhyML are available on the project web site, http://why3.lri.fr. However, the rest of this paper does not assume any further knowledge of Why3.

4   Cursors

A cursor [5] is a data structure that implements iteration via a function, say next, that is called each time we need to get the next element, if there is one. It is thus an iteration paradigm where the control is given to the *consumer*, which calls next whenever needed, contrary to other paradigms where control is given to the *producer* of the iteration. Cursors are broadly used in C++ and Java, for instance.

We adopt a model where we interact with the cursor via two functions: has_next returns a Boolean indicating the existence of a next element in the iteration; and next advances to the next element and returns it. The latter operation updates the cursor by a side effect[1]. A typical client code looks like this:

```
c ← create_cursor(...)
while has_next(c) do
  x ← next(c)
  ...
```

In Java, the "for each" loop construct for (E x: ...) is nothing more than syntactic sugar for the above.

---

[1] This is not mandatory. A cursor can be implemented as a persistent structure [6].

In this section we describe the use of predicates *enumerated* and *completed* to formally specify what is a cursor (Sect. 4.1), to verify a cursor implementation (Sect. 4.2), and to verify a client code that uses a cursor (Sect. 4.3).

4.1 Cursor Specification

We assume two data types to be given: a type `elt` for the elements enumerated by the cursor, and a type `collection` for the collection whose elements are enumerated.

```
type elt
type collection
```

The term "collection" is to be taken broadly here. It does not necessarily designate a data structure but rather any data needed for the iteration specification. We model the cursor type as follows:

```
type cursor model {
          collection: collection;
  mutable    visited: seq elt;

}
```

The field `collection` is used to stock the collection of elements that is to be iterated by the cursor. The field `visited` contains the sequence of the elements enumerated by the cursor so far. This field is marked as mutable, to account for the imperative nature of the cursor. Finally, the `cursor` type is marked as being a *model type*. It means this is an abstract data type from the programming point of view. In particular, client code cannot access the `visited` field, preventing any modification of its contents. The specification, however, is free to refer to cursor's field and typically will.

Next, we introduce the two predicates *enumerated* and *completed* to specify the cursor's behavior.

```
predicate enumerated (c: cursor) = ...
predicate completed  (c: cursor) = ...
```

Now we can provide suitable contracts to functions `has_next` and `next`. They are introduced as unimplemented functions with the keyword `val`.

```
val has_next (c: cursor) : bool =
  requires { enumerated c }
  ensures  { result ↔ not (completed c) }
```

In other words, function `has_next` decides whether the predicate `completed` holds. The second operation, `next`, is specified as follows:

```
val next (c: cursor) : elt
  requires { enumerated c }
  requires { not (completed c) }
  writes   { c }
  ensures  { enumerated c }
  ensures  { c.visited = snoc (old c.visited) result }
```

A call to next is only allowed when the iteration is not yet completed (the second requires). The postcondition guarantees that the returned element is appended at the end of the visited sequence. This side effect is expressed with the writes clause.

The postcondition of next also guarantees that the visited sequence satisfies the enumerated predicate. Functions has_next and next also require predicate enumerated as a precondition. This is a way to ensure that the cursor remains in a consistent state. Suppose for instance that the cursor is enumerating the elements of an array. Nothing prevents us from mutating the array while the cursor is being used. If we do so, however, the enumerated predicate will not hold anymore and, consequently, we will not be able to call functions has_next and next anymore.

In practice, we also need to provide operations to create cursors. Such an operation looks as follows:

```
val create_cursor (t: collection) : cursor
  ensures { result.visited = empty }
  ensures { enumerated result }
  ensures { result.collection = t }
```

It returns a fresh cursor whose visited sequence is empty (first postcondition) and which is in a consistent state (second postcondition).

Collection modification. Taking an example of a cursor to traverse the elements of an array we can imagine the following code:

```
let c = create_cursor a in
a [0] ← 42;
let x = next c in
...
```

that modifies the array a after creating the cursor c. However, if we try to prove this program we will no be able to prove the precondition of function next, namely coherent c. The array has been modified and so has the cursor as it contains the array in the collection field.

4.2   Cursor Implementations

To validate our approach, we have implemented and verified several cursors using Why3. These examples include iterators for collections, such as arrays, and lists, and sets, as well as a symbol generator, the in-order traversal of a binary tree, the DFS traversal of a graph, and a cursor that merges the ordered sequences generated by two other cursors. For each cursor, we have

- refined the cursor data type, to add data specific fields. If we consider the cursor for an array, for instance, the refinement is as follows:

```
type cursor = { ghost mutable    visited: seq elt;
                      mutable      index: int;
                              collection: array elt; }
```

Table 1. Experimental results.

cursor	loc	los	time (sec)
gensym	12	30	0.03
array	12	23	0.05
list	15	28	0.40
set	12	22	13.74
binary tree	36	72	0.21
merge	36	75	2.83
dfs	48	85	11.02
total	171	335	

(a) Cursor Implementations

program	loc	los	time (sec)
array sum	8	12	0.70
list length	8	4	0.03
search	8	10	0.10
same fringe	36	72	0.21
check path	11	4	1.25
merge cursors	36	75	2.83
mjrty	32	22	1.67
total	139	199	

(b) Cursor Clients

- strengthen the **enumerated** predicate, so that it acts as a gluing invariant as well. For the array example, the gluing invariant adds the property that the **index** field is equal to the length of **visited**.

```
predicate enumerated (c: cursor) =
   (forall i. 0 ≤ i < length c.visited → c.visited[i] = c.array[i]) ∧
   c.index = length c.visited
```

- implemented and verified operations **next**, **has_next**, and **create_cursor**.

Table 1a shows the lines of code, the lines of specification (functions contracts, invariants, and auxiliary lemmas), and the total verification time (in seconds) for each cursor. All verification conditions are discharged automatically, using a combination of the SMT solvers Alt-Ergo, Z3, and CVC4.

4.3 Cursor Clients

We have also implemented and verified a number of client programs that make use of the cursors presented in the previous section. We do this in a modular way, *i.e.*, the client programs are only using the cursor interface (from Sect. 4.1) and have no access to the underlying implementation.

Our programs include summing the elements of an array, computing the length of a list, searching for a particular element in some abstract collection, solving the "same fringe" problem (comparing two binary trees using two in-order traversal cursors), checking for the existence of a path in a graph using a DFS cursor, merging two ordered sequences, and implementing Boyer & Moore's "mjrty" algorithm [2] using array cursors.

Table 1b shows the lines of code, the lines of specification, and the total verification time (in seconds) for each program. All verification conditions are discharged automatically. Source files are available online.

5   Higher-Order Iterators

In programming languages featuring first-class functions, iteration is commonly implemented as a higher-order function that takes as argument a function to be applied to each element of the enumerated sequence. In an imperative language, such a function can be as simple as

$$\texttt{iter} : (elt \to unit) \to collection \to unit$$

where *elt* is the type of the iteration elements, *collection* is the type of the collection to be iterated over, and *unit* is a type with no meaningful values. If the elements of a collection c are $x_1, \ldots, x_n$, in that order, then a call to iter f c simply amounts to evaluate $f(x_1), \ldots, f(x_n)$ sequentially. Assuming the elements of c are integers, we can sum them using

$$s \leftarrow 0;\ \texttt{iter}\ (\lambda x.\, s \leftarrow s + x)\ c$$

where λ introduces an anonymous function. The recent introduction of closures in languages such as C++ and Java eases this style of programming.

Higher-order iterators coexist with cursors, allowing the user to choose the paradigm that suits best. The main difference between the two is that control is given to the producer in the case of a higher-order iterator, while it is given to the consumer in the case of a cursor.

In this section we describe a methodology to specify and verify higher-order iterators using *enumerated* and *completed* predicates. As we did for cursors, we intend to verify both implementations of iter functions (Sect. 5.1), and client code using iter functions (Sect. 5.2). One way to tackle the verification of higher-order functions is to use a higher-order (program) logic, in such a way that we can quantify over the specification of function arguments. There exist already several systems in which we can do so; we will discuss those in Sect. 6. We consider here a different approach, which only requires first-order logic. This is possible thanks to the *abstraction barrier* provided by the *enumerated/completed* predicates. On both sides of this interface, we are making distinct first-order program proofs, one for the implementation of iter and one for each call to iter.

Currently, Why3 does not support the use of effectful higher-order code. To circumvent this limitation, we have developed a prototype tool that reads both implementations and uses of higher-order iterators, together with specification and possible annotations, and turns them into regular Why3 programs to be verified.

5.1   Verifying an Iterator

Given an implementation of some iter function, our approach consists in automatically building a first-order function iter_correct whose correctness implies that of iter. Once function iter_correct is verified, we do not need it anymore.

We obtain function iter_correct by specializing the code of iter for a particular function that appends the element it receives (the next element of the iteration) to a sequence stored in a global variable visited. Then we can verify the resulting code against the specification given by the predicates *enumerated* and *completed*.

Let us consider the case of the in-order traversal of a binary tree, the type of which is:

```
type tree = E | N tree elt tree
```

In our prototype, we implement in-order traversal as follows:

```
let rec iter (f: elt → unit) (t: tree) : unit
  with { enumerated (visited, t) = ...
         completed  (visited, t) = ... }
= match t with
  | E        → ()
  | N l x r → iter f l; f x; iter f r
  end
```

The iteration specification is introduced with the keyword with, as the pair of the two predicates enumerated and completed (whose definition is omitted here). In this case, iter is defined recursively, as it is the simplest way to do. Yet this is not mandatory. Our technique applies as well to iterative implementations. From this definition, we automatically generate the following Why3 function iter_correct, together with its specification.

```
val visited: ref (seq elt)

let iter_correct (t0: tree)
  requires { !visited == empty ∧ enumerated (empty, t0) }
  ensures  { enumerated (!visited, t0) ∧ completed (!visited, t0) }
= let f x = visited := snoc !visited x in
  let rec iter0 (t: tree) : unit =
    match t with
    | E        → ()
    | N l x r → iter0 l; f x; iter0 r
    end in
  iter0 t0
```

This function takes a tree t0 as argument. It stands for the original argument of iter. The specification expresses that if we start with an empty visited sequence, then we end up with a completed iteration for the tree t0. To verify this code, we have to equip function iter0 with suitable annotations. This part is not done automatically, as it depends on the implementation of iter and the nature of *enumerated* and *completed*.

Using our prototype tool, we have verified several implementations of iterators, including traversals of arrays, lists, trees, and abstract collections. The resulting verification conditions are all discharged automatically by SMT solvers.

5.2   Using an Iterator

As we did for the implementation of the iter function, we propose a methodology to verify a client code using iter by translating it to a first-order program. Predicates *enumerated* and *completed* are used to specify the iteration, and the client code has no access to the implementation of iter. Our idea is to transform the client code by replacing the use of iter with a while loop that uses a cursor. This cursor is specified exactly as in Sect. 4.1. Once again abstraction is the key: the client code only relies on the iteration specification, and not on the way it is implemented.

Let us illustrate the idea on an example. We consider a program that takes a list as an argument and returns a list containing the same elements without repetitions. It uses an iter function to traverse the input list and a hash table to store the elements we have seen so far. Considering the following type for lists

```
type list = Nil | Cons elt list
```

we can use our prototype to define the following client program (assuming hash table operations provided by a module H):

```
let uniq (l: list) : list
  ensures { distinct result }
  ensures { forall x. mem x result ↔ mem x l }
= let h = H.create () in
  let r = ref Nil in
  iter (fun x →
          if not (H.mem x h) then begin H.add x h; r := Cons x !r end)
       l;
  !r
```

The code first declares a new hash table h and a reference r to hold the output list. The consumer function checks, each time it is called, whether the element x is not yet in the hash table. If so, it adds x both to the table h and to the list r. When the iteration completes, we return the contents of r.

To verify function uniq, we need to equip the iteration with a suitable "loop" invariant. We use here the term "loop" in a loose way, to refer to the iteration performed by the iter function. To allow this invariant to refer to the sequence of already enumerated elements, we add an extra ghost argument v to the consumer function. The code now looks as follows:

```
iter (fun (ghost v) x →
        invariant { ...user loop invariant... }
        if not (H.mem x h) then begin H.add x h; r := Cons x !r end)
```

For this program, a suitable invariant is the following:

```
distinct !r ∧ (forall x. mem x v ↔ mem x !r) ∧
(forall x. H.contains h x ↔ mem x !r)
```

It states that at each step of the iteration the accumulator r contains exactly the elements enumerated so far, without repetition. The last clause states that the elements in the hash table are exactly the elements of r.

We now turn the uniq program into a first-order implementation uniq_correct that uses a cursor to perform the same iteration as the iter function. The following is the Why3 code resulting from this transformation (as produced automatically by our prototype tool):

```
let uniq_correct (l: list elt) : list elt
  ensures { distinct result }
  ensures { forall x. mem x result ↔ mem x l }
= let h = H.create () in
  let r = ref Nil in
  let _c = create_cursor l in
  while has_next _c t do
    invariant { enumerated _c }
    invariant { let v = _c.visited in ...user loop invariant... }
    let x = next _c l in
    if not (H.mem x h) then begin H.add x h; r := Cons x !r end
  done;
  !r
```

The invariant `enumerated _c` is automatically added to the loop[2]. The second invariant is the one that was given by the user, where `v` is bound to the sequence contained in the cursor. The cursor functions `create_cursor`, `next`, and `has_next` are given the same contracts as in Sect. 4.1. The body of the consumer function is turned into the loop body, and `x` is bound to the next iteration element, as returned by `next`.

Then we can feed the program `uniq_correct` to Why3 for verification. In this case, all verification conditions are discharged automatically by SMT solvers. This implies that the original higher-order `uniq` program is correct with respect to its specification, provided function `iter` is implemented and proved correct w.r.t. the same *enumerated/completed* specification. The latter can be done using the technique presented in the previous section.

It is worth pointing out that the consumer function passed to `iter` is free to have side effects. (In the example above, it does, as it fills the hash table.) In particular, it could jeopardize the iteration by mutating data on which the iteration relies. This is not an issue, though, since we have to prove the preservation of the loop invariant `enumerated`. In this respect, the situation is not different from the use of cursors, as described in Sect. 4.1.

6   Related Work

The idea of formally specifying and proving cursors is not new. Weide presents a formal specification for the cursors' behavior [16] using the *RESOLVE* language [10]. A collection is modeled as a finite set (in the mathematical sense) and a cursor is specified using a `past` sequence corresponding to our `visited` and another `future` sequence corresponding to remaining elements. A third sequence, `original`, contains the set of elements of the collection. Under such formalization, a cursor can only be used with finite collections and the traversal is necessarily deterministic. The author also presents a mechanism to ensure coherence, by

---

[2] Here we use a definition of `enumerated` that takes as argument a cursor. This can be easily derived from the definition of `enumerated` that was given to specify the iterator.

means of extra operations over cursors, Start_Iterator and Finish_Iterator, that should limit all the cursor uses. In this way, and contrary to our approach, the validity of a cursor can only be verified once the traversal is finished.

In the literature we can find many cursors formalization and proof examples under the more general context of data structures library verification. One example is that of the EiffelBase2 library [12], a container library for the Eiffel language. The verification task is performed using the AutoProof system. However, EiffelBase2 offers no generic presentation of cursors.

Many tools exist that tackle the verification of higher-order effectful programs, in particular of higher-order iterators. These are normally based on rich specification logics and type systems. Liquid Types [13] is a type system with refinement types extracted from a decidable logic. This type system is used to infer simple "loop invariants" from a given code. In our case, the user supplies the loop invariant and, contrary to the Liquid Types approach, we apply and prove an iterator client without access to the iterator implementation, in a modular way.

Vazou *et al.* [15] present a technique to verify a call to a foldr function (another iterator, very close to iter) over lists. This technique consists in annotating the program with a dependent type that expresses an invariant about the list of already processed elements. We provide a similar invariant when calling an iter function. The main difference is that our approach is not limited to lists: using predicates *enumerated* and *completed* we can specify many kinds of iteration.

Dependent types and monad structures are used in the F* tool [14] as the theoretical basis to tackle the proof of higher-order programs with effects. F* can be used both as a programming language and as a proof assistant, featuring a higher-order specification and programming language. This tool has been used to verify many complex effectful programs including cryptographic protocols and the mechanization of lambda calculi metatheory. Even though F* is able to use SMT solvers during the proving process, it seems that the verification of nontrivial (effectful) higher-order programs is out of the realm of automatic provers. In particular, the specification of a higher-order iterator is very similar to what one would write in a general-purpose proof assistant like Coq.

The CFML tool [3] uses characteristic formulas to verify OCaml code within the Coq proof assistant. Characteristic formula is a higher-order formula that can be generated from a source code and its specification, and that describes the semantics of a given program. Using a proof assistant based on higher-order logic, the characteristic formula can be exploited to prove complex properties about that program. Up to now, CFML has been used to verify several nontrivial higher-order imperative programs, including higher-order iterators over mutable data structures. However, the specification used to describe a higher-order iterator is always tied to a specific collection data type.

Ynot [11] is a library for the Coq proof assistant that can be used to write and verify imperative programs. It is based on Hoare Type Theory and the use of monads and separation logic to reason about effects. An implementation of imperative finite maps has been verified with Ynot, including a *fold*-like (effect-ful) iterator. The theoretical techniques employed by Ynot seem to make difficult its use in an automatic proof process.

7   Conclusion and Perspectives

In this paper we presented an approach to specify programs performing itera-tions. Our proposal consists in specifying two predicates *enumerated* and *com-pleted* characterizing the sequence of already enumerated elements. Our specifi-cation allows, notably, non-deterministic and infinite iterations. This approach can be applied to different iteration paradigms.

To validate our idea, we applied it to the specification of two particular forms of iteration, namely cursors and higher-order iterators. We wrote several exam-ples of iterators and client codes for each paradigm. Using the Why3 deductive verification tool we were able to formally prove that these implementations are correct. It is worth noting that our approach to specify an iteration via pred-icates `enumerated` and `completed` is not tied to Why3. Any other deductive verification tool could be used instead.

To verify higher-order iterators, we proposed a mechanical translation of a higher-order code (either an iterator implementation or a client code) into a first-order program. The specification of this first-order program is automatically derived from the predicates *enumerated* and *completed*, and the correctness of the generated code implies that of the initial higher-order code.

Perspectives. On a short term perspective, we intend to extend Why3 with a `for` loop á la Java based on cursors. This will be of particular interest for a longer-term project of verifying a realistic graph library with Why3. Indeed, graph algorithms heavily rely on the use of iterators, for example to traverse vertices of a graph or neighbors of a vertex. It remains to show that our specification of iteration is well suited for the verification of such algorithms, particularly in a context where we seek proofs as most automatic as possible.

Besides, we think that our proposal could apply as well to other iteration par-adigms, such as streams (implemented as lazy lists) or generators (implemented as coroutines). We intend to explore this question in the future.

Acknowledgments. We thank Clément Fumex, Chantal Keller, Claude Marché, Andrei Paskevich, Vitor Pereira, François Pottier, and Simão Melo de Sousa for their comments on earlier versions of this paper.

References

1. Bobot, F., Filliâtre, J.C., Marché, C., Paskevich, A.: Let's verify this with Why3. Int. J. Softw. Tools Technol. Transf. (STTT) **17**(6), 709–727 (2015)
2. Boyer, R.S., Moore, J.S.: Mjrty: A fast majority vote algorithm. In: Automated Reasoning: Essays in Honor of Woody Bledsoe, pp. 105–118 (1991)

3. Charguéraud, A.: Characteristic formulae for the verification of imperative programs. In: Proceeding of the 16th ACM SIGPLAN International Conference on Functional Programming (ICFP), pp. 418–430. ACM, Tokyo, Japan, September 2011
4. Clochard, M., Filliâtre, J.-C., Marché, C., Paskevich, A.: Formalizing semantics with an automatic program verifier. In: Giannakopoulou, D., Kroening, D. (eds.) VSTTE 2014. LNCS, vol. 8471, pp. 37–51. Springer, Heidelberg (2014)
5. Coplien, J.O.: Advanced C++ Programming Styles and Idioms. Addison-Wesley, Reading (1992)
6. Filliâtre, J.C.: Backtracking iterators. In: ACM SIGPLAN Workshop on ML, Portland, Oregon, September 2006
7. Filliâtre, J.-C.: One logic to use them all. In: Bonacina, M.P. (ed.) CADE 2013. LNCS, vol. 7898, pp. 1–20. Springer, Heidelberg (2013)
8. Filliâtre, J.-C., Gondelman, L., Paskevich, A.: The spirit of ghost code. In: Biere, A., Bloem, R. (eds.) CAV 2014. LNCS, vol. 8559, pp. 1–16. Springer, Heidelberg (2014)
9. Filliâtre, J.-C., Paskevich, A.: Why3 — where programs meet provers. In: Felleisen, M., Gardner, P. (eds.) ESOP 2013. LNCS, vol. 7792, pp. 125–128. Springer, Heidelberg (2013)
10. Kulczycki, G.: A language for building verified software components. In: Favaro, J., Morisio, M. (eds.) ICSR 2013. LNCS, vol. 7925, pp. 308–314. Springer, Heidelberg (2013)
11. Nanevski, A., Morrisett, G., Shinnar, A., Govereau, P., Birkedal, L.: Ynot: reasoning with the awkward squad. In: Proceedings of ICFP 2008 (2008)
12. Polikarpova, N., Tschannen, J., Furia, C.A.: A fully verified container library. In: Bjørner, N., de Boer, F. (eds.) FM 2015. LNCS, vol. 9109, pp. 414–434. Springer, Heidelberg (2015)
13. Rondon, P.M., Kawaguchi, M., Jhala, R.: Liquid types. In: Gupta, R., Amarasinghe, S.P. (eds.) PLDI 2008, Tucson, AZ, USA, 7–13 June 2008, pp. 159–169. ACM (2008)
14. Swamy, N., Hriţcu, C., Keller, C., Rastogi, A., Delignat-Lavaud, A., Forest, S., Bhargavan, K., Fournet, C., Strub, P.Y., Kohlweiss, M., Zinzindohoue, J.K., Zanella-Béguelin, S.: Dependent types and multi-monadic effects in F*. In: 43rd ACM Symposium on Principles of Programming Languages (POPL), pp. 256–270. ACM, January 2016
15. Vazou, N., Rondon, P.M., Jhala, R.: Abstract refinement types. In: Felleisen, M., Gardner, P. (eds.) ESOP 2013. LNCS, vol. 7792, pp. 209–228. Springer, Heidelberg (2013)
16. Weide, B.W.: SAVCBS 2006 challenge: specification of iterators. In: Proceedings of the 2006 Conference on Specification and Verification of Component-Based Systems, SAVCBS 2006, NY, USA, pp. 75–77. ACM, New York (2006)

A Proof Infrastructure for Binary Programs

Ashlie B. Hocking[1]([⊠]), Benjamin D. Rodes[1], John C. Knight[1],
Jack W. Davidson[2], and Clark L. Coleman[2]

[1] Dependable Computing, Charlottesville, VA, USA
{ben.hocking,ben.rodes,john.knight}@dependablecomputing.com
[2] Zephyr Software LLC, Charlottesville, VA, USA
{jwd,clc}@zephyr-software.com

Abstract. Establishing properties of binary programs by proof is a
desirable goal when the properties of interest are crucial, such as those
that arise in safety- and security-critical applications. Practical development of proofs for binary programs requires a substantial infrastructure
to disassemble the program, define the machine semantics, and actually undertake the required proofs. At the center of these infrastructure
requirements is the need to document semantics in a formal language. In
this paper we present a work-in-progress proof infrastructure for binary
programs based on AdaCore and Altran's integrated development and
verification environment, SPARKPro. We illustrate the infrastructure
with proof of a security property.

1 Introduction

Establishing properties of binary programs by proof is a desirable goal receiving
significant attention recently [2,4–6]. Any approach to proving software properties requires a comprehensive infrastructure that: (a) defines the semantics of
the target machine architecture, (b) translates binary programs into a representation suitable for proof based on the defined machine architecture semantics,
and (c) operates on translated binary representations to generate proof.

Many languages could be used to define machine semantics, and many proof
tools exist. Our infrastructure is based on an application of AdaCore and Altran's
integrated development and verification environment, SPARKPro [1] and our
custom binary-to-SPARK-Ada translator. SPARKPro was chosen for many reasons:

- The SPARK Ada language [1] has been designed for proof and includes syn-
  tactic structures to enable definition of the necessary verification conditions.
- SPARK Ada is familiar to many in the community and simple to use.
- SPARKPro proof tools provide the capability to establish necessary proofs.
- SPARKPro has industrial-strength support thereby allowing the technology
  to be adopted by practitioners.
- SPARKPro provides an executable specification that can be tested.

© Springer International Publishing Switzerland 2016
S. Rayadurgam and O. Tkachuk (Eds.): NFM 2016, LNCS 9690, pp. 337–343, 2016.
DOI: 10.1007/978-3-319-40648-0_25

In this paper, we present a work-in-progress binary proof infrastructure based on SPARKPro. We illustrate the infrastructure with an example binary program and prove the program possesses a desired security property.

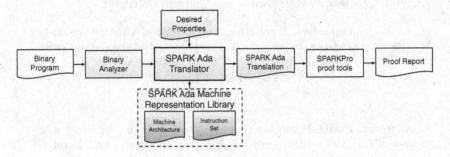

Fig. 1. Architecture of proof infrastructure for binary programs. The SPARK Ada Machine Representation is the focus of this paper, and light gray elements indicate other supporting aspects of our work.

2 Proof Infrastructure

Figure 1 shows the architecture of our proof infrastructure. A binary program is first processed by a static analyzer to disassemble the program and recover important program structures. Of particular importance in the analysis is the recovery of function boundaries and control structures such as conditions and loops. A translator then converts the binary program to a SPARK Ada representation. The translator accesses semantics of the target machine architecture and instruction set, both defined within our SPARK Ada library. It also accesses a description of desired program properties to prove and merges them into the representation of the subject program. Finally, the composite representation of the subject program and desired properties is submitted to the SPARK prover.

The proof infrastructure could be applied to any instruction set architecture (ISA); however, our current research focuses on X86–64. Figure 2 shows a high-level organization of the two semantic definitions of the X86–64 ISA.

Central to the machine semantics are registers. The integer registers are represented as Ada integers with modulus 2^{64} (Unsigned64). As shown in Fig. 3, a general-purpose X86–64 register (e.g., RAX) can be accessed multiple ways. RAX is modeled as Unsigned64 and is directly accessed for reading and writing. EAX is modeled by read/write functions as shown in Fig. 4. The read function (EAX) returns the lower 32-bits of RAX and Write_EAX sets those bits, while setting the upper bits to zero. AL, and AH and AX are specified similarly, except with appropriate bits preserved instead of set to zero. Each function includes a postcondition in the SPARK Ada syntax describing the expected result. These postconditions are verified by the SPARKPro proof tools. Flag registers (OF, SF, ZF,

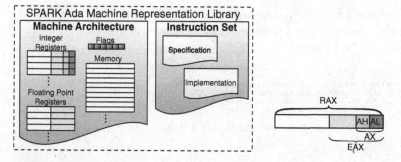

Fig. 2. X86–64 Semantic Definition Library

Fig. 3. RAX register and alternate access methods

```
133 function EAX return Unsigned32 with
134   Global => (Input => RAX),
135   Post => (EAX'Result = Unsigned32(RAX and 16#00000000FFFFFFFF#));
136 procedure Write_EAX(Val : in Unsigned32) with
137   Global => (In_Out => RAX),
138   Post => ((EAX = Val) and ((RAX and 16#FFFFFFFF00000000#) = (16#0000000000000000#)));
```

Fig. 4. EAX specification

AF, CF, and PF) are modeled as `Boolean`. Floating-point registers (e.g., `XMM` and `YMM`) are not currently modeled.

Memory is modeled as an array of 2^{64} 8-bit elements. The declaration of this array is shown in Fig. 5, along with 16-bit reads and writes operating on the memory array.

```
12 type Mem_Array is array (Unsigned64) of Unsigned8;
13 Memory: Mem_Array := Mem_Array'(others => 0);
14 function ReadMem16(addr: in Unsigned64) return Unsigned16 with
15   Global => (Input => Memory),
16   Post => (((ReadMem16'Result and 16#00FF#) = Unsigned16(Memory(addr))) and
17           ((ReadMem16'Result and 16#FF00#) = Unsigned16(Memory(addr+1))*16#100#));
18 procedure WriteMem16(addr : in Unsigned64; Val : in Unsigned16) with
19   Global => (In_Out => Memory),
20   Post => ((ReadMem16(addr) = Val) and (for all i in Unsigned64 =>
21     (if ((i /= addr) and (i /= addr + 1)) then (Memory(i) = Memory'Old(i)))));
```

Fig. 5. Memory type specification

Many X86–64 instructions are modeled as SPARK Ada functions operating on memory and registers. For example, the instruction `setnbe` is specified as shown in Fig. 6. In some cases, instructions match an operator in Ada (e.g., addition), and for those instructions the Ada operator is used directly. Similarly, jump instructions are modeled using Ada control statements (e.g., loops). Other approaches to modeling jumps are possible, but difficult to prove. For example, a binary program could be modeled as an array of instructions and a location counter that is used as an array pointer. Jump instructions could then set the instruction counter accordingly. The lack of loop details, however, would make synthesis of loop invariants and subsequent proof almost impossible.

```
622  procedure setnbe__CL with
623    Global => (Input => (ZeroFlag, CarryFlag), In_Out => RCX),
624    Post => (if ((not CarryFlag) and (not ZeroFlag)) then (CL = 1) else (CL = 0));
```

Fig. 6. Specification of setnbe

3 Example

To illustrate the proof infrastructure and to highlight areas of current work, we examine an example challenge function for security, zero_array, the C representation of which is shown in Fig. 7. The zero_array function is passed a pointer to an array and a size parameter. The function proceeds to zero out size elements of the array. This function presents a typical security challenge since zero_array might result in a buffer overflow that could corrupt, among other things, function return addresses depending on the value of the size parameter.

```
24  void zero__array(int *array, int size) {
25    for (int i = 0; i < size; i++) array[i] = 0;
26  }
```

Fig. 7. Implementation of zero_array

In an example program (not illustrated) zero_array is called from two different functions, each of which passes a pointer to an array of a different size. In the program, the size parameter is always set to the size of the array, i.e., while zero_array is potentially dangerous, its use in this example does not introduce a security vulnerability. The example program was compiled with gcc and the raw disassembled binary as produced by objdump was examined.[1]

The SPARK Ada representation of the zero_array function is shown in Fig. 8, with the associated disassembled code included as comments. Line 19 of Fig. 8 represents the mov instruction as Write_EAX; however, for lines 9–11, instead of modeling the test instruction as a procedure, the result of test (i.e., assignment of flag registers) is represented explicitly in the translated code. Additionally, the binary analysis detects write-after-write situations affecting flags. For example, the flags that would be set by the add instruction (lines 23–24) are not read prior to the following cmp instruction, so there is no need to model the setting of these flags.

---

[1] The binary analyzer uses a combination of objdump and IDA Pro.

```
 6  procedure zero_array is
 7  begin
 8      --100000ed4: test esi,esi
 9      X86.ZeroFlag := (X86.ESI = 0);
10      X86.SignFlag := (X86.ESI > X86.MaxSignedInt32);
11      X86.OverflowFlag := False;
12      --100000ed6: jle 100000eec <_zero_array+0x18>
13      if (X86.ZeroFlag or X86.SignFlag /= X86.OverflowFlag) then
14          --100000eec: f3 c3 repz ret
15          X86.RSP := X86.RSP + 8;
16          return;
17      end if;
18      --100000ed8: mov eax,0x0
19      X86.Write_EAX(0);
20      loop
21          --100000edd: DWORD PTR [rdi+rax*4],0x0
22          X86.WriteMem32(X86.RDI +(X86.RAX*4), 0);
23          --100000ee4: add rax,0x1
24          X86.RAX := X86.RAX + 1;
25          --100000ee8: cmp esi,eax
26          X86.ZeroFlag := ((X86.ESI - X86.EAX) = 0);
27          X86.SignFlag := (X86.ESI < X86.EAX);
28          X86.OverflowFlag := ((X86.SignFlag and (X86.EAX > X86.MaxSignedInt32) and
29          (X86.ESI <= X86.MaxSignedInt32)) or ((not X86.SignFlag) and
30          (X86.ESI > X86.MaxSignedInt32) and (X86.EAX <= X86.MaxSignedInt32)));
31          --100000eea: jg 100000edd <_zero_array+0x9>
32          exit when(not(X86.ZeroFlag=False and X86.SignFlag=X86.OverflowFlag));
33      end loop;
34      --100000eec: repz ret
35      X86.RSP := X86.RSP + 8;
36      return;
37  end zero_array;
```

Fig. 8. SPARK Ada representation of `zero_array`

The loop on line 20 and the `if` statement on line 13 are examples of control structures recovered by the static analyzer from analysis of jump instructions.

To prove security properties about the SPARK Ada representation, constraints are added to the initial version of the representation (not illustrated). So as to prove the integrity of other items on the stack, the constraint in this example is that the loop index of `zero_array` will not exceed the `size` parameter. With this constraint in the example, using the SPARKPro prover (`gnatprove`) with the `cvc4` backend we are able to prove that the example program will not overwrite any function's return address.

This proof requires approximately 8 seconds to complete when using all 8 cores of a MacBook Pro (Retina, Mid 2012). We plan to publish further discussion of automatic constraint development in the future.

4   Related Work

Zhao et al. [6] propose binary software fault isolation techniques (ARMor) based on a model of the ARM ISA [3] and Hoare logic. Their approach modifies a binary program by inserting guards at possibly dangerous instructions. Proofs are then generated about security of the modified code. XFI is an approach similar to Zhao et al. developed to support binary programs on Windows [2]. XFI's verification is based primarily on the defined properties of security guards. Software modifications simplify the development of constraints and proofs; however, modifications add overhead and do not allow isolation of weaknesses in the original binary program. In our approach, binary modifications are not necessary, but could be used as a last resort when proofs cannot be established.

AUSPICE is also an approach based on a model of the ARM ISA using Hoare logic [5]. AUSPICE supports security property verification for binary programs without the need for modifications. To avoid manual development of invariants and function pre-/post-conditions, AUSPICE makes simplifying assumptions. In particular, machine-code instructions are not allowed to alter memory addresses greater than the current function's frame pointer address. This restriction is not practical for most real-world programs.

Prior versions of the Binary Analysis Platform (BAP) support some security analysis through manual insertion of predicates into intermediate representations of the binary program [4]. This approach is limited to intraprocedural analysis of functions that do not call other functions. Further, the BAP approach does not complete proofs unless loops are unrolled and the code is free of indirect jumps. More recent versions of BAP no longer appear to support formal analysis.

5 Conclusion

Reverse engineering of binary programs into a formal language and including formal specifications of desired properties admits the possibility of proving those properties. We have presented our infrastructure based on SPARKPro for proving properties about binary programs. Binary programs are analyzed and translated into SPARK Ada. Properties are specified using SPARK Ada and proven using the SPARKPro toolchain. We illustrated the application of our approach with an example binary program, proving an important security property.

The SPARKPro toolchain has the advantage of being able to run multiple proofs in parallel with most proofs discharged automatically. Additionally, the SPARK Ada representation can be compiled into an executable program that could allow for verification by testing for representational accuracy. A current disadvantage of the toolchain is that, when proofs are not discharged automatically, completing the proof manually can be difficult. We plan to discuss specific details of translating binary programs and producing constraints for security properties in future publications; however, the work presented here lays the foundation for and focuses the direction of further research and development.

Acknowledgments. This research was developed with funding from the Defense Advanced Research Projects Agency (DARPA) under contract W31P4Q–14–C–0086. The views, opinions, and/or findings expressed are those of the author(s) and should not be interpreted as representing the official views or policies of the Department of Defense or the U.S. Government. The authors thank the software engineers of AdaCore, in particular, Yannick Moy for providing support.

References

1. Barnes, J.: SPARK: The Proven Approach to High Integrity Software. Altran Praxis, Bath (2012)
2. Erlingsson, U., Abadi, M., Vrable, M., Budiu, M., Necula, G.C.: XFI: software guards for system address spaces. In: Proceedings of the 7th Symposium on Operating Systems Design and Implementation, OSDI 2006, pp. 75–88. USENIX Association, Berkeley (2006)
3. Fox, A., Myreen, M.O.: A trustworthy monadic formalization of the ARMv7 instruction set architecture. In: Kaufmann, M., Paulson, L.C. (eds.) ITP 2010. LNCS, vol. 6172, pp. 243–258. Springer, Heidelberg (2010)
4. Jager, I., Brumley, D.: Efficient directionless weakest preconditions (cmu-cylab-10-002). CyLab, p. 27 (2010)
5. Tan, J., Tay, H.J., Gandhi, R., Narasimhan, P.: AUSPICE: automatic safety property verification for unmodified executables. In: Gurfinkel, A., et al. (eds.) VSTTE 2015. LNCS, vol. 9593, pp. 202–222. Springer, Heidelberg (2016). doi:10.1007/978-3-319-29613-5_12
6. Zhao, L., Li, G., De Sutter, B., Regehr, J.: ARMor: fully verified software fault isolation. In: Proceedings of the Ninth ACM International Conference on Embedded Software, EMSOFT 2011, pp. 289–298, NY. ACM, New York (2011)

Hierarchical Verification of Quantum Circuits

Sidi Mohamed Beillahi$^{(\boxtimes)}$, Mohamed Yousri Mahmoud, and Sofiène Tahar

Department of Electrical and Computer Engineering,
Concordia University, Montreal, Canada
{beillahi,mo_solim,tahar}@ece.concordia.ca

Abstract. In this paper, we introduce the idea of hierarchical verification for quantum circuits, where we use a powerful language, higher-order logic, to reason about quantum circuits formally. We propose a formal modeling and verification approach that captures quantum models built hierarchically from primitive optical quantum gates. The analysis and verification of composed circuits is done seamlessly based on dedicated mathematical foundations formalized in the HOL Light theorem prover. In order to demonstrate the effectiveness of the proposed infrastructure, we present the formal analysis of the controlled-phase gate and Shor's factoring quantum circuits.

1 Introduction

Since it has been proved that classical machines cannot simulate quantum physics in polynomial times [11], scientists were working to develop new computers which employ quantum physics. Throughout their research, quantum technologies showed a good potential to provide solutions to several challenges such as secure communication and faster computation. Quantum optics is considered as one of the promising approaches for realizing "universal" quantum machines [6].

Despite the fact that quantum computers are not yet commercially available, their realisation requires the development of comprehensive tools for the modeling and verification of quantum devices. Due to the inherent complexity of quantum circuits, numerical simulations are incomplete: the computation space increases exponentially with the size of the circuit. Nevertheless, a number of tools have been proposed for simulation of quantum circuits. For instance, in [4] quantum gates are described as matrices and applied to quantum states using matrix-vector multiplication, however, a time-out is reached when simulating 15 qubits (quantum bits) circuits. Hence, we believe that there is a dire need of comprehensive and expressive computer-aided design and verification tools for quantum systems that cover both the mathematics and the principles of quantum physics.

Higher-order-logic (HOL) theorem proving is an effective approach to analyze engineering systems, thanks to its solid mathematics. Therefore, we believe that HOL can assist in the modeling and verification of quantum computers. In this paper, we propose to use the HOL Light theorem prover [5] to handle the hierarchical verification of quantum circuits thanks to its rich support for

© Springer International Publishing Switzerland 2016
S. Rayadurgam and O. Tkachuk (Eds.): NFM 2016, LNCS 9690, pp. 344–352, 2016.
DOI: 10.1007/978-3-319-40648-0_26

multivariate calculus and Hilbert spaces theories [9] which are essential to reason about quantum optics.

Our ultimate goal is to build the necessary tools to formally model and verify quantum circuits composed of primitive quantum gates, that are built using only optical components, in a hierarchical fashion. The first step towards this goal is to formally define in HOL the required mathematics, including the notions of projection, tensor product, and tensor product projection. We then apply these definitions to formally model and verify quantum primitive gates and circuits. We use this approach to formally model and verify the controlled-phase (CZ) gate circuit [6] and the Shor's factorization circuit of number 15 [1]. The source code of our formalization is available for download at [2].

In [8], the authors formalized the controlled-not (CNOT) gate. However, they did not provide the bi-linearity of tensor product and other important properties which are required to model and verify composed quantum circuits. In [12], a quantum process calculus is used to model linear optical quantum systems. It was applied to model the CNOT gate. The main limitation of this work is that the beam splitters parameters are considered as real numbers, however, they often need to be complex numbers as in the case of quantum interferometer [10].

2   Formalization of Tensor Product and Projection

For quantum optics the state of a quantum system is a probability density function which provides the probability of the number of photons inside the optical beam, typically written as $|\psi\rangle$. The set of quantum pure states (i.e., states which form the basis for a quantum states space) are called fock states. An optical beam in a fock state $|n\rangle$, where $n = 0, 1, 2, \ldots$, means that the light stream exactly contains n photons. Given an n-beam quantum state where each $|\psi\rangle_k$, $k \in [1; n]$, describes the quantum state of single mode beam k, then the joint state of the n optical beams is $|\psi\rangle_1 \otimes |\psi\rangle_2 \otimes \ldots \otimes |\psi\rangle_n$ (sometimes we use $|\psi_1, \psi_2, \ldots, \psi_n\rangle$), where $\otimes$ operation is the tensor product.

2.1   Formalization of Tensor Product

Given the quantum state $|\psi\rangle_1 \ldots |\psi\rangle_n$ of n optical beams, the function that describes the joint probability of the n beams is then the point-wise multiplication of all the states, which refers to the optical states tensor product. Hence, we define the tensor product for an n-beam quantum state as follows: $\lambda\ y_1 \ldots y_n.\ (|\psi\rangle_1 \otimes \ldots \otimes |\psi\rangle_n)(y_1 \ldots y_n) = |\psi\rangle_1 y_1 * \ldots * |\psi\rangle_n y_n$. We therefore define the tensor product for n beams in HOL, recursively, as:

Definition 1 (Tensor Product)
$\vdash$ tensor 0 mode $= (\lambda y.\ 1)\ \wedge$
tensor n + 1 mode $= (\lambda y.\ ((\text{tensor n mode})\ y) * (\text{mode}\$(n + 1)\ y\$(n + 1)))$

where the symbol $ denotes the vector indexing operator $(a\$i \Leftrightarrow a(i))$. mode is a vector of size n that contains n modes. The basic case of zero mode $n = 0$ is a trivial case; it is a constant function (i.e., $y \to 1$) and it guarantees a terminating definition. Next, we prove that this tensor satisfies the bi-linearity property:

Theorem 1 (Tensor: Bi-Linearity)

$\vdash$ 0 < k $\leq$ n + 1 $\land$ mode$k = a1 % x1 + a2 % x2 $\Rightarrow$
tensor n + 1 mode = a1 % tensor n + 1 (λi. if i = k then x1 else mode$i)
  + a2 % tensor n + 1 (λi. if i = k then x2 else mode$i)

where the symbol % denotes the scalar multiplication. Note that the number of modes is $n + 1$ as this property does not hold for 0 where tensor is the constant function. The two assumptions $0 < k \leq n + 1$ and mode$k = a1 % x1 + a2 % x2 ensure that the element k is part of the tensor and is a combination of two vectors. The proof is based on using induction where the base case is trivial and in the inductive step we use the lemma k $\leq$ n + 2 $\Leftrightarrow$ (k $\leq$ n + 1 $\lor$ k = n + 2) then using the induction hypothesis for the first and the definition of tensor for the second.

An important property for the manipulation of the tensor product is when we have a tensor constructed out of two elementary tensors. In this case, this property states that a tensor $v_1 \otimes \ldots \otimes v_m \otimes u_1 \otimes \ldots \otimes u_n = (v_1 \otimes \ldots \otimes v_m) \otimes (u_1 \otimes \ldots \otimes u_n)$.

Theorem 2 (Tensor: Multiplication)

$\vdash$ tensor m + n mode =
  (λy. ((tensor m mode) y) $*$ (tensor n (λi. mode$(i + m))) ($\lambda$i. y$(i + m)))

A typical usage of this theorem is to separate elementary tensors for the sake of conducting quantum transformations independently from each other. Then using the same theorem, we can return back to the initial tensor.

2.2 Formalization of Linear Projection

In linear algebra, a projection is a linear transformation p from a vector space to itself that maintains the idempotent property; $p^2 = p$. In the quantum context, for a pure state $|\psi\rangle$, the projection is defined as $p = |\psi\rangle \langle\psi|$ which is a self-adjoint and linear transformation. In particular, for a quantum circuit design, the expected circuit output is the projection of all possible outputs over the appropriate fock states. For example, let us consider the state $|\phi\rangle = \frac{1}{3}|n\rangle + \frac{1}{3}|n-1\rangle + \frac{1}{3}|n+1\rangle$ and the projection $p_n = |n\rangle \langle n|$. The result of the projection of $|\phi\rangle$ is $p_n(|\phi\rangle) = |n\rangle \langle n|(\frac{1}{3}|n\rangle + \frac{1}{3}|n-1\rangle + \frac{1}{3}|n+1\rangle) = \frac{1}{3}|n\rangle$, because the fock states form an orthonormal basis. Therefore, we define the projection on fock states as follows:

Definition 2 (Linear Projection)

$\vdash \forall$ x. (proj $|$n$\rangle_{sm}$) x $= \langle n_{sm}|x\rangle$ % $|$n$\rangle_{sm}$

where proj $|$n$\rangle_{sm}$ is the projection over the fock state and accepts as parameter x. We have proven the three requirements for this projection which are linearity, idempotent and self-adjoint properties. Next we show the first two properties:

Theorem 3 (Projection: Linearity)

$\vdash$ is_sm sm $\Rightarrow \forall$ x y a.
    (proj $|$n$\rangle_{sm}$) (a1 % x + a2 % y) = a1 % (proj $|$n$\rangle_{sm}$) x + a2 % (proj $|$n$\rangle_{sm}$) y

where the assumption is_sm sm is used to maintain the requirement that the optical mode sm is indeed the single mode used.

Theorem 4 (Projection: Idempotent)

$\vdash$ is_sm sm $\Rightarrow \forall$x. (proj $|$n$\rangle_{sm}$) ((proj $|$n$\rangle_{sm}$) x) = (proj $|$n$\rangle_{sm}$) x

2.3 Formalization of Tensor Product Projection

In some realization of quantum optics, the gates are implemented using *ancillas* which are extra qubits that are used for detecting the correct output [7]. During the design process of a quantum circuit, the ancilla is measured after it leaves the circuit. The correct output is known whenever the detector registers the expected ancilla. In our formalization, we implement the process of detecting the expected ancillas in the outputs of a quantum circuit as the tensor product projection of the outputs. We combine the tensor product and linear projection together to obtain the tensor product projection. By doing this, we will eliminate the undesirable outputs and keep only the "correct" output. In addition, we will have the projected state multiplied by a scalar value which is the success probability of the circuit. We define the projection of multi-mode states as follows:

Definition 3 (Tensor Projection)

$\vdash$ is_tensor_proj m_proj $\Leftrightarrow \forall$ mode1 mode2 n.
    is_linear_cop (m_proj (tensor n mode1)) $\wedge$
  m_proj (tensor n mode1) (tensor n mode2) =
            tensor n (λi. ((proj mode1\$i) mode2\$i))

where is_linear_cop op ensures that the operator op is indeed a linear operator. Using this definition, we prove a crucial property in the analysis of quantum circuits, which states that $(p_1 \otimes ... \otimes p_n)(u_1 \otimes ... \otimes u_n) = p_1(u_1) \otimes ... \otimes p_n(u_n)$:

Theorem 5 (Tensor Projection: Multiplication)

$\vdash$ is_tensor_proj m_proj $\wedge 1 \leq$ n $\Rightarrow$
(m_proj tensor m + n mode1) tensor m + n mode2 =
(λy. ((m_proj tensor m mode1) tensor m mode2) y $*$
(m_proj tensor n (λi. mode1\$(i + m)) tensor n (λi. mode2\$(i + m))) (λi. y\$(i + m)))

This property is very useful when projecting a multi-mode state which is applied to parallel quantum gates as the case for the controlled-phase gate. Using the tensor product lemma $v_1 \otimes ... \otimes 0 \otimes ... \otimes v_n = 0$, we prove the following property:

Theorem 6 (Tensor Projection: Fock States)

⊢ is_tensor_proj m_proj ∧ 0 < k ∧ mode1$k = $|m1\rangle_{sm}$ ∧ mode2$k = $|m2\rangle_{sm}$ ∧
m1 ≠ m2 ∧ is_sm sm ∧ k ≤ n + 1 ⇒
(m_proj tensor n + 1 mode1) tensor n + 1 mode2 = 0

This theorem is very important for the measurement of photons as it indicates that for two multi-mode states, where in the first state, the single mode k contains the fock state $|m1\rangle$ and in the second state, the single mode k contains the fock state $|m2\rangle$. If $m1$ and $m2$ are different, then the projection of the first multi-mode state over the other is zero. By this, we have covered the required mathematics for dealing with the verification and analysis of quantum circuits.

3   Hierarchical Verification: Applications

In this section, we will demonstrate the idea of hierarchical verification of quantum circuits based on the formalization of primitive gates, reported in [3], by formally verifying the controlled-phase (CZ) gate and Shor's factoring of number 15 circuits.

3.1   Verification of CZ Gate

A CZ gate is constructed using two non-linear sign (NS) gates [3] and two beam splitters, as shown in Fig. 1. The CZ gate transforms the input $|x, y\rangle$ to the output $e^{i\pi x \cdot y}|x, y\rangle$, $x, y \in \{0, 1\}$. The success probability of measuring the ancilla state $|1, 0\rangle$ in both NS gates is $\frac{1}{16}$ [3]. We define the CZ gate as follows:

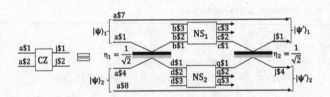

Fig. 1. Controlled-phase gate circuit

Definition 4 (CZ Gate)

⊢ is_cz (a, j, ten) ⇔ (∀ b c d q k l m p.
ns_gate(d, m, p, q, ten) ∧ ns_gate(b, l, k, c, ten) ∧
beam_splitter($\frac{1}{\sqrt{2}}, \frac{1}{\sqrt{2}}, \frac{1}{\sqrt{2}}, -\frac{1}{\sqrt{2}}$, ten, a$1, 1, a$4, 4, b$1, 1, b$4, 4) ∧
beam_splitter($\frac{1}{\sqrt{2}}, \frac{1}{\sqrt{2}}, \frac{1}{\sqrt{2}}, -\frac{1}{\sqrt{2}}$, ten, c$1, 1, c$4, 4, j$1, 1, j$4, 4) ∧
(q$1 = c$4 ∧ q$2 = c$5 ∧ q$3 = c$6) ∧ (b$4 = d$1 ∧ b$5 = d$2 ∧ b$6 = d$3)

Note that we rename the input and output ports for the second NS gate in order to match the order of the modes in the definition of NS, instead of $|b\$4, b\$5, b\$6\rangle$ and $|c\$4, c\$5, c\$6\rangle$ we have $|d\$1, d\$2, d\$3\rangle$ and $|q\$1, q\$2, q\$3\rangle$, respectively. We formally verified the CZ operations and its success probability for the four possible combinations of inputs, among which we provide here one of them.

Theorem 7 (CZ Gate: Input: $|1,1\rangle$)

$\vdash$ `let constraints = is_tensor_proj m_proj $\wedge$ is_tensor ten $\wedge$`
`is_cz (a, j, ten) in`
`let` $|2, 1, 0, 0, 1, 0, 0, 0\rangle_{cq} =$ `tensor` $8\,(\lambda i.$ `if i = 1 then` $|2\rangle_{c\$1}$ `elseif i = 2 then`
$|1\rangle_{c\$2}$ `elseif i = 5 then` $|1\rangle_{q\$2}$ `else` $|0\rangle_{c\$3})$ `in`
`let` $|0, 1, 0, 2, 1, 0, 0, 0\rangle_{cq} =$ `tensor` $8\,(\lambda i.$ `if  i = 2 then` $|1\rangle_{c\$2}$ `elseif i = 4 then`
$|2\rangle_{q\$1}$ `elseif i = 5 then` $|1\rangle_{q\$2}$ `else` $|0\rangle_{c\$3})$ `in`
`let` $|1, 1, 0, 1, 1, 0, 0, 0\rangle_{cq} =$ `tensor` $8\,(\lambda i.$ `if i = 1 then` $|1\rangle_{c\$1}$ `elseif i = 2 then`
$|1\rangle_{c\$2}$ `elseif i = 4 then` $|1\rangle_{q\$1}$ `elseif i = 5 then` $|1\rangle_{q\$2}$ `else` $|0\rangle_{c\$3})$ `in`
`let` $|1, 1, 0, 1, 1, 0, 0, 0\rangle_{ab} =$ `tensor` $8\,(\lambda i.$ `if i = 1 then` $|1\rangle_{a\$1}$ `elseif i = 2 then`
$|1\rangle_{b\$2}$ `elseif i = 4 then` $|1\rangle_{a\$4}$ `elseif i = 5 then` $|1\rangle_{b\$5}$ `else` $|0\rangle_{b\$3})$ `in`
`let` $|1, 1, 0, 1, 1, 0, 0, 0\rangle_{cj} =$ `tensor` $8\,(\lambda i.$ `if i = 1 then` $|1\rangle_{j\$1}$ `elseif i = 2 then`
$|1\rangle_{c\$2}$ `elseif i = 4 then` $|1\rangle_{j\$4}$ `elseif i = 5 then` $|1\rangle_{c\$5}$ `else` $|0\rangle_{c\$3})$ `in`
`constraints` $\Rightarrow$ (`m_proj` $|2, 1, 0, 1, 0, 0, 0, 0\rangle_{cq}$ + `m_proj` $|0, 1, 0, 1, 2, 0, 0, 0\rangle_{cq}$ +
`m_proj` $|1, 1, 0, 1, 1, 0, 0, 0\rangle_{cq})$ $(|1, 1, 0, 1, 1, 0, 0, 0\rangle_{ab}) = -\frac{1}{4}$ % $|1, 1, 0, 1, 1, 0, 0, 0\rangle_{cj}$

Note that the output of the CZ gate has been projected over three different states. This is because that we have two photons at the input ($|1,1\rangle$) which results in three possibilities at the input of the two parallel NS gates: (1) two photons go through the first NS gate; (2) two photons go through the second NS gate; and (3) one photon goes through the first NS gate and the other goes through the second NS gate. The verification of the CZ gate has been done using Theorem 6 in order to subdivide the main tensor product projection to two tensor product projections, where each is fed to an NS gate. This completes the analysis of the CZ for the input "11". The analysis for the inputs "01", "00", and "10" follows the same pattern. The actual physical implementations of the CZ gate have 8 input modes. However, the CZ is a 2-qubits gate, where each logical qubit is represented by two optical modes and the rest of the modes are ancillas. Therefore in order to facilitate the use of this gate in complex quantum circuits, we developed an input/output behavioral description:

Definition 5 (CZ Behavioral Description)

Input : $|1, 1\rangle_L \equiv$ (`m_proj` $|2, 1, 0, 1, 0, 0, 0, 0\rangle_{cq}$ + `m_proj` $|0, 1, 0, 1, 2, 0, 0, 0\rangle_{cq}$ +
`m_proj` $|1, 1, 0, 1, 1, 0, 0, 0\rangle_{cq})$ $|1, 1, 0, 1, 1, 0, 0, 0\rangle_{ab}$
Output : $|1, 1, 0, 1, 1, 0, 0, 0\rangle_{cj} \equiv |1, 1\rangle_L$

3.2   Verification of Shor's Factorization

Shor's integer factorization is a quantum algorithm to compute the two primes factor of a given integer much faster than classical algorithms. Our objective here is to show the formal modeling and verification of a compiled version of Shor's factoring of number 15 [1] using the previously presented formalization. The task of the underlying circuit is to find the minimum integer r that satisfies $a^r \ mode \ N = 1$, where $N = 15$ and a is a randomly chosen co-prime integer to N, in our case $a = 2$. r is called the order of a modulo N, from which we compute the desired prime factors; $(a^{\frac{r}{2}} - 1)$ and $(a^{\frac{r}{2}} + 1)$. The circuit is composed of six Hadamard [3] and two CZ gates, as shown in Fig. 2, and has 4 inputs/outputs. Inputs are initialized to the state; $|\psi\rangle_{in} = |0,0,1,0\rangle_{x1f1f2x2}$. From the computed output, $|\psi\rangle_{out} = |.,.,.,.\rangle_{\dot{x}1\dot{f}1\dot{f}2\dot{x}2}$, we extract the variable $z = |.,.,0\rangle_{\dot{x}1\dot{x}2}$, then we obtain $r = a^z \ mod \ 15$. Accordingly, we formally define the structure of the circuit and verify its operation as follows:

Definition 6 (Shor Circuit)
$\vdash$ shor $(x1, x2, f1, f2, \ddot{f}1, \ddot{f}2, j1, j2, ten) \Leftrightarrow (\forall \ b \ d. \ j2\$2 = \ddot{x}2 \ \land$
is_hadamard$(x1, b\$2, ten) \land$ is_hadamard$(f1, b\$1, ten) \land$ is_cz$(d, j2, ten) \land$
is_hadamard$(x2, d\$2, ten) \land$ is_hadamard$(f2, d\$2, ten) \land$ is_cz$(b, j1, ten) \land$
$j1\$2 = \ddot{x}1 \land$ is_hadamard$(j1\$1, \ddot{f}1, ten) \land$ is_hadamard$(j2\$1, \ddot{f}2, ten))$

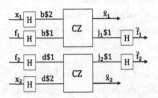

Fig. 2. Shor's factoring of 15 circuit

Theorem 8 (Shor' Factoring of 15)
$\vdash$ let constraints = is_tensor_proj m_proj $\land$ is_tensor ten $\land$
shor $(x1, x2, f1, f2, \ddot{f}1, \ddot{f}2, j1, j2, ten)$ in
let $|0,0,1,0\rangle_{f1x1f2x2} = $ tensor4 $(\lambda i. \ \text{if } i = 1 \text{ then } |0\rangle_{f1} \text{ elseif } i = 2 \text{ then } |0\rangle_{x1}$
elseif $i = 3$ then $|1\rangle_{f2}$ else $|0\rangle_{x2})$ in
let $|0,0,0,1\rangle_{\ddot{f}1\ddot{x}1\ddot{f}2\ddot{x}2} = $ tensor4 $(\lambda i. \ \text{if } i = 1 \text{ then } |0\rangle_{\ddot{f}1} \text{ elseif } i = 2 \text{ then } |0\rangle_{\ddot{x}1}$
elseif $i = 3$ then $|0\rangle_{\ddot{f}2}$ else $|1\rangle_{\ddot{x}2})$ in
let $|0,0,1,0\rangle_{\ddot{f}1\ddot{x}1\ddot{f}2\ddot{x}2} = $ tensor4 $(\lambda i. \ \text{if } i = 1 \text{ then } |0\rangle_{\ddot{f}1} \text{ elseif } i = 2 \text{ then } |0\rangle_{\ddot{x}1}$
elseif $i = 3$ then $|1\rangle_{\ddot{f}2}$ else $|0\rangle_{\ddot{x}2})$ in
let $|1,1,0,1\rangle_{\ddot{f}1\ddot{x}1\ddot{f}2\ddot{x}2} = $ tensor4 $(\lambda i. \ \text{if } i = 1 \text{ then } |1\rangle_{\ddot{f}1} \text{ elseif } i = 2 \text{ then } |1\rangle_{\ddot{x}1}$
elseif $i = 3$ then$|0\rangle_{\ddot{f}2}$ else $|1\rangle_{\ddot{x}2})$ in
let $|1,1,1,0\rangle_{\ddot{f}1\ddot{x}1\ddot{f}2\ddot{x}2} = $ tensor4 $(\lambda i. \ \text{if } i = 1 \text{ then } |1\rangle_{\ddot{f}1} \text{ elseif } i = 2 \text{ then } |1\rangle_{\ddot{x}1}$
elseif $i = 3$ then $|1\rangle_{\ddot{f}2}$ else $|0\rangle_{\ddot{x}2})$ in
constraints $\Rightarrow |0,0,1,0\rangle_{f1x1f2x2} \doteq \frac{1}{32} \ \% \ (|1,1,1,0\rangle_{\ddot{f}1\ddot{x}1\ddot{f}2\ddot{x}2} + |1,1,0,1\rangle_{\ddot{f}1\ddot{x}1\ddot{f}2\ddot{x}2}$
$+ \ |0,0,1,0\rangle_{\ddot{f}1\ddot{x}1\ddot{f}2\ddot{x}2} + |0,0,0,1\rangle_{\ddot{f}1\ddot{x}1\ddot{f}2\ddot{x}2})$

Here the circuit outputs two categories of solutions; (1) $|000\rangle$ or $|100\rangle$ which are expected failures of the algorithm [1]; (2) $|010\rangle$ or $|110\rangle \equiv z = 2$ or $z = 6$ which give $r = 4$ from which we obtain the 5 and 3 prime numbers. The verification of the compiled Shor's circuit has been done using Theorem 3 to subdivide the tensor to four tensors, and apply Hadamard transformation on each elementary tensor.

4   Conclusion and Discussion

In this paper, we reported a novel application of formal methods to enable the hierarchical modeling and verification of quantum circuits. We presented the higher-order logic formalization of mathematical foundations such as tensor product, linear projection, and tensor product projection. Then we showed how they can be applied for the hierarchical modeling and analysis of composed quantum circuits using the CZ gate and Shor's 15 factoring circuits.

One of the important outcomes of this work is the efficiency that the tensor projection brought to our formalization: if we tackled the NS gate without the projection (such as in [8,12]), we will have 10 possible outputs (with only one correct output) which dramatically affects the CZ analysis that contains two parallel NS gates which in turn produce $10*10 = 100$ possible outputs. Moreover, it gets worse when it comes to the Shor's circuit where we have two CZ gates and at the level of inputs of each gate we have four possible inputs, which means at the output of these gates we have $(4*100)*(4*100) = 16.10^4$ possible outputs. Thanks to the projection properties, such as projection linearity and projection of two orthogonal tensor products, we were able to reduce the possible outputs to consider only the correct ones. This is very important for scalability reasons, especially for larger circuits which contain many quantum gates. We believe this to be a significant feature of our formalization compared to before mentioned related works, e.g., [8,12]. The reported mathematical foundation can be used to reduce the complexity in the implementation of design verification tools for quantum optics circuits analysis.

In future work, we plan to apply the formalization developed in this paper to perform a formal synthesis of quantum circuits and to apply our methods on other quantum systems, such as Grover's algorithm.

References

1. Politi, A., Matthews, J.C.F., O'Brien, J.L.: Shor's quantum factoring algorithm on a photonic chip. Science **325**(5945), 1221 (2009)
2. Beillahi, S.M., Mahmoud, M.Y.: Hierarchical Verification of Quantum Circuits (2016). http://hvg.ece.concordia.ca/projects/optics/hvqc.html
3. Beillahi, S.M., Mahmoud, M.Y., Tahar, S.: Optical Quantum Gates Formalization in HOL Light. Technical report, ECE Department, Concordia University, Montreal, QC, Canada, February 2016
4. Viamontes, G.F., Rajagopalan, M., Markov, I.L., Hayes, J.P.: Gate level simulation of quantum circuits. In: ASP-DAC, pp. 295–301 (2003)
5. Harrison, J.: HOL light: a tutorial introduction. In: Srivas, M., Camilleri, A. (eds.) FMCAD 1996. LNCS, vol. 1166, pp. 265–269. Springer, Heidelberg (1996)

6. Knill, E., Laflamme, R., Milburn, G.J.: A scheme for efficient quantum computation with linear optics. Nature **409**, 46–52 (2001)
7. Kok, P., Munro, W.J., Nemoto, K., Ralph, T.C., Dowling, J.P., Milburn, G.J.: Linear optical quantum computing with photonic qubits. Rev. Mod. Phys. **79**, 135–174 (2007)
8. Mahmoud, M.Y., Panangaden, P., Tahar, S.: On the formal verification of optical quantum gates in HOL. In: Núñez, M., Güdemann, M. (eds.) FMICS 2015. LNCS, vol. 9128, pp. 198–211. Springer, Heidelberg (2015)
9. Mahmoud, M.Y., Aravantinos, V., Tahar, S.: Formalization of infinite dimension linear spaces with application to quantum theory. In: Brat, G., Rungta, N., Venet, A. (eds.) NFM 2013. LNCS, vol. 7871, pp. 413–427. Springer, Heidelberg (2013)
10. Mandel, L., Wolf, E.: Optical Coherence and Quantum Optics. Cambridge University Press, Cambridge, UK (1995)
11. Feynman, R.P.: Simulating physics with computers. Int. J. Theor. Phys. **21**(6–7), 467–488 (1982)
12. Franke-Arnold, S., Gay, S.J., Puthoor, I.V.: Quantum process calculus for linear optical quantum computing. In: Dueck, G.W., Miller, D.M. (eds.) RC 2013. LNCS, vol. 7948, pp. 234–246. Springer, Heidelberg (2013)

Correctness and Certification

Semantics for Locking Specifications

Michael D. Ernst[1], Damiano Macedonio[2], Massimo Merro[2(✉)],
and Fausto Spoto[2]

[1] Computer Science and Engineering, University of Washington, Seattle, WA, USA
[2] Dipartimento di Informatica, Università degli Studi di Verona, Verona, Italy
massimo.merro@univr.it

Abstract. Lock-based synchronization disciplines, like Java's
@GuardedBy, are widely used to prevent concurrency errors. However,
their semantics is often expressed informally and is consequently ambiguous. This article highlights such ambiguities and overcomes them by
formalizing two possible semantics of @GuardedBy, using a reference
operational semantics for a core calculus of a concurrent Java-like language. It also identifies when such annotations are actual guarantees
against data races. Our work aids in understanding the annotations and
supports the development of sound tools that verify or infer them.

1 Introduction

Data races are common errors in concurrent programs which occur when a shared
data structure is manipulated by different threads, without synchronization, with
consequent unpredictable or erroneous software behavior. Such errors are difficult
to understand, diagnose, and reproduce. They are also difficult to prevent: testing
tends to be incomplete due to nondeterministic scheduling choices, and model-
checking scales poorly to real-world code.

The simplest approach to prevent data races is to follow a *lock-based synchronization discipline*: always hold a given lock when accessing a shared data
structure. Since a lock can be held by at most one thread at any time, this
discipline ensures data-race freedom. However, it is easy to violate a locking discipline, so tools that verify adherence to the discipline are desirable. These tools
require a *specification language* to express the intended locking discipline.

The focus of this paper is on the formal definition of such a specification
language, its semantics, and the guarantees that it gives against data races.

In Java, the most popular specification language for expressing a locking discipline is the @GuardedBy [15]. Informally, if the programmer annotates a field f
as @GuardedBy(E) then a thread may access f only while holding the monitor
corresponding to the *guard expression* E. The @GuardedBy annotation was proposed by Goetz [11] as a documentation convention only, without tool support.
It has been adopted by practitioners; GitHub contains about 35,000 uses of the
annotation in 7,000 files of distinct projects. Tool support now exists in Java

Partially funded by Joint Project 2011 "Statical Analysis for Multithreading".

© Springer International Publishing Switzerland 2016
S. Rayadurgam and O. Tkachuk (Eds.): NFM 2016, LNCS 9690, pp. 355–372, 2016.
DOI: 10.1007/978-3-319-40648-0_27

PathFinder [18], the Checker Framework [8], Houdini/rcc [1], IntelliJ [22], and Julia [16].

All of these tools, except for [1], rely on the previous informal definition of @GuardedBy(E) [15]. However, such an informal description is prone to many ambiguities. Suppose a field f is annotated as @GuardedBy(E), for some guard expression E. (1) The definition above does not clarify how an occurrence of the self-reference variable this in E should be interpreted in client code; this actually depends on the context in which f is accessed. (2) It does not define what an *access* is. (3) It does not say whether a synchronization block must use the guard expression E as written in the annotation or whether a different expression that evaluates to the same value is permitted. (4) It does not indicate whether the lock that must be taken is the value of E at the time of synchronization or that at the time of field access: side effects on E might make a difference here. (5) It does not clarify whether the lock on the guard E must be taken when accessing the field *named* f or the *value* bound to f. The latter ambiguity is particularly important. The interpretation of @GuardedBy based on names is adopted in most tools appearing in the literature [1,16,18,22], whereas the interpretation based on values seems to be less common [8,16]. As a consequence, it is interesting to understand whether and how these two possible interpretations actually protect against data races on the annotated field.

The main contribution of this article is the formalization of two different semantics for annotations of the form @GuardedBy(E) *Type* f: a *name-protection* semantics, in which accesses to the annotated *field* f need to be synchronized on the guard expression E, and a *value-protection* semantics, in which accesses to a *value* referenced by f need to be synchronized on E. The semantics clarify all the above ambiguities, so that programmers and tools know what those annotations mean and which guarantees they entail. We then show that both the name-protection and the value-protection semantics can protect against data races under proper restrictions on the variables occurring in the guard expression. The name-protection semantics requires further constraints — the protected field must not be aliased and the guard expression E must be final, i.e. immutable.

Finally, we have used our formalization to extend the Julia static analyzer [16] to check and infer @GuardedBy annotations in arbitrary Java code. Our companion paper [10] presents the implementation in Julia together with experiments that show how the tool scales to large real software. Julia allows the user to select either name-protection or value-protection. For instance, in the code of Google Guava [12] (release 18), the programmer put 64 annotations on fields; 17 satisfy the semantics of name protection; 9 satisfy the semantics of value protection; the others do not satisfy any. Julia automatically infers all annotations for name-protection and 5 of those that satisfy the value-protection semantics.

In this extended abstract proofs are omitted; full details can be found in [9].

Outline. Section 2 discusses the informal semantics of @GuardedBy by way of examples. Section 3 introduces a calculus for a concurrent fragment of Java. Section 4 gives formal definitions for both the name-protection and value-protection semantics in our calculus. Section 5 shows which guarantees they provide against data races. Section 6 describes the implementation in Julia. Section 7 discusses related work and concludes.

2   Informal Semantics of @GuardedBy

This section illustrates the use of @GuardedBy by example. Figure 1 defines an observable object that allows clients to concurrently register listeners. Registration must be synchronized to avoid data races: simultaneous modifications of the ArrayList might result in a corrupted list or lost registrations. Synchronization is needed in the getListeners() method as well, or otherwise the Java memory model does not guarantee the inter-thread visibility of the registrations.

The interpretation of the @GuardedBy(this) annotation on field listeners requires resolving the ambiguities explained in Sect. 1. The intended locking discipline is that every use of listeners should be enclosed within a construct synchronized (*container*) {...}, where *container* denotes the object whose field listeners is accessed (ambiguities (1) and (2)). For instance, the access original.listeners in the copy constructor is enclosed within synchronized (original) {...}. This contextualization of the guard of synchronized blocks is not clarified in any informal definitions of @GuardedBy (ambiguity (3)). Furthermore, it is not clear if a definite alias of original can be used as synchronization guard at line 5. It is not clear if original would be allowed to be reassigned between lines 5 and 6 (ambiguity (4)). Note that the copy constructor does not synchronize on this even though it accesses this.listeners. This is safe so long as the constructor does not leak this. This paper assumes that an escape analysis [5] has established that constructors do not leak this. The @GuardedBy(this) annotation on field listeners suffers also from ambiguity (5): it is not obvious whether it intends to protect the *name* listeners (*i.e.*, the name can be only used when the lock is held) or the value currently bound to listeners (*i.e.*, that value can be only accessed when the lock is held). Another way of stating this is that @GuardedBy can be interpreted as a *declaration annotation* (a restriction on uses of a name) or as a *type annotation* (a restriction on values associated to that name).

The code in Fig. 1 seems to satisfy the name-protection locking discipline expressed by the annotation @GuardedBy(this) for field listeners: every use of listeners occurs in a program point where the current thread locks its container, and we conclude that @GuardedBy(this) name-protects listeners. Nevertheless, a data race is possible, since two threads could call getListeners() and later access the returned value concurrently. This cannot be avoided when critical sections *leak* guarded data. More generally, name protection does not prevent data races if there are aliases of the guarded name (such as a returned value in our example) that can be used in an unprotected manner. The value-protection semantics of @GuardedBy is not affected by aliasing as it tracks accesses to the value referenced by the name, not the name itself.

Any formal definition of @GuardedBy must result in mutual exclusion in order to ban data races. If f is @GuardedBy(E), then at any program point where a

```
1   public class Observable {
2     private @GuardedBy(this) List<Listener> listeners = new ArrayList<>();
3     public Observable() {}
4     public Observable(Observable original) { // copy constructor
5       synchronized (original) {
6         listeners.addAll(original.listeners);
7     } }
8     public void register(Listener listener) {
9       synchronized (this) {
10        listeners.add(listener);
11    } }
12    public List<Listener> getListeners() {
13      synchronized (this) {
14        return listeners;
15  } } }
```

Fig. 1. This code has a potential data race due to aliasing of the `listeners` field.

thread accesses f (or its value) that thread must hold the lock on E. Let $\mathcal{P}$ be the set of such program points where f is accessed. Mutual exclusion requires two conditions: (i) E can be evaluated at all program points $P \in \mathcal{P}$, and (ii) these evaluations, at a given instant of time, always yield the same value at all $P \in \mathcal{P}$.

Point (i) is syntactic and related to the fact that E cannot refer to variables or fields that are not always in scope or visible at all program points in $\mathcal{P}$. This problem exists for both name protection and value protection, but is more significant for the latter, that is meant to protect values that flow in the program through arbitrary aliasing. For instance, the annotation `@GuardedBy(listeners)` cannot be used for value protection in Fig. 1, since the name `listeners` is not visible outside class `Observable`, but its value flows outside that class through method `getListeners()` and must be protected also if it accessed there. For this, we support a special variable `itself` that refers to the current value of f. For instance, for value protection, the code in Fig. 1 should be rewritten as in Fig. 2.

```
1   public class Observable {
2     private @GuardedBy(itself) List<Listener> listeners = new ArrayList<>();
3     public Observable() {}
4     public Observable(Observable original) { // copy constructor
5       synchronized (original.listeners) {
6         listeners.addAll(original.listeners);
7     } }
8     public void register(Listener listener) {
9       synchronized (listeners) {
10        listeners.add(listener);
11    } }
12    public List<Listener> getListeners() {
13      synchronized (listeners) {
14        return listeners;
15  } } }
```

Fig. 2. Value protection prevents data races; see `itself` in the guard expression.

Point (ii) is semantical and related to the intent of providing a guarantee of mutual exclusion. This point bans the use of a variable in E that, although in scope and visible at every program point in $\mathcal{P}$, might have different values at distinct program points. We need this requirement for both semantics, but it translates into two distinct constraints on the guard E for each semantics. As we will see in Sect. 5, a simple restriction that allows us to satisfy (ii) is to allow only variables `itself`, pointing to the value of the guarded field itself, and variable `this`, pointing to the container of the guarded field, when that container can be identified unambiguously. These two variables have the same value at every program point and this is why we only allow them in E. Moreover, in the semantics for name protection we will require that E only refers to final fields, since the instant of time when the field name is locked and that when the field value gets dereferenced might be arbitrarily away. This latter restriction is not needed for the semantics for value protection, since it requires that a thread holds the lock on the value of a field exactly when that value is accessed.

Thus, in Fig. 2 value protection bans data races on `listeners` since the guard `itself` can be evaluated everywhere (point (i)) and always yields the value of `listeners` itself (point (ii)). Here, the `@GuardedBy(itself)` annotation requires all accesses to the value of `listeners` to occur only when the current thread locks the same monitor — even outside class `Observable`, in a client that operates on the value returned by `getListeners()`. In Fig. 3, instead, field `listeners` is `@GuardedBy(guard)` according to both name protection and value protection, but the value of `guard` is distinct at different program points: no mutual exclusion guarantee exists and data races on `listeners` occur.

```
1   public class Observable {
2     private @GuardedBy(guard) List<Listener> listeners = new ArrayList<>();
3     private Object guard1 = new Object();
4     private Object guard2 = new Object();
5     public Observable() {}
6     public Observable(Observable original) { // copy constructor
7       Object guard = guard1;
8       synchronized (guard) {
9         listeners.addAll(original.listeners);
10    } }
11    public void register(Listener listener) {
12      Object guard = guard2;
13      synchronized (guard) {
14        listeners.add(listener);
15  } } }
```

Fig. 3. Mutable guard expressions may lead to data races.

3   A Core Calculus for Multithreaded Java

Our calculus is a variant of RACEFREEJAVA [1]. We begin with some preliminary notions. A *partial function* f from A to B is denoted by $f : A \rightharpoonup B$, and its *domain* is dom(f). The symbol ϕ denotes the empty function; $\{v_1 \mapsto t_1, \ldots, v_n \mapsto t_n\}$ denotes a function f such that $f(v_i) = t_i$ for $i \in 1..n$;

$f[v_1 \mapsto t_1, \ldots, v_n \mapsto t_n]$ denotes the update of f, where $\text{dom}(f)$ is enlarged for every i such that $v_i \notin \text{dom}(f)$. A *poset* is a structure $\langle A, \leq \rangle$ where A is a set and $\leq$ is a partial order. For $a \in A$, we define $\uparrow a \stackrel{def}{=} \{a' : a \leq a'\}$. A *chain* is a totally ordered poset.

3.1 Syntax

Letters $f, g, x, y, \ldots$ range over a set of variables Var that includes $\texttt{this}$. Variables identify either local variables in methods or instance variables (*fields*) of objects. Symbols $m, p, \ldots$ range over a set $MethodName$ of method names. There is a set Loc of memory locations, ranged over by l. Symbols $\kappa, \kappa_0, \kappa_1, \ldots$ range over a set of *classes* (or *types*) $Class$, ordered by a *subclass relation* $\leq$; $\langle Class, \leq \rangle$ is a poset such that for all $\kappa \in Class$ the set $\uparrow \kappa$ is a finite chain. If $m \in MethodName$, then $\kappa.m$ denotes the implementation of m inside class κ, if any. The partial function $lookup(\,) : Class \times MethodName \rightharpoonup Class$ formalizes *Java's dynamic method lookup*, *i.e.* the runtime process of determining the class containing the implementation of a method on the basis of the class of the receiver object: $lookup(\kappa, m) \stackrel{def}{=} min(\uparrow \kappa.m)$ if $\uparrow \kappa.m \neq \emptyset$ and is undefined otherwise, where $\uparrow \kappa.m \stackrel{def}{=} \{\kappa' \in \uparrow \kappa \mid m \text{ is implemented in } \kappa'\}$ is a finite chain since $\uparrow \kappa.m \subseteq \uparrow \kappa$.

Let us provide the syntax of our core language.

$$
\begin{aligned}
E ::= \; & x \;\mid\; l \;\mid\; E.f \;\mid\; \kappa \langle f_1 = E_1, \ldots, f_n = E_n \rangle \\
C ::= \; & \texttt{let } x = E \texttt{ in } C \;\mid\; E.f := E \;\mid\; C; C \;\mid\; \texttt{skip} \;\mid\; E.m(\,) \;\mid\; \\
& \texttt{spawn } E.m(\,) \;\mid\; \texttt{sync}(E)\{C\} \;\mid\; \texttt{monitor\_enter}(l) \;\mid\; \texttt{monitor\_exit}(l)
\end{aligned}
$$

Expressions Exp, ranged over by E, are given by variables, locations, field accesses, and object allocation, $\kappa \langle f_1 = E_1, \ldots, f_n = E_n \rangle$, to create an object of class κ and initialize each field f_i to the value of E_i. For simplicity, we only have classes and no primitive types, so the only possible *values* are locations.

Commands Com are ranged over by C. *Method bodies*, ranged over by B, are $\texttt{skip}$-terminated commands. Formally, $B :: = \texttt{skip} \mid C; \texttt{skip}$. The set of classes is $Class \stackrel{def}{=} \{\kappa : MethodNames \rightharpoonup B \mid \text{dom}(\kappa) \text{ is finite}\}$. The binding of fields to their defining class is not relevant in our formalization. Given a class κ and a method name m, if $\kappa(m) = B$ then κ implements m with body B. With "$\texttt{this}$" we denote the standard self-reference variable. In our syntax, self-reference binding is implicit; methods have no formal parameters and/or return value.

Terms containing locations (such as $l.f$ or $\texttt{monitor\_enter}(l)$) cannot be used by the programmer: they are introduced by the semantics.

We write $U\{E_1/x_1, \ldots, E_n/x_n\}$ to denote the capture-free substitution of expressions E_i, for all free occurrences of x_i, within $U \in Com \cup Exp$, for all $i \in 1..n$.

A *program* is a finite set of classes including a special class *Main* that only defines a method *main* where the program starts: $Main \stackrel{def}{=} \{main \mapsto B_{main}\}$.

```
1   public class K {
2     private C x = new C();
3     private C y = new C();
4     private C z = new C();
5     private Object h = new Object();
6     public void m() {
7       this.z = this.x;
8       synchronized (this.z) {
9         this.h = this.z.f;
10        this.z = this.y;
11      }
12      this.z.f = new Object();
13  } }
14  class C {
15    Object f = new Object();
16  }
```

	name protection	value protection
field x	−	@GuardedBy(itself)
field y	@GuardedBy(this.x)	−
field z	−	−

Fig. 4. Running example.

Example 1. Figure 4 gives our *running example* in Java. In our core language, the body of method m is translated as follows: $B_\mathtt{m} = \mathtt{this.z} := \mathtt{this.x}; \mathtt{sync}(\mathtt{z})$ $\{\mathtt{this.h} := \mathtt{this.z.f}; \mathtt{this.z} := \mathtt{this.y}\}; \mathtt{this.z.f} := \mathtt{Object}\langle\rangle; \mathtt{skip}$, with classes $\mathtt{K} \stackrel{def}{=} \{\mathtt{m} \mapsto B_\mathtt{m}\}$, $\mathtt{C} \stackrel{def}{=} \phi$, and $\mathtt{Object} \stackrel{def}{=} \phi$.

3.2 Semantic Domains

Threads, ranged over by T, are constituted by a sequence of commands C and a set $\mathcal{L} \subseteq Loc$ of locations that it currently locks, formally $T ::= \lceil C \rceil \mathcal{L}$. We use letters P and Q to denote a *pool of threads*. Formally, $P, Q ::= T^*$.

A *running program* consists of a pool of threads that share a memory. Initially, a single thread runs the *main* method. The $\mathtt{spawn}\ E.m(\ )$ command adds a new thread to the existing ones. A *memory* μ maps a finite set of already allocated memory locations into *objects*.

An object o is a triple containing the object's class, the object's state binding its fields to their corresponding values, and a lock, *i.e.*, an integer counter incremented whenever a thread locks the object (locks are re-entrant).

Definition 1. *Let us define: Object* $\stackrel{def}{=}$ *Class* $\times$ *State* $\times \mathbb{N}$ *and Memory* $\stackrel{def}{=} \{\mu : Loc \rightharpoonup Object \mid \text{dom}(\mu) \text{ is finite}\}$, *with selectors class*$(o) \stackrel{def}{=} \kappa$, *state* $(o) \stackrel{def}{=} \sigma$ *and lock*$^\#(o) \stackrel{def}{=} n$, *for every* $o = \langle\kappa, \sigma, n\rangle \in Object$. *We also define* $o[f \mapsto l] \stackrel{def}{=} \langle\kappa, \sigma[f \mapsto l], n\rangle$ *and lock*$^+(o) \stackrel{def}{=} \langle\kappa, \sigma, n+1\rangle$ *and lock*$^-(o) \stackrel{def}{=} \langle\kappa, \sigma, \max(0, n-1)\rangle$.

The *evaluation of an expression* E in a memory μ, written $[\![E]\!]^\mu$, yields a pair $\langle l, \mu'\rangle$, where l is the runtime value of E, and μ' is the memory resulting from the evaluation of E. Given a pair $\langle l, \mu\rangle$ we define $loc(\langle l, \mu\rangle) = l$ and $mem(\langle l, \mu\rangle) = \mu$.

Definition 2 (Evaluation of Expressions). *The evaluation function has the type* $[\![\ ]\!] : (Exp \times Memory) \rightharpoonup (Loc \times Memory)$ *and is defined as:*

$$[\![l]\!]^\mu \stackrel{\text{def}}{=} \langle l, \mu \rangle \quad [\![E.f]\!]^\mu \stackrel{\text{def}}{=} \langle state(\mu'(l))(f), \mu' \rangle, \; where \; [\![E]\!]^\mu = \langle l, \mu' \rangle$$

$$[\![\kappa \langle f_1 = E_1, .., f_n = E_n \rangle]\!]^\mu \stackrel{\text{def}}{=} \langle l, \mu_n[l \mapsto \langle \kappa, \sigma, 0 \rangle] \rangle, \; where$$

(1) $\mu_0 = \mu$ and $\langle l_i, \mu_i \rangle = [\![E_i]\!]^{\mu_{i-1}}$, for $i \in [1..n]$
(2) l is fresh in μ_n, that is $l \notin \text{dom}(\mu_n)$
(3) $\sigma \in State$ is such that $\sigma(f_i) = l_i$ for $i \in [1..n]$, while $y \notin \text{dom}(\sigma)$ elsewhere.

We assume that $[\![\,]\!]$ is undefined if any of the function applications is undefined.

In the evaluation of the object creation expression, a fresh location l is allocated and bound to an unlocked object whose environment σ binds its fields to the values of the corresponding initialization expressions.

3.3 Structural Operational Semantics

We define a *reduction semantics* on *configurations* of the form $\langle P, \mu \rangle$. We write $\langle P, \mu \rangle \to \langle P', \mu' \rangle$ for representing an execution step. We write $\to^*$ to denote the reflexive/transitive closure of $\to$, and $\to^i$ for i consecutive reduction steps.

Table 1. Structural operational semantics for sequential commands.

$$\frac{[\![E]\!]^\mu = \langle l, \mu' \rangle}{\langle \lceil \texttt{let } x = E \texttt{ in } C \rceil \mathcal{L}, \mu \rangle \to \langle \lceil C\{{}^l/_x\} \rceil \mathcal{L}, \mu' \rangle} \; \text{[let]}$$

$$\frac{[\![E]\!]^\mu = \langle l, \mu' \rangle \quad [\![E']\!]^{\mu'} = \langle l', \mu'' \rangle \quad o = \mu(l) \quad o' \stackrel{\text{def}}{=} o[f \mapsto l'] \quad \mu''' \stackrel{\text{def}}{=} \mu''[l \mapsto o']}{\langle \lceil E.f := E' \rceil \mathcal{L}, \mu \rangle \to \langle \lceil \texttt{skip} \rceil \mathcal{L}, \mu''' \rangle} \; \text{[field-ass]}$$

$$\frac{\langle \lceil C_1 \rceil \mathcal{L}, \mu \rangle \to \langle \lceil C_1' \rceil \mathcal{L}', \mu' \rangle \quad C_1 \neq \texttt{spawn } E.p()}{\langle \lceil C_1; C_2 \rceil \mathcal{L}, \mu \rangle \to \langle \lceil C_1'; C_2 \rceil \mathcal{L}', \mu' \rangle} \; \text{[seq]}$$

$$\frac{-}{\langle \lceil \texttt{skip}; C \rceil \mathcal{L}, \mu \rangle \to \langle \lceil C \rceil \mathcal{L}, \mu \rangle} \; \text{[seq-skip]}$$

$$\frac{[\![E]\!]^\mu = \langle l, \mu' \rangle \quad \kappa' = lookup(class(\mu'(l)), m) \quad \kappa'(m) = B}{\langle \lceil E.m(\,) \rceil \mathcal{L}, \mu \rangle \to \langle \lceil B\{{}^l/_{\texttt{this}}\} \rceil \mathcal{L}, \mu' \rangle} \; \text{[invoc]}$$

Table 1 deals with sequential commands. Rule [seq] assumes that the first command is not of the form spawn $E.p(\,)$; this case is treated separately. In rule [invoc] the receiver E is evaluated and the method implementation is looked up from the dynamic class of the receiver. The body of the method is then executed after binding this to the receiver.

Table 2 focuses on concurrency and synchronization. The spawn of a new method is similar to a method call, but the method body runs in its own new

Table 2. Structural operational semantics for concurrency and synchronization.

$$\frac{[\![E]\!]^\mu = \langle l, \mu' \rangle \quad \kappa' = lookup(class(\mu'(l)), p) \quad \kappa'(p) = B}{\langle \lceil \texttt{spawn } E.p(\ ); C \rceil \mathcal{L}, \mu \rangle \ \rightarrow\ \langle \lceil B\{^l/_{\texttt{this}}\} \rceil \emptyset.\lceil C \rceil \mathcal{L}, \mu' \rangle} \quad \text{[spawn]}$$

$$\frac{[\![E]\!]^\mu = \langle l, \mu' \rangle}{\langle \lceil \texttt{sync}(E)\{C\} \rceil \mathcal{L}, \mu \rangle \ \rightarrow\ \langle \lceil \texttt{monitor\_enter}(l); C; \texttt{monitor\_exit}(l) \rceil \mathcal{L}, \mu' \rangle} \quad \text{[sync]}$$

$$\frac{lock^\#(\mu(l)) = 0 \quad \mathcal{L}' \stackrel{def}{=} \mathcal{L} \cup \{l\} \quad \mu' \stackrel{def}{=} \mu[l \mapsto lock^+(\mu(l))]}{\langle \lceil \texttt{monitor\_enter}(l) \rceil \mathcal{L}, \mu \rangle \ \rightarrow\ \langle \lceil \texttt{skip} \rceil \mathcal{L}', \mu' \rangle} \quad \text{[acquire-lock]}$$

$$\frac{l \in \mathcal{L} \quad \mu' \stackrel{def}{=} \mu[l \mapsto lock^+(\mu(l))]}{\langle \lceil \texttt{monitor\_enter}(l) \rceil \mathcal{L}, \mu \rangle \ \rightarrow\ \langle \lceil \texttt{skip} \rceil \mathcal{L}, \mu' \rangle} \quad \text{[reentrant-lock]}$$

$$\frac{lock^\#(\mu(l)) > 1 \quad \mu' \stackrel{def}{=} \mu[l \mapsto lock^-(\mu(l))]}{\langle \lceil \texttt{monitor\_exit}(l) \rceil \mathcal{L}, \mu \rangle \ \rightarrow\ \langle \lceil \texttt{skip} \rceil \mathcal{L}, \mu' \rangle} \quad \text{[decrease-lock]}$$

$$\frac{lock^\#(\mu(l)) = 1 \quad \mathcal{L}' \stackrel{def}{=} \mathcal{L} \setminus \{l\} \quad \mu' \stackrel{def}{=} \mu[l \mapsto lock^-(\mu(l))]}{\langle \lceil \texttt{monitor\_exit}(l) \rceil \mathcal{L}, \mu \rangle \ \rightarrow\ \langle \lceil \texttt{skip} \rceil \mathcal{L}', \mu' \rangle} \quad \text{[release-lock]}$$

$$\frac{\langle T, \mu \rangle \ \rightarrow\ \langle P, \mu' \rangle}{\langle P_1.T.P_2, \mu \rangle \ \rightarrow\ \langle P_1.P.P_2, \mu' \rangle} \quad \text{[thread-pool]}$$

thread with an initially empty set of locked locations. Note that if a sequence of commands starts with a $\texttt{spawn}$ then rule [spawn] is the only rule which can be used. In rule [sync] the location l associated to the guard E is computed; the computation can proceed only if a lock action is possible on l. The lock will be released only at the end of the critical section C. Rule [acquire-lock] models the entering of the monitor of an unlocked object. Rule [reentrant-lock] models Java's *lock reentrancy*. Rule [decrease-lock] decreases the lock counter of an object that still remains locked, as it was locked more than once. When the lock counter reaches 0, rule [release-lock] can release the lock of the object. Rule [thread-pool] lifts the execution to a pool of threads.

Definition 3 (Operational Semantics of a Program). *The initial configuration of a program is* $\langle P_0, \mu_0 \rangle$ *where* $P_0 \stackrel{def}{=} \lceil B_{main}\{^{l_{init}}/_{\texttt{this}}\} \rceil \emptyset$, $\mu_0 \stackrel{def}{=} \{l_{init} \mapsto \langle Main, \phi, 0 \rangle\}$ *and* $Main = \{main \mapsto B_{main}\}$ *The operational semantics of a program is the set of traces of the form* $\langle P_0, \mu_0 \rangle \rightarrow^* \langle P, \mu \rangle$.

Example 2. The implementation in Example 1 becomes a program by defining B_{main} as: $\texttt{K}\langle \texttt{x} = \texttt{C}\langle \texttt{f} = \texttt{Object}\langle\rangle\rangle, \texttt{y} = \texttt{C}\langle \texttt{f} = \texttt{Object}\langle\rangle\rangle, \texttt{z} = \texttt{C}\langle \texttt{f} = \texttt{Object}\langle\rangle\rangle,$ $\texttt{h} = \texttt{Object}\langle\rangle\rangle.\texttt{m}(); \texttt{skip}.$

The operational semantics builds the following maximal trace from $\langle P_0, \mu_0\rangle$:

1. $\rightarrow^* \langle \lceil l.z := l.x; \text{ sync(z)}\{l.h := l.z.f; \ l.z := l.y\}; \ l.z.f := \text{Object}\langle\rangle; \text{ skip; skip}\rceil\emptyset, \mu_1\rangle$
   with $\mu_1 \stackrel{def}{=} \mu_0[l \mapsto o, l_1 \mapsto o_1, l_2 \mapsto o_2, l_3 \mapsto o_3, l_4 \mapsto o_4, l'_1 \mapsto o_4, l'_2 \mapsto o_4, l'_3 \mapsto o_4];$
   $o \stackrel{def}{=} \langle \text{K}, \{x \mapsto l_1, y \mapsto l_2, z \mapsto l_3, h \mapsto l_4\}, 0\rangle; \ o_i \stackrel{def}{=} \langle \text{C}, \{f \mapsto l'_i\}, 0\rangle, \text{ for } i \in 1..3;$
   $o_4 \stackrel{def}{=} \langle \text{Object}, \phi, 0\rangle$

2. $\rightarrow^* \langle \lceil \text{sync(z)}\{l.h := l.z.f; \ l.z := l.y\}; l.z.f := \text{Object}\langle\rangle; \text{ skip; skip}\rceil\emptyset, \mu_2\rangle$
   with $\mu_2 \stackrel{def}{=} \mu_1[l \mapsto o[z \mapsto l_1]]$

3. $\rightarrow^* \langle \lceil l.h := l.z.f; \ l.z := l.y; \text{ monitor\_exit}(l_1); \ l.z.f := \text{Object}\langle\rangle; \text{ skip; skip}\rceil\{l_1\}, \mu_3\rangle$
   with $\mu_3 \stackrel{def}{=} \mu_2[l_1 \mapsto lock^+(o_1)]$

4. $\rightarrow^* \langle \lceil l.z := l.y; \text{ monitor\_exit}(l_1); \ l.z.f := \text{Object}\langle\rangle; \text{ skip; skip}\rceil\{l_1\}, \mu_4\rangle$
   with $\mu_4 \stackrel{def}{=} \mu_3[l \mapsto o[z \mapsto l_1][h \mapsto l'_1]]$

5. $\rightarrow^* \langle \lceil \text{monitor\_exit}(l_1); \ l.z.f := \text{Object}\langle\rangle; \text{ skip; skip}\rceil\{l_1\}, \mu_5\rangle$
   with $\mu_5 \stackrel{def}{=} \mu_4[l \mapsto o[z \mapsto l_2, h \mapsto l'_1]]$

6. $\rightarrow^* \langle \lceil l.z.f := \text{Object}\langle\rangle; \text{ skip; skip}\rceil\emptyset, \mu_6\rangle, \text{ with } \mu_6 \stackrel{def}{=} \mu_5[l_1 \mapsto o_1]$

7. $\rightarrow^* \langle \lceil \text{skip}\rceil\emptyset, \mu_7\rangle, \text{ with } \mu_7 \stackrel{def}{=} \mu_6[l_2 \mapsto o_2[f \mapsto l''_2], l''_2 \mapsto o_4].$

Our formal semantics allows us to prove the correctness of the locking mechanism: two threads never lock the same location (*i.e.* object) at the same time.

Proposition 1 (Locking correctness). *Let* $\langle P_0, \mu_0\rangle \rightarrow^* \langle \lceil C_1\rceil \mathcal{L}_1 ... \lceil C_n\rceil \mathcal{L}_n, \mu\rangle$ *be an arbitrary trace. For any* $i, j \in \{1 \ldots n\}$, $i \neq j$ *entails* $\mathcal{L}_i \cap \mathcal{L}_j = \emptyset$.

4   Two Semantics for @GuardedBy Annotations

This section gives two distinct formalizations for locking specifications of the form `@GuardedBy(E)` `Type` `f`, where E is a guard expression allowed by the language, possibly using a special variable `itself` that stands for the protected field `f`.

In a *name-protection* interpretation, a thread must hold the lock on the value of the guard expression E whenever it *accesses* (reads or writes) the *name* of the guarded field `f`. Definition 4 formalizes the notion of *accessing an expression* when a given command is executed. For our purposes, it is enough to consider a single execution step; thus the accesses in $C_1; C_2$ are only those in C_1. When an object is created, only its creating thread can access it. Thus field initialization cannot originate data races and is not considered as an access. The access refers to the value of the expression, not to its lock counter, hence `sync(E){C}` does not access E. For accesses to a field f, Definition 4 keeps the exact expression used for the container of f, that will be used in Definition 5 for the contextualization of `this`.

Definition 4 (Expressions Accessed). *The set of expressions accessed in a single execution step is defined as follows:*

$$\mathrm{acc}(l) \stackrel{def}{=} \emptyset \qquad \mathrm{acc}(\kappa\langle f_1{=}E_1, \dots, f_n{=}E_n\rangle) \stackrel{def}{=} \bigcup_{i=1}^n \mathrm{acc}(E_i)$$

$$\mathrm{acc}(\mathtt{let}\ x = E\ \mathtt{in}\ C) \stackrel{def}{=} \mathrm{acc}(E) \qquad\qquad \mathrm{acc}(E.f) \stackrel{def}{=} \mathrm{acc}(E) \cup \{E.f\}$$

$$\mathrm{acc}(C_1; C_2) \stackrel{def}{=} \mathrm{acc}(C_1) \qquad\qquad \mathrm{acc}(E.f := F) \stackrel{def}{=} \mathrm{acc}(E.f) \cup \mathrm{acc}(F)$$

$$\mathrm{acc}(E.m()) \stackrel{def}{=} \mathrm{acc}(E) \qquad\qquad \mathrm{acc}(\mathtt{spawn}\ E.m()) \stackrel{def}{=} \mathrm{acc}(E)$$

$$\mathrm{acc}(\mathtt{monitor\_enter}(l)) \stackrel{def}{=} \emptyset \qquad\qquad \mathrm{acc}(\mathtt{monitor\_exit}(l)) \stackrel{def}{=} \emptyset$$

$$\mathrm{acc}(\mathtt{sync}(E.f)\{C\}) \stackrel{def}{=} \mathrm{acc}(E) \qquad\qquad \mathrm{acc}(\mathtt{sync}(x)\{C\}) \stackrel{def}{=} \emptyset$$

$$\mathrm{acc}(\mathtt{skip}) \stackrel{def}{=} \emptyset \qquad\qquad \mathrm{acc}(\mathtt{sync}(l)\{C\}) \stackrel{def}{=} \emptyset$$

$$\mathrm{acc}(\mathtt{sync}(\kappa\langle f_1 = E_1, \dots, f_n = E_n\rangle)\{C\}) \stackrel{def}{=} \mathrm{acc}(\kappa\langle f_1{=}E_1, \dots, f_n{=}E_n\rangle).$$

We say that C accesses a field f if and only if $E.f \in \mathrm{acc}(C)$, for some E.

Definition 5 formalizes when a field f is name-protected by `@GuardedBy(`E`)` in a program. In Sect. 2 we have discussed the reasons for using the special variable `itself` in the guard expressions when working with a value-protection semantics. In the name-protection semantics, `itself` denotes just an alias of the accessed name: `@GuardedBy(itself)` *Type* `f` is the same as `@GuardedBy(f)` *Type* `f`.

Definition 5 (Name-protection @GuardedBy). *A field f in a program is name protected by* `@GuardedBy(`E`)` *if and only if for any trace of that program*

$$\langle P_0, \mu_0\rangle \rightarrow^* \langle P_1.T.P_2, \mu\rangle \rightarrow \langle P_1.\hat{T}.P_2, \hat{\mu}\rangle$$

where $T = \lceil C \rceil \mathcal{L}$, whenever C accesses f, i.e. $E'.f \in \mathrm{acc}(C)$, for some E', with $[\![E']\!]^\mu = \langle l', \mu'\rangle$ and $l'' = state(\mu'(l'))f$, we have $loc([\![E\{^{l',l''}/_{\mathtt{this,itself}}\}]\!]^{\mu'}) \in \mathcal{L}$.

Definition 5 evaluates the guard expression E at those program points where f is accessed, in order to verify that its lock is held by the current thread. Thus, E is evaluated in a memory μ' obtained by the evaluation of the container of f, that is E'. Actually, we evaluate E only after having replaced the occurrences of the variable `this` with l', *i.e.* the evaluation of E', and the occurrences of `itself` with l'', *i.e.* the evaluation of f.

Example 3. In Example 2, field `y` is name protected by `@GuardedBy(this.x)`. It is accessed during the 5th macro-step, when $[\![\mathtt{this.x}\{^l/_{\mathtt{this}}\}]\!]^{\mu_4} = [\![l.\mathtt{x}]\!]^{\mu_4} = \langle l_1, \mu_4\rangle$, and l_1 is locked. Fields `x` and `z` are name protected by `@GuardedBy(`E`)`, for *no E*, as they are accessed at macro-step 2, when no location is locked.

An alternative semantics for `@GuardedBy` protects the values held in a field rather than the field name. In this *value-protection* semantics, a field f is `@GuardedBy(`E`)` if wherever a thread dereferences a location l eventually bound to f, it holds the lock on the object obtained by evaluating E at that point. In object-oriented parlance, *dereferencing a location l* means accessing the object stored at l in order to read or write a field. In Java, accesses to the lock counter are synchronized at a low level and the class tag is immutable, hence their accesses cannot give rise to data races and are not relevant here. Dereferences (Definition 6) are very different from accesses (Definition 4). For instance, statement `v.f := w.g.h` accesses expressions `v`, `v.f`, `w`, `w.g` and `w.g.h` but dereferences only the locations held in `v`, `w` and `w.g`: locations bound to `v.f` and `w.g.h` are left untouched. Definition 6 formalizes the set of locations dereferenced by an expression or command to access some field and keeps track of the fact that the access is for reading ($\Rightarrow$) or writing ($\Leftarrow$) the field. Hence dereference tokens are $l.f\Leftarrow$ or $l.f\Rightarrow$, where l is a location and f is the name of the field that is accessed in the object held in l.

Definition 6 (Dereferenced Locations). *Given a memory μ, the dereferences in a single reduction are defined as follows:*

$$\text{deref}(l)^\mu \stackrel{def}{=} \emptyset \qquad \text{deref}(E.f)^\mu \stackrel{def}{=} \{loc\,([\![E]\!]^\mu)\,.f\Rightarrow\} \cup \text{deref}(E)^\mu$$

$$\text{deref}(\kappa\langle f_1 = E_1, \ldots, f_n = E_n\rangle)^\mu \stackrel{def}{=} \bigcup_{i=1}^n \text{deref}(E_i)^\mu$$

$$\text{deref}(\texttt{let } x = E \texttt{ in } C)^\mu \stackrel{def}{=} \text{deref}(E)^\mu \qquad\qquad \text{deref}(\texttt{skip})^\mu \stackrel{def}{=} \emptyset$$

$$\text{deref}(\texttt{sync}\,(E)\{C\})^\mu \stackrel{def}{=} \text{deref}(E)^\mu \qquad\qquad \text{deref}(C_1; C_2)^\mu \stackrel{def}{=} \text{deref}(C_1)^\mu$$

$$\text{deref}(\texttt{monitor\_enter}\,(l))^\mu \stackrel{def}{=} \emptyset \qquad\qquad \text{deref}(\texttt{monitor\_exit}\,(l))^\mu \stackrel{def}{=} \emptyset$$

$$\text{deref}(E.f := E')^\mu \stackrel{def}{=} \{loc\,([\![E]\!]^\mu)\,.f\Leftarrow\} \cup \text{deref}(E')^\mu$$

$$\text{deref}(E.m(\,))^\mu \stackrel{def}{=} \text{deref}(E)^\mu \qquad\qquad \text{deref}(\texttt{spawn } E.m(\,))^\mu \stackrel{def}{=} \text{deref}(E)^\mu$$

We define $\text{derefloc}(C)^\mu \stackrel{def}{=} \{l \mid \exists f \text{ s.t. } l.f\Leftarrow \in \text{deref}(C)^\mu \vee l.f\Rightarrow \in \text{deref}(C)^\mu\}$.

Definition 7 formalizes when a field f is value-protected by `@GuardedBy(E)` in a program. Intuitively, for any execution trace t we collect the set $\mathcal{F}$ of locations that have ever been bound to a guarded field f in t. Then, we require that whenever a thread dereferences one of those locations, that thread must hold the lock on the object obtained by evaluating the guard E.

Definition 7 (Value-protection @GuardedBy). *A field f in a program is value-protected by @GuardedBy(E) if and only if for any trace of that program*

$$\langle P_0, \mu_0\rangle \rightarrow^i \langle P_i, \mu_i\rangle = \langle P.T.Q, \mu_i\rangle \rightarrow \langle P.T'.Q, \mu_{i+1}\rangle \rightarrow \cdots$$

letting $T = \lceil C\rceil \mathcal{L}$; letting $\mathcal{F} = \bigcup_{j>0}\{state(\mu_j(l))f \mid l \in \text{dom}(\mu_j) \wedge state(\mu_j(l))f\downarrow\}$ be the set of locations eventually associated to field f; letting $\Delta_f = \text{derefloc}(C)^{\mu_i} \cap \mathcal{F}$ be those locations in $\mathcal{F}$ dereferenced at the $i{+}1$-th step of the trace above. Then, for every $l \in \Delta_f$ it follows that $loc\,([\![E\{^l\!/_{\texttt{itself}}\}]\!]^{\mu_i}) \in \mathcal{L}$.

Note that $\mathcal{F}$ contains all locations eventually bound to f, at any time, in the past or the future, not just those bound in the last configuration $\langle P_i, \mu_i\rangle$. This is because value-protection `@GuardedBy(E)` is a kind of type annotation that predicates on the values held in the annotated field, and the properties of such values must remain unchanged as they flow through the program.

Note also that the only variable allowed in the guard expression E is `itself`. This is because there is no value that we can bind to the container `this` of the guarded value (in Definition 5, instead, we had the value of E'). It is actually possible that the value of the guarded field f might be held in more fields of distinct containers, hence the unique identification of the value of `the` container `this` becomes impossible here.

Example 4. In Example 2 field x is value protected by `@GuardedBy(itself)`. This because $\Delta_\texttt{x} = \{l_1\}$ and l_1 is dereferenced only at macro-step 4, when the corresponding object o_1 is accessed to obtain the value of its field f. At that program point, l_1 is locked by the current thread. Fields y and z are value protected by @GuardedBy(E), for *no* E, since $\Delta_y = \{l_2\}$, $\Delta_z = \{l_1, l_2\}$, and l_2 is dereferenced at macro-step 7, when the thread holds no locks.

The two semantics for @GuardedBy are incomparable: neither entails the other. In Example 2 field x is value protected by @GuardedBy(itself), but is not name protected. Field y is name protected by @GuardedBy(this.x), but is not value protected.

5   Protection Against Data Races

In this section we provide sufficient conditions that ban data races when @GuardedBy annotations are satisfied, in either of the two versions. Intuitively, a *data race* occurs when two threads dereference the same location l, at the same time, to access a field of the object stored at l, and at least one modifies the field.

Definition 8 (Data race). *Let* $\langle P_0, \mu_0 \rangle \to^* \langle P, \mu \rangle = \langle P_1.T_1.P_2.T_2.P_3, \mu \rangle$, *with* $T_i = \lceil C_i \rceil \mathcal{L}_i$, *for* $i \in 1..2$. *A data race occurs at a location l during the access to some field f in $\langle P, \mu \rangle$, only if*

- $\langle P, \mu \rangle \to \langle P_1.T_1'.P_2.T_2.P_3, \mu' \rangle$, *for some* $T_1' \neq T_1$
- $\langle P, \mu \rangle \to \langle P_1.T_1.P_2.T_2'.P_3, \mu'' \rangle$, *for some* $T_2' \neq T_2$

where $l.f \!\!\Leftarrow\, \in \mathrm{deref}(C_1)^\mu$ *and* $(l.f \!\!\Leftarrow\, \in \mathrm{deref}(C_2)^\mu$ *or* $l.f \!\!\Rightarrow\, \in \mathrm{deref}(C_2)^\mu)$.

In Sect. 2 we said that accesses to fields (or their value) that are @GuardedBy(E) occur in mutual exclusion if the guard E is such that it can be evaluated at distinct program points and its evaluation always yields the same value. This implies that E cannot contain local variables as they cannot be evaluated at distinct program points. Thus, we restrict the variables that can be used in E. However, itself can always be used since it refers to the location being dereferenced. For the name-protection semantics, this can also be used, since it refers to the container of the guarded field, as long as it can be uniquely determined; for instance, if there is no aliasing. Indeed, Sect. 2 shows that name protection without aliasing restrictions does not ban data races, since it protects the name but not its value, that can be freely aliased and accessed through other names, without synchronization. In a real programming language, *aliasing* arises from assignments, returned values, and parameter passing. Our simple language has no returned values and only the implicit parameter this.

Definition 9 (Non-aliased fields). *A field f is* non-aliased *in a program if and only if for any trace* $\langle P_0, \mu_0 \rangle \to^* \langle P, \mu \rangle$ *of that program, there are no l', l'', and g such that* $state(\mu(l'))f = state(\mu(l''))g$, *and* $l' = l''$ *entails* $f \neq g$.

Field aliasing can be inferred through a may-alias analysis (that is, a must-non-alias analysis) or prevented by syntactic restrictions, as currently done by

Julia. Although the precision of this aliasing analysis might in principle affect the precision of the results, it must be said that programmers who use name protection do not alias the protected fields. When they do it, the field is not actually data race free, hence simple syntactic restrictions are enough in practice.

However, as discussed in Sect. 2, to ensure the soundness of the name-protection semantics we need a further assumption: the value of the guard expression must not change during program execution.

Definition 10 (Final expressions). *An expression E where the only allowed variables are* this *and* itself *is said to be* final *in a program if for every trace $\langle P_0, \mu_0 \rangle \rightarrow {}^i \langle P_i, \mu_i \rangle$ of that program, for all $0 \leq p \leq q \leq i$ and for all $l, l' \in \mathrm{dom}(\mu_p)$, $[\![E\{{}^{l,l'}/_{\mathtt{this,itself}}\}]\!]^{\mu_p} = \langle l_1, \mu_1 \rangle$ and $[\![E\{{}^{l,l'}/_{\mathtt{this,itself}}\}]\!]^{\mu_q} = \langle l_2, \mu_2 \rangle$ entails $l_1 = l_2$.*

We can now prove that, for non-aliased fields and final guard expressions, the name-protection semantics of @GuardedBy protects against data races.

Theorem 1 (Name-protection semantics vs. data race protection). *Let E be a final expression in a program, and f be a* non-aliased *field that is name protected by* @GuardedBy(E). *Let E contain no variable distinct from* itself *and* this. *Then, no data race can occur at those locations bound to f, at any execution trace of that program.*

As argued in Sect. 2, the assumptions on non-aliased fields and final guard expressions are not necessary in the value-protection semantics as this locking discipline protects directly the value of the guarded field f.

Theorem 2 (Value-protection semantics vs. data race protection). *Let E be an expression in a program, and f be a field that is value-protected by* @GuardedBy(E). *Let E have no variable distinct from* itself. *Then no data race can occur at those locations bound to f, during any execution of the program.*

Both results are proved by contradiction, by supposing that a data race occurs and showing that two threads would lock the same location, against Proposition 1.

6   Implementation in Julia

The Julia analyzer infers @GuardedBy annotations. The implementation is based on the theory of this article, while the theoretical results were inspired by actual case studies. The user selects name-protection or value-protection semantics.

As formalized in Sect. 4, a field f is @GuardedBy(E) if, at *all* program points P where f is accessed (for name protection) or one of its locations is dereferenced (for value protection), the value of E is locked by the current thread. The inference algorithm of Julia builds on two phases: (i) compute the set $\mathcal{P}$ of program points where f is accessed; (ii) find expressions E locked at all program points $P \in \mathcal{P}$.

Point (i) is obvious for name protection, since accesses to f are syntactically apparent in the program. For value protection, the set $\mathcal{P}$ is instead undecidable, since there might be infinitely many objects potentially bound to f at runtime, that flow through aliasing. Hence Julia overapproximates the set $\mathcal{P}$ by abstracting objects into their *creation point* in the program: if two objects have distinct creation points, they must be distinct. The number of creation points is finite, hence the approximation is finitely computable. Julia implements creation points analysis as a concretization of the class analysis in [21], where objects are abstracted in their creation points instead of just their class tag.

Point (ii) uses the *definite aliasing* analysis of Julia, described in [19]. At each synchronized(G) statement, that analysis provides a set L of expressions that are definitely an alias of G at that statement (*i.e.*, their values coincide there, always). Julia concludes that the expressions in L are locked by the current thread after the synchronized(G) and until the end of its scope. Potential side-effects might however invalidate that conclusion, possibly due to concurrent threads. Hence, Julia only allows in L fields that are never modified after being defined, which can be inferred syntactically for a field. For name protection, viewpoint adaptation of this is performed on such expressions (Definition 5). These sets L are propagated in the program until they reach the points in $\mathcal{P}$. The expressions E in point (ii) are hence those that belong to L at *all* program points $\mathcal{P}$.

Since @GuardedBy(E) annotations are expected to be used by client code, E should be visible to the client. For instance, Julia discards expressions E that refer to a private field or to a local variable that is not a parameter, since these would not be visible nor useful to a client.

The supporting creation points and definite aliasing analyses are sound, hence Julia soundly infers @GuardedBy(E) annotations that satisfy the formal definitions in Sect. 4. Such inferred annotations protect against data races if the sufficient conditions in Sect. 5 hold for them.

More detail and experiments with this implementation, in the value-protection semantics, can be found in [10]. There, we have analyzed 15 large open-source programs, including parts of Eclipse and Tomcat, for a total of 1,290,060 non-blank lines of code. Julia has often inferred the annotations already present in code (if any), while the annotations not inferred by Julia have often been proved to be programmers' mistakes (either fields that are not actually guarded as expected, or they are guarded in a way that do not prevent data races).

7 Conclusions, Future and Related Work

Coming back to the ambiguities sketched in Sect. 1, we have clarified that: (1) this in the guard expression must be interpreted as the container of the guarded field and consistently contextualized (Definition 5). (2) An access is a field use for name protection (Definitions 4 and 5). A value access is a dereference (field get/set or method call) for value protection; copying a value is not an access in this case (Definitions 6 and 7). (3) The value of the guard expression must be locked when a name or value is accessed, regardless of how it is accessed in the synchronized block (Definitions 5 and 7). (4) The lock must be held on the value of the guard expression as evaluated at the access to the guarded field (name or value) (Definitions 5 and 7). (5) Either the *name* or the *value* of a field can be guarded, but this choice leads to very different semantics. Namely, in the *name-protection* semantics, the lock must be held whenever the field's name is accessed (Definitions 4 and 5). In the *value-protection* semantics, the lock must be held whenever the field's value is accessed (Definitions 6 and 7), regardless of what expression is used to access the value. Both semantics yield a guarantee against data races, though name protection requires an aliasing restriction on the field and final guard expressions (Theorems 1 and 2).

This work could be extended by enlarging the set of guard expressions that protect against data races. For instance, it could be extended with static fields. We believe that the protection results in Sect. 5 still hold for them. Another aspect to investigate is the scope of the protection against data races. In this article, a single location is protected (Definition 8), not the whole tree of objects reachable from it: our protection is shallow rather than deep. Deep protection is possibly more interesting to the programmer, since it relates to a data structure as a whole, but it requires to reason about boundaries and encapsulation of data structures.

The work of Abadi et al. [1] is the closest to ours. It proposes a type system for detecting data races in Java programs by means of @GuardedBy type annotations, according to a name-preservation semantics. Theoretical results are stated on a significant concurrent subset of Java, RACEFREEJAVA, which shares many similarities with our calculus. The main result of the paper is that well-typed programs do not have data races. This result relies on a few constraints: (i) like us, in GuardedBy(E) annotations, E must be final, so this is the only admitted variable in E; (ii) unlike us, in blocks sync(E){C}, E must be final; (iii) unlike us, field updates are admissible (typable) only if they are guarded by some final expression; (iv) unlike us, Java lock reentrancy is not admitted; (v) unlike us, the limitation (i) is overcome by extending the type system to allow fields of a class to be protected by locks external to that class. Note that non-aliasing is not required in [1], although this seems to be a consequence of the (quite) strong requirement (iii) that field updates can *only* occur on annotated fields.

We refer to [1] for a careful review of tools developed for detecting data races.

There are many other formalizations of concurrent fragments of Java, such as [2,7]. Our goal here is the semantics of annotations such as @GuardedBy. Hence we kept the semantics of the language to the minimum core needed for the formalization of those program annotations. Another well-known formalization is Featherweight Java [14], a functional language that provides a formal kernel of sequential Java. It does not include threads, nor assignment. Thus, it is not adequate to formalize data races, which need concurrency and assignments. A similar argument applies to Middleweight Java [4] and Welterweight Java [20]. The need of a formal specification for reasoning about Java's concurrency and for building verification tools is recognized [6,17] but we are not aware of any formalization of the semantics of Java's concurrency annotations.

Our formalization will support tools based on model-checking such as Java PathFinder [18] and Bandera [3,13], on type-checking such as the Checker Framework [8] and Houdini/rcc [1], or on abstract interpretation such as Julia [16].

Acknowledgments. We thank Ruggero Lanotte for valuable comments on an early draft. This material is based on research sponsored by DARPA under agreement numbers FA8750-12-2-0107, FA8750-15-C-0010, and FA8750-16-2-0032.

References

1. Abadi, M., Flanagan, C., Freund, S.: Types for safe locking: static race detection for Java. ACM TOPLAS **28**(2), 207–255 (2006)
2. Ábrahám-Mumm, E., de Boer, F.S., de Roever, W.-P., Steffen, M.: Verification for java's reentrant multithreading concept. In: Nielsen, M., Engberg, U. (eds.) FOSSACS 2002. LNCS, vol. 2303, pp. 5–20. Springer, Heidelberg (2002)
3. Bandera: About Bandera. http://bandera.projects.cis.ksu.edu
4. Bierman, G.M., Parkinson, M.J.: Effects and effect inference for a core java calculus. ENTCS **82**(7), 82–107 (2003)
5. Blanchet, B.: Escape analysis for java: theory and practice. ACM TOPLAS **25**(6), 713–775 (2003)
6. Bogdanas, D., Rosu, G.: K-java: a complete semantics of java. In: ACM SIGPLAN-SIGACT POPL, pp. 445–456, Mumbai, India (2015)
7. Cenciarelli, P., Knapp, A., Reus, B., Wirsing, M.: From sequential to multi-threaded java: an event-based operational semantics. In: Johnson, M. (ed.) AMAST 1997. LNCS, vol. 1349, pp. 75–90. Springer, Heidelberg (1997)
8. Dietl, W., Dietzel, S., Ernst, M.D., Muslu, K., Schiller, T.W.: Building and using pluggable type-checkers. In: Taylor, R.N., Gall, H.C. (eds.) ICSE 2011 (2011)
9. Ernst, M.D., Macedonio, D., Merro, M., Spoto, F.: Semantics for locking specifications. CoRR abs/1501.05338 (2015)
10. Ernst, M., Lovato, A., Macedonio, D., Spoto, F., Thaine, J.: Locking discipline inference and checking. In: ICSE 2016, Austin, TX, USA (2016)
11. Goetz, B., Peierls, T., Bloch, J., Bowbeer, J.: Java Concurrency in Practice. Addison Wesley, Boston (2006)
12. Google: Guava: Google Core Libraries for Java 1.6+. https://code.google.com/p/guava-libraries
13. Hatcliff, J., Dwyer, M.B.: Using the bandera tool set to model-check properties of concurrent java software. In: Larsen, K.G., Nielsen, M. (eds.) CONCUR 2001. LNCS, vol. 2154, p. 39. Springer, Heidelberg (2001)
14. Igarashi, A., Pierce, B.C., Wadler, P.: Featherweight java: a minimal core calculus for Java and GJ. ACM TOPLAS **23**(3), 396–450 (2001)
15. Javadoc for @GuardedBy. https://jsr-305.googlecode.com/svn/trunk/javadoc/javax/annotation/concurrent/GuardedBy.html
16. Julia, S.: The Julia Static Analyzer. http://www.juliasoft.com/julia
17. Long, B., Long, B.W.: Formal specification of java concurrency to assist software verification. In: Dongarra, J. (ed.) IPDPS 2003. IEEE Computer Society (2003)
18. NASA: Java PathFinder. http://babelfish.arc.nasa.gov/trac/jpf
19. Nikolić, D.J., Spoto, F.: Definite expression aliasing analysis for java bytecode. In: Roychoudhury, A., D'Souza, M. (eds.) ICTAC 2012. LNCS, vol. 7521, pp. 74–89. Springer, Heidelberg (2012)

20. Östlund, J., Wrigstad, T.: Welterweight java. In: Vitek, J. (ed.) TOOLS 2010. LNCS, vol. 6141, pp. 97–116. Springer, Heidelberg (2010)
21. Palsberg, J., Schwartzbach, M.I.: Object-oriented type inference. In: Paepcke, A. (ed.) OOPSLA 1991, pp. 146–161. ACM SIGPLAN Notices, ACM, New York (1991)
22. Pech, V.: Concurrency is hot, try the JCIP annotations (2010). http://jetbrains. dzone.com/tips/concurrency-hot-try-jcip

From Design Contracts to Component Requirements Verification

Jing Liu[1]([✉]), John D. Backes[2], Darren Cofer[2], and Andrew Gacek[2]

[1] Advanced Technology Center, Rockwell Collins, Cedar Rapids, USA
jing.liu@rockwellcollins.com
[2] Advanced Technology Center, Rockwell Collins, Minneapolis, USA
{john.backes,darren.cofer,andrew.gacek}@rockwellcollins.com

Abstract. During the development and verification of complex airborne systems, a variety of languages and development environments are used for different levels of the system hierarchy. As a result, there may be manual steps to translate requirements between these different environments. This paper presents a tool-supported export technique that translates high-level requirements from the software architecture modeling environment into observers of requirements that can be used for verification in the software component environment. This allows efficient verification that the component designs comply with their high-level requirements. It also provides an automated tool chain supporting formal verification from system requirements down to low-level software requirements that is consistent with certification guidance for avionics systems. The effectiveness of the technique has been evaluated and demonstrated on a medical infusion pump and an aircraft wheel braking system.

Keywords: Design contracts · Specification model · Design model · AGREE · Simulink · Requirements-based verification · Certification

1 Introduction

As part of the software development process for complex avionics systems, system requirements are iteratively decomposed, allocated, and refined to lower level requirements for software and hardware components. Different verification processes are used to provide evidence that these components satisfy their requirements. The focus of all development and verification activities in the avionics domain is to ensure that a system meets its requirements and contains no unintended functionality.

Requirements at different levels of the system hierarchy may be specified using different languages and development environments. Even when formal methods tools are used to verify requirements, there may be manual steps to translate requirements between these different environments. The work presented in this paper attempts to close the gap between verification at the system level and the component level.

© Springer International Publishing Switzerland 2016
S. Rayadurgam and O. Tkachuk (Eds.): NFM 2016, LNCS 9690, pp. 373–387, 2016.
DOI: 10.1007/978-3-319-40648-0_28

We present a tool-supported technique that translates requirements from a system-level reasoning framework into observers of requirements for software components. The observers that the tool produces can be verified using a model checker specialized to the software component development language. Our work closes the gap between high-level requirements captured with the software architecture and low-level requirements for component implementation. This ensures consistency of the verification results and improves productivity and accuracy through the use of automation to eliminate manual steps. Furthermore, making these property observers available during the design process supports early verification of the software components.

In previous work, we have developed a compositional analysis environment [1,2] based on the Architecture Analysis and Design Language (AADL) [3]. AADL can be used to model both the hardware and software aspects of the system, but in this work we have limited our attention to the software architecture. In our compositional analysis approach, the AADL model is augmented with assume-guarantee contracts to capture both system-level requirements and the requirements for the software components.

In the present work, we link the component contracts to their implementations in Simulink® [4], a framework developed by MathWorks® and integrated with MATLAB®. Simulink provides a graphical programming environment for modeling, simulation, code generation, testing, and formal analysis. It is widely used in the avionics industry. By automatically translating formal contracts for software component behavior into specifications that can be checked in the Simulink environment, we now support a complete top-to-bottom development process with formal verification of all requirements. Furthermore, the design of our approach is sufficiently general that it can be adapted to support other software development environments and languages.

Since our objective is the production of high-assurance software for avionics, we must be cognizant of how this approach will fit into a certification context. As we will show, our approach has been designed to be consistent with new certification guidance related to the use of formal methods and model-based development processes.

The rest of the paper is organized as follows. Section 2 provides background information related to the development and analysis environment, including certification considerations. Section 3 describes the contract translation process in detail. Section 4 evaluates the techniques in an avionics system case study and a medical device system case study. Section 5 describes related work and Sect. 6 presents concluding remarks.

2   Preliminaries

In this section, we describe the overall design flow and introduce some terminology associated with the certification context. We also describe the system architecture modeling environment and the software component modeling environment that we are using.

2.1   Design Flow from Architecture to Component

One of our goals is to transition the tools we have developed into use by the system and software engineers who develop avionics products. Therefore, we need to understand how the tools and the models they produce will fit into the certification process.

Certification guidance for software in commercial aircraft is found in DO-178C, *Software Considerations in Airborne Systems and Equipment Certification* [5]. The process described in DO-178C is essentially a waterfall model in which system requirements are allocated to hardware and software, becoming high-level requirements for each. High-level requirements are refined to become a software design, consisting of software architecture and low-level requirements from which individual software components can be developed.

DO-178C is accompanied by several supplement documents which provide guidance for the use of specific technologies, including formal methods (DO-333 [6]) and model-based development (DO-331 [7]). DO-333 describes how software life-cycle artifacts such as high and low-level requirements can be expressed as formal properties and how formal analysis tools can be used to satisfy many certification objectives. DO-331 provides guidance on how software life-cycle artifacts expressed as different types of models fit into the certification process. A case study showing how different formal methods can be used to satisfy certification objectives is found in [8], including a model-based example that uses Simulink [4] and Simulink Design Verifier™ [9].

DO-331 describes the relationships between models at the system and software levels, and distinguishes between *specification models* and *design models*. A specification model represents high-level requirements that provide an abstract representation of functional, performance, interface, or safety characteristics of software components. Specification models do not define software design details or prescribe a specific software implementation or architecture. Design models prescribe software component internal data structures, data flow, and/or control flow. They may include low-level requirements or architecture, and may be used to produce source code directly.

Figure 1 provides an overview of our proposed design flow, connecting it to the terminology used in a DO-178C process. On the left side of Fig. 1, system requirements allocated to software (generally in textual form) are refined to a collection of high-level software requirements and used to construct an architecture model in AADL. This process is described in more detail in the next section. The AADL model is a design model (in DO-331 terminology) because it contains information such as data flows, message types, and execution rates and priorities, that will be used to produce source code and configure the operating system. High-level requirements associated with each level of the architecture and software components represented in the architecture are captured into formal design contracts using the Assume Guarantee Reasoning Environment (AGREE) [1]. Compositional verification is used to show that contracts (requirements) at each level satisfy the contract of the level above.

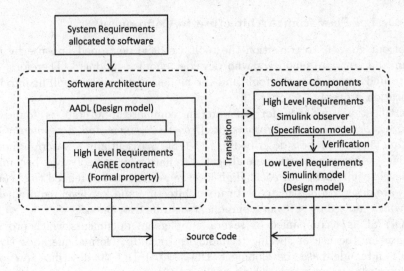

Fig. 1. Architecture to component design flow

On the right side of the figure, software components are implemented and verified. Simulink models describe the detailed behaviors and are used to generate source code for each component. They are therefore considered low-level requirements and also design models (in DO-331 terms). High-level requirements for each component are represented as specification models (in DO-331 terms). These models are observers that produce a true output whenever their corresponding property (specified over the component inputs and outputs) is true. A model checker such as the one provided by Simulink Design Verifier can be used to show that the design model satisfied the high-level requirements defined by the specification model.

Clearly there is a gap between the methods, tools, and models of the software architecture and those for the software components. In the past, high-level requirements for the software components have been manually captured as observers in Simulink before they can be used for verification [10]. The manual process may be error-prone, and it can be difficult and costly to keep the models in sync. The work we describe in this paper bridges this gap by automating the translation of high-level requirements associated with the architecture model into Simulink observers that can be verified in the Simulink environment.

2.2 Architecture Description and Design Contracts

The Architectural Analysis and Design Language (AADL) [3] is a architecture modeling language for embedded, real-time, distributed systems. It was approved as an SAE Standard in 2004, and its standardization committee has active participation from many academic and industrial partners in the aerospace industry. It provides the constructs needed to model both hardware and software in embedded systems such as threads, processes, processors, buses, and memory.

It is sufficiently formal for our purposes, and is extensible through the use of language annexes that can initiate calls to separately developed analysis tools.

The Assume Guarantee Reasoning Environment (AGREE) [1] is a language and tool for compositional verification of AADL models. It is implemented as an AADL annex that allows AADL models to be annotated with assume-guarantee behavioral contracts. A contract contains a set of assumptions about the component's inputs and a set of guarantees about the component's outputs. The assumptions and guarantees may also contain predicates that reason about how the state of a component evolves over time.

AGREE uses a syntax similar to Lustre [11] to express a contract's assumptions and guarantees. AGREE translates an AADL model and its contract annotations into Lustre and then queries a user-selected model checker to perform verification. The goal of the analysis is to prove that each component's contract is satisfied by the interaction of its direct subcomponents as described by their respective contracts. Verification is performed at each layer of the architecture hierarchy and details of lower level components are abstracted away during verification of higher level component contracts. This compositional approach allows large systems to be analyzed efficiently.

Component contracts at the lowest level of the architecture are assumed to be true by AGREE. Verification of these component contracts must be performed outside of the AADL/AGREE environment. In a traditional software development process, components will be developed to meet the high-level requirements corresponding to these contracts and verified by testing or code review. However, there are two problems with this approach:

1. Verification methodologies like test and code review are not exhaustive. Errors in these activities can cause the compositional verification that AGREE performs to be incorrect.
2. Manual translation of an AGREE contract into a property for verification at the component level can be time-consuming and error-prone.

Our solution to these problems is to automatically translate AGREE contracts of software components into expressions in the development language of the component software. A formal verification tool that reasons about artifacts expressed in this language can then be used to verify that the contracts hold. The remainder of the paper describes this solution in detail.

2.3 Component Requirements and Verification

The following tools and features are used to capture component level requirements and perform verification.

Simulink. Simulink [4], developed by MathWorks and integrated with MATLAB, provides a graphical programming environment for modeling, simulation, code generation, testing, and analysis. It is widely used in the Avionics industry. It is used to capture low-level component design models and requirements.

Simulink Design Verifier. The Simulink Design Verifier (SLDV) tool [9], provides a model checker for the Simulink environment. SLDV can verify properties expressed with MATLAB functions, Simulink blocks, or Stateflow diagrams. The first is a textual language while the last two are graphical.

Simulink Observer. A Simulink observer is a component in a Simulink model which observes the behavior of another component and computes a Boolean value indicating if the latter component is satisfying its requirements. A Simulink observer along with the component it observes can be verified using SLDV to show that the component under observation always satisfies its requirements. Using DO-331 terminology, the Simulink observer is a specification model that captures high-level requirements, while the component it observes is a design model that captures low-level requirements. Our tool generates Simulink observers using a MATLAB function block which encapsulates a MATLAB function. A MATLAB function consists of statements written in the MATLAB scripting language, an imperative, dynamically typed language. In addition to a main function, a MATLAB function block can contain other local functions defined in the same block. Unlike the other graphical language alternatives, the textual representation of a MATLAB function makes the export easier to control and maintain.

3 Detailed Approach

This section details our approach for automatically constructing a specification model from high level requirements.

3.1 Export Scheme Overview

The requirements used to generate each specification model come directly from a component contract specified in AGREE. Each specification model is a Simulink observer implemented as a MATLAB function. The observer's interface is generated from the component's features described in the AADL model.

Table 1 provides a summary of the constructs that appear in an AGREE contract and their mapping in MATLAB. Our process can translate any AGREE specification. The specification model generation process is divided into two major steps, as depicted in Fig. 2:

1. The tool produces an intermediate specification in Lustre. The Lustre language [11] is a synchronous dataflow language for modeling reactive systems, with formalisms similar to temporal logics [12]. The AGREE grammar and the Lustre grammar are very similar. This makes Lustre well suited as a common intermediate language to feed into different formal analysis or translation engines. A number of common translation steps are performed to create this intermediate format. For example, variable assignments are put into dataflow order, all function calls are inlined, and nested temporal expressions are decoupled.

Table 1. Mapping between AGREE and MATLAB constructs

AGREE constructs	MATLAB constructs
Component contract[a]	Simulink observer
Component inputs and outputs[a]	Inputs to the Simulink observer[b]
Assume statement	Proof assumption
assume "B input range": $Input < 20$	sldv.assume ($Input < 20$)
Guarantee statement	Proof objective
guarantee "B output range":	sldv.prove($Output < (Input + 15)$)
$Output < Input + 15$	
Equation statement	Assignments
eq $Active : bool = not\ Sync.Active$	$Active = not(Sync.Active)$
If-then-else expression	Generated local function
$if\ Error\ then\ false\ else\ Active$	$ifFunction(Error, false, Active)$
AGREE basic data types	MATLAB built-in data types[b]
int	(u)int8, (u)int16, (u)int32
real	single, double
bool	boolean
Record types (on inputs and outputs)	Simulink bus objects
AGREE operators	MATLAB operators or function calls
$-$, not, $<>$, and, or	$-$, $\sim$, $\sim=$, &&, $\|$
$+, -, *, /, >, <, >=, <=$	$+, -, *, /, >, <, >=, <=$
mod operator	mod function
$=$ (equal operator)	isequal function[c]
div (integer divide operator)	/ with operands typecast to integer types
$\Rightarrow$	generated local $impliesFunction$
$\rightarrow$	generated local $arrowFunction$[d]
pre	persistent variable for the operand[d]

[a]This information comes from the component type in AADL.
[b]Data size selection based on user input (Sect. 3.3).
[c]Use isequal function rather than == to apply to structure types.
[d]The translation for $\rightarrow$ and pre operators need persistent variables (Sect. 3.2).

2. From the intermediate Lustre a MATLAB function is produced. The MATLAB function is specified by an abstract syntax tree (AST). This allows for structured, easily extendable export. MATLAB specific features introduced in this translation include constructing valid MATLAB identifiers with no duplications and turning local structures in the intermediate output into local variables to eliminate any dynamically allocated structures.

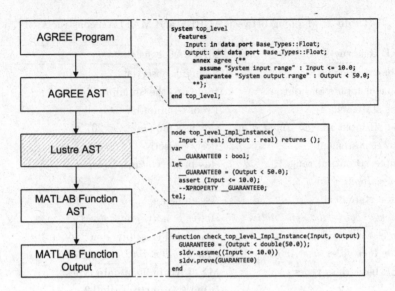

```
system top_level
  features
    Input: in data port Base_Types::Float;
    Output: out data port Base_Types::Float;
    annex agree {**
      assume "System input range" : Input <= 10.0;
      guarantee "System output range" : Output < 50.0;
    **};
end top_level;
```

```
node top_level_Impl_Instance(
  Input : real; Output : real) returns ();
var
  __GUARANTEE0 : bool;
let
  __GUARANTEE0 = (Output < 50.0);
  assert (Input <= 10.0);
  --%PROPERTY __GUARANTEE0;
tel;
```

```
function check_top_level_Impl_Instance(Input, Output)
  GUARANTEE0 = (Output < double(50.0));
  sldv.assume((Input <= 10.0))
  sldv.prove(GUARANTEE0)
end
```

Fig. 2. Implementation scheme

3.2 Translation for Temporal Operations

There are two types of temporal operations used in AGREE:

- The $\rightarrow$ operation evaluates to its left-hand side expression when the transition system is in its initial state. Otherwise it evaluates to its right-hand side expression. For example, the expression: $true \rightarrow false$ is $true$ in the initial state and $false$ otherwise.
- The pre operation takes a single expression as an argument and returns the value of this expression in the previous state of the transition system. For example, the expression: $x = (0 \rightarrow pre(x) + 1)$ constrains the current value of variable x to be 0 in the initial state; otherwise it is the value of x in the previous state incremented by 1.

In the model's initial state the value of the pre operation on any expression is undefined. Every occurrence of a pre operator must be in a subexpression of the right hand side of the $\rightarrow$ operator. The pre operation can be performed on expressions containing other pre operators, but there must be $\rightarrow$ operations between each occurrence of a pre operation. For example, the expression: $true \rightarrow pre(pre(x))$ is not well-formed, but the expression: $true \rightarrow pre(x \rightarrow pre(x))$ is well-formed.

To represent temporal constructs, the Simulink observer needs to differentiate the behavior at the initial state from the other states. It also needs to remember variable values from the previous calls to the function.

We make use of persistent variables to record the previous state of the function's variables across multiple calls. A single persistent Boolean variable, *first_time*, is used for all → expressions to indicate whether or not the function is being called for the first time. Additionally, a persistent variable is created for each unique *pre* expression[1]. We refer to these variables as the "*pre* variables". The Simulink unit delay block could also be used to remember previous variable values by placing the graphical block outside of the MATLAB function for each "*pre* variable". However, the block needs to be placed outside of the MATLAB function, requiring any "*pre* variable" to become an input to the function; the graphical representation also makes it harder to automate.

The persistent variables used to model the → and *pre* operations appear in the following contexts in the Simulink observer:

1. **Declaration.** Each of these persistent variables is declared at the beginning of the function. MATLAB is dynamically typed, so the type of these variables is determined during their initialization.
2. **Initialization.** The initialization of a persistent variable occurs immediately after its declaration. The built-in function "isempty", e.g., *isempty* (*first_time*), is used to determine whether or not the variable has been initialized. The *pre* variables are initialized to the default value for their type (e.g., true for booleans, 0 for integers, and 0 for floating points). Because all occurrences of *pre* operators are guarded by → operators, this initial value is never used. This initialization takes place for the sole purpose of allowing the Simulink code generator to function properly.
3. **Use.** Each of these persistent variables is used in place of its corresponding *pre* expression.
4. **Update.** Before the observer function returns, all of the *pre* variables are updated to the current value of their expression. For example, the persistent variable for the expression *pre*(x) is updated to the value of x. The *first_time* variable is always set to false before the observer function returns.

3.3 Translation for Data Types

Here we note differences between the data types of AGREE and MATLAB.

Constants. Any constant numbers (integers or floats) that appear in a MATLAB function are assumed to be *double* precision floating point numbers. Therefore, explicit typecasts are needed when translating constants from the AGREE specifications.

Arbitrary Data Size vs. Fixed Data Size. AGREE assumes that integer and real valued variables have arbitrary size. However, MATLAB's primitive data types for integers are of bounded size (integers are represented by 8-bit, 16-bit, or 32-bit 2's complement numbers). Integer valued variables in AGREE are translated into fixed size integers in MATLAB. Similarly, MATLAB uses floating point arithmetic to represent non-integers. Real valued variables in AGREE are

---

[1] For example, if the term *pre*(x) appears multiple times in the AGREE contract, we only create a single persistent variable for this expression.

translated to floating point variables in MATLAB. The size/precision of the translated variables can be changed easily by users.

This mismatch in types can cause differences in semantics for some contracts described in AGREE and their corresponding Simulink observers. Moreover, we note that SLDV interprets floating point variables as real variables as well. So it suffers from the same mismatch in semantics for floating point vs. real numbers. In the future we plan to allow users to specify bit-vector types in AGREE.

3.4 Workflow

We have implemented the export scheme as an extension to AGREE, available at [13]. The export process has the following steps:

1. **Select Data Types.** Users may select one of the MATLAB/Simulink supported integer types (i.e., (u)int8, (u)int16, (u)int32) to represent integers from the AGREE specification and one of the MATLAB supported floating point types (i.e., single, double) to represent reals from the AGREE specification.
2. **Export Design Contracts.** For any component with an AGREE contract, the user can invoke the tool to translate the contract into a MATLAB function.
3. **Update Simulink Model.** A script file provided by the toolset automatically packages the MATLAB function generated above as a MATLAB function block and connects the function block to the inputs and outputs of the component's Simulink model. The augmented Simulink model contains both a design model and a specification model that observes the design model.
4. **Invoke Simulink Design Verifier (SLDV).** Users can invoke SLDV on the verification model generated in the above step. SLDV checks to see if all properties in the MATLAB function are true, and provides counterexamples for the ones that are falsified.

4 Case Studies

In this section, we evaluate and demonstrate the effectiveness of the export techniques in two case studies: (1) an avionics braking and steering control unit and (2) a medical infusion pump. The workflow was tested with the latest version of the AGREE toolset and MATLAB Release 2015b.

As our export tool has not yet been qualified [14], for each case study, the specification model generated by the tool is manually reviewed against the original contracts and design information in AGREE and AADL to assess if the high-level requirements have been maintained.

4.1 Avionics Braking and Steering Control Unit

Overview. The avionics Braking and Steering Control Unit (BSCU) is a computer located in an aircraft's Wheel Braking System (WBS), controlling the

"Normal braking, Autobrake, Nose Wheel Steering Aid and Antiskid functions" [15]. The specification of the BSCU came from prior verification efforts [15] based on the report of an Airbus A-320 accident which occurred on May 21, 1998 [16]. In that accident, both the normal and alternate braking systems failed on landing. The loss of the normal braking system was caused by logic disagreement in the BSCU.

The BSCU system consists of two functionally identical channels, with only one channel being active at a time. When a fault is detected in the active channel, the standby channel becomes active if it is not faulty. Each channel contains a command function unit (COM component) and a monitor function unit (MON component). Both the COM and MON components compute the braking pressure to be applied based on their braking mode. Their outputs are compared at the MON function unit, and a fault will be logged when there is a disagreement between the outputs.

The COM and MON units operate in four braking modes: MANUAL, LO, MED, MAX. In MANUAL mode, the computed breaking pressure is mainly determined by the pressure on the brake pedal applied by the pilot. Other modes are Autobrake modes selected when pilot presses one of the LO, MED, or MAX buttons on the AUTO BRK panel, providing low, medium, and maximum levels of deceleration. Each unit starts in the MANUAL mode, and can transition to another mode when the associated button is pressed once; pressing the same button again transitions the unit back to MANUAL mode.

For this specific case study, the system architecture was previously modeled in AADL, and the design contracts between the components were specified in AGREE. Prior work [15] has found a disagreement in detecting a button push between the COM and MON component. The problem was remedied by updating the design contracts in the architecture model.

For this case study, we created Simulink models for the COM and MON components. This was a manual design process to interpret the high-level requirements into a design model. The behaviors of the COM and MON models were intended to satisfy all AGREE contracts for the COM and MON components in AADL.

For each component, we exported the design contract to a Simulink observer and connected it to the corresponding Simulink model. We ran Simulink Design Verifier (SLDV) on the augmented model to discover which properties were validated and which were not. For the falsified properties, SLDV produced a counterexample.

Results and Findings. Two types of falsified properties were found during the verification process. The first type was caused by a discrepancy on the behavior of the initial step. The second type was due to a discrepancy on the value of a global parameter used to indicate if the component is currently in an active channel. In both cases, the Simulink design model failed to interpret the specific design detail as presented in AGREE. Such discrepancies were missed from the first round of manual review of the models. After updating the Simulink model to match the design contracts, all properties specified in the Simulink observer were verified.

Investigation of the counterexamples was carried out by comparing the values of the intermediate signals computed in the model and in the Simulink observer during the simulation of the counterexamples. Having the specification model and design model co-located in the same environment allowed the simulation to compare their values during runtime.

The verification results demonstrate the benefit of using formal verification over manual review or simulation/testing, as it reasons about all execution paths and identifies design flaws that can be missed by other methods.

Automatically exporting AGREE contracts to Simulink observers allows fast turn-around in verification. The verification of the Simulink design model can be conducted as soon as the model is created. This supports early and frequent verification starting from the design phase. It also reduces errors that are easily introduced from manual interpretations, especially for large components with complex contracts.

4.2   Generic Patient Controlled Analgesic Infusion Software

Overview. The Generic Patient Controlled Analgesic (GPCA) infusion pump system [10] is a medical cyber-physical system "used for controlled delivery of liquid drugs into a patient's body according to a physician's prescription (the set of instructions that governs infusion rates for a medication)." [10]. It allows patients to administer a controlled amount of drug (typically a pain medication) themselves. It consists of four main components: Alarm, Infusion, Mode, and Logging. They are used to monitor the exceptional conditions and notify the clinician, determine the flow of drug, manage the mode, and log the status of the system. Detailed information on GPCA requirements can be found in [17].

The workflow for this case study was similar to the BSCU case study, except that the Simulink design models for the components, as well as the Simulink observer for the properties of the design models, had been manually created in prior work [17]. In this case study, we reused the design model created for each component, and we replaced the existing (manually created) Simulink observers with the ones generated by our tool from the corresponding AGREE contracts. The updated models were then verified using Simulink Design Verifier and the verification results from both models were compared.

Results and Findings. For both the manual and auto version of the Simulink observer, the verification results identified falsified properties due to the design model not behaving as expected. The verification time between the two versions were comparable (within 10 s). Some properties were undecided after reaching the maximum analysis time (set at 1200 s) for both versions.

Although the manually created versions of the Simulink observers are still a work in progress, we can make the following observations:

1. The manual properties tended to address the simpler, more straightforward contracts in AGREE, and they often missed modeling the temporal constructs

from AGREE (i.e., *pre* and → operators). Automation now allows us to easily translate even the complex contracts.

2. The manual properties tended to lag behind the AGREE contract updates, resulting in different verification results between the manual and automated versions for the same AGREE contract. Automation makes it easy to keep all the models synchronized.
3. The manual properties used Simulink unit delays outside of the MATLAB function to interpret the *pre* operator, a translation that preserves the meaning but is not easy to automate.
4. The manual properties selected signals from bus elements outside of the MATLAB function, while the auto translated properties did bus element selection inside the MATLAB function. The latter is a design choice that is easier to automate and maintain.

We found the benefits of automatically connecting the created Simulink observer to the design model through a counterexample. In this counterexample, one input port to the design model and the Simulink observer was a duplicate (different port numbers and treated as different ports) instead of a replicate (same port number and treated as the same port). This made the observer not a synchronous one, and yielded different verification results from the version that had the Simulink observer auto connected.

We also found design details introduced in the Simulink model that did not conform to the interface design in AGREE. For example, for an input port of record type in AGREE, its counterpart in Simulink (of Simulink bus type) had additional elements and elements with different names. While it is understandable that the design model may introduce new details needed for the component, any new design details that affect the interface should be synchronized with the AGREE model.

5   Related Work

The idea of auto generating test cases from higher level requirements has been the subject of intensive study in both the academia and industry [18–20]. Creating properties for formal verification from higher level requirements, has been performed manually [10,21], through patterns [22], and automatically [23,24]. The unique contribution of our work is a method for automatically exporting high-level requirements from a system-level reasoning framework as property observers in a component-level modeling framework. This enables formal verification of the component requirements as they are developed, bridging the gap between system-level and component-level reasoning. The compositional reasoning framework OCRA [25] has similar goals as AGREE. Both frameworks reason hierarchically about a system of components with connections and contracts. However, as far as we know, there are no tools to translate OCRA contracts to observers in specification languages commonly used in the avionics industry.

6   Conclusions

In this paper we have described a method for translating design contracts for components in an AADL software architecture model into specification models that can be verified at the component level. We have provided tool support for export as Simulink observers that can be verified using the Simulink Design Verifier. Moreover, our approach is sufficiently general that other component development environments could be easily targeted. This approach is built upon the AGREE compositional analysis framework that allows verification of requirements during architecture development, prior to software component implementation. Applying the technique on an avionics system and a medical device system has shown that the design contracts from the architecture model were faithfully exported, and saved time and reduced errors compared to the manual effort. Our approach also allowed verification to proceed in parallel with software development.

Possible future work includes qualifying the export tool in accordance with avionics certification guidelines [14] and enhancing the usability of the tool by supporting automatic re-verification when design contracts are updated.

Acknowledgments. This work was funded by NASA under contract NNA13AA21C (Compositional Verification of Flight Critical Systems). We would like to thank Chad Van Fleet, Anitha Murugesan, and Mike Whalen for their valuable feedback during this work.

References

1. Cofer, D., Gacek, A., Miller, S., Whalen, M.W., LaValley, B., Sha, L.: Compositional verification of architectural models. In: Goodloe, A.E., Person, S. (eds.) NFM 2012. LNCS, vol. 7226, pp. 126–140. Springer, Heidelberg (2012)
2. Whalen, M.W., Gacek, A., Cofer, D.D., Murugesan, A., Heimdahl, M.P.E., Rayadurgam, S.: Your "what" is my "how": Iteration and hierarchy in system design. IEEE Softw. **30**, 54–60 (2013)
3. Feiler, P.H., Gluch, D.P.: Model-Based Engineering with AADL: An Introduction to the SAE Architecture Analysis & Design Language, 1st edn. Addison-Wesley Professional, Boston (2012)
4. MathWorks: Simulink (2016). http://www.mathworks.com/products/simulink/
5. RTCA DO-178C: Software Considerations in Airborne Systems and Equipment Certification, Washington, DC (2011)
6. RTCA DO-333: Formal Methods Supplement to DO-178C and DO-278A, Washington, DC (2011)
7. RTCA DO-331: Model-Based Development and Verification Supplement to DO-178C and DO-278A, Washington, DC (2011)
8. Cofer, D., Miller, S.P.: Formal methods case studies for DO-333, NASA contractor report NASA/CR-2014-218244 (2014)
9. MathWorks: Simulink   (2016).   http://www.mathworks.com/products/sldesignverifier/

10. Murugesan, A., Whalen, M.W., Rayadurgam, S., Heimdahl, M.P.: Compositional verification of a medical device system. In: ACM International Conference on High Integrity Language Technology (HILT) 2013. ACM (2013)
11. Halbwachs, N., Caspi, P., Raymond, P., Pilaud, D.: The synchronous dataflow programming language LUSTRE. Proc. IEEE **79**, 1305–1320 (1991)
12. Huth, M., Ryan, M.: Logic in Computer Science: Modelling and Reasoning about Systems, 2nd edn. Cambridge University Press, Cambridge (2004)
13. Backes, J., et al.: AGREE toolset (2016). http://loonwerks.com/tools/agree.html
14. RTCA DO-330: Software Tool Qualification Considerations, Washington, DC (2011)
15. Miller, S.P., Bhattacharyya, S., Tinelli, C., Smolka, S., Sticksel, C., Meng, B., Yang, J.: Formal verification of quasi-synchronous systems. Final Technical report delivered Air Force Research Laboratory (2015)
16. Accident, C.A., Incident Investigation Commission (CIAIAC), S.: Technical report: Accident occurred on 21 May 1998 to Aircraft Airbus A-320-21 Registration G-UKLL At Ibiza Airport, Balearic Islands (1998)
17. CriSys Group: Generic patient controlled analgesia infusion pump project (2016). http://crisys.cs.umn.edu/gpca.shtml
18. Wang, C., Pastore, F., Goknil, A., Briand, L., Iqbal, Z.: Automatic generation of system test cases from use case specifications. In: Proceedings of the 2015 International Symposium on Software Testing and Analysis, ISSTA 2015, pp. 385–396. ACM, New York (2015)
19. Ibrahim, R., Saringat, M., Ibrahim, N., Ismail, N.: An automatic tool for generating test cases from the system's requirements. In: 7th IEEE International Conference on Computer and Information Technology, CIT 2007, pp. 861–866 (2007)
20. Escalona, M.J., Gutierrez, J.J., Mejías, M., Aragón, G., Ramos, I., Torres, J., Domínguez, F.J.: An overview on test generation from functional requirements. J. Syst. Softw. **84**, 1379–1393 (2011)
21. Miller, S.P., Tribble, A.C., Whalen, M.W., Heimdahl, M.P.E.: Proving the shalls: early validation of requirements through formal methods. Int. J. Softw. Tools Technol. Transf. **8**, 303–319 (2006)
22. Bozzano, M., Cimatti, A., Katoen, J., Katsaros, P., Mokos, K., Nguyen, V.Y., Noll, T., Postma, B., Roveri, M.: Spacecraft early design validation using formal methods. Reliab. Eng. Syst. Saf. **132**, 20–35 (2014)
23. Silva, W., Bezerra, E., Winterholer, M., Lettnin, D.: Automatic property generation for formal verification applied to hdl-based design of an on-board computer for space applications. In: 2013 14th Latin American Test Workshop (LATW), pp. 1–6 (2013)
24. Soeken, M., Kuhne, U., Freibothe, M., Fe, G., Drechsler, R.: Automatic property generation for the formal verification of bus bridges. In: 2011 IEEE 14th International Symposium on Design and Diagnostics of Electronic Circuits Systems (DDECS), pp. 417–422 (2011)
25. Cimatti, A., Tonetta, S.: Contracts-refinement proof system for component-based embedded systems. Sci. Comput. Program. Part 3 **97**, 333–348 (2015)

A Hybrid Architecture
for Correct-by-Construction Hybrid
Planning and Control

Robert P. Goldman[1]([⊠]), Daniel Bryce[1], Michael J.S. Pelican[1],
David J. Musliner[1], and Kyungmin Bae[2]

[1] SIFT, LLC, Minneapolis, MN, USA
{rpgoldman,dbryce,mpelican,musliner}@sift.net
[2] Carnegie-Mellon University, Pittsburgh, PA, USA
kquine@gmail.com

Abstract. This paper describes Hy-CIRCA, an architecture for verified, correct-by-construction planning and execution for hybrid systems, including nonlinear continuous dynamics. Hy-CIRCA addresses the high computational complexity of such systems by first planning at an abstract level, and then progressively refining the original plan. Hy-CIRCA integrates the dReal nonlinear SMT solver with enhanced versions of the SHOP2 HTN planner and the CIRCA Controller Synthesis Module (CSM). SHOP2 computes a high level nominal mission plan, the CIRCA CSM develops reactive controllers for the mission steps, accounting for disturbances, and dReal verifies that the plans are correct with respect to continuous dynamics. In this way, Hy-CIRCA decomposes reasoning about the plan and judiciously applies the different solvers to the problems they are best at.

1 Introduction

In this paper we describe Hy-CIRCA, an architecture for verified, correct-by-construction planning and execution for hybrid systems, including nonlinear continuous dynamics (see Fig. 1). Hy-CIRCA addresses the high computational complexity of nonlinear hybrid systems by first planning at an abstract level, and then progressively refining the original plan. During this refinement process, Hy-CIRCA incorporates formal verification at increasing levels of fidelity.

Hy-CIRCA is an extension of our Playbook[1] approach for controlling multiple autonomous agents to cover hybrid discrete/continuous planning and control, with nonlinear continuous dynamics. The Playbook approach aims to make it easy for users to exert supervisory control over multiple autonomous systems by "calling a play" [9]. The Playbook approach is implemented by combining (1) a human-machine interface for commanding and monitoring the autonomous systems; (2) a hierarchical planner for translating commands into executable plans; and (3) a smart executive to manage plan execution by coordinating the

---

[1] Playbook® is a registered trademark of SIFT, LLC.

© Springer International Publishing Switzerland 2016
S. Rayadurgam and O. Tkachuk (Eds.): NFM 2016, LNCS 9690, pp. 388–394, 2016.
DOI: 10.1007/978-3-319-40648-0_29

control systems of the individual autonomous agents, tracking plan execution, and triggering replanning when necessary.

Hy-CIRCA integrates the dReal nonlinear SMT solver [4] with enhanced versions of the SHOP2 [11] planner and the CIRCA Controller Synthesis Module (CSM) [6,10]. The planning process in Hy-CIRCA proceeds in 5 steps: (1) SHOP2 computes an approximate, nominal mission plan. While computing this plan, Hy-CIRCA also computes a hybrid automaton model of the plan, featuring more expressive continuous dynamics. (2) dReal solves this hybrid model, establishing the correctness of the plan, and refining it by computing values for its continuous parameters. This mission plan uses projection to handle resources and find paths to the goal state. However, it is still an open-loop plan. (3) To build an executable plan, Hy-CIRCA extracts specifications for closed-loop, hard real-time supervisory controllers that will achieve each step of the plan and reject disturbances from outside sources of change (e.g., adversaries or nature). (4) Based upon these specifications, CIRCA CSM plans the supervisory controllers. The CSM uses an over-approximating abstraction of the continuous dynamics. (5) Finally, dReal ensures correctness of the controllers by verifying they meet the specifications, using a higher-fidelity nonlinear hybrid model.

Hy-CIRCA has superficial similarities with established three layer architectures (TLAs) for robotics, but those typically feature deliberative planning, reactive programming for a smart executive, and then a platform control interface [5]. The TLA provides a combination of open-loop projective planning to efficiently reason about mission goals and manage resources, with closed-loop, event-driven interaction with low-level platform control. In most TLAs, considerations of continuous and hybrid dynamics are confined to the executive layer, the executive is usually manually programmed rather than automatically synthesized, and the relationship between the planning and executive layers is *ad hoc*. TLAs contrast with hierarchical schemes such as CHARON [1], that are homogeneous across abstraction layers, permitting systematic reasoning about relations between components in terms of traces and trace refinements. Hy-CIRCA shares the ability to systematically reason about relations between layers, and permits higher-level behaviors to constrain synthesis of lower-level behaviors.

As the first step in developing Hy-CIRCA, we have constructed a proof-of-concept implementation of key parts of Hy-CIRCA, and tested it on a demonstration problem involving multi-agent firefighting using uninhabited aerial vehicles (UAVs). In this paper, we describe this aerial firefighting scenario and how Hy-CIRCA meets its challenges.

Our contributions include: a method of using the SHOP2 planner to perform hybrid automaton model construction; a logical formalization of the SHOP2-generated plan as a hybrid system, for use in the dReal SMT solver; techniques for extracting controller specifications from an HTN plan; and techniques for verifying the correctness of CIRCA closed-loop controllers on hybrid systems.

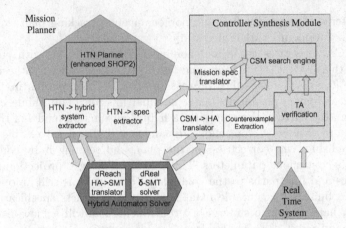

Fig. 1. Hy-CIRCA synthesizes hybrid controllers to satisfy mission specifications expressed in high-level temporal logic through two-way interactions between the Mission Planner, the Controller Synthesis Module, and the Hybrid Automaton Solver.

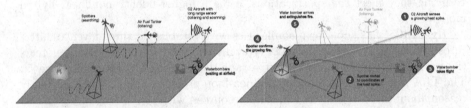

Fig. 2. Multiple-UAV firefighting scenario.   **Fig. 3.** Plan to extinguish a fire.

2   Scenario of Use

The following motivating use case illustrates how the Hy-CIRCA architecture can be used for hybrid planning and control of multiple-platform packages of autonomous systems. In this multi-UAV firefighting scenario (see Fig. 2), the fleet of UAVs includes *waterbombers* that drop water or retardant on a fire, *spotters* that localize the fires and transmit targeting coordinates to the waterbombers, *C2 aircraft* that coordinate operations and have long-range sensors that detect possible fires, and *tankers* that provide in-air refueling.

The mission's objective is to extinguish a fire that has just been spotted by the long-range, low-accuracy sensors on a C2 aircraft. An airborne fire manager on the C2 aircraft uses his Playbook interface to call the *extinguish* play, tailoring the play to the situation by incorporating information about the location of the suspected fire, the assets available to the team, and their current state/location. Given the plan library and any tailored parameters from the operator, Hy-CIRCA first invokes the SHOP2 HTN planner to generate a complete set of tasks for the mission. The first step in the mission plan (see Fig. 3) is for a spotter to go to the vicinity of the suspected fire to confirm its existence. After confirmation, the fire can be extinguished by dropping a load of retardant from a waterbomber. SHOP2 also plans a route for the waterbomber to reach the area of the fire to extinguish the fire. In order for the waterbomber to correctly target the fire, it must get a stream of location information from a spotter as it drops the retardant.

SHOP2 chooses a take-off time for the waterbomber that attempts to get it to the fire area shortly after the spotter has arrived. This will avoid fuel waste that would occur in a plan where the waterbomber arrives first and must loiter, waiting for the spotter. But we don't want the waterbomber to arrive too late: even though the spotter uses less fuel than the waterbomber, we still don't want to waste its fuel, or keep it from other uses. Note that this means that the problem has *required concurrency* [3]. Required concurrency is a feature of more difficult temporal planning/scheduling problems in which there are "too early," as well as "too late" constraints. Problems with required concurrency differ from simpler temporal problems whose temporal aspect can be solved by choosing the earliest feasible activity start times.

SHOP2's plan is only approximate, because of limits in its computations about real continuous quantities such as fuel (in particular, its inability to solve systems of simultaneous equations). But SHOP2 can more efficiently solve the discrete sequencing problems than dReal, and it can invoke special solvers to synthesize waypoint sequences.

Once the initial plan has been computed, Hy-CIRCA uses the higher fidelity reasoning offered by dReal to refine it. As a side-effect of computing its plan, Hy-CIRCA's version of SHOP2 builds a hybrid systems SMT problem. Hy-CIRCA uses dReal to solve this problem, where a solution is a satisfying trajectory through the high-dimensional hybrid space. By solving that problem, dReal will synthesize continuous parameters for the mission plan. In our tests, dReal solved a system of nonlinear constraints to choose the fuel and flame retardant loads for the waterbomber, and refined the mission schedule based on more accurate models of flight than those used by SHOP2.

The mission plan guides the operation of the autonomous systems, but is not sufficient for their closed-loop control. Hy-CIRCA uses an enhanced version of the CIRCA Controller Synthesis Module (CSM) to automatically synthesize controllers for the platforms (waterbombers, spotters, etc.) in the mission. These controllers will constitute the smart executives for those platforms.

The first step of the controller synthesis process is to generate controller specifications from the mission plan. These specifications include both temporal logic invariants and goals. For our current Hy-CIRCA proof of concept, we extracted the specifications for the waterbomber aircraft in the mission. These specifications include control operations used in flight, representations of known disturbances, temporal logic representations of the goals ("eventually the fire should be extinguished"), temporal logic invariants ("the waterbomber must release its load within k time units from receiving a target message from the spotter"), and signal temporal logic (STL) [8] hybrid invariants ("the vehicle must always maintain a fuel reserve of at least n gallons").

The CIRCA CSM uses these inputs to synthesize a closed-loop, real-time discrete outer-loop controller for each platform. Note that these controllers will perform coordinated actions, directed by the mission plan that has been translated into temporal logic specifications. For example, the spotter will repeatedly transmit targeting information until the waterbomber has dropped its load. Similarly, the waterbomber will wait in the vicinity of the fire until it has received the targeting information, and is constrained to drop its load before the targeting information becomes stale.

The CIRCA CSM reasons about continuous processes only as approximated by upper and lower bounds on temporal durations. For example, its reasoning about whether it can reach the target quickly enough is based on whether it can initiate the motion soon enough, and is verified in terms of time bounds on its flight processes.

For more accurate reasoning about the control of continuous processes, Hy-CIRCA re-checks the controller using dReal. We developed a technique for translating the CIRCA controllers and STL invariants into a hybrid automaton representation that can be checked by dReach (a preprocessor translating hybrid automata for dReal) and dReal. We tested this algorithm by translating the waterbomber controller into a hybrid automaton, the STL invariants into a separate automaton, forming the product, and then checking reachability. The reachability computation was done using dReach's translation from automaton to dReal SMT formulas. E.g., in one of our tests, we checked the invariant that the waterbomber would always have an adequate fuel reserve.

If Hy-CIRCA finds that an invariant cannot be verified, it will use a process of culprit extraction to translate the counterexample into information that the CIRCA CSM can use to guide backjumping and repair the synthesized controller [7]. We have developed a method for performing this culprit extraction. We tested the approach on an example where the waterbomber's controller originally generated a plan that involved monitoring a fuel level warning, which is signaled when a threshold fuel level is reached (like the fuel level warning in a car). The original synthesized controller would go into a special fuel-conserving flight mode and return to base if the low fuel warning was triggered. In some missions, where the flight radius is lower, this controller will be verified to work correctly.

However, if the flight radius is longer, then dReal will detect that a failing state can be reached if the fuel warning goes off when the aircraft is beyond some distance d from base. From this counterexample, Hy-CIRCA can extract a culprit that indicates that the controller using the special return-to-base flight mode is not safe. This will cause the CSM to backjump and choose the (more expensive) recovery action of in-air refueling. The resulting revised controller then will be verified by dReal.

3   Conclusions and Future Work

We have described our Hy-CIRCA framework for integrated planning, controller synthesis, and verification for nonlinear hybrid domains. Hy-CIRCA decomposes complex mission planning into strategy planning with SHOP2, controller synthesis with CIRCA, and verification with dReach. Some of the most challenging and novel aspects of this framework are how the tools integrate to solve the overall problem. For instance, SHOP2 and dReal interact to solve planning and scheduling with numeric resources. SHOP2 and CIRCA collaborate to synthesize low-level controllers for high-level actions that must satisfy temporal properties. CIRCA and dReach cooperate to verify the controllers with respect to the underlying nonlinear continuous change.

As we continue to develop the Hy-CIRCA framework, the important remaining issues concern how to automatically divide the overall problem among the Hy-CIRCA components and how to effectively evaluate these decisions. We recognize that the division of decision making between the tools is an important area for future research, especially given that we have recently made advances in scaling dReal's discrete decision-making capabilities [2]. We have designed algorithms for SHOP2/CSM and CSM/dReach integration, and tested them on cases drawn from the firefighting scenario. We are about to begin a second phase of the project to complete the integration and extend our set of experiments. We are also working to extend the capabilities of the system in a number of areas. In order to handle the full generality of the temporal specifications handled by the Hy-CIRCA CSM, we are improving the native finite trace verification of temporal logic specifications in the CSM. The current timed automaton verifier in the CSM only checks safety conditions. We will extend it to handle liveness conditions, as well. While the basics of liveness checking are well understood, our algorithms for extracting nogoods – used for backjumping – need extension in order to accommodate counterexamples to liveness goals.

Acknowledgments. Thanks to the anonymous reviewers, Laura Humphrey, Sicun Gao, and Soonho Kong for comments and advice. This material is based upon work supported by the U.S. Air Force (AFRL) under Contract No. FA9550-15-C-0030. Any opinions, findings and conclusions, or recommendations expressed in this material are those of the authors and do not reflect the views of the U.S. Air Force (AFRL).

References

1. Alur, R., Dang, T., Esposito, J., Fierro, R., Hur, Y., Ivančić, F., Kumar, V., Lee, I., Mishra, P., Pappas, G.J., Sokolsky, O.: Hierarchical hybrid modeling of embedded systems. In: Henzinger, T.A., Kirsch, C.M. (eds.) EMSOFT 2001. LNCS, vol. 2211, p. 14. Springer, Heidelberg (2001)
2. Bryce, D., Gao, S., Musliner, D.J., Goldman, R.P.: SMT-based nonlinear PDDL+ planning. In: Proceedings National Conference on Artificial Intelligence, pp. 3247–3253 (2015)
3. Cushing, W., Kambhampati, S., Mausam, Weld, D.S.: When is temporal planning really temporal? In: Veloso, M.M. (ed.) Proceedings of the 20th International Joint Conference on Artificial Intelligence, pp. 1852–1859 (2007)
4. Gao, S., Kong, S., Clarke, E.M.: dReal: an SMT solver for nonlinear theories over the reals. In: Bonacina, M.P. (ed.) CADE 2013. LNCS, vol. 7898, pp. 208–214. Springer, Heidelberg (2013)

5. Gat, E.: Three-layer architectures. In: Kortenkamp, D., Bonasso, R.P., Murphy, R. (eds.) Artificial Intelligence and Mobile Robots. AAAI Press/MIT Press, Cambridge, MA (1998)

6. Goldman, R.P., Musliner, D.J., Pelican, M.J.S.: Exploiting implicit representations in timed automaton verification for controller synthesis. In: Tomlin, C.J., Greenstreet, M.R. (eds.) HSCC 2002. LNCS, vol. 2289, p. 225. Springer, Heidelberg (2002)

7. Goldman, R.P., Pelican, M.J.S., Musliner, D.J.: Guiding planner backjumping using verifier traces. In: Zilberstein, S., Koehler, J., Koenig, S. (eds.) Proceedings of the Fourteenth International Conference on Automated Planning and Scheduling, pp. 279–286, June 2004

8. Maler, O., Nickovic, D.: Monitoring temporal properties of continuous signals. In: Lakhnech, Y., Yovine, S. (eds.) FORMATS/FTRTFT 2004. LNCS, vol. 3253, pp. 152–166. Springer, Heidelberg (2004)

9. Miller, C.A., Goldman, R.P., Funk, H.B., Wu, P., Pate, B.: A playbook approach to variable autonomy control: application for control of multiple, heterogeneous unmanned air vehicles. In: AHS 60th Annual Forum Proceedings, pp. 2146–2157. American Helicopter Society, Alexandria, VA, June 2004

10. Musliner, D.J., Durfee, E.H., Shin, K.G.: CIRCA: a cooperative intelligent real-time control architecture. IEEE Trans. Syst. Man Cybern. 23(6), 1561–1574 (1993)

11. Nau, D., Au, T.C., Ilghami, O., Kuter, U., Murdock, J.W., Wu, D., Yaman, F.: SHOP2: an HTN planning system. J. Artif. Intell. Res. 20, 379–404 (2003)

Author Index

Printed in the United States
by Baker & Taylor Publisher Services

Printed in the United States
By Bookmasters